CHANNEL FOUR RACING

COMPLETE A–Z OF
HORSE RACING

Sean Magee

First published 2001 by Channel 4 Books
an imprint of Pan Macmillan Ltd
Pan Macmillan, 20 New Wharf Road, London, N1 9RR
Basingstoke and Oxford
Associated companies throughout the world
www.panmacmillan.com

Associated companies throughout the world

ISBN 07522 1948 0

A CIP catalogue record for this book is available from
the British Library.

Designed and typeset by Production Line
Printed and bound by Mackays of Chatham plc, Chatham, Kent

This book accompanies the Channel 4 Racing coverage
produced by Highflyer Productions for Channel 4.
Executive Producers: John Fairley and Andrew Franklin

INTRODUCTION

Click onto a website and you'll frequently be offered a page marked 'FAQ' – 'Frequently Asked Questions'. It is in the spirit of addressing Frequently Asked Questions about horse racing that this volume is published.

The entries cannot presume to supply answers to every single racing question you might come up with – the word 'complete' in its title refers of course to its covering the complete alphabet from A to Z, rather than any unsustainable claim of being completely comprehensive – but it can tackle the more likely. Where and when was Frankie Dettori born? How many races did Pilsudski win? What is a 'teaser', or a 'sex allowance', or an 'auction race'? The intention has been to provide information most likely to interest viewers of Channel Four Racing, and thus there is a bias towards current and recent horses and personalities rather than the historically remote, and towards British and Irish racing rather than further-flung arenas.

This book supplements and builds on *The Channel Four Book of Racing*, first published in 1989 and updated in 1995, and the three *Channel Four Racing Guides* published in 1998 and 1999 – *Form and Betting*, *Racecourses* and *Racehorses*.

A few words of explanation and justification:

• Cross references to other entries are indicated by the use of **bold type**. The system of cross-referencing is neither consistent nor comprehensive and has been dictated by this consideration: if in the context of an entry it is felt that the reader might like to find out more by pursuing the cross-reference, one has been marked; if that is unlikely, no cross-reference is indicated. If in doubt, have a look anyway.

• The boxes of race results for major races cover all Group One races on the Flat in Great Britain, the major handicaps on the Flat regularly covered by Channel Four Racing, the principal jump races and a handful of big overseas events. Each of these boxes consists of seven columns, listing: year; name of winning horse; age of winning horse; winning trainer; winning jockey; starting price of winning horse; number of runners. The country where the winning horse has been trained is given after the trainer's name when there has not been a 'home' win, in the form *GB* (Great Britain), *IRE* (Ireland), *FRA* (France), *GER* (Germany), *JAP* (Japan), *AUS* (Australia) and *USA* (USA). In the column giving starting prices (or, as appropriate in the case of the Japan Cup and Prix de l'Arc de Triomphe, local pari-mutuel returns), market leaders are indicated by F (favourite), JF (joint favourite), CF (co-favourite), and – in the sole case of the Arc – CPF (coupled favourite). The latest result listed in these boxes is that of the Nassau Stakes at Goodwood on 4 August 2001: big races run in Britain after that were too late for inclusion. (Although Michael Stoute was knighted in 1998, the result boxes leave him as plain 'M. Stoute' for races he won after being so honoured, for the sake of consistency.)

• Distances for major races have been rounded up or down to the nearest half furlong, since to describe the distance of the Derby as 1 mile 4 furlongs 10 yards (the distance at which it was officially run in 2001) or the Nassau Stakes as 1 mile 1 furlong 192 yards seems excessively pedantic. An exception has been made in the case of the St Leger, where to round down the traditional distance of 1 mile 6 furlongs 132 yards would be heresy, a sin far worse than pedantry.

- The term 'Classic' when used without an adjective indicating nationality signifies one of the five Classic races run in England.
- On the whole, sponsors' names have been omitted from traditional race names – not out of any disrespect for sponsors but in an attempt to render the text less ponderous than would otherwise be the case.
- The information in the book is as up-to-date as we can make it at the end of July 2001.
- A word about the lists of leading jockeys, owners and trainers. Anyone who dabbles in racing statistics will have experienced acute frustration that the criteria for what constitutes champions are inconstant. On the Flat, before the coming of all-weather racing the jockeys' championship was decided on the number of winners ridden during the season, which stretched from late March to mid November. All-weather racing changed the shape of the racing year: in 1994 it was decreed that the Flat season would run from 1 January to 31 December, and that for the first time winners ridden on the artificial surfaces would count towards the jockeys' title – a change not lost on one **Lanfranco Dettori**. The title is currently decided on winners ridden (on both turf and all-weather surfaces) during the turf season which runs from late March to early November, so that all-weather wins outside that period do not count towards the championship: this explains how Kevin Darley won the 'official' title in 2000 with 152 winners, while he actually rode

155 winners in Great Britain during the calendar year 2000. Trying to bring consistent criteria to the ranking of owners and trainers is even more aggravating. There are no quasi-official championships in these categories, and sources divide between counting all prize money won and just counting win money, and even then there are discrepancies between sources. The tables in this book dodge the issue by omitting actual prize money won for owners and trainers.
- One for the truly obsessive. The name of the 1965 Derby winner is variously given in racing books as Sea-Bird, Sea-Bird II, Sea Bird and Sea Bird II. Here he is Sea Bird II, since that is how he was named in the Epsom racecard on 2 June 1965, the only occasion he ever raced in Britain.

This book cannot and does not presume to provide the answer to Everything You Always Wanted To Know About Horse Racing But Were Afraid To Ask, but Channel Four Racing aims to supply answers to further questions about the sport – people, horses, rules, procedures, the hyphen in Sea Bird II's name – via our website. E-mail your queries to racing@channel4.com and we'll do our best to answer them (although please bear in mind that we cannot calculate your winnings for you, nor can we adjudicate in betting disputes): we can't guarantee success, but we'll have a go. Meanwhile, we hope you'll find the information in the pages that follow illuminating and useful.

Acknowledgements

The text of this book has been gone over by more anoraks than you'd find in your local Millets. Very special thanks to Phillip Jones for hunting down the truth with such zeal, and to Chris Pitt (whose wonderful book about defunct racecourses, *A Long Time Gone*, deserves every plug) and his wife Mary for cheerfully putting me right. It is traditional at this point to assert that any remaining errors are the responsibility of the compiler alone and I am happy to follow that custom, tempting as it is to ask: if there are mistakes remaining, why did my carefully assembled team of anoraks not pick them up? …Thanks also to Gillian Bromley and Charlie Webster for so elegantly squeezing a quart into a pint pot; to Sandy Holton at Channel Four for all that champagne (oh yes, and for years of support); to Paull Khan at Weatherbys and John Maxse at the Jockey Club for so promptly answering queries; to Steve Cannon and Robert Cooper for advice on their respective fields of expertise; to Andrew Franklin at Channel Four Racing; and to Emma Tait and Verity Willcocks at Channel Four Books.

A

ABDULLAH, KHALID

Saudi Arabian prince (though in Britain he races as plain 'Mr Khalid Abdullah') whose extensive worldwide owning and breeding operations have made him one of the most influential figures in world racing. When Known Fact took the 1980 Two Thousand Guineas on the disqualification of Nureyev he became the first Arab-owned English Classic winner, and since then the Abdullah colours (green, pink sash and cap, white sleeves) have been carried to success in all five English Classics and in top contests around the world by such horses as the brilliant milers Rousillon and Warning; Rainbow Quest, who won the Coronation Cup and Prix de l'Arc de Triomphe in 1985; Derby winners Quest For Fame (1990) and Commander In Chief (who also won the Irish Derby in 1993); Prix du Jockey-Club winner Sanglamore (1990); **Zafonic**, explosive winner of the 1993 Two Thousand Guineas; and **Xaar**, whose seven-

length victory in the 1997 Dewhurst Stakes was one of the greatest two-year-old performances in living memory. But Khalid Abdullah's greatest horse to date has undoubtedly been **Dancing Brave**, winner in 1986 of the Two Thousand Guineas, Eclipse Stakes, King George VI and Queen Elizabeth Diamond Stakes and Prix de l'Arc de Triomphe, and a controversial runner-up to Shahrastani in the Derby. Abdullah's Juddmonte Studs operation has bases in Berkshire, Suffolk, Co. Meath and Kentucky.

ABERNANT

Trained by **Noel Murless**, this grey colt was a grandson of the flying filly Mumtaz Mahal, from whom he inherited the blinding speed which won him 14 of his 17 races between 1948 and 1950. As a two-year-old he won five races including the Chesham Stakes, Champagne Stakes and Middle Park Stakes. At three he was narrowly beaten by Nimbus in the Two Thousand Guineas and then went on to prove himself one of the greatest of all sprinters by winning such races as the King's Stand Stakes, July Cup, King George Stakes and Nunthorpe Stakes, and he consolidated his reputation as a four-year-old, when his victories included repeat wins in the July Cup, King George Stakes and Nunthorpe. The Abernant Stakes, named in his memory, is run over six furlongs at Newmarket's Craven Meeting in April. He died in 1970 aged 24.

ACCEPTORS

Horses entered for a race who stand their ground after **forfeit stages** have been reached.

ACCUMULATOR

Bet involving several horses: the returns from each winning selection are staked on the next.

Khalid Abdullah's Classic winners

Two Thousand Guineas
   1980 Known Fact
   1986 Dancing Brave
   1993 Zafonic

One Thousand Guineas
   1999 Wince

Oaks
   1997 Reams Of Verse

Derby
   1990 Quest For Fame
   1993 Commander In Chief

St Leger
   1991 Toulon

ACEY-DEUCEY

Riding style, principally on the left-handed racetracks of the USA, where the jockey rides with the left stirrup leather longer than the right in order to keep balanced while the horse is negotiating the left-hand turns.

ACROSS THE CARD

Used of races run at the same time at different meetings.

ACTION

How a horse moves. Action can furnish significant clues about how that horse will perform on the **going**: if it strides out well and 'pokes its toe' on the way down to the start, that suggests that it is at ease on the ground. But if it moves scratchily ('goes down short'), it is clearly uncomfortable on the going – and likely to be even more uncomfortable at racing speed. A high knee action suggests that the horse needs soft ground. When a horse 'loses its action' – for example, on the helter-skelter downhill run to Tattenham Corner at Epsom – the rhythm of its gallop is disrupted.

ADDED MONEY

Money contributed towards the value of a race by sponsors or the racecourse, and added to the entry fees of owners to supply the prize money for that race.

AFFIRMED

The most recent winner of the American Triple Crown, Affirmed etched his place in American racing history with three hard-fought victories over his great rival **Alydar**.

Ridden in all three of the 1978 Triple Crown races by US prodigy **Steve Cauthen**, he won the Kentucky Derby by one and a half lengths, the Preakness by a neck and the Belmont Stakes, after a famously hard-fought duel, by a head. (In all, Affirmed and Alydar raced against each other ten times, with the final tally reading: Affirmed 7, Alydar 3.) Affirmed, named Horse of the Year in 1978 and 1979, posted a career record of 22 wins from 29 starts, with 14 of those wins

coming at Grade One level. On his death at the age of 26 in January 2001 the tributes were led by Cauthen: 'He was probably the most intelligent horse I was ever around. He had a lot of common sense, he loved to run and battle, and he was an easy horse to ride. I just appreciated his company.' An even more fitting epitaph might be the observation of his trainer Laz Barrera after Affirmed had exploded from the starting gate to beat **Spectacular Bid** in the 1979 Jockey Club Gold Cup: 'When Affirmed breaks like that you can put the beans on the fire – you're gonna eat for sure.'

AGA KHAN

Grandson of the Aga Khan whose horses won the Derby five times, and son of Petite Etoile's owner Prince **Aly Khan,** the present Aga Khan – full title His Highness Prince Karim, the Aga Khan – was born in 1936 and is Imam (spiritual leader) of the Ismaili sect of Shia Muslims. He developed his racing interests during the 1970s (when his horses included the brilliant French-trained colt **Blushing Groom**, third to The Minstrel in the 1977 Derby), and early the following decade hit the Classic jackpot with the great Shergar, winner in 1981 of the Derby (by 10 lengths), Irish Derby and King George VI and Queen Elizabeth Diamond Stakes. The Aga Khan won the Derby twice more in the 1980s with Shahrastani (1986) and Kahyasi (1988), but things went very sour after the disqualification of his 1989 Oaks winner Aliysa: her post-race specimen had proved positive to a derivative of the prohibited substance camphor, and after a lengthy dispute with the Jockey Club all the Aga Khan's horses were removed from Britain in 1991. However, changes in British testing procedures brought the familiar colours (green, red epaulets) back to the country in 1995, and in 2000 Sinndar added a fourth Derby for the Aga Khan, going on to win the Irish Derby and Arc in brilliant style. Other of his notable performers in recent years include 1982 Arc winner Akiyda, 1988 Two Thousand Guineas winner Doyoun, the brilliant miler Sendawar, 1999 Ascot Gold Cup winner Enzeli and Kalanisi, winner in 2000 of the

The Aga Khan's English Classic winners

Two Thousand Guineas
1988   Doyoun

Derby
1981   Shergar
1986   Shahrastani
1988   Kahyasi
2000   Sinndar

Champion Stakes and Breeder's Cup Turf (his Lashkari had won the inaugural running of the Turf in 1984). The Aga Khan's breeding interests are divided between Ireland and France and include the Gilltown Stud in Co. Kildare (where Sinndar stands as a stallion) and the Haras de Bonneval. He was leading owner in Britain in 1981 and 2000.

AGE

A racehorse born in the northern hemisphere has its official birthday on 1 January (1 August in the southern hemisphere): on 1 January following its foaling it becomes a yearling, the following 1 January a two-year-old, and so on. The youngest age at which horses race on the Flat is two; they can race over hurdles at three and over fences at four. A two-year-old on the Flat, or a hurdler running at three in the autumn or four in the spring, is often referred to as a 'juvenile'. The Thoroughbred racehorse matures at about five.

On the Flat it has tended to be unusual for a top horse to continue racing beyond the age of four: all the English Classics (Two Thousand Guineas, One Thousand Guineas, Oaks, Derby and St Leger) are confined to three-year-olds, and the fees which a high-class horse can command as a stallion exceed the prize money he is likely to earn by continuing racing. That said, there has been an encouraging trend in recent years for a few of the best horses to be kept in training at five or even six, sometimes with spectacular results:

- Six-year-old **Swain** became the oldest horse ever to win the King George VI and Queen Elizabeth Diamond Stakes at Ascot when beating High-Rise in 1998.
- **Singspiel** won the Dubai World Cup, Coronation Cup and International Stakes in 1997 at five.
- **Pilsudski,** having won the Breeders' Cup Turf at four, excelled himself at five, winning the Eclipse Stakes, Irish Champion Stakes, Champion Stakes and Japan Cup in 1997.
- **Cigar** was six when he won the inaugural Dubai World Cup in 1996.
- **Daylami** won the Coronation Cup, King George, Irish Champion Stakes and Breeders' Cup Turf at five in 1999.

Such cases are still the exception, as most owners of the very best horses understandably want to get them off to stud when they are at the top of the market and can command high covering fees: for example, of the 10 Derby winners between Generous in 1991 and Sinndar in 2000, all but High-Rise (1998) were retired at the end of their three-year-old careers. Equally understandably, racegoers want to watch the top horses in action for as long as they can, and the chance of seeing the likes of Pilsudski, Swain and Daylami on the track well beyond their Classic year has made the Flat scene infinitely more interesting to racing fans than it was when nearly all of the star performers were prematurely retired.

On the Flat, any horse running at six years old or over is thought to be fairly long in the tooth, though steeplechasers will carry on typically to about 12 – often beyond – and are usually held to be in their prime at eight or nine. Oldest horse in the twentieth century to win the Grand National was Sergeant Murphy, 13 when landing the 1923 running, while the oldest winners of the Cheltenham Gold Cup were 12: since the Second World War, Silver Fame (1951) and What A Myth (1969) have won at that age. Oldest Champion Hurdle winners have been **Hatton's Grace** (1950) and **Sea Pigeon** (1981), both 11. At the other end of the age scale, youngest Grand National winner in the twentieth century was Lutteur III at the age of five in 1909 – and no horse as young can win the modern race, since the National is now for six-year-olds and over. (Since the Second World War no horse younger than eight or older than 12 has won the National.) Five-year-olds may still run in the Cheltenham Gold Cup, but none has won it since **Golden Miller** (1932), shortly preceded by Patron Saint (1928) and Red Splash (1924). Before the war four horses won the Champion Hurdle at four (including the great **Brown Jack** in 1928), but in the post-war period the youngest winners have been five – most recently **See You Then** in 1985.

The oldest horse to win a Group One race on the Flat in Europe since the **Pattern** was introduced in 1971 is My Best Valentine, eight when landing the Prix de l'Abbaye at Longchamp in 1998.

There is no record of a horse in Britain winning a race at older than 18, and of those who have scored at that venerable age special mention must be made of Wild Aster, who in 1919, in his nineteenth year, won three hurdle races in the space of a week. More familiar to current racing fans is the memory of Sonny Somers, a grand old chaser trained by Fred Winter who won twice in 1980 at 18.

The oldest horse to have taken part in a race in Britain is Creggmore Boy, who ran in the Furness Selling Handicap Chase at Cartmel in June 1962 at the age of 22: he finished fourth.

Thoroughbreds can live to about 30 – **Hyperion** was still active at stud at that age, and Gunner B, sire of 2001 Grand National winner Red Marauder, was still covering mares at the age of 28. Some last even longer. The Australian gelding Tango Duke is reported to have been 42 on his death in 1978.

AGED

Term, rarely used nowadays, denoting a horse over six years old.

AINTREE

Ormskirk Road, Aintree, Liverpool L9 5AS
Tel.: 0151 523 2600; fax: 0151 522 2920
E-mail: aintree@rht.net
Web: www.aintree.co.uk

The most familiar of all racecourses, its landmarks – **Becher's Brook**, the Chair, Valentine's Brook, the Melling Road, the Elbow – are known to millions outside racing whose experience of the sport extends no further than one race: the **Grand National**.

There are two distinct circuits, both left-handed. The Grand National course is two and a quarter miles round, the longest circuit of any British track, and completely flat. The National is the highlight of the three-day Aintree festival meeting in early April, and the same course is used for big races on each of the other days: the John Hughes Trophy (commemorating one of the great clerks of the course) over two and three-quarter miles, and the Fox Hunters' Chase over the same distance for hunter–chasers. Several other important races are run at this very high-quality meeting, including the Martell Cup, the Melling Chase and the Aintree Hurdle. These three races are all run on the Mildmay Course, at one and a half miles round much sharper than the National circuit. The final two bends are tight, and horses tend to go very fast round here, making it a course for the fast, nippy type, whereas the National course very much favours the galloper – and the Grand National itself demands bold, accurate jumping and buckets of stamina besides.

On the Mildmay Course the steeplechase fences are constructed in the orthodox way from birch, while on the Grand National course they are built from thorn dressed with spruce.

In 1992 the November meeting, which had been abandoned some years previously, was revived: the major race at that meeting is the Becher Handicap Chase, run over three miles three furlongs of the National course; it starts by the Canal Turn, and Valentine's Brook is the first fence.

There was racing in the Liverpool area in the sixteenth century, though the contest which became the Grand National did not begin life until the 1830s. Since the Second World War Aintree has had its ups and downs, and great uncertainty over the course's future during changes of ownership in the 1960s and 1970s led to the gradual dilapidation of facilities: it was ironic that the greatest National performance of modern times, that of **Crisp** in 1973, came in a running of the race which many expected to be the last. But in 1975 Ladbrokes came to the rescue and started rapidly to shake things up. Flat racing, latterly a very dismal affair at the course, was dropped after the meeting in April 1976, and Ladbrokes continued to make improvements during their seven-year lease, which lasted until 1982, when a public appeal was launched. Eventually the course reached the safe haven of ownership by the Jockey Club, and is now under the umbrella of **Racecourse Holdings Trust**.

From those dark days when it seemed odds-on that the historic Grand National course would disappear into the hands of property developers, Aintree has staged a remarkable recovery, and the Grand National Festival is now the biggest fixture of the British jumping year after Cheltenham. The Queen Mother Stand was opened in 1991 alongside the old and elegant County Stand, and the Princess Royal Stand, replacing the old grandstand, in 1998.

ALDANITI
See **Bob Champion**.

ALEXANDRA PARK
The only racecourse within the confines of Greater London when it was closed down in 1970, since when it has been followed into oblivion by Wye – in Kent – (1974), Lanark (1977) and Teesside Park (1981). 'Ally Pally' was highly popular with the local crowd, but a fixture list heavy with evening meetings did not suit the levy-hungry racing world of the 1960s (when betting shops were not open in the evening), and the course's fortunes shrivelled to the point where sport could no longer be sustained there. The track itself, a large circle off which ran a spur to form the home straight (hence its nickname 'The Frying Pan'), cried out for specialists, and horses such as Induna, Cantab and Cider Apple were a familiar sight here. Races were run over just three distances: five furlongs (a dog-leg course with the start on another spur off the circle), one mile 160 yards (start in front of the stands, go round the circle and come back) and one mile five furlongs (ditto, but go round the circle a second time and *then* come back). You can still see the outline of the track, and John McCririck, like so many Londoners of a certain age, waxes all sentimental over the place:

I've told the Booby that when I die, there's to be no period of national mourning. No state funeral, or 69-gun salute. The nation, in its grief, mustn't come to a standstill. I know very well there's a space allotted for me in Westminster Abbey. A stonemason is already sculpting my monument. But I'll have none of this. The Booby understands that I'm to be cremated, and the ashes scattered where the furlong pole used to stand at Alexandra Park.

ALLEGED
Trained in Ireland by **Vincent O'Brien** and co-owned by **Robert Sangster**, the American-bred Alleged was defeated only once in 10 races, his big-race victories including back-to-back wins in the Prix de l'Arc de Triomphe in 1977 and 1978. After winning on his single outing as a two-year-old in 1976, Alleged won his first four races at three (including the Royal Whip at The Curragh at 33–1 and a runaway victory in the Great Voltigeur Stakes at York) before meeting his sole defeat at the hands of the Queen's great filly Dunfermline after a memorable home-straight duel for the St Leger. He picked up the winning thread by landing the 1977 Arc from Balmerino under an inspired front-running ride by **Lester Piggott**, then ran just three times as a four-year-old, easily winning the Royal Whip at The Curragh and the Prix du Prince d'Orange before becoming the first horse since Ribot in 1956 to score an Arc repeat, cruising home under another confident Piggott ride to win from Trillion and Dancing Maid. Alleged returned to the USA to stand as a stallion at a valuation of $16 million. His progeny included dual Classic-winning filly Midway Lady and 1985 Irish Derby winner Law Society. He died in June 2000 at the age of 26.

ALLEZ FRANCE

Owned by **Daniel Wildenstein** and trained by Albert Klimscha and then Angel Penna, this great French racemare was wildly popular in her adopted land, though strictly speaking she was a native of the USA, where she was bred. The best ever offspring of the great 1965 Derby winner Sea Bird II, she notched up 13 victories from 21 races between 1972 and 1975, eight of them Group One: two out of two as a two-year-old; three as a three-year-old, including the Poule d'Essai des Pouliches, Prix de Diane and Prix Vermeille (as well as finishing runner-up to Rheingold in the Arc); five out of five as a four-year-old in 1974, including the Prix Ganay and Arc (beating Comtesse de Loir by a head); and another three (including a second Ganay) as a five-year-old. She was second in the Champion Stakes on both occasions she ran in England: to Hurry Harriet in 1973 and to Rose Bowl in 1975. Allez France was put down at the age of 19 in December 1989 following an accident at stud in Kentucky.

ALLOWANCE

A deduction in the weight a horse is set to carry in a race – on the grounds, for example, of being a filly or mare (fillies are 'allowed' 5lb from colts in the Derby), or being a **maiden**, or being ridden by an **apprentice** or **conditional** jockey: the rider can claim a weight allowance depending on how many winners he or she has ridden.

ALL-WEATHER RACING

Although the term 'all-weather' comes in for a good deal of stick whenever meetings on artificial surfaces are cancelled for reasons relating to the climate, racing on substances other than turf has made a big impact on horse racing in Great Britain – and although nobody pretends that all-weather racing is very high up the scale of Turf glamour, form shrewdies are well aware that with some horses all-weather form stands up remarkably well, and have profited accordingly.

All-weather racing in Britain crept upon a mostly indifferent racing public when Niklas Angel won the William Hill Claiming Stakes at Lingfield Park on 30 October 1989. The following day saw the first all-weather fixture at Southwell, and four years later the two pioneer courses were joined by Wolverhampton: the first fixture there on 27 December 1993 included two races under floodlights, the first illuminated horse races in Britain.

While racing on artificial surfaces has long been a feature of the sport overseas, there had been resistance to the notion in Britain. But in the early 1980s there was increasing concern – especially in the betting industry – about the number of fixtures being lost to adverse weather in the depths of winter: no racing meant significantly less business in betting shops, and turnover took a dive. January and February 1985 saw no fewer than seventy-two days' scheduled racing lost to the climate, and the Jockey Club launched an investigation into the feasibility of a limited amount of all-weather sport. In November 1985 the go-ahead was given, and the carefully laid plans came to fruition at Lingfield Park at eleven o'clock on a Monday morning nearly four years later.

Attempts at all-weather jump racing were short-lived. Jockeys disliked the lack of 'give' in the surface, which could make falls – for horses and riders alike – more painful and more serious than the same accidents would have been on turf. Adverse publicity was attracted by a spate of equine deaths on all-weather tracks, and all-weather jumping was suspended in February 1994. It never came back.

Racing surfaces on the three all-weather tracks are made from compounds of specially graded sand stabilized with synthetic fibres: Lingfield Park is replacing its Equitrack with Polytrack, while Southwell and Wolverhampton use Fibresand.

ALSO RAN

A horse not placed in a race (that is, not in the first three or four) is described as 'also ran' – from the heading under which some newspapers list such horses.

ALYCIDON

Owned by Lord Derby and trained by Walter Earl, Alycidon was the finest stayer of the late

1940s in Britain, winning 11 of his 17 races – including the Princess of Wales's Stakes and Jockey Club Stakes as a three-year-old in 1948 – and going through his four-year-old career in 1949 unbeaten in five outings, including the Ormonde Stakes, Ascot Gold Cup (which he won by five lengths from Black Tarquin, who had beaten him in the 1948 St Leger), Goodwood Cup and Doncaster Cup. Among his offspring were Alcide, winner of the 1958 St Leger and 1959 King George VI and Queen Elizabeth Stakes, and the great filly Meld, who landed the One Thousand Guineas, Oaks and St Leger in 1955. He died in 1972.

ALYDAR

The only horse in history to come second in all three legs of the American Triple Crown – beaten one and a half lengths in the Kentucky Derby, a neck in the Preakness and a head in the Belmont Stakes, behind **Affirmed** every time. After a career in which he won 14 of his 26 races, Alydar became a very successful stallion – significantly more successful than his great rival – and sired such horses as Alysheba (winner of the 1987 Kentucky Derby and Preakness), Easy Goer (1989 Belmont Stakes winner and runner-up to Sunday Silence in a famous Breeders' Cup Classic the same year), Alydaress (1989 Irish Oaks) and Cacoethes (third to Nashwan in 1989 Derby and narrowly beaten by the same horse in that year's King George). He was put down in November 1990.

ALY KHAN

Son of the 'old' Aga Khan who owned Derby winners Blenheim, Bahram, Mahmoud, My Love and Tulyar, Prince Aly Khan owned the winners of three English Classics, all in 1959. His best colt was Two Thousand Guineas winner Taboun, but he will be most remembered as owner of the great filly **Petite Etoile**, winner of 14 races including the One Thousand Guineas and Oaks. He was killed in a car crash near Paris in May 1960, a few days before Petite Etoile won the first of her two Coronation Cups. A darling of the gossip columns, Aly Khan was for a while married to the film actress Rita Hayworth, following the break-up of his first marriage to the Hon. Mrs Loel Guinness, mother of his son Karim, the present **Aga Khan**.

AMATEUR JOCKEYS

Riders who take part in races without receiving a fee (distinguishable by being labelled 'Mr', 'Mrs' or 'Miss' as appropriate in the list of jockeys in a race), are an integral part of the jump racing scene, and a rarer feature on the Flat. There are two categories of licensed amateur riders. Category A amateur riders may ride in any Flat or National Hunt race confined to amateur riders, while category B riders may ride against licensed professional jockeys under National Hunt Rules. (On the Flat there are no races – other than novelty events – in which amateurs may ride against professionals.) Many top jump jockeys have begun their riding careers as amateurs. Channel Four Racing's own **John Oaksey** was a notable amateur rider – champion amateur over jumps in the 1957–8 and 1970–71 seasons – but failed by just three-quarters of a length to land the greatest jumping prize of all when Carrickbeg was caught on the line by Ayala in the 1963 Grand National. Despite that reverse, John (who rode as John Lawrence before succeeding to his father's title) proved that the best amateurs can land the big races, winning the 1958 Whitbread and Hennessy Gold Cups on Taxidermist.

Since the Second World War the Grand National has been won by amateur jockeys five times (Captain Bobby Petre on Lovely Cottage in 1946, Tommy Smith on Jay Trump in 1965, Charlie Fenwick on Ben Nevis in 1980, Dick Saunders on Grittar in 1982 and Marcus Armytage on Mr Frisk in 1990); the Cheltenham Gold Cup twice (Dick Black on Fortina in 1947 and Jim Wilson on Little Owl in 1981); and the Champion Hurdle also twice (Alan Lillingston on Winning Fair in 1963 and Colin Magnier on For Auction in 1982).

On the Flat the amateur race with the highest profile is the Moët & Chandon

Silver Magnum, run over the full Derby course at Epsom on August Bank Holiday Monday. The race, first held in 1963 and known as 'The Amateurs' Derby' ever since, has been won by some notable horses (including **Sea Pigeon** in 1978) and notable riders (including John Oaksey four times, Philip Mitchell four times, Bill O'Gorman, Nick Gaselee, **Dermot Weld** and **Luca Cumani**).

AMISS

A term used to describe the condition of a mare in season.

AMRULLAH

Legendary loser who failed to win in 74 outings on the Flat, over hurdles and over fences. He first ran in a two-year-old maiden race at Newmarket in October 1982, when he was unplaced behind Tolomeo (who went on to win the Arlington Million in 1983), and last ran in a novices' chase at Fontwell Park in March 1992. An 80,000 guineas yearling trained initially by **Guy Harwood**, then briefly by **Peter Easterby** and for most of his career by John Bridger, he was placed often enough in good-class company to earn over £26,000 in prize money, but he just would not stir himself enough to win (the closest he came was defeat by a neck). Towards the end of his career he became something of a racing celebrity for the wrong reasons, but **Timeform** failed to see the joke, awarding him the dreaded 'double squiggle' as a mark of incorrigible unreliability and sniffily branding him 'thoroughly irresolute'. The announcement of his retirement from action (if that is quite the right word) was the subject of the 'And Finally . . . ' section of *News At Ten*.

ANGLO-IRISH JUMPS CLASSIFICATIONS

Jumping equivalent of the International Classifications, first published in 2000. Classifications are categorised under chasing or hurdling by distance range: thus in the 2001 rankings First Gold headed the three-mile chasers, Istabraq the two-mile hurdlers.

ANTE-POST BETTING

Betting well in advance of the event. Most of the big races of the calendar produce a lively ante-post market, with races such as the Derby attracting business months – or even years – in advance. In the *Channel Four Racing Guide to Form and Betting*, John McCririck has a few hints about ante-post betting:

- *Be wary of a long-distance ante-post punt on a horse whose chances might be diminished by extremes of going: you cannot tell far in advance that he'll have conditions in his favour on the day.*
- *Be careful about serious ante-post betting in a race where the draw is known to be a significant factor, such as the Lincoln Handicap or the Ayr Gold Cup.*
- *The more inside knowledge you have about running plans the better. Be as sure as you can be that the horse is actually being aimed at the race in question.*
- *Remember that wisest of old betting sayings: 'You can't go skint taking a profit.' If the horse you've backed ante-post at 50–1 shortens to 6–4 favourite, you could theoretically lay that horse at 2–1 yourself and be guaranteed a profit. Theoretically – but not legally, unless you have a bookmaker's licence. When you find yourself the happy possessor of a 50–1 voucher about a 6–4 chance, make the most of it by backing other horses in the race.*
- *Don't throw away your voucher as soon as the horse is withdrawn. If the race is abandoned (and even the Derby was threatened in 1983), all ante-post bets are refunded.*

ANY TO COME

Betting term indicating that all or part of the returns from one bet are to be reinvested on another: for example, '£10 win Bacchanal, any to come £5 win First Gold' involves an initial stake of £10 on Bacchanal, with the subsequent and separate bet being struck on First Gold only if there are sufficient returns from that first bet.

APPRENTICE JOCKEY

Young jockey on the Flat tied by annually renewed contract to a licensed trainer, under whose guidance he or she learns race riding. An apprentice cannot ride in a race until he or she has reached 16 years of age, and cannot remain an apprentice beyond the age of 24. When the race conditions so stipulate, an apprentice may claim an **allowance** of 7lb until he or she has ridden the winners of 10 races, 5lb up to 50 winners, and 3lb up to 75 winners. Naturally it is unusual for such inexperienced jockeys to ride winners of the biggest races, but it does happen. The last English Classic winner to be ridden by an apprentice was Time Charter in the 1982 Oaks, partnered by Billy Newnes. Jamie

Spencer was still an apprentice in Ireland when he won the 1998 Irish One Thousand Guineas on Tarascon. (In jump racing the equivalent of the apprentice is the **conditional jockey**.)

AQUEDUCT

Racecourse in the Queens borough of New York City. The Breeders' Cup was run at the track in 1985 (the second staging of the Cup), when Pebbles won the Turf to become the first British-trained winner of a Breeders' Cup race.

ARAZI

'If there is a third certainty after death and taxes,' wrote Geoff Lester in the *Sporting Life* on 2 May 1992 when looking forward to that day's big race in the USA, 'it is that Arazi will win the 118th Kentucky Derby at Churchill Downs.' He didn't, but before the race you could see Lester's point. Owned by American aerospace magnate Allen Paulson and trained in France by **François Boutin**, Arazi had blazed a meteoric trail as a juvenile in 1991. After finishing runner-up on his debut, he won six races off the reel in France, including the Prix Robert Papin, Prix Morny, Prix de la Salamandre and Grand Criterium. After his facile win in the Criterium a half-share in the horse was sold to Sheikh Mohammed, but Paulson's colours were still carried by Arazi in his final outing, the Breeders' Cup Juvenile at Churchill Downs, against the best two-year-olds in the USA. That day Arazi turned in a performance which almost defied belief. Ridden by Pat Valenzuela and drawn on the outside, he was second last at the first turn, by the stands, and as the field swung into the back stretch seemed to be disliking the American experience intensely. But halfway down the back straight Arazi was suddenly transformed, weaving his way from the outside to the inner, slaloming past rival after rival until at the top of the home turn he had only the top US two-year-old Bertrando to beat. Swinging wide into the straight, Arazi swept past Bertrando and barrelled up the home stretch to put more and more distance between himself and his

Champion apprentices since 1975		
Year	Jockey	Wins
1975	A. Bond	66
1976	D. Dineley	54
1977	J. Bleasdale	67
1978	K. Darley	70
1979	Philip Robinson	51
1980	Philip Robinson	59
1981	B. Crossley	45
1982	W. Newnes	57
1983	M. Hills	39
1984	T. Quinn	62
1985	G. Carter and W. Ryan	37
1986	G. Carter	34
1987	G. Bardwell	27
1988	G. Bardwell	39
1989	L. Dettori	75
1990	J. Fortune	46
1991	D. Holland	79
1992	D. Harrison	56
1993	D. Harrison	40
1994	S. Davies	45
1995	S. Sanders	61
1996	D. O'Neill	79
1997	R. Ffrench	77
1998	C. Lowther	72
1999	R. Winston	49
2000	L. Newman	63

toiling rivals. His official winning distance was five lengths, but it was the manner of the performance which put Arazi's Breeders' Cup Juvenile into the list of all-time great races. Future possibilities looked limitless, but Arazi's three-year-old career was a deep disappointment. After winning easily on his reappearance at Saint-Cloud, he returned to Churchill Downs for the Kentucky Derby but could finish only eighth behind Lil E Tee after looking poised to win at the home turn. He ran three more times in Europe, winning just once (the Prix du Rond-Point at Longchamp) before travelling to Gulfstream Park for the Breeders' Cup Mile, finishing eleventh behind Lure. He was then retired to the Dalham Hall Stud in Newmarket, from where he was exported to Japan.

ARCHER, FRED

Born in 1857 very near the present site of Cheltenham racecourse, Fred Archer rode 2,748 winners on the Flat from the 8,084 races in which he rode – a strike rate better than one in three – in a famous career which began in 1869 (when he rode his first winner in a steeplechase at Bangor-on-Dee at the age of 12, weighing out at 4st 11lb) and ended tragically with his suicide at the age of 29 in 1886. Champion jockey 13 times (for 13 successive years between 1874 and 1886), he rode the winners of 21 Classics, including the Derby five times – on Silvio (1877), **Bend Or** (1880, riding with one arm all but useless, having been savaged by a horse less than a month before), Iroquois (1881), Melton (1885) and **Ormonde** (1886). A notoriously ruthless rider who once put his own brother over the rails during a race, he fought a constant battle with the scales, aided by a notoriously strong purgative known as 'Archer's mixture': 'I tried it myself when I was riding races,' recalled trainer George Lambton, 'and from my own experience I should say it was made of dynamite.' In October 1886 Archer wasted fiercely to ride St Mirin in the Cambridgeshire, put up 1lb overweight and was beaten a head. The wasting had brought on a fever, but he carried on riding, visiting Lewes for what

proved to be his final ride, and then returned to Newmarket, where on 8 November 1886 he shot himself in a fit of depression and delirium.

ARGENTINA

Minor in world racing terms but the principal racing nation in South America, Argentina has produced one very famous horse in the shape of Forli, who after a glittering three-year-old career in his native land in 1966 was sold to the USA, where he made his mark on the track before standing at stud at Claiborne Farm in Kentucky. His offspring included Forego (American champion racehorse in 1974, 1975 and 1976), Thatch and Home Guard. The two principal racecourses in Argentina are both in Buenos Aires: Palermo and San Isidro.

ARKLE

Three times Cheltenham Gold Cup winner, widely considered the greatest chaser ever, Arkle was a freak. The bare facts of his career – winner of 22 of his 26 steeplechases, including the Cheltenham Gold Cup in 1964, 1965 and 1966, the Hennessy Gold Cup in 1964 and 1965, the Whitbread Gold Cup and King George VI Chase in 1965, the Irish National in 1964 – tell only part of the story. For Arkle was so transcendentally good that the rules of handicapping in Ireland had to be changed to allow for his superiority, with one set of weights framed to include 'Himself' (as he was widely known in his home country), another to be applied when he wasn't running.

By Archive out of Bright Cherry, Arkle was bred in modest circumstances and foaled in 1957 in Co. Dublin. He was bought by **Anne, Duchess of Westminster** at public auction as a three-year-old for 1,150 guineas and put into training with **Tom Dreaper**. In his first two outings in December 1961 (both amateur riders' races on the Flat) he was beaten; then, in a novice hurdle at Navan in January 1962, he scored at 20–1, prompting Dreaper to remark to his wife Betty as they came down from the stands, in one of racing's great understatements: 'Do you know, I think we've got something there!'

Some inkling of exactly what they had got soon began to emerge. After three more wins over hurdles Arkle was sent across to Cheltenham for his debut over fences. He won it – and everything else he took part in for the remainder of the 1962-3 season.

This was clearly an exceptional young horse; but so too was his exact contemporary **Mill House** – Irish-bred like Arkle, but trained in Lambourn by **Fulke Walwyn** – who at just six years of age had scored a precocious victory in the 1963 Cheltenham Gold Cup. The rivalry between these two great horses made the mid-1960s a golden age of British steeplechasing. Their first meeting, in the 1963 Hennessy Gold Cup at Newbury, saw Arkle lose his chance when slipping after the final ditch; Mill House powered home to an easy victory, with Arkle only third. Thus the scene was set for the famous Cheltenham Gold Cup in March 1964, perhaps the most keenly anticipated horse race since the Second World War. Mill House was favourite at 13–8 on, with Arkle at 7–4, while the only other runners, King's Nephew and Pas Seul, were priced at 20–1 and 50–1 respectively. By the second circuit the big two had the race to themselves; then, on the run to the last, Arkle – ridden as in all his chases by **Pat Taaffe** – cruised into the lead and charged up the hill to win by five lengths.

When the pair met again in the following autumn's Hennessy Gold Cup, Arkle had it all his own way, sweeping imperiously to victory while Mill House crumpled to finish only fourth. A week later the champion delivered one of his greatest performances in the Massey-Ferguson Gold Cup at Cheltenham (now the Tripleprint Gold Cup), failing only narrowly, under the crushing burden of 12st 10lb, to pin back two very high-class and lightly weighted horses, Flying Wild and Buona Notte. Undaunted, he went on through that season to win the Leopardstown Chase in Ireland, a second Cheltenham Gold Cup from Mill House, and the Whitbread under 12st 7lb.

Perhaps his greatest race of all came in November 1965, in the Gallaher Gold Cup at Sandown Park. This was the fifth time he and Mill House had raced against each other, and this time Arkle displayed stunning acceleration on the final turn to surge past his rival (who was eventually passed by Rondetto to finish third), to whom he was conceding 16lb, and go on to win in a time which beat the course record by 17 seconds.

Arkle looked invincible. He won the Hennessy again, the King George VI Chase (the running in which the great two-mile chaser Dunkirk was killed), the Leopardstown Chase and a third Gold Cup. He had amassed a huge popular following, drew vast crowds every time he raced, was deluged with fan mail (some addressed simply to 'Arkle, Ireland') and even had a song recorded about him by Dominic Behan. And he was still only nine years old.

But, though no one knew it as the 1966–7 season opened, there were to be only three more races. First time out, in the Hennessy, Arkle was beaten half a length by Stalbridge Colonist, to whom he was conceding 35lb. Victory in the SGB Chase at Ascot re-established the normal state of affairs, and the 1966 King George was widely seen as a formality: his starting price at Kempton was 9–2 on. Here disaster struck. Leading over the last, Arkle was passed on the run-in by Dormant, a horse whom in the normal course of events he could have picked up and carried. The reason for this sensational outcome was not far to seek: Arkle was badly lame and could scarcely hobble into the unsaddling enclosure. He had cracked the pedal bone in his off-fore hoof, and would never race again.

Arkle retired to the Duchess of Westminster's Irish home, Bryanstown, where he remained until, stiffness in the joints causing him increasing discomfort, on 31 May 1970 he was put down. He was 13. On his death John Oaksey wrote in *Horse and Hound*: 'Now he is gone and we must search for others to warm our blood on winter afternoons, to fill the stands and set the crowds on fire. No doubt we shall find them – but they will be pale shadows of the real thing. For those who saw Arkle will never forget the sight and, until they see another like him, will never believe that two such miracles can happen in a lifetime.'

Arkle's skeleton can be seen in the Irish Horse Museum at the **Irish National Stud**.

ARLINGTON MILLION

First run in 1981, this 10-furlong event at Arlington Park, Chicago, enjoyed a very high status as an international race until the increasing importance of the **Breeders' Cup** (inaugurated 1984) seemed to push it from the limelight. None the less, the roll of honour contains one of the all-time greats – the American horse **John Henry**, who won the inaugural running by a nose from The Bart in 1981 (with Lester Piggott-ridden Madam Gay third), and staged a repeat three years later when beating Royal Heroine in 1984. In 1983 John Henry was beaten a neck by Tolomeo, trained in Newmarket by **Luca Cumani** and ridden by **Pat Eddery**, whose starting price of a shade over 38–1 long stood as an irrefutable argument for taking the local odds when backing British horses overseas: British bookmakers had the horse as low as 6–1. In 1985 the Arlington Million saw another famous victory for a British raider when Teleprompter – owned by Lord Derby, trained by Bill Watts and ridden by Tony Ives – became the first English-trained gelding to win a Group One or Grade One race anywhere in the world. Teleprompter's win was all the more remarkable as it came less than a month after a fire had destroyed the Arlington Park grandstand. The Arlington Million forms one leg of the **Emirates World Series**.

ASCOT

Ascot, Berkshire SL5 7JN
Tel.: 01344 622211; fax: 01344 628299
E-mail: enquiries@ascot.co.uk
Web: www.ascot.co.uk

Early in 1711 Queen Anne, the ample-girthed 46-year-old monarch, was taking a carriage ride through the forest near Windsor Castle when she came upon a large clearing. Immediately registering that this was the ideal place to indulge her love of equestrian sport (though she was by then too stout to follow the family tradition and ride in races herself), she ordered the clearing to be prepared for horse racing, and the next time the court was in Windsor that summer, racing at Ascot was under way – with 'Her Majesty's Plate of 100 guineas' on 11 August 1711. Today the founder of the course is commemorated in the opening race of the Royal Meeting: the Queen Anne Stakes.

From that beginning, Ascot developed through the eighteenth century into one of the major racing venues in the land, and the Royal Meeting into one of the great social occasions of the year. George IV instituted the tradition of the carriage procession up the course in 1825.

Gold Cup day – 'Ladies' Day' – remains the social pinnacle of Royal Ascot, but for racing purists the key events of the meeting are the other three Group One races: the **St James's Palace Stakes** for three-year-old colts over the round mile (known at Ascot as the 'Old Mile') on the Tuesday; the **Prince of Wales's Stakes** over a mile and a quarter on the Wednesday; and the **Coronation Stakes** for three-year-old fillies on the Friday.

But the great appeal of Royal Ascot as a race meeting is the overall quality of the fare, with those four Group One events taking their place alongside many other major races:

- the Royal Hunt Cup (straight mile) and Wokingham Stakes (six furlongs), highly competitive handicaps which form the major betting mediums of the week;
- high-class sprint races in the King's Stand Stakes (five furlongs) and Cork and Orrery Stakes (six furlongs);
- major two-year-old races such as the Coventry Stakes (six furlongs) and, for fillies, the Queen Mary Stakes (five furlongs);
- major middle-distance races for three-year-olds over a mile and a half: the King Edward VII Stakes (colts and geldings) and Ribblesdale Stakes (fillies);
- Hardwicke Stakes (one and a half miles) for four-year-olds and upwards aspiring to the top rank of middle-distance horses.

Quality is the watchword for the rest of the Ascot year too. The **King George VI and Queen Elizabeth Diamond Stakes**, run over one and a half miles in late July, is arguably – whatever may be claimed of the Derby – the single most important Flat race of the year in this country, attracting the top horses from different generations and invariably an event of the highest class. The other two Group One races at Ascot are both run over the Old Mile at the Ascot Festival in late September: the **Queen Elizabeth II Stakes** for three-year-olds and upwards, and the **Fillies' Mile** for two-year-old fillies. The September meeting also has the Royal Lodge Stakes (Group Two) over the round mile for staying two-year-olds.

National Hunt racing at Ascot began in April 1965, the new track having received a turf transplant from Hurst Park, which had closed down in 1962. For some racegoers jump racing here lacks immediacy and the true excitement of the winter game at its best, as the chase and hurdles courses are inside the Flat track, and thus somewhat remote from the stands: jumping at Ascot has been famously described as 'like Blackpool with the tide out'. But, as on the Flat, the standard of racing is very high. Principal events include the Victor Chandler Chase (two miles) in January; the Ascot Chase (two miles three and a half furlongs) in February; the First National Gold Cup (two miles three and a half furlongs) in November; and the Tote Silver Cup Chase (three miles and half a furlong) in December. The last-named began life in 1965 as the SGB Chase, and under that name the following year was the last race ever won by **Arkle**.

The reason why Ascot attracts such quality under both codes lies in the nature of the course itself, a wide track with good sweeping bends. The circuit is in the shape of a right-handed triangle about a mile and six furlongs round, on to which runs the straight mile (on which all races shorter than a mile are run); the Old Mile starts on a spur and takes in one bend into the home straight. The run from the home turn is less than three furlongs, and Ascot is no course for a jockey to be well off the pace turning in – as plenty have found to their cost.

From the long bend beyond the winning post, the round course has a gentle uphill rise and then sweeps downhill, which makes this a particularly telling part of the course for steeplechasers, who on that stretch have to negotiate two plain fences and a very trappy open ditch before the ground levels out approaching the water jump. At the end of that straight the runners reach Swinley Bottom, where the course sweeps round to join the Old Mile and make a steadily uphill run. The ground levels out at the home turn, then rises towards the winning post before falling shortly before the line. The straight mile begins slightly downhill then undulates gently until joining the round course.

Brough Scott rode his last winner under Rules at Ascot: Kitaab in the Shadwell Estates Private Handicap on 25 September 1992. It was Brough's first winner for twenty-one years. John Oaksey finished fourth on Kabayil in the same race, his last ride under Rules in Britain: 'As we turned into the straight I looked up and the winning post appeared to be about four miles away. I realised then it was time to hang up my riding boots.'

Despite that short home straight, Ascot is very much a course for the galloping type, for there are no sudden gradients to unbalance a horse. When the ground is heavy Ascot puts a strong emphasis on stamina, and in any conditions it is a track where the horse needs to get the trip well.

Ambitious plans are afoot to transform Ascot, with new stands and a new alignment of the course due over the next few years. What will not change is the sheer quality which characterises both the place and the horses who grace its famous turf.

ASCOT GOLD CUP

Group One: four-year-olds and over:
2½ miles (Royal Ascot)

In terms of racing quality the Gold Cup, the longest Group One race of the Flat season in Britain, is no longer the foremost race of the Royal Meeting – the St James's Palace Stakes, Coronation Stakes and Prince of Wales's

Ascot Gold Cup winners since 1990

1990	Ashal	4	H. Thomson Jones	R. Hills	14–1	11
1991	Indian Queen	6	Lord Huntingdon	W. R. Swinburn	25–1	12
1992	Drum Taps	6	Lord Huntingdon	L. Dettori	7–4F	6
1993	Drum Taps	7	Lord Huntingdon	L. Dettori	13–2	10
1994	Arcadian Heights	6	G. Wragg	M. Hills	20–1	9
1995	Double Trigger	4	M. Johnston	J. Weaver	9–4	7
1996	Classic Cliché	4	S. bin Suroor	M. Kinane	3–1	7
1997	Celeric	5	D. Morley	Pat Eddery	11–2	13
1998	Kayf Tara	4	S. bin Suroor	L. Dettori	11–1	16
1999	Enzeli	4	J. Oxx *IRE*	J. Murtagh	20–1	17
2000	Kayf Tara	6	S. bin Suroor	M. Kinane	11–8F	11
2001	Royal Rebel	5	M. Johnston	J. Murtagh	8–1	12

Stakes, the fixture's other Group One events, are richer in terms of the class of horse competing – but for socialites and dedicated followers of fashion Gold Cup Day remains the high point of the meeting: Ladies' Day.

The Gold Cup itself began its long and distinguished history with the victory of three-year-old Master Jacky in 1807 and soon became one of the classiest races in the calendar: in 1829, for example, the field included two Derby winners, an Oaks winner, a St Leger winner and the previous year's Gold Cup winner. From 1845 until 1853 the race was run as The Emperor's Plate to acknowledge the annual donation of £500 prize money by Emperor Nicholas I of Russia, but that arrangement was brought to an abrupt halt by the Crimean War, and in 1854 it was the Ascot Gold Cup again – won by the first Triple Crown winner, West Australian. Before the end of the century two other Triple Crown winners had gone on to win the Gold Cup – **Gladiateur** in 1866 and Isinglass as a five-year-old in 1895 – and other famous names to grace the roll of honour in the nineteenth century include **The Flying Dutchman** (1850), **St Simon** (1884) and **Persimmon** (1897).

The first half of the twentieth century produced many historic runnings, including the sensational defeat of **Pretty Polly** by Bachelor's Button in 1906 and perhaps the most famous Gold Cup of all in 1936, when Omaha, winner of the American Triple Crown the previous year, was beaten a short head by 1935 Oaks winner Quashed after a gruelling duel up the straight.

Since the Second World War winners of the Ascot showpiece have included the finest stayers of the age, including dual winners Fighting Charlie (1965 and 1966), Le Moss (1979 and 1980), Ardross (1981 and 1982), Gildoran (1984 and 1985), Sadeem (1989 and 1990), Drum Taps (1992 and 1993) and Kayf Tara (1998 and 2000). (Rock Roi could so easily have been another dual winner, but instead has the deeply unfortunate distinction of having been first past the post in the Gold Cup twice and having lost on both occasions: disqualified for failing the dope test in 1971 and for interfering with second-past-the-post Erimo Hawk in 1972.)

Pride of place in the parade of Gold Cup winners, however, must go to **Sagaro**, the only horse to have won the race three times – in 1975, 1976 and 1977. And on the human front, special homage must be paid to Sagaro's partner **Lester Piggott**, who in all won the Ascot Gold Cup no fewer than 11 times.

ASMUSSEN, CASH

Born Brian Keith Asmussen in Agar, South Dakota, in 1962, Cash Asmussen (in 1977 he formally adopted his nickname given to him by his father) became one of the leading jockeys on the international stage, famed for the coolness with which he rode waiting races – a coolness summed up by his description of being in 'the cat-bird seat' when poised to strike on one the best horses he has ridden, 1991 Prix de l'Arc de Triomphe winner Suave Dancer. To date the only foreigner to become champion jockey in France, he was leading rider there five times: 1985, 1986, 1988, 1989 and 1990. Despite landing big races around the world on such star performers as In The Wings, Soviet Star, April Run, Mairzy Doates (Japan Cup 1981), Kingmambo, Hernando, Dream Well, Spinning World (Breeders' Cup Mile 1997) and **Montjeu**, Cash Asmussen never won an English Classic. In spring 2001 he announced that his riding career was over.

AUCTION RACE

Race on the Flat confined to horses bought as yearlings at public auction: the weights carried reflect the sale price of each runner, with the most expensive carrying the highest weight and the cheapest the lowest. For example, the White Swan Maiden Auction Stakes at Pontefract in October 2000 was restricted to two-year-olds sold or **bought in** as yearlings by public auction, or as two-year-olds at the **Breeze-Up** Sales, for 9,000 guineas or less, with colts and geldings to carry 8st 11lb, fillies 8st 6lb, with 1lb allowed for each 1,000 guineas below 9,000 guineas paid for the horse at the sale: the winner Captain Gibson carried 8st 5lb, having been bought for 3,000 guineas.

See also **median auction race**.

AUSTRALIA

Recent rapid improvements in equine air travel have put Australia well within reach of European horses looking to challenge for the top Antipodean races, but Australia has long been one of the major racing nations, in terms both of domestic racing and of influence on the world scene through the export of bloodstock and of top jockeys.

There are some 500 racecourses in Australia, of which the best known to European racing fans are Flemington and Caulfield in Melbourne, Rosehill and Randwick in Sydney, and Morphettville,

Victoria Park and Cheltenham in Adelaide. The **Melbourne Cup**, run on the first Tuesday of November, is one of the greatest racing occasions in the world.

The most famous Australian racehorse of all time was undoubtedly **Phar Lap**, while trainers Colin Hayes, **Tommy Smith** and Bart Cummings all reached legendary status well beyond their native land.

The influence of Australia in breeding has tended to be felt more in jump racing than on the Flat – for example, the great chaser **Crisp** was Australian-bred – but recently, again thanks to improved conditions of equine air travel, it has become common for some European-based stallions to be transported to the southern hemisphere to carry on their duties down under: such horses have become known as 'shuttle stallions'.

Another area in which Australia has made a distinct mark on world racing is in the succession of top-notch jockeys to come out of that country. **Scobie Breasley**, champion in Britain four times, was the most famous son of Wagga Wagga, while other great Australian riders to have made their mark in Europe in the last half century include Edgar Britt (who won every English Classic except the Derby), Ron Hutchinson, Jack Purtell, Garnie Bougoure (rider of Ragusa and Noblesse), Bill Pyers, **George Moore** (rider of **Royal Palace** and Busted), Pat Glennon (who won the Derby on **Sea Bird II** in 1965), **Bill Williamson** ('Weary Willie'), Neville Sellwood (who won the Derby on Larkspur in 1962), Gary Moore (son of George) and Brent Thomson. The tradition has continued in very recent memory with the riding of Craig Williams, who won his first Group One race in Britain on Tobougg in the Dewhurst Stakes in October 2000.

The system of betting in Australia is unique among the major racing nations of the world: on course the bookmakers compete with the Tote, while off course there is a Tote monopoly.

AUSTRALIAN CHEEKER

A variation on the standard bridle fitted to racehorses, the Australian cheeker is a rubber strip which is attached to the browband, runs down the horse's nose and is connected to the bit to keep it high in the mouth.

AUTEUIL

Racecourse in Paris, principal venue of jump racing in France and home of the Grand Steeple-Chase de Paris (famously won by **Fred Winter** and **Mandarin** in 1962) and the Grande Course de Haies (French equivalent of the Champion Hurdle – the race in which **Dawn Run** was killed in 1986). The obstacles confronting chasers on this very tight figure-of-eight circuit are a far cry from the standard issue in Britain: they include two water jumps, a bank and 'Le Bullfinch' – a rail, ditch and fence on top of a stone wall.

AUTUMN DOUBLE

Traditional name for the two big handicaps run at Newmarket in the autumn – the Cambridgeshire, run over one mile one furlong at Newmarket in early October, and the Cesarewitch, over twice that distance a fortnight later.

AWAY MEETING

For the racegoer, an 'away meeting' is a fixture that day other than than the one you're at.

AYR

Whitletts Road, Ayr KA8 0JE
Tel.: 01292 264179; fax: 01292 610140
E-mail: info@ayr-racecourse.co.uk
Website: www.ayr-racecourse.co.uk

Two events dominate the racing year at Ayr, and they could hardly be more different: the marathon **Scottish Grand National**, a handicap steeplechase run in April as the jumping season enters its final days, and the **Ayr Gold Cup** over six furlongs, with a very large field of bullet-fast handicappers powering down the straight.

The circuit at Ayr is a left-handed oval of about a mile and a half round, with mild undulations but suitable for the long-striding, galloping sort of horse. On the Flat, five- and six-furlong races are straight and start from a spur, and the run from the home turn is half a mile. The hurdle and chase courses are inside the Flat, but similarly favour the long-striding horse.

The facilities at Ayr are excellent – spacious stands, plenty of roomy bars – and the atmosphere friendly; even on the biggest days racegoers do not feel overcrowded. One particularly attractive feature for patrons of the members' enclosure nestles among the trees at the far end of the paddock: Western House, which must be just about the most civilised racecourse building in the country, housing bars and restaurants but with the feel of a large country house.

The only time an English Classic has been run outside England was when the 1989 St Leger was transferred from Doncaster to Ayr after subsidence in the track caused the abandonment of the meeting at the Yorkshire course.

Racing on the current site dates from 1907 – the lovely old grandstand built then remains a feature of the course – though horses were raced at Ayr as long ago as the sixteenth century. Modern developments include a new weighing room, first used in 1995, and the Princess Royal Stand, opened the following year.

AYR GOLD CUP

Handicap; three-year-olds and upwards;
6 furlongs (Ayr)

The Ayr Gold Cup always provides both one of the big betting races and one of the great sights of the Flat season – a huge field of closely handicapped sprinters charging down Ayr's wide, straight six furlongs. But the race we know today is a very far cry from the very first Ayr Gold Cup – run in 1804 in two heats over two miles at the old course at Belleisle, with the stipulation that runners had to be bred and trained in Scotland. The heats format was soon dropped, though the distance of the race remained at two miles.

In 1907 Ayr racecourse moved to its current location, and the following year the Ayr Gold Cup was reconstituted as a six-

Ayr Gold Cup winners since 1990

1990	Final Shot	3	M. H. Easterby	J. Lowe	12–1	29
1991	Sarcita	3	D. Elsworth	B. Doyle	14–1	28
1992	Lochsong	4	I. Balding	F. Arrowsmith	10–1	28
1993	Hard To Figure	7	R. Hodges	R. Cochrane	12–1	29
1994	Daring Destiny	3	K. Burke	J. Tate	18–1	29
1995	Royal Figurine	4	M. Fetherston-Godley	D. Holland	8–1	29
1996	Coastal Bluff	4	D. Barron	J. Fortune	3–1F	28
1997	Wildwood Flower	4	R. Hannon	Dane O'Neill	14–1	29
1998	Always Alight	4	K. Burke	J. Egan	16–1	29
1999	Grangeville	4	I. Balding	K. Fallon	11–1	28
2000	Bahamian Pirate	5	D. Nicholls	A. Nicholls	33–1	28

furlong handicap – in which guise it has been won by many of the biggest names of the sprinting division.

The 1967 running produced the largest field in the history of the race – 33 runners – and one of the very best winners in the shape of **Peter O'Sullevan**'s great chestnut sprinter Be Friendly, then a three-year-old whose credentials included victory in the King's Stand Stakes at Royal Ascot: ridden by Geoff Lewis, Be Friendly started at 100–8 and scored by an easy two lengths. He went on to win many more big races (including the Prix de l'Abbaye and the first two runnings of the **Sprint Cup** at Haydock).

But perhaps the greatest of all Ayr Gold Cups came in 1975, when the gigantic Roman Warrior, trained locally by Nigel Angus, carried the mammoth burden of 10st and after a tremendous battle on the far side of the track wore down the favourite Lochnager – while Stewards' Cup winner Import was finishing well clear on the stands side. As Import and Roman Warrior scorched across the line separated by the width of the track it was impossible to know which had won, but the photograph delivered the verdict: Roman Warrior by a short head. No wonder Timeform described Roman Warrior as 'a colossus of a horse with a heart to match'.

If Roman Warrior was a colossus, the no less adored **Lochsong** was the incarnation of racing speed, and her Ayr Gold Cup win as a four-year-old in 1992 brought the flying filly a unique handicap treble, adding the Ayr race to victory in the Stewards' Cup and Portland Handicap. Showing that characteristically uncompromising style of racing which was soon to make her one of the most popular racehorses of the modern era, she broke smartly and looked in little danger of being beaten, winning by two lengths from Echo-Logical.

Other great sprinters to have won the Ayr Gold Cup include Blue Cashmere, sent out to score in 1973 by a youthful trainer named **Michael Stoute**; another Stoute stalwart in Vaigly Great, who in 1978 defied 9st 6lb to win as a three-year-old; and the indestructible grey Hard To Figure, who became the oldest horse to win since the war when landing the 1992 renewal at the age of seven, and in all ran in the race six times.

The Ayr Gold Cup was first sponsored (by Burmah Castrol Oil) in 1972, was supported by Ladbrokes from 1979 until 2000, and came under Tote sponsorship in 2001.

In 1992 Ladbrokes inaugurated the Ayr Silver Cup, a race over the same course and distance for horses who cannot run in the Ayr Gold Cup after the elimination procedure.

B

BACKHANDER

If a jockey gives a horse a 'backhander' he is not offering it a bribe but administering a stroke of the whip on the quarters with the whip in the 'rest' position rather than twirled through the fingers into the usual hitting position.

BACKING

In the context of **breaking in** – that is, teaching a horse to be ridden – backing is the process of getting the horse used to having a human being on its back. A stable lad or lass will lean across the horse, then gently lay across its back for a few moments. Once the pupil has become used to this sensation the lad or lass will sit quietly astride, and the big breakthrough has been achieved.

BACKWARD

Used of a horse not as mature or developed as it should be. A typical sign of a backward two-year-old is that its limbs are not yet in proportion to the rest of its body.

BAD

In racing idiom, a horse which finishes 'a bad third' is a very long way behind the horse in front of it. Years ago 'bad' was an official distance: for example, the official distances in the 1951 Grand National – won by Nickel Coin from Royal Tan and the remounted Derrinstown – were 'six lengths, bad'.

BADEN-BADEN

Web: www.baden-galopp.de

The most prestigious racecourse in Germany, situated a little outside the spa town whose name it bears, is notable for its autumn festival meeting which features the Group One Grosser Preis von Baden over 2,400 metres (one and a half miles) for three-year-olds and upwards. In 2000 this prestigious prize joined the **Emirates World Series** and, with a purse equivalent to £322,581 going to the winning owner, was the richest race ever run in Germany. The prize was matched by the class of the field, with the race going to Samum (who had won the German Derby earlier in the season) with the likes of Fruits Of Love, Daliapour, Holding Court and Mutafaweq behind him. Winners of the Grosser Preis von Baden in recent years include such familiar horses as Glint Of Gold (1982), the Australian colt Strawberry Road (1984), Acatenango (1986 and 1987), subsequent Arc winner Carroll House (1988), the indomitable **Pilsudski** (1996), Borgia (1997) and another dual winner Tiger Hill (1998 and 1999). Baden-Baden is also the venue for Germany's major yearling sale. The course – which is principally known for Flat racing but also stages good sport over jumps – is left-handed, about a mile and a quarter round, with a dog-leg six-furlong sprint course.

BAHRAM

Owned by the Aga Khan (grandfather of the present **Aga Khan**) and trained by Frank Butters, Bahram was unbeaten in nine races in 1934 and 1935. As a juvenile he won the National Breeders' Produce Stakes at Sandown Park (starting at 20–1), the Rous Memorial Stakes at Goodwood, the Gimcrack Stakes at York, and the Boscawen Stakes and Middle Park Stakes at Newmarket. As a three-year-old he went straight to the Two Thousand Guineas, which he won at 7–2, and then headed for the Derby, for which he started 5–4 favourite and ran out a comfortable two-length winner. Next came victory in the St James's Palace Stakes at Royal Ascot. Ridden in the St

Leger by **Charlie Smirke** as his regular jockey Freddie Fox was injured, Bahram started at 11–4 on and cruised to a five-length victory to become the first Triple Crown winner since Gainsborough in 1918. At stud Bahram sired several good horses, including 1942 Two Thousand Guineas winner Big Game, before being sold in 1940 to the USA, moving on to Argentina in 1946. He died in 1956. Trainer Frank Butters observed: 'As Bahram was very lazy, and never beaten, not even I ever knew how good he was.'

BAILEY, JERRY

Born in Dallas, Texas, on 29 August 1957, Jerry Bailey rode quarter horses in match races at the age of 12 and notched up his first winner on his very first ride in Thoroughbred racing, Fetch, at Sunland Park, New Mexico. By the end of 2000 he had ridden over 4,000 winners worldwide and firmly established himself in the Premier League of international jockeys. His big-race victories include three of the first six runnings of the Dubai World Cup, on his most celebrated mount **Cigar** (1996), Singspiel (1997) and Captain Steve (2001); 11 Breeders' Cup races, including the Classic on Black Tie Affair (1991), Arcangues (1993), Concern (1994) and Cigar (1995); the Kentucky Derby on Sea Hero (1993) and Grindstone (1996); and the runaway victory of **Dubai Millennium** in the Prince of Wales's Stakes at Royal Ascot in June 2000, when he was brought in to replace Frankie Dettori, who was recovering from a plane crash earlier that month. He was inducted into the Racing Hall of Fame in the USA in 1995, the year he won ten races on Cigar.

BAILEY, KIM

Web: www.kcbaileyracing.com

Now based in Preston Capes, Northampton-shire, where he moved in 1999 after a long spell in Upper Lambourn, Kim Bailey was born in 1953, son of trainer Ken Bailey. After learning the trade at the feet of Humphrey Cottrell, Tim Forster and Fred Rimell, Kim took out his first licence in 1978. His three best horses – the trio who brought him the distinction of having sent out the winners of

jump racing's three top races – have been Mr Frisk, who won the Grand National in 1990 in record time and went on to land the Whitbread Gold Cup; Master Oats, winner of the Cheltenham Gold Cup in 1995 and many other big races including the Welsh National run at Newbury in January 1995; and 1995 Champion Hurdle winner Alderbrook. Another familiar name trained by Kim Bailey was the popular chaser Docklands Express (Whitbread Gold Cup 1991).

Of jumps trainers holding a licence at the start of 2001, only Kim Bailey and Toby Balding have trained winners of the Grand National, Cheltenham Gold Cup and Champion Hurdle.

BALDING, IAN

Web: www.kingsclere.com

Younger brother of trainer Toby and father of BBC racing presenter Clare, Ian Balding (born 7 November 1938) trained one of the all-time great horses in **Mill Reef**, who in 1971 won the Derby, Eclipse Stakes, King George VI and Queen Elizabeth Stakes and Prix de l'Arc de Triomphe. A Cambridge rugby blue, he rode some 70 winners as an amateur under National Hunt Rules and took out his first trainer's licence in 1964. Thanks to the exploits of Mill Reef, he was leading trainer in 1971. While Mill Reef has been his only Classic winner to date, Ian Balding has trained many well-known horses, including Silly Season (Champion Stakes 1964), Glint Of Gold (second in Shergar's 1981 Derby) and Diamond Shoal (Grand Prix de Saint-Cloud 1983) – all of whom ran in the colours of his principal patron **Paul Mellon** – and other familiar names such as Mrs Penny (Prix de Diane 1980), Selkirk (Queen Elizabeth II Stakes 1991) and the flying filly **Lochsong**. He has sent out many winners for the Queen from his stables at Kingsclere, not far from Newbury in Berkshire.

BALDING, TOBY

Web: www.tobybalding.co.uk

Gerald Barnard Balding – better known as Toby – was born in September 1936 and first took out a licence in 1957. While he has had some notable successes on the Flat (for example when winning the Stewards' Cup and Ayr Gold Cup with Green Ruby in 1986), he is better known for his exploits over jumps, having won the Grand National twice (with Highland Wedding in 1969 and Little Polveir in 1989), the Champion Hurdle twice (with Beech Road in 1989 and Morley Street in 1991) and the Cheltenham Gold Cup with Cool Ground in 1992. As well as being a noted judge of a horse, Toby Balding has a pretty good eye for a jockey: in 1994 he appointed as his conditional jockey a young Irishman named **Tony McCoy**. His yard is at Fyfield, near Andover in Hampshire.

BALLING

Term describing how snow forms into hard lumps inside a horse's shoe, making it very difficult for him to keep his footing.

BALLINROBE

Ballinrobe, Co. Mayo

Tel.: 092 41052 (racedays)

Fax: 092 41406 (racedays)

With a circuit of a little over one mile and mild undulations, Ballinrobe, 28 miles north-west of Galway, is a course for the handy type of horse. It stages race on the Flat and over jumps, and the major races here are the Harp Lager Chase in June and the Heineken Chase in July. While there has been racing in the Ballinrobe area since the eighteenth century, the present racecourse was opened in 1921.

BALLOT

If more horses stand in the entries by the time of declaration (the day before the race) than can be accommodated by the safety factor at the course, some horses need to be eliminated. In handicaps horses are eliminated from the lowest weight up, but for a wide range of other races the field is thinned by balloting out the required number of runners. Exemptions are usually allowed for certain horses (such as previous winners). The balloting operation takes place at Weatherbys.

BALLYMOSS

The greatest Irish-trained horse of the 1950s was owned by John McShain (head of the American construction company which had built the Pentagon) and trained by **Vincent O'Brien**. From four outings as a two-year-old in 1956 he won just once. As a three-year-old he was unplaced in the Madrid Free Handicap and then sprang a surprise when winning the Trigo Stakes at Leopardstown at 20–1 (his stable companion Gladness was unplaced odds-on favourite). This upturn in his form strengthened O'Brien's long-held conviction that Ballymoss had a serious chance in the 1957 Derby, though the conviction was not widely shared by the betting public: at Epsom he started at 33–1 but defied those odds when finishing runner-up to hot favourite Crepello. Ballymoss then landed the Irish Derby in a canter, was beaten in the Great Voltigeur Stakes at York on unsuitably soft ground, and won the St Leger from Court Harwell – the first ever Irish-trained horse to win the Doncaster Classic. Having been beaten in the Champion Stakes, he had done enough for that season.

In 1958 Ballymoss was beaten by Doutelle in the Ormonde Stakes at Chester and then embarked on a glorious sequence of four big middle-distance races. Ridden in all four by **Scobie Breasley**, Ballymoss won the Coronation Cup, Eclipse Stakes, King George VI and Queen Elizabeth Stakes and Prix de l'Arc de Triomphe – the first Irish-trained horse to win the Arc. He then travelled to the USA for the Washington DC International – in those days the only big American target for European horses – and in a notoriously rough race could finish only third.

Champion sire in 1967 thanks to the achievements of his son **Royal Palace**, Ballymoss died in 1979 at the age of 25.

BANDAGES

Cotton bandages are sometimes wrapped round a horse's legs to provide protection and support (in much the same way that a human runner may wear an athletic support) during a race. Naturally they are used more often for jumpers than on the Flat – where their presence can raise suspicions of unsoundness.

BANGOR-ON-DEE

Bangor-on-Dee, near Wrexham, Clwyd LL13 0DA
Tel.: 01978 780323
Fax: 01978 780985
E-mail: racing@bangordee.sagehost.co.uk
Web: www.bangordee.co.uk

Apart from being one of the quintessential **gaff tracks** – those small courses which form the backbone of National Hunt racing in Britain – Bangor-on-Dee has two perverse claims to fame: it is the only racecourse in the country which has no building which even purports to be a grandstand; and it is not the other Bangor in north Wales, the university town near Anglesey. Tradition has it that many a horsebox driver has merrily driven his charges to the latter Bangor, only to discover his mistake too late to get to the course in time.

The lack of a grandstand does not represent a serious hardship for Bangor-on-Dee racegoers, as they can enjoy excellent vantage points on the hill which slopes down towards the track. None the less, watching a race from the paddock area at Bangor can be a curious experience as your main view of the finish is head-on. For a decent side-on view you need to take up position in the large picnic area beyond the course buildings.

Fred Archer, one of the greatest jockeys of all time, rode the first winner of his career in a steeplechase at Bangor in 1869. Aged 12 (the same age as Lester Piggott was when he rode his first winner), Archer weighed out at 4st 11lb before winning on Maid Of Trent.

The circuit is about one and a half miles round. Its sharp bends and mostly level terrain favour the nippy sort of horse rather than the relentless galloper, and it can pay to follow previous course winners here.

While it would be stretching a point to claim that the course stages any major races, quality of sport is not everything, and Bangor-on-Dee is a highly enjoyable place to experience the very roots of the jumping game – especially if you have a well-stocked picnic hamper in the car.

BANKER

A punter's most confident bet – as in 'Istabraq has to be the Cheltenham banker.'

BAR

If a betting show is concluded '20–1 bar', that indicates that the horses not listed stand at 20–1 or longer.

BARRY, RON

Champion jump jockey in the 1972–3 season with the then record total of 125 winners, and champion again the following season, Ron Barry was one of the finest jump jockeys of his time, famed for his fearlessness and gung-ho attitude both in and out of the saddle. He was born in Co. Limerick on 28 February 1943, served his apprenticeship with Tommy Shaw and then moved to Britain: his first winner was Final Approach in a novice hurdle at Ayr on 19 October 1964. He won the 1973 Cheltenham Gold Cup on that hugely popular white-faced chaser **The Dikler**, who caught **Pendil** right on the post to win by a short head, and on the same horse landed the 1974 Whitbread Gold Cup on the disqualification of **John Oaksey** and Proud Tarquin. Another notable victory was on Grand Canyon in the Colonial Cup in South Carolina in 1976. But he was never placed in the Grand National, and the nearest he came to landing the Champion Hurdle was second place on Easby Abbey behind Comedy Of Errors in 1973. Ron Barry retired in 1983 and is now an Inspector of Courses for the Jockey Club (as are other former jump jockeys Richard Linley and Peter Hobbs).

BATH

Lansdown, Bath, Somerset BA1 9BU
Tel.: 01225 424609
Fax: 01225 444415

At 780 feet above sea level, Bath is the highest Flat course in the country. Although its location is much loftier than its status – Bath is unarguably in the minor league of Flat tracks – the course is famed for the quality of its downland turf. Over the years it has proved an ideal testing ground for promising two-year-olds before they graduate to the more prestigious tracks.

The left-handed circuit is just over a mile and a half round, and although the turns at each end of the track are fairly tight, the course is generally galloping rather than sharp in nature. The run-in from the home turn rises all the way to the winning post, and bends notice-ably to the left about two furlongs out, which can cause bunching and puts a premium on skilful jockeyship: it can be rewarding for punters to pay close attention to which riders have done well at Bath over the years.

A particularly appealing feature of Bath from the spectator's point of view is that, since the shape of the course is that of a squashed sausage, the crowd in the stands has a very close-up view of the action even when the runners are on the far side.

BEASLEY, BOBBY

One of only four jockeys since the Second World War to have won the Grand National, Cheltenham Gold Cup and Champion Hurdle (the other three are **Fred Winter**, **Willie Robinson** and **Richard Dunwoody**), Bobby Beasley is a grandson of the legendary Harry Beasley (who won the Grand National on Come Away in 1891 and had his final ride in public in 1935 at the age of 83). He landed jumping's Big Three within just three years – Gold Cup in 1959 on Roddy Owen, Champion Hurdle in 1960 on Another Flash, Grand National in 1961 on the grey Nicolaus Silver – but later a combination of increasing weight and alcohol addiction brought about his premature retirement from the saddle. He fought his way back, and in 1974 landed a second Cheltenham Gold Cup on the brilliant but wayward **Captain Christy**. Bobby Beasley, described by Ivor Herbert as 'the complete jockey: strong and stylish, a beautiful horseman and as brave as a lion', retired at the end of the 1973–4 season.

BEAVERBROOK, LADY

Lady Beaverbrook's colours – beaver-brown, maple-leaf green crossbelts and cap – were a familiar sight on British racecourses from the time she took up racing on the death of her husband Max, proprietor of the *Daily Express*, in 1964 until her own death at the age of 85 in 1994. Her best horse was **Bustino**, who won the 1974 St Leger and 1975 Coronation Cup and ran second to Grundy in 'The Race of the Century', the 1975 King George VI and Queen Elizabeth Diamond Stakes, while she also struck Classic success with Minster Son (St Leger 1988) and Mystiko (Two Thousand Guineas 1991). Lady Beaverbrook won the King George ten years after Bustino's heroic effort with Petoski in 1985, and her other top-class horses included the highly popular and durable sprinter Boldboy; Relkino, second to Empery in the 1976 Derby and winner of the Benson and Hedges Gold Cup that year; Niniski, who won the Irish St Leger and Prix Royal-Oak in 1979; Easter Sun, winner of the Coronation Cup in 1982; and Terimon, 500–1 runner-up to Nashwan in the 1989 Derby and winner in 1991 of the International Stakes at York.

BECHER'S BROOK

The most famous steeplechase obstacle in the world, Becher's Brook is jumped as the sixth fence on the first circuit of the Grand National at Aintree and the twenty-second on the second. It takes its name from Captain Martin Becher, who in the 1839 Grand Liverpool Steeplechase – the prototype Grand National – was riding a horse named Conrad across an obstacle described as 'a strong paling, next a rough, high jagged hedge, and lastly a brook about six feet wide'. Conrad hit the 'paling' hard and deposited his rider in the brook, whence he emerged with the observation that 'water is no damned use without brandy' and proceeded to remount, only to be dunked again at the next brook (now known as Valentine's). Today the fence itself is 4ft 10in high on the take-off side but features a steep drop over the brook on the landing side which catches out the unwary, though Becher's is a good deal fairer than it was before modifications were made following the deaths of Brown Trix and Seeandem there in 1989. Before those modifi-cations, the drop was noticeably more severe on the inner, with a slope leading up from the brook, whereas now there is less difference between inner and outer.

BEESWAX
Slang for betting tax.

BELLEWSTOWN
Bellewstown. Drogheda. Co. Louth
Tel.: 041 23614 (racedays only) or 23425

One of Ireland's most ancient and most scenic racecourses, Bellewstown stages just one meeting a year, early in July. Steeplechases are no longer run here, so the regular fare is a mixture of Flat and hurdles. The course is left-handed and undulating, approximately nine furlongs round.

Although the racing at Bellewstown is usually of a pretty humble standard, Bellewstown will live for ever in the folklore of Irish racing on account of the 'Yellow Sam Coup', the betting stroke masterminded by Barney Curley – owner, trainer and famed gambler – which took place there in 1975. Yellow Sam was carefully backed off course, and in order to stem the flow of money into the on-course market, and thus keep the price long, one of Curley's associates commandeered the single telephone box in the village, thus preventing off-course money getting through. 'There was this heavily built man,' according to Curley himself, 'a tough sort of guy, who suddenly discovered that a close relation of his was seriously ill and he had to keep in constant touch with the hospital. Once he had the phone in his hand he was not going to let go. He was broad enough in the beam not to permit anyone past him into the box.' The horse did his bit, Yellow Sam pulling off a major touch by winning at a starting price of 20–1 – though in running you could only get 2–1!

BELMONT PARK
Racetrack in the Jamaica district of New York on Long Island, where the current track was founded as a right-handed circuit in 1905: it was only in 1921 that the direction was reversed to the present anti-clockwise. In addition to the **Belmont Stakes**, third leg of the US Triple Crown, the course stages all three races in the fillies' Triple Crown: Acorn Stakes, Mother Goose Stakes and Coaching Club American Oaks. The great filly Ruffian won all three in 1975, then in a match at Belmont against Kentucky Derby winner Foolish Pleasure she broke down soon after the start and had to be put down. Her grave is by the Belmont Park winning post. The course was closed in 1963 on account of serious structural defects in the grandstand, and Belmont's fixtures were shared between Saratoga and Aqueduct until the track re-opened in 1968. Belmont Park has hosted the **Breeders' Cup** twice: in 1990 (when a memorable programme included such sensations as Dayjur jumping the shadow and losing the Sprint, Go For Wand's death in the Distaff and Lester Piggott's victory on Royal Academy in the Mile) and 1995 (when Ridgewood Pearl won the Mile and **Cigar** the Classic). The Breeders' Cup is due to return to Belmont Park in 2001.

BELMONT STAKES

In 1990 Go And Go. trained by Dermot Weld and ridden by Michael Kinane. became the first European-based winner of a US Triple Crown race when winning the Belmont Stakes by eight and a quarter lengths.

Third leg of the **US Triple Crown**, the Belmont Stakes is run over one and a half miles at **Belmont Park**, New York. The Belmont is the oldest of the Triple Crown races, having been first run in 1867 at the now defunct Jerome Park in the Bronx. It is also the longest, and the extra distance can prove too much for horses going for the elusive treble after landing the Kentucky Derby and Preakness. Northern Dancer, for example, won the first two legs in 1964 but failed in the Belmont, and more recently such well-known horses as Spectacular Bid (1979), Alysheba (1987), Sunday Silence (1989), Silver Charm (1997), Real Quiet (1998) and Charismatic (1999) have suffered the same fate. Undoubtedly the most sensational recent running was the 1973 race, won by **Secretariat** by 31 lengths. (For winners since 1990, *see* **US Triple Crown**.)

BEND OR

Bred and owned by the first Duke of Westminster and trained by Robert Peck, Bend Or was one of the greatest horses of the late nineteenth century. Ridden by **Fred Archer**, with one arm out of action following a savaging by a horse a month earlier, he won the 1880 Derby by a head from Robert The Devil. His other victories included the St James's Palace Stakes in 1880 and the Epsom Gold Cup – now the Coronation Cup – by a neck from Robert The Devil and the Champion Stakes in 1881. As a stallion his best son was the great 1886 Triple Crown winner Ormonde, while his daughters included Ornament, dam of **Sceptre**. **Arkle** traces to Bend Or on both sides of his pedigree, and Arkle's owner **Anne, Duchess of Westminster** was the fourth wife of the second Duke of Westminster, grandson of Bend Or's owner and always known as 'Bendor'. ('Bend Or' is a heraldic term meaning a diagonal band [bend] in gold [or] across a shield.)

BENTINCK, LORD GEORGE

Born in 1802, Lord George Bentinck was a highly influential member of the **Jockey Club** and left a lasting mark on horse racing in Britain through a number of significant reforms at a time when the sport was very ill-regulated. He can be credited with the organisation of race meetings in roughly the form we know them today – by outlawing the custom of the winning owner giving a present to the judge after a big race; seeking a more efficient way of starting races than the prevailing one where the starter simply shouted 'Go!' as soon as the field had made a rough line; devising the system of different enclosures at racecourses; and establishing such familiar aspects of racing as number boards and allotting each horse a number on the racecard. Many of these developments were introduced at Goodwood, a course with which he was closely associated. As an owner he had many successes, but divested himself of his racing interests in 1846 to concentrate on politics and died in 1848 at the age of 46, having suffered a heart attack while on a country walk. He lived just long enough to see Surplice, whom he had bred but had sold at the dispersal of his bloodstock, win the 1846 Derby – a setback which occasioned his famous outburst to Benjamin Disraeli in the library of the House of Commons: 'All my life I have been trying for this, and for what have I sacrificed it?'

BETTING SHOPS

Betting shops were made legal in the United Kingdom in 1961, the first shops opening on 1 May that year. Before then betting on horses could legally take place only on a racecourse or through a credit account; illegal betting, though, was rife, with 'bookies' runners' operating in pubs and clubs and on street corners, and it was in an attempt to end this illicit activity that Home Secretary R. A. Butler brought in legislation – the Betting and Gaming Act – which made betting shops possible. Butler noted in his memoirs that 'the House of Commons was so intent on making "betting shops" as sad as possible, in order not to deprave the young, that they ended up more like undertakers' premises.' Indeed, the general ambience of betting shops was deliberately kept seedy and inhospitable for decades; but in 1986 new legislation allowed a general brightening up and, most significantly, the transmission of races live on television to shops which took the service from **Satellite Information Services**. Even coffee machines appeared, and the notion of a betting shop as an establishment into which no respectable person should ever stray had at last disappeared. Now, with evening opening and Sunday opening, betting shops are almost becoming respectable outposts of the leisure industry, a move accelerated early in 1995 when they were at last allowed to show their interiors to high-street passers-by, rather than skulking guiltily behind solid display boards in the shop windows.

There are around 9,000 betting shops in Britain, responsible for a large proportion of the £7,500 million bet off course every year.

BEVERLEY

The Grandstand. York Road. Beverley. East Yorkshire HU17 8QZ

Tel.: 01482 867488

Fax: 01482 863892

E-mail: info@beverleyracecourse.co.uk

Web: www.goracing.co.uk

There has been horse racing on the Westwood, an area of common land just outside the cathedral town of Beverley, since 1690, and today the same land is the site of an unpretentious, well-run Flat racecourse with a strong local following.

The round course is a right-handed oval just over one mile three furlongs in circumference, with five-furlong sprints starting from a chute: runners in five-furlong races negotiate a slight right-hand bend as that chute meets the round course, and spend most of the race on a steady uphill rise, which means that the trip takes some getting, especially for early-season two-year-olds. The round course is mostly galloping in nature, but there is a downhill run along the back straight and the run-in from the home turn is less than three furlongs, favouring the well-balanced horse.

BHB

See **British Horseracing Board**.

BIDDLECOMBE, TERRY

Terry Biddlecombe was born in 1941 and rode in point-to-points and as an amateur before turning professional in 1960: his first winner under Rules was on Burnella in a novice hurdle at Wincanton in March 1958. He joined trainer **Fred Rimell**'s yard for the 1962–3 season and stayed there for the best part of a decade before turning freelance in 1972. It was on the Fred Rimell-trained Woodland Venture that Biddlecombe won his sole Cheltenham Gold Cup in 1967, while other big-race success came his way with horses such as Charlie Potheen, Coral Diver, Red Thorn, Game Spirit and Gay Trip, on whom he twice won the Mackeson Gold Cup (1969 and 1971) but whose Grand National victory in 1970 he was forced to miss through injury, Pat Taaffe coming in for the winning

ride. Biddlecombe and Gay Trip ran a close second to Well To Do in the 1972 Grand National, but he was never to win the Aintree showpiece. Famed for his cavalier approach and his exceptional strength in a finish, Terry Biddlecombe was champion jump jockey for three seasons – 1964–5, 1965–6 and 1968–9 (when he shared the title with Bob Davies) and retired in 1974 having ridden 905 winners. After a period spent in Australia, Terry Biddlecombe returned to Britain and is now again a highly popular player on the jumping scene, working with his wife, trainer **Henrietta Knight**.

BIRTHDAY (HORSE'S)

Whatever the date on which it was actually born, a racehorse becomes one year older on 1 January – the official birthday of all Thoroughbreds foaled in the northern hemisphere.

A filly by Nashwan out of the 1990 One Thousand Guineas. Oaks and Irish Derby winner Salsabil was foaled on 1 January 1992. Had she been born one day earlier she would have officially become a yearling on the second day of her life. Named Firdous. the filly never raced.

Thus on the stroke of midnight which brings in New Year's Day all foals become yearlings, all yearlings become two-year-olds, all two-year-olds become three-year-olds, and so on. (In the southern hemisphere the official birthday of the Thoroughbred racehorse is 1 August.)

BIT

The metal bar which forms the mouthpiece of a bridle. Bits come in all sorts of varieties, but the common racing bit is the snaffle – two pieces linked in the middle. When a horse is 'on the bit' (or 'on the bridle') he is going well within himself (**Sea Bird II** famously won the Derby in 1965 without coming off the bit). When 'off the bit' (or 'off the bridle') he is being pushed along. Sometimes you will hear that a horse has 'picked up his bit', which indicates a change of gear from cruising to increasing the tempo. Similarly, 'dropped his bit' is the equine equivalent of downing tools.

BLACK TYPE

When a sales catalogue gives the racing record of a mare and her progeny, a Group race or a Listed race is printed in bold type to advertise its status. Thus the amount of 'black type' in an entry proclaims the overall quality of that pedigree. You will often hear a trainer say of a filly that he or she is 'hoping to get some black type' with her – that is, hoping to win or be placed in a Group or Listed race and thus underline her potential as a broodmare.

BLAZE

A patch of white running down a horse's face.

BLEEDER

A horse prone to **breaking blood vessels**. (Horses have been called 'bleeders' in other contexts.)

BLINKERS

A horse's field of vision is nearly 360 degrees – useful for a creature which has evolved to be constantly on the look-out for predators – and the fitting of blinkers significantly reduces the level of lateral vision, thus compelling the horse to focus straight ahead and (so the theory goes) keep its mind on the job. The blinkers themselves (and related equipment such as **visor** and **eyeshield**) consist of a hood which is fitted to the upper part of the horse's head and has over each eye either a 'full cup', blocking off lateral vision entirely, or, to allow some degree of sideways vision, a 'half cup'. Horses wearing blinkers have traditionally had their integrity questioned – time was when a pair of blinkers was known as the 'rogue's badge' – but plenty of perfectly genuine horses have worn them. **Earth Summit** in 1998 was the most recent horse to win the Grand National wearing blinkers, and who could question *his* genuineness? It is often the case that a horse wearing blinkers in a race for the first time will show a marked improvement in form.

BLISTERING

A treatment for inflammation of the tendons, in which concentrated sulphuric acid is applied to the skin of the affected leg. This causes acute inflammation which promotes healing by increasing blood supply and blood flow.

BLOWER

Before the days of mobile phones, off-course money was sent into the on-course betting ring by means of the 'blower', a dedicated phone line between off-track bookmakers and the course. Thus the betting report on a race might allude to 'blower money'.

BLOW UP

A horse is said to 'blow up' in a race when it rapidly runs out of breath.

BLUSHING GROOM

Owned by the **Aga Khan** and trained in France by François Mathet, Blushing Groom won five of his six races as a two-year-old in 1976, including a defeat of the very highly rated English juvenile J. O. Tobin in the Grand Criterium at Longchamp. As a three-year-old in 1977 he won the Poule d'Essai des Poulains so impressively that he became hot favourite for the Derby, but after looking all over the winner a quarter of a mile out ran out of gas and could finish only third behind The Minstrel and Hot Grove. He was then beaten by Flying Water in the Prix Jacques le Marois and retired, winner of seven of his ten races. As a stallion he is notable for being the sire of 1985 Arc winner Rainbow Quest and of **Nashwan**, winner of the Two Thousand Guineas, Derby, Eclipse and King George VI and Queen Elizabeth Diamond Stakes in 1989, as well as notable fillies such as Al-Bahathri and Snow Bride, who, ironically, benefited from the disqualification of the Aga Khan's Aliysa following the post-race dope test to be credited with winning the 1989 Oaks. Blushing Groom died in 1991.

BOARD PRICE

The price relayed to betting shops during pre-race market moves and displayed there on the board or, more likely, the television screen: a punter can take this price and be on at those odds, regardless of starting price.

BOARDSMAN
The person who enters prices on to the board (though in most betting shops nowadays price fluctuations are shown on screens rather than marked up on a board).

BOGEY
The horse which represents the biggest liability in a bookmaker's book.

BOLD RULER
One of the great American racehorses of the 1950s but perhaps most famous as the sire of **Secretariat**, Bold Ruler won seven of his ten races as a two-year-old in 1956, then the following year counted the Preakness Stakes among his eleven victories at three and was named Horse of the Year. At four he won five more races but was then injured in the Brooklyn Handicap and retired to the **Claiborne** Farm in Kentucky. He was champion sire for seven consecutive years from 1963 to 1969 and again in 1973 (Secretariat's *annus mirabilis*), and was put down in 1971.

BOLGER, JIM
Jim Bolger was born in Co. Wexford on Christmas Day 1941. After working as an accountant in the offices of a Dublin car dealer he switched his attention to racing, and took out his first trainer's licence in 1976. To the end of 2000 he has won just one English Classic – the 1991 Oaks with 50–1 shot Jet Ski Lady – but he has long been a major force in his native land, winning big races with fillies such as Give Thanks (who brought him his first Irish Classic in the 1983 Irish Oaks), Park Appeal, Park Express, Polonia, Condessa and Flame Of Tara (a fine racehorse who achieved lasting fame as dam of Salsabil). But his best horse has been St Jovite, runner-up to Dr Devious in the 1992 Derby before slamming that colt by twelve lengths in the Irish Derby and then going on to land the King George VI and Queen Elizabeth Diamond Stakes at Ascot. Based at Coolcullen in Co. Carlow, Jim Bolger was champion trainer in Ireland by prize money won in 1991 and 1992, and by number of winners trained in 1990, 1992, 1994 and 1996: his 1990 total of 125 domestic winners remains, at the end of 2000, an Irish record.

BOOKMAKERS
The term 'bookmaker' for a person who constructs a 'book' on the outcome of a horse race was first coined in the 1860s. Today the bookmaking industry is divided between on-course bookies, who play their trade from pitches in the various enclosures, and off-course bookmakers operating through betting shops or credit companies. The 'Big Three' bookmaking companies are Ladbrokes (which claims to have a market share of approximately a quarter of the High Street market), William Hill and Coral Eurobet, with the next level of the industry being occupied by such names as Victor Chandler and Stanley Leisure. At the lowest rung are small businesses which may have just one betting shop. Variations include the **Tote** and bookmakers who concentrate on **spread betting**.

BOOTS
Leather boots are a common accoutrement for jumpers, offering protection from knocks when taking fences and hurdles, and from overreaching – that is, when the horse's hind foot strikes into one of his forefeet.

BOTTLE
Betting slang for 2–1.

BOTTLE AND A HALF
Betting slang for 5–2.

BOTTOMLESS
Very heavy going is often referred to as 'bottomless'.

BOUGHT IN
At the auction after a **selling race**, the declaration 'bought in' at the conclusion of the bidding indicates that the horse's existing connections have bought it back.

BOUSSAC, MARCEL

Monsieur Marcel Boussac, born in 1889, made his fortune from textiles and used it to build one of the Europe's greatest racehorse breeding operations. He won the French Derby with Ramus in 1922 and went on to see countless big races won in his colours of orange, grey cap, including five English Classics: the 1940 Two Thousand Guineas with Djebel; the 1950 Derby with Galcador; the 1950 Oaks with Asmena; the 1950 St Leger with Scratch II; and the 1951 St Leger with Talma II. In addition he won the Ascot Gold Cup four times – with Caracalla II (1946), Arbar (1948), Elpenor (1954) and Macip (1956); the Eclipse Stakes twice – with Djeddah (1949) and Argur (1953) – and the Champion Stakes three times, with Djeddah in 1949 and Dynamiter in 1951 and 1952. By the time his colt Acamas won the Prix du Jockey-Club in 1978 the Boussac empire was in decline: that year the bloodstock was sold to the Aga Khan and the stud to Stavros Niarchos. Marcel Boussac died in 1980, and the Prix Marcel Boussac is run at Longchamp at the Arc meeting in early October.

BOUTIN, FRANÇOIS

The death of François Boutin in February 1995 at the age of 58 deprived the European racing scene of one of its most prominent figures, a trainer whose famous charges included **Miesque** and **Arazi**. Born in 1937, Boutin learned his trade as assistant to Sea Bird II's trainer Etienne Pollet, and took out his first licence in 1964. Classic success in England came early with the easy 1968 Oaks victory of La Lagune, a filly he had bought for just £2,500, and the following year he won the Champion Stakes with Flossy. Nonoalco brought Boutin another English Classic in the 1974 Two Thousand Guineas, but in 1980 his brilliant colt Nureyev was controversially disqualified after finishing first past the post in the first colts' Classic after barging Posse when making his run. Boutin also won the Two Thousand Guineas with Zino, who scraped home from Wind And Wuthering by a head in 1982, and the One Thousand in

1987 with the brilliant filly Miesque, who went on to win the Breeders' Cup Mile in two successive years, 1987 and 1988. The Breeders' Cup brought Boutin probably his greatest moment with the sensational victory of Arazi in the Juvenile at Churchill Downs in 1991, while his victories in French Classics included the 1976 Prix du Jockey-Club with Caracolero, and he won the Irish Derby with Malacate in 1976. But perhaps Boutin's greatest horse was **Sagaro**, who with Lester Piggott won the Ascot Gold Cup three times: 1975, 1976 and 1977.

BOX-WALKER

A horse who constantly walks round and round its box – a sign of nervous agitation.

BOYD-ROCHFORT, CECIL

Captain Sir Cecil Boyd-Rochfort trained winners of all five English Classics, clocking up 13 Classic victories in all. Born in 1887, he took out his first licence in 1923, and by the time he retired in 1968 had sent out 1,169 winners in Britain – including winners of 57 races for King George VI, whose trainer he became in 1943, three for the then Queen

---

Cecil Boyd-Rochfort's Classic winners

Two Thousand Guineas
  1958 Pall Mall
One Thousand Guineas
  1933 Brown Betty
  1946 Hypericum
  1955 Meld
Derby
  1959 Parthia
Oaks
  1944 Hycilla
  1955 Meld
St Leger
  1936 Boswell
  1941 Sun Castle
  1948 Black Tarquin
  1953 Premonition
  1955 Meld
  1958 Alcide

Elizabeth, and 136 for the present Queen. Horses he trained for the Queen included Pall Mall (Two Thousand Guineas 1958), the very fine middle-distance horse Aureole (second to Pinza in the 1953 Derby and winner the following year of the Coronation Cup and King George VI and Queen Elizabeth Stakes), Doutelle, Above Suspicion and Almeria. He won the Derby once, with Sir Humphrey de Trafford's colt Parthia in 1959, but the best horses to have benefited from his perfectionist standards were Meld, winner of the One Thousand Guineas, Oaks and St Leger in 1955, and Alcide, winner of the 1958 St Leger and 1959 King George. On his retirement in 1968 he passed over his yard at Freemason Lodge, Newmarket, to his stepson **Henry Cecil**, whose widowed mother he had married a few weeks before Henry's birth. Cecil Boyd-Rochfort died in 1983, aged 95.

BOSRA SHAM

A highly attractive chestnut filly with a large white blaze, Bosra Sham was owned by Wafic Said and trained by Henry Cecil. She won both her races at two in 1995 – notably the Fillies' Mile at Ascot – and in 1996 was indisputably the champion of her sex, winning the One Thousand Guineas despite suffering foot trouble during her preparation and annihilating her rivals in the Champion Stakes, winning by two and a half lengths from Halling. Kept in training at four, she sauntered home in her seasonal debut at Sandown Park and scorched in to win the Prince of Wales's Stakes by eight lengths from Alhaarth. Then she was controversially beaten in the Eclipse Stakes when rider Kieren Fallon managed to get her boxed in up the Sandown Park straight, and finished last of four behind Singspiel when odds-on favourite for the International Stakes at York: one of her shoes flew off halfway through the race (narrowly missing Michael Kinane on Desert King), which provided an explanation for an uncharacteristically downbeat run which saw the end of a fine career dogged by foot problems. Bosra Sham retired the winner of seven of her ten races.

BRADLEY, GRAHAM

Controversy, popularity and big-race triumph attended Graham Bradley in almost equal measure throughout his career. Born at Wetherby in 1960, he joined trainer Tony **Dickinson** as conditional jockey and rode his first winner on Talon in a novices' hurdle at Sedgefield on 11 March 1980. He became second-string jockey to Robert Earnshaw for the Dickinson yard, where son Michael took over on the retirement of Tony, and rode many winners for Michael and subsequently for Mrs Monica Dickinson, notably the 1982 Hennessy Gold Cup and 1983 Cheltenham Gold Cup on Bregawn (the Gold Cup in which Michael Dickinson trained the first five home), 1983 Sun Alliance Hurdle on Sabin du Loir, 1984 Welsh National on Righthand Man and 1985 King George VI Chase on Wayward Lad. He also won the 1985 Irish National on Rhyme 'N' Reason, 1986 Welsh National on Stearsby and 1997 Hennessy Cognac Gold Cup on Suny Bay (whose trainer Charlie Brooks had given Bradley's career a new lease of life by appointing him stable jockey in 1991). But apart from Bregawn his only other success in the 'Big Three' of jump racing came when Collier Bay won the 1996 Champion Hurdle. That Wayward Lad, probably the best horse he rode regularly, gave his name to Bradley's autobiography highlights what the jockey himself called his 'image problem' – constant brushes with the racing authorities over supposed misdemeanours, from a two-month suspension for placing a bet in the ring at Cartmel in 1982 when a raw young jockey, to being charged – charges that were subsequently dropped – in 1999 as part of a long-running race-fixing investigation. A jockey of exceptional style and panache – his ride on Morley Street in the 1993 Aintree Hurdle won him an award for the riding performance of the season – Graham Bradley retired from the saddle in November 1999 having ridden 738 winners in Britain, and was soon highly successful in his new career as a bloodstock agent.

BREAKING BLOOD VESSELS

Bleeding from a horse's nostrils indicates a haemorrhage in the lungs caused by strenuous exertion. The horse will be 'scoped' – subjected to endoscopic examination of the airways – to assess the nature of the damage, and can be treated by drugs and by a period of rest, of anything from a few days to several months, depending on the severity of the problem. While it will not necessarily recur every time the horse races, a tendency to break blood vessels is always a cause for concern as it will markedly affect performance.

BREAKING DOWN

A horse is said to have broken down when it has been severely affected by strain or rupture in the tendons – the bands of strong tissue which attach muscles to bones – of the lower leg. All the muscles in the horse's foreleg are above the knee, and are attached to the bones of the pastern and hoof by tendons. Obviously, these tendons are subjected to great strain when a horse is galloping, and are placed under particular stress by jumping. Unlike muscles, tendons cannot stretch much, and so are vulnerable to damage under extreme pressure. Uneven going, tired muscles and jolts to the leg all increase the likelihood of tendon strain, which in severe cases causes the tendons to elongate and tear or give way completely. A common method of treating tendon strain is 'firing', based on the principle that the scar tissue that will form in response to the application of heat is stronger than the damaged tissue. First a local anaesthetic is applied to the area; then red-hot irons are applied to the damaged tendon. In bar or line firing the iron is drawn across the skin in lines about an inch apart; in pin firing the iron is inserted through the skin into the tissue of the tendon; acid firing involves the application of concentrated sulphuric acid to the skin. Unpleasant as such treatments sound, they are held by many to be very effective, despite opposition in some quarters within the veterinary profession. In 1991 firing was outlawed by the Royal College of Veterinary Surgeons, but professional support for the practice was such that the ban was allowed to lapse, and firing is now in common use once more. A less common method of treating damaged forelegs is the implantation of carbon fibres to strengthen the tendons: the Queen Mother's chaser Special Cargo underwent such treatment and after an absence of two years returned to racing and beat Lettoch and Diamond Edge in the memorable Whitbread Gold Cup of 1984.

BREAKING IN

A yearling bought at the autumn sales and expected to run on the Flat as a two-year-old will go from the sales to the yard of its new trainer, where the process of breaking in will begin immediately. On the other hand, a horse who is to be kept as a 'store' for racing over jumps without racing on the Flat first will probably not begin his first lessons until much later: Arkle was not broken in until he was nearly four. Whenever it happens, breaking in – an unfortunate term for a process intended to imbue the young pupil with trust and compliance – tends to follow a certain pattern. The horse will have worn a halter or headcollar and become accustomed to being led from his days as a very young foal and will be used to human company, but breaking in even a good-natured and well-handled youngster is both a tricky and a crucial operation, and for this reason is usually entrusted to a highly experienced stable lad. For the same reason the process cannot be rushed, normally taking two to three weeks.

First the horse must get used to the feel of a **bit** in his mouth. At the next stage, long reins are attached to the bit on either side and the horse is taught to walk with the lad behind him; then he learns to lunge – to walk and trot in circles on the end of a single long rein. In both long-reining and lungeing, the horse learns to respond to the voice of the handler as well as to pressure on his mouth through the reins and bit. Once the horse is responding well to the signals he is receiving, he is introduced to the roller, a padded girth fitted in the position where there will later be a saddle: the reins are fitted through rings on the roller to replicate the feel of the rider's hands on the reins. Next, the roller is replaced by a saddle, so that the horse can become accustomed to a larger item on his back. Eventually comes the big moment when the horse is 'backed' – introduced for the first time to a rider. Like everything else in breaking in, this is done in careful stages. Then the horse will be lunged with the lad on top, and finally, when it is clear that the horse accepts the presence of the rider as normal, the lunge rein will be removed and the horse will be 'ridden away'. Now he must no longer look to instructions from the ground, but must obey the signals given from the saddle.

Restricted at first to quiet walking and trotting, the youngster will soon be got used to being ridden in company by engaging in a gentle canter up the gallops, usually with an older horse to show the way.

That is the traditional procedure, but times are changing, and new methods of teaching a young horse are beginning to be more widely adopted – and, significantly, described as 'starting' rather than 'breaking'. These rely to a large extent on the work of Monty Roberts, the American guru of 'starting' horses who is often described as 'the original horse whisperer'. The key to Roberts's method has been to encourage rather than subordinate, to adopt a slow, softly-softly approach which gives the horse complete confidence and, crucially, makes the horse come to the teacher, rather than have the teacher force his or her attentions on the horse.

The first stages of breaking in, or starting, will be much the same for a horse destined for any equestrian discipline; but the potential racehorse must also learn some very specific skills particular to his intended calling. For a horse who will run on the Flat, there is the requirement of getting used to the starting stalls. Using a set of stalls kept for the purpose on the training grounds, the yearling is led quietly into the stalls with his rider, at first walking straight through and then pausing in the stall before walking, and then trotting, out when the front doors are opened. When he is used to that he will be ridden out of the stalls more forcefully and be allowed to canter for a few hundred yards.

On the Flat or over jumps, every racehorse must learn the art of keeping himself balanced while negotiating bends and how to stretch out at the gallop. It is not until these crucial stages are broached that the trainer will learn the potential racing ability of his charge.

BREASLEY, SCOBIE

Winner of four Classics plus a host of other big races, champion jockey on the Flat four times and a rider of exceptional skill and judgement of pace, Scobie Breasley was in the vanguard of the group of Australian jockeys who graced British racing in the 1950s and 1960s. Born Arthur Edward Breasley in Wagga Wagga, New South Wales, in 1914, he took his nickname from the trainer Jim Scobie and rode his first winner, Noogee, at Melbourne in 1928. He moved to England in 1950 and was soon on the Classic scoreboard, with Ki Ming in the 1951 Two Thousand Guineas and Festoon in the 1954 One Thousand Guineas.

Scobie Breasley married his wife May on 5 November 1935 – the day his great rival Lester Piggott was born.

It was over a decade before he rode his next Classic winner, landing the 1964 Derby on Santa Claus at the age of 50 and following up with a second Derby win two years later on Charlottown in 1966. Those were his only four English Classics, but he won plenty of other big races, including the Coronation Cup, Eclipse Stakes, King George and Prix de l'Arc de Triomphe on the great **Ballymoss** in 1958, while other notable horses with whom he was associated were Pipe Of Peace and Reform, both trained by Sir Gordon Richards. Scobie Breasley was champion jockey in 1957, 1961, 1962 and 1963 (when he rode 176 winners, one more than his long-time rival Lester Piggott) and retired in 1968 having ridden 2,160 winners in Britain. The high point of his subsequent training career was the victory of Steel Pulse in the 1972 Irish Derby, and after spells training in England, France and America he retired from the sport in 1980.

BREAST GIRTH

A length of webbing which fits around the horse's chest and, kept in place by a neckstrap, is attached to each side of the saddle to prevent the saddle slipping backwards. (Sometimes known as a 'breast plate'.)

BREEDERS' CUP

Web: www.breederscup.com

'Why, John – I didn't know you smoked pot!' The reaction of 85-year-old American breeder John Galbreath to John Gaines's suggestion of a richly endowed annual programme of championship races clustered on the same afternoon's card was typical. Gaines was a prominent breeder in the USA, but many thought his idea that North America should put on a racing equivalent of the Superbowl or World Series completely scatty. Yet the sceptics were soon silenced as his vision came to fruition in November 1984 and then proved so successful that the Breeders' Cup was soon acknowledged as the sport's biggest day. Indeed, this extravaganza where the best horses from around the globe meet for huge prizes has changed the whole shape of the racing year, and is now in effect the world championship of racing.

The Breeders' Cup programme – which is financed by the breeding industry worldwide and takes place in late October or early November (the timing and venue change from year to year) – now consists of eight races. The exact distances may vary slightly according to the host track, but this was the card at Churchill Downs in 2000:

Breeders' Cup Distaff for three-year-old and upwards fillies and mares: 1 mile 1 furlong, dirt

Breeders' Cup Juvenile Fillies for two-year-old fillies: 1 mile 1/2 furlong, dirt

Breeders' Cup Mile for three-year-olds and upwards: 1 mile, turf

Breeders' Cup Sprint for three-year-olds and upwards: 6 furlongs, dirt

Breeders' Cup Filly & Mare Turf for three-year-old and upwards fillies and mares: 1 mile 3 furlongs, turf

Breeders' Cup Juvenile for two-year-old colts and geldings: 1 mile 1/2 furlong, dirt

Breeders' Cup Turf for three-year-olds and upwards: 1 1/2 miles, turf

Breeders' Cup Classic for three-year-olds and upwards: 1 1/4 miles, dirt

British-trained Breeders' Cup winners

1985 *Turf*	Pebbles (Clive Brittain)
1991 *Sprint*	Sheikh Albadou (Alex Scott)
1994 *Mile*	Barathea (Luca Cumani)
1996 *Turf*	Pilsudski (Michael Stoute)
1999 *Turf*	Daylami (Saeed bin Suroor)
2000 *Turf*	Kalanisi (Michael Stoute)

Irish-trained Breeders' Cup winners

1990 *Mile*	Royal Academy (Vincent O'Brien)
1995 *Mile*	Ridgewood Pearl (John Oxx)

French-trained Breeders' Cup winners

1984 *Turf*	Lashkari (Alain de Royer-Dupré)
1986 *Mile*	Last Tycoon (Robert Collet)
1987 *Mile*	Miesque (François Boutin)
1988 *Mile*	Miesque (François Boutin)
1990 *Turf*	In The Wings (André Fabre)
1991 *Juvenile*	Arazi (François Boutin)
1991 *Turf*	Miss Alleged (Pascal Bary)
1993 *Classic*	Arcangues (André Fabre)
1994 *Turf*	Tikkanen (Jonathan Pease)
1997 *Mile*	Spinning World (Jonathan Pease)

Breeders' Cup venues

1984	Hollywood Park, California
1985	Aqueduct, New York
1986	Santa Anita, California
1987	Hollywood Park, California
1988	Churchill Downs, Kentucky
1989	Gulfstream Park, Florida
1990	Belmont Park, New York
1991	Churchill Downs, Kentucky
1992	Gulfstream Park, Florida
1993	Santa Anita, California
1994	Churchill Downs, Kentucky
1995	Belmont Park, New York
1996	Woodbine, Toronto
1997	Hollywood Park, California
1998	Churchill Downs, Kentucky
1999	Gulfstream Park, Florida
2000	Churchill Downs, Kentucky
2001	Belmont Park, New York

Most valuable of the eight races is the Classic, whose sterling equivalent of £1,710,621 to the winning owner in 2000 made it the second most valuable horse race in the world after the **Dubai World Cup**.

As befits a fixture of this quality and value, the history of the Breeders' Cup is awash with performances and moments which will live long in racing's memory:

- The 1985 Turf going to **Pebbles**, first British-trained winner of a Breeders' Cup race
- **Dancing Brave**'s shock defeat in the 1986 Turf
- Famous finishes in the Classic: Ferdinand and Alysheba in 1987, Sunday Silence and Easy Goer in 1989, Tiznow and **Giant's Causeway** in 2000
- **Miesque** winning back-to-back runnings of the Mile in 1987 and 1988
- The unforgettable 1990 Breeders' Cup afternoon: **Dayjur** jumping the shadow, the death of Go For Wand, and Lester Piggott winning the Mile on Royal Academy
- **Arazi**'s sensational slalom to victory in the 1991 Juvenile
- Barathea and Frankie Dettori scorching home in the 1994 Mile
- **Cigar** raising the roof in the 1995 Classic
- **Pilsudski** landing the 1996 Turf under Walter Swinburn
- Dettori's disgrace when **Swain** veered away from the whip to lose the 1998 Classic . . .

- . . . and Dettori's delight when **Daylami** stormed clear in the 1999 Turf

There's simply no single day's racing in the world like the Breeders' Cup – which from 2001 will be officially named the Breeders' Cup World Thoroughbred Championships.

The Breeders' Cup Steeplechase was run from 1986 to 1993 at a variety of locations – Fair Hill, Maryland; Far Hills, New Jersey; Belmont Park, New York – and won by some familiar names: Morley Street, trained by Toby Balding, in 1990 and 1991; Highland Bud (formerly a good hurdler in England) in 1989 and 1992; and Lonesome Glory in 1993. Between 1987 and 1999 the race was not run. It was renewed at Far Hills in 2000, when prize money of $250,000 made it the richest steeplechase in the USA.

BREEDING

The breeding business underpins the whole sport of horse racing, for the Thoroughbred racehorse is a very specialised animal, carefully bred for a particular purpose – to win races. But the apparently straightforward requirement to breed a horse which can run fast has to be balanced by other considerations, such as soundness (a horse which keeps breaking down under the pressures of training and racing is not much of a prospect) and temperament (a horse not mentally

Breeders' Cup winners since 1990

Year	Sprint	Mile	Turf	Classic
1990	Safely Kept	Royal Academy *IRE*	In The Wings *FRA*	Unbridled
1991	Sheikh Albadou *GB*	Opening Verse	Miss Alleged *FRA*	Black Tie Affair
1992	Thirty Slews	Lure	Fraise	A.P. Indy
1993	Cardmania	Lure	Kotashaan	Arcangues *FRA*
1994	Cherokee Run	Barathea *GB*	Tikkanen *FRA*	Concern
1995	Desert Stormer	Ridgewood Pearl *IRE*	Northern Spur	Cigar
1996	Lit de Justice	Da Hoss	Pilsudski *GB*	Alphabet Soup
1997	Elmhurst	Spinning World *FRA*	Chief Bearhart *CAN*	Skip Away
1998	Reraise	Da Hoss	Buck's Boy	Awesome Again
1999	Artax	Silic	Daylami *GB*	Cat Thief
2000	Kona Gold	War Chant	Kalanisi *GB*	Tiznow

equipped to cope with the strain of racing will not perform to the best of its physical ability).

The racehorse we know today is the result of some three centuries of careful breeding. By the sixteenth century the type of horse most commonly used for racing in what is now the British Isles was the 'hobby', a small but extremely tough and durable animal which had been imported from Spain to Ireland, whence it had become popular for racing in England. But the desire to add more speed to the bloodlines led, towards the end of the seventeenth century, to the import from the Near East of the three famous Arab stallions whose influence has made the English Thoroughbred the standard breed for the sport in all major racing countries of the world: the **Byerley Turk**, the **Darley Arabian** and the **Godolphin Arabian**. Every single modern Thoroughbred traces his or her ancestry to one of this trio.

Horse races in the eighteenth century were usually run over what we would consider exceptionally long distances (around four miles) and in heats: the winners would go through to run off for the prize. But towards the end of the century significant changes took place. Races for two-year-olds were instituted, encouraging breeders to produce more precocious types rather than solely horses who would not run until they were mature at four or five. Handicaps were introduced, to make racing a more interesting betting medium. And what became the Classics, for three-year-olds only, were first staged: the St Leger in 1776, the Oaks in 1779 and the Derby in 1780. (The Two Thousand Guineas was first run early the following century, in 1809, with the inaugural One Thousand five years later in 1814.)

Shorter races called for horses who could run faster, and there was more emphasis on early development. Racehorses became bigger. The Darley Arabian had stood 15 hands high, the Godolphin Arabian just 14 hands 3 inches and the diminutive Gimcrack 14 hands 1 inch; Eclipse, at 15 hands 3 inches, was considered tall. By the middle of the nineteenth century the average Thoroughbred was about six inches taller

than the founding fathers of the breed.

Since the Second World War the increasing importance and influence of American bloodlines have seen the ideal middle distance of the Classic horse on the Flat shift from a mile and a half (the distance of the Derby at Epsom) to a mile and a quarter (the distance of the Kentucky Derby): connections of a potential stallion looking to attract US breeders will want their horse to have won over 10 furlongs if possible. Another recent trend is a move away from extreme precocity towards a longer racing career for the best horses. It is no longer crucial for a Derby candidate to have shown serious form as a two-year-old.

Horses bred for National Hunt racing are given more time to mature before being subjected to the rigours of racing. The earliest age at which a horse may run over hurdles is three, and many a potential steeplechaser is kept as a 'store', not going into training until the age of four or five. While breeding for the Flat is dominated by a few super-rich operations such as those of the **Maktoum brothers**, other major Arab owner-breeders, the **Aga Khan** and the **Coolmore Stud**, breeding racehorses is still much more than a private playground for the super-rich. The history of National Hunt racing is littered with examples of cheaply bred horses who have hit the heights on the racecourse: **Desert Orchid**, for example, was home-bred by James Burridge from a mare whose dam he had purchased for 175 guineas.

At whatever level, the real fascination of breeding is in the choice of mating, as enthralling and unpredictable in horses as it can be in humans. All sorts of theories have been tried out in the quest for the perfect racehorse, but for a realistic approach one can hardly put it better than the late John Hislop, breeder of the great Brigadier Gerard: 'All that the breeder can do is to try to arrange matters so that there is a reasonable chance of the right genetic shakeup emerging, and hope for the best.' The 'right genetic shakeup' would be a balance of temperamental and physical attributes that embodied speed, stamina, toughness, conformation and resolution in their ideal proportions.

Breeding on an international scale is an immensely complex business, but the fundamental cycle of the breeding year in Britain is fairly straightforward. On 15 February begins the 'covering season', which lasts five months until 15 July. The owner of the mare will have decided, usually after much research, advice and pondering, which stallion he wishes to mate her with. Major breeders may send a mare to a stallion whom they themselves own or in whom they have an interest, but in any event the stallion will normally be standing at a stud, to which the mare will be sent. The gestation period of a Thoroughbred being about eleven months (320–360 days), she may well be carrying a foal conceived the previous year; in this case she will arrive shortly before that foal is due, give birth at the stud and then await the next covering. She will come into season ('on heat') about eight to ten days after foaling, and thereafter at three-weekly intervals.

If the mare appears to be in season, the next stage is to introduce her to a 'teaser', a stallion – in some cases, but not all, sterile – kept by the stud for the purpose of gauging the mares' sexual response. The teaser flirts with the mare by nibbling her across the 'trying board' over which they are introduced, and if she reacts favourably he is led away to repeat this frustrating task with another mare while the vet examines this one. The reason why the stallion who will actually cover the mare is not allowed to engage in this foreplay himself is to protect him – and his owners' investment: for if the mare is not receptive she may show her reluctance with considerable violence, and a swift bite or kick could cause considerable damage to millions of pounds' worth of horseflesh. Some stallions, moreover, can do with a warm-up act, being less than entirely psychologically committed or biologically suited to their calling: **The Tetrarch**, one of the most brilliant racehorses the Turf has ever seen, had a singular lack of interest in sex while at stud, though he managed to produce several good offspring, and more recently the stud career of the great

American horse **Cigar** was a disaster: he proved infertile, and was taken out of stud duties.

If the mare's reactions to the teaser show that the time is right for the covering to go ahead, she is washed off in the appropriate area (to prevent the spread of infection), her tail is bandaged and she is fitted with felt shoes on her hind feet in case she should lash out. The stallion is then led into the covering barn to meet his mate. One groom holds the mare's upper lip in a twitch (a loop of rope attached to a stick) to keep her still while another lifts one of her forelegs to make it difficult for her to kick out. He releases it as she is mounted, when the stallion man, who looks after the stallion and supervises the mating, helps his charge achieve efficient penetration. The whole covering operation should take a minute or two.

If the mare does not conceive at that covering, the procedure is repeated when she is next in season, and a stallion will sometimes cover the same mare several times. (He will often need to cover several mares in a day, as it cannot be accurately predicted well in advance exactly when any mare will be receptive.) Although a pregnancy can be detected as early as 14 days after covering, the mare will not normally return to her owner until the pregnancy has become properly established, around two months after mating. She will then remain at home while the foal develops, returning to the stud the following year in time to give birth.

Covering fees for stallions vary considerably according to the status of the stallion involved. A nomination (the right to send a mare to be covered by a particular stallion) to **Sadler's Wells**, currently the most influential stallion in the world, is not available to any Tom, Dick or Harry breeder, but had you set your sights a little lower for the 2001 covering season you could, subject to availability and the acceptability of your mare, have had her covered by **Giant's Causeway** for a six-figure fee; if your pocket does not stretch to that, how about Singspiel, ultra-tough winner of many big races around the world including the Dubai World Cup and Japan Cup, for a mere £20,000, or the 1985 Derby winner Slip Anchor for a trifling £4,000?

There is usually a 'no foal, no fee' condition which stipulates that the fee is payable only if the mare is certified in foal on 1 October of the year in which the covering took place. Sometimes other arrangements apply, under which, for example, the breeder pays half the fee at covering and half when conception is confirmed, or part of the fee is held back until a live foal is born.

The very best male racehorses are often 'syndicated' for stud purposes, which means that ownership is divided into shares, each worth an equal portion of the total valuation of the horse.

The owners of top stallions usually put a ceiling on the number of mares their prized investment may cover in a season – not because of the risk of exhaustion to the horse but on the grounds that too many offspring would undermine the value of the stock. Other stallions have had to be more vigorous: Be My Native, winner of the Coronation Cup in 1983, covered 325 mares at the Grange Stud in Co. Cork during 1994, and it is common for National Hunt sires to be kept very busy.

Lammtarra was the first Derby winner to be the produce of a Derby winner and an Oaks winner. The 1995 Epsom hero was by Nijinsky, winner of the Derby in 1970, out of Snow Bride, promoted to first place in the 1989 Oaks on the disqualification of Aliysa for failing the dope test.

When to have a mare covered, and thus when her foal is to be born, can be a difficult question. A foal conceived at a covering in March should be born the following February, whereas a June mating would mean (assuming a full-term pregnancy) a May foal. Taking into account the rule by which every Thoroughbred's official birthday falls on the 1 January preceding its biological birthday, deciding on the ideal timing involves weighing up different factors: an early foal may mature sooner than others of its generation, and thus possibly have the advantage over them in juvenile races; but a later foal will have the benefit of better grass and climate when it is very young, which may give its physical development a better start.

A commercial breeder may sell the foal later in the year of its birth, or may wait until the following year, when the youngster will be sold as a yearling and go into training with a view to racing on the Flat the year after as a two-year-old. The business of buying foals and then selling them on as yearlings is known as pinhooking.

The top yearling sales, where trainers, owners and bloodstock agents compete at auction for the best young horses, form a great international circus, starting at the Keeneland sales in Kentucky in July, moving on to Deauville in France and the Goffs' sales in Ireland, and culminating in the October sales held at Newmarket by the famous firm of **Tattersalls**, founded in 1766 and the world's most renowned bloodstock auctioneers. The competition in these contests for the Classic winners of the future can be extremely hot, and periodically (especially when fuelled by a head-to-head battle between two or more of the dominant players) sends prices sky-high. In recent years the market has settled down somewhat, with the realisation that yearling prices were bearing little relation to the likely returns from either racing or breeding; but back in the mid-1980s the hothouse atmosphere of the sale ring saw some crazy sums changing hands. The current record price paid for a yearling at the sales was set when Seattle Dancer – a son of Nijinsky – was sold to the Robert Sangster group of breeders for $13.1 million in 1985. The colt turned out to be a reasonably good racehorse, but – hardly surprisingly, set such a target – recouped only a small portion of his purchase price in prize money on the track.

Even that could not be said of the famous Snaafi Dancer, the Northern Dancer colt who caused a sensation when sold to Sheikh Mohammed at the Keeneland sales in 1983 for $10.2 million (then the world record price) after a prolonged sale-ring battle with Sangster. Snaafi Dancer went into training with John Dunlop, where it rapidly became apparent that, as a racehorse, he was completely useless. He then was shipped off to stud in Canada, where he proved equally useless as a stallion.

See also **studs**.

BREEZE-UP

A 'breeze-up sale' is a bloodstock sale at which the lots are put through their paces in front of prospective purchasers, cantering over about three furlongs of the course at which the sale is being held. ('Breeze' is racing jargon for going an easy pace.)

BRIGADIER GERARD

Winner of 17 of his 18 races between 1970 and 1972, Brigadier Gerard was home-bred – by the unfashionable sire Queen's Hussar out of La Paiva – by his owners John and Jean Hislop and sent to trainer **Dick Hern** at West Ilsley. Four wins from four races as a two-year-old in 1970 (the last of these the Middle Park Stakes at Newmarket) made the colt an outstanding prospect for the 1971 Two Thousand Guineas, but in that race he was opposed by two horses officially rated his superior as juveniles, **Mill Reef** and My Swallow, and The Brigadier (who did not have a preliminary outing) started third favourite at 11–2. Ridden as in all his races by **Joe Mercer**, Brigadier Gerard powered down the stands side to win by three lengths from Mill Reef. He ran five more times in 1971, winning the St James's Palace Stakes at Royal Ascot, Sussex Stakes at Goodwood, Goodwood Mile, Queen Elizabeth II Stakes at Ascot and Champion Stakes at Newmarket.

He remained in training as a four-year-old and straight away resumed the winning habit, mopping up the Lockinge Stakes at Newbury, Westbury Stakes at Sandown Park (nowadays named the Brigadier Gerard Stakes in his honour), Prince of Wales's Stakes at Royal Ascot and Eclipse Stakes. The last three of those races were over a mile and a quarter, widely thought to be the limit of the horse's stamina, but the Hislops were adventurous campaigners, and Brigadier Gerard was stepped up to one and a half miles for the 1972 King George VI and Queen Elizabeth Stakes at Ascot. Here his connections' boldness was rewarded with a hard-fought victory over Parnell and Riverman to give him 15 wins out of 15 races.

Mill Reef had also remained in training, and another clash between these two greats in the inaugural Benson and Hedges Gold Cup over a mile and a quarter at the York August meeting was eagerly awaited. Then an injury to Mill Reef during his preparation seemed to leave the race at The Brigadier's mercy. He started at 3–1 on, but Roberto, ridden by Panamanian jockey Braulio Baeza and starting at 12–1 (an insulting price for the current Derby winner) scorched out of the gate and led all the way to win by three lengths: 'He must have been stung by a bee,' commented Jean Hislop.

Brigadier Gerard, whose sire was Queen's Hussar, was named after an Arthur Conan Doyle character: an officer in the Hussars de Conflan in Napoleon's army.

Brigadier Gerard may have been beaten at last but he remained a hugely popular performer, and racegoers poured into Ascot to see him right his crown with a six-length victory over Sparkler in the Queen Elizabeth II Stakes – then flocked to Newmarket for the Champion Stakes, raising the roof when he outgalloped Riverman in a glorious finale to a glorious racing career as the finest miler of the post-war period in Europe. His time at stud was less distinguished, with only one English Classic winner to his name: Light Cavalry (1980 St Leger). Brigadier Gerard died in October 1989 at the age of 21.

BRIGHTON

Freshfield Road, Racehill, Brighton, East Sussex BN2 2XZ
Tel.: 01273 603580
Fax: 01273 673267
E-mail: info@brighton-racecourse.co.uk
Web: www.brighton-racecourse.co.uk

Somehow Brighton racecourse has never quite managed to shrug off the reputation it acquired in Graham Greene's 1938 novel

Brighton Rock as the stamping ground of razor-toting gangs, but nowadays the chance of bumping into Richard Attenborough on the raceday held during the Labour Party conference is greater than that of encountering Pinkie, the character he played in the film of the novel. Yet like the town, the racecourse retains a slight air of raffishness.

One of the four tracks in the country which is not a circuit (the others are Epsom Downs, Newmarket and York), the left-handed course is in the shape of a hammered-out horseshoe a fraction short of a mile and a half in length. Runners tackling the longest distance raced over here, one mile three furlongs 196 yards (called one and a half miles before the course was properly measured), go uphill from the start for about half a mile, negotiating left-hand turns, then, turning for home about five furlongs out, run downhill until a quarter of a mile out, when the ground rises again.

Operatic Society, one of the most popular geldings on the Flat since the war, ran 14 times at Brighton and won seven races on the course, where there are now a bar and a race named after him.

Uphill and downhill, sweeping left-hand turns – sounds familiar? . . . The terrain of Brighton has distinct similarities with that of the Derby course at Epsom Downs, and time was when Brighton was considered a course on which trainers could assess the agility and balance of their Classic hopefuls. With a series of valuable trials taking place elsewhere, Brighton has lost favour in this respect in recent years, and the last horse to run prominently in the Derby after flexing his muscles around here was Cacoethes, third to Nashwan in 1989: his seasonal debut had been in a minor race at Brighton.

The undulations make Brighton a course for the nimble and quick-actioned rather than the long-striding type of horse.

With much of the action skirting a housing estate, Brighton is not the most scenic track in the country, but it commands wonderful views of the English Channel, and with many of its fixtures catering for large holiday crowds, the atmosphere is usually one of relaxed jollity.

BRING DOWN

In jumping, a horse is deemed to have been 'brought down' if it falls through no mistake of its own – for, instance, if it is crashes into a horse which has fallen in front of it.

BRITISH HORSERACING BOARD

42 Portman Square, London W1H 6EN
Tel.: 020 7396 0011
Fax: 020 7935 0131
E-mail: info@bhb.co.uk
Web: www.thebhb.co.uk

The British Horseracing Board – BHB – was launched as the governing authority of British racing in June 1993 with the following formal aims and objectives: 'The British Horseracing Board will strive to secure and maintain significant improvements to the finances of the spectator sport, entertainment industry and betting medium of Flat and Jump horseracing. It will aim to do this for the benefit of all those who invest and work in Racing and derive enjoyment from it, and in order to enhance British Racing's competitive position internationally.' Broadly, the BHB has taken over the role of racing's governing body from the **Jockey Club**, and its jurisdiction covers such areas as the fixture list and race planning, funding, training and education, marketing and the promotion of racing to potential owners, sponsors and racegoers. The board has a chairman (currently **Peter Savill**) and 11 directors – four appointed by the Jockey Club, three by the Industry Committee, and two each by the Racehorse Owners' Association and the Racecourse Association – and its standing committees are the Industry Committee, the Race Planning Committee, the British Horseracing Training Board and the Finance Committee.

BRITISH RACING SCHOOL

Snailwell Road, Newmarket, Suffolk CB8 7NU
Tel.: 01638 665103
Fax: 01638 560929
E-mail: enquiries@brs.org.uk
Web: www.brs.org.uk

Based in Newmarket, the British Racing School was founded in 1983 with the aim of providing school leavers with the opportunity to learn the rudiments of stablecraft and jockeyship before being placed with trainers.

BRITTAIN, CLIVE

Born in 1933, Clive Brittain worked as a stable lad (and latterly head lad) for the great Newmarket trainer **Noel Murless** for many years before taking out his own licence in 1972. His fondness for going for the top prizes with less-than-obvious contenders has been likened to Don Quixote tilting at windmills, but the results have been much more effective than those of his fictional counterpart, and he has scored many notable coups around the globe. He sent out the wonderful filly **Pebbles** to become the first ever British-trained winner of a Breeders' Cup race when lifting the Turf at Aqueduct in 1985; his Bold Arrangement was the first ever British-trained runner in the Kentucky Derby when runner-up to Ferdinand in 1986; his Jupiter Island was the first British-trained winner of the Japan Cup in 1986; and his exceptionally durable Luso won 10 races in four countries. Clive Brittain has won every Classic except the Derby: the Two Thousand Guineas (Mystiko, 1991); the One Thousand Guineas (Pebbles, 1984; Sayyedati, 1993); the Oaks (User Friendly, 1992); and the St Leger (Julio Mariner, 1978; User Friendly, 1992). Yet though the Derby has to date eluded him, the performance of his colt Terimon in the 1989 running epitomised the Clive Brittain spirit: unconsidered in the market, the colt ran second to Nashwan at 500–1, the longest-priced horse ever placed in a Classic.

BROODMARE

Filly or mare kept at stud for breeding purposes.

BROOKSHAW, TIM

Born in 1929, Tim Brookshaw was one of the strongest and bravest National Hunt riders of the post-war period. He was champion jockey in 1958–9, the season in which he performed his most famous feat of horsemanship when riding **Wyndburgh** into second place in the Grand National – beaten only one and half lengths by Oxo – despite having a stirrup leather break at second Becher's (nine fences from home) and riding the last mile and a half with no stirrups: the following morning he confessed to feeling 'a bit stiff'. While he never won the National, Cheltenham Gold Cup or Champion Hurdle, he took the 1963 Scottish National on Pappageno's Cottage. A fall at Aintree in December 1963 left him paralysed from the waist down, but some good came out of this misfortune: the Farrell Brookshaw Fund was set up to assist him and fellow jockey Paddy Farrell, whose career was also brought to a halt that season, and from that fund evolved the **Injured Jockeys' Fund**. It took more than paralysis to dampen Tim Brookshaw's indomitable spirit: he returned to the saddle in jockeys' show jumping competitions, and in April 1977 took part in a charity Flat race at Navan. One of the true greats of his trade, he died in 1981. Steve Brookshaw, trainer of 1997 Grand National winner Lord Gyllene, is Tim Brookshaw's nephew.

BROWBAND

Part of the bridle which goes round the top of the horse's head and fits under its forelock. Stops the headpiece slipping backwards.

BROWN JACK

One of the greatest and most popular stayers of the twentieth century, Brown Jack was bred in Ireland, and after two unsuccessful outings as a three-year-old in that country (he did not run at two) was sold to Sir Harold Wernher for £750, with an extra £50 to be paid if the horse ever won a race. In the event, he won 25 of his 65 races between 1927 and 1934.

Brown Jack made his English debut in September 1927 over hurdles at Bournemouth, finishing third. He won his next race, over hurdles at Wolverhampton, and developed into such a fine hurdler that by the end of the 1927–8 season he had won seven races, notably the second ever running of the Champion Hurdle at Cheltenham, for which the four-year-old Brown Jack started at 4–1 and earned Sir Harold £680. That Champion Hurdle victory caught the eye of the great jockey **Steve Donoghue**, who suggested to Brown Jack's then trainer Aubrey Hastings that the horse should run on the Flat. Rarely in racing has better advice been given. By the end of his illustrious career Brown Jack had won 18 races on the level from 55 outings, including the Ascot Stakes (1928), Goodwood Cup (1930), Doncaster Cup (1930), Chester Cup (1931, carrying 9st 6lb) and Ebor Handicap (1931, under 9st 5lb).

Philip Larkin's famous poem about old racehorses in a field, 'At Grass', was inspired by his watching a film about Brown Jack's retirement.

But the Queen Alexandra Stakes at Royal Ascot, at two and three-quarter miles the longest distance in the Flat calendar, was the race which Brown Jack really made his own. He first won this marathon in 1929, three days after finishing runner-up in the Ascot Stakes at the same meeting, and proceeded to repeat the achievement five times in a row. The scenes following his sixth victory at the age of 10 in 1934 have been famously described by Steve Donoghue, who rode him in most of his races on the Flat, including all six victories in the Queen Alexandra: 'Never will I forget the roar of that crowd as long as I live. Ascot or no Ascot, they went mad. I have never seen so many hats flung in the air, and I have never heard such shrieks of joy in my life.' Ivor Anthony, who following the death of Aubrey Hastings in 1929 had trained Brown Jack for most of his career, had not been able to watch the race, and had sat under a tree in the paddock until the noise from the crowd told him that Brown Jack had duly won. The horse never raced again.

Brown Jack, a great character who liked nothing better than leaning against his manger and having a kip, died at his owner's home in 1948.

BRUISED FOOT

The underside of the foot is quite sensitive in many Thoroughbreds and can fairly easily be damaged. If a horse steps on a large stone it may well bruise the sole, and will feel sore and unwilling to put its weight on that foot. A sharp stone or spike – anything that actually punctures the sole – can cause a more serious problem by allowing infection to enter the foot, leading to the build-up of pus. The resulting pressure inside the hoof will cause the horse considerable discomfort and he will be noticeably lame. An infected foot will need to be treated with antibiotics and poulticing: the application of a hot compress to draw the pus out of the foot.

BRUSH PRICKER

An attachment to a horse's bit in the form of a small brush. If the horse hangs in the direction of the brush he will feel a mild pricking pain and (so the theory goes) straighten up. High-profile instances of the benefit of fitting a brush pricker include Belmez, whose bridle was so adorned when he won the King George VI and Queen Elizabeth Diamond Stakes in 1990, and 1999 Grand National winner Papillon, who wore one for some of his races.

BUCKLE, FRANK

Until Lester Piggott won the St Leger on Commanche Run in 1984, no jockey in history had ridden more Classic winners than Frank Buckle, whose record of 27 had stood since 1827. Those 27 wins consisted of: Two Thousand Guineas five times; One Thousand Guineas six times; Derby five times; Oaks nine times; and St Leger twice. Born in 1766, Buckle rode in his first race in 1783 (weighing out at 3 stone 13 pounds) and his last at the age of 65 in 1831. He died the following year.

BUCKPASSER

Forced to miss the US Triple Crown races in 1966 on account of injury, his exploits none the less proclaimed Buckpasser one of the best American horses of the post-war period. He won nine of his 11 races as a two-year-old, and at three was beaten only once in 14 outings and was voted Horse of the Year: in the Arlington Classic he set a new world record for a mile. At four he won three from six, and retired winner of 25 of his 31 races, unplaced only once. As a stallion at Claiborne Farm in Kentucky his offspring included 1980 One Thousand Guineas winner Quick As Lightning. Buckpasser died of a heart attack in 1978 at the age of 15.

BUDGETT, ARTHUR

Arthur Budgett was only the second person in racing history to breed, own and train two winners of the Derby, after William I'Anson in the mid-nineteenth century. Born in 1916, Budgett took out a training licence in 1939, though he did not win a Classic until 30 years later when his Blakeney – a son of Windmill Girl, whom he had trained to become a very high-class filly, second in the 1964 Oaks – landed the Derby, a victory which helped Budgett become champion trainer in 1969. His second success came with Morston – also a son of Windmill Girl – in 1973. Other well-known horses trained by Arthur Budgett include Commissar, Blast, Derring-Do, Huntercombe, Petty Officer, Dominion and Daring Boy.

BUG

American slang for an **apprentice** jockey.

BULL, PHIL

When Phil Bull died in June 1989 at the age of 79, racing in Britain lost one of its most influential personalities and one of its shrewdest brains. Instantly recognisable on the racecourse by his large white beard and ever-present huge cigar, Bull left a permanent mark on racing – and earned the undying gratitude of millions of punters – by founding the **Timeform** organisation.

Phil Bull was born in 1910. It is said that his father, a Salvation Army captain, was drawn to betting after a religious slogan he had posted on a wall in Doncaster asking 'What shall we do to be saved?' was answered by an anonymous scrawler, 'Back Doricles for the St Leger.' Captain Bull took the advice, collected

at 40–1, and passed on to his son a love of racing and betting. A mathematics graduate of the University of Leeds and subsequently a maths teacher in London, Bull adopted the the pseudonym William K. Temple and started a service for punters called Temple's Racetime Analysis, based on the then revolutionary method of studying the horses' times in races. In the 1940s he began publishing the *Best Horses* series, which became the *Racehorses* annuals, cornerstone of any serious racing library.

Phil Bull was not a man amused by what he saw as petty bureaucracy. When in 1984 Weatherbys declined to register the name Ho Chi Minh for a colt he owned, on the grounds that 'it is Jockey Club policy to tread warily when there there is any risk of causing ill feeling' and it was considered that 'Ho Chi Minh's influence and following is still strong enough to warrant such caution', Bull fired off a stinging riposte comparing this rejection with the allowed naming of the chaser Henry Kissinger – and then registered the name as Ho Mi Chinh.

Among the best horses he owned were Orgoglio (Champagne Stakes 1951), Pheidippides (Gimcrack Stakes 1957) and Sostenuto (Ebor Handicap 1962), and he bred the good miler Romulus (winner of the Sussex Stakes and Queen Elizabeth II Stakes in 1962). A man of forthright opinions eloquently expressed, Phil Bull is well summed up by the jacket blurb on the biography by Howard Wright: 'A man who made a fortune out of betting on horses, a writer and publisher of international repute, a successful racehorse breeder and owner, a political thinker and philosopher, and a longtime campaigner for reform in the sport of racing.'

BUMPER

The popular term for a National Hunt Flat race – that is, a race under National Hunt Rules where the runners do not jump any obstacles. Bumpers, which are usually confined to four-, five- and six-year-olds who have not run on the Flat, have long been a common feature of racing in Ireland but were introduced to British racing only in the 1970s.

By winning the Tote Festival Bumper, last race on the last day of the Cheltenham Festival in 1992, and the Trafalgar House Novices' Hurdle, first race on the first day of the 1993 Festival, Montelado achieved the highly unusual feat of winning two consecutive Cheltenham Festival races.

Principal bumper of the season is the Festival Bumper at the Cheltenham National Hunt Festival: first run in 1992, this has in its short life produced winners of the calibre of Dato Star (1995), Florida Pearl (1997), Alexander Banquet (1998) and Monsignor (1999). Although bumpers rarely set the racegoer's pulse quivering – they tend to be placed at the end of the day's programme when fainthearts are scurrying towards the car park to make a quick getaway – they are now a very fertile breeding ground for champions, and many a future winner can be spotted having his early education in a bumper in the gathering gloom.

BUNBURY, SIR CHARLES

The great Turf reformer Sir Charles Bunbury (1740–1821), who became Steward of the **Jockey Club** in 1768, was extremely influential both in building up the authority of the Club and in improving the speed of the Thoroughbred by introducing shorter races for younger horses: it was during his regime that the Classics were founded. But Bunbury's firmest claim to Turf immortality is his part in the naming of the Derby: if legend is to be believed, he and the 12th Earl of Derby, having come up with the idea for the race, tossed a coin to decide whose name the new event should carry. Had that coin come down the other way, Galileo would have won the Irish Bunbury, and Everton and Liverpool would twice a year lock horns in a local Bunbury. But Sir Charles had rapid consolation for losing the toss: his colt Diomed won the first ever running of the Derby on 4 May 1780. The Bunbury Cup is a competitive one-mile handicap run at the July Meeting at Newmarket, where the one-mile distance on the July Course is formally known as the Bunbury Mile.

BURLINGTON BERTIE

Betting slang for 100–30.

BURST

When a horse **breaks a blood vessel** it is often said to have 'burst'.

BUSTINO

Bustino wrote his name on the Classic roll of honour when landing the 1974 St Leger, but his Turf immortality is ensured by his heroic role as runner-up to **Grundy** in 'The Race of the Century', the King George VI and Queen Elizabeth Diamond Stakes at Ascot in July 1975. A son of Busted, Bustino could be expected to be a late developer, and connections – owner **Lady Beaverbrook** and trainer **Dick Hern** – were careful to give him a quiet time as a two-year-old: he had just one race as a juvenile, running third in the Acomb Maiden Stakes at York in August 1973. He reappeared as a three-year-old in the Classic Trial at Sandown Park and beat Snow Knight, then defeated Sin Y Sin and Snow Knight in the Lingfield Derby Trial. Such performances made him a leading candidate for the Derby and at Epsom he started 8–1 third favourite, but he could finish only fourth behind 50–1 shock winner Snow Knight, who comprehensively reversed Sandown and Lingfield form. Bustino then ran second to Sagaro in the Grand Prix de Paris at Longchamp and beat Irish Derby winner English Prince in the Great Voltigeur Stakes at York. Such form was good enough to make him hot favourite for the St Leger, which he won easily from Giacometti and his own pacemaker, Riboson.

Bustino's four-year-old campaign consisted of just two races. He won the Coronation Cup in record time after a tremendous duel up the straight with the French horse Ashmore; and then came the King George. Bustino, who started second favourite at Ascot behind Derby winner Grundy and was assisted by two pacemakers to exploit his reserves of stamina, took up the running before the home turn and simply would not cave in once Grundy came at him. Grundy gradually got his nose in front, but Bustino fought back, and the pair served up a pulsating duel before Grundy prevailed by half a length.

Plans to train Bustino for the Prix de l'Arc de Triomphe were thwarted by an injury on the gallops and he never ran again, retiring the winner of five of his nine races (in all of which he was ridden by **Joe Mercer**). As a stallion he sired good horses such as Easter Sun, Bustomi, Bedtime, Paean and Terimon, but his most influential offspring was the filly Height Of Fashion, dam of Nashwan, Unfuwain and Nayef. Bustino, a magnificent stamp of a horse with a racing record to match, died in October 1997 at the age of 26.

BUTE

Phenylbutazone ($C_{19}H_{20}N_2O_2$) – commonly shortened to 'bute' following its trade names Butazolidin and Butazone – is an anti-inflammatory drug given to horses to ease musculoskeletal disorders. While the use of bute on racehorses is unrestricted in most states of the USA, in Britain it is a prohibited substance, and must not be traceable in a horse's system in the post-race dope test.

See also **Lasix**.

BUZZER

Horse for which there is significant support in the betting market.

BYERLEY TURK

One of the three founding stallions of the Thoroughbred breed (*see also* **Darley Arabian**, **Godolphin Arabian**), the Byerley Turk was foaled around 1680 and, according to some reports, saw action at the Battle of the Boyne before being sent to stud in Co. Durham. Among his distinguished descendants is **The Tetrarch**, 'The Spotted Wonder' who was unbeaten in seven races as a two-year-old in 1913, and recent Derby winners Blakeney and Dr Devious.

C

CAMBRIDGESHIRE

Handicap; three-year-olds and upwards;

1 mile 1 furlong (Newmarket, Rowley Mile)

The Cambridgeshire, nowadays a regular fixture in the top ten betting races of the year, was first run in 1839. In those far-flung days there were fewer opportunities for top-class horses, and it was not unusual for the race to attract Classic winners: Triple Crown winner Gladiateur was unplaced in 1865, as were other Derby winners Favonius in 1871 and St Gatien in 1885, while La Fleche, winner of the fillies' Triple Crown in 1892, won the Cambridgeshire under 8st 10lb the same year; Hannah, winner of the fillies' Triple Crown in 1871, was unplaced in 1872 and 1873. Shortly after that, three horses won the Cambridgeshire and the **Cesarewitch**, over twice the distance, in the same year: Rosebery (1876), Foxhall (1881) and Plaisanterie (1885). These days such combinations are all but inconceivable, but the Cambridgeshire does occasionally throw up an improving horse who graduates to the highest level.

There's no better example of this in recent memory than Halling, who won as a three-year-old in 1994, then developed into a tip-top ten-furlong horse, winning the Eclipse Stakes and International Stakes in both 1995 and 1996. Lear Spear, winner in 1998, won the prestigious Prince of Wales's Stakes at Royal Ascot at 20–1 the following year. For all that the race is often won by a top-class horse, the essence of the Cambridgeshire is the highly competitive handicap, and its history has been peppered with major betting coups. Risen Moon, trained by Barry Hills, landed a hefty touch in 1990, and in 1997 the Sir Mark Prescott-trained winner Pasternak was backed down to 4–1 starting price from 11–1 in the morning, reportedly taking £5 million from the bookies. There have been six dual winners of the Cambridgeshire: Hackler's Pride (1903 and 1904), Christmas Daisy (1909 and 1910), Sterope (1948 and 1949), Prince de Galles (1969 and 1970), Baronet (1978 and 1980) and Rambo's Hall (1989 and 1992).

Cambridgeshire winners since 1990

1990	Risen Moon	3	B. Hills	S. Cauthen	7–1F	40
1991	Mellottie	6	Mrs M. Reveley	J. Lowe	10–1	29
1992	Rambo's Hall	7	J. Glover	D. McKeown	9–2F	30
1993	Penny Drops	4	Lord Huntingdon	D. Harrison	7–1F	33
1994	Halling	3	J. Gosden	L. Dettori	8–1CF	30
1995	Cap Juluca	3	R. Charlton	R. Hughes	11–1	39
1996	Clifton Fox	4	J. Glover	N. Day	14–1	38
1997	Pasternak	4	Sir Mark Prescott	G. Duffield	4–1F	36
1998	Lear Spear	3	D. Elsworth	N. Pollard	20–1	35
1999	She's Our Mare	6	A. Martin *IRE*	F. Norton	11–1	33
2000	Katy Nowaitee	4	P. Harris	J. Reid	6–1	35

CAMERA PATROL

The camera patrol – which films races for subsequent scrutiny by the racecourse stewards – was introduced to England in 1960, having been a familiar part of the American racing scene for many years before that. 'Scout' cameras, which offer the additional evidence of film taken from the rear of the field, first came into use in 1965. Nowadays cameras are sited around the racecourse so that they can pick up every part of the race, and record crucial stages – such as the finishing straight – from various angles: these varying perspectives can often be crucial in the stewards' unravelling of exactly what happened. Filming of races in this way comes under the remit of **RaceTech**, whose pictures are often deployed into Channel Four Racing coverage: for example, the head-on shots which form a rapid element of post-race analysis come from the RaceTech service.

CANADA

Racing in Canada is closely linked with the sport in the neighbouring USA, with the best horses regularly crossing the border. Canada's main track is **Woodbine** in Toronto, venue of the 1996 Breeders' Cup and home of the Canadian International and of North America's oldest continuously running stakes race – the Queen's Plate, first run in 1860 at the old Woodbine track (now named Greenwood). The Queen's Plate, over one and a quarter miles on dirt, forms the first leg of the Canadian Triple Crown, followed by the Prince of Wales's Stakes over nine and a half furlongs on dirt at Fort Erie and the Breeders' Stakes over one and half miles on turf at Woodbine. All three races have been won by New Providence (1959), Canebora (1963), With Approval (1989), Izvestia (1990) and Dance Smartly (1991: she went on to win the Breeders' Cup Distaff that year). The influence of Canada on world racing has been considerable, not least through the exploits – both on the track and at stud – of **Northern Dancer**, bred in Canada by E. P. Taylor. His son **Nijinsky** was also Canadian-bred.

CANADIAN

See **Super Yankee**.

CANADIAN INTERNATIONAL

The Canadian International, over one and a half miles on turf at Woodbine in October, was first run in 1938, though it was not until the early 1970s that it reached its present position as one of the most prestigious international races in the world: it now forms the Canadian leg of the **Emirates World Series**. In 1973 it was won by the immortal **Secretariat**, and the following four years went to horses very familiar to European racing fans: in 1974 to **Dahlia**, in 1975 to 1974 Derby winner Snow Knight (by then in training in the USA), in 1976 to Prix du Jockey-Club winner Youth and in 1977 to Exceller, winner of that year's Coronation Cup. (Dahlia, Youth and Exceller were all trained in France by **Maurice Zilber**.) In 1983 the International was won by **Walter Swinburn** on the filly All Along, second leg of a wonderful quartet of big-race wins that autumn which began with the Arc and concluded with the Turf Classic at Aqueduct and the Washington, DC International at Laurel Park. Infamy won for **Luca Cumani** in 1988, the first time the race had gone to a British-based trainer, and since then four more British stables have won: **Paul Cole** with Snurge in 1992 (on the disqualification of first-past-the post Wiorno), **Singspiel** for **Michael Stoute** in 1996, Royal Anthem for **Henry Cecil** in 1998 and Mutafaweq for **Saeed bin Suroor** in 2000.

CANNON BONE

In a horse's leg, the cannon bone is the bone between the knee and the fetlock.

CAPTAIN CHRISTY

Winner of the 1974 Cheltenham Gold Cup and the King George VI Chase in 1974 and 1975, Captain Christy was one of the finest chasers of the modern age. Bred in County Cork and bought as a foal for just 290 guineas, Captain Christy was the best horse trained by **Pat Taaffe**, whom he joined in 1972 after an unexceptional time running in amateur races on the Flat and a promising early career over hurdles. In the 1972–3 season he improved to become one of the best hurdlers in the British Isles, winning four on the trot (including the valuable Sweeps Hurdle at Leopardstown), finishing third behind Comedy Of Errors in the 1973 Champion Hurdle, then winning the Scottish Champion Hurdle. By now his regular jockey was **Bobby Beasley**, back in the saddle after his struggle with the bottle, and the combination reached the pinnacle when Captain Christy was put over fences in the 1973–4 season, winning every chase in which he completed the course, including the 1974 Gold Cup from The Dikler despite nearly pitching over when blundering at the last fence. Ridden by Bobby Coonan following the departue of Bobby Beasley to England, Captain Christy won his first King George VI Chase at Kempton in December 1974, beating hot favourite Pendil by eight lengths, and his second (this time ridden by Gerry Newman as Coonan was injured) the following year, slamming Bula by 30 lengths with a performance which had journalists' juices flowing to a rare degree. For John Oaksey it was 'the finest performance seen in a three-mile chase since Arkle retired', for Peter Willett 'one of the great performances of steeple-chasing history', and for *Stud & Stable* magazine 'one of the greatest ever steeple-chasing performances'. Captain Christy was still only eight years old when winning the 1975 King George and looked destined for true greatness, but sustained a leg injury soon after that spectacular display and it proved his final run that season. But despite what some books pronounce, it was not the last seen of this fine horse. In November 1978, at the age of 11 and now trained by Francis Flood, he ran in the Troytown Chase at Navan, finishing sixth at 25–1. Even that was not the end, and in February 1980 13-year-old Captain Christy ran last of five behind Anaglog's Daughter in the P. Z. Mower Chase at Thurles – a sad end to a great career, which had also seen him runner-up in the Grand Steeple-Chase de

Paris and fourth in the **Colonial Cup** in 1975. He died in 1984, aged 17.

CARBERRY, TOMMY

Tommy Carberry, born in 1941, was apprenticed to trainer Dan Moore in 1955, then moved to ride on the Flat for J. J. Lenehan as he was deemed too light for jumping. He was champion apprentice in Ireland in 1958 and 1959, but once the weight started piling on he returned to Moore (and sealed the relationship by marrying his daughter Pamela). His first big win in England came on the grey mare Flying Wild in the 1964 Massey-Ferguson Chase at Cheltenham – the running best remembered for Arkle's heroic performance when third under 12st 10lb, beaten a fraction over a length – and thereafter Tommy Carberry was a familiar name in the big races. He landed the Cheltenham Gold Cup in successive years on **L'Escargot** (1970 and 1971) and the Grand National on the same horse in 1975 (beating Red Rum 15 lengths), a few weeks after winning a third Gold Cup on Ten Up. He thought he had landed a fourth when Tied Cottage passed the post eight lengths clear of Master Smudge in 1980, only to be disqualified for failing the dope test. Tommy Carberry's other big Cheltenham wins came in the 1973 Two Mile Champion Chase on Inkslinger (on which horse he had won the **Colonial Cup** in South Carolina in 1971) and the 1977 Triumph Hurdle on Meladon. On his retirement from the saddle he took up training, his most notable victory coming with Bobbyjo, ridden by his son Paul, in the 1999 Grand National. (In 1998 Bobbyjo had won the Irish Grand National, a race Tommy won as a jockey on Brown Lad in 1975 and 1976.)

CARBINE

Great Australian racehorse who won the 1890 **Melbourne Cup** carrying 10st 5lb and beating 38 opponents. He also landed the Sydney Cup two years running (1889 and 1890), and in all won 33 of his 43 career races.

CARBON IMPLANTS
See **breaking down.**

CARLISLE

Durdar Road, Carlisle, Cumbria CA2 4TS
Tel.: 01228 522973
Fax: 01228 591827
E-mail: info@carlisle-races.co.uk
Web: www.carlisle-races.co.uk

Carlisle is such a roller-coaster of a course that parts of the action down the far side can be viewed only from the upper reaches of the charming but roofless grandstand, erected when the course was established on its present site in the first decade of the twentieth century. The undulations make Carlisle a particularly testing track under both Flat and National Hunt codes, especially when the going gets heavy (as it frequently does during the jumping season). The right-handed circuit is pear-shaped, a little over 12 furlongs round. Beyond the winning post the track sweeps downhill, then rises for a while before levelling out about a mile from home. But the straight involves a steep rise until just before the post, so stamina is always at a premium here. The Carlisle Bell, run in late June, dates from the reign of Elizabeth I.

CARPET

Betting slang for 3–1.

CARPET AND A HALF

Betting slang for 7–2.

CARSON, WILLIE

William Fisher Hunter Carson was born in Stirling, Scotland, on 16 November 1942 and apprenticed first to Gerald Armstrong at Middleham, then to Sam Armstrong at Newmarket. He rode his first winner on Pinkers Pond in an apprentice race at Catterick on 19 July 1962. Champion jockey five times – 1972, 1973, 1978, 1980 and 1983 – he rode 17 Classic winners in England and a host of top-notch horses, including **Troy** (Derby, Irish Derby, King George and Benson and Hedges Gold Cup 1979), **Nashwan** (Two Thousand Guineas, Derby, Eclipse and King George 1989), Henbit (Derby 1980), Erhaab (Derby 1994, when Carson was fifty-one years old), **Dunfermline** (Oaks and St Leger 1977), Sun Princess (Oaks and St Leger 1983), Salsabil

Willie Carson's Classic winners

Two Thousand Guineas
1972 High Top
1980 Known Fact
1987 Don't Forget Me
1989 Nashwan
One Thousand Guineas
1990 Salsabil
1991 Shadayid
Derby
1979 Troy
1980 Henbit
1989 Nashwan
1994 Erhaab
Oaks
1977 Dunfermline
1980 Bireme
1983 Sun Princess
1990 Salsabil
St Leger
1977 Dunfermline
1983 Sun Princess
1988 Minster Son

(One Thousand Guineas, Oaks and Irish Derby 1990) and the great sprinter **Dayjur**, wretchedly unlucky to lose the 1990 Breeders' Cup Sprint but winner that year of the King's Stand Stakes at Royal Ascot, Nunthorpe Stakes at York, Sprint Cup at Haydock Park and Prix de l'Abbaye at Longchamp. Carson also won the King George on Ela-Mana-Mou (1980) and Petoski (1985), which with Troy and Nashwan gives him four victories in that race. He announced his retirement in March 1997, having ridden 3,828 winners in Britain (which puts him fourth in the all-time British ranking behind **Gordon Richards**, **Lester Piggott** and **Pat Eddery**), and now works as a presenter for BBC television racing coverage, as well as acting as British racing manager for the **Thoroughbred Corporation**.

Willie Carson became the first man to ride a Classic winner he had bred himself when landing the 1988 St Leger on Minster Son.

CARTMEL

Cartmel, Cumbria LA11 6QF

Tel.: 01539 536340

There is nowhere in the racing world like Cartmel. On the edge of a small Lakeland village otherwise famed for its priory, the course snuggles up on one side against the stone walls at the end of delightful cottage gardens, on the other against dense woodland. The track itself is the shortest and oddest in jump racing, the quality of the racing is bargain-basement, the facilities are basic in the extreme (there is no covered grandstand), it is effectively impossible for any racegoer to get an uninterrupted view of the races themselves – and yet crowds swarm to Cartmel in their tens of thousands: on Spring Bank Holiday Monday 1997, for example, a crowd of over 21,000 crammed into the course. For many of this host, the racing is a peripheral activity. They drive their cars into the infield, spread out their picnics, visit the large funfair which occupies half the course, and generally have a great day out in the open air – one punctuated every half hour by a handful of racehorses whizzing by on the outside of the picnic area. The circuit at Cartmel mirrors the quirkiness of the occasion. Little over a mile round, left-handed, mildly undulating and very tight, it demands a compact, nippy sort of horse. The steeplechase fences are sited very irregularly, and one of Cartmel's most disorientating features is that when the runners take the last fence they are going away from the stand: they have still to come round the final bend and up the chute which forms the finishing straight – at half a mile the longest run-in on any chasing course. Tradition has it that racing at Cartmel began in the Middle Ages when the monks at the priory started racing their mules across the sands, and there was organised racing on the present site in the late nineteenth century. For many years Cartmel raced only at its two-day Whitsun meeting; then another two days were added at August Bank Holiday weekend, and it was on August Bank Holiday Monday 1974 that Cartmel ensured its place in the history of great betting stings when an obscure horse named **Gay Future** won the Ulverston Novices' Hurdle.

CAST IN BOX

A horse is said to have been 'cast in his box' if he lies down in his stable and then rolls over in such a way that he is trapped by the legs – often against a wall or under the manger – and cannot get up without assistance. The experience will probably leave him stiff and distressed, especially since it is most likely to occur at night when he may be struggling to free himself for several hours before human assistance arrives. Often a cast horse can only be extricated by being pulled out from the wall or corner with ropes, a process which can add to the trauma.

CATTERICK

Catterick Bridge, Richmond, North Yorkshire

DL10 7PE

Tel.: 01748 811478

Fax: 01748 811082

E-mail: jamesh@aol.com

Web: www.goracing.co.uk

The Flat circuit at Catterick is just under nine furlongs round, undulating and with tight bends – tailor-made for the nippy starter with a catch-me-if-you-can approach; there is never much time to make up lost ground before the next bend, and the course's sharpness militates against the big, long-striding sort of horse.

Gods Solution, owned by Peter Jones (now chairman of the Tote), won the same six-furlong handicap at Catterick's early-season meeting six times: 1985–9 and 1991. In 1990 the race was renamed the Gods Solution Handicap in his honour, but he could finish only third. The following year, as a ten-year-old, Gods Solution picked up the winning thread in the race for his eighth course win and was promptly retired. A bar in the new grandstand commemorates his Catterick achievements.

The five-furlong course starts with a downhill stretch and is very fast. The jumping circuit is longer than the Flat at about one and a quarter miles, and down the back straight runs parallel with but completely detached from the Flat course. But as with the Flat, the course does not favour the galloping type of horse but rather the nifty sort who can set off sharply. The speed at which jumpers tear round Catterick makes this an awkward place for a novice chaser – if you're tempted to bet in a novice chase here, make sure your selection comes from a yard which is known for schooling its young horses well. Racing was staged at Catterick as long ago as the seventeenth century, with regular fixtures on the site of the present course dating back to 1783. Facilities at the course had a major boost with the opening of a new grandstand in July 1998.

CAULFIELD CUP

One of Australia's most prestigious races, the Caulfield Cup is run over one and a half miles for three-year-olds and upwards at Caulfield, Melbourne, in October. The race was first run in 1879 and has been won by some of the great Australian horses, including Tulloch, who won in record time in 1957. First ever winner trained outside Australasia was the seven-year-old Taufan's Melody, trained at Arundel by Lady Herries and ridden by **Ray Cochrane** to win a rough race in 1998 by a short nose at 66–1, thereby eliciting this gracious post-race comment from third-placed jockey Shane Dye: 'Taufan's Melody is a third-rater in England – it's an embarrassment to Australian racing.' Taufan's Melody narrowly avoided giving further embarrassment when close-up fourth in the **Melbourne Cup** the following month.

CAUTHEN, STEVE

One of the most popular jockeys of the modern period, Steve Cauthen was born in Kentucky on 1 May 1960, and rode his first winner on Red Pipe at River Downs shortly after his sixteenth birthday on 17 May 1976. Before long he had become a riding phenomenon, showing a precocity unknown since the early career of **Lester Piggott**. In 1977 his 487 winning mounts in the USA earned over $6 million in prize money and brought the young rider the predictable label of The Six Million Dollar Man – though he was known more simply as The Kid. In 1978 he won the Triple Crown on **Affirmed**, and in 1979 accepted an offer from top owner **Robert Sangster** to come and ride for him in England. Cauthen won on his first English ride – Marquee Universal at Salisbury on 7 April 1979 – and within a month had landed his first Classic in England when Tap On Wood beat Kris and Young Generation to win the Two Thousand Guineas. He rode 51 winners in Britain that first season, and in 1984 became champion jockey, the first American to do so since **Danny Maher** in 1913. In 1985 he became first rider to the powerful **Henry Cecil** stable, and rode four Classic winners for Cecil that year: on Slip Anchor he won the Derby with a brilliantly judged ride from the front (thereby becoming the only jockey to have won the Derby and Kentucky Derby), and on the great filly **Oh So Sharp** he landed the One Thousand Guineas, Oaks and St Leger. A second Derby and a second St Leger came with Reference Point in 1987, and in all he won ten Classics. Other big-race success came with horses like Old Vic (Prix du Jockey-Club and Irish Derby 1989), Indian Skimmer (Prix de Diane 1987), **Time Charter** (Coronation Cup 1984), **Pebbles** (Eclipse Stakes 1985), **Triptych** (International Stakes 1987 and

---

Steve Cauthen's Classic winners

Two Thousand Guineas
  1979 Tap On Wood

One Thousand Guineas
  1985 Oh So Sharp

Derby
  1985 Slip Anchor
  1987 Reference Point

Oaks
  1985 Oh So Sharp
  1988 Diminuendo
  1989 Snow Bride (awarded race
       on disqualification of Aliysa
       after post-race dope test)

St Leger
  1985 Oh So Sharp
  1987 Reference Point
  1989 Michelozzo

Coronation Cup 1988, the latter a masterclass in a jockey galvanising a less-than-committed partner), In The Groove (International Stakes and Champion Stakes 1990, Coronation Cup 1991) and Cormorant Wood (Champion Stakes 1983, Benson and Hedges Gold Cup 1984). He announced his retirement early in 1993, having ridden the winners of 1,704 races in Britain, 954 in the USA, and many others around the world.

CAZALET, PETER

Leading trainer in the 1949–50, 1959–60 and 1964–5 seasons and a man whose influence in securing the enthusiasm of the **Queen Mother** for National Hunt racing left the sport a lasting benefit, Peter Cazalet was born in 1907. He rode as an amateur over fences between 1932 and 1938 and took up training at Fairlawne, the magnificent estate near Tonbridge in Kent, in 1939. He never won any of the 'Big Three' races of National Hunt racing, and his litany of hard-luck stories in the Grand National was heart-breaking: in 1936 Davy Jones, ridden by **Anthony Mildmay**, ran out between the last two fences when in a winning position after the reins broke; in 1948 Mildmay was attacked by cramp when looking like winning on Cromwell; and worst of all, the Queen Mother's **Devon Loch** slithered to defeat 50 yards from certain victory in 1956. But Cazalet won the King George VI Chase four times, with the Queen Mother's Manicou (1950), Statecraft (1951), Rose Park (1956) and Lochroe (1958; the same horse was beaten a length by Pas Seul in the 1960 Gold Cup). Other fine horses he trained included the brilliant two-mile chaser Dunkirk, who won the Two Mile Champion Chase and Mackeson Gold Cup in 1965 and was killed when taking on **Arkle** in the 1965 King George. It was to Cazalet that the Queen Mother, having been introduced to the sport by Lord Mildmay, sent her jumping horses, and he enjoyed great success with the likes of Monaveen, Manicou, Double Star, Silver Dome (who provided her first win over the Grand National fences when winning the 1964 Becher Chase), Makaldar, Laffy, Antiar,

The Rip and – at least until that fateful slide – Devon Loch. Peter Cazalet died in 1973, having trained over 1,100 winners, some 250 of them for the Queen Mother.

CECIL, HENRY

Of Flat trainers currently holding a licence, none can match the Classic-winning record – 23 – of Henry Richard Amherst Cecil. He was born on 11 January 1943, ten minutes before his identical twin brother David. A fortnight before his birth his father had been killed in action in North Africa, and in 1944 his widowed mother married Captain **Cecil**

Henry Cecil's Classic winners

Two Thousand Guineas
1975 Bolkonski
1976 Wollow

One Thousand Guineas
1979 One In A Million
1981 Fairy Footsteps
1985 Oh So Sharp
1996 Bosra Sham
1997 Sleepytime
1999 Wince

Derby
1985 Slip Anchor
1987 Reference Point
1993 Commander In Chief
1999 Oath

Oaks
1985 Oh So Sharp
1988 Diminuendo
1989 Snow Bride (awarded race
     on disqualification of Aliysa
     after the post-race dope test)
1996 Lady Carla
1997 Reams Of Verse
1999 Ramruma
2000 Love Divine

St Leger
1980 Light Cavalry
1985 Oh So Sharp
1987 Reference Point
1989 Michelozzo

Boyd-Rochfort. Henry Cecil became Boyd-Rochfort's assistant trainer in 1964 and took charge of the famous stables at Freemason Lodge in 1968 on the Captain's retirement, his first winner coming when Celestial Cloud (ridden by Bill O'Gorman, later a trainer) won the Newby Maiden Stakes for amateur riders at Ripon on 17 May 1969. The same year Cecil won his first big races, the Eclipse Stakes with Wolver Hollow and the Observer Gold Cup (now the Racing Post Trophy) with Approval. He won his first English Classic with Bolkonski in the 1975 Two Thousand Guineas and took the race again with Wollow in 1976, the first year he was champion trainer. On the retirement of Sir **Noel Murless** (whose daughter Julie he had married 10 years earlier: they divorced in 1990), he moved into Murless's stables at Warren Place in Newmarket. Leading trainer again in 1978 and 1979, he set a twentieth-century record for winners trained (128) in 1979. It was not until 1985 that Cecil won his first Derby, with Slip Anchor, following up in the premier Classic with Reference Point (1987), Commander In Chief (1993) and Oath (1999). Cecil has long been hailed as the consummate trainer of fillies ('I think you've just got to take them very gently, rather like women'), and notable females to have thrived in his care include **Oh So Sharp** (fillies' Triple Crown winner 1985), **Bosra Sham** (One Thousand Guineas and Champion Stakes 1996, Prince of Wales's Stakes 1997 – by eight lengths), Indian Skimmer (Prix de Diane 1987, Irish Champion Stakes and Champion Stakes 1988), One In A Million (One Thousand Guineas and Coronation Stakes 1979), Fairy Footsteps (One Thousand Guineas 1981), Diminuendo (Oaks, Irish Oaks – dead heat – and Yorkshire Oaks 1988), Ramruma (Oaks, Irish Oaks and Yorkshire Oaks 1999) and Love Divine (Oaks 2000). He has also trained some famous stayers, including Le Moss, who landed the Ascot Gold Cup, Goodwood Cup and Doncaster Cup in both 1979 and 1980, and Ardross, who won the Gold Cup in 1981 and 1982 (thus giving his trainer four successive wins in the Ascot showpiece) and was beaten a head by Akiyda in the 1982 Prix de l'Arc de Triomphe, a race Cecil has never won. (Ardross was runner-up to Le Moss in all three legs of the 'Stayers' Triple Crown' in 1980, at the time trained not by Cecil but by Kevin Prendergast in Ireland.) Other top-class horses to have graced Warren Place under Henry Cecil include Old Vic (Prix du Jockey-Club and Irish Derby 1989), Belmez (who beat Old Vic a neck in the 1990 King George VI and Queen Elizabeth Diamond Stakes), King's Theatre (King George 1994) and the great miler Kris, who won 14 of his 16 races between 1978 and 1980 (including the 1979 St James's Palace Stakes, Sussex Stakes and Queen Elizabeth II Stakes and 1980 Lockinge Stakes). He has been leading trainer ten times: in 1976, 1978, 1979, 1982, 1984, 1985, 1987, 1988, 1990 and 1993.

CENTURY
Betting slang for £100.

CESAREWITCH
Handicap; three-year-olds and upwards; 2¼ miles (Newmarket, Rowley Mile)

Like the **Cambridgeshire**, its partner in the Autumn Double, the Cesarewitch was first run in 1839, and takes its unusual name from the heir to the throne of Russia. The 21-year-old Tsarevich, destined to become Emperor Alexander II, had recently visited Newmarket and donated £300 to the Jockey Club, which used the gift as prize money for a new long-distance handicap which would bear an anglicised version of the donor's title. The Tsarevich's sponsorship of the race ran until 1849, when difficulties between Britain and Russia which culminated in the Crimean War made his support politically awkward. But the name lives on.

Just as the Cambridgeshire in its early days often attracted Classic horses, the list of Cesarewitch results contains the names of some seriously good horses. Bloomsbury, second in 1840, had won the Derby the previous year, and in 1880 Robert The Devil, beaten a head by Fred Archer and Bend Or in a famous Derby finish, won the Newmarket marathon (and the Champion Stakes two days later!). But to St Gatien in 1884 goes the unique distinction of having won both the Derby (in which he dead-heated with Harvester) and the Cesarewitch: what price that feat will ever be repeated? ... To modern racegoers the Cesarewitch is both marvellous and daft: marvellous because it invariably brings together a large field of top staying handicappers and provides a wonderful betting medium, daft because most of it is run completely out of sight of the spectators in the enclosures, and the fun of watching the early stages of the race is to catch glimpses of the field in the extreme distance, making their way to the course's one bend 10 furlongs from home. Yes, you can watch on the big screen the other side of the course from the stands, but somehow it's not quite the same as catching the live action – and the Cesarewitch is the epitome of the occasional eccentricity of racing in Britain.

Recent runnings have produced many memorable moments: John Cherry and Lester Piggott winning under 9st 13lb in 1976; the mare Double Dutch battling home from Chelsea Girl under 9st 10lb in 1989; **Vintage Crop**, trained in Ireland by Dermot Weld and backed from 25–1 earlier in the week to 5–1 favourite, powering to an eight-length victory under Walter Swinburn in 1992 (he went on to land the Melbourne Cup in 1993); Spirit Of Love winning for Mark Johnston by nine lengths in 1998; and nine-year-old Top Cees becoming the oldest winner when taking the

race at the third attempt in 1999 (on the July Course while the Millennium Stand was being built at the Rowley Mile).

CHAMPION, BOB

Bob Champion rode 421 winners in a career as a jump jockey which lasted from 1968 to 1982, but will always be remembered for just one: the 1981 Grand National on Aldaniti, perhaps the most emotionally charged National of all. Less than two years earlier Champion had been diagnosed with testicular cancer at the age of 31. After a long and harrowing struggle through chemotherapy he regained his health and, against all the odds, his riding career: he won on his comeback ride in a Flat race in the USA, and resumed his career in Britain at Stratford in August 1980, registering his first winner back – Physicist at Fontwell Park – in September 1980. His recovery had been underpinned by a determination to ride Aldaniti in the Grand National, but the horse himself had had his own problems, having broken down in November 1979. Aldaniti was nursed back to health by trainer **Josh Gifford** and won his comeback race at Ascot, then started 10–1 second favourite for the Grand National behind 8–1 shot Spartan Missile, ridden by 54-year-old amateur John Thorne. By the end of the first circuit Aldaniti had taken the lead, and as the challengers fell away only two horses – Royal Mail and Spartan Missile – looked likely to spoil the fairytale. But try as they might they

Cesarewitch winners since 1990

1990	Trainglot	3	J. FitzGerald	W. Carson	13–2	25
1991	Go South	7	J. Jenkins	N. Carlisle	33–1	22
1992	Vintage Crop	5	D. Weld *IRE*	W. R. Swinburn	5–1F	24
1993	Aahsaylad	7	J. White	J. Williams	12–1	31
1994	Captain's Guest	4	G. Harwood	A. Clark	25–1	32
1995	Old Red	5	Mrs M. Reveley	L. Charnock	11–1	21
1996	Inchcailloch	7	J. King	R. Ffrench	20–1	26
1997	Turnpole	6	Mrs M. Reveley	L. Charnock	16–1	31
1998	Spirit Of Love	3	M. Johnston	O. Peslier	11–1	29
1999	Top Cees	9	I. Balding	K. Fallon	7–1	32
2000	Heros Fatal	6	M. Pipe	G. Carter	11–1	33

could not peg back Aldaniti and Bob Champion, who plugged on up the run-in to win by four lengths from Spartan Missile, with Royal Mail third. Champion rode Aldaniti again in the 1982 Grand National, but they got no further than the first fence.

In 1983 the Bob Champion Cancer Trust was founded, with Aldaniti playing a major part in its fund-raising activities: in 1987 the horse was ridden from Buckingham Palace to Liverpool by a succession of 250 riders who had each guaranteed at least £1,000 in sponsorship – a venture which raised nearly £1 million.

Aldaniti died in March 1997 at the age of 27. On his retirement from the saddle Bob Champion trained in Newmarket, quitting in 1998. He suffered a heart attack in early 2001, but is continuing his work raising millions of pounds for the Trust. His book *Champion's Story*, written with Jonathan Powell, attracted sales worthy of such an inspirational tale, and was made into the film *Champions*, starring John Hurt.

CHAMPION HURDLE

Grade One hurdle; four-year-olds and
upwards; 2 miles and ½ furlong
(Cheltenham)

The first running of the Champion Hurdle on 9 March 1927 was worth just £365 to the winner; the 2000 running which gave **Istabraq** his third successive victory in the

race brought his owner **J. P. McManus** £145,000. Blaris, ridden by ace hurdle jockey George Duller, won the inaugural race as 11–10 favourite, and before the Second World War two other winners stand out. **Brown Jack**, who had started his hurdling career at Bournemouth, won the 1928 race – his last run over hurdles before concentrating on a Flat career which made him one of the most popular horses of all time. Insurance, owned by **Dorothy Paget**, won in 1932 and 1933 to become the first dual winner. Miss Paget won again with Solford in 1940 and Distel in 1946. The decade after the ending of the Second World War saw a dual winner in National Spirit (1947 and 1948) and the first two triple winners, **Hatton's Grace** (1949, 1950, 1951) and **Sir Ken** (1952, 1953, 1954), a feat matched by **Persian War** (1968, 1969, 1970), **See You Then** (1985, 1986, 1987) and **Istabraq** (1998, 1999, 2000). But for sheer competitiveness at the highest level the golden period of the Champion Hurdle ran from early 1970s to the early 1980s. Persian War's attempt to land a record fourth foundered when in 1971 he finished runner-up to the new champion in the form of Fred Winter-trained Bula – who himself reigned for two years, winning again in 1972 and then finishing fifth behind Comedy Of Errors in 1973. Trained by Fred Rimell, Comedy Of Errors would in due course become another dual winner, but between his victories in

Champion Hurdle winners since 1990

1990	Kribensis	6	M. Stoute	R. Dunwoody	95–40	19
1991	Morley Street	7	G. Balding	J. Frost	4–1F	24
1992	Royal Gait	9	J. Fanshawe	G. McCourt	6–1	16
1993	Granville Again	7	M. Pipe	P. Scudamore	13–2	18
1994	Flakey Dove	8	R. Price	M. Dwyer	9–1	15
1995	Alderbrook	6	K. Bailey	N. Williamson	11–2	14
1996	Collier Bay	6	J. Old	G. Bradley	9–1	16
1997	Make A Stand	6	M. Pipe	A. McCoy	7–1	17
1998	Istabraq	6	A. O'Brien *IRE*	C. Swan	3–1F	18
1999	Istabraq	7	A. O'Brien *IRE*	C. Swan	4–9F	14
2000	Istabraq	8	A. O'Brien *IRE*	C. Swan	8–15F	12
2001	no race (foot-and-mouth epidemic)					

1973 and 1975 was inserted that of Lanzarote, trained like Bula by Fred Winter and ridden by Richard Pitman to beat Comedy Of Errors three lengths. Comedy Of Errors regained the crown in 1975 (only horse to do so), and then came the glorious era of **Night Nurse** (1976 and 1977), **Monksfield** (1978 and 1979) and **Sea Pigeon** (1980 and 1981). For three consecutive years Monksfield and Sea Pigeon came to the last flight together, and their ferocious battle to the line in 1979, which the diminutive entire Monksfield won by three-quarters of a length, was arguably the greatest Champion Hurdle finish of all. Sea Pigeon got the upper hand in 1980 and (with Monksfield departed from the scene) followed up in 1981, **John Francome** producing one of his greatest ever rides: Sea Pigeon was only the second 11-year-old to win the race, emulating Hatton's Grace in 1951. (It was not only the winners who made the late 1970s such a golden period for the Champion Hurdle: supporting acts like Beacon Light, Dramatist, Kybo and especially the directionally challenged Bird's Nest played their part in creating such memorable races.) **Dawn Run**, whose greatest Cheltenham moment was still to come, beat Cima in a weak renewal in 1984 (first mare to win since African Sister in 1939), and **See You Then** dominated a less than top-notch hurdling division for the next three years, while the 1990s saw the influence of the Flat: Kribensis, owned by Sheikh Mohammed and trained by Michael Stoute,

beat Nomadic Way, owned by Robert Sangster and trained by Barry Hills, in 1990; Royal Gait, a top-class stayer on the Flat also owned by Sheikh Mohammed and trained by James Fanshawe, won in 1992; and Alderbrook, who boasted very good form on the level, took the 1995 running for Kim Bailey. The millennium turned with the race dominated by Istabraq, whose three wins in 1998, 1999 and 2000 have placed ever more strain on the roof of the Cheltenham grandstand and who was robbed of the opportunity to make it a historic quartet in 2001 only by the outbreak of foot-and-mouth disease.

CHAMPION STAKES

Group One; three-year-olds and upwards; 1¼ miles (Newmarket, Rowley Mile)

The Champion Stakes, first run in 1877, is the last big middle-distance race of the year in Britain, and is unique among the big 10-furlong events around the globe in its course being completely straight, putting an emphasis on resolution and stamina which occasionally finds out even the best horses at the end of a long hard season. Many of the all-time greats have run in the race. The likes of **Bend Or** (1881), **Sceptre** (1903), **Pretty Polly** (1905, from a solitary opponent), Triple Crown winner Gay Crusader (1917), and more recently **Petite Etoile** (1959), **Brigadier Gerard** (1971, by a scrambled short head from Rarity, and 1972, beating Riverman in a glorious farewell), Rose Bowl

Champion Stakes winners since 1990

Year	Winner	Age	Trainer	Jockey	SP	Ran
1990	In The Groove	3	D. Elsworth	S. Cauthen	9–2	10
1991	Tel Quel	3	A. Fabre FRA	T. Jarnet	16–1	12
1992	Rodrigo de Triano	3	P. Chapple-Hyam	L. Piggott	11–8F	10
1993	Hatoof	4	Mme C. Head FRA	W. R. Swinburn	5–2F	12
1994	Dernier Empereur	4	A. Fabre FRA	S. Guillot	8–1	8
1995	Spectrum	3	P. Chapple-Hyam	J. Reid	5–1	8
1996	Bosra Sham	3	H. Cecil	Pat Eddery	9–4	6
1997	Pilsudski	5	M. Stoute	M. Kinane	evensF	7
1998	Alborada	3	Sir M. Prescott	G. Duffield	6–1	10
1999	Alborada	4	Sir M. Prescott	G. Duffield	5–1	13
2000	Kalanisi	4	M. Stoute	J. Murtagh	5–1	15

(1975), **Time Charter** (1982), **Pebbles** (1985, beating Derby winner Slip Anchor), **Triptych** (1986 and 1987), Indian Skimmer (1988), **Bosra Sham** (1996), **Pilsudski** (1997) and another dual winner Alborada (1998 and 1999) all etched their names deep into the roll of honour. But the Champion Stakes can be a cruel race for horses at the end of their tether. **Nijinsky**, looking to redeem his reputation after his first ever defeat in the Arc, simply compounded the gloom in 1970 when failing to catch Lorenzaccio – a race which was uncannily like the 2000 running, when **Montjeu**, likewise unexpectedly defeated in that year's Arc, also came to Newmarket on a redeeming mission, only to find the ultra-gutsy Kalanisi half a length too good. But whether the great horses win or lose, one characteristic unites every running of the Champion Stakes and makes it one of the most keenly anticipated races of the year: sheer quality.

Of the 25 runnings of the Champion Stakes between 1976 and 2000, 14 were won by fillies or mares.

CHANGE LEGS

When a horse adjusts its galloping action, it is said to 'change legs'. In its faster paces, a horse will 'lead' with one of its forelegs, the last of its legs to strike the ground during the cycle of the stride. On a left-hand track the horse should lead with its near foreleg (that is, its left front leg), and if it is uneasy on the ground it will change to leading with the other leg, especially when under pressure towards the end of the race. Changing legs is generally an indication of tiredness, inexperience or (on a switchback course like Epsom Downs) difficulty keeping balance.

CHANNEL FOUR RACING

Teddington Studios, Broom Road, Teddington, Middlesex TW11 9NT
Tel.: 020 8781 2770
Fax: 020 8781 2762
E-mail: racing@channel4.com
Web: www.channel4.com/racing

The Channel Four Racing presenters

• *Mike Cattermole* has worked for Timeform, as a journalist on the *Sporting Life* and more recently *Raceform Update*, and as a presenter on the Racing Channel. He also acts as a course commentator.

• *Alastair Down*, now senior presenter on Channel Four Racing, was voted Racing Journalist of the Year by his peers in 1994 and 1999. He worked for the *Sporting Life* until that newspaper shut in 1998, and now writes regular columns for the *Racing Post* and *Sunday Mirror*.

• *John Francome*: see separate entry.

• *Graham Goode* started as a racecourse commentator in 1967, becoming senior commentator for ITV in 1981. He is a director of Nottingham racecourse.

• *Lesley Graham* worked as a corporate solicitor before joining the Channel Four Racing team in 1993. She is married to Newmarket trainer Neil Graham.

• *Simon Holt* worked as a journalist on the *Sporting Life* and began racecourse commentating in 1988. He joined the Channel Four Racing team in 1994.

• *John McCririck* went to Harrow School, then moved into the world of private handicapping and bookmaking. He joined the *Sporting Life* in 1972 – initially as coursing correspondent – and wrote for that paper until 1983. He was named Specialist Writer of the Year in 1978, Campaigning Journalist of the Year in 1979 and Sports Presenter of the Year in 1992. Mrs Jenny McCririck is referred to by her husband as 'The Booby' for reasons best not gone into . . .

• *Jim McGrath* is managing director of Timeform. He joined ITV in 1981 and subsequently moved to Channel Four Racing. Jim has owned many good racehorses, and among his successes as breeder is top-class miler Decorated Hero, third in the 1997 Breeders' Cup Mile.

(continued overleaf)

The Channel Four Racing presenters

- *John Oaksey*: see separate entry.

- *Walter Swinburn*: see separate entry.

- *Derek Thompson* started his broadcasting career on BBC radio in 1973 and has been presenting racing on television since 1982. He worked as assistant trainer to Denys Smith and later to Pierre Sanoner in Chantilly, and the pinnacle of his riding career came when he rode Classified to victory in a charity race at Plumpton in 1981, with the Prince of Wales in second place. (*See* royalty.)

And, lest we forget ...

- *Brough Scott* retired from his Channel Four Racing duties on Whitbread Gold Cup day at Sandown Park in April 2001. Brough rode exactly 100 winners as an amateur and then professional jockey between 1963 and 1971: he won the 1968 Imperial Cup at Sandown Park on Persian Empire, and was third in the Champion Hurdle that year on Black Justice. He has been a leading sports journalist for over 30 years, and writes regular columns for the *Racing Post* and *Sunday Telegraph*.

Channel Four Racing began life covering midweek meetings in 1984, and since 1985 all racing on the independent network has been on Channel Four. *The Morning Line* was first broadcast on 7 October 1989 – Cambridgeshire day at Newmarket – and Channel Four now covers over 100 days' racing a year, including the Cheltenham National Hunt Festival and the majority of Group One races on the Flat. The Channel Four Racing presenters as of summer 2001 are shown in the box.

CHANNON, MICK

After retiring from a footballing career which saw him win 46 caps and score 21 goals for England between 1973 and 1978, as well as give long and distinguished service to Southampton (for whom he made 507 League appearances) and other clubs, Mick Channon (born November 1948) turned his attention to horse racing. He worked as assistant to John Baker and Ken Cunningham-Brown before taking out his own licence in 1990. Now based in West Ilsley, he has become one of the very few men to have reached the top in two different sports. Piccolo, awarded the 1994 Nunthorpe Stakes on the disqualification of Blue Siren, was his first Group One winner and went on to win the King's Stand Stakes at Royal Ascot in 1995, and he has won major two-year-old races with such horses as Tobougg (Prix de la Salamandre and Dewhurst Stakes 2000), Seazun (Cheveley Park Stakes 1999), Bint Allayl (Queen Mary Stakes at Royal Ascot and Lowther Stakes at York 1998) and Josr Algarhoud (Gimcrack Stakes at York 1998).

CHANTILLY

Home of the Prix du Jockey-Club and Prix de Diane – French equivalents of the Derby and Oaks – Chantilly, about 25 miles north of Paris, boasts the spectacular backdrop of Les Grands Ecuries ('the great stables'), part of a huge chateau built in the eighteenth century by the Prince de Condé, anxious that when he was reincarnated as a horse (as he surely would be) there should be suitable stabling. Chantilly is a flat, right-handed course, with a long sweeping turn into the straight, and stages one Group One race apart from the two Classics: the Prix Jean Prat, run in June over nine furlongs for three-year-olds. The area is also a major training centre.

CHELTENHAM
Prestbury Park, Cheltenham, Gloucestershire
GL50 4SH
Tel.: 01242 513014 (for bookings: 01242 226226)
Fax: 01242 224227
E-mail: cheltenham@rht.net
Web: www.cheltenham.co.uk

Set in glorious Cotswold countryside, with Cleeve Hill looming at the far end of the course to form a natural backdrop, Cheltenham is the spiritual home of National

Hunt racing. The entire jumping season is dominated by and geared towards one meeting here, the National Hunt Festival in March: three days of the very best steeple-chasing and hurdling (and one National Hunt Flat race), top horses, vast crowds, hordes of Irish visitors, huge excitement. No wonder the ailing Irishman, when told by his doctor that he had three days to live, asked if those three days could be at Cheltenham in mid-March . . .

Highlight of the first day – Tuesday – is the **Champion Hurdle** over an extended two miles, the undisputed championship event for the best hurdlers. Wednesday features the **Queen Mother Champion Chase** over two miles for the cream of the chasing speed merchants. Thursday is **Cheltenham Gold Cup** day itself, with a crowd of over 50,000 squeezing into the course to produce an atmosphere unlike any other occasion in racing. As with Royal Ascot on the Flat, the strength of the National Hunt Festival is its depth, and the three peaks are supported by a host of other major races:

- three big races for novice hurdlers: the Triumph Hurdle (two miles), top four-year-old hurdle of the season; the Supreme Novices' Hurdle (two miles); and the Royal & SunAlliance Novices' Hurdle (two miles five furlongs);
- major novice chases in the shape of the Arkle Trophy (two miles) and the Royal & SunAlliance Novices' Chase (three miles one furlong);
- the Stayers' Hurdle (three miles and half a furlong) and the Vincent O'Brien County Hurdle (two miles one furlong);
- more big steeplechases in the National Hunt Chase (three miles one furlong), the Mildmay of Flete Challenge Cup (two miles $4^{1}/_{2}$ furlongs), the Cathcart Challenge Cup (two miles five furlongs) and the Foxhunter Chase (three miles $2^{1}/_{2}$ furlongs).

The rest of the Cheltenham year is pretty good as well. In November the course stages the **Thomas Pink Gold Cup** – previously the Mackeson, and briefly the Murphy's – a steeplechase over an extended two and a half miles which marks the effective beginning of the serious core of the jumping season. The same meeting sees the Sporting Index Chase over three miles seven furlongs of the cross-country course built in the infield of the main track and first used in 1995: purists shake their heads at the sight of stay-for-ever chasers belting round this curious circuit of natural hedges, banks and timber – a sort of mongrel bred from the La Touche Cup course at Punchestown and the Velka Pardubicka track in the Czech Republic. The December meeting has the Tripleprint Gold Cup over two miles five furlongs, companion race to the Thomas Pink Gold Cup; this event began life in 1963 as the Massey-Ferguson Gold Cup and under various names has been won by horses of the quality of **Flyingbolt, Pendil** and Dublin Flyer. Pegwell Bay and the dashing grey Senor El Betrutti are the only horses to have won the November and December highlights in the same year. The December meeting also features the Bula Hurdle, named after the great dual Champion Hurdler trained by Fred Winter. The pre-Festival meeting at the end of January is regularly used by Gold Cup aspirants for a dress rehearsal.

There are three distinct circuits at Cheltenham in addition to the infrequently used cross-country course. Racing switches between the Old Course and the New Course through the season so that the ground is given time to recover from each meeting, and the characteristics of both are broadly the same: a left-handed oval about one and a half miles round, with long straights and no sharp bends. From the stands the runners sweep left and head out into the country, turning at the far end of that straight to negotiate a stiff uphill climb, from the peak of which they sweep sharply downhill – fences on this stretch are particularly problematic – before making the turn towards home. (That downhill stretch is further from the stands on the New Course, which is slightly longer than the Old.) Two fences are jumped in the straight on the New Course, just one on the Old, but from the last on either circuit the run to the winning post is an exceptionally tough uphill haul, and the complexion of many a

Cheltenham race has changed on the run-in as tired horses meet that rising ground. In addition, there is an extension which bisects the downhill stretch of the main courses, and in 1991 this extension was joined to the New Course to form a circuit known as the Park Course, used at early-season meetings and a less demanding proposition for horses than having to slog all the way to the top of the hill.

The opening of the new Tattersalls grandstand in 1997 marked another stage in an extensive development programme which has seen major changes over the years: the parade ring, for example, is now a prominent feature of the Cheltenham racegoing experience, as the paddock incorporates the winner's enclosure (a layout followed at several other courses) and the winner returns to face his or her adoring public massed on the terraces. Cheltenham may be looking to the future, but it has due respect for the past. Statues of **Arkle**, **Golden Miller** and **Dawn Run** face the parade ring. The Arkle Bar, a traditional meeting place, is not just another racecourse bar named after a great horse but almost a museum, with plenty of cuttings and souvenirs recalling the greatest career of all – including those famous envelopes addressed to 'Arkle, Ireland'. And no visit is complete without a decent spell in the Hall of Fame, an extensive and very well-mounted exhibition of the feats of the horses and people who have made Cheltenham the shrine it is today.

Although a permanent course was laid out at the current site in 1902, there had been racing at Prestbury, the adjacent village, as far back as 1831: the Grand Annual Steeplechase, still an event on the Festival programme, was run there in 1834. The first Gold Cup was run in 1924, the inaugural Champion Hurdle three years later.

CHELTENHAM GOLD CUP

Grade One steeplechase; five-year-olds and upwards; 3 miles 2½ furlongs (Cheltenham)

Since 12 March 1924, when the inaugural running was won by Red Splash, ridden by Fred Rees, the Cheltenham Gold Cup has developed to its current standing as the undisputed showpiece of the jumping season, a race whose history is so powerful and evocative that the names of its most famous winners – equine and human – are like beacons illuminating the history of the sport:

- **Easter Hero**, winner in 1929 and 1930;
- **Golden Miller**, who won five consecutive runnings between 1932 and 1936 and put the race firmly on the map as one of the highlights of the racing year: the famous 1935 running when he beat his great rival Thomond II by three-quarters of a length has been described as the greatest Gold Cup ever run – at least until 1964 . . .

Cheltenham Gold Cup winners since 1990

1990	Norton's Coin	9	S. Griffiths	G. McCourt	100–1	12
1991	Garrison Savannah	8	Mrs J. Pitman	M. Pitman	16–1	14
1992	Cool Ground	10	G. Balding	A. Maguire	25–1	8
1993	Jodami	8	P. Beaumont	M. Dwyer	8–1	16
1994	The Fellow	9	F. Doumen *FRA*	A. Kondrat	7–1	15
1995	Master Oats	9	K. Bailey	N. Williamson	100–30F	15
1996	Imperial Call	7	F. Sutherland *IRE*	C. O'Dwyer	9–2	10
1997	Mr Mulligan	9	N. Chance	A. McCoy	20–1	14
1998	Cool Dawn	10	R. Alner	A. Thornton	25–1	17
1999	See More Business	9	P. Nicholls	M. Fitzgerald	16–1	12
2000	Looks Like Trouble	8	N. Chance	R. Johnson	9–2	12
2001	no race (foot-and-mouth epidemic)					

- **Prince Regent**, winner in 1946 at 7–4 on;
- **Cottage Rake**, triple winner 1948–50;
- **Mill House** in 1963 – the arrival of 'The Big Horse', who looked a world-beater until his famous 1964 Gold Cup clash with . . .
- **Arkle**, who conquered Mill House by five lengths in 1964 – 'This is the champion! This is the best we've seen for a long time!', sang out Peter O'Sullevan's immortal call of a famous race – and followed up in 1965 (beating Mill House 20 lengths) and (despite an almighty mistake at the fence in front of the stands first time round) 1966;
- **L'Escargot** winning in 1970 (at 33–1) and 1971 (at 7–2);
- **The Dikler** beating **Pendil** a short head in 1973;
- Midnight Court winning in 1978 – a running postponed from March to April after snow wiped out racing on the original date – to bring a once-in-a-career Gold Cup victory both to trainer **Fred Winter** (who rode the winner three times) and to jockey **John Francome**;
- Michael Dickinson's quintet of Bregawn, Captain John, **Wayward Lad**, Silver Buck and Ashley House filling the first five places in 1983;
- **Dawn Run** becoming the first horse to win the Champion Hurdle and Gold Cup after an unbelievable rally up the hill in 1986, unleashing the biggest bedlam ever seen at Cheltenham;
- **Desert Orchid** in 1989 clawing his way up the hill in desperate going to beat Yahoo;
- **Norton's Coin** winning at 100–1 in 1990;
- The Fellow winning for **François Doumen** at the fourth attempt in 1994, after being beaten a short head by Garrison Savannah in 1991 and the same distance by Cool Ground in 1992;
- Imperial Call winning from Rough Quest in 1996, an Irish victory which triggered a rare old hooley in the unsaddling enclosure – appropriate celebration of winning the biggest and best steeplechase in the calendar.

CHEPSTOW

Chepstow, Gwent NP6 5YH
Tel.: 01291 622260
Fax: 01291 625550
E-mail: enquiries@chepstow-racecourse.co.uk
Web: www.chepstow-racecourse.co.uk

Chepstow is one of the more modern courses in Britain, having been opened in 1926 – although there has been racing in the locality since the eighteenth century. At just short of two miles round, the left-handed circuit is tailor-made for the doughty stayer. Its back straight and home straight are each long enough to tax the determination and stamina of even the stoutest horse, but it is extremely undulating, and thus not ideal for the long-striding galloper. On the Flat, there is a straight mile, and all distances shorter than one mile are run on the straight course. But it is as a jumping track that Chepstow really excels, and never more so than when it stages one of the very big races – and best racegoing occasions – of the jumping year: the Welsh National just after Christmas. The race starts right in front of the stands and takes in two complete circuits of the course to make its trip of three miles five and a half furlongs a true test of stamina – notably up the home straight, where there are five fences to be jumped.

Chepstow hosts several other significant National Hunt races. The Rehearsal Chase in early December is a valuable opportunity for staying chasers to warm up for the King George at Kempton; the Persian War Novices' Hurdle in February commemorates the triple Champion Hurdle winner; the John Hughes Grand National Trial in February provides pointers to the Aintree marathon; and in April the Welsh Champion Hurdle is often a consolation prize for horses who have missed out in the 'real' championship at Cheltenham the previous month.

CHESTER

Chester, Cheshire CH1 2LY
Tel.: 01244 304600
Fax: 01244 304649
E-mail: sales@chester-races.com
Web: chester-races.co.uk

Chester racecourse is an oval – not far off a circle – a few yards over one mile round, which makes this the shortest Flat circuit in the country. About half the left-handed circuit is bordered by the River Dee; the short straight after the winning post runs parallel to the railway line; and the stands and home straight nestle up against the city's old Roman walls, from which skint racing fans and casual passers-by can enjoy a wonderful view of the sport for free. The surface is completely flat, runners are never far from the next turn, and the home straight is under two furlongs long. So good jockeyship can be crucial at Chester: punters do well to follow pilots who have proved that they have mastered its curiosities.

Chester is popularly known as the Roodeye or Roodee – from an old phrase meaning the meadow ('eye') of the cross ('rood'). A stone cross, the pedestal of which remains, stood on the site.

The May Meeting – the course's and the city's great annual event – is noted for its Classic trials: the Chester Vase (one and a half miles), Cheshire Oaks (one mile three furlongs) and Dee Stakes (one and a quarter miles). Chester, like Epsom, requires nimbleness and balance in a racehorse, and it is no coincidence that horses which act well here can go on to greater things at the Surrey course. In 1959 Parthia won the Dee Stakes before landing the Derby, but the Chester Vase tends to be a stronger race: in recent years Henbit and Shergar both won this before going on to Epsom success, and other notable winners since then have been Law Society, Unfuwain, Old Vic and Belmez; Quest For Fame, second to Belmez in 1990, won that year's Derby. But for all those dreams of Classics, the big race of the May Meeting – and thus of the Chester year – is the Chester Cup over two and a quarter miles, which amounts to two and a quarter circuits of the track, passing the winning post three times. The other big race of the May Meeting is the Ormonde Stakes over one mile five furlongs, which since the war has been won by three Derby winners: Tulyar before his Epsom

victory in 1952, and Blakeney (1970) and Teenoso (1984) as four-year-olds.

Chester racecourse is the oldest horseracing venue in Britain: there were races here early in the reign of Henry VIII, and the Silver Bell run for at the invitation of the mayor on Shrove Tuesday 1540 was the first recorded regular prize.

CHESTNUT (1)
A chestnut horse has a reddish coat, on a colour scale from light gold to dark liver; mane and tail are of similar hue to the coat or (occasionally) very light – 'flaxen'.

CHESTNUT (2)
On a horse's leg, the chestnut is the bony, horny growth situated just above the knee on the inside of the foreleg and below the hock on the inside of the hind leg. The exact pattern of the chestnut is unique to the individual horse.

CHEVELEY PARK STAKES
Group One; two-year-old fillies; 6 furlongs (Newmarket, Rowley Mile)
The Cheveley Park Stakes was first run in 1899 and named after the Newmarket estate owned by Colonel Harry McCalmont (owner of 1893 Triple Crown winner Isinglass): the first winner was Lutetia, ridden by **Tod Sloan**. The great **Pretty Polly** won at 100–8 on in 1903 – her sixth straight win as a juvenile – and two days later won the Middle Park Stakes. Fifinella, winner in 1915, won both Derby and Oaks the following year (the last filly to do so). The essence of the Cheveley Park Stakes is to indicate likely candidates for the One Thousand Guineas over the same course (but another quarter of a mile) the following spring, on the basis that a filly who has the speed, balance and resolve to win the Cheveley Park on Newmarket's yawning Rowley Mile in the autumn should be well qualified to take on the Classic seven months later. Since the Second World War nine winners of the race have gone on to win the Guineas: Belle Of All (1950), Zabara (1951), Night Off (1964), Fleet (1966), Humble Duty (1969), Waterloo

Cheveley Park Stakes winners since 1990

1990	Capricciosa	2	M. V. O'Brien *IRE*	J. Reid	7–1	11
1991	Marling	2	G. Wragg	W. R. Swinburn	15–8F	9
1992	Sayyedati	2	C. Brittain	W. R. Swinburn	5–2	4
1993	Prophecy	2	J. Gosden	Pat Eddery	12–1	6
1994	Gay Gallanta	2	M. Stoute	Pat Eddery	14–1	10
1995	Blue Duster	2	D. Loder	M. Kinane	4–5F	5
1996	Pas de Reponse	2	Mme C. Head *FRA*	F. Head	7–1	8
1997	Embassy	2	D. Loder	K. Fallon	5–2	8
1998	Wannabe Grand	2	J. Noseda	Pat Eddery	3–1F	9
1999	Seazun	2	M. Channon	T. Quinn	10–1	14
2000	Regal Rose	2	M. Stoute	L. Dettori	11–2	13

(1971), Ma Biche (1982), Ravinella (1987) and Sayyedati (1992).

CHING AND A HALF

Betting slang for 11–2.

CHURCHILL DOWNS

Web: www.churchilldowns.com

Louisville, Kentucky, has two major claims to sporting fame: it is the birthplace of Muhammad Ali; and it is the home of the USA's most famous racetrack, Churchill Downs, home of the **Kentucky Derby** and frequent host of the **Breeders' Cup**. Instantly recognisable by the twin spires set on top of the grandstand, Churchill Downs staged the Breeders' Cup in 1988, 1991 (the year of **Arazi**'s famous win in the Juvenile), 1994 (when Barathea won the Mile), 1998 and 2000 (when Kalanisi won the Turf and **Giant's Causeway** just failed in the Classic).

CIGAR

Cigar raked in prize money of US$9,999,813 in a career which saw him equal the US record of 16 consecutive victories, set by **Citation** in 1948, and win two of the most valuable races in the world – the **Breeders' Cup** Classic and the **Dubai World Cup**. A son of 1984 Champion Stakes winner Palace Music, Cigar was bred by his owner Allen Paulson and trained for most of his career by Bill Mott. His early races were mostly on turf courses and gave no hint that he was anything out of the ordinary

– he won just one race on grass – but when towards the end of his four-year-old year in 1994 he started concentrating on races on dirt, his fortunes started to soar: his last two races that season produced two victories, including a seven-length triumph in the Grade One NYRA Mile (since renamed the Cigar Mile).

As a five-year-old he won 10 successive races, culminating in the Breeders' Cup Classic at Belmont Park from L'Carriere. By this time he had become a national hero; but the international stage beckoned, and after winning his first race of 1996 at Gulfstream Park Cigar was sent to the Middle East for the inaugural running of the Dubai World Cup – which he won in gutsy style after a memorable duel up the straight with compatriot Soul Of The Matter. That race, Cigar's only outing outside North America, marked his fourteenth consecutive victory, and Citation's record of 16 in a row, set half a century earlier, was in sight. Win number 15 duly came in the Massachusetts Handicap at Suffolk Downs; then, in July 1996, Cigar went to Arlington Park, Chicago, for the Arlington Citation Challenge, a race specially framed for his record attempt. He won by three and a half lengths. The record was matched; but sadly he was not able to better it, thwarted by Dare And Go in the Pacific Classic at Del Mar in his next race. Nevertheless, he resumed the winning habit in the Woodward Stakes at Belmont, before being narrowly beaten by Skip Away in the Jockey Club Gold Cup at the same track and suffering another defeat in what turned out to be his final race, the Breeders' Cup Classic at Woodbine, Toronto, where he was beaten a nose and a head by Alphabet Soup and Louis Quatorze. It was a downbeat ending to a phenomenal career, with 12 of his 19 victories (from 33 races) coming in Grade One events.

Cigar proved infertile after being retired to the Ashford Stud in Kentucky and now resides at the Kentucky Horse Park in Lexington. A tough, battling campaigner who always dug deep in his races, his appeal was summed up by one journalist seeking to explain the defeats once the horse was past his best: Cigar, he said, 'was only human'.

CITATION

US Triple Crown winner in 1948, Citation won 32 of his 45 races between 1947 and 1951, including 16 in a row in 1948 (a record sequence equalled in 1996 by **Cigar**). He was the first horse to earn over $1 million in prize money, but was disappointing at stud. Citation died in 1970 at the age of 23.

CLAIBORNE FARM

Web: www.claibornefarm.com

One of the most famous studs in Kentucky, Claiborne has been home to many Turf legends after their racing careers. **Sir Ivor**, **Nijinsky** and **Secretariat** stood here as stallions, as did other influential sires like Danzig and Mr

Prospector. It was at Claiborne that **Triptych** met her untimely end in May 1989.

CLAIM, CLAIMER

'Claimer' in racing parlance has two distinct senses – a **claiming race** (see next entry) and an **apprentice** or **conditional jockey** who is still able to claim a weight allowance. By the same token, a prospective new owner 'claims' a horse out of a race by agreeing to pay the advertised amount, and a young jockey 'claims' a weight allowance until he or she has ridden a stipulated number of winners.

CLAIMING RACE

A claiming race (or 'claimer') is a lowly event in which any runner may be claimed afterwards for an advertised sum, and if the owner of any runner wishes it to carry less than the maximum weight the price at which it may be claimed is accordingly reduced. Thus the conditions for a claiming race may stipulate that the top weight to be carried is 9st 9lb and the maximum claiming price is £12,000, with a 1lb weight allowance for each £1,000 taken off the claiming price. If you put a claiming price of £6,000 on your horse when entering it, it will carry 9st 3lb. Claims for any individual horse are decided by ballot, and a maximum of one claim is allowed per prospective buyer. An owner can make a 'friendly claim' and attempt to claim his own horse back.

Leading Classic jockeys

name	first/last	2000	1000	Derby	Oaks	St Leger	total
Lester Piggott	1954/1992	5	2	9	6	8	30
Frank Buckle	1792/1827	5	6	5	9	2	27
Jem Robinson	1817/1848	9	5	6	2	2	24
Fred Archer	1874/1886	4	2	5	4	6	21

Leading Classic trainers

name	first/last	2000	1000	Derby	Oaks	St Leger	total
John Scott	1827/1863	7	4	5	8	16	40
Robert Robson	1793/1827	6	9	7	12	0	34
Matthew Dawson	1853/1895	5	6	6	5	6	28
John Porter	1868/1900	5	2	7	3	6	23

CLASSIFICATION OF RACES
See **grading of races**.

CLASSICS

The Classics in England are confined to three-year-olds and are, in chronological order as run in 2001:

- **Two Thousand Guineas** over one mile at Newmarket for colts and fillies in early May;
- **One Thousand Guineas** over one mile at Newmarket for fillies only in early May;
- **Oaks** over one and a half miles at Epsom Downs for fillies only in early June;
- **Derby** over one and a half miles for colts and fillies at Epsom Downs in early June;
- **St Leger** for colts and fillies over one mile six furlongs 132 yards at Doncaster in mid September.

In order of founding, the sequence reads St Leger (1776), Oaks (1779), Derby (1780), Two Thousand Guineas (1809) and One Thousand Guineas (1814), but they were not referred to collectively as 'the Classics' until the 1880s, and their position as the landmarks of the Flat season came about by evolution rather than planning. These races offer to three-year-old colts and fillies the challenge of having the speed to beat the best of the generation over a mile at Newmarket in the spring, the agility and stamina to do so again over one and a half miles of very different terrain at Epsom in the summer, and the stamina and resilience to win over a mile and three-quarters at Doncaster in the autumn. (For the races popularly held to be the most significant as prep races for the Classics, *see* **trial races**.) Other countries have equivalent races to the Classics in England (see, for example, **France**), and the term 'classic' has come generally to apply to big races: you might, for instance, hear the Cheltenham Gold Cup or King George VI Chase referred to as 'jumping classics'.

Winners of the Classics since the Second World War (1)

year	2000 Guineas	1000 Guineas	Derby	Oaks	St Leger
1946	Happy Knight	Hypericum	Airborne	Steady Aim	Airborne
1947	Tudor Minstrel	Imprudence	Pearl Diver	Imprudence	Sayajirao
1948	My Babu	Queenpot	My Love	Masaka	Black Tarquin
1949	Nimbus	Musidora	Nimbus	Musidora	Ridge Wood
1950	Palestine	Camaree	Galcador	Asmena	Scratch II
1951	Ki Ming	Belle Of All	Arctic Prince	Neasham Belle	Talma II
1952	Thunderhead II	Zabara	Tulyar	Frieze	Tulyar
1953	Nearula	Happy Laughter	Pinza	Ambiguity	Premonition
1954	Darius	Festoon	Never Say Die	Sun Cap	Never Say Die
1955	Our Babu	Meld	Phil Drake	Meld	Meld
1956	Gilles de Retz	Honeylight	Lavandin	Sicarelle	Cambremer
1957	Crepello	Rose Royale II	Crepello	Carrozza	Ballymoss
1958	Pall Mall	Bella Paola	Hard Ridden	Bella Paola	Alcide
1959	Taboun	Petite Etoile	Parthia	Petite Etoile	Cantelo
1960	Martial	Never Too Late II	St Paddy	Never Too Late II	St Paddy
1961	Rockavon	Sweet Solera	Psidium	Sweet Solera	Aurelius
1962	Privy Councillor	Abermaid	Larkspur	Monade	Hethersett
1963	Only For Life	Hula Dancer	Relko	Noblesse	Ragusa
1964	Baldric II	Pourparler	Santa Claus	Homeward Bound	Indiana
1965	Niksar	Night Off	Sea Bird II	Long Look	Provoke
1966	Kashmir II	Glad Rags	Charlottown	Valoris	Sodium
1967	Royal Palace	Fleet	Royal Palace	Pia	Ribocco

Winners of the Classics since the Second World War (2)

year	2000 Guineas	1000 Guineas	Derby	Oaks	St Leger
1968	Sir Ivor	Caergwrle	Sir Ivor	La Lagune	Ribero
1969	Right Tack	Full Dress II	Blakeney	Sleeping Partner	Intermezzo
1970	Nijinsky	Humble Duty	Nijinsky	Lupe	Nijinsky
1971	Brigadier Gerard	Altesse Royale	Mill Reef	Altesse Royale	Athens Wood
1972	High Top	Waterloo	Roberto	Ginevra	Boucher
1973	Mon Fils	Mysterious	Morston	Mysterious	Peleid
1974	Nonoalco	Highclere	Snow Knight	Polygamy	Bustino
1975	Bolkonski	Nocturnal Spree	Grundy	Juliette Marny	Bruni
1976	Wollow	Flying Water	Empery	Pawneese	Crow
1977	Nebbiolo	Mrs McArdy	The Minstrel	Dunfermline	Dunfermline
1978	Roland Gardens	Enstone Spark	Shirley Heights	Fair Salinia	Julio Mariner
1979	Tap On Wood	One In A Million	Troy	Scintillate	Son Of Love
1980	Known Fact	Quick As Lightning	Henbit	Bireme	Light Cavalry
1981	To-Agori-Mou	Fairy Footsteps	Shergar	Blue Wind	Cut Above
1982	Zino	On The House	Golden Fleece	Time Charter	Touching Wood
1983	Lomond	Ma Biche	Teenoso	Sun Princess	Sun Princess
1984	El Gran Senor	Pebbles	Secreto	Circus Plume	Commanche Run
1985	Shadeed	Oh So Sharp	Slip Anchor	Oh So Sharp	Oh So Sharp
1986	Dancing Brave	Midway Lady	Shahrastani	Midway Lady	Moon Madness
1987	Don't Forget Me	Miesque	Reference Point	Unite	Reference Point
1988	Doyoun	Ravinella	Kahyasi	Diminuendo	Minster Son
1989	Nashwan	Musical Bliss	Nashwan	Snow Bride	Michelozzo
1990	Tirol	Salsabil	Quest For Fame	Salsabil	Snurge
1991	Mystiko	Shadayid	Generous	Jet Ski Lady	Toulon
1992	Rodrigo de Triano	Hatoof	Dr Devious	User Friendly	User Friendly
1993	Zafonic	Sayyedati	Comm. In Chief	Intrepidity	Bob's Return
1994	Mister Baileys	Las Meninas	Erhaab	Balanchine	Moonax
1995	Pennekamp	Harayir	Lammtarra	Moonshell	Classic Cliché
1996	Mark Of Esteem	Bosra Sham	Shaamit	Lady Carla	Shantou
1997	Entrepreneur	Sleepytime	Benny The Dip	Reams Of Verse	Silver Patriarch
1998	King Of Kings	Cape Verdi	High-Rise	Shahtoush	Nedawi
1999	Island Sands	Wince	Oath	Ramruma	Mutafaweq
2000	King's Best	Lahan	Sinndar	Love Divine	Millenary
2001	Golan	Ameerat	Galileo	Imagine	

CLENCH

A clench (or clinch) is the nail which fixes a horse's shoe (or **plate**) to its hoof.

CLERK OF THE COURSE

Racecourse official, appointed by the course executive, responsible to the stewards for the general arrangements of a race meeting. The duties broadly cover the conduct of the fixture, including the condition of the course, the framing of the racing programme, going reports and other matters relating directly to the racing itself.

CLERK OF THE SCALES

Racecourse official responsible for weighing out the jockeys before the race and weighing them back in after it. Should any jockey fail to weigh in or weigh in at an unacceptable level, the Clerk of the Scales must lodge an objection. His other responsibilities include: jurisdiction of the racecourse number board; registering of overweight, allowances, horses' headgear, changes of colours and other relevant information; and making a return at the end of the racing day with details of results, weights carried, stewards' decisions, fines inflicted and any other data required for the official record of that day's racing.

CLONMEL
Powerstown Park Racecourse, Clonmel,
Co. Tipperary
Tel./fax: 052 25719
E-mail: news@sportingpress.iol.ie
Web: www.ireland.iol.ie/sportingpress

The town of Clonmel lies at the foot of the Comeragh Mountains in the valley of the River Suir, and the racecourse – locally known as Powerstown Park – sits in a high picturesque setting. The circuit is right-handed, about a mile and a quarter round, and has a stiff uphill finish. Some top-class jump races are run here, notably the Morris Oil Chase in November: when Dorans Pride won this in 2000, he was doing so for the fourth year in succession.

CLOSE-COUPLED
A close-coupled horse has a shorter than usual span of belly between its forelegs and hind legs and gives a more compact appearance than the long-backed, 'rangy' type.

CLUB
The Members' Enclosure of a racecourse is colloquially referred to as the 'Club' enclosure, since many racegoers in there would be annual members. But it is usually possible to buy admission to the Club on a daily basis.

COCHRANE, RAY
Ray Cochrane retired from the saddle on medical advice at the age of 43 in October 2000, on account of injuries incurred in the Newmarket plane crash on 1 June that year which killed pilot Patrick Mackey and badly injured passengers Cochrane and Frankie Dettori. Born in Ulster in June 1957, Cochrane was apprenticed to trainers Barry

Hills and Ron Sheather, riding his first winner on Roman Way at Windsor in August 1974. (He also rode over jumps, notching up the first of his eight winners over hurdles on Wanlockhead at Newton Abbot in August 1977.) He won three Classics in England – the 1986 One Thousand Guineas and Oaks on Midway Lady and 1988 Derby on Kahyasi – and landed plenty of other big races at home and abroad, including the 1988 Irish Derby on Kahyasi, 1989 Irish One Thousand Guineas on Ensconse, 1999 Poule d'Essai des Pouliches on Valentine Waltz, 1988 Canadian International on Infamy, 1989 Coronation Cup on Sheriff's Star, 1989 Champion Stakes on Legal Case, 1991 Queen Elizabeth II Stakes and 1992 Lockinge Stakes on Selkirk, and – his most notable win overseas – the 1998 Caulfield Cup in Australia on Taufan's Melody, when he incurred a one-month suspension and a fine of nearly £8,000 after the horse had wandered off a true line in the closing stages. Following the Newmarket crash (after which he was much praised for his heroism in pulling Dettori from the wreckage) he returned to the saddle, winning on his comeback ride on Glowing at Newmarket on 21 July 2000, but a fall galloping a horse at Salisbury at the end of August sidelined him again, and this time there would be no return. Shortly after his retirement he announced that he would be working as Frankie Dettori's agent.

COCKLE
Betting slang for £10, or 10–1.

CO-FAVOURITE
If three or more horses share the lowest price in the market, they are co-favourites (as opposed to one horse being favourite, and two being joint favourites).

Of the ten runners in the Law Society Legal Handicap Hurdle at Hexham on 29 April 1991, *seven* were co-favourites at 6–1, including the winner Fingers Crossed. Ponder the implications of that when next backing an unnamed favourite . . .

COLE, PAUL

Born in 1941, Paul Cole was assistant to Richmond Sturdy and to George Todd before taking out his first training licence in 1968. He started his training career in Lambourn, moving to his present base at the historic yard of Whatcombe (near Wantage in Oxfordshire) in 1985. His first Classic victory came with Snurge in the 1990 St Leger, and the following year he had a glorious time with Generous (owned by his principal patron **Fahd Salman**), who in 1991 won the Derby, Irish Derby and King George VI and Queen Elizabeth Diamond Stakes and made a major contribution to putting Cole at the top of the trainers' table that year. Generous has undoubtedly been his best horse, but other familiar names he has trained are Knight's Baroness (Irish Oaks 1990), Ibn Bey (Irish St Leger 1990, and runner-up to Unbridled in that year's Breeders' Cup Classic), and the grey filly Ruby Tiger, winner of the Nassau Stakes in 1991 and 1992.

COLIC

The severe abdominal pain in equines known as colic can arise from a variety of causes, including lack of blood supply to the intestines (due to parasitic worm larvae around the blood vessels), impacted foodstuffs or displacements of the bowel. The horse's digestive system is arranged in such a way that it cannot vomit, so any obstruction has to be shifted if the condition is to be eased and serious damage, or even death, prevented. It is usually treated with pain-killing drugs and bowel lubricants, but displacements may call for surgery.

COLLAR

A stretch of a racecourse is described as 'against the collar' when it is stiffly uphill – the long haul from the back straight at Towcester, for example.

COLONIAL CUP

Web: www.carolina-cup.org

The Colonial Cup is an invitation race run over two and three-quarter miles at Springdale racecourse in Camden, South Carolina, in November. The race was first run in 1970 and has often attracted serious challengers from Britain and Ireland. Grand Canyon, trained at Chichester by Derek Kent, won in 1976 (the first time the race had gone to an overseas raider) and 1978, ridden both times by **Ron Barry**. In the inaugural running in 1970 **L'Escargot** came fourth, **Captain Christy** filled the same place in 1975, and the 1974 Champion Hurdler Lanzarote also ran fourth behind Grand Canyon in 1976. Early winners Inkslinger (1971) and Soothsayer (1972) crossed the Atlantic to make their mark on chasing in Europe: Inkslinger joined Irish trainer Dan Moore, for whom he won the Two Mile Champion Chase at Cheltenham in 1973, and Soothsayer went to **Fred Winter** and finished second to Ten Up in the 1975 Cheltenham Gold Cup. The 2000 running, won by Romantic, carried prize money of $100,000.

COLOUR (HORSES)

A Thoroughbred horse's colour is registered at birth, though colouring can occasionally change with age. The basic colours are:

- *Bay* All shades of brown, with the 'points' (muzzle, mane, tail and extremities of the legs) black. Bay is by far the most common colour found in Thoroughbreds.
- *Brown* Distinctly brown all over.
- *Black* Distinctly black all over.
- *Chestnut* A range of shades from a light golden colour to a dark 'liver' chestnut.
- *Grey* A range from pure white to dark grey. Grey horses tend to get whiter as they get older. About 3 per cent of racehorses are greys.
- *Roan* A combination of red, white and yellow or black, white and yellow hairs which gives a washy appearance.

Colour is sometimes held to be an indication of a horse's temperament. A bright or 'flashy' chestnut (in particular a filly) is often thought to be unreliable, and there is a theory – belied by such performers as **Eclipse** and The Minstrel, an exceptionally brave winner of the Derby in 1977 under the full Lester Piggott treatment – that you cannot trust a chestnut with four white legs.

COLOURS, RACING

Racing colours were first used on jockeys in 1762, according to the Jockey Club order, 'for the greater convenience of distinguishing the horses in running, as also for the prevention of disputes arising from not knowing the colours worn by each rider'. In those days subtle shades could be accepted: the then Duke of Devonshire registered his colours as 'straw', and the current Duke keeps the same colours. In similar tone, **Lord Howard de Walden**'s colours were apricot, and those of Canadian-born **Lady Beaverbrook** maple leaf-green and beaver-brown. Nowadays colours are registered at Weatherbys, and new owners are restricted to 18 basic hues: white, grey, pink, red, maroon, light green, emerald green, dark green, light blue, royal blue, dark blue, mauve, purple, yellow, orange, beige, brown and black). Design of colours has been standardised: the cap, for example, must be plain, hooped, striped, check, spots, quartered, star, diamond, stars or diamonds. Single colours are extremely stylish and tend to go to major players: in addition to the straw and apricot mentioned above, royal blue belongs to **Godolphin,** dark blue to Mrs Susan Magnier (*see* **John Magnier**), dark green to the late Prince **Fahd Salman.** The auction in recent years of new registrations of single colours generated a great deal of interest and a great deal of money for racing charities: Mrs Magnier paid £69,000 for all-pink at an auction at Sotheby's in March 2000, while other shades offered as a single colour have included bronze, black, aquamarine and mauve. White belongs to Ahmed Ali.

COLT

Male horse up to and including the age of four. (A horse is said to be 'colty' or acting in a 'coltish' manner if he refuses to behave with due decorum in the parade ring.)

COME ON FOR THE RACE

A horse who is expected to 'come on for the race' is expected to put up a better performance next time out – for reasons such as being fitter, or running less **green.**

COMPANIONS (OF HORSES)

Thoroughbreds tend to be highly strung, nervous individuals, and in many cases the presence of another creature proves a calming influence. Often the companion is another equine. The great filly **Pebbles** had a particularly soft spot for a fellow inmate of Clive Brittain's yard, the gelding Come On The Blues, and many other well-known horses have found a pony or donkey a good friend. **Arkle** was accompanied by a donkey named Nellie when recuperating from his career-ending injury, and the friendship of another great Irish chaser for a donkey resulted in disaster: *see* **Cottage Rake.** Many stables have a resident goat for the calming-down role – **Foinavon**, winner of the grotesque 1967 Grand National, and 1994 Lincoln Handicap heroine Our Rita were both goat-lovers. Top-class chaser Remittance Man was very attached to sheep, as was the great mare **Allez France:** rumour has it that the stable vet was exasperated by having to spend more time on that sheep than on the horses, and as soon as Allez France had departed to stud in the USA, the barbecue was lit . . . Sunnyhill, a chaser in Ireland in the 1950s, was more original in his tastes, bestowing his affections on a goose, and 1929 Grand National winner Gregalach went everywhere with a rough-haired terrier. But the idea does not always work: when Celtic Shot, Champion Hurdler in 1988, was put in a field with a flock of sheep he proceeded to savage any that wandered too close. For an equally unharmonious relationship, *see* **St Simon.**

COMPUTER STRAIGHT FORECAST

A betting-shop wager (usually abbreviated to CSF) which involves predicting the first two in a race in correct order. The bet is so called because the dividend is calculated by computer, using a formula too complex for mortal man to comprehend.

CONDITION

Racing euphemism for flesh and muscle. A horse is said to be 'carrying plenty of condition' if it is well muscled (or sometimes just too fat!), and to be 'losing condition' if it is too skinny.

CONDITIONER

US colloquial term for a trainer.

CONDITIONAL JOCKEY

A conditional jockey is the jumping equivalent of an **apprentice** on the Flat. Conditionals can (when race conditions permit) claim an allowance of 7lb until they have won 15 races, then 5lb until they have won 35 races, then 3lb until they have won 65 races. A conditional loses the right to claim an allowance at the age of 26.

CONDITIONS RACE

A Flat race which is not a **handicap**, nor a **selling** or **claiming** race, nor a **maiden** race or a **novice** race. (A 'conditions stakes', according to the definition in the Rules, is 'a Flat race which has not been awarded Pattern or Listed status, is not a Handicap or a Novice race, is not restricted to Maidens, is not governed by Selling or Claiming provisions and is not restricted to Apprentice or Amateur riders if less than £7,500 is added to stakes.')

CONFORMATION

A horse's build; *see* **paddock inspection**.

CONNECTIONS

Horse's owner and trainer.

COOLMORE STUD

Web: www.coolmore.com

Coolmore, near Fethard in County Tipperary, is the leading stud farm in Europe, home of **Sadler's Wells**, greatest stallion of the age, and many other luminaries including 1999 Arc and 2000 King George winner **Montjeu**, Grand Lodge (sire of 2000 Derby, Irish Derby and Arc winner Sinndar), 'The Iron Horse' **Giant's Causeway**, 1992 Derby winner Dr Devious, 1997 Two Thousand Guineas winner Entrepreneur, 1997 Arc winner Peintre Celebre, Spectrum (sire of 2001 Two Thousand Guineas winner Golan, himself due to stand at Coolmore from 2002), Danehill, Bluebird, Desert King, Turtle Island and Night Shift. In all the stud has over 50 stallions in Ireland, the USA (where at Coolmore's Ashford Stud the star turns include 1990 Breeders' Cup Mile winner Royal Academy, Kentucky Derby winners Fusaichi Pegasus and Thunder Gulch, 1998 Two Thousand Guineas winner King Of Kings and the great milers Lure and Spinning World), South America, Japan and Australia. Coolmore pioneered the notion of dual-hemisphere stud duties, sending Irish-based stallions to Australia for the covering season there. The stud was established in 1975, when a partnership of trainer **Vincent O'Brien**, owner–breeder **Robert Sangster** and stallion master **John Magnier** (O'Brien's son-in-law) took over an existing 350-acre property and built it to bloodstock pre-eminence. Be My Guest, a son of Northern Dancer trained by O'Brien to win the 1977 Waterford Crystal Mile at Goodwood, was one of the first Coolmore stallions, became champion sire in 1982 and was still active for the 2001 covering season at the age of 30. The current management of Coolmore is headed by John Magnier, with **Michael Tabor** and trainer **Aidan O'Brien** close associates.

CORK

Mallow, Co. Cork

Tel.: 022 50207

Fax: 022 50213

Founded in 1924, the racecourse was known as Mallow until being renamed Cork in 1997, when the refurbished track, complete with a smart and well-appointed new grandstand and a much improved racing surface, was opened following its purchase by the Racing Board. The circuit is right-handed, about 12 furlongs round, flat and galloping, and the setting would be delightful but for the vast sugar refinery belching smoke beyond the back straight.

CORONATION CUP

Group One; four-year-olds and upwards; 1½ miles (Epsom Downs)

The Coronation Cup was first run in 1902 to mark the coronation of Edward VII, and throughout its history has tended to attract small but exceptionally high-class fields, as befits a race aimed at the top older horses embarking on a midsummer middle-distance

Coronation Cup winners since 1990

1990	In The Wings	4	A. Fabre FRA	C. Asmussen	15–8F	6
1991	In The Groove	4	D. Elsworth	S. Cauthen	7–2	7
1992	Saddlers' Hall	4	M. Stoute	W. R. Swinburn	5–4F	9
1993	Opera House	5	M. Stoute	M. Roberts	9–4JF	8
1994	Apple Tree	5	A. Fabre FRA	T. Jarnet	12–1	11
1995	Sunshack	4	A. Fabre FRA	Pat Eddery	10–1	7
1996	Swain	4	A. Fabre FRA	L. Dettori	11–10F	4
1997	Singspiel	5	M. Stoute	L. Dettori	5–4F	5
1998	Silver Patriarch	4	J. Dunlop	Pat Eddery	7–2	7
1999	Daylami	5	S. bin Suroor	L. Dettori	9–2	7
2000	Daliapour	4	M. Stoute	K. Fallon	11–8F	4
2001	Mutafaweq	5	S. bin Suroor	L. Dettori	11–2	6

campaign. Three very great fillies won the race twice: **Pretty Polly** in 1905 and 1906, **Petite Etoile** in 1960 and 1961, and **Triptych** in 1987 and 1988 (she was also beaten a short head by Saint Estephe in 1986). Nine Derby winners have won the Coronation Cup the year after an even more notable Epsom triumph, of whom the five since the Second World War are Relko (1964), Charlottown (1967), **Royal Palace** (1968), **Mill Reef** (1972) and Roberto (1973). Most recent Classic winners to have won the Coronation Cup are Silver Patriarch (1998, St Leger 1997) and Mutafaweq (2001, St Leger 1999). But the recent roll of honour also includes horses who were not forward enough to figure in the Classics as three-year-olds but enjoyed ever more glittering careers as they got older: **Swain** won as a four-year-old in 1996, and Opera House (1993), **Singspiel** (1997) and **Daylami** (1999) as five-year-olds.

CORONATION STAKES
Group One; three-year-old fillies; 1 mile
(Royal Ascot)

The fillies' equivalent of the St James's Palace Stakes, the Coronation Stakes was first run in 1840 to mark the coronation of Queen Victoria (which had actually taken place in

Coronation Stakes winners since 1990

1990	Chimes Of Freedom	3	H. Cecil	S. Cauthen	11–2	7
1991	Kooyonga	3	M. Kauntze IRE	W. O'Connor	3–1	8
1992	Marling	3	G. Wragg	W. R. Swinburn	8–11F	7
1993	Gold Splash	3	Mme C. Head FRA	G. Mosse	100–30	5
1994	Kissing Cousin	3	H. Cecil	M. Kinane	13–2	10
1995	Ridgewood Pearl	3	J. Oxx IRE	J. Murtagh	9–2	10
1996	Shake The Yoke	3	E. Lellouche FRA	O. Peslier	evensF	7
1997	Rebecca Sharp	3	G. Wragg	M. Hills	25–1	6
1998	Exclusive	3	M. Stoute	W. R. Swinburn	5–1	9
1999	Balisada	3	G. Wragg	M. Roberts	16–1	9
2000	Crimplene	3	C. Brittain	P. Robinson	4–1JF	9
2001	Banks Hill	3	A. Fabre FRA	O. Peslier	4–1JF	13

1838). Like the colts' race, it was elevated to Group One status in 1988 and tends to command small but very select fields, with the form of runners linked closely with that of the early-season Classics in England, Ireland and France. The immortal **Pretty Polly** won at 5–1 on in 1904, and since the Second World War the Coronation Stakes has eight times gone to the winner of the One Thousand Guineas: Belle Of All (1951), Zabara (1952), Happy Laughter (1953), Festoon (1954), Meld (1955), Fleet (1967), Humble Duty (1970) and One In A Million (1979). But perhaps the best running in the last 20 years came in 1984, when One Thousand Guineas heroine Pebbles was beaten by Irish One Thousand winner Katies after a long-drawn-out tussle. Notable winners from the last decade include Kooyonga (1991) and Ridgewood Pearl (1995), both trained in Ireland: Kooyonga won the 1992 Eclipse Stakes, and Ridgewood Pearl went on to win the Breeders' Cup Mile the same season as her Ascot triumph. Geoff Wragg-trained winner Marling (1992) won the Sussex Stakes the same season.

CORONET

The top of a horse's foot, where hoof meets hair.

COTTAGE RAKE

Triple winner of the Cheltenham Gold Cup – 1948, 1949 and 1950 – and winner of the 1948 King George VI Chase, Cottage Rake was one of the finest chasers of the first decade following the end of the Second World War. Bred in Mallow, County Cork, he spent his formative years turned out on a bog, going into training at the age of five with a promising young trainer at nearby Churchtown named **Vincent O'Brien**, who by the end of Cottage Rake's career had sent him out to win 12 steeplechases, one hurdle and three races on the Flat, including the Irish Cesarewitch in 1947. He won his first Gold Cup by a length and a half from Happy Home in 1948; his second by two lengths from Cool Customer in 1949; and his third by ten lengths from Finnure in 1950. After the end

of the 1949–50 season he was the victim of a freak accident. He and his donkey companion were let out every day in a field, and on one occasion the cattle who spent the night in the field were inadvertently left in when Cottage Rake and his pal arrived the following morning. The donkey ambled off among the cattle, and when Cottage Rake could not locate his friend he panicked. Belting round the field in search of the donkey, he slipped and damaged a tendon. He recovered but was never again the same horse, eventually moving to the stable of Gerald Balding (father of Ian and Toby) in England and ending his career in a chase worth £204 at Wolverhampton in December 1953, three weeks short of his fifteenth birthday. He died in 1961. Cottage Rake was partnered in all his big steeplechase victories by Aubrey Brabazon, a great Irish jockey whose partnership with the triple Gold Cup winner was immortalised in a famous racing rhyme:

Aubrey's up, the money's down
The frightened bookies quake
Come on, me lads and give a cheer
Begod, 'tis Cottage Rake!

COUP

In betting parlance, a coup is a successful bet – usually on a hefty scale, and not invariably pulled off within the exact letter of the law – landed by astute planning. Often a coup will be brought about by the horse being carefully prepared for a race in such a way that the bookmakers have a less accurate idea of its chance than those who are betting on it, and will consequently let it be backed at an over-generous price; the history of the Turf is peppered with occasions when a massive amount of money invested has caused a dramatic reduction in the odds of a horse. But the coup which pushes against – and sometimes through – the bounds of legality is easier to pull off in a small race which will attract little attention, and the most sensational frauds of the post-war era have taken place in minor events. A selling race at Bath on 16 July 1953 was won by a horse named Francasal at 10–1; but investigations revealed that the winner was not Francasal but a **ringer** named Santa Amaro. The main perpetrators of the affair were convicted and gaoled. When Flockton Grey won a two-year-old maiden race at Leicester in March 1982 by 20 lengths at 10–1 heads were scratched and tongues started wagging with equal ferocity. Juveniles simply do not win that easily; could this really be a two-year-old? No: Flockton Grey was actually a three-year-old named Good Hand – and again the long arm of the law descended on the perpetrators. Then there was In The Money, who landed a gamble when winning a selling hurdle at Newton Abbot in August 1978 on his first outing for two seasons. The day after the race he was reportedly so lame that he was put down, but this turned out to be a case of destroying the evidence in another ringer case: poor In The Money had been switched for a horse called Cobblers March. The most ingenious coup of all merits its own entry: *see* **Gay Future**.

COUPLED

In France and some other countries where betting is principally on the pari-mutuel system, horses in the same ownership are coupled for betting purposes, so that a coup cannot be pulled by the 'wrong' horse winning. In the 2000 Prix de l'Arc de Triomphe the Aga Khan's colt Sinndar started 6–4 second favourite. His pacemaker Raypour, also owned by the Aga Khan, was coupled with Sinndar in the on-course pool and thus also started at 6–4, though his true chance was better represented by the odds quoted by British bookmakers on the morning of the race: 200–1.

COVERING

In the language of the bloodstock business, covering is the act of mating: *see* **breeding**.

In the northern hemisphere the covering season lasts five months, from 15 February to 15 July; in the southern hemisphere it commences on 1 September.

COX PLATE

Australian leg of the **Emirates World Series**, the Cox Plate is a weight-for-age event for three-year-olds and upwards run on turf over one and a quarter miles at Moonee Valley, Melbourne, in late October, as the city (and all Australia) gears up for the running of the **Melbourne Cup** on the first Tuesday in November. First run in 1922, the race was won by **Phar Lap** in 1930 and 1931, by Tulloch in 1960, and by Kingston Town in 1980, 1981 and 1982. Strawberry Road, winner in 1983, was runner-up to **Pebbles** in the Breeders' Cup Turf at Aqueduct in 1985, and the great New Zealand-trained mare Sunline won in 1999 and again – this time by seven lengths – in 2000, a victory which made her the highest stakes-winning horse in Australasian racing history.

CRIB-BITER

A horse who gnaws away at his crib (manger) – or anything else he can get his teeth round, such as the stable door – is doing so to calm himself down and counter nervous agitation.

CRISP

Crisp won nine steeplechases in Britain, but will be for ever remembered by British racing fans – and by millions more who watched on television – for one defeat, his heroic but unavailing front-running effort in the 1973 Grand National, when after building up an enormous lead he was caught in the shadow of the post and beaten by **Red Rum**. Owned and bred by Sir Chester Manifold, one of the most powerful figures in Australian racing, Crisp was foaled in Australia in 1963. After winning two races on the Flat, five hurdles and six chases (including the Carolina Hunt Cup in the USA), he came to England as a seven-year-old in 1970 to be trained by **Fred Winter**. He won his first race at Wincanton in the manner of a top-class horse, and proved his quality when winning the Two Mile Champion Chase at the 1971 Cheltenham Festival by 25 lengths. In 1972 he won the Coventry Chase at Kempton Park (now the Racing Post Chase) and finished fifth behind Glencaraig Lady in the Gold Cup, and in 1973 ran third behind Inkslinger in the Two Mile Champion Chase. Crisp's ideal distance seemed to be around two and a half miles, but many felt that sheer class gave him a major chance over the four and a half of the Grand National, and on 31 March 1973 the ten-year-old started 9–1 joint favourite with Red Rum for the Aintree marathon despite being asked to hump 12st, joint top weight with **L'Escargot**. Red Rum, who had been building a name for himself as a very useful chaser in the north, carried just 10st 5lb. Crisp, ridden by **Richard Pitman**, was in the front rank from the start; by the Canal Turn he was out on his own, and the next five minutes produced the greatest display of galloping and jumping in Grand National history – and the most heart-rending climax. On the second circuit, Crisp soared over the big ditch at the nineteenth, winged the next two and then took Becher's in his stride, still 30 lengths clear. On the run from the Canal Turn back towards the stands he was keeping up his gallop – but then the petrol gauge started to flicker. At the second last Crisp was still some 15 lengths ahead of Red Rum but his stride was shortening. In the grandstand Fred Winter turned to Crisp's owner and muttered, 'I'm afraid, Sir Chester, we are going to be beaten' – as Crisp sent the gorse flying at the last and set off up the run-in, desperately tired under his top weight and with his lightly weighted rival closing inexorably. Three strides from the line Red Rum got his head in front and won by three-quarters of a length in a time which shattered the previous record for the race by nearly 20 seconds.

Crisp had put up the greatest of Grand National performances, but had lost. He met Red Rum again in a two-horse race at Doncaster the following November: they started at level weights, and Crisp won effortlessly by eight lengths in what proved the final victory of his career. In the 1974–5 season he appeared six times but failed to win, though for a brief moment at the Railway Fences in the 1975 Whitbread Gold Cup he set Sandown Park on a roar when moving into a challenging position, only to blunder his chance away at the second last and finish fourth behind April Seventh. He did not run again, and spent an honourable retirement in Northumberland, where he

died at the age of 22 in 1985 while out hunting. His best epitaph comes from John Oaksey, who rode in that famous race (finishing sixth on Proud Tarquin) and in the following day's *Sunday Telegraph* wrote that Crisp had 'earned a sort of immortality wherever men admire brave horses.'

CROSS-COUNTRY RACES

McGregor The Third won three times over the Cheltenham cross-country course (including the first two runnings of the Sporting Index Chase in 1995 and 1996), but in the 1998 running his jockey Tony Dobbin mistook the course after the third last fence – an occupational hazard on such a circuit – and McGregor The Third could finish only fifth.

Although cross-country steeplechases have been popular in Ireland with the La Touche Cup at **Punchestown**, and the Velka Pardubicka at **Pardubice** in the Czech Republic has long fascinated British jumping followers, cross-country chases under Rules came to Britain only with the first running of the Sporting Index Chase at **Cheltenham** in November 1995. This event, which has grown in popularity over the years, involves horses and jockeys negotiating a convoluted course over three miles seven furlongs, laid out in the infield of the more orthodox Cheltenham circuits and involving such obstacles as a ditch and bank, a double bank with hedges, timber rails and an 'Aintree' jump which replicates the Canal Turn on the Grand National course.

CRUDWELL

Crudwell was named after a village in Wiltshire, a couple of miles from the village of Oaksey.

Crudwell was the last horse in Britain to win 50 races: seven on the Flat, four over hurdles and 39 steeplechases, including the Welsh Grand National (ridden by **Dick Francis**) in 1956. Foaled in 1946 and trained throughout his career by Frank Cundell, Crudwell notched up his first victory over 12 furlongs at Leicester on 28 March 1950 and his fiftieth at Wincanton on 15 September 1960 when, ridden by Michael Scudamore (father of Peter), he won the Somerset Chase at the age of 14. He did not race again. The Crudwell Cup, a steeplechase commemorating a highly durable and popular horse, is run at Warwick.

CRUMP, NEVILLE

Middleham-based Captain Neville Crump trained the winners of three Grand Nationals – Sheila's Cottage (1948), Teal (1952) and Merryman II (1960) – and a host of other big steeplechases. Born in 1910, he rode in point-to-points and as an amateur under Rules, and took out his first trainer's licence in 1937. In addition to those three Nationals he won the Whitbread Gold Cup three times, with Much Obliged in the inaugural running in 1957, Hoodwinked (1963) and the peripatetic Dormant, who was receiving 3st from Mill House when winning in 1964. (Dormant got through trainers like Big Mac goes through cigars, and was in the care of his owner Mrs Doris Wells-Kendrew – though nominally trained by her husband – when beating Arkle in the 1966 King George VI Chase.) Crump won the Scottish Grand National five times (Wot No Sun 1949, Merryman II 1959, Arcturus 1968, Salkeld 1980 and Canton 1983), the Hennessy Gold Cup with Springbok in 1962, the Welsh Grand National with Skyreholme in 1951 and Narvik in 1980, and the Mackeson Gold Cup with Cancello in 1976, and was leading trainer in the 1951–2 and 1956–7 seasons. Neville Crump retired from training in 1989 and died in January 1997 at the age of 86.

Neville Crump was famed for his forthright attitude. When his opinion was sought regarding whether a little-known member of the aristocracy would make a suitable steward at Aintree, he replied: 'Absolutely perfect. He can't see, can't hear, and he knows f*** all about racing.'

CUMANI, LUCA

Born in Milan in April 1949, Luca Cumani rode 85 winners as an amateur in Italy, France and Britain (where he won the Moët & Chandon Silver Magnum at Epsom on Ian Balding-trained Meissen in 1972). His training career in Britain started with a spell as assistant to **Henry Cecil** in the mid-1970s, and he took out his first full licence in 1976. His biggest successes have come with Derby winners Kahyasi (who also won the Irish Derby) in 1988 and High-Rise in 1998, and he won the St Leger in 1984 with Commanche Run, **Lester Piggott**'s record twenty-eighth Classic victory. (Commanche Run beat Oh So Sharp in the 1985 Benson and Hedges Gold Cup.) Apart from those Classic winners, his best horses have included Barathea (Irish Two Thousand Guineas and Breeders' Cup Mile 1994), Markofdistinction (Queen Anne Stakes and Queen Elizabeth II Stakes 1990), Only Royale (Yorkshire Oaks 1993 and 1994), Tolomeo (Arlington Million 1983), Infamy (Canadian International 1988), Legal Case (Champion Stakes 1989), Second Set (Sussex Stakes 1991), One So Wonderful (International Stakes 1998) and Endless Hall (Singapore Airlines International Cup 2001). For all that array of success with his horses, Luca Cumani has earned the everlasting gratitude of the racing public in Britain for the role he played in nurturing the career of his compatriot **Frankie Dettori**. It was to Cumani's Newmarket yard that Frankie came as apprentice in 1987, and the trainer formed a steadying influence during the rockier moments of the young phenomenon's early years in Britain. He provided Frankie's first two Group One winners: Markofdistinction in the Queen Elizabeth II Stakes and Shamshir in the Fillies' Mile in consecutive races at Ascot in September 1990.

CUMMINGS, BART

Legendary Australian trainer, born in 1927, who won the **Melbourne Cup** 11 times (a record) between Light Fingers in 1965 and Rogan Josh in 1999. He has also trained the winner of the **Caulfield Cup** six times.

CURB

Condition of a horse's hock where the plantar ligament thickens; treated by rest.

CURRAGH

The Curragh, Co. Kildare
Tel.: 045 441205
Fax: 045 441442
E-mail: info@curragh.ie
Web: www.curragh.ie

The Curragh is to Ireland what Newmarket is to England – the national headquarters of Flat racing, a major training centre and home of an internationally renowned racecourse. All five Irish Classics are run here, plus three other Group One races (Tattersalls Gold Cup, Moyglare Stud Stakes and National Stakes), making The Curragh the venue for eight of Ireland's ten Group One events (*see* Pattern). The Curragh – the word is a modern rendition of *cuireach*, the Gaelic word for racecourse – has a history stretching back to the third century AD, when the vast plain on which the racecourse now stands was the site of chariot races. Fast forward 1,500 years to the eighteenth century and The Curragh has become the venue for regular horse races, with stables being built on the edge of the plain to accommodate a growing number of horses. A coffee house in nearby Kildare saw the founding of the Turf Club before the end of the eighteenth century, and by the middle of the nineteenth the Club had become the effective manager of the racecourse as well as the governing body of the sport in Ireland. Today The Curragh manages to combine the magic of its ancient origins with the characteristics of a major international racecourse. The main track is horseshoe-shaped, right-handed, wide and, with no sharp bends and an uphill finish, perfect for the long-striding horse. Off that track come chutes to accommodate starts for races of under 10 furlongs. As well as having Ireland's premier racecourse, The Curragh is also the country's major training centre, with the yards of leading trainers such as **John Oxx**, **Dermot Weld**, Kevin Prendergast and Michael Grassick nearby.

CUT

Colloquial term for the act of **gelding**.

CUT IN THE GROUND

Informal term referring to going softer than good.

D

DAHLIA

One of the most popular racemares of the post-war period, Dahlia won races at the top level over five seasons and in five different countries. Owned and bred by **Nelson Bunker Hunt** and trained in France by **Maurice Zilber**, she first made the headlines in Britain with a devastating turn of foot to win the 1973 Irish Oaks – beating hotly fancied Oaks winner Mysterious – and just a week later produced an even more sensational burst of acceleration to demolish a top-class field (including Roberto, **Rheingold**, Hard To Beat and Weaver's Hall) in the King George VI and Queen Elizabeth Stakes at Ascot. That season she started to make her mark on the global stage, as well as advertise her extraordinary toughness, when winning the Washington, DC International. In 1974 she won the Grand Prix de Saint-Cloud and then, ridden by Lester Piggott, became the first horse to win the King George twice (beating Highclere). The following month she won the Benson and Hedges Gold Cup (now the International Stakes) at York and later in the year landed more big money in North America in the Man O' War Stakes and the Canadian International. In 1975 she finished third in the King George behind **Grundy** and **Bustino**, then won a second Benson and Hedges (with Grundy well back in fourth). For her 1976 campaign she moved to California to be trained by **Charlie Whittingham**, for whom she won the Hollywood Invitational Handicap. On the domestic front her great rival was another much-loved French mare **Allez France**, who finished in front of Dahlia on each of the eight occasions they met. On her retirement, winner of 15 of her 48 races, her earnings of approximately $1.5 million comprised a world record for a filly or mare.

As a broodmare she produced several top-class performers, and died in Kentucky in April 2001 at the age of 31.

DALHAM HALL STUD

Newmarket base of Sheikh Mohammed's **Darley Stud Management**. Stallions standing there for 2001 are Diktat, Halling, Lujain, Machiavellian, Mark Of Esteem, Polish Precedent and **Singspiel**. **Dubai Millennium** had covered the majority of his first book of mares at the stud before his untimely death in April 2001.

DAM

Mother of horse.

DANCING BRAVE

A son of Lyphard, bred in the United States and bought by his owner **Khalid Abdullah** for 200,000 guineas as a yearling, Dancing Brave was trained in Sussex by Guy Harwood, who made sure that the horse was not over-exposed as a two-year-old in 1985: he contested just two small races, both of which he won. In 1986 Dancing Brave warmed up for the Two Thousand Guineas with a smooth victory in the Craven Stakes at Newmarket, then returned to the same course for the Classic itself and charged home three lengths clear of Green Desert. Next stop Epsom for the Derby – and a race brimming with controversy. Despite worries about his stamina over the trip of a mile and a half, Dancing Brave was sent off 2–1 favourite, with Dante Stakes winner Shahrastani second market choice at 11–2. Those doubts about the colt's staying power prompted **Greville Starkey** to keep the favourite well back, and Dancing Brave was still third last at Tattenham Corner. Once the field hit the home straight Starkey pulled the Guineas winner to the outside and Dancing Brave started to devour the ground. But Shahrastani was by now in full flight and not stopping, and as the final furlongs slipped away it became horribly obvious to Dancing Brave's legion of supporters that his jockey had been cutting it very fine – too fine, as Shahrastani kept up his gallop all the way to the finish, and despite Dancing Brave's surge was still half a length to the good at the line. Arguments raged about whether Dancing Brave should have won, but the cold fact of the entry in the form book was that the colt had suffered his first defeat.

A four-length victory over **Triptych** in the Eclipse Stakes eased the pain a little, and then came the re-match with Shahrastani in the King George VI and Queen Elizabeth Diamond Stakes at Ascot. It was no contest: Dancing Brave – now ridden by Pat Eddery – set the record straight by sweeping past not only Shahrastani but also Shardari and Triptych, leaving the Derby winner back in fourth.

Then, after a facile victory in his prep race at Goodwood (in which Dancing Brave was such a stone-cold certainty that no starting prices were returned), came the Arc. Red-hot opposition included Bering, winner of the Prix du Jockey-Club; German challenger Acatenango, who had won his last 12 races; the redoubtable mare Triptych; Shardari, who since the King George had won the International at York; and Shahrastani again. By any standards this was one of the best renewals of Europe's biggest race for many a year. Cool as ever despite the quality of the opposition, Pat Eddery waited until all the other jockeys had made their moves, then produced Dancing Brave for a sweeping run up the outside to win from Bering. It was a devastating performance.

Champion of Europe; but there were other worlds to conquer, and Dancing Brave – who had been syndicated for stud purposes even before the Eclipse Stakes at a valuation of £14 million – travelled to California in an attempt to end his career in a blaze of glory in the Breeders' Cup Turf at Santa Anita. He started at 2–1 on but could finish only fourth behind Manila: yet another case of a great horse being taken to the well once too often. The colt did not race again, and retired winner of eight of his ten races.

He spent five years at stud in Britain – his fertility affected by his contracting Marie's Disease – before being sold to Japan, where he was already established as a stallion when in 1993 his son Commander In Chief, product of his third crop in Britain, won the Derby. Dancing Brave died in August 1999 at the age of 16.

DARLEY, KEVIN

Kevin Darley was born in Tettenhall, Staffordshire, in 1960. Apprenticed to trainer Reg Hollinshead, he rode his first winner on Dust Up at Haydock Park on 5 August 1977 (his seventeenth birthday) and was champion apprentice in 1978. He was runner-up to Pat Eddery in the jockeys' championship in 1993, third behind Frankie Dettori and Jason Weaver in 1994, runner-up to Dettori in 1995 and third behind Kieren Fallon and Dettori in 1997, before finally landing the title for the first time in 2000. The best horse he has yet ridden is Celtic Swing, on whom he won the Prix du Jockey-Club in 1995 after being narrowly beaten by Pennekamp in the Two Thousand Guineas, and his championship year in 2000 was highlighted by Group One wins in Britain on Pipalong (Haydock Sprint Cup) and Observatory (who beat Giant's Causeway in the Queen Elizabeth II Stakes).

DARLEY ARABIAN

One of the three founding sires of the Thoroughbred breed, and far more influential than the other two, the **Godolphin Arabian** and the **Byerley Turk**: the great majority of modern Thoroughbreds trace back to him, principally through his great-great-grandson **Eclipse**. The Darley Arabian was foaled in 1700 and sent to England as a four-year-old.

DARLEY STUD MANAGEMENT

Web: www.darleystallions.com

Darley Stud Management is the blanket name for the breeding interests of Sheikh

Mohammed Al **Maktoum**. At the beginning of the 2001 breeding season there were 36 stallions standing in seven countries.

DARLING, FRED

Fred Darling, born in 1884, was one of the most successful trainers of the twentieth century. He began his career with a small string of jumpers which he trained for Lady de Bathe (better known as Lily Langtry), then spent a spell in Germany before returning to Britain just before the start of the First World War to take over the famous yard at Beckhampton, Wiltshire, where his father Sam Darling had trained. He trained 19 Classic winners, including seven of the Derby: Captain Cuttle (1922), Manna (1925), Coronach (1926), Cameronian (1931), Bois Roussel (1938), Pont L'Eveque (1940) and Owen Tudor (1941). He also trained Sun Chariot, winner of the fillies' Triple Crown in 1942. Fred Darling died in 1953 a few days after Pinza, whom he had bred, had won the Derby.

DAVIES, BOB

Born in 1946, Bob Davies rode his first winner in 1966, and after riding for two seasons as an amateur turned professional for the 1967–8 season. He was champion jump jockey for three seasons: 1968–9 (in only his second season as a professional he shared the title with Terry Biddlecombe), 1969–70 and 1971–2, and won the Grand National on Lucius in 1978. He retired from the saddle in 1981 and is now Clerk of the Course at Ludlow.

DAWN RUN

By the great jumping sire Deep Run, Dawn Run was foaled on a farm in County Cork and sold at auction as a three-year-old for 5,800 guineas to Mrs Charmian Hill, then 62 years old and famed throughout Ireland as 'The Galloping Granny': in 1973 Mrs Hill had become the first woman in Ireland to ride against men under Rules. Dawn Run was put into training with Paddy Mullins and made her debut in a bumper at Clonmel in May 1982, ridden by her indefatigable owner.

They were beaten, but two races later won at Tralee – Mrs Hill's last ride.

Dawn Run soon developed into a very good hurdler indeed, good enough to be a serious contender for the Sun Alliance Novices' Hurdle at the 1983 Cheltenham Festival. Second there to Sabin Du Loir, she then went to Aintree to win a valuable handicap hurdle under top weight and the following day finished runner-up to Gaye Brief, the current Champion Hurdler, in the Sun Templegate Hurdle. Such a schedule was already proclaiming her a mare of extraordinary toughness.

Early the following season her trainer's son Tony Mullins, who had ridden the mare in most of her races, was replaced by **Jonjo O'Neill**, and the partnership reversed placings with Gaye Brief in the Christmas Hurdle at Kempton Park in December 1983 before landing the Irish Champion Hurdle. With Gaye Brief sidelined by injury Dawn Run started odds-on favourite for the 1984 Champion Hurdle, and won narrowly from Cima. Later that season she won the Grande Course de Haies at Auteuil in Paris to complete a hat-trick of English, Irish and French hurdling crowns.

Dawn Run is one of three great Cheltenham horses commemorated by statues at the course. The others are Golden Miller and Arkle.

She was switched to steeplechasing for the 1984–5 season but, hampered by injury, managed only one run that term, at Navan in November 1984: nevertheless, she made it a winning one. It was over a year before she was seen out again, and though sights were firmly set on the Cheltenham Gold Cup, her preparation was far from ideal. In her final prep race at Cheltenham she unseated Tony Mullins at the ditch at the top of the hill, and again Jonjo O'Neill was called up for the big occasion.

And what an occasion the 1986 Gold Cup turned out to be! After being headed between the last two fences, Dawn Run staged a remarkable rally up the run-in to collar

Wayward Lad close home and trigger such scenes of delirious excitement that 15 years later there are still Cheltenham racegoers looking for their hats. A unique feat had been achieved by a mare whose connections and whose own dogged character epitomised the gigantic Irish contribution to jump racing, and Cheltenham's euphoria was unbounded.

After the hysteria came anti-climax, followed by tragedy. Dawn Run fell at the first fence in the Whitbread Gold Label Cup at Liverpool, then won a match over two miles at Punchestown against Buck House, winner of the Queen Mother Champion Chase. In early June 1986 she was second in the Prix la Barka at Auteuil, and at the end of that month attempted a repeat victory in the Grand Course de Haies. This time she was ridden by French jockey Michel Chirol, and the mare was a close-up third when at the fifth last hurdle she fell heavily, broke her neck and died instantly. Winner of 21 of her 35 races, she was just eight years old when she died.

DAY, PAT

When Pat Day won on Camden Park at Churchill Downs in Kentucky on 31 May 2001, he became only the third jockey in US racing history to ride 8,000 winners, following **Bill Shoemaker** and **Laffit Pincay**. Born in October 1953, Day rode his first winner in 1973. He has landed the Kentucky Derby on Lil E Tee (1992), the Preakness Stakes five times and the Belmont Stakes three times, and has ridden a record eleven Breeders' Cup winners, including the Classic on Wild Again (1984), Unbridled (1990), Awesome Again (1998) and Cat Thief (1999).

DAYJUR

Owned by Sheikh Hamdan Al **Maktoum** (who had bought him for $1.65 million as a yearling) and trained by **Dick Hern** to win seven of his 11 races (in all of which he was ridden by **Willie Carson**), Dayjur was one of the finest sprinters seen in Britain in modern times. He won one of his two races as a two-year-old in 1989, and in 1990 won five consecutive Pattern races: the Temple Stakes at Sandown Park, King's Stand Stakes at Royal Ascot, Nunthorpe Stakes at York, Sprint Cup at Haydock and Prix de l'Abbaye at Longchamp. He then went to Belmont Park in New York for the Breeders' Cup Sprint. That he was running for the first time on dirt, and for the first time round a bend, caused much hilarity among the local horse-players, but Dayjur very nearly had the last laugh, losing narrowly and in the most bizarre circumstances. Having scorched round the bend as if he were on rails, he barrelled up the straight in the lead and looking certain to win – only to jump a shadow across the track a hundred yards from the wire, causing him to lose momentum and cede the advantage to Safely Kept. Dayjur fought back, then leapt at another shadow right on the line, and was beaten a head. He did not run again, retiring to stud in Kentucky.

DAYLAMI

A handsome grey who raced with tremendous zest, Daylami won seven Group or Grade One races and underlined the value of keeping top-class horses in training rather than rushing them off to stud. He was bred by the **Aga Khan**, in whose colours he raced when trained in France by Alain de Royer-Dupré to win two of his three races as a two-year-old in 1996, and the Poule d'Essai des Poulains (French Two Thousand Guineas) in 1997. In October 1997 Daylami was sold to Sheikh Mohammed and thereafter raced in the Godolphin colours, in 1998 winning the Tattersalls Gold Cup at The Curragh, Eclipse Stakes at Sandown Park and Man O'War Stakes at Belmont Park and finishing fourth behind stable companion **Swain** in the King George and third to Alborada in the Champion Stakes. But Daylami's real *annus mirabilis* came as a five-year-old in 1999, when he won the Coronation Cup from Royal Anthem, sprinted away from top-class rivals to win the King George by five lengths from stable companion Nedawi and the Irish Champion Stakes by nine lengths from Dazzling Park, then ended his career in glorious style by winning the Breeders' Cup Turf at Gulfstream Park – thereby becoming the first

European-trained winner of a Breeders' Cup race at the Florida track. His exploits in 1999 were enough to make him the top horse in the inaugural **Emirates World Series**. Winner of nine of his 19 races, Daylami retired to stand at the Aga Khan's Gilltown Stud in Ireland – back where he was born.

DEAD HEAT

A dead heat is declared by the judge when two horses are deemed to have passed the line exactly together. A punter who has backed either of those horses receives the full odds to half the stake. So £5 on a horse which started at 10–1 and dead-heated for first place would return £27.50 – winnings of £25 plus the return of half the stake (£2.50). (The practice of running off a dead heat – that is, the horses involved racing again for first prize – was not completely stopped until 1931.) Since the introduction of photo-finish technology in the late 1940s there has been no recorded case of a triple dead heat in Britain, though before that there had been several races where the human eye could not distinguish among the first three home.

DEATH IN ACTION

There are around 200 equine fatalities on racetracks in Britain every year, and around one in 200 horses competing in National Hunt races is either killed outright or humanely put down on the course. There are several causes – a broken back, neck or leg after blundering at a jump or falling; a heart attack during the race; a leg snapping while racing along the level – and as soon as the vet has ascertained that there is no hope of healing and connections have agreed, the horse is despatched very quickly. It may seem callous to destroy a horse so readily and with so little thought of repairing the damage and nursing him through a long convalescence, but the brutal fact is that the chances of the animal recovering from a broken limb are very remote indeed – it is not easy for a horse to make a good patient – and putting him down is usually kinder than trying to keep him alive.

All too many well-known jumpers have been killed in action in recent memory. Lanzarote in the 1977 Cheltenham Gold Cup, Dawn Run in the Grand Course de Haies at Auteuil in 1986 and One Man in the Mumm Melling Chase at Aintree in 1998 were very high-profile casualties, while other good jumpers to have paid the ultimate price have been Gloria Victis, The Outback Way, Alverton, Brownes Gazette, Celtic Ryde, Ekbalco, Forgive'N Forget, Golden Cygnet, Killiney, Noddy's Ryde, Ten Plus, Royal Gait, Pegwell Bay, Cahervillahow, Rushing Wild, Shadow Leader, Monsieur Le Cure and Young Kenny. Other famous horses, such as Bula and Mighty Mogul, have had to be put down due to serious injuries sustained on the track.

It is not only in National Hunt racing that deaths in action occur: the Breeders' Cup, world showpiece of Flat racing, has seen fatal accidents in running, notably the deaths of the great American filly Go For Wand in the Distaff at Belmont Park in 1990 and of Richard Hannon's July Cup winner Mr Brooks, ridden by Lester Piggott, in the Sprint at Gulfstream Park in 1992. Vicious Circle was put down after injuring himself in the Ascot Gold Cup in June 2001.

DEAUVILLE

Racecourse on the Normandy coast, one of the premier venues in France. It is here that the French racing world decamps in August for the big yearling sales and a race meeting which features three Group One races: the Prix Maurice de Gheest (six and a half furlongs), Prix Jacques le Marois (one of Europe's top mile races, won in 1999 by **Dubai Millennium**) and Prix Morny (for two-year-olds over six furlongs).

DECLARATIONS

For most races, horses are entered five days in advance of the race and declared to run (at **Weatherbys**) the day before. Big races where entries close well in advance may have a confirmation stage five days before the race, then a final declaration stage on the eve of the race (two days before the running of a Group One event).

DERBY

Group One: three-year-old colts and fillies:
1½ miles (Epsom Downs)

Derby Day is a famous sporting occasion, but it also remains a great annual celebration, when tens of thousands of people swarm on to Epsom Downs, just a few miles outside London, to eat, drink, be merry and catch a glimpse – if they can – of what doggedly claims, in the face of fierce competition, to be the greatest horse race in the world. Traditionally, this is a day when class differences are disregarded, as the entire spectrum of society from the royal family down joins together for a day at the races.

What they said about the Derby

'The Derby is a little like your first experience of sex – hectic, strenuous, memorably pleasant and over before you know it.'

Bill Bryson

'The trouble with the Derby is that the bastards are all trying.'

A head lad, to writer Jeffrey Bernard

'Anyone who doesn't consider the Epsom Derby one of the greatest sporting events in the world must be out of his mind.'

John Galbreath,
owner of 1972 winner Roberto

'The Thoroughbred exists because its selection has depended not on experts, technicians or zoologists, but one piece of wood: the winning post of the Epsom Derby.'

Federico Tesio, legendary Italian breeder

'On Derby Day, a population rolls and scrambles through the place that may be counted in millions.' Charles Dickens, 1851

'For one reason or another, business or pleasure, a large part of the inhabitants of the civilised world is accustomed to spend some of the leisure hours of the spring picking the Derby winner. It is a blameless pleasure, which has kept more men out of trouble than it has led astray.'

Guy Griffith and Michael Oakeshott

This tradition goes back a long way. In the middle of the nineteenth century, the halcyon days of the Derby were seen as pure festivity, half of London seemed to take the day off and make for Epsom, and for many decades Parliament suspended business on Derby Day so that MPs could join the tumultuous throng on the Downs. Writers such as Dickens, Trollope and Henry James saw the Derby Day crowd as a microcosm of British society, and artists took the opportunity to depict a broad sweep of the population: of dozens of nineteenth-century depictions of the occasion, William Frith's great painting *Derby Day* is the best known.

Such a tumultuous occasion would have been far from the thoughts of the 12th Earl of Derby and **Sir Charles Bunbury** when they hatched the plan which led to the first running of the race on 4 May 1780, and whether or not the story is true that they tossed a coin to see which man's name would be given to the race, it seems that the Earl was the principal proponent of the idea. For it was he who had organised the first running of the Oaks the previous year, an experiment considered such a success that it was decided to repeat the formula of a race at Epsom for three-year-olds, this time for both colts and fillies and to be run over a mile. (The distance was not increased to a mile and a half until 1784.) That first Derby was won – fittingly – by Sir Charles Bunbury's **Diomed**, and Bunbury was to win it twice more, with Eleanor and Smolensko.

The history of the Derby has oozed drama. In 1844, the first horse past the post had been entered as the three-year-old Running Rein. He was, in fact, a four-year-old named Maccabaeus, who had come under extreme suspicion the previous year when winning a two-year-old race at Newmarket as a three-year-old, the intrigue being masterminded by his owner Goodman Levy. A group of prominent Turf figures headed by **Lord George Bentinck** tried to prevent 'Running Rein' taking part in the Derby, but the stewards decided that he should be permitted to run. He won from Orlando, whose owner duly sued Mr Wood, in whose name Running Rein had competed. The judge in the case, remarking that 'if gentlemen condescended to race with blackguards, they must condescend to expect to be cheated,' found against Wood, and the race went to Orlando. It is almost incidental to record the other happenings in this Derby. Another runner, Leander, was struck into by Running Rein and broke his leg. When he had been put down the vet examined his jaw and found him to be a four-year-old, though his indignant German owners claimed that he was actually six! The favourite, Ugly Buck, was the victim of deliberate foul riding, and the second favourite was both 'got at' the night before and pulled by his jockey to prevent his winning just in case the doping had not worked. Those were the days . . .

Perhaps the most sensational Derby of all was the 1913 race. The militant suffragette Emily Davison ran on to the course in front of King George V's horse Anmer as the runners came round Tattenham Corner, and died four days later from her injuries. Anmer was towards the rear of the field at the time, and meanwhile up front a furious race was developing. At the post the 6–4 favourite Craganour beat the 100–1 outsider Aboyeur by a head after a good deal of deliberate barging, but the stewards objected to the winner and the race was awarded to Aboyeur.

A much happier occasion was the Coronation Derby in 1953. There was plenty of support both for Aureole, owned by the newly crowned Queen, and for Pinza, ridden by **Gordon Richards**, just knighted and the greatest jockey of his age but still unsuccessful in the Derby after 27 attempts: Pinza won by four lengths from Aureole – possibly the most popular Derby result of all.

Nearly half a century has passed since Pinza's emotional triumph, but the magic and drama of the Derby persists: Lester Piggott winning as an 18-year-old on Never Say Die in 1954 . . . seven horses falling on the run to Tattenham Corner in 1962 . . . Scobie Breasley winning at last on Santa Claus in 1964 . . . the majestic **Sea Bird II** swooping home in 1965 . . . **Sir Ivor**'s unbelievable turn of foot in 1968 . . . **Nijinsky** striding home with contemptuous ease in 1970, and **Mill Reef** almost as easily in 1971 . . . driving finishes between Roberto (Piggott again) and **Rheingold** in 1972, and The Minstrel (yet another Piggott winner) and Hot Grove in 1977 . . . **Shergar** by ten lengths in 1981 . . . Secreto short-heading **El Gran Senor** in 1984 . . . **Dancing Brave**'s failure to peg back Shahrastani in 1986 . . . **Lammtarra** and Walter Swinburn sweeping up the outside in 1995 . . . pulsating finishes between Benny The Dip and Silver Patriarch in 1997 and High-Rise and City Honours in 1998 . . . Sinndar collaring Sakhee in 2000 . . . the imperious **Galileo** in 2001.

Derby winners since 1990

1990	Quest For Fame	3	R. Charlton	Pat Eddery	7–1	18
1991	Generous	3	P. Cole	A. Munro	9–1	13
1992	Dr Devious	3	P. Chapple-Hyam	J. Reid	8–1	18
1993	Commander In Chief	3	H. Cecil	M. Kinane	15–2	16
1994	Erhaab	3	J. Dunlop	W. Carson	7–2F	25
1995	Lammtarra	3	S. bin Suroor	W. R. Swinburn	14–1	15
1996	Shaamit	3	W. Haggas	M. Hills	12–1	20
1997	Benny The Dip	3	J. Gosden	W. Ryan	11–1	13
1998	High-Rise	3	L. Cumani	O. Peslier	20–1	15
1999	Oath	3	H. Cecil	K. Fallon	13–2	16
2000	Sinndar	3	J. Oxx IRE	J. Murtagh	7–1	15
2001	Galileo	3	A. O'Brien *IRE*	M. Kinane	11–4JF	12

(For a list of all winners since the Second World War, *see* Classics.)

DESERT ORCHID

Not many racehorses find their way into the Chancellor of the Exchequer's Budget speech, but it is a mark of how intense the public adulation of 'Dessie' became that Norman Lamont sought to ingratiate himself with the electorate by mentioning the great grey in the House of Commons in 1991. A poll had shown that while 84 per cent of people had heard of Dessie only 77 per cent had heard of Lamont, and the Chancellor saw his chance: 'Desert Orchid and I have a lot in common. We are both greys, vast sums of money are riding on our performance, the opposition hopes we will fall at the first fence, and we are both carrying too much weight.' Ho ho, very droll . . .

It is not difficult to understand why Desert Orchid touched a public nerve. His bold, front-running style of racing, his flamboyant, attacking attitude towards jumping fences, and his sheer physical appearance – a big, headstrong grey oozing power and enthusiasm – made up a heady cocktail. In a racing career which spanned nearly nine years he rarely let down his fans or his connections: owner Richard Burridge, trainer **David Elsworth** and regular jockeys Colin Brown, Simon Sherwood (who won on nine out of his ten rides on the horse) and latterly **Richard Dunwoody**.

But the glory days were a far cry from his racecourse debut, in a novices' hurdle at Kempton Park in January 1983: he fell at the final obstacle, and for a while, as he failed to rise from the ground, it seemed that his first race would be his last. But he was only winded, and after 10 minutes prostrate heaved himself up to continue his way into the hearts of the racing public. That first season he failed to win from four runs, but in the 1983–4 term developed into a very fine hurdler, winning six of his seven starts before running unplaced behind **Dawn Run** in the Champion Hurdle. The following year was less productive, but the switch from hurdling to chasing in winter 1985 proved an immediate success, with victories in several top novice events.

By Boxing Day 1986 Desert Orchid was already one of the most popular chasers in training, but he was thought to be a two-mile specialist rather than a horse who would excel at the top-level staying events, and he was allowed to start at 16–1 for the three-mile King George VI Chase at Kempton Park against the likes of **Wayward Lad**, Forgive'N Forget and Combs Ditch. His performance belied the odds, and after a sensational display of front running had left those distinguished rivals toiling in his wake as he won by 15 lengths, Dessie was firmly in the top flight.

Desert Orchid ran once on the Flat. Ridden by Brian Rouse, he finished tenth of 11 runners behind Longboat in the Sagaro Stakes at Ascot in May 1985.

In the 1987 King George he finished second to Nupsala, then later that season won the Chivas Regal Cup at Aintree and raised the roof at Sandown Park when beating Kildimo in the 1988 Whitbread Gold Cup. A second King George victory in 1988 put him right up there with the best post-war chasers, but to seal his place in the pantheon he needed to win the Cheltenham Gold Cup, and therein lay a problem. Cheltenham had never been one of Desert Orchid's favourite places, and the fact that he had not won there was widely attributed to his dislike of left-handed tracks, the single win at Aintree being his only anti-clockwise victory to date. On Gold Cup day 1989 his chances seemed further diminished by a deluge of rain and snow that turned the track into a quagmire – heavy conditions which the horse hated. But he overcame all adversities, battling up the hill to get the better of Yahoo just before the post in one of the most emotional races of the modern era.

Now a national institution – complete with his own fan club – Desert Orchid continued his winning ways. In the 1989–90 season he won a third King George VI Chase and put up a brilliant weight-carrying performance when humping 12st 3lb to victory in the Racing Post Chase at Kempton. He finished third behind **Norton's Coin** and Toby Tobias in the Gold Cup, but then went on to win the Irish Grand National at Fairyhouse – his only victory outside Britain – under 12st. The following season he won a record fourth King George amid scenes of huge enthusiasm at Kempton, lugged 12st to victory in the Agfa Diamond Chase at Sandown – in what turned out to be his last win – and again finished third in the Gold Cup, this time behind Garrison Savannah and The Fellow. By the time of his sixth consecutive King George on Boxing Day 1991 Dessie was a few days short of his thirteenth birthday, and the power was beginning to fade. But he still managed to hog the limelight – falling at the third last fence when out of contention, then galloping Dunwoody-less past the stands to a wildly appreciative farewell from his adoring fans.

Desert Orchid retired winner of 34 of his 72 races, but he was not to disappear from the racing scene. In retirement his public appearances became a regular feature of the big occasions, and his continuing popularity was nowhere more evident than on his annual trip to Kempton for the King George VI Chase: on Boxing Day 2000, a few days short of his twenty-second birthday, he yet again drew rapturous applause from the Kempton crowd when thundering back past the stands after the parade.

DETTORI, LANFRANCO

Frankie Dettori was born in Milan in December 1970, son of the great Italian jockey Gianfranco Dettori, who had won the Two Thousand Guineas on Bolkonski in 1975 and Wollow in 1976. Frankie's first winner came on a horse named Rif at Turin on 16 November 1986, but it was when he moved to England to serve his apprenticeship at Newmarket with fellow Italian **Luca Cumani** that the flame of his career really started to blaze. He rode his first winner in Britain on Lizzy Hare (named after Cumani's secretary) at Goodwood on 9 June 1987. In 1989 he was champion apprentice, with 75 winners; and the following year, at the age of 19, he became the first teenager to ride a century of winners in Britain since Lester Piggott – an older 19 – in 1955. That season he came fourth in the jockeys' championship with 141 wins to his credit, and he kept up the momentum in the following years, scoring 94

in 1991, 101 in 1992 and 149 in 1993 (third in the championship behind Pat Eddery and Kevin Darley). It was an extraordinary start to a riding career, the more so because along with quantity was coming quality. His association with the great sprinting filly **Lochsong** captivated the racing public, securing an affection that public was already predisposed to bestow on account of Dettori's naturally ebullient demeanour. He was champion jockey for the first time in 1994 with the huge total of 233 winners, having stolen a march on his rivals by notching up a good number in all-weather races early in the year before the 'season proper' got under way. But 1994 was also a year of huge achievement on the quality scale, with more big sprint wins on Lochsong (including a second Prix de l'Abbaye), his first win in an English Classic (after being beaten a short head in both Guineas that year) when Balanchine won the Oaks, a first Irish Derby on the same filly, and then a memorable victory in the Breeders' Cup Mile on Barathea. In 1995 he was champion jockey again, won his second English Classic on Moonshell in the Oaks, his third on Classic Cliché in the St Leger, and partnered **Lammtarra** to win the King George VI and Queen Elizabeth Diamond Stakes and the Arc. By now Frankie Dettori was in the foothills of sporting superstardom, and at Ascot on 28 September 1996 he was catapulted to the summit. All his seven rides that day won – Wall Street, Diffident, Mark Of

Frankie Dettori's Classic winners

Two Thousand Guineas
   1996 Mark Of Esteem
   1999 Island Sands
One Thousand Guineas
   1998 Cape Verdi
Oaks
   1994 Balanchine
   1995 Moonshell
St Leger
   1995 Classic Cliché
   1996 Shantou

Esteem (on whom he had won the Two Thousand Guineas earlier that year), Decorated Hero, Fatefully, Lochangel and Fujiyama Crest. Those seven winners delivered a 25,095–1 accumulator for Frankie freaks, and he entered the history books as the first jockey ever to go through a seven-race card. More important, the feat made Frankie – and racing – front-page news, and the boost to the public image of racing was immense: he even had a stint as guest presenter on *Top of the Pops*. Since that magical moment Dettori has maintained his place both as the public face of jockeyship and as one of its very finest practitioners. His role as stable jockey for **Godolphin** has brought him countless big race victories – including the King George in 1998 on **Swain** and 1999 on **Daylami**, the 1998 Ascot Gold Cup on Kayf Tara (to add to two earlier Gold Cups, on Drum Taps in 1992 and 1993), the 1999 Breeders' Cup Turf on Daylami, and a glorious all-the-way victory on the mighty **Dubai Millennium** in the 2000 Dubai World Cup. But it has not all been plain sailing. In June 2000 the plane in which he and **Ray Cochrane** were taking off from Newmarket to fly to the races crashed, killing pilot Patrick Mackey and leaving both jockeys badly injured. Frankie, being Frankie, bounced back, and by the end of the season normal service had been resumed.

DEVON AND EXETER
Name until 1992 of the racecourse now known simply as Exeter.

DEVON LOCH
Although he won eight steeplechases, Devon Loch reached true racing immortality – for once that word is not an exaggeration – as the most famous loser in racing history. Owned by the **Queen Mother**, trained by **Peter Cazalet** and ridden by **Dick Francis**, he started 100–7 joint fourth favourite for the 1956 Grand National on 24 March 1956 in front of a huge crowd which included his owner. After tracking the leaders on the first circuit Devon Loch began a forward move, and by the second Canal Turn had slipped into

second place, going noticeably well. When front-runners Armorial III and Much Obliged fell two fences later he found himself in the lead, and still had the advantage as he approached the last fence, a length and a half in front of the toiling E.S.B. Full of running, Devon Loch jumped the fence and set off down the run-in, the crowd going wild at the certain prospect of a royal victory in the Grand National. Round the Elbow he came, still galloping strongly, and then as he passed the water jump on the inside of the course, with about 50 yards still to cover, disaster struck. Cue Dick Francis:

In one stride he was bounding smoothly along, a poem of controlled motion; in the next, his hind legs stiffened and refused to function. He fell flat on his belly, his limbs splayed out sideways and backwards in unnatural angles, and when he stood up he could hardly move . . . the rhythm was shattered, the dream was over, and the race was lost.

Explanations for this extraordinary collapse abounded – Francis himself thought the horse was scared by the wall of noise greeting him as he came up the straight – but Devon Loch kept his own counsel. After his racing career he spent a brief time as trainer's hack to Noel Murless before being moved to Sandringham, and he died, his name etched for ever in racing history, at the age of 16 in 1962.

DE WALDEN, HOWARD

Lord Howard de Walden was famous for the ingenuity with which he named his horses. Kris was by Sharpen Up out of Doubly Sure: a 'kris' is a double-edged Malaysian dagger. Diesis was by the same sire and out of the same dam as Kris: a 'diesis' is the double-dagger sign used in printing.

Lord Howard de Walden had one of the most eye-catching and familiar sets of colours to be seen on British racecourses in the twentieth century – apricot – and the quality of his horses matched his silks. On the Flat, his best horses were the 1985 Derby winner Slip

Anchor and Kris, a brilliant miler whose victories included the St James's Palace Stakes, Sussex Stakes and Queen Elizabeth II Stakes in 1979. He also won big races with Diesis (Middle Park Stakes and Dewhurst Stakes in 1982), Grand Lodge (Dewhurst Stakes 1993, St James's Palace Stakes 1994), Oncidium (Coronation Cup 1965) and Paean (Ascot Gold Cup 1987). His best jumper was Lanzarote, who won the 1974 Champion Hurdle and was killed in the 1977 Cheltenham Gold Cup. Three times Senior Steward of the Jockey Club, Lord Howard de Walden died in 1999 at the age of 86.

DEWHURST STAKES

Group One: two-year-old colts: 7 furlongs
(Newmarket, Rowley Mile)

Britain's most important race for two-year-olds, the Dewhurst Stakes was first run in 1875, founded by Tom Gee, owner of the Dewhurst Stud in Sussex. His intention was to create a race which would attract the sort of horse who the following year would go on to contest the Classics, and he did not have long to wait to see that aim fulfilled. First winner was Kisber, who won the Derby in 1876. Second winner was Chamant, who won the Two Thousand Guineas. Third winner Pilgrimage landed the rare double of the Two Thousand Guineas and One Thousand Guineas. And the fourth Dewhurst winner was Wheel Of Fortune, who went on to win the One Thousand Guineas and Oaks.

So the first four winners netted six Classics: not bad! By the time of the First World War, the Dewhurst roll of honour included subsequent Triple Crown winners **Ormonde** and Rock Sand, St Leger winner Bayardo, Derby winner Lemberg and Two Thousand Guineas winners Louvois and Kennymore. **Hyperion** won the Dewhurst in 1932 and the Derby the following year, and in the 1950s that distinguished double was achieved by Pinza (Dewhurst 1952) and Crepello (1956: he also won the Two Thousand Guineas). The race had a quiet period in the 1960s before hitting the heights again in 1969 with **Nijinsky**, who started at 3–1 on to beat five opponents in the Dewhurst (which he did easily) and in 1970 went on to win the Triple Crown. **Mill Reef** won the Dewhurst in 1970 and the Derby in 1971, and through the mid-1970s the Newmarket race enjoyed a dizzy reputation, with wins for such horses as **Grundy** (1974), Wollow (1975, ridden by Gianfranco Dettori: he won the 1976 Two Thousand Guineas) and The Minstrel (winner of the Dewhurst in 1976 and the Derby, Irish Derby and King George in 1977). **El Gran Senor** beat subsequent Prix de l'Arc de Triomphe winner Rainbow Quest in 1983 and the following year won the Two Thousand Guineas and Irish Derby.

The 1990s saw the best traditions of the Dewhurst continuing, with victories for subsequent Derby winners Generous – who started at 50–1 in 1990 – and Dr Devious

Dewhurst Stakes winners since 1990

Year	Winner		Trainer	Jockey	Odds	Ran
1990	Generous	2	P. Cole	T. Quinn	50–1	8
1991	Dr Devious	2	P. Chapple-Hyam	W. Carson	3–1F	9
1992	Zafonic	2	A. Fabre *FRA*	Pat Eddery	10–11F	11
1993	Grand Lodge	2	W. Jarvis	Pat Eddery	9–4F	10
1994	Pennekamp	2	A Fabre *FRA*	T. Jarnet	5–2JF	7
1995	Alhaarth	2	W. Hern	W. Carson	4–7F	4
1996	In Command	2	B. Hills	M. Hills	10–1	8
1997	Xaar	2	A. Fabre *FRA*	O. Peslier	11–8F	7
1998	Mujahid	2	J. Dunlop	R. Hills	25–1	7
1999	Distant Music	2	B. Hills	M. Hills	4–6F	5
2000	Tobougg	2	M. Channon	C. Williams	7–4F	10

(1991), and brilliant Two Thousand Guineas winners **Zafonic** (1992) and Pennekamp (1994). In 1997 Zafonic's son **Xaar** – like Pennekamp trained in France by André Fabre – turned in one of the great juvenile performances of recent years to win by seven lengths. The record of the race says it all: this is *the* two-year-old race of the season.

DICK, DAVE

Dave Dick is the only jockey to have won both legs of the Spring Double: he won the Lincoln on Gloaming in 1941 and the Grand National on E.S.B. in 1956. Born in 1924 and apprenticed to his trainer father Dave Dick senior, he rode on the Flat until increasing weight led him to concentrate on the National Hunt game. He won the Cheltenham Gold Cup on the novice Mont Tremblant in 1952 and the Whitbread on Pas Seul in 1961, and the 1965 Two Mile Champion Chase (now the Queen Mother) on the exhilarating front-runner Dunkirk: the first time he rode Dunkirk the horse had turned in a typical barnstorming performance, and Dick's comment on returning to unsaddle was a simple 'Blimey!' But the race for which he will best be remembered is the one where the winner is usually forgotten: the 1956 Grand National which saw the collapse of **Devon Loch**. It was Dave Dick who rode the winner that day, E.S.B., and for years afterwards he would joke with Devon Loch's rider Dick Francis that 'I would have won anyway.' Dave Dick was famed for his devotion to wine, women and song (though not necessarily in that order): when at the start of one Grand National he was faced with an evangelist carrying a banner reading 'Repent or your sins will find you out', he observed, 'If that's the case, I won't get as far as the first.' Dave Dick died at the age of 76 in February 2001.

DICKINSON FAMILY

The Dickinson family enjoyed a high level of success in jumps racing during the 1970s and 1980s. Tony Dickinson, born in 1915, was a very successful rider in point-to-points (as was his wife Monica, the former Miss Birtwistle), and for the 1967–8 season took out a permit to train a few jumpers – which he did so effectively that he became a public trainer for the 1968–9 term. He kept the number of horses in the yard to a manageable level, but won many big races with such horses as Gay Spartan (who won the 1978 King George VI Chase), Silver Buck (1979 King George), Broncho II, Winter Rain and I'm A Driver.

In 1980 Tony Dickinson retired and the stable at Harewood, not far from Leeds, passed to his son Michael Dickinson, who had enjoyed a successful career as a jump jockey until injured in 1978. Michael proved to have inherited the family skill at handling racehorses, sending out Silver Buck to win the 1980 King George and 1982 Cheltenham Gold Cup (with his Bregawn second), and saddling 12 winners in one day on Boxing Day 1982. In 1983 he pulled off possibly the greatest feat ever produced by a jumps trainer, when the first five horses home in the Gold Cup were all trained by him: Bregawn, Captain John, **Wayward Lad**, Silver Buck and Ashley House. Wayward Lad, third in that famous race, played a significant role in the Dickinson family fortunes by winning the King George VI Chase three times (1982, 1983 and 1985), which meant that Dickinson-trained horses had lifted that race on six of the seven runnings between 1978 and 1985 (the race was abandoned in 1981). At the end of 1984 Michael, champion trainer in 1981–2, 1982–3 and 1983–4, was tempted away from Yorkshire to set up as **Robert Sangster**'s private trainer at Manton. The new arrangement did not work out: in November 1986 it was announced that he and Sangster were to part company, and Dickinson moved to the USA.

Meanwhile the Harewood operation had been kept firmly in the family, with Michael's mother Monica Dickinson taking over the licence and ushering in yet another period of success. She won the Welsh National in 1984 with Righthand Man, and in 1985 the Queen Mother Champion Chase with Badsworth Boy (his third win in the race, having won for Michael in 1983 and 1984), Whitbread Gold Cup with By The

Way and King George with Wayward Lad. When she retired in 1989, jump racing in Britain did not seem the same without a Dickinson sending out winners. But we had not heard the last of Michael, and he showed that his move to America had not blunted his skills by sending out Da Hoss to win the Breeders' Cup Mile in 1996 and 1998.

Tony Dickinson died in June 1991, aged 75.

DIOMED

First winner of the Derby in 1780. Owned by **Sir Charles Bunbury**, he started 6–4 favourite. The Diomed Stakes is run over one mile at Epsom on Derby Day.

DISHING

The action of a horse throwing in one or both of his forelegs to the side as he walks. This usually suggests a less than perfect conformation, though it will not mean that the horse cannot gallop perfectly well.

DISTANCE, A

In the official record of a race, 'a distance' is a measure in excess of 30 lengths. The official distances for the 2001 Grand National, won by Red Marauder from Smarty and the remounted Blowing Wind and Papillon, were: distance, distance, distance.

DISTANCE, THE

'The distance' is an unidentified spot 240 yards (that is, just over a furlong) from the winning post. (You will sometimes hear a race commentator announce that the field is 'coming to the distance', or, if the runners have passed that point, 'below the distance'.) This eccentric measurement derives from match races in the seventeenth and eighteenth centuries. A horse finishing more than 240 yards behind the horse in front was judged to have been 'distanced' and disqualified from further heats of that match: the practice was brought in to prevent riders giving a horse a deliberately easy race in order to keep it fresh for the next heats. A 'distance judge' would be positioned 240 yards from the finish.

See also **Eclipse**.

DISTANCES, THE

The official declared margins between the horses at the end of a race. In Britain the distances are short head, head, neck, half a length, three-quarters of a length, length, one and a quarter lengths, one and a half lengths, one and three-quarter lengths – and then ascend in halves and whole lengths up to 30, beyond which is **a distance**. Nowadays the distances are automatically computed by the **photo finish** equipment, so the judge simply has to read them off the monitor in his or her box.

DIVIDING RACES

If more horses are down to run in a race than can be accommodated by the safety factor on the racecourse, certain races are divided into two (or more) separate races – known as 'divisions'.

DOER

A 'good doer' is a horse whose eats enthusiastically and is not fussy about his food.

DOG

An untrustworthy horse.

DONCASTER

The Grandstand, Leger Way, Doncaster, South Yorkshire DN2 6BB
Tel.: 01302 320066
Fax: 01302 323271
E-mail:
administration@doncasterracing.co.uk
Web: www.doncasterracing.co.uk

Home of the **St Leger**, first run in 1776 and oldest of the Classics, Doncaster is a racecourse steeped in history. There were races run on the Town Moor – where the course is still situated, though the first two St Legers were run on the adjacent Cantley Common – in the late sixteenth century, and ever since then the sport has been an important facet of Doncaster life: today the St Leger fixture is the northern equivalent of Derby Day, with a large funfair dispensing jollity alongside the racetrack, a huge crowd and general air of merriment.

Doncaster is acknowledged to be one of the fairest and best racing surfaces in the country.

The circuit is left-handed and pear-shaped, a little under two miles round, with the 'sharp end' of the pear after the winning post providing the only tight bend; the other turn is a very long, sweeping curve which need cause no interruption to the rhythm of a galloping horse. The only significant undulation on the circuit is a small rise and fall – Rose Hill – about 10 furlongs out, and the run from the home turn up the wide straight is just under five furlongs. Thus Doncaster is the ideal venue for the long-striding galloper, a place where a horse needs to see out every yard of the trip.

The jumping course has in its time been criticised for the perceived easiness of the steeplechase fences; like the Flat track, it is a place for the galloping rather than the nippy type of animal. From the last fence to the winning post is a little over one furlong.

Doncaster provides the book-ends of the Flat season proper. All-weather racing may have been on the go since the very beginning of the year, but it is the first turf fixture at Donny in late March that heralds the traditional 'Start of the Flat'. That meeting features the **Lincoln Handicap**, one of the big betting races of the year, with a large field hammering up the straight mile. At the other end of the season, the November meeting with the November Handicap (one and a half miles) marks the close of the Flat on turf.

But Doncaster's greatest race, and greatest occasion, is unarguably the St Leger, high point of the four-day September meeting which also features the Champagne Stakes over seven furlongs and the Flying Childers Stakes over five furlongs, both for two-year-olds. The May Hill Stakes over the round mile is a Group Three event for staying two-year-old fillies, and older fillies have a Group Three race over the full St Leger distance in the Park Hill Stakes. The Doncaster Cup (first run in 1766 and thus older than the Classics) over two and a quarter miles is the final leg of the 'Stayers' Triple Crown', following on from the Ascot Gold Cup and the Goodwood Cup.

Doncaster's other Group One event, apart from the St Leger, is the **Racing Post Trophy** over the round mile in October, only Group One two-year-old contest over a mile and the last Group One of the season in Britain.

DONOGHUE, STEVE

Steve Donoghue, born in 1884, dominated the jockeys' championship during and following the First World War, taking the title 10 times, annually from 1914 until 1923, when he tied with the then apprentice Charlie Elliott. The cry of 'Come on, Steve!' was a familiar shout for long after. Donoghue rode the winners of 14 Classics, including the Derby six times, on Pommern (1915), Gay Crusader (1917), Humorist (1921), Captain Cuttle (1922), Papyrus (1923) and Manna (1925). His name will for ever be associated with two other immortals of the Turf – **The Tetrarch**, who ran only as a two-year-old but whose achievements in that one year (1913) give him a claim to be the fastest horse ever seen in England, and **Brown Jack**, on whom Donoghue won the Queen Alexandra Stakes at Royal Ascot for six consecutive years from 1929 to 1934. Their final victory gave rise to some of the most emotional scenes ever seen on a British racecourse: 'Never will I forget the roar of that crowd as long as I live,' wrote Donoghue; 'All my six Derbys faded before the reception that was awaiting Jack and myself as we set out to return to weigh in. I don't think I was ever so happy in my life.' He retired from riding in 1937 and embarked on a not conspicuously successful career as a trainer; he died suddenly in 1945.

DOPING

There are two reasons for doping (or 'nobbling') a horse: to make it go faster, or to make it go slower. While the horse's own connections have an obvious motive for artificially enhancing its performance, when a horse is shown to have been chemically slowed down suspicion falls on those connected with betting. If a bookmaker *knows* that a horse is not going to win, he can take money for that horse without any fear of having to pay out later. Techniques for the detection of banned drugs are becoming ever more effective, and doping consequently rarer. None the less, it does happen. The 'race fixing' enquiry which so absorbed racing in 1999 was partly centred on two proven instances of horses having been 'got at' in March 1997: Avanti Express at Exeter and Lively Knight at Plumpton. Higher-profile cases of doping to lose include Playschool in the 1988 Cheltenham Gold Cup (though the post-race test proved negative) and Bravefoot in the 1990 Champagne Stakes at Doncaster (positive). The temptation to administer a prohibited substance in order to enhance performance is tempered by the likelihood of being found out – and suffering an extreme penalty. Most horses (but not all) that win a race in Britain are subject to a routine post-race test (usually of urine), and the specimens are sent to the Horseracing Forensic Laboratory in Newmarket for analysis. Not until a horse's specimen has been cleared will the prize money be released to connections. If a horse has run inexplicably badly, the stewards may order a routine dope test.

DOUBLE

Bet combining two horses in different races. If the first wins, the returns (winnings plus stake) go on the second.

DOUBLE CARPET

Betting slang for 33–1.

DOUMEN, FRANÇOIS

François Doumen has changed the face of modern jump racing. While Irish horses running in the top British races have always been a feature of the sport, French raiders used to be very rare – so rare that when Doumen sent Nupsala over to run in the 1987 King George VI Chase he was allowed to start an unconsidered 25–1 outsider. Nupsala won by 15 lengths from Desert Orchid, and British jumping was never quite the same again. Since firing that bolt from the blue François Doumen – born in 1940 – has become a familiar and highly popular figure on the jumping scene in Britain, with his horses regularly taking the top prizes across the Channel. The Fellow won the King George in 1991 and 1992, having been beaten a short head in the Cheltenham Gold

Cup in each of those years: by Garrison Savannah in 1991 and Cool Ground in 1992. Fourth behind Jodami in the 1993 Cheltenham showpiece (when reportedly the heaviest-backed horse in Cheltenham history), he finally won the crown he so richly deserved when beating Jodami in the 1994 Gold Cup. Doumen won a fourth King George VI Chase with Algan in 1994 (the year Barton Bank fell at the last when well clear) and a fifth in 2000 with the brilliant First Gold, who was denied a crack at the Gold Cup by the foot-and-mouth epidemic. Other major jumping prizes snaffled for France include the 2000 Triumph Hurdle with Snow Drop. But it is not only as a jumps trainer that François Doumen excels. His gelding Jim And Tonic is a tip-top performer on the Flat, winner of the Hong Kong Cup in 1999 and the Dubai Duty Free at Nad Al Sheba on Dubai World Cup day 2001.

DOWN ROYAL

Maze, Co. Antrim BT27 5BW
Tel.: 028 9262 1256
Fax: 028 9262 1433
E-mail: info@downroyal.com
Web: www.downroyal.com

Down Royal – one of two racecourses in Northern Ireland – is a historic place: Down Royal Corporation of Horse Breeders (Maze Racecourse) was incorporated by Royal Charter granted by King James II on 22 December 1685 'for the improvement of horse breeding in the County of Down'. These days improvements of another sort are under way at this progressive racecourse, notably the inauguration of a highly valuable early-season steeplechase, the James Nicholson Wine Merchant Champion Chase. The first running of this race in November 2000 was worth IR£68,750 to the winning owner and attracted a very high-class field: that year's Gold Cup hero Looks Like Trouble put in a brilliant display to win from Dorans Pride, with Florida Pearl back in fourth. Down Royal is also home to the Ulster Harp Derby, Northern Ireland's biggest Flat race. The circuit is about a mile and seven furlongs round, right-handed and galloping in a nature.

DOWNPATRICK

Ballyduggan Road. Downpatrick. Co. Down
BT30 7SP
Tel.: 028 4484 2054
Fax: 028 4484 2227

Downpatrick is a tight, undulating right-handed track about 11 furlongs round, with a stiff uphill finish. The major race here is the Jameson Ulster National.

DRAW

The draw is the numbered position in the starting stalls that a horse must take up at the start of a Flat race. (There is no draw for jumps races as the minimum distance is two miles and the starting position makes little difference over long distances.) Facing from the start towards the finish, number 1 is always on the left-hand side. The draw is made at **Weatherbys** the day before the race by a random number generator within the declarations computer programme; previously a bingo machine was used. On some courses the draw, especially over short distances, has a marked effect on a horse's chance: the shape and conformation of the track means that some draws are advantageous. For example, the tight left-handed turns of Chester favour horses with a low – that is, inside – draw. A horse drawn high in a big field at Chester would have further to run to get to the winning post!

DREAPER. TOM

Tom Dreaper was one of the greatest Irish trainers of the twentieth century – probably the greatest – and his most famous charge **Arkle** was *certainly* the greatest racehorse. Born in 1898, Dreaper rode in point-to-points, and in 1930 bought a farm named Greenogue, at Kilsallaghan, not far from Dublin Airport, where he started training a few horses alongside his farming. In 1938 he was sent four horses belonging to leading owner J. V. Rank, among them Prince Regent, whom Dreaper trained to win the 1946 Cheltenham Gold Cup. At the Goffs sales in Dublin in 1960 he bought a three-year-old bay gelding by Archive on behalf of Anne, Duchess of Westminster, and the rest is history: Arkle won three Cheltenham Gold Cups, two Hennessys, the Irish National, the Whitbread, the King George and many other big races, and was hailed as the greatest steeplechaser of all time. Dreaper's other great horse at this time was **Flyingbolt** (whose win in the 1966 Irish National was one of the trainer's 10 victories in Ireland's biggest steeplechase), and he won the Gold Cup for a fifth time in 1968 with Fort Leney. (After Tom Dreaper's death in 1975 his wife Betty – who had effectively trained Arkle for a year when Tom was ill – married Fort Leney's widowed owner Sir John Thomson.) The Dreapers' son Jim, who as an amateur rider had been beaten a neck on Black Secret in the 1971 Grand National, took over the yard on his father's retirement. He won the Gold Cup with Ten Up (in the Arkle colours) in 1975 and trained Brown Lad to win three Irish Nationals.

DROP HANDS

A jockey lowers his hands – and the reins – on to the horse's neck to relax the horse and reduce speed after the winning post, or when all realistic chance of winning has gone. Dropping hands prematurely can land a rider in very hot water. Royston Ffrench was stood down for 14 days when allowing Happy Diamond to relax too early at Doncaster in July 2000 and being caught close home by McGillicuddy Reeks, thereby turning certain victory into unlikely defeat, and Darryl Holland received similar punishment when dropping his hands too soon on Island House at Chester in May 2001 and allowing Adilabad to win by a short head.

DUAL FORECAST

The Dual Forecast was a Tote bet in which the punter nominates first and second horse, to finish in either order. It has now been replaced by the **Exacta**.

DUBAI

See **United Arab Emirates**.

DUBAI MILLENNIUM

Though he ran in just 10 races, beaten only once, this was certainly the best horse yet to race for **Godolphin**, and arguably the best middle-distance horse of the last quarter of a century. Bred by his owner Sheikh Mohammed (and originally named Yaazer), he was trained as a two-year-old in 1998 by David Loder at Newmarket and ran just once that year, turning in a hugely promising performance under **Frankie Dettori** (who rode the horse in all bar his last race) when winning a maiden race at Yarmouth by five lengths. He was transferred to the Godolphin team to be trained by Saeed bin Suroor, and started his three-year-old campaign by winning a conditions stakes at Doncaster. A facile victory in the Predominate Stakes at Goodwood suggested a serious chance in the 1999 Derby: he went off 5–1 favourite at Epsom but finished only ninth behind Oath. After that setback the rest of his short career was a triumphal progress. He won the Prix Eugene Adam at Maisons-Laffitte and the Prix Jacques le Marois at Deauville, ending his three-year-old season with an easy victory in the Queen Elizabeth II Stakes at Ascot. He was now established as a colt of the very highest order, but his real date with destiny was to be the 2000 running of the Dubai World Cup, the event for which he had been renamed. After winning his prep race at Nad Al Sheba – his first run on dirt – he met a top-class international field for the World Cup and produced a performance which for once justified the description 'awesome', taking the lead from the start and going further and further ahead to win by six lengths from the American horse Behrens. Now Dubai Millennium was more than a great horse: he was one of the greatest – possibly *the* greatest – of the modern era.

With Dettori sidelined by his plane crash, **Jerry Bailey** came over from the USA to ride Dubai Millennium in the Prince of Wales's Stakes at Royal Ascot – for which, extraordinarily, he did not start favourite. The brilliant French miler Sendawar was preferred in the market, but the race was another display of front-running power from Dubai Millennium, who scorched round Ascot and won unchallenged by eight lengths. The following month **Montjeu** won the King George VI and Queen

Elizabeth Diamond Stakes equally imperiously, and the racing world was abuzz with the prospect of the two horses meeting. Sheikh Mohammed proposed a match for $6 million, but the very day after that challenge had been announced Dubai Millennium broke a hind leg on the Newmarket gallops, and his racing career was over. Saved for breeding, he took up stallion duties at the Dalham Hall Stud with a book of some 100 mares for 2001, but had covered only 82 when struck down with the disease grass sickness. Despite the best veterinary attention he could not be saved, and he died on 29 April 2001. The tributes to a truly great horse flowed in, but perhaps the best epitaph was Sheikh Mohammed's comment when Dubai Millennium was at the height of his powers: 'There is no horse like this horse.'

DUBAI WORLD CUP

Web: www.dubaiworldcup.com
Grade One; four-year-olds and upwards;
1¼ miles (2000 metres) on dirt (Nad Al Sheba, Dubai)

Opening leg of the **Emirates World Series**, the Dubai World Cup is the richest horse race in the world. Like so much that has catapulted Dubai to the centre of the world racing stage, the race was principally the brainchild of Sheikh Mohammed, and the idea was simple: to stage a contest so staggeringly valuable and under such suitable conditions of surface (dirt), distance (one and a quarter miles) and timing (spring) that it would become a natural target for the very best middle-distance horses around the globe. The race got off to a spectacular start in 1996 by attracting the most famous horse in the world, the American superstar **Cigar**, who went into the inaugural Dubai World Cup unbeaten in 13 races on dirt. He came out of it unbeaten in 14, having seen off Soul Of The Matter in a memorable eyeball-to-eyeball duel up the straight, with the main English challenger Pentire back in fourth. The following year produced another perfect winner in the shape of the ultra-tough five-year-old **Singspiel**, trained at Newmarket by Michael Stoute and running in Sheikh

Dubai World Cup winners since 1996

1996	Cigar	6	W. Mott USA	J. Bailey	–	11
1997	Singspiel	5	M. Stoute GB	J. Bailey	–	12
1998	Silver Charm	4	Bob Baffert USA	G. Stevens	–	9
1999	Almutawakel	4	S. bin Suroor	R. Hills	–	8
2000	Dubai Millennium	4	S. bin Suroor	L. Dettori	–	13
2001	Captain Steve	4	Bob Baffert USA	J. Bailey	–	12

Mohammed's own maroon and white colours. In 1998 the World Cup line-up included Godolphin's six-year-old **Swain** (who at that stage had won a hatful of big races, including the first of his King Georges at Ascot) and the grey American colt Silver Charm, who the previous year had landed the Kentucky Derby and Preakness and narrowly failed to secure the Triple Crown in the Belmont: the race shook down to a monumental duel between these two, the grey just prevailing by a short head. The 1999 running kept the prize very much in the family, going to Almutawakel, owned by Sheikh Mohammed's brother Sheikh Hamdan and trained under the Godolphin banner by Saeed bin Suroor.

But it was the Dubai World Cup in 2000 which truly sealed the race's position as a showcase for the very best in world horse racing with the sensational pillar-to-post victory of the great Godolphin colt **Dubai Millennium** – renamed with just such a destiny in mind – who powered home by six lengths under Frankie Dettori in one of the greatest exhibitions of sheer galloping power ever witnessed. There was nothing of Dubai Millennium's quality in the 2001 renewal, but the victory of US-trained Captain Steve over Japanese challenger To The Victory underlined the true international nature of the race – and brought jockey Jerry Bailey his third Dubai World victory from six runnings. The 2001 running had guaranteed prize money of £4 million, with £2,400,000 going to winning owner Mike Pegram.

(While British bookmakers issue prices on the World Cup, there is no legal betting in Dubai, and thus no official betting returns are shown on the table of results above. The table also considers Almutawakel and Dubai Millennium to be trained in Dubai, as they were prepared for the race in that country.)

DUFFIELD, GEORGE

At the start of the 2001 Flat season George Duffield was 54, the oldest jockey riding in Britain. Born in 1946, he served his apprenticeship with Jack Waugh and rode his first winner on Syllable at Yarmouth on 15 June 1967. After years as one of the most popular and consistent jockeys around, riding plenty of winners for his main retainer Sir Mark Prescott, Duffield finally got onto the Classic scoreboard in 1992 with the Clive Brittain-trained filly User Friendly, who won the Oaks and St Leger, and was beaten a neck by Subotica in the Arc; she also won the Irish Oaks and Yorkshire Oaks. His other big wins include the Eclipse Stakes twice, on Environment Friend in 1991 and Giant's Causeway in 2000, and the Champion Stakes in 1998 and 1999 on Alborada.

DUNDALK

Dowdallshill, Dundalk, Co. Louth
Tel.: 042 937 1271
Fax: 042 937 1271

Dundalk racecourse is situated at the foot of the Cooley Mountains, beside Carlingford Lough. It is a left-handed, undulating circuit of one and a quarter miles, and the major races here are the Rossbracken Handicap Chase and the Mickey McArdle Novices' Chase.

DUNFERMLINE

Dunfermline showed exquisite timing by winning Her Majesty the Queen the fourth Classic of her years as an owner at the very height of the Jubilee celebrations in 1977 – and later that year delivered a fifth. Dunfermline, a bay filly by **Royal Palace** trained by **Dick Hern**, failed to win in three outings as a two-year-old in 1976 (though she was runner-up in the May Hill Stakes at Doncaster and the Fillies' Mile at Ascot). She started her three-year-old campaign in highly encouraging style by winning the Pretty Polly Stakes at Newmarket, then turned in a resolute performance to win the Oaks from Freeze The Secret (though her task was made easier by the withdrawal of hot favourite Durtal, who gashed herself against a rail when depositing Lester Piggott on the way to the start and was withdrawn). Dunfermline was beaten in the Yorkshire Oaks, then lined up for the St Leger against the brilliant Vincent O'Brien colt **Alleged**, who started at 7–4 on; Dunfermline was 10–1. Early in the straight Dunfermline, ridden as in the Oaks by **Willie Carson**, took on Alleged, and furiously as he tried Lester Piggott on the colt could not shake her off. She gradually got the upper hand and won by a length and a half. Dunfermline never won again, finishing fourth behind Alleged in the Arc and failing to win in three outings as a four-year-old; but on St Leger day 1977 she was perhaps the best horse the Queen has ever owned. Dunfermline died in January 1989 aged 15.

DUNLOP, JOHN

Website: www.jldunlop.enta.net

John Leeper Dunlop was born in 1939 and took out his first trainer's licence in 1966, after being assistant to Gordon Smyth: his first winner came in April 1966. In a long career he has won a string of big races, including two Derbys – Shirley Heights in 1978 (he also won the Irish Derby) and Erhaab in 1974 – and handled several notable horses, including the filly Salsabil, who in 1990 won the One Thousand Guineas, Oaks and Irish Derby, and the great sprinter Habibti, winner of the July Cup and Nunthorpe Stakes in 1983. He was leading trainer in 1995. John Dunlop trains at Castle Stables, Arundel in West Sussex (within the grounds of Arundel Castle), and

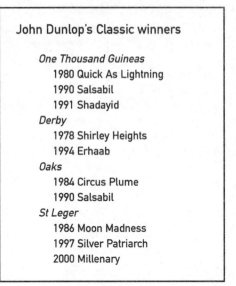

John Dunlop's Classic winners

One Thousand Guineas
1980 Quick As Lightning
1990 Salsabil
1991 Shadayid
Derby
1978 Shirley Heights
1994 Erhaab
Oaks
1984 Circus Plume
1990 Salsabil
St Leger
1986 Moon Madness
1997 Silver Patriarch
2000 Millenary

has one of the largest strings in British racing: 198 horses are listed as being under his care in *Horses in Training 2001*, many of whom are owned by his principal patron Sheikh Hamdan Al **Maktoum**. His son Ed Dunlop trains in Newmarket.

DUNWOODY, RICHARD

Born in Belfast in January 1964, Richard Dunwoody first sat on a pony at the age of two, led up a horse at a race meeting at Gowran Park at the age of seven ('Is he not a bit young?', the stipendiary steward asked his father) and had his first ride under Rules in August 1982, with his first winner coming on Game Trust in a hunter-chase at Cheltenham on 4 May 1983. Within just seven years of that initial victory Dunwoody had joined Fred Winter, Willie Robinson and Bobby Beasley as the only jockeys since the war to have won the big treble of jump racing, taking the Grand National on West Tip in 1986, the Cheltenham Gold Cup on Charter Party in 1988 and the Champion Hurdle on Kribensis in 1990. But the horse with whom he became most closely associated was **Desert Orchid**: taking over the ride on the grey on the retirement of Simon Sherwood, he won seven races on Dessie, including the King George VI Chase in 1989 and 1990. By the time a second Grand

National was landed with Miinnehoma in 1994 Dunwoody had established himself as one of the great jump jockeys of the age. After three consecutive years as runner-up to **Peter Scudamore**, he was champion jockey for the first time in 1992–3, and the following term just beat **Adrian Maguire** after a sensationally close contest which went to the very last meeting of the season.

He was champion again in 1994–5, and on 5 April 1999 rode Yorkshire Edition to win a novices' hurdle at Wincanton to register his 1,679th winner, thus beating Scudamore's record and becoming the winningmost jump jockey of all. On his retirement from the saddle in December 1999 Richard Dunwoody – a rider of supreme style – had ridden 1,699 winners.

E

EACH WAY

An each way bet is betting on the horse either to win or to be placed; the standard definition of 'placed' is

- to finish in the first two in races of five, six or seven runners; or
- to finish in the first three in races of eight or more runners; or
- to finish in the first four in handicaps with 16 or more runners.

These stipulations can vary from one bookmaker to another, and some pay out on the fifth place in very competitive big races. The odds for a place are normally one-quarter or one-fifth the odds for a win, depending on the nature of the race and the number of runners.

An each-way bet is in fact two bets – one for the win and one for the place – and consequently the stake will be twice the unit of the bet: thus a bet of £5 each way costs £10. A bet of £5 each way (with the place odds one-quarter the win odds) on a horse which wins at 10–1 returns winnings of £62.50 (£50 win plus £12.50 place, as the winning horse is also placed) plus your stake of £10 – a total return (tax-free) of £72.50. If the horse is second you win £12.50 and have your stake on the place bet returned, but lose your £5 win bet: so your return on the £10 invested is £17.50.

Obviously it is not worth backing a horse each way if its odds are much less than 5–1, as the amount you will make on the place bet if it is placed but does not win will not cover your loss on the win bet: it should be clear that an on-course each-way bet at 4–1, one-quarter the odds a place, will yield no gain and no loss if the horse is placed but does not win.

EAR 'OLE

Betting slang for 6–4 (derived from the **tic-tac** sign).

EARLY DOORS

Early exchanges in the betting market.

EAR PLUGS

Nervous horses may be fitted with ear plugs to shield them from the noise of the racecourse – but one of the Jockey Club's more beguiling instructions states that 'when any horse runs in a race with ear plugs of any type, such plugs must not be removed during the course of the race'. Quite so; but wouldn't it take a pretty nifty jockey even to try?

EARTH SUMMIT

Trained by Nigel Twiston-Davies and owned by a partnership which included Nigel Payne (press officer at Aintree) and Ricky George (who scored the winning goal for non-League Hereford against Newcastle in the FA Cup in 1971), and famously did not include football commentator John Motson (who declined the opportunity to participate), Earth Summit won 10 of his 41 races and is the only horse ever to have won the Scottish National (1994), Welsh National (1997) and Grand National – 1998, after a relentless slog with Suny Bay in very heavy ground.

EASTER HERO

Winner of 20 steeplechases, including the Cheltenham Gold Cup in 1929 and 1930, Easter Hero also made an indelible mark on the Grand National, for bad reasons and good. In the 1928 Aintree marathon he built up a big lead in the first mile but slipped on taking off at the Canal Turn (then an open ditch) and straddled the fence, causing such mayhem in the following pack that only nine of his 41 rivals managed to get over: the race was won by 100–1 shot Tipperary Tim. The following year Easter Hero carried top weight of 12st 7lb in a field of 66 runners and was going like the winner when he twisted a shoe at second Valentine's, causing him great pain as he led over the last mile – only to be caught at the last fence by 100–1 outsider Gregalach and finish second, beaten six lengths. He started favourite for the 1931 National but was brought down at second Becher's – and was brought out again the very next day to dead-heat in the Champion Chase. He spent his retirement on the Virginia farm of J. H. Whitney, who had owned him for the latter part of his career, and died in 1948 at the age of 28.

EASTERBY, MICK

Web: www.mickeasterby-racing.co.uk

M. W. (Michael William) Easterby trains at Sheriff Hutton, near York, and is the younger brother of **Peter Easterby**. He took out his first licence in 1961 and won his first big race with Boismoss in the 1967 Cesarewitch. His only Classic came with Mrs McArdy in the 1977 One Thousand Guineas, but his best horse has been the great sprinter Lochnager, who won the King's Stand Stakes, July Cup and William Hill Sprint (now the Nunthorpe Stakes) in 1976.

EASTERBY, PETER

M. H. (Miles Henry) Easterby, always known as Peter, was born in 1929. He took out his first trainer's licence in 1950 and made his presence felt both on the Flat – with horses such as Old Tom (Lincoln Handicap 1965) and Goldhill (King's Stand Stakes 1965) – and over jumps, winning the Cheltenham Gold Cup in 1979 with Alverton and in 1981 with Little Owl. He trained two dual Champion Hurdlers: **Night Nurse** (1976 and 1977) and **Sea Pigeon**, who won 37 races including two Champion Hurdles (1980 and 1981), two Chester Cups (1977 and 1978) and the 1979 Ebor Handicap. On his retirement in 1995 Peter Easterby's yard near Malton was taken over by his son Tim, who has been responsible for such good horses as Barton.

EBF

See **European Breeders' Fund**.

EBOR HANDICAP

Handicap; three-year-olds and upwards; 1¾ miles (York)

The Ebor is one of the great races of the year – a highly competitive handicap attracting a large and good-class field, a major betting heat which forms the centrepiece of York's biggest fixture. Named after the Roman title for the city of York – Eboracum – the Ebor was first run in 1843. It was soon boasting top-class winners, including dual Ascot Gold Cup

Ebor Handicap winners since 1990

1990	Further Flight	4	B. Hills	M. Hills	7–1JF	22
1991	Deposki	3	M. Stoute	F. Norton	12–1	22
1992	Quick Ransom	4	M. Johnston	D. McKeown	16–1	22
1993	Sarawat	5	R. Akehurst	T. Quinn	14–1	21
1994	Hasten To Add	4	Sir M. Prescott	G. Duffield	13–2F	21
1995	Sanmartino	3	B. Hills	W. Carson	8–1	21
1996	Clerkenwell	3	M. Stoute	F. Lynch	17–2	21
1997	Far Ahead	5	L. Eyre	T. Williams	33–1	21
1998	Tuning	3	H. Cecil	K. Fallon	9–2F	21
1999	Vicious Circle	5	L. Cumani	K. Darley	11–1	21
2000	Give The Slip	3	Mrs A. Perrett	Pat Eddery	8–1	22

winners The Hero (1849) and Isonomy (1879), and Lily Agnes (1875), one of the great racemares of the late ninteenth century. **Brown Jack** won the Ebor in 1931, while since the Second World War notable winners have included Vincent O'Brien's great mare Gladness (who carried 9st 7lb to a six-length victory under Lester Piggott in 1958) and **Sea Pigeon**, who at the age of nine in 1979 beat Gladness's weight-carrying record for the race when humping 10st – most of it Jonjo O'Neill – to a short-head victory over Donegal Prince, who was receiving 40lb. Sir Montagu won the Ebor in 1976 from subsequent Cheltenham Gold Cup winner Alverton and went on to win the Prix Royal-Oak (French St Leger), while other notable winners are Jupiter Island (1983), who won the Japan Cup in 1987, Kneller (1988), who won the Doncaster Cup and Jockey Club Cup later the same year, and the ever-popular grey **Further Flight** (1990).

ECLIPSE

Foaled in 1764 and named after the great eclipse of the sun in the year of his birth, Eclipse was bred by the Duke of Cumberland, and on the Duke's death in 1765 was bought by William Wildman, a Smithfield meat salesman, for 75 guineas. His new owner was in no hurry to race Eclipse, and the horse was given ample time to mature, going into serious training only at the age of five.

In April 1769 Wildman held a trial on Banstead Downs, near Epsom; it was to be kept secret, but none the less – according to a contemporary report – some touts did their best to get a sneak preview of this new prospect. Turning up too late to see the action, instead 'They found an old woman who gave them all the information they wanted. On inquiring whether she had seen a race, she replied she could not tell whether it was a race or not, but she had just seen a horse with a white leg running away at a monstrous rate, and another horse a great way behind, trying to run after him; but she was sure he never would catch the white-legged horse if he ran to the world's end.'

A month later Eclipse – the 'horse with a white leg' – had his first outing in public, at Epsom in a race of four-mile heats. Starting favourite at 4–1 on following rumours of the trial, he won the first heat with ease, prompting an Irish gambler called Dennis O'Kelly to bet that he could predict the placings of the runners in the next heat in their correct finishing order. When his challenge was taken up he uttered the phrase which was to become part of racing language: 'Eclipse first, the rest nowhere.' His prediction – that all the other runners would be 'distanced' by Eclipse (that is, finish over 240 yards behind him) – was proved triumphantly correct, and O'Kelly went on to purchase a half share in the horse for 650 guineas; later he bought the other half too, by which time the price had risen to 1,100 guineas: no mean sum for the eighteenth century.

In 18 races Eclipse was never whipped or spurred; yet he was never headed, let alone beaten. Retiring to stud in 1771, he sired three of the first five Derby winners, and died in 1789. Today the skeleton of Eclipse is one of the prize exhibits at the **National Horseracing Museum** in Newmarket.

ECLIPSE STAKES

Group One; three-year-olds and upwards;
1¼ miles (Sandown Park)

Earliest race of the season when the top middle-distance three-year-olds meet the best of the older generations, the Eclipse Stakes was the first £10,000 race ever staged in England: its inaugural running in 1886 was worth more than twice the value of that year's Derby. By the turn of the century the Eclipse had established its position as one of the key events of the Flat season, and the 1900 race underlined its quality: it was won by Diamond Jubilee, who had already won the Two Thousand Guineas and Derby that year and would go on to land the St Leger and thus the Triple Crown. The 1903 Eclipse proved one of the most famous races of all time, when Ard Patrick and **Sceptre** drew clear of Rock Sand (who would win the Triple Crown that year) in a pulsating finish. Ard Patrick prevailed by a neck, and it was this race which prompted the great trainer George Lambton to make his famous observation that

Eclipse Stakes winners since 1990

1990	Elmaamul	3	W. Hern	W. Carson	13–2	7
1991	Environment Friend	3	J. Fanshawe	G. Duffield	28–1	7
1992	Kooyonga	4	M. Kauntze *IRE*	W. O'Connor	7–2F	12
1993	Opera House	5	M. Stoute	M. Kinane	9–2	8
1994	Ezzoud	5	M. Stoute	W. R. Swinburn	5–1	8
1995	Halling	4	S. bin Suroor	W. R. Swinburn	7–1	8
1996	Halling	5	S. bin Suroor	J. Reid	100–30	7
1997	Pilsudski	5	M. Stoute	M. Kinane	11–2	5
1998	Daylami	4	S. bin Suroor	L. Dettori	6–4F	7
1999	Compton Admiral	3	G. Butler	D. Holland	20–1	8
2000	Giant's Causeway	3	A. O'Brien *IRE*	G. Duffield	8–1	8
2001	Medicean	4	M. Stoute	K. Fallon	7–2	8

'About the best thing in racing is when two good horses single themselves out from the rest of the field and have a long-drawn-out struggle.' Between the wars three Derby winners landed the Eclipse – Coronach (1926) and Blue Peter (1939) as three-year-olds, Windsor Lad (1935) at four – and post-war runnings have seen the tradition of sheer excellence continued. Horses in that period who won Derby and Eclipse in the same season are Tulyar (1952), St Paddy (1961), **Mill Reef** (1971) and **Nashwan** (1989), while **Royal Palace** won at Sandown the year after Epsom: he beat Taj Dewan and **Sir Ivor** in a famous finish in 1968. Other big names on the post-war roll of honour include **Ballymoss** (1958), Ragusa (1964), Busted (1967), **Brigadier Gerard** (1972), Star Appeal (1975), Ela-Mana-Mou (1980), **Sadler's Wells** (1984), **Pebbles** (1985 – first filly ever to win the race) and **Dancing Brave** (1986); dual winners Mtoto (1987 – beating Derby winner Reference Point – and 1988) and Halling (1995 and 1996); **Pilsudski** (1997), **Daylami** (1998) and **Giant's Causeway**, who eyeballed out Kalanisi in a desperate struggle in 2000.

EDDERY, PAT

Son of Irish jockey Jimmy Eddery (who had ridden Panaslipper into second place in the 1955 Derby and won the Irish Derby on the same horse), Pat was born in County Kildare on 18 March 1952. At the age of 13 he was apprenticed to Seamus McGrath, and in 1967 moved to England to complete his apprenticeship with Frenchie Nicholson. He was 17 when he rode his first winner – Alvaro at Epsom on 24 April 1969. He was champion apprentice in 1971, and the following year joined **Peter Walwyn**, for whom he rode his first Classic winner,

Pat Eddery's Classic winners

Two Thousand Guineas
    1983 Lomond
    1984 El Gran Senor
    1993 Zafonic
One Thousand Guineas
    1996 Bosra Sham
Derby
    1975 Grundy
    1982 Golden Fleece
    1990 Quest For Fame
Oaks
    1974 Polygamy
    1979 Scintillate
    1996 Lady Carla
St Leger
    1986 Moon Madness
    1991 Toulon
    1994 Moonax
    1997 Silver Patriarch

Polygamy in the 1974 Oaks. Eddery was champion jockey in 1974 for the first time, and in all has won the title on 11 occasions (the same number as Lester Piggott): 1974-7, 1986, 1988-91, 1993 and 1996. He was champion in Ireland in 1982 while riding as stable jockey for **Vincent O'Brien**. In addition to the Classic winners highlighted in the box opposite, he has won the King George VI and Queen Elizabeth Diamond Stakes twice (**Grundy** in 1975 and **Dancing Brave** in 1986), two Breeders' Cup races (**Pebbles** in the 1985 Turf and Sheikh Albadou in the 1991 Sprint), the Irish Derby four times (Grundy in 1975, **El Gran Senor** in 1984, Law Society in 1985 and Commander In Chief in 1993) and the Prix de l'Arc de Triomphe four times (Detroit in 1980, then three consecutive runnings between 1985 and 1987 with Rainbow Quest, Dancing Brave and Trempolino), as well as countless other big races around the world. His 4,000th winner came with Silver Patriarch's victory in the 1997 St Leger, and by the beginning of the 2001 Flat season he was closing fast on the domestic career total of Lester Piggott, whose 4,493 winners in Britain was bettered only by the 4,870 of Sir Gordon Richards.

EL GRAN SENOR

Of the eight races he ran, El Gran Senor was beaten in only one, doing enough in those few outings to proclaim himself one of the very best colts of the modern period. Trained at Ballydoyle by Vincent O'Brien, he ran in the colours of Robert Sangster and was ridden in all his races by Pat Eddery. As a two-year-old in 1983 he won a maiden race at Phoenix Park, then the Railway Stakes and the National Stakes at The Curragh before travelling to Newmarket to beat Rainbow Quest in the Dewhurst Stakes and install himself as market leader for the 1984 Two Thousand Guineas. Sent off hot favourite for that Classic, he produced a wonderful performance to win from Chief Singer and Lear Fan, and then attention turned to the Derby. Debate raged about whether El Gran Senor, a brilliant miler, would stay the extra half mile

at Epsom, but on the day he went off 11-8 on favourite. It was an extraordinary race. With two furlongs to go El Gran Senor was pulling all over his rivals: it was simply a matter of when Eddery would release the brake and let him saunter to a facile victory. Then the little considered Secreto – trained by Vincent O'Brien's son David – joined issue with the favourite and suddenly El Gran Senor had a real fight on his hands. Despite Eddery's urgings Secreto just would not be shrugged off, and after a fierce battle all the way to the line El Gran Senor was beaten a short head. Despite that setback, El Gran Senor was tried again at a mile and a half in the Irish Derby, and got back on the winning trail by beating Rainbow Quest in what proved to be his last race. He was retired to stand at stud in Maryland alongside his sire **Northern Dancer** and is now in Kentucky.

ELECTRICAL TIMING

The official time of a race in Britain on the Flat is recorded by a system controlled by **RaceTech** and linked to the starting stalls and photo-finish systems. When the starter presses the button which releases the front gates of the starting stalls, the breaking of the electrical circuit sets off the electronic timing system and the time is plotted on the photo-finish strip. (Since starting stalls are not used for jumps races, timing for these is compiled by Raceform's watch-holders.)

ELEF

Betting slang for 11-1.

ELEF A VIER

Betting slang for 11-4.

ELLIOTT. CHARLIE

Champion jockey in 1923 (sharing the title with Steve Donoghue) and in 1924 while still an apprentice, Charlie Elliott was a leading jockey for a quarter of a century, though his career was dwarfed by the achievements of his contemporary **Gordon Richards**. He rode 14 Classic winners, including Derby winners Call Boy (1927), Bois Roussel (1938) and Nimbus (1949). Charlie Elliott died in 1979.

ELSWORTH, DAVID

Born in 1939, David Elsworth, now based at Whitsbury in Hampshire, took out his first licence to train in 1978. While his best-known charge has been the great chaser **Desert Orchid**, whom Elsworth trained throughout his racing career, he has had plenty of other good horses through his hands. Over jumps Rhyme 'N' Reason won the 1988 Grand National; Barnbrook Again won the Queen Mother Champion Chase twice (1989 and 1990); Heighlin won the 1980 Triumph Hurdle, and Oh So Risky the same race in 1991; then there was the good chaser Combs Ditch and the staying hurdler Floyd. On the Flat his best horse has been In The Groove, who won the Irish One Thousand Guineas, International Stakes and Champion Stakes in 1990 and Coronation Cup in 1991, while other popular Elsworth-trained horses have been Lear Spear (Cambridgeshire 1998) and the doughty stayer Persian Punch. Elsworth trained 1999 Two Thousand Guineas winner Island Sands as a two-year-old, only to see the colt snapped up by Godolphin and win the Newmarket Classic with Saeed bin Suroor as trainer. He was leading jumps trainer in the 1987–8 season.

EMIRATES WORLD SERIES

Web: www.racingseries.com

Inaugurated in 1999 and the brainchild of Sheikh Mohammed, the Emirates World Series is an unofficial 'world championship of racing' in which horses, jockeys, owners and trainers are given points for their placings in a series of major races around the globe. (The points system covers the first six places in each race on the basis of 12 points to the winner, 6 to the second, 4 to the third, 3 to the fourth, 2 to the fifth and 1 to the sixth.)

The addition of the Prix de l'Arc de Triomphe in 2001 to the original programme brings the series up to 12 races:

- *Dubai World Cup* (Nad Al Sheba, Dubai, March)
- *King George VI and Queen Elizabeth Diamond Stakes* (Ascot, Great Britain, July)
- *Arlington Million* (Arlington Park, USA, August)
- *Grosser Preis von Baden* (Baden-Baden, Germany, September)
- *Irish Champion Stakes* (Leopardstown, Ireland, September)
- *Prix de l'Arc de Triomphe* (Longchamp, France, October)
- *Canadian International* (Woodbine, Canada, October)
- *Cox Plate* (Moonee Valley, Australia, October)
- *Breeders' Cup Turf* (Belmont Park USA, October)
- *Breeders' Cup Classic* (Belmont Park, USA, October)
- *Japan Cup* (Tokyo, Japan, November)
- *Hong Kong Cup* (Sha-Tin, Hong Kong, December)

ENIN

Betting slang for 9–1.

ENIN TO ROUF

Betting slang for 9–4.

ENTIRE

An ungelded male horse – also known as a 'full' horse. It is unusual, though by no means unheard of, for a successful jumping horse to be an entire rather than a gelding. The last entire to win the Grand National was

---

Emirates World Series winners 1999–2000

year	horse	jockey	trainer	owner
1999	Daylami	L. Dettori	S. bin Suroor	Godolphin
2000	Fantastic Light	L. Dettori	S. bin Suroor	Godolphin

Battleship in 1938, and the last entire to win the Cheltenham Gold Cup was Fortina in 1947. More recently, the good and gutsy chaser Kadastrof, who won several races for trainer Robin Dickin, was an entire. Hurdlers are more likely to be 'full horses' than chasers, and in recent memory the Champion Hurdle has been won by entires **Monksfield** (1978 and 1979) and Alderbrook (1995).

ENTRIES

Unless the conditions stipulate to the contrary, entries for a race are made to **Weatherbys** five days before the race is run (thus would be made on Monday for a race the following Saturday). If fewer than eight entries are received, that race may be re-opened. Entry for certain big events closes well in advance of the race: for example, the 2001 Martell Grand National closed on 24 January 2001, and the 2001 Vodafone Derby way back on 1 December 1999. For some races a supplementary entry is allowed for, whereby for a hefty premium a horse can be entered very late. For example, a week before the race, the fee for supplementing for the 2001 Vodafone Derby was £75,000.

EPSOM DOWNS

Epsom, Surrey KT18 5LQ
Tel.: 01372 726311
Fax: 01372 748253
E-mail: epsom@rht.net
Web: www.epsomderby.co.uk

Epsom Downs, home of the Derby and Oaks, is one of the most historic racecourses in the world – and that history is inextricably linked with the town above which the racecourse perches, affording modern racegoers spectacular views of London. By the middle of the seventeenth century Epsom had become one of the most frequented spa towns in England, its waters notable for their purgative effect. As the town became a magnet for those craving the medicinal properties of the area, so horse races on the Downs became part of local social activity; and although Epsom's status as a spa town declined during the eighteenth century, racing on the Downs continued. The first running of the **Oaks** took place in 1779,

with the inaugural **Derby** on 4 May the following year. That 1780 race was a far cry from today's familiar event, with its climb up the hill, helter-skelter charge down to Tattenham Corner and the final surge up the straight: the first Derby was run over a dog-leg course of just one mile (the distance of the race was not increased to a mile and a half until 1784), starting to the east of the present Tattenham Corner.

The present Derby course, which has been used for the race since 1872, starts opposite the stands. After leaving the stalls the field gets into its stride over a short uphill run into a gradual right-hand bend, then shifts across to the opposite running rail and continues towards the top of Tattenham Hill, 502 feet above sea level. From there the runners engage a sweeping left-handed descent into Tattenham Corner, where, a little under four furlongs from the winning post, they swing into the straight. The gradient in the straight is a gradual downwards incline until the ground levels out and rises slightly just before the winning post. But that home straight poses a particularly trappy problem for the tired young horse trying to get home: its camber. The ground slopes down from the stands side towards the infield, causing tired horses to hang to their left.

The original Epsom grandstand, which was opened in 1830 and stood for nearly a century, was for a time during the 1840s the home of a young girl named Isabella Mayson, whose stepfather Henry Dorling was Clerk of the Course. She was to achieve lasting fame as Mrs Beeton.

The course has long been the subject of debate: do its ups and downs, its right- and left-hand bends, provide the ultimate test of the athleticism of the Thoroughbred racehorse, or is Epsom a crazy terrain over which to stage serious horse racing? Australian jockey Mick Goreham, who rode in the 1974 Derby, had forthright views: 'It's the queerest course I've ever ridden on. It's not just the hill but the angle. I never expected to see anything like that. And to think you run the greatest race in the world on it. I feel most trainers back home would take one look at it and put their horses right back in the box!'

Although Epsom's three major races – Derby, Oaks and **Coronation Cup** – are all run over that mile and a half, the course also supplies distances of five, six and seven furlongs, one mile and half a furlong, and one and a quarter miles. Races over six and seven furlongs start from spurs off the round course, while the straight five furlongs starting beyond Tattenham Corner provides the fastest sprint track in the world. It was in the Tadworth Handicap over this course in 1960 that Indigenous, carrying 9st 5lb and ridden by Lester Piggott, established the fastest ever time for five furlongs – 53.6 seconds.

Over any distance, the key requirement of an Epsom horse is balance, the ability to stay on an even keel over the course's unusual contours. But over the Classic distance that sense of equilibrium must be complemented by adaptability. The ideal Derby or Oaks horse has the speed to take up and hold a position in the early stages of the race, the agility to go uphill and then steeply downhill and, when the strain of the closing stages begins to bite, the fortitude to keep going up that cambered straight.

Although the terrain itself retains its historic contours, the facilities at Epsom have undergone significant changes in recent years. A new parade ring has been laid out immediately behind the Queen's Stand, which was opened in 1992 as a state-of-the-art facility, and the mammoth old grandstand has – not before time – undergone extensive refurbishment.

Derby Day is Epsom's greatest occasion by a distance. It may be a far cry from the jamboree the Victorians knew, when the running of the Derby annually triggered an unofficial public holiday, but it is still a very special day. Huge numbers of racegoers make their way to Epsom Downs – many of them in the open-topped buses which line the inside rail in the straight, tens of thousands to picnic on the hill or spend the afternoon at the funfair, and a select few arrayed in morning dress to hob-nob in the Queen's Stand. The other big Epsom occasion is Oaks Day, which since 1995 has been on the Friday, the eve of Derby Day. As well as the Oaks, the fillies' equivalent of the Derby, this programme includes the Coronation Cup, for four-year-olds and upwards over the Derby course. The Epsom Spring Meeting, revived in 1997 after several years in the fixture-list wilderness, includes the Blue Riband Trial, a useful opportunity for Derby candidates to try out their abilities over the course, and the Great Metropolitan and the City and Suburban, both handicaps now a shadow of their former distinguished selves. Evening racing has become very popular at Epsom Downs, and the August Bank Holiday Monday fixture includes the Moët & Chandon Silver Magnum – the 'Amateurs' Derby' for gentleman riders over the full Classic distance – which was first run in 1963 and was won four times by John Oaksey.

Epsom is also a training centre, with trainers such as Philip Mitchell and Simon Dow having yards in the vicinity.

EUROPEAN BREEDERS' FUND

Stanstead House, The Avenue, Newmarket, Suffolk CB8 9AA
Tel.: 01638 667960
Fax: 01638 667270
E-mail: ebf@dial.pipex.com
Web: www.ebfhorseracing.com

The European Breeders' Fund (EBF), which was established in 1983, is the largest individual sponsor in British racing. The fund takes the form of a scheme whereby stallion owners in the five major European racing countries (Great Britain, France, Ireland, Germany and Italy), plus Switzerland, each put up a sum of money equal to the average value of a nomination to each of their stallions in the year in question. The money raised is used to support races (whose names carry the 'EBF' abbreviation), to provide breeders' prizes, and to fund veterinary research.

EVENING RACING

Evening meetings, now such a popular feature of the racing scene, were born at Hamilton

Park on 18 July 1947 and have grown to the point where 162 evening fixtures – Flat and jumps – were scheduled for 2001. A variation on the standard evening meeting, which ideally takes place as a balmy summer twilight falls, came with the introduction of floodlit racing at Wolverhampton in December 1993.

EVENS, EVEN MONEY

Betting term when the chance of winning is perceived as exactly equal to the chance of losing – in other words, 1–1.

EXACTA

Tote bet which requires you to pick the first and second horse in a race in correct finishing order.

EXES

Betting slang for 6–1.

EXETER

Kennford, near Exeter, Devon EX6 7XS
Tel.: 01392 832599
Fax: 01392 833454
E-mail: exeterraces@eclipse.co.uk

Named 'Devon and Exeter' until dropping the redundant first two words in 1992, Exeter is an unassuming, friendly little track highly popular with summertime holidaymakers in the West Country. The right-handed course, nearly two miles round, undulates severely – so severely that a stretch at the beginning of the far straight is obscured from the view of most observers in the stands. The fences are held to be fairly stiff, and the run from the home turn is an uphill half mile. So you need a horse here who has plenty of balance to cope with the undulations, and who won't shirk the issue in the closing stages.

Exeter prides itself on being one of the oldest courses in the country: there are records of meetings nearby as long ago as 1738, and evidence exists that there was racing here in the early seventeenth century. Nowadays the sport is fairly modest, but the course can boast one very high-class early-season steeplechase in the Haldon Gold Cup, run in late October or early November over two miles one and a half furlongs: winners include Panto Prince, Sabin Du Loir (who won the race twice), Waterloo Boy and Viking Flagship.

EYE-COVER

Equine headgear used on a horse with defective vision: one of the eyes is completely covered over.

EYE-SHIELD

Equine headgear sometimes used in **all-weather racing**: the cups over the eyes are made of mesh or a transparent material which protects the horse's eyes from kickback.

F

FABRE, ANDRÉ

André Fabre, born in December 1945 and a licensed trainer since 1977, dominates the training ranks in France: when he was champion trainer in that country in 2000, having sent out 101 winners to earn his patrons FFr23,659,400, he was taking the title for the thirteenth consecutive season.

While André Fabre was a law student in Paris he earned money by working as a plumber.

Fabre rode more than 250 winners as an amateur jump jockey – he won the Grand Steeplechase de Paris on Corps A Corps in 1977 – and in the early years as a trainer concentrated on jumpers, switching his attention to the Flat in 1984. From his yard in Chantilly he has sent out countless big-race winners around the world: he has to date won four Classics in England (Toulon in the 1991 St Leger, **Zafonic** in the 1993 Two Thousand Guineas, Intrepidity in the 1993 Oaks, Pennekamp in the 1995 Two Thousand Guineas); two Breeders' Cup races (In The Wings in the 1990 Mile and Arcangues in the 1993 Classic); and the Prix de l'Arc de Triomphe five times (Trempolino in 1987, Subotica in 1992, Carnegie in 1994, Peintre Celebre in 1997 and Sagamix in 1998).

FACE

Betting slang for 5–2 (from the **tic-tac** sign).

FACES

Punters in the betting ring whom the bookmakers regard as being particularly well informed.

FAIRYHOUSE

Fairyhouse Club Limited, Rataoth, Co. Meath
Tel.: 01 825 6167
Fax: 01 825 6051

Best known as the home of the Irish Grand National on Easter Monday, Fairyhouse is one of Ireland's leading racecourses, boasting a fine modern stand and a high-class racing programme, especially over jumps. The right-handed circuit is about one and three-quarter miles round, ideal for the long-striding, galloping sort of horse.

FAKENHAM

Fakenham, Norfolk NR21 7NY
Tel.: 01328 862388
Fax: 01328 855908

Fakenham is the modern name for the racecourse known until 1963 as the West Norfolk Hunt. A left-handed square-shaped track of about one mile round, this is very much a course for front-runners and for the nifty, compact horses who need to take their chances where their long-striding rivals are less comfortable. The short circuit and the tightness of the bends mean that fields tend to go very fast here, and the undulations further militate against the galloping type of horse.

Going racing at Fakenham is an experience not dissimilar from going to a **point-to-point**, with a certain informality, strong connections to the surrounding community and a crowd drawn very much from the locality. The racing will not be top-class, but nobody minds, and there is always a very convivial atmosphere.

FALLON, KIEREN

Kieren Fallon was born in Crusheen, County Clare, in February 1965 and rode his first winner on Piccadilly Lord at Navan on 18 June 1984; his first winner in Britain (where he moved to be apprenticed to Jimmy FitzGerald) was Evichstar at Thirsk on 16 April 1988. In 1993 Fallon joined forces with trainer Lynda Ramsden and became one of the most successful jockeys in the north, though his career was not without controversy. In 1994 he was suspended for six months for pulling rival jockey Stuart Webster off his horse after a rough race at Beverley, and it was Fallon's ride on Lynda Ramsden-trained Top Cees in the Swaffham Handicap at Newmarket in April 1995 which led to the High Court libel case in early 1998 when the jockey, the trainer and her husband Jack won damages against the *Sporting Life*. Given Fallon's profile at the time, it occasioned surprise in some quarters when he was made stable jockey to the powerful **Henry Cecil** yard from the start of the 1997 term, but the rider gave the best possible riposte to the sceptics by becoming champion jockey that season, landing the title again in 1998 and 1999. Those first three seasons with Cecil brought Fallon five Classic winners – Sleepytime (One Thousand Guineas 1997), Reams Of Verse (Oaks 1997), Wince (One Thousand Guineas 1999), Ramruma (Oaks 1999) and Oath (Derby 1999) – but the golden relationship turned very sour in July 1999, when amid a flurry of rumour Fallon lost his job with Cecil – though he still ended the season champion. Fallon had proved himself too good a rider to be removed from top-class action for long, and by the beginning of the 2000 season was stable jockey to Cecil's Newmarket rival **Sir Michael Stoute**: the new partnership struck Classic gold early that season when King's Best scored a scintillating victory in the Two Thousand Guineas. A terrible fall from Alhawa in the Ascot Stakes at Royal Ascot saw him sidelined for the rest of the season, but in spring 2001 he returned to the saddle and resumed his place as stable jockey to Sir Michael Stoute, winning the Two Thousand Guineas on Golan – his seventh Classic.

FALLS

A jump jockey can expect to have a fall approximately once in every 12 rides, although a small proportion of falls result in serious injury. None the less, race riding is an extremely dangerous way of earning your living, and the racing has its melancholy list of jockeys – both Flat and jumping – who have paid the ultimate price. Manny Mercer, brother of Joe, was killed when thrown on the way to the start at Ascot in 1959, while Brian Taylor, who won the 1974 Derby on Snow Knight, was killed in a fall in a race at Hong Kong in December 1984. Also on the Flat, Joe Blanks was killed at Brighton in 1981, and Steve Wood at Lingfield Park in May 1994. Falls on the Flat are often more serious than over jumps since they are so sudden and unexpected. Over jumps, recent casualties include Doug Barrott, who died after a fall at Newcastle in 1973, Viv Kennedy (at Huntingdon in August 1988), Philip Barnard (Wincanton on Boxing Day 1991) and Richard Davis (Southwell in July 1996).

FARRIER

The blacksmith: an essential member of racing's backroom team. Most big stables employ their own; smaller stables would rely on regular visits from an outside farrier. A farrier is on duty at every race meeting in order to carry out last-minute repairs if necessary.

See also **plate**.

FASIG-TIPTON

American sale company based near Lexington, Kentucky, whose yearling **sales** are second in importance in the USA only to **Keeneland**.

FAVOURITE

Shortest-priced horse in the betting market. It may be tempting for the indolent punter simply to back favourites, but statistics show that this will be unprofitable in the long run. Out of every five races, roughly two are won by the favourite or joint favourite.

FEEDING (HORSES)

A racehorse is usually fed twice a day (early morning and early evening), and its intake of food is carefully adjusted according to its individual needs and tastes and to its racing and training programme. The traditional basic diet is corn – oats (too much of which can get a horse over-excited) – and hay, though many trainers now feed their charges on 'racehorse cubes', manufactured compounds which ensure a balanced diet of high-quality feed. The drawback of cubes is that they can be contaminated by prohibited substances, and the trainer feeding cubes has less control over exactly what he is giving his horses. Also commonly fed are sugar beet (dried, and then rehydrated by soaking), linseed, molasses, and carrots and apples. A bran mash is a sort of porridge in which the bran is supplemented with oats, treacle or other ingredients to make it more appetising, and perhaps some Epsom salts as a laxative.

Unsupervised eating can cause problems, and not only ones of nutritional balance: No Bombs, a good hurdler, once filched his lad's Mars Bar, thereby giving himself a dose of the prohibited substance theobromine which the 'work, rest and play' delicacy contains. He ran, won, failed the dope test and forfeited the race.

Other additives may be less conventional. **Arkle**'s basic feed when in training was a mixture of mash and dry oats mixed up with six eggs and supplemented by two bottles of Guinness, and **Mandarin** enjoyed a Mackeson: in retirement he had two bottles a day delivered to him from the local pub in Lambourn, courtesy of the late Colonel Bill Whitbread, whose company sponsors the famous handicap chase in which he was three times runner-up.

FEELING THE GROUND

A horse is said to be 'feeling the ground' if he is uncomfortable on the going and thus reluctant to exert himself to the full.

FENCES

In a steeplechase (apart from **cross-country** events under Rules such as the Sporting Index

Chase at Cheltenham) there are three basic sorts of fence: plain fence, open ditch and (on some courses) water jump. Jockey Club regulations stipulate that there must be at least 12 fences in the first two miles of a steeplechase, at least two of which must be open ditches, with three fences for each additional half mile.

FETLOCK

In a horse's leg, the joint at the lower end of the cannon bone, above the pastern.

FIBRESAND

The artificial racing surface used on the **all-weather** tracks at Southwell and Wolverhampton. It consists of specially graded sand stabilised with synthetic fibres.

FIDDLER

Bookmaker who will lay only a small bet.

FIELD, THE

Runners in a race.

FILLIES' MILE

Group One; two-year-old fillies; 1 mile (Ascot)

The race which in 2000 was run as the Meon Valley Stud Fillies' Mile began life back in 1973 as the Green Shield Stakes and was won by Lester Piggott on the Queen's filly Escorial. After being lost to waterlogging in 1974, it became the Argos Star Fillies' Mile in 1975, with Hoover taking over sponsorship in 1978. The race was promoted from Group Three to Group Two in 1986, and to Group One in 1990. Whatever its Group status, this race has long enjoyed a reputation for identifying contenders for the following year's Classic campaign, and the list of winners bristles with fillies who have gone on to Classic success: Quick As Lightning (1979: One Thousand Guineas 1980); **Oh So Sharp** (1984: One Thousand Guineas, Oaks and St Leger 1985); Diminuendo (1987: Oaks 1988); **Bosra Sham** (1995: One Thousand Guineas 1996); and Reams Of Verse (1996: Oaks 1997). Other Classic-winning fillies have been placed in the Fillies' Mile, notably **Dunfermline**, second in 1976, who went on to win the

Fillies' Mile winners since 1990

1990	Shamshir	2	L. Cumani	L. Dettori	11–2	12
1991	Culture Vulture	2	P. Cole	T. Quinn	5–2F	7
1992	Ivanka	2	C. Brittain	M. Roberts	6–1	8
1993	Fairy Heights	2	N. Callaghan	C. Asmussen	11–1	11
1994	Aqaarid	2	J. Dunlop	W. Carson	11–2	9
1995	Bosra Sham	2	H. Cecil	Pat Eddery	10–11F	6
1996	Reams Of Verse	2	H. Cecil	M. Kinane	5–1	8
1997	Glorosia	2	L. Cumani	L. Dettori	10–1	8
1998	Sunspangled	2	A. O'Brien *IRE*	M. Kinane	9–1	8
1999	Teggiano	2	C. Brittain	L. Dettori	11–8F	6
2000	Crystal Music	2	J. Gosden	L. Dettori	4–1	9

1977 Oaks and St Leger. Height Of Fashion, winner in 1981 and owned like Dunfermline by the Queen, was the dam of **Nashwan**. The idea of this race is to pinpoint top staying fillies of the future, and in that it has been conspicuously successful.

FILLY
Female horse up to and including the age of four.

The last filly to be placed in the Derby was Nobiliary, runner-up to Grundy in 1975.

FIRING
Method for treating tendon strain by applying red-hot irons to the damaged area. *See* **breaking down**.

FITZGERALD, MICK
'Sex will be an anti-climax after that': Mick Fitzgerald's euphoria after winning the 1996 Grand National on Rough Quest has entered every dictionary of sporting quotations, but within racing Fitzgerald had long before that been admired as a jockey exceptionally stylish in the saddle and exceptionally articulate out of it. Born in Cork in May 1970, Fitzgerald served his apprenticeship with Richard Lister and John Hayden before moving to England, where he rode his first winner on Lover's Secret at Ludlow on 20 December 1988. From that beginning he made rapid progress to his present position as one of the top jump

jockeys, and his association with trainer **Nicky Henderson** has assured a steady stream of high-class winners. But his greatest victories so far have not been for Henderson: Terry Casey trained Rough Quest, whose hugely impressive win from Encore Un Peu in the 1996 Grand National provoked *that* comment, and **Paul Nicholls** trained See More Business, on whom Fitzgerald won the 1999 Cheltenham Gold Cup and King George VI Chase.

FIVEFOLD
In betting, a five-horse **accumulator**.

FLAGMAN
The flagman is the figure – usually dressed in a white coat – who stands about half a furlong down the course from the start, ready to wave down the field if the starter indicates a false start and wants the field recalled. This rather specialised pursuit had gone on for decades without anybody noticing until Aintree on 3 April 1993, when the unfortunate Ken Evans became the first flagman to become a public figure: the problems starting the Grand National that year focused on whether he had or had not performed his function correctly. Matthew Engel, reporting that notorious occasion in the *Guardian*, wrote that 'there was no trouble at all finding a scapegoat. Ken Evans, the £28-a-day flagman, was singled out. He was supposed to wave his flag in front of the horses in

response to the starter's red flag. At 3.50 p.m. on Saturday the flagman's duties would have been as obscure as those of a sagger-maker's bottom-knocker to 99.9 per cent of the nation; by 4.30 everyone was lucidly expert on his technical failings.'

FLAGS, BETWEEN THE

A horse described as having run 'between the flags' has been running in a **point-to-point**.

FLAG START

While Flat races are usually started from starting stalls, and jump races by some form of starting gate or tape, a flag start – where the runners are sent on their way by the starter raising and then lowering a red flag – can take place if for some reason the usual methods cannot apply (for example, if very heavy going means that starting stalls cannot be deployed). When the the start of the 1975 Two Thousand Guineas was disrupted by striking stable lads so that the stalls could not be used, the runners were moved to the front of the stalls and the race started by flag.

FLASHY

A horse described as being of a 'flashy' **chestnut** colour is bright chestnut with a good deal of white about his body – on his head and feet. There has long been a popular prejudice against such colouring and a suggestion that it indicates a lack of relia-bility, but horses such as **Grundy** and The Minstrel, both of whom might have been described as flashy, showed no lack of resolve in their many big-race wins.

FLAT

In Britain the Flat season officially runs from 1 January to 31 December. In the winter months action on the Flat is confined to **all-weather** surfaces, and what many still regard as the 'Flat season proper' runs from late March (with the Lincoln meeting at Doncaster) to early or mid-November (with the November Handicap at the same course).

FLIMPING

Giving under the odds; underpaying.

FLYINGBOLT

It was Flyingbolt's misfortune to be a contem-porary of the greatest Irish chaser of them all, his illustrious stable companion **Arkle**. Without Arkle around, he would have swept all before him in the mid-1960s and been hailed as one of the all-time greats. As it is, he has the distinction of being officially the second-best jumper of that generation, at his peak rated by the Irish handicapper only 2lb inferior to Arkle. Flyingbolt was a tall, flashy chestnut with a large white blaze, reportedly very cussed with those about him. Trained like Arkle by **Tom Dreaper** near Dublin, he ran up a sequence of four consecutive hurdle races in the 1963–4 season, culminating in the first division of the Gloucestershire Hurdle at Cheltenham (the equivalent of the novices' hurdle which today opens the Festival meeting). He was switched to fences and went through the next season unbeaten, again winning at the Cheltenham National Hunt Meeting: the Cotswold Chase (today the Arkle). The 1965–6 season was Flyingbolt's greatest. After a warm-up hurdle at Phoenix Park he won the Carey's Cottage Chase at Gowran Park, the Black and White Gold Cup at Ascot, the Massey Ferguson Gold Cup at Cheltenham (now the Tripleprint) and the Thyestes Chase at Gowran Park – all impor-tant races. Then in March 1966 he wrote his name even deeper into Cheltenham Festival history by winning the Two Mile Champion Chase on the Tuesday in a canter from Flash Bulb and Flying Wild, and turning out again on the Wednesday to line up 15–8 favourite for the Champion Hurdle. He was going like a winner when knocked back by a mistake four out, and though he had taken the lead by the second last he had to give best on the run-in to Salmon Spray and Sempervivum. He then returned to Ireland to win the Irish Grand National under 12st 7lb. A line through the mare Height O'Fashion, second in that race and second to Arkle on her previous outing, put Flyingbolt just 2lb inferior to 'Himself', and in the next handicap for which they were both entered Arkle was allotted 12st 7lb, Flyingbolt 12st 5lb. Despite that elevated status, Flyingbolt was never the same horse again. Training problems overtook him and he was moved to Britain to be trained first by Ken Oliver (under whose charge he was second to Titus Oates in the 1969 King George VI Chase) and then by Roddy Armytage. Flyingbolt spent his retirement in a field in Oxfordshire with another great Dreaper stalwart, 1968 Gold Cup winner Fort Leney, and died in 1983 aged 24. The key question, of course, is what would have happened if Flyingbolt had met Arkle in a race. **Pat Taaffe**, who rode them both, had no doubt: 'Flyingbolt was a front runner; Arkle would have been able to sit on his tail and beat him for speed.'

FLYING CHILDERS

Sometimes described as the first truly great racehorse – though he is recorded as having run in only two races! He ran in a match over four miles at Newmarket in April 1721, and another over six miles the following October, winning both. He is said to have been capable of covering 25 feet at a stride. The Flying Childers Stakes, for two-year-olds over five furlongs, is run at Doncaster on St Leger day.

FLY-JUMP

A fly-jump is when, without warning, a horse suddenly jumps into the air – as if stung by a horse fly.

FOAL

A Thoroughbred horse is a foal from the date of its birth until 1 January the following year, when it becomes a yearling.

FOINAVON

Originally owned by Anne, Duchess of Westminster, Foinavon was named after a mountain on her estate in Sutherland (as were her famous champion **Arkle** and another of her good chasers Ben Stack). Sent into training with Tom Dreaper in Ireland, the horse proved to have plenty of ability but very little inclination to make good use of it: in a chase at Baldoyle he fell when in the lead at the third last fence and lay prostrate. Connections rushed over to tend the stricken horse – only to find that he was lying on the ground contentedly picking at the grass around him. Exasperated by such behaviour, the Duchess sold Foinavon for 2000 guineas to be trained at Compton in Berkshire by John Kempton, for whom he became a regular – if forlorn – contender in many of the big races: he was a remote fourth in the 1966 King George VI Chase (Arkle's last race), and warmed up for the 1967 Grand National by running last in the Cheltenham Gold Cup at 500–1. Foinavon's starting price of 100–1 at Aintree seemed about right as the runners, led by loose horse Popham Down (who had fallen at the first fence) poured over Becher's Brook on the second circuit: he was well in arrears. But at the twenty-third – the smallest fence on the Grand National course – Popham Down decided he had had enough, ran up the take-off side of the fence and caused mayhem. All the front-runners were brought to a halt, and the horses following cannoned into those in the front. Foinavon, ridden by John Buckingham, was at this stage so far behind that Buckingham was able to see what was happening and steer his mount to the outside, popping him over the one part of the fence not seething with bodies and setting off for home. By the time the favourite Honey End had disentangled himself and made off in pursuit it was too late: Foinavon came home in glorious, if unlikely, isolation and won by 15 lengths. (The Tote paid 444–1.) He should not have won the Grand National – but he did, and the fence between Becher's Brook and the Canal Turn on the Grand National course is now officially known as the Foinavon Fence.

Foinavon ran several more times after he was catapulted to unlikely fame at Aintree (he was brought down at the water jump in the 1968 National), and in October 1968 won a three-mile chase at Uttoxeter under curiously similar circumstances. He jumped badly and by the seventh fence was tailed off. At the second last the leader, Jenin, was hampered by a loose horse and fell, while the only other survivor, Paddynoggin, was carried out in the mêlée. This left Foinavon clear, and he ambled home to win by a distance from the remounted Jenin.

FOLKESTONE

Westenhanger, Hythe, Kent CT21 4HY
Tel.: 01303 266407
Fax: 01303 260185
E-mail: info@lingfieldpark.co.uk
Web: www.folkestone-racecourse.co.uk

Although not universally popular with all racing professionals (its sharp nature and less than state-of-the-art facilities are uncongenial to some trainers and jockeys), Folkestone has its charms, including its very own goldfish pond – a tranquil spot by which to contemplate one's losses. The only track in Kent since the closure of Wye in 1974, the current course has staged racing since 1898. About one mile and three furlongs round and fairly undulating, the right-handed circuit here is tight, and with a home straight of just two and a half furlongs, it is no place for a horse to lay too far off the pace. Accordingly it favours the handy, sharp type rather than the resolute galloper.

FONTWELL PARK

Fontwell, near Arundel, West Sussex
BN18 0SX
Tel.: 01243 543335
Fax: 01243 543904
E-mail: brooke@fontwellpark.co.uk
Web: www.fontwellpark.co.uk

The steeplechase track at Fontwell Park – where racing has taken place since 1924 – is one of Britain's two figure-of-eight courses (the other is Windsor), with all the fences on the criss-cross diagonals; the hurdle course, just over one mile round, forms a left-handed oval outside the chase track. Hence your ideal Fontwell horse will be compact, handy, and – especially in the case of chasers – not prone to bouts of dizziness from being so often on the turn. Its peculiarities make it an excellent venue at which to apply the 'horses for courses' theory, though any Fontwell specialist these days will have to go some to beat the record of the chaser Certain Justice, who won 14 races on this track, the last in 1965.

Although the standard of sport here does not rival that at Cheltenham or Sandown Park, Fontwell is a delightful place to go racing, with good facilities and excellent viewing. The key spot for those wishing to experience steeplechasing in the raw is at the central angle of the figure-of-eight, where you can revel in intimate views of several fences and still nip back up the hill for a close-up of the finish. But if the twists and turns of a chase here are confusing to spectators, think what it can be like for a jockey. It's not unusual for even a leading rider to lose count of how many times the field has gone round, and many a pilot has ridden a finish one circuit too early.

A particular feature of the stands area at Fontwell is the little classical garden tucked away beyond the winning post, a real haven of tranquillity complete with rotunda bearing an inscription in stained glass: 'Be ye therefore followers of God as dear children.' Not many racecourses can claim such closeness to the Almighty.

FOOTBALL

There has long been a close link between the sports of football and horse racing. Many well-known footballers have shown a keen interest in the Turf, and some have taken this interest further than just racegoing. Plenty of footballers and managers have owned horses: for instance, the good hurdler Auetaler is owned by a partnership of Liverpool players and former players including Steve McManaman and Robbie Fowler, while Manchester United manager Sir Alex Ferguson has had an interest in several horses and is a keen racegoer. England internationals Francis Lee and **Mick Channon** both took up training careers, and Channon has become one of the leading trainers in the country. Footballers are also recalled in horses' names. Bobby Moore ran in the 1969 and 1970 Champion Hurdles as pacemaker for winner Persian War, while more recently four-legged versions of Frank Leboeuf and Dennis Bergkamp have been seen in action. (*See also* **Quixall Crossett**.)

FORDHAM, GEORGE

Second only to **Fred Archer** in reputation in the nineteenth century, George Fordham rode the winners of 16 Classics, including the

Derby on Sir Bevys in 1879. Born in 1837, he rode his first winner at Brighton in 1851 and in 1853 weighed just 3st 12lb when winning the Cambridgeshire on Little David. He died in 1887 at the age of 50.

FOREARM

A horse's forearm is the upper part of his foreleg.

FORECAST

Bet involving predicting the first two in a race. The now discontinued Tote 'dual forecast' required nominating the first two in either order, while a 'straight forecast' – now the **Exacta** – requires getting the first two in correct order. *See* **computer straight forecast**.

FORFEIT LIST

The Forfeit List, published in the *Racing Calendar*, is a record of those who have outstanding debts under the Rules of Racing – for example, a trainer who has not paid a fine prescribed by a disciplinary hearing. Remaining on the list renders the offender liable to be **warned off**.

FORFEIT STAGES

When a race has an entry timetable longer than the standard five days, the schedule has built-in 'forfeit stages' at which unless the horse is withdrawn he remains in the race and the owner pays an additional fee. For example, the conditions for the 2001 Whitbread Gold Cup won by Ad Hoc stated '£150 stake, £250 extra unless forfeit declared by April 10th, £200 extra if entry confirmed' – that is, the owner paid £150 to enter, and an extra £250 if the entry was upheld on 10 April, plus a further £200 to have the entry confirmed. If the horse were withdrawn at the 10 April stage, the £150 entry fee would be forfeited.

FORSTER, TIM

Captain Tim Forster, who died in April 1999 at the age of 65, was a trainer very much of the 'old school', where training was under-pinned by a military discipline and where horses were big, strong, strapping steeple-chasers. He started training in 1962, and in his early years had charge of one of the most popular hunter–chasers ever, Baulking Green. He considered steeplechasing the only *real* horse racing – he once observed that were he an MP he would bring in a bill to get hurdling banned! – and over a long career won most of the big chases of the calendar. The Grand National went to Forster three times, with Well To Do, who won in his own colours in 1972; Ben Nevis, ridden by American amateur Charlie Fenwick in 1980; and Last Suspect in the Arkle colours of Anne, Duchess of Westminster, in 1985.

Legend has it that Tim Forster's riding instructions to Charlie Fenwick before his Grand National victory on Ben Nevis were: 'Keep remounting.'

Among his other well-known horses were Royal Marshall II, who won the Hennessy Gold Cup in 1974 and King George VI Chase in 1976; Pegwell Bay, first horse to win both Cheltenham's big autumn handicap chases (then the Mackeson and the A. F. Budge) in 1988; Martha's Son, who won the Queen Mother Champion Chase and Mumm Melling Chase in 1997; and the massively popular Dublin Flyer, who won a hatful of races including the Tripleprint Gold Cup in 1994 and John Hughes Memorial Trophy and Mackeson Gold Cup in 1995. Forster retired in 1998, having trained winners of 1,346 races, and handed over his stables in Shropshire (where he had moved from his base at Letcombe Basset in Oxfordshire) to his assistant Henry Daly.

FORTH, JOHN

The oldest man to ride a Derby winner, being over 60 (his precise age is not known) when winning on Frederick, whom he also trained, in 1829.

FORWARD

A horse is said to be 'forward' if he appears to be developing and maturing at a rate faster than average.

See also **backward**.

FOURFOLD
In betting, a four-horse **accumulator**.

FRACTURES OF THE KNEE
There are 10 bones in a horse's knee joint. Repeated stress on the front aspect of these bones can result in 'chip' or 'slab' fractures, which occur most commonly in young horses at the end of a race when the muscles are fatigued, making the knees less stable. The chips of bone can be surgically removed and the larger slabs screwed back into place. The horse must then be rested. Premature resumption of work will only exacerbate the condition.

FRAME (1)
The skeletal structure of a horse.

FRAME (2)
The first four places in a race. The numbers of first, second, third and fourth home are (on most racecourses) displayed to racegoers in a metal frame. Thus a placed horse is said to have 'made the frame' or be 'in the frame'.

FRANCE
One of the three major racing nations of Europe, alongside Britain and Ireland, France sends a steady stream of challengers to Britain for the big races – Flat and jumps alike.

There are 257 racecourses in France, many of them country tracks which have little bearing on the larger picture of European racing. Most familiar to racing fans this side of the Channel are **Longchamp**, **Chantilly**, Maisons-Laffitte, **Saint-Cloud** and the jumping track at **Auteuil**, in or near Paris; **Deauville** in Normandy; and Cagnes-sur-Mer near Nice, where many British trainers run their horses at the big February meeting. The major training centres are at Maisons-Laffitte and at Chantilly, not far from Paris; here are based several of the French trainers familiar to Channel Four Racing viewers, such as **François Doumen, André Fabre, Criquette Head-Maarek** and **John Hammond**. French jockeys have traditionally been on the receiving end of a fair amount of stick when riding in Britain (*see* **Head family**), and that tradition has been carried on by none other than John McCririck, who criticised Adam Kondrat after his losing rides on The Fellow in the Cheltenham Gold Cup in 1991, 1992 and 1993. When The Fellow and Kondrat finally won the Cheltenham showpiece in 1994 Big Mac graciously pointed out that they had won because Kondrat had heeded the advice that Mac himself had been so generously offering.

Around 4,000 Thoroughbred foals are born each year in France, and the influence of the

Winners of the French Classics since 1990

year	Poulains	Pouliches	Jockey-Club	Diane	Royal-Oak
1990	Linamix	Houseproud	Sanglamore	Rafha	Braashee / Indian Queen
1991	Hector Protector	Danseuse du Soir	Suave Dancer	Caerlina	Turgeon
1992	Shanghai	Culture Vulture	Polytain	Jolypha	Assessor
1993	Kingmambo	Madeleine's Dream	Hernando	Shemaka	Raintrap
1994	Green Tune	East Of The Moon	Celtic Arms	East Of The Moon	Moonax
1995	Vettori	Matiara	Celtic Swing	Carling	Sunshack
1996	Ashkalani	Ta Rib	Ragmar	Sil Sila	Red Roses Story
1997	Daylami	Always Loyal	Peintre Celebre	Vereva	Ebadiyla
1998	Victory Note	Zalaiyka	Dream Well	Zainta	Tiraaz
1999	Sendawar	Valentine Waltz	Montjeu	Daryaba	Amilynx
2000	Bachir	Bluemamba	Holding Court	Egyptband	Amilynx
2001	Vahorimix	Rose Gypsy	Anabaa Blue	Aquarelliste	

country on breeding around the world is immense. A noticeable trend is the number of French-breds now making their mark on the British jumping scene.

There are no bookmakers in France, all wagering taking place through the pari-mutuel system of pool betting.

The French equivalents of the Classics run in England are:

- *Poule d'Essai des Poulains* (French Two Thousand Guineas) run over 1 mile at Longchamp;
- *Poule d'Essai des Pouliches* (French One Thousand Guineas), run over 1 mile at Longchamp;
- *Prix du Jockey-Club* (French Derby), run over $1^1/_2$ miles at Chantilly;
- *Prix de Diane* (French Oaks), run over $1^1/_4$ miles at Chantilly;
- *Prix Royal-Oak* (French St Leger) run over $1^3/_4$ miles at Longchamp.

Other major French races which regularly attract overseas raiders include:

- *Prix Ganay* for four-year-olds and upwards over 1 mile $2^1/_2$ furlongs at Longchamp;
- *Grand Prix de Paris* for three-year-olds and upwards over $1^1/_4$ miles at Longchamp;
- *Grand Prix de Saint-Cloud* for three-year-olds and upwards over $1^1/_2$ miles at Saint-Cloud;
- *Prix Jacques le Marois* for three-year-olds and upwards over 1 mile at Deauville;
- *Prix de l'Abbaye* for two-year-olds and upwards over 5 furlongs at Longchamp;
- *Prix du Cadran* for four-year-olds and upwards over $2^1/_2$ miles at Longchamp;
- *Grand Criterium* for two-year-olds over 1 mile at Longchamp.

(For a list of all French Group One races, *see* **Pattern**.)

FRANCE GALOP

Web: www.france-galop.com

The ruling body of French racing, based in Boulogne. France Galop is the modern name for that mouthful: *Société d'encouragement pour l'amélioration des races de chevaux de galop en France*.

FRANCIS, DICK

Born in Pembrokeshire in 1920, Dick Francis rode his first winner on Wrenbury Tiger in a hunter–chase at Bangor-on-Dee on 3 May 1947, and his last on Crudwell at Leicester on 7 January 1957. He was champion jump jockey in the 1953–4 season and rode 345 winners (though never managed to land any of jump racing's Big Three), but his career in the saddle is most notable for a famous loser: **Devon Loch**, who slithered to a halt 50 yards from certain victory for the Queen Mother in the 1956 Grand National. On his retirement Francis turned his hand to writing – he was a racing correspondent for the *Sunday Express* for many years and published his autobiography *The Sport of Queens* in 1957 – and is now world-famous as an author of crime novels, most of them based in or around the world of racing. His first novel was *Dead Cert*, published in 1962, and his latest *Shattered*, published in 2000.

FRANCOME, JOHN

It's not hard to appreciate why John McCririck insists on dubbing his Channel Four Racing colleague John Francome the 'Greatest Jockey'. Statistically he literally was that – for a while. On his retirement from the saddle in 1985 he had ridden 1,138 winners in Britain, a record for a jump jockey not passed until Peter Scudamore beat it in November 1989. But Francome's greatness was about far more than dry numbers: it was his sheer style, his horsemanship and his unsurpassed ability to get a horse jumping fluently which made him, in many observers' opinion – and despite plenty of fierce opposition both before his career and after – the greatest jump jockey of the lot.

The son of a Swindon builder, John Francome was born on 13 December 1952. He won junior international honours in the show-jumping ring and in 1969 joined the Lambourn yard of **Fred Winter**, with whom he remained for the whole of his riding career. His first ride in public, Multigrey in a three-mile hurdle at Worcester on 2 December 1970, brought him his first winner. His second ride in public brought him a broken wrist. On the retirement of Richard Pitman in 1975 John took over as Winter's stable jockey, and was champion jockey for the first time in the 1975–6 season. In all he won the championship seven times: 1975–6, 1978–9, 1980–1, 1981–2 (sharing the title with Peter Scudamore, who had built up a big lead before being injured and ruled out for the rest of the season: Francome stopped riding when he reached Scu's total), 1982–3, 1983–4 and 1984–5. He won the Cheltenham Gold Cup on Midnight Court in 1978 and the Champion Hurdle, after riding a masterly waiting race, on **Sea Pigeon** in 1981, but the nearest he came to winning the Grand National was second on Rough And Tumble in 1980. Other famous horses he rode included Bula, Burrough Hill Lad (on whom he won the Hennessy Gold Cup and King George VI Chase in 1984), Brown Chamberlin (Hennessy Gold Cup 1983), **Wayward Lad** (King George VI Chase 1982) and Lanzarote. He retired late in the 1984–5 season and spent a brief spell as a trainer before making another change of direction to concentrate on broadcasting and writing.

FREEDMAN, LOUIS

Louis Freedman's colours of yellow, black spots, yellow sleeves and cap have been one of the most familiar sets of racing silks in the big Flat races. His first top-class horse was I Say, third to Sea Bird II in the 1965 Derby and winner of the 1966 Coronation Cup, and he had Classic success with Polygamy (Oaks 1974) and Reference Point (Derby and St Leger 1987: he also won the King George VI and Queen Elizabeth Diamond Stakes). He also owned the good fillies Lucyrowe, Attica Meli and Mil's Bomb. He died in 1998 at the age of 81, and his racing interests – based at the Cliveden Stud in Berkshire – are carried on by his son Philip.

FULL

A 'full' horse is an **entire**, a male who has not been gelded.

FULL BROTHER/SISTER

A horse is a full brother (or sister) to another horse if they share both sire and dam.

FURLONG

One eighth of a mile – 220 yards.

FURTHER FLIGHT

A grey son of 1974 Cambridgeshire winner Flying Nelly owned by Simon Wingfield Digby and trained by Barry Hills, Further Flight won the Group Three Jockey Club Cup at Newmarket every year between 1991 and 1995 – the only horse to have won the same Pattern race five years in a row – and for good measure was third in the 1997 running at the grand old age of 11. In all Further Flight won 24 of his 70 races over 11 seasons' racing (1988 to 1998); in addition to that monopoly of the Jockey Club Cup, his big-race victories included the Ebor Handicap (1990), Goodwood Cup (1991 and 1992) and Doncaster Cup (1992). He was put down in July 2001 at the age of 15.

G

GAFF TRACK

In jump racing parlance, the 'gaffs' are the small tracks – places like Ludlow, Sedgefield or Taunton – which form the backbone of the sport. ('Gaff' is an old slang word for a fair.)

GAINSBOROUGH STUD

Web: www.gainsborough-stud.com

The Gainsborough Stud, near Newbury in Berkshire, is the centre of the breeding operation of Sheikh Maktoum Al **Maktoum**. Stallions standing there for 2001 are Cadeaux Genereux, Green Desert and Zilzal. The Sheikh's breeding operation in the USA is based at Gainsborough Farms in Kentucky.

GALGO JR

Winningmost horse in racing history, Galgo Jr won 137 races – all in his native Puerto Rico – between 1930 and 1936. In all he raced 159 times, and finished out of the first four only once.

GALILEO

When Galileo forged clear of Fantastic Light to land the King George VI and Queen Elizabeth Diamond Stakes at Ascot in July 2001 the burning question was: just how great is he? This book goes to press before a definitive answer is known, but after the King George most observers considered Galileo one of the very best middle-distance horses of modern times. By **Sadler's Wells** out of 1993 Arc winner Urban Sea, owned by Mrs Susan Magnier and **Michael Tabor** and trained in Ireland by **Aidan O'Brien**, Galileo ran once as a two-year-old in 2000, winning a Leopardstown maiden by fourteen lengths. At three he won twice more at Leopardstown before displaying a blistering turn of foot to win the Derby by 3½ lengths from Golan,

then followed up by winning the Irish Derby by four lengths from Morshdi en route to his first clash with the older generation at Ascot. **Michael Kinane**, who rode Galileo in both Derbies and the King George, was unequivocal: 'Not many horses are truly great but this one is.' Just how great, you will know better than I …

GALLOPING TRACK

A racecourse is described as 'galloping' if its terrain – long straights, easy turns – encourages the long-striding sort of horse, as opposed to the nippier sort able to whizz around tight bends.

GALWAY

Ballybrit, Co. Galway
Tel.: 091 753870
Fax: 091 752592
E-mail: galway@iol.ie
Web: www.iol.ie/galway-races

Home of the great festival meeting in late July/early August which features the Galway Plate (2¾ mile handicap chase) and the Galway Hurdle (2 miles). The festival lasts six days and presents a fabled challenge to the stamina – and in particular to the livers – of the thousands who attend, not only for a feast of sport but for one of Irish racing's most vibrant social occasions. The course itself is right-handed, with a steep rise to the finish.

GAY FUTURE

The most ingenious betting **coup** of modern times concerned a gelding named Gay Future, who won the Ulverston Novices' Hurdle at Cartmel on 26 August 1974, Bank Holiday Monday. The essence of this intricate story is that an unnamed horse had been sent by the planners of the coup, based in Ireland, to the stables of trainer Anthony Collins at Troon in Scotland. Collins had entered a horse called Gay Future and another horse, Racionzer, in the race at Cartmel, and two other horses – Opera Cloak and Ankerwyke – in races at other courses on the same day and both starting within half an hour of the Cartmel race. On that Bank Holiday morning members of the syndicate who were staging the coup, masterminded by Cork building contractor Tony Murphy, placed bets in a variety of betting shops in London on doubles connecting Gay Future with Opera Cloak or with Ankerwyke: doubles are deemed by bookmakers to be 'mugs' bets', and these wagers would not have aroused suspicion.

Meanwhile the 'real' Gay Future, who had been prepared for the race in Ireland by trainer Edward O'Grady, had been brought over the Irish Sea, swapped for the horse in Collins's charge, and sent off to Cartmel for the race. Neither Ankerwyke nor Opera Cloak reached the courses where they were supposed to be running (it transpired that they had never left their trainer's stable). When one leg of a double is a non-runner the bet becomes a single on the remaining horse, so a large amount of money was then running on Gay Future: the conspirators stood to win around £300,000. But the 'blower' system transmitting off-course money to the course betting market was not operating to Cartmel that very busy Bank Holiday Monday (as the planners of the coup had cleverly been aware), and by the time the bookmakers realised what was afoot they could get his price down only by dispatching a representative to the course to bet on him there.

As the bookies' man struggled towards the Lakeland track, the coup was coming to fruition. Before he had entered the paddock at Cartmel, Gay Future's flanks had had soap flakes rubbed into them to give the impression that he was sweating freely and so put off on-course punters, and the other Collins horse, Racionzer, was well supported in the betting ring to allay suspicion regarding the stable's supposed second string. Gay Future duly delivered the goods by strolling home 15 lengths in front of his rivals at 10–1. Smelling a rat, most of the betting shops who had taken the bets withheld payment, though some later regarded the matter as a legitimate coup and paid out. The police launched a prosecution: Collins and Murphy were convicted of conspiracy to defraud the bookmakers, and fined. Conflicting views were aired about whether the matter should ever have been brought to court, but Murphy and his co-conspirators achieved mythic status in the annals of betting. A film entitled *Murphy's Stroke* chronicled their deeds (trainer Jim Old had a ride-on part as Gay Future's jockey) and a bar in a Cork hotel was named after a horse who, for not quite orthodox reasons, had entered racing legend.

GELDING

A gelding is a horse that has been castrated (in racing jargon, 'cut'). The operation commonly takes place in the autumn of the horse's second year, although many others are gelded later, after their racing performances have shown that they have little future at stud. The gelding operation is performed under sedation and then local anaesthetic, using a clamping and cutting device, and is quite painless.

Arcadian Heights became the first gelding to win a Group One race in Great Britain when taking the Ascot Gold Cup in 1994.

Geldings are barred from taking part in the Classics (the rationale being that for the good of the breed all Classic winners should be able to pass on their qualities), but most of the big Flat races are open to them, and old geldings such as Teleprompter or **Further Flight** won a place in the affections of the racing public unmatched by all but a very few Classic winners, however brilliant their transient glory. To some it may seem strange that the likes of **Arkle** or **Desert Orchid** could not procreate, but had they not been gelded they would not have achieved what they did in steeplechasing. While the common explanation for gelding a potential chaser – that the ungelded or 'full' horse might be understandably reluctant to launch himself over four and a half feet of packed birch – is certainly plausible, of more pressing relevance is that an entire is likely to have his mind on other things as he matures and will find it difficult to stand up to the wintry rigours of the jumping game – or, indeed, a prolonged racing life on the Flat.

See also entire; rig.

GENUINE

A genuine horse is one who is perceived as always doing its best, running consistently to form. An 'ungenuine' horse cannot be trusted to run to form, and is thus a source of exasperation to punters.

GERMANY

In the pecking order of European racing, Germany comes fourth, behind Britain, France and Ireland and in front of Italy – but German-trained horses have made their mark in many of the big races around the world. Star Appeal, trained by Theodore Greiper, won the Eclipse Stakes and Prix de l'Arc de Triomphe (at odds of 119–1) in 1975. More recently, Lando, trained by Heinz Jentzsch, won the 1995 Japan Cup, and the filly Borgia, trained by Bruno Schutz, ran third to Peintre Celebre in the 1997 Arc and the following month was runner-up to Chief Bearhart in the Breeders' Cup Turf at Hollywood Park. (The following season she was trained by André Fabre.) Tiger Hill finished third in the 1998 Prix de l'Arc de Triomphe, Sumitas was runner-up to Dubai Millennium in the Prince of Wales's Stakes at Royal Ascot in 2000, and the same year Catella was third in the Breeders' Cup Filly & Mare Turf: all three were trained by Peter Schiergen.

There are 44 racecourses in Germany, of which the best known in Britain are **Baden-Baden** (home of the Grosser Preis von Baden), Hamburg (where the Deutsches Derby is run in July), Düsseldorf, Munich and Cologne (venue for the Preis von Europa, won in 2000 by John Dunlop-trained Golden Snake).

GIANT'S CAUSEWAY

Few horses have won the level of respect, admiration and sheer awe which was accorded to Giant's Causeway during the colt's campaign in 2000. A product of the great Coolmore Stud breeding operation, trained by **Aidan O'Brien** and ridden in all but one of his races by **Michael Kinane**, Giant's Causeway was unbeaten in three races as a juvenile, including the Prix de la Salamandre, but in 2000 was beaten in both the Two Thousand Guineas (runner-up to King's Best) and Irish Two Thousand Guineas (runner-up to Bachir). He was then launched on a midsummer campaign which saw him win five Group One races in a row and proclaim himself one of the toughest colts in living memory, well deserving the epithet of 'The Iron Horse' with which he was regaled as his triumphant progress continued. He won the St James's Palace Stakes at Royal Ascot by a head from Valentino; the Eclipse Stakes at Sandown Park (ridden by **George Duffield**) by a head from Kalanisi, after a furious battle in the final furlong; the Sussex Stakes at Goodwood by three-quarters of a length from Dansili; the International Stakes at York by a head from Kalanisi, after a battle every bit as furious as the Eclipse; and the Irish Champion Stakes by half a length from Greek Dance. Giant's Causeway's colours were finally lowered when Observatory, under an inspired Kevin Darley ride, came wide to beat him half a length in the Queen Elizabeth II Stakes at Ascot, but still this gritty horse had not finished. In the Breeders' Cup Classic at Churchill Downs he turned in a sensational performance in his first race on dirt, failing by only a neck to beat Tiznow after yet another titanic tussle. That performance was enough to raise his covering fee at Coolmore Stud, where he took up duties in 2001, from a previously announced IR75,000 guineas to IR100,000 guineas, making him one of the most valuable stallions in the world.

GIFFORD. JOSH

Josh Gifford was born in 1941, apprenticed to Cliff Beechener and then Fred Armstrong, and rode 51 winners on the Flat, including Trentham Boy in the 1956 Manchester November Handicap and Curry in the 1957 Chester Cup. Increasing weight led him to switch to riding over jumps, and he joined trainer **Ryan Price**, riding his first National

Hunt winner on Kingmaker in a novice hurdle at Wincanton on 17 December 1959. On the retirement of **Fred Winter**, Gifford took over as Price's stable jockey. He was champion rider under National Hunt Rules four times: 1962–3, 1963–4, 1966–7 (with the then record total of 122) and 1967–8, and rode the winners of many big races: four of the first five runnings of the Schweppes Gold Trophy (Rosyth in 1963 and 1964, Le Vermontois in 1966, and Hill House in 1967), the 1962 Triumph Hurdle on Beaver II, the Welsh National on Forty Secrets the same year, the Mackeson Gold Cup on Charlie Worcester in 1967 and the Whitbread Gold Cup on Larbawn in 1969. But he never won any of jumping's 'Big Three': on Honey End he was second to **Foinavon** in the notorious 1967 Grand National and on Major Rose second to **Persian War** in the 1970 Champion Hurdle, but he never had a ride in the Cheltenham Gold Cup. On his retirement from the saddle in 1970 Gifford took over the jumping side of Ryan Price's operation at Findon in Sussex and embarked on a highly successful career as a trainer. By far his most famous moment came when Aldaniti won that emotional Grand National under **Bob Champion** in 1981: Champion has acknowledged that Gifford's assurance that he would keep his old job as stable jockey sustained him through the dark days of his cancer. Other top-class horses trained by Josh Gifford include the hurdler Kybo; Approaching, winner of the Hennessy Gold Cup in 1978; Deep Sensation, winner of the Tote Gold Trophy in 1990 and the Queen Mother Champion Chase in 1993; and Bradbury Star, winner of the Mackeson Gold Cup in 1993 and 1994.

GIMCRACK

A small iron-grey colt foaled in 1760, Gimcrack ran in 36 races between 1764 and 1771 and won 26 of them; he also took part in a 'match against time' in France in 1766, covering $22\frac{1}{2}$ miles in one hour. His name is commemorated in the Gimcrack Stakes for two-year-olds at the August Meeting at York – where, ironically, he was beaten in the two races he contested.

GLADIATEUR

Owned by Count de Lagrange and trained at Newmarket by Tom Jennings, Gladiateur won the Two Thousand Guineas before going to Epsom, where his victory in 1865, as the first French-bred winner of the Derby, earned him the sobriquet 'The Avenger of Waterloo'. He then won the Grand Prix de Paris and the St Leger – and thus the Triple Crown. In 1866 he won the Ascot Gold Cup by 40 lengths. A huge statue of Gladiateur stands just inside the main entrance to **Longchamp** racecourse.

GODOLPHIN

Web: www.godolphin.com

Fired by his conviction that 'in the race for excellence there is no finishing line', Sheikh Mohammed bin Rashid al **Maktoum** devised the Godolphin operation both to challenge received European wisdom about the most effective way to train and race horses, and to establish the tiny Emirates state of Dubai as a major player in world racing. In both respects his experiment has proved spectacularly successful. At the root of the idea is the notion that horses will benefit from the warmth and sun of Dubai, and the European team winters there before returning to Newmarket to be primed for the big races. Since all the Maktoum brothers feed their horses into the

---

Godolphin's Classic winners

Two Thousand Guineas
  1996 Mark Of Esteem
  1999 Island Sands
One Thousand Guineas
  1998 Cape Verdi
Derby
  1995 Lammtarra
Oaks
  1994 Balanchine
  1995 Moonshell
St Leger
  1995 Classic Cliché
  1998 Nedawi
  1999 Mutafaweq

Godolphin operation, it is often the case that a good two-year-old in their ownership, having announced his or her ability on the track, will be commandeered from the original trainer to join Godolphin for the rest of the racing career.

The first horses to race under the Godolphin banner ran in 1994, and the operation very nearly hit the Classic jackpot at the first time of asking: Balanchine was beaten a short head by Las Meninas in the One Thousand Guineas. Balanchine went on to win the Oaks and the Irish Derby that year in the care of Godolphin's trainer Hilal Ibrahim, but in 1995 a new trainer was installed in the shape of **Saeed bin Suroor**, and the success accelerated. In 1995 Lammtarra won the Derby for Godolphin (though he raced in the colours of Saeed Maktoum al Maktoum, Sheikh Maktoum al Maktoum's son), then went on to add the King George and Arc, Moonshell won the Oaks, and Classic Cliché the St Leger. In 1996 Godolphin carried on the Classic momentum when Mark Of Esteem won the Two Thousand Guineas with Frankie Dettori, now established as the operation's principal jockey in Europe, sporting the familiar royal blue colours. Since then the list of big winners is quite mind-boggling: Halling (Eclipse Stakes 1995 and 1996, International Stakes 1995 and 1996), Swain (King George 1997 and 1998, Irish Champion Stakes 1998), **Daylami** (Eclipse Stakes 1998, King George, Irish Champion Stakes and Breeders'Cup Turf 1999), Intikhab (Queen Anne Stakes at Royal Ascot by eight lengths in 1998), Kayf Tara (Ascot Gold Cup 1998 and 2000), Cape Verdi (One Thousand Guineas 1998), **Dubai Millennium** (Queen Elizabeth II Stakes 1999, Dubai World Cup and Prince of Wales's Stakes 2000), Almutawakel (Dubai World Cup 1999), Fantastic Light (Hong Kong Cup 2000 and Prince of Wales's Stakes 2001) – in addition to the Classic winners listed in the box. Godolphin was leading owner in the first two stagings of the **Emirates World Series** in 1999 and 2000, and has been leading owner in Britain in 1996, 1998 and 1999.

GODOLPHIN ARABIAN

One of the three founding sires of the Thoroughbred breed, the Godolphin Arabian was foaled in 1724 and – according to some contemporary accounts – discovered in Paris pulling a water cart. Although his influence has not been as profound as that of the **Darley Arabian**, he is the direct ancestor of several famous racehorses, including the great American horse **Man O' War** and the 1964 Derby winner Santa Claus.

GOFFS

Web: www.goffs.com

Founded in 1866 and based at Kill, County Kildare, Goffs is the leading bloodstock **sales** company in Ireland. Its principal yearling sale is the Orby Sale in October. Among the horses who have passed through the Goffs sales ring over the years are Arkle, Red Rum, Hatton's Grace and Monksfield.

GOING

The 'going' is the condition of the ground. On turf, there are seven official states of the going in Britain: hard; firm; good to firm; good; good to soft; soft; and heavy. On **all-weather** surfaces, there are three categories of going: fast; standard; and slow. The Clerk of the Course will give advance assessments of the state of the ground (published in the racing press) in the few days leading up to each meeting to alert trainers to likely conditions, and will declare the official going on the day – though this can alter during the programme, for example in the case of a torrential downpour. Normally one category will cover the course, though sometimes the official statement will allow for variations on different parts of the track: for example, 'good, good to soft in the back straight'.

The going is usually measured by the traditional method of the Clerk of the Course shoving a stick into the ground, though some courses supplement gut feeling with a numerical reading obtained by using the Penetrometer, a device developed in France whereby a weight is dropped down a metal rod at various parts of the course. Some trainers complain that some clerks of the course give misleading information on going in order to encourage connections to run their horses (for example, a trainer of the average chaser is more likely to run his horse if the going is good to soft than if it is good to firm); the Jockey Club's instruction to courses is that they should aim – though naturally, given the climate, they can do no more than aim – to produce good ground for jump racing and good to firm for Flat racing. Most courses now use some artificial means of watering to help produce the desired ground – either portable sprays or an in-built system whereby jets of water are played on to different parts of the course.

Take heed of Jim McGrath's expert observations in the *Channel Four Racing Guide to Form and Betting*:

Horses, like humans, are built in different ways, and their actions – their manner of running – also differs. For simple physical reasons, few are able to turn in the same level of performance on firm and heavy ground. As a horse's racing record builds up, astute punters construct a picture of which going suits it ideally.

But it also pays to appreciate the difference between the same status of going at different courses, as this can influence how you assess a performance. Chepstow, for example, often becomes especially heavy when conditions are very wet, as does Aintree. The last few years have seen runnings of the Grand National in ground so heavy that only a few horses have managed to complete [six in 1994, six again in 1998, and just four – two of which were remounted – in 2001]... Lingfield Park is another course where conditions become very testing in heavy ground.

When weighing up form in such circumstances, punters must take into account that fields will almost invariably return strung out – and that the distances separating the runners at the finish don't truly reflect their relative merits.

On the other hand, there is rarely genuinely soft going at Newmarket, a course which drains well, and Doncaster doesn't often get seriously testing for Flat racing. A little course knowledge can definitely be of some help.

GOLDEN MILLER

Foaled near Dublin in 1927 and sold as a yearling at public auction for 120 guineas, Golden Miller was sold on as an unbroken three-year-old to trainer Basil Briscoe for 500 guineas. He ran his first race at three in a two-mile hurdle at Southwell in September 1930, and at Leicester on his third outing scored his first win, thereby confounding some in the Briscoe yard who had thought the young horse slow, clumsy and unwilling. The Hon. **Dorothy Paget**, then a newcomer to racehorse ownership, reportedly spent £12,000 to acquire Golden Miller and the hurdler Insurance before the 1931–2 season, and her investment was rewarded the following March when on the same afternoon Golden Miller won his first Cheltenham Gold Cup – at the tender age of five – and Insurance the first of his two Champion Hurdles.

Golden Miller ran up a sequence of five straight wins the following year, including a second Gold Cup from Thomond II, before going to Liverpool for the 1933 Grand National, the first of his five runs in the race. Starting 9–1 favourite, he blundered badly at second Becher's and finally unshipped jockey Ted Leader at the Canal Turn. By the time he returned for another attempt in 1934 he had won a third Gold Cup, beating Avenger and the previous year's National winner Kellsboro' Jack: carrying 12st 2lb round Aintree and starting 8–1 second favourite, he won by five lengths to become the only horse ever to win the Gold Cup and the Grand National in the same year.

Golden Miller ran three times on the Flat – at Warwick and Newmarket in April 1931. and at Liverpool in March 1932.

He proceeded to run up another five-timer the next season, culminating in the famous battle with Thomond in the Gold Cup. From the third last, down the hill and all the way up the straight, Thomond and Golden Miller were at it hammer and tongs, until close home the Miller edged ahead and won by three-quarters of a length. Then it was back to Liverpool – and disaster. At 2–1 the shortest-priced favourite in Grand National history, Golden Miller was already trailing by the eleventh fence, where he attempted to refuse and then, having been persuaded to cross the jump, unshipped Gerry Wilson. The following day he came out again for the Champion Chase – and this time unseated Wilson at the first fence. Owner–trainer relations, strained at the best of times, snapped, and Briscoe demanded the removal of the Paget horses from his yard. So it was under the care of Owen Anthony that Golden Miller won his fifth consecutive Cheltenham Gold Cup in 1936, beating Royal Mail (who would win the 1937 National) and Kellsboro' Jack. But again the National proved a fiasco, with Golden Miller brought down at the first fence, then remounted before refusing at the eleventh – his bogey fence from the previous year. The 1937 Gold Cup was lost to the weather, but Golden Miller was yet again in the line-up at Liverpool for the Grand National. He refused at – guess – the eleventh.

By the beginning of the 1937–8 season Golden Miller was still only 10, but his powers were on the wane, and in the 1938 Gold Cup – ridden by Frenchie Nicholson, father of David – he had to accept the runner-up berth, two lengths behind Morse Code. It was the only time Golden Miller was beaten at Cheltenham. Spared another disagreement with the eleventh fence in the National, Golden Miller ran just once more, in a handicap chase at Newbury nearly a year after his last Gold Cup. He finished unplaced, and was retired, winner of 29 of his 55 races. With Insurance as his grazing companion, he spent his retirement at Miss Paget's Elsenham Stud in Essex, where he was put down in January 1957 after suffering a heart attack.

GOLIATH

Combination bet linking eight selections in 247 bets:

- 28 doubles
- 56 trebles
- 70 four-horse accumulators
- 56 five-horse accumulators
- 28 six-horse accumulators
- 8 seven-horse accumulators
- 1 eight-horse accumulator.

GONE IN ITS COAT

A horse is said to have 'gone in its coat' once it has started to grow its winter coat. In fillies, this tends to signal an imminent loss of form.

GOODWOOD

Goodwood, Chichester, West Sussex PO18 0PS
Tel.: 01243 755022
Fax: 01243 755025
E-mail: racing@goodwood.co.uk
Web: www.goodwood.co.uk

The shape of the Goodwood track, dictated by its position along the rim of the downs, is unique among British racecourses: a straight six furlongs to which a triangular loop is attached by two bends (officially the Top and the Lower), one of which is used for some races, the other for others. Thus a race over one mile starts on the right-hand side of the triangular loop and joins the home straight by means of the Lower Bend – that is, the bend nearer the stands; a race over one mile one furlong starts near the top of the loop on the left and gets to the straight by means of the Lower Bend, whereas a race over 10 furlongs starts at the same place but uses the Top Bend. Over a mile and a half, the race begins very near that start but goes round the top of the loop, using the Top Bend. Races over two and a half miles start near the stands, the runners going the reverse way up the straight before turning left up the Lower Bend, round the top of the loop, and returning to the straight by the Top Bend.

Confused? So, sometimes, are the poor souls who have to doll off the course to indicate to runners in each race where they should be going, and mistakes have been known to occur: the Festival Stakes won by Mtoto in May 1988 was declared void when it was discovered that the horses had been directed on to the Lower Bend rather than the Top, thereby cutting a considerable amount off their intended journey. It can also be confusing to jockeys: during the running of the Goodwood Cup a few years ago Greville Starkey on the leader helped his fellow riders by making elaborate hand-signals as the runners switched from the left-hand to the right-hand rail.

The course is undulating, especially in the straight, where the six-furlong course begins on such a stiff uphill rise that the stalls for that distance cannot be easily seen from the stands, whereas five-furlong races are run mostly downhill: Goodwood has a very fast course over the minimum distance. The luxuriant downland turf here provides one of the best racing surfaces in the country.

The July Meeting, which takes place at the very end of that month – the week after the running of the King George VI and Queen Elizabeth Diamond Stakes at Ascot – and usually spills over into August, is the high point of the Goodwood year, both in the quality of the sport and in social cachet. If the emblem of Royal Ascot is the top hat, at this meeting the panama comes into its own, and the atmosphere is traditionally one of genteel relaxation. It was not always so. Until 1906 morning dress was the order of the day at the July Meeting, but that year Edward VII turned up wearing – horror of horrors! – a lounge suit, giving as an excuse his opinion that Goodwood was 'a garden party with racing tacked on'. Since then the idea of Glorious Goodwood as a sort of garden party with a purpose has persisted, though nowadays it has more of the atmosphere of a festival of quality racing.

The high point of the five-day July Meeting comes on the Wednesday with the running of the **Sussex Stakes**, a top-class event over one mile which provides Goodwood with one of its two Group One races: the other is the **Nassau Stakes** over 10 furlongs for fillies and mares on the Saturday. For punters (as opposed to purists), the high spot of the July Meeting is the Stewards' Cup, a six-furlong handicap which has long been one of the key betting heats of the whole season. The other major races at the July Meeting include the Gordon Stakes over one and a half miles, a sound trial for the St Leger; the Richmond Stakes (six furlongs) for two-year-olds; and the five-furlong King George Stakes, won twice by **Lochsong**. The traditional centrepiece of the meeting is the Goodwood Cup over two miles, middle leg of the 'Stayers' Triple Crown' between Ascot and Doncaster.

Goodwood's major meeting in the earlier part of the season comes in May, where the main interest is in the Predominate Stakes and Lupe Stakes, trials respectively for the Derby and Oaks. The August meeting features the Celebration Mile, first run in 1967 and boasting a roll of honour which includes Classic winners Humble Duty, Brigadier Gerard, Known Fact, To-Agori-Mou, Harayir and Mark Of Esteem.

Goodwood's facilities are excellent. The stands are modern and well appointed, and if you don't like crowds you can still watch the racing from beyond the winning post on Trundle Hill, the venue where the less advantaged racegoing public traditionally went to watch the toffs promenading around in the Richmond Enclosure.

Racing was first staged at Goodwood, on the private estate belonging to the Duke of Richmond, in 1802, and the Goodwood Cup first run in May 1812. The main fixture switched to July in 1814, and for over a century and a half that was about all the racing that Goodwood offered each year. New autumn fixtures were introduced in 1965, and the May Meeting in 1968. A new parade ring and weighing room complex was opened in July 2001.

GOSDEN, JOHN

Son of trainer 'Towser' Gosden, John Gosden was born in 1951. After working as assistant trainer to **Noel Murless** and then to **Vincent O'Brien**, he began his training career in California in 1980, and sent out Royal Heroine to win the Mile at the inaugural Breeders' Cup at Hollywood Park in 1984. He returned to Britain in 1988 to continue his career at Newmarket, first tasting Classic success when Shantou won the 1996 St Leger, and landing the 1997 Derby when Benny The Dip short-headed Silver Patriarch. His third Classic came with Lahan in the One Thousand Guineas in 2000. Other well-known horses trained by Gosden include Catrail, Keen Hunter, Muhtarram, Presenting,

Tamure, Wolfhound, Decorated Hero and Observatory. In 1999 he moved from Newmarket to train on the famous estate at Manton, near Marlborough in Wiltshire.

GOWRAN PARK
Gowran, Co. Kilkenny
Tel.: 056 26225
Fax: 056 26173

A right-handed, undulating track suited to the galloping sort of horse, Gowran Park maintains a high standard of racing, featuring events such as the Thyestes Chase, run in January, and the Red Mills Trial Hurdle. Many famous names have run here, including **Arkle** and **Foinavon**. The first ever racecourse commentary in Ireland took place at Gowran Park in 1952.

GRADING OF RACES
Both on the Flat and over jumps, all races are graded into classes, reflecting their value and importance. On the Flat, there are seven classifications, from Class A (**Pattern** and **Listed** races – that is, the cream of the year's events) down to Class G (**selling races** with small amounts of prize money, and apprentice and amateur races of similar value). Over jumps, there are eight ranks, from Class A (races run under the jumping Pattern) down to Class H (hunter-chases and National Hunt Flat Races – 'bumpers' – of low value).

GRAKLE NOSEBAND
A noseband formed by two straps that cross over on the horse's nose (in place of the more common single noseband) which prevents its pulling excessively. It is named after the 1931 Grand National winner Grakle.

GRAND
Betting slang for £1,000.

GRAND NATIONAL
Grade Three steeplechase; six-year-olds and upwards; 4½ miles (Aintree)

Four and a half miles, 30 fences including **Becher's Brook**, Valentine's Brook and the Chair, countless tales of romance and heroism, and guaranteed racing immortality for the winner – there's simply no race in the world like the Grand National.

Sixty-six horses lined up for the 1929 Grand National, largest field ever for a race in Britain. They had to start in two rows.

Exactly when the race we now know as the Grand National was first run is a matter of some scholarly dispute, hingeing on whether the long-distance steeplechases run near Liverpool between 1836 and 1838 were run at Maghull or, as has recently been asserted with some authority, at nearby Aintree. But there is no disputing that 'The Grand Liverpool Steeplechase' was run at Aintree in 1839 – 'four miles across country', the conditions including the stipulation: 'no rider to open a gate or ride through a gateway, or more than 100 yards along any road, footpath or driftway'. The race was won by **Lottery**, whose name is so appropriate as the first winner of what became the nation's annual flutter that the niceties of the historical record seem irrelevant. That 1839 running involved the runners negotiating 29 obstacles, including a 5ft stone wall in front of the stands and a 'strong paling, next a rough, high jagged hedge, and lastly a brook about six feet wide' which after the dunking of one notable rider would henceforth be known as Becher's Brook.

Three Channel Four Racing presenters have ridden in the Grand National. John Oaksey rode in the race 11 times, completing on four occasions – including 1963, when on Carrickbeg he was beaten by just three-quarters of a length by Pat Buckley on Ayala. John Francome rode in the race 10 times, completing on six occasions: he was third on Rough And Tumble behind Rubstic in 1979, and second on the same horse to Ben Nevis in 1980. Brough Scott had just the one National ride, falling at the 21st fence on Time in 1965.

By the end of the nineteenth century the Grand National had worked its way into the public affection as a race with a unique

Grand National winners since 1990

1990	Mr Frisk	11	K. Bailey	Mr M. Armytage	16–1	38
1991	Seagram	11	D. Barons	N. Hawke	12–1	40
1992	Party Politics	8	N. Gaselee	C. Llewellyn	14–1	40
1993	race void (two false starts)					
1994	Miinnehoma	11	M. Pipe	R. Dunwoody	16–1	36
1995	Royal Athlete	12	Mrs J. Pitman	J. Titley	40–1	35
1996	Rough Quest	10	T. Casey	M.Fitzgerald	7–1F	27
1997	Lord Gyllene	9	S. Brookshaw	A. Dobbin	14–1	36
1998	Earth Summit	10	N. Twiston-Davies	C. Llewellyn	7–1F	37
1999	Bobbyjo	9	T. Carberry *IRE*	P. Carberry	10–1	32
2000	Papillon	9	T. Walsh *IRE*	R. Walsh	10–1	40
2001	Red Marauder	11	N. Mason	R. Guest	33–1	40

character. It completely dominated National Hunt racing, and the turn of the century produced one of the immortals of the game in the shape of **Manifesto**, who ran in the National eight times, winning in 1897 and 1899, finishing third twice (on the second occasion at the age of 15) and fourth once.

A rapid scamper through the next century of Grand National history brings impressions as rapid as the field streaming over the first fence: Ambush II, owned by the Prince of Wales, providing the only royal winner in 1900 . . . Sergeant Murphy winning at the age of 13 in 1923 . . . 100–1 shot Tipperary Tim and the remounted Billy Barton the only finishers in 1928 after **Easter Hero** had caused mayhem at the Canal Turn . . . **Golden Miller** winning in 1934 . . . the minute entire Battleship beating Royal Danieli by a head in 1938 . . . **Vincent O'Brien**'s three consecutive wins in the 1950s with Early Mist, Royal Tan and Quare Times . . . the collapse of the Queen Mother's horse **Devon Loch** on the run-in in 1956 . . . Jay Trump and Freddie fighting out a desperate finish in 1965 . . . the perversity of **Foinavon** winning in 1967 because he was so far behind at the twenty-third fence . . . the gallant **Crisp** being worn down relentlessly by **Red Rum** in 1973 . . . Red Rum's historic third win in 1977 . . . **Bob Champion** defying cancer to win on Aldaniti in 1981 . . . the fiasco of the two false starts leading to the void race in 1993 . . . bomb scare and evacuation in 1997 . . . right up to the mud-caked slog of Red Marauder and Smarty splashing home in 2001.

For a description of the Grand National course, *see* **Aintree**.

GREEN

When used of a horse: inexperienced. (There is a story of the owner being told by the trainer that his horse is green, and replying indignantly, 'Well, he was brown the last time I saw him.') In a race, signs of greenness in a horse – most common in an inexperienced two-year-old – include **changing his legs**, looking at the crowd or other distractions, and generally not catching on immediately that the business of a racehorse is to get his head down and race.

GREY

About 3 per cent of racehorses are grey, ranging from pure white to dark grey. Grey horses tend to get lighter as they get advanced in years (compare photographs of the young Desert Orchid with the older).

Last grey horse to win the Grand National: Nicolaus Silver in 1961.

Last grey horse to win the Derby: Airborne in 1946.

Last grey horse to win the Cheltenham Gold Cup: Desert Orchid in 1989.

GROUP RACES
See **Pattern (Flat)**.

GRUNDY

A bright chestnut colt owned by Carlo Vittadini, trained by **Peter Walwyn** and ridden in all his races by **Pat Eddery**, Grundy was unbeaten in four outings as a two-year-old in 1974, culminating in a six-length victory over Steel Heart in the Dewhurst Stakes. His early-season preparation in 1975 was interrupted when he was kicked in the face one morning by a stable companion, and he had not fully recovered when beaten by Mark Anthony in the Greenham Stakes. He started favourite for the Two Thousand Guineas but went down narrowly to Bolkonski (ridden by Frankie Dettori's father Gianfranco), then won the Irish Two Thousand Guineas at The Curragh. Next stop was Epsom for the Derby, where he started 5–1 second favourite behind hot favourite Green Dancer and stormed home by three lengths from the filly Nobiliary. A straightforward win in the Irish Derby set Grundy up for a showdown between the generations in the King George VI and Queen Elizabeth Diamond Stakes at Ascot on 26 July 1975, when his rivals included the cream of European middle-distance horses: the four-year-old **Bustino**, winner of the St Leger and Coronation Cup; the great mare **Dahlia**, who had won the previous two runnings of the King George; Star Appeal, winner of that year's Eclipse Stakes (and later to land the Arc); Ashmore, On My Way, Dibidale, Libra's Rib, Card King – and two unconsidered outsiders named Kinglet and Highest. But those last two held the key to a fascinating tactical plan: they were both running as pacemakers for Bustino, a proven stayer whose main hope was to expose any chink in Grundy's stamina. As the stalls opened Highest shot off into the lead, taking the field along at a furious pace until, with little over half a mile covered, he fell back and let Kinglet take over. Kinglet led until half a mile from home, when Joe Mercer on Bustino, sensing that the pacemaker was running out of steam, sent his horse on. Bustino swept into the straight the best part of three lengths clear as Eddery galvanised Grundy to go in pursuit. Gradually Grundy got to Bustino's quarters, and then forged half a length clear. But Bustino was not finished with, and he clawed back the lost ground to get to within a neck of Grundy – before the younger horse, straining to the point of exhaustion, found slightly more and stayed on to win by half a length. It was acclaimed as 'The Race of the Century', but it left its mark. Bustino never ran again, and Grundy flopped badly behind Dahlia when 9–4 on for the Benson and Hedges Gold Cup at York the following month. He was then retired to the National Stud in Newmarket, where he stood until being sold to Japan in 1983. He died in May 1992 at the age of 20.

GUEST, RAYMOND

Raymond Guest's colours – chocolate, pale blue hoops and cap – were associated with many famous horses, including the winners of two Derbys, two Cheltenham Gold Cups and a Grand National. His best horse was **Sir Ivor**, winner of the Two Thousand Guineas, Derby, Champion Stakes and Washington, DC International in 1968, though Guest had won his first Derby six years earlier in 1962 with Larkspur. An American who for many years was US ambassador to Ireland, he won one Triple Crown race in his native land: the 1965 Preakness with Tom Rolfe. Over jumps, his best horse was **L'Escargot**, winner of the Cheltenham Gold Cup in 1970 and 1971 and the Grand National in 1975. Raymond Guest died in December 1991 at the age of 84.

GUINEA

In old money, a guinea was one pound one shilling – £1.05 in modern terms. Bloodstock sales in Britain and Ireland (including the auction after a **selling race**) are still conducted in guineas. The most expensive yearling sold at Tattersalls in 2000, a colt by Sadler's Wells out of Darara, went for 3,400,000 guineas – £3,570,000 in real money.

GULFSTREAM PARK

Racetrack in Florida, USA, venue for the **Breeders' Cup** in 1989, 1992 and 1999.

H

HALF-BREDS

Not all the racehorses we see in action over jumps are pure Thoroughbreds (only Thoroughbreds may race on the Flat). Some have elements of other breeds in their genes: for instance, The Fellow, winner of the 1994 Cheltenham Gold Cup, is a French Saddlebred – *selle français* – a purpose-bred strain evolved through selective breeding with non-Thoroughbreds.

HALF-BROTHER/SISTER

A horse is described as a half-brother (or half-sister) to another horse if they are by different stallions but share the same dam. (Horses by the same stallion but out of different dams are *not* described as half-brothers.)

HAMILTON PARK

Bothwell Road, Hamilton, Lanarkshire
ML3 0DW
Tel.: 01698 283806
Fax: 01698 286621
E-mail: morag@hamilton-park.co.uk
Web: www.hamilton-park.co.uk

With marked undulations and a very stiff uphill finish, Hamilton Park puts the emphasis on stamina. The six-furlong course is dead straight, and all distances above six furlongs involve the right-handed pear-shaped loop attached to the straight course: fields for the longest distance run here, one mile five furlongs nine yards, start right in front of the stands then run 'the wrong way' away from the enclosures before veering left on to that loop. When the ground gets heavy here it can be very heavy, making the longer trips a real endurance test.

Since racing first took place in the area in the late eighteenth century, Hamilton has had a rather on–off sort of history – including a period when racing was discontinued for a while after only three horses arrived to compete at a two-day meeting in 1793! Racing was revived in 1800, then lapsed again for most of the nineteenth century, a new course opening in the Park in 1888, and folding in 1907. The current track was first used in 1926.

Hamilton Park was the first course in Great Britain in modern times to stage an evening race meeting – on 18 July 1947. The first race was at 6 p.m., and a crowd of 18,000 racegoers turned up. It was also the first course to stage a Saturday morning programme, on 8 May 1971 (thus avoiding competition with the Arsenal v. Liverpool Cup Final that afternoon).

HAMMOND, JOHN

John Hammond was born in Bromley, Kent, in 1960, educated at Rugby and Trinity College, Dublin, and started his racing career working for Susan Piggott's bloodstock business, moving on to become assistant to Newmarket trainer Patrick Haslam and adding to his experience by working for Jim Dreaper in Ireland and **André Fabre** in France. He took out his first training licence in France in 1987, and four years later had a hugely successful campaign with Suave Dancer, who won the Prix du Jockey-Club, Irish Champion Stakes and Prix de l'Arc de Triomphe. His other charges have included Dear Doctor, Polar Falcon, Sought Out and Dolphin Street, but the best horse to have been trained at his Chantilly stable has been **Montjeu**, winner in 1999 of the Prix du Jockey-Club, Irish Derby and Prix de l'Arc de Triomphe, and in 2000 of the King George VI and Queen Elizabeth Diamond Stakes.

HAND (1)

The unit by which a horse's height is measured – at the shoulder. A hand is four inches.

HAND (2)

Betting slang for 5–1.

HANDS

A jockey is said to have 'good hands' if he or she is a notably sensitive and sympathetic rider, to whom horses respond.

HANDICAP

A handicap is a race in which the weight each horse is to carry is individually allotted by the official **handicapper**, who adjusts the weights according to past performance – the goal being to give all horses in a race a theoretically equal chance of winning. The BHB handicappers maintain a list of official ratings for every horse (from 0 to 140 for the Flat, 0 to 175 for National Hunt), so that handicaps can be framed very speedily. The ratings are revised weekly, but if a horse wins a race after the weights for a future race have been allotted he may incur a **penalty** for that later race in order to take account of the improvement in performance not yet reflected in his official rating. Weights are allotted from the highest (which will be specified in the race conditions) down to the lowest in accordance with the handicapper's assessment of each horse's chance, the lowest-ranked horse being allotted a weight which reflects its perceived chance compared with the top-ranked (and top-weighted) horse, however low such a weight may be and even if it is below the lowest weight actually to be carried in the race. This is the 'long handicap'.

Any horse whose weight is so low that it is below the minimum to be carried is said to be **'out of the handicap'**. If at the five-day or overnight declaration stage the highest-weighted horse still left in the race has less than the originally stipulated top weight to be carried, that horse's weight is raised to the level of the original minimum top weight and all the other weights are raised by the same amount – so a horse originally out of the handicap may then be racing off a true weight in relation to the new top weight.

Some handicaps are restricted to horses within a set range of ratings: for example, a handicap designated '0–70' would be open only to horses rated no higher than 70 on the BHB scale, and thus would afford an opportunity for a lower-class horse to chalk up a win.

By their very nature handicaps cannot be expected to sort out the very best horses, as the purest races can only be run on level terms. But by the same token they are excellent betting races: the big handicaps always attract large fields and the very notion of handicapping makes for open betting. Traditionally the major handicaps of the Flat season are the **Lincoln** at Doncaster, the Royal Hunt Cup (Royal Ascot), Stewards' Cup (Goodwood), **Ebor** (York), **Ayr Gold Cup**, **Cambridgeshire** and **Cesarewitch** (both Newmarket) and November Handicap (Doncaster). Many of the landmarks of the jumping season are handicaps, including the **Thomas Pink Gold Cup** (Cheltenham), **Hennessy Cognac Gold Cup** and **Tote Gold Trophy** (both Newbury), the **Whitbread Gold Cup** (Sandown Park) – and, of course, the **Grand National**.

See also **limited handicap; nursery; rated stakes; out of the handicap**.

HANDICAPPER (1)

Official (under the jurisdiction of the BHB) responsible for allotting ratings.

HANDICAPPER (2)

A horse whose racing tends to be confined to handicaps rather than better-class races. (You may hear a pundit refer to a horse aspiring to run in a Group race as being 'no better than a handicapper'.)

HANDICAPPER (3)

In the USA, 'handicapper' is used to describe a form student.

HANG

In a race, a horse is said to 'hang' when he fails to run in a straight line – or shows an inclination not to keep straight.

HANNON, RICHARD

Born in 1945 and now training at East Everleigh, near Marlborough in Wiltshire, he took out his first licence in 1970, and had his first winner, Ampney Prince, at Newbury on 17 April that year. (Ampney Prince was a son of Ampney Princess, who had been trained by his father Henry.) Hannon now has one of the largest strings in the country, with over 160 horses in training in 2001. He has won the Two Thousand Guineas three times –with Mon Fils (1973), Don't Forget Me (1987) and Tirol (1990), and his other good horses included the flying filly Lyric Fantasy – who won the Nunthorpe Stakes as a two-year-old in 1992 (when Hannon was champion trainer) – and Mr Brooks, winner of the 1992 July Cup. Legend has it that in a previous life Richard Hannon was drummer with the pop group The Troggs, but no one seems entirely sure, and he isn't saying.

Writer Jeffrey Bernard told a famous Richard Hannon story in his book *Talking Horses*:

His wife had triplets, two boys and a girl. One night after his wife and children had gone to bed, Richard was downstairs enjoying a drink with a merry band of lunatic, punting-mad Irishmen when he had a brilliant idea. He crept upstairs, got hold of the triplets, brought them down to the sitting room and arranged them on the sofa. 'Now,' he announced, 'we're going to play Find The Lady.' When Hannon's companions had finished betting on which triplet was the odd girl out, he removed their nappies with the panache of a bullfighter about to administer the coup de grace. But that wasn't the end of the game. 'All out of the room,' Hannon bellowed, 'while I shuffle them!'

HARWOOD, GUY

Guy Harwood, born in 1939, rode 14 winners under National Hunt Rules and took out his first training licence in 1966, having previously been assistant to **Bryan Marshall**. He gradually worked his way to the top of the tree through the performances of horses like Jan Ekels (who won the Queen Elizabeth II Stakes at Ascot in 1973), but his greatest triumphs came in the 1980s. His best horse was the great **Dancing Brave**, who in 1986 won the Two Thousand Guineas, Eclipse Stakes, King George VI and Queen Elizabeth Diamond Stakes and Prix de l'Arc de Triomphe, and he enjoyed further big-race success with such horses as To-Agori-Mou (Two Thousand Guineas and Queen Elizabeth II Stakes 1981), Recitation (Poule d'Essai des Poulains 1981), Kalaglow (Eclipse and King George 1982), Lear Fan (Prix Jacques le Marois 1984), Rousillon (Sussex Stakes 1985) and Warning (Sussex Stakes and Queen Elizabeth II Stakes 1988). On his retirement in 1998 his stable at Pulborough in Sussex was passed to his daughter Amanda Perrett.

HATTON'S GRACE

The first horse to win three Champion Hurdles, Hatton's Grace was bred in Tipperary and sold at Goffs for just 18 guineas, probably on account of his singularly unprepossessing looks. He was first trained by Barney Nugent, then in 1948 moved to **Vincent O'Brien**. His first Champion Hurdle in 1949 was only his third run for this new trainer, but he won by six lengths at 100–7. The following year he started 5–2 favourite and won by a length and a half from Harlech, and as an eleven-year-old in 1951 he came to the last flight half a length behind National Spirit, who had won the race in 1947 and 1948. National Spirit overjumped and crashed to the ground, leaving Hatton's Grace to win unchallenged. He ran in the race again in 1952, but was unplaced behind the rising star Sir Ken, who would himself become a triple Champion Hurdler. Hatton's Grace – who also won the Irish Cesarewitch twice and the Irish Lincolnshire Handicap – took up steeplechasing at the advanced age of 12 and won a race at Leopardstown shortly after his thirteenth birthday. He was then retired, one of the most popular horses in Irish racing history. As Aubrey Brabazon, who had partnered Hatton's Grace to the first two of his Champion Hurdles, observed: 'It was probably because he was such a miserable and scraggy-looking devil that they took him to their hearts.'

HAYDOCK PARK

Newton-le-Willows, Merseyside WA12 0HQ
Tel.: 01942 725963
Fax: 01942 270879
E-mail: haydockpark@rht.net
Web: www.haydock-park.com

The circuit at Haydock Park is a left-handed oval one mile five furlongs round, with a right-hand dog-leg halfway down the back straight. There is a slight rise up the home straight (which is nearly four and a half furlongs long), but generally Haydock is flat with good bends, an ideal stage for the galloping sort of horse. Races of five and six furlongs take place on the straight course. For jump racing, the chase track is inside the Flat course, and the hurdles course inside that – which makes the hurdles circuit the shortest and sharpest of the three.

Lester Piggott rode his first winner at Haydock Park: The Chase in the Wigan Lane Selling Handicap on 18 August 1948. He was 12 years old. Haydock was also the venue of Lester's last winner on British soil: Palacegate Jack on 5 October 1994. He was 58 years old.

Haydock Park stages a single Group One race on the Flat: the **Sprint Cup**, run over six furlongs in September, while other major Flat events include the Lancashire Oaks (July), the Old Newton Cup (also July), first run nearby in 1751, and the Rose of Lancaster Stakes (August). But it is as a jumping track that Haydock Park really excels. The fences are notably well built and some have a drop on the landing side, making the course an ideal place for Grand National preparations: in each of the five years that **Red Rum** ran in the Grand National, his last outing before Liverpool was at Haydock. Among the big jump races are the Tommy Whittle Chase over three miles in December (won by **One Man** in 1995), the Peter Marsh Chase (three miles in January), Champion Hurdle Trial (two miles in January), Long Distance Hurdle (two miles 7½ furlongs in January), De Vere Gold Cup (3 miles 4½ furlongs in February), and Swinton Handicap Hurdle (two miles in May).

HEAD LAD

The head lad is one of the key people in a training stable, responsible for the smooth running of the place in all aspects relating directly to the horses and to the stable lads and lasses who look after them. Many of today's top trainers learned their trade working as head lad – **Barry Hills** with John Oxley, for example, and **Clive Brittain** with **Noel Murless**.

HEAD FAMILY

Alec Head, born in 1924, was apprenticed to his father Willie Head and rode on the Flat and over hurdles. He was runner-up in the 1947 Champion Hurdle on Le Paillon (who was trained by his father and went on to win that year's Prix de l'Arc de Triomphe) and the same year started training himself. From his base at Chantilly he sent out the winners of three Classics in England – the Derby with Lavandin in 1956, One Thousand Guineas with Rose Royale II in 1957 and Two Thousand Guineas with Taboun in 1959 – and his other big-race successes in England included Vimy in the 1955 King George VI and Queen Elizabeth Stakes, two of the first three runnings of the Queen Elizabeth II Stakes with Hafiz II (1955) and Midget II (1957), the 1959 Eclipse Stakes with Saint Crespin III and the 1960 Ascot Gold Cup with Sheshoon. He won the Prix de l'Arc de Triomphe four times, with Nuccio (1952), Saint Crespin III (1959), Ivanjica (1976) and Gold River (1981).

The dynasty continued with Alec's son Freddie Head, born in 1947, who became one of the leading jockeys in France. He won the Prix du Jockey-Club on Goodly (1969, trained by his grandfather Willie), Roi Lear (1973, trained by his father), Val de l'Orne (1975, trained by his father) and Youth (1976), and the Prix de l'Arc de Triomphe on Bon Mot (1966, trained by his grandfather), San San (1972), Ivanjica (1976, trained by his father) and Three Troikas (1979, trained by his sister Criquette). Freddie Head won three Classics in England: the 1982 Two Thousand Guineas on Zino, 1983 One Thousand Guineas on Ma Biche and 1987 One Thousand Guineas on

Miesque (the great filly on whom he also won back-to-back Breeders' Cup Miles in 1987 and 1988). But to some English racegoers he is still best remembered for his ride round Tattenham Corner on Lyphard in the 1972 Derby, when, according to writer Roger Mortimer, he 'went so wide that he appeared desirous of visiting relatives in Putney'.

Alec Head's daughter Criquette Head-Maarek is a leading Chantilly trainer. Born in 1948 and christened Christiane, she took out her first licence in 1977, and has made a particular name for herself as a trainer of fillies, winning the One Thousand Guineas three times, with Ma Biche (1983), Ravinella (1988) and Hatoof (1992). She won the Prix de l'Arc de Triomphe with the filly Three Troikas (owned by her mother) in 1979, becoming the first lady trainer to land the Arc. Her other good horses include Sigy, winner of the 1978 Prix de l'Abbaye, 1996 July Cup winner Anabaa, and Bering, winner of the Prix du Jockey-Club in 1986 and runner-up to Dancing Brave in that year's Arc.

HEADQUARTERS
Informal name for **Newmarket** – the headquarters of British horse racing.

HEART TROUBLE
Racing can put great stress on a horse's heart, and detection of a heart murmur or another heart condition casts a serious shadow over a racing career. Recent veterinary research has suggested that as many as 60 per cent of racehorses have some form of heart murmur, although in only a small fraction of cases is this marked enough to impair performance. Large horses tend to be more affected by heart trouble than small. Some well-known horses have overcome heart complaints, including two post-war Cheltenham Gold Cup winners in the shape of Knock Hard and Fort Leney.

HEDGING
Hedging a bet is reducing your liability. The most common way this is done is when a bookmaker has more to lose if a horse wins than he is comfortable with. He hedges by backing that horse with another bookmaker: thus if the horse wins he has money coming in to cover some (or, if the odds are favourable, all) of the money he is paying out.

HEIGHT (OF HORSES)
A horse is measured, at the shoulder, in 'hands' – a hand being four inches. The usual height for a mature Thoroughbred is around 16 hands (5 feet 4 inches), though some notable horses have been at the extremes of the height scale, including 1992 Grand National winner Party Politics, a giant at over 18 hands.

HEINZ
Combination bet linking six selections in 57 bets:

- 15 doubles
- 20 trebles
- 15 four-horse **accumulators**
- 6 five-horse accumulators
- 1 six-horse accumulator.

See also **Super Heinz**.

HENDERSON, NICKY
Nicky Henderson, born in 1950, worked as assistant trainer to **Fred Winter** between 1974 and 1978, and rode 75 winners as an amateur jockey, including the Fox Hunters' Chase at Aintree on Happy Warrior in 1977. He took out his first trainer's licence in 1978 and has handled a succession of top-class jumpers, notably **See You Then**, who won the Champion Hurdle in 1985, 1986 and 1987. His best steeplechaser has been Remittance Man, winner of the Arkle Chase in 1991 and the Queen Mother Champion Chase in 1992. Other noteworthy Henderson charges have been The Tsarevich (second in the 1987 Grand National), Bacchanal, winner of the Stayers' Hurdle at Cheltenham in 2000, Marlborough, who won the Tote Gold Trophy – the steeplechase version – at Sandown Park in 2001, and three winners of the more traditional Tote Gold Trophy, the valuable handicap hurdle at Newbury: Sharpical (1998), Geos (2000) and Landing Light (2001).

He trains at Seven Barrows, just outside Lambourn.

HENNESSY COGNAC GOLD CUP

Grade Three steeplechase: five-year-olds and upwards: 3 miles 2½ furlongs (Newbury)

The Hennessy is to the autumn what the Whitbread Gold Cup is to the spring – a highly competitive race for the best staying chasers which always generates a healthy ante-post market and draws a huge crowd to the racecourse. For the inaugural race in 1957 that course was not Newbury but Cheltenham, and the first Hennessy went to **Mandarin** – an appropriate winner, as he was owned by Madame Kilian Hennessy, whose family firm sponsored the race. The second running went to Taxidermist, ridden by a 29-year-old amateur named John Lawrence – now John Oaksey – who cajoled an extraordinary turn of foot from his mount up the final hill after they had been sixth at the final fence to beat Kerstin by, in the winning rider's words, 'the length of a cigarette end'. Kerstin herself, by then a Cheltenham Gold Cup winner, took the 1959 race. The Hennessy moved to Newbury in 1960 (Knucklecracker the first winner there), and the 1960s produced a string of memorable races: the giant **Mill House** powering down the straight to win in 1963, with Arkle back in third; **Arkle** winning the 1964 and 1965 runnings effortlessly, then going down to the grey Stalbridge Colonist (who was receiving 2½ stone) after a great battle in 1966. The quality of the Hennessy established by heroes of that stature has been maintained since by the victories of horses like Charlie Potheen (1972), Bachelor's Hall (1977), Diamond Edge (1981), Bregawn (1982), Brown Chamberlin (ridden by John Francome to win in 1983), Burrough Hill Lad (1984: also ridden by John Francome), **One Man** (1994) and Suny Bay (1997).

There is an Irish race named the Hennessy Cognac Gold Cup, run over three miles at **Leopardstown** in February: Florida Pearl won in 1999 and 2000.

HEREFORD

Roman Road, Holmer, Hereford HR4 9QU
Tel.: 01432 273560
Fax: 01432 352807
E-mail: info@hereford-racecourse.co.uk
Web: www.hereford-racecourse.co.uk

Hereford is a right-handed, square-shaped track of about one and a half miles round, with gentle undulations including a downhill run towards the home straight. Its bends are mostly easy and thus it favours the galloping horse, but many jockeys consider the fences here to be stiff, and sound jumping can be at a premium, especially in novice chases. Racing at Hereford, which has been taking place in the great cathedral city since at least the late eighteenth century, tends to cater for the lower class of chaser or hurdler, but the course enjoys a strong local following and

Hennessy Cognac Gold Cup winners since 1990

1990	Arctic Call	7	O. Sherwood	J. Osborne	5–1	13
1991	Chatam	7	M. Pipe	P. Scudamore	10–1	15
1992	Sibton Abbey	7	G. Hubbard	A. Maguire	40–1	13
1993	Cogent	9	A. Turnell	D. Fortt	10–1	9
1994	One Man	6	G. Richards	A. Dobbin	4–1	16
1995	Couldnt Be Better	8	C. Brooks	D. Gallagher	15–2	11
1996	Coome Hill	7	W. Dennis	J. Osborne	11–2	11
1997	Suny Bay	8	C. Brooks	G. Bradley	9–4F	14
1998	Teeton Mill	9	Miss V. Williams	N. Williamson	5–1	16
1999	Ever Blessed	7	M. Pitman	T. Murphy	9–2F	13
2000	King's Road	7	N. Twiston-Davies	J. Goldstein	7–1	17

On 1 May 1975 there were so many runners at Hereford for what had been planned as an evening meeting that several races had to be divided. In the end the programme started at 1.30 p.m. and consisted of 14 races – the greatest number yet held on a single card in Britain. Off-time of the last was 8.02 p.m.

racegoers occasionally get the chance to glimpse a top-notch horse: 1982 Cheltenham Gold Cup winner Silver Buck, for example, won here twice in the 1979–80 season.

HERN, DICK

William Richard Hern was born in 1921. From 1952 to 1957 he was assistant to Michael Pope, and was then taken on by Major Lionel Holliday as private trainer: it was for Major Holliday that Hern trained his first Classic winner, Hethersett in the 1962 St Leger. He moved to West Ilsley in Berkshire at the end of 1962, and from that famous stable sent out a steady procession of big-race

---

Dick Hern's Classic winners

Two Thousand Guineas
1971 Brigadier Gerard
1989 Nashwan
One Thousand Guineas
1974 Highclere
1995 Harayir
Derby
1979 Troy
1980 Henbit
1989 Nashwan
Oaks
1977 Dunfermline
1980 Bireme
1983 Sun Princess
St Leger
1962 Hethersett
1965 Provoke
1974 Bustino
1977 Dunfermline
1981 Cut Above
1983 Sun Princess

---

winners, including **Brigadier Gerard**, beaten only once in 18 races and winner of the 1971 Two Thousand Guineas from Mill Reef. Hern's other top horses included Derby winners **Troy** (1979), Henbit (1980) and **Nashwan** (1989); **Bustino**, winner of the 1974 St Leger and runner-up to Grundy in the 1975 King George at Ascot; Sun Princess, winner of the Oaks and St Leger in 1983; Highclere (1974 One Thousand Guineas and Prix de Diane); and the phenomenally fast sprinter **Dayjur**, sensationally pipped in the 1990 Breeders' Cup Sprint at Belmont Park after jumping a shadow in the straight. His horses won the King George five times: Brigadier Gerard (1972), Troy (1979), Ela-Mana-Mou (1980), Petoski (1985) and Nashwan (1989). In 1984 Dick Hern was badly injured in a hunting accident which left him partly paralysed, and in 1988 a serious heart problem caused his licence to be temporarily granted to his assistant Neil Graham (now husband of Lesley): it was in Neil Graham's name that the stable's Minster Son won the 1988 St Leger. The West Ilsley stables were owned by the Queen, and the termination of Hern's lease there attracted a great deal of controversy – and sympathy for the departing trainer. But with the help of Sheikh Hamdan Al **Maktoum**, one of his principal patrons and owner of Nashwan, he started a new operation at Kingwood, just outside Lambourn, and carried on the Classic tradition from the new base when Harayir won the 1995 One Thousand Guineas. Leading trainer in 1962, 1972, 1980 and 1983, he retired from training at the end of the 1997 season.

HEXHAM

High Yarridge, Hexham, Northumberland NE46 2JP
Tel.: 01434 606881
Fax: 01434 605814
E-mail: hexrace@aol.com
Web: www.hexham-racecourse.co.uk

Set 800 feet above sea level and commanding glorious views across the Northumbrian countryside, Hexham is one of the most scenic courses in the country. In the eighteenth century races were held down in Hexham itself, but the site in High Yarridge was established late in the nineteenth, and those who make the steep climb from the town are rewarded not only with stunning vistas, but with a course whose homely rural charm is hard to match anywhere.

Bobby Renton, trainer of 1950 Grand National winner Freebooter and for a while of Red Rum, had his last ride in a race at Hexham on 30 September 1963 when he was 75 years old.

Unsurprisingly, given its situation, the track itself – left-handed, and one and a half miles round – is undulating, with a stiff climb out of the back straight. In steeplechases, the finish is along a spur which bypasses three fences in the straight. The fences are fairly easy but this is a testing track, with that climb to the home turn putting demands on a horse's stamina and resolution.

HIDE, EDWARD

Born in Shropshire in 1937, Edward Hide rode his first winner on Ritornello at Chepstow in September 1951. His last victory in Britain – Hi-Tech Leader at Nottingham on 13 August 1985 – was the 2,591st domestic winner of his career, placing him at the time of his retirement sixth in the list of winning-most British riders. He rode six Classic winners: Cantelo (St Leger 1959), Pia (Oaks 1967), Waterloo (One Thousand Guineas 1972), Mrs McArdy (One Thousand Guineas 1977), Morston (Derby 1973) and Julio Mariner (St Leger 1978). He was leading jockey in the north no fewer than 16 times.

HILLS FAMILY

Web: www.barryhills.com

This British racing dynasty began with the birth of Barrington William Hills – Barry Hills – in 1937, son of Tom Rimell's head lad. He was an apprentice with trainer George Colling, riding nine winners, then worked for Fred Rimell and became head lad to John Oxley at Newmarket. Legend has it that he was such a shrewd backer of horses (particularly Oxley's Frankincense, 100–8

winner of the 1968 Lincoln Handicap) that he was able to squirrel away a hefty nest egg, put to good use when he was granted his first trainer's licence in 1969, setting up shop in Lambourn. Within four years Hills had reached the big time, winning the 1973 Prix de l'Arc de Triomphe with **Rheingold**. To date he has won three Classics – 1978 One Thousand Guineas with Enstone Spark, 1979 Two Thousand Guineas with Tap On Wood (ridden by **Steve Cauthen** in his first season riding in Britain) and 1994 St Leger with Moonax – and a host of other major races. Hawaiian Sound, beaten a head by Shirley Heights in the 1978 Derby (one of four runners-up Hills has had in the premier Classic), won the Benson and Hedges Gold Cup in 1978, and Cormorant Wood took that race in 1984 and the Champion Stakes in 1983. Gildoran won the Ascot Gold Cup twice (1984 and 1985). Sir Harry Lewis won the 1987 Irish Derby. And then there were Handsome Sailor, top miler Distant Relative, the highly popular **Further Flight**, Irish One Thousand Guineas winners Nicer (1993) and Hula Angel (1999), top sprinter Royal Applause, and leading two-year-olds Auction House and Distant Music. After a spell on the estate at Manton, Barry Hills returned to the Lambourn area, where he now trains around 160 horses from his new, purpose-built complex.

Of Barry's sons, the eldest, John, trains in Upper Lambourn – his best horse to date has been Broadway Flyer, winner of the Chester Vase and Gordon Stakes in 1994 – and the twins Michael and Richard, born in 1963, are both top jockeys. Michael Hills rode rode his first winner on Sky Thief at Nottingham on 13 August 1979. His biggest victory came on Shaamit in the 1996 Derby, and he rode Pentire to win the King George VI and Queen Elizabeth Diamond Stakes in the same year. He was also the regular partner of Further Flight. Richard Hills, who rode his first winner on Border Dawn at Doncaster on 26 October 1979, won his first Classic on Harayir in the 1995 One Thousand Guineas and is now retained by that filly's owner Sheikh Hamdan Al Maktoum. Other big victories in the

Sheikh's colours came on Almutawakel in the 1999 Dubai World Cup and the One Thousand Guineas in 2000 on Lahan, while he landed the 1999 St Leger for Godolphin on Mutafaweq.

HOBDAY
See **whistling and roaring**.

HOCK
The joint in a horse's hind leg between the stifle and the pastern. Although it corresponds visually to the knee in the front leg, it is in fact equivalent to the ankle in a human.

HOD
Bookmaker's large leather satchel – once a familiar sight bulging with readies, though in modern joints in the betting ring the receptacle for all that cash is much more discreet.

HOLLYWOOD PARK
Racetrack in Los Angeles, California: venue of the **Breeders' Cup** in 1984 (the inaugural running), 1987 and 1997.

HONG KONG
Horse racing is big business in Hong Kong. Betting turnover in the former colony in the financial year 1999/2000 was HK$83.4 billion, and significant moves are afoot to make Hong Kong a force in world horse racing, both by sending home raiders overseas and by staging highly valuable races which will attract the best horses from around the world. Fairy King Prawn's victory in the Yasuda Kinen in Japan in June 2000 was the first win in an international race for a Hong Kong horse; Indigenous (who had run unplaced behind **Daylami** when the first Hong Kong-trained runner in the King George VI and Queen Elizabeth Diamond Stakes in 1999) was second in the 1999 Japan Cup; and Fairy King Prawn was beaten a whisker by Jim And Tonic in the Dubai Duty Free at Nad Al Sheba on Dubai World Cup day 2001. The Hong Kong Cup, run at Sha Tin in December, forms the final leg of the **Emirates World Series**: the race was won in 1999 by Jim And Tonic, trained in France by **François** Doumen**, and in 2000 by Godolphin's Fantastic Light, and is scheduled to carry a purse of HK$14 million in 2001. Sha Tin, a racecourse built on reclaimed land and opened in 1978, hosts most of Hong Kong's big races. The other racecourse here is Happy Valley, where racing has taken place since 1846. At both tracks average daily attendance is around 50,000 – further testimony to the firm grip which racing has on the Hong Kong population.

HOOD
A hood is a piece of equine headgear similar to **blinkers**, but leaving the eyes clear and covering the ears.

HORSERACE BETTING LEVY BOARD
See **Levy Board**.

HORSES FOR COURSES
A maxim based on the notion that certain horses will run well on certain tracks. Punters do well to take this into account, especially on notoriously quirky tracks such as Chester, Epsom or Windsor. Any horse running on a course where it has won before is worthy of consideration, for it is clearly able to act effectively on that track; exactly how much importance you attach to such evidence depends on both horse and course.

HOUGHTON SALE
The Houghton Yearling Sale, held by **Tattersalls** at Newmarket in late September/early October, is the premier yearling sale in Europe.

HUNT, NELSON BUNKER
A Texas oil magnate who made a considerable fortune by cornering the world market in silver and proceeded to lose a good deal of it when the market crashed, Hunt owned many very well-known horses. Perhaps the greatest was **Dahlia**, dual winner of both the King George VI and Queen Elizabeth Stakes (1973 and 1974) and the Benson and Hedges Gold Cup (1974 and 1975). In 1976 Bunker Hunt won the Derby with Empery and the French equivalent, the Prix du Jockey-Club, with

Youth. His other well-known horses included Nobiliary, the last filly to be placed in the Derby when second to Grundy in 1975, and 1977 Coronation Cup winner Exceller, and he owned a share of 1968 Arc winner **Vaguely Noble**. He was leading owner in Britain in 1973 and 1974.

HUNTER–CHASE

According to the Rules of Racing, a hunter-chase is 'a weight-for-age Steeple Chase confined to horses certified by a Master of Hounds to have been hunted and to amateur riders'. The two major hunter-chases of the year are the Christies Foxhunter Chase at the Cheltenham Festival, and the Martell Fox Hunters' Chase at Aintree over the Grand National fences. Most recent horse to win both of these is Cavalero, who won at Aintree in 1998 and Cheltenham in 2000 to join an elite band of hunter-chasers which includes Spartan Missile, Rolls Rambler, Grittar, Eliogarty, Call Collect and Double Silk. Some horses graduate from hunter-chases to running in the big races under Rules – the aforementioned Grittar, for example, won the 1982 Grand National – while fields for hunter–chases often include an old favourite retired from the rigours of competing at the highest level: for example, Rough Quest, brilliant winner of the 1996 Grand National, won a hunter–chase at the age of 13 at Newbury in March 1999.

HUNTINGDON

Brampton. Huntingdon. Cambridgeshire
PE18 8NN
Tel.: 01480 453373
Fax: 01480 455275
E-mail: huntingdon@rht.net
Web: www.huntingdon-racecourse.com

Huntingdon's right-handed circuit of one and a half miles round is flat and fast, with easy bends and well-made fences – including an open ditch right in front of the stands which provides one of the viewing highlights here. Although not in the premier league of jumping tracks, Huntingdon stages some very good races, notably the Peterborough Chase over two miles $4\frac{1}{2}$ furlongs in November.

This always attracts a small but high-class field: recent winners include Sabin Du Loir (who beat **Norton's Coin** and **Desert Orchid**), Remittance Man, Martha's Son, Dublin Flyer, **One Man** (who beat Viking Flagship) and Edredon Bleu. The Sidney Banks Novices' Hurdle, run in February, is a good pre-Cheltenham outing for staying novice hurdlers: 1998 winner French Holly duly went on to land the Royal & SunAlliance Hurdle at the Cheltenham Festival.

There has been racing on the present Huntingdon course since 1886, and the facilities are neat, compact and very well ordered.

HURDLE

The standard design of obstacle to be jumped in a hurdle race is a wooden frame like a sheep hurdle into which are woven gorse and birch. Hurdles must not measure less than 3ft 6in from the top bar to the bottom bar. In the first two miles of a hurdle race there must be a minimum of eight flights of hurdles, with an additional flight every complete quarter mile beyond that. Experiments have been carried out with the use of a different design of hurdles, more like small steeplechase fences, which supposedly encourage the jumping horse to arch his back, and thus make easier the transition from hurdles to steeplechases fences later in his career.

HYPERION

Foaled in 1930, bred and owned by the 17th Earl of Derby, Hyperion was so small at birth that it was debated whether he should be allowed to survive. But he gradually grew into a fine – if still very diminutive – young horse, a chestnut with four white stockings. As a two-year-old in 1932 he won two of his five races outright and dead-heated in another, and was not considered in the top bracket. But he went through his three-year-old season in 1933 unbeaten: he won the Chester Vase, the Derby (by four lengths), the Prince of Wales's Stakes and the St Leger (easily by three lengths). At the end of that season his trainer George Lambton stopped training for Lord Derby: Hyperion came under the care of Colledge Leader, and the colt was never as good as he had been at three, being beaten in his main target, the Ascot Gold Cup. At stud he was a huge success, covering mares until the year he died, siring the winners of 748 races and producing some very good offspring, including 1941 Derby winner Owen Tudor; the great Sun Chariot, winner of the fillies' Triple Crown in 1942; and the Queen's 1953 Derby runner-up and 1954 King George winner Aureole. In his old age he was fascinated by aeroplanes: gazing intently out of his box, he would follow their flight across the sky until they disappeared from sight. He died in 1960 at the age of 30. A magnificent John Skeaping statue of Hyperion stands outside the Jockey Club Rooms in Newmarket High Street.

I

IDENTIFICATION (HORSES)

Since the temptation to switch one horse for one of very similar looks but greatly superior ability might just prove too much for some people, the identification of horses is very closely monitored. Every Thoroughbred is issued with a 'passport' which describes his colouring and markings and must accompany that horse to the races and be offered for examination on entering the racecourse stables. Since 1999 every Thoroughbred foal born in the British Isles has had implanted in its neck a 12mm microchip which when scanned reveals a 15-digit reference number.

'IGGINS

This Josh Gifford-trained gelding, who first ran in 1995, is the only horse in British racing history whose name began with a mark of punctuation rather than a letter of the alphabet. His initial apostrophe caused such problems to newspaper databases that a rule was brought in that names must henceforth begin with a letter.

INBREEDING

In the bloodstock business, inbreeding is when a particular horse or family of horses appears on both sides of a pedigree, the theory being that this can strengthen some chosen feature.

INJURED JOCKEYS' FUND

1 Lynx Court, Victoria Way, Newmarket,
 Suffolk CB8 7SH
Tel.: 01638 662246
Fax: 01638 668988
E-mail: ijfund@aol.com
Web: www.ijf.org.uk

The Injured Jockeys' Fund was founded in 1964, back in the Dark Ages when a jockey whose career had been brought to an untimely halt – temporary or permanent – through injury had to fend for himself. Paddy Farrell and **Tim Brookshaw**, two well-known jump jockeys, suffered injuries which left them paralysed, and the Farrell Brookshaw Appeal was launched to help them – thanks in large measure to the efforts of top amateur jockey John Lawrence, now **John Oaksey**. Farrell and Brookshaw suggested that the Fund be developed to assist all jockeys in similar plight, and thus was born the IJF. The Fund exists to provide help to all injured jockeys, professional or amateur, jumping or Flat, who have been licensed to ride under the Rules of Racing, and the help offered takes many forms, including the provision of housing. A particularly popular part of the IJF's drive to secure funds is its highly popular annual Christmas card, tens of thousands of which are sold annually – a good number on freezing racecourses in the run-up to the festive season by Chicky Oaksey (wife of the Noble Lord) and her team of helpers. Brough Scott and John Oaksey are currently on the Fund's board of trustees.

INSPECTOR OF COURSES

Jockey Club official whose responsibility is to inspect and monitor safety aspects at racecourses. Some well-known former jockeys, including Ron Barry and Richard Linley, are inspectors of courses.

INTELLIGENCE

Just how 'intelligent' is the racehorse? Most racing fans would like to think that their favourite horses are very clued up about what they are doing and the response they are triggering in spectators, but the harsh reality is somewhat different. According to the book *The Nature of Horses* by Stephen Budiansky (strongly recommended for those who want to know more about a horse than whether he'll win the 2.30 at Market Rasen), 'The good news is that horses have a relatively large brain for an animal of their size. The bad news is that they use most of it just to keep their feet in the right place.' The horse's brain is about the size of an adult human fist and on average weighs about 650 grams – around 0.14 per cent of body weight, compared with about 2 per cent in a human. Whatever the brain size, what matters is what is performed and achieved with it, and the question of 'intelligence' in a horse is difficult to define. A horse does not have the intellectual capacity to solve the Picture Puzzle or get interfered with in running as he knows he's expected at Chepstow next week; nor does he know where the winning post is. In a range of tests, horses were shown to learn approximately as quickly as tropical aquarium fish, guinea pigs and octopuses. But it has also been shown by animal behaviourists that once a horse has managed to learn something it has an excellent memory with which to retain that lesson.

But how intelligent do we want our equine heroes to be? To describe a horse as a 'thinker' is not generally intended as a compliment: rather, it implies a level of individuality which renders him suspect as a racehorse, since he will be bright enough to slow down when it hurts. In any event, once we start to talk in terms of horses thinking, or of showing courage or determination or other more specific human traits such as playing up to the crowd, we are entering dangerous territory. We cannot know what a horse is feeling or what is motivating him, and yet we have to talk of horses in human terms because there is no other suitable vocabulary. Timeform may have described **Pilsudski** as 'game and genuine', and **Amrullah** as 'thoroughly irresolute'; in both cases the judgement boils down to a matter of consistency, or lack of it. 'Unreliability' in a horse means that his form cannot be taken at face value every time he runs: at some times he will run better than at

others. But the whole basis of form study is shaky if horses are not consistent, and therefore consistency – or genuineness – is a quality rightly prized in a racehorse.

The key to the psychology of the racehorse is, of course, that it is a beast of flight: its natural instinct is to put as much distance as it can, as fast as it can, between itself and any predator. When your hero lugs himself up the Cheltenham hill, he is not trying to get to the winning post, he is trying to get away from his pursuers.

INTERNATIONAL CLASSIFICATIONS

The International Classifications are the annual ratings, agreed by a committee of **handicappers** from the participating countries, of the best horses to have raced on the Flat around the world. (The National Hunt equivalent are the **Anglo-Irish Jumps Classifications**.) The scheme was inaugurated by Britain, Ireland and France in 1977 and now covers 10 countries – Britain, Ireland, France, Germany, Italy, the USA, Canada, Dubai, Japan and Hong Kong – with South Africa and Australia likely to be incorporated in the near future. Ranked horses are grouped in the categories:

- two-year-olds;
- three-year-olds, divided into the distances sprint, mile, intermediate ($9\frac{1}{2}$ furlongs plus), long (11 furlongs plus), and extended (14 furlongs plus);
- four-year-olds and upwards, divided into the same categories as the three-year-olds.

INTERNATIONAL STAKES
Group One: three-year-olds and upwards:
1 mile 2½ furlongs (York)

In its short life the International Stakes has seen fields of the highest class and drama galore. The race's early reputation for producing the unexpected began with its first running – as the Benson and Hedges Gold Cup – in August 1972, when the mighty **Brigadier Gerard** met with his first and only defeat at the hands of Roberto. An odds-on favourite went down again in the second running: **Rheingold** started at 6–4 on but could finish only third behind 14–1 shot Moulton. The 1974 running saw another odds-on favourite in the shape of the great filly **Dahlia**, who restored order to the race's reputation by winning, and she was back in 1975, this time a supposed supporting act to Derby and King George winner **Grundy**, the fourth odds-on favourite in a row. Poor Grundy had clearly not got over 'The Race of the Century' against **Bustino** at Ascot the previous month, and trailed in fourth as Dahlia and Lester Piggott notched up back-to-back victories.

The International Stakes, in its various guises, has proved something of a graveyard for odds-on favourites. In the 29 runnings between 1972 and 2000, 13 horses started odds on and nine were beaten: Brigadier Gerard (1–3 in 1972), Rheingold (4–6 in 1973), Grundy (4–9 in 1975), Trepan (10–11 in 1976), Artaius (8–11 in 1977), Oh So Sharp (2–5 in 1985), Cacoethes (2–5 in 1989), Stagecraft (5–6 in 1991) and Bosra Sham (4–5 in 1997). During the same period the four odds-on winners were Dahlia (8–15 in 1974), Troy (1–2 in 1979), Assert (4–5 in 1982) and Giant's Causeway (10–11 in 2000).

Since those dramatic opening years, the hallmark of this race – renamed the International Stakes in 1986 – has been class, with four Classic winners following Roberto on to the roll of honour: Wollow (Two Thousand Guineas 1976), **Troy** (Derby 1979),

Commanche Run (St Leger 1984: he beat 5–2 on hotpot **Oh So Sharp** in the 1985 race) and Rodrigo de Triano (1992). Dahlia's feat of winning the race twice has been emulated by Ezzoud (1993 and 1994) and Halling (1995 and 1996), while other notable heroes and heroines of the York showpiece include **Triptych** (1987), **Singspiel** (1997) and **Giant's Causeway**, whose head victory over Kalanisi in 2000 upheld the race's tradition not only of class but of thrilling finishes.

INTERNET

The rapid development of the internet has begun to be felt in the world of horse racing. Most racecourses have websites dispensing a range of information. Studs advertise their stallions and facilities on the web, and some sales companies are using the new technology to conduct international 'virtual auctions'. Websites run by newspapers and other organisations allow access to a stupendous range of information. The internet has added a whole new dimension to betting, with many bookmakers now making available the means to bet at the click of a mouse (providing your credit card or switch card is handy), and a particular innovation in betting over the net is the growth of sites where an individual can act as punter or layer. There is even a site devoted to British racing's favourite loser, **Quixall Crossett**. And don't forget Channel Four's own website – www.channel4.com – and the Channel Four Racing e-mail address:

International Stakes winners since 1990

1990	In The Groove	3	D. Elsworth	S. Cauthen	4–1	9
1991	Terimon	5	C. Brittain	M. Roberts	16–1	6
1992	Rodrigo de Triano	3	P. Chapple-Hyam	L. Piggott	8–1	12
1993	Ezzoud	4	M. Stoute	W. R. Swinburn	28–1	11
1994	Ezzoud	5	M. Stoute	W. R. Swinburn	4–1	8
1995	Halling	4	S. bin Suroor	W. R. Swinburn	9–4F	6
1996	Halling	5	S. bin Suroor	L. Dettori	6–4F	6
1997	Singspiel	5	M. Stoute	L. Dettori	4–1	4
1998	One So Wonderful	4	L. Cumani	Pat Eddery	6–1	8
1999	Royal Anthem	4	H. Cecil	G. Stevens	3–1JF	12
2000	Giant's Causeway	3	A. O'Brien *IRE*	M. Kinane	10–11F	6

racing@channel4.com. Internet technology is developing and spreading so rapidly that it pays to keep up with the latest moves: to that end, the weekly 'Net Prophet' column in the *Racing Post* is strongly recommended.

IRELAND

Web: www.irish-racing.com

As long ago as the seventeenth century it was recognised that the geography, geology and climate of Ireland were singularly well suited to the breeding of horses. 'The soil is of a sweet and plentiful grass,' wrote Sir William Temple in 1673, 'which will raise a large breed; and the hills, especially near the sea-coasts, are hard and rough and so fit to give them shape and breath and sound feet.' Much Irish pasture is rich in limestone, which produces particular strength of bone in a horse, and as a large and healthy bloodstock industry developed in Ireland, so the special affinity of the Irish with the horse produced not only fine horses but fine horsemen and women to go with them.

In November 2001 the state-owned Horse Racing Ireland is taking over the functions of the Irish Horseracing Authority as governing body of Irish racing. The **Turf Club** is the Irish equivalent of the Jockey Club.

There are 27 racecourses in Ireland, ranging from the major venues such as The Curragh and Leopardstown to the tiny country tracks like Kilbeggan and the once-a-year racing on the beach at Laytown. In racing terms there is no border between Ireland and Ulster: those 27 courses include the Northern Ireland pair of Down Royal and Downpatrick.

Ireland is a major **breeding** country. **Coolmore Stud** in Tipperary is the largest stallion station in Europe, and most of the big owner–breeders – including the Aga Khan and the Maktoums – have studs in Ireland, their young horses thriving on that sweet and plentiful grass. At the other end of the spectrum are farmers who might keep a mare or two and breed on a very small scale.

Irish horsemen have made a huge impact on racing around the globe. There are trainers such as **Vincent O'Brien** and **Paddy Prendergast**, and more recently **Dermot Weld**, **Aidan O'Brien** and **John Oxx**. There is a steady procession of jockeys bred in Ireland or Northern Ireland who, either from their home base or after moving overseas, have reached the top of the tree. On the Flat, there are names like **Pat Eddery**, **Michael Kinane**, **Johnny Murtagh**, **John Reid**, **Kieren Fallon** and Richard Hughes. Over jumps, it seems that the majority of jockeys who have made their mark on the sport in Britain since the Second World War are of Irish extraction: **Tim Molony**, **Pat Taaffe**,

Winners of the Irish Classics since 1990

year	2000 Guineas	1000 Guineas	Derby	Oaks	St Leger
1990	Tirol	In The Groove	Salsabil	Knight's Baroness	Ibn Bey
1991	Fourstars Allstar	Kooyonga	Generous	Possessive Dancer	Turgeon
1992	Rodrigo de Triano	Marling	St Jovite	User Friendly	Mashaallah
1993	Barathea	Nicer	Comm. In Chief	Wemyss Bight	Vintage Crop
1994	Turtle Island	Mehthaaf	Balanchine	Bolas	Vintage Crop
1995	Spectrum	Ridgewood Pearl	Winged Love	Pure Grain	Strategic Choice
1996	Spinning World	Matiya	Zagreb	Dance Design	Oscar Schindler
1997	Desert King	Classic Park	Desert King	Ebadiyla	Oscar Schindler
1998	Desert Prince	Tarascon	Dream Well	Winona	Kayf Tara
1999	Saffron Walden	Hula Angel	Montjeu	Ramruma	Kayf Tara
2000	Bachir	Crimplene	Sinndar	Petrushka	Arctic Owl
2001	Black Minnaloushe	Imagine	Galileo	Lailani	

Willie Robinson, Ron Barry, Tommy Stack, Jonjo O'Neill, Richard Dunwoody, and currently Charlie Swan, **Norman Williamson**, **Mick Fitzgerald**, Ruby Walsh, Paul Carberry and **Tony McCoy**.

That so many top jump jockeys are Irish should occasion little surprise, since steeplechasing is especially close to the Irish heart: the word itself comes from the day in 1752 when Edmund Blake and Cornelius O'Callaghan rode a race in County Cork from Buttevant Church to the steeple of the church at Doneraile, four and a half miles away. Nowadays the twin peaks of the jumps season in Ireland are two major festival meetings: Punchestown in April and Galway (featuring the Galway Plate) in late July. Outside these meetings, the major Irish races over jumps are:

- **Irish Grand National** at Fairyhouse;
- *Hennessy Cognac Gold Cup* at Leopardstown (the Irish equivalent of the Cheltenham Gold Cup);
- *AIG Europe Champion Hurdle* at Leopardstown;
- *Pierse Handicap Hurdle* (formerly the Ladbroke) at Leopardstown.

On the Flat, there are 10 Group One events in Ireland: the five Irish Classics described below, plus:

- *Tattersalls Gold Cup* for older horses (The Curragh, May);
- *Phoenix Stakes* for two-year-olds (Leopardstown, August);
- **Irish Champion Stakes** (Leopardstown, September);
- *Moyglare Stud Stakes* for two-year-old fillies (The Curragh, September);
- *National Stakes* for two-year-olds (The Curragh, September).

The programme of Irish Classics closely follows that in Britain, with the races so timed that a horse can run in the British version and then go on to the Irish. All five are run at The Curragh.

The *Irish Two Thousand Guineas* (one mile, for three-year-old colts and fillies) was first run in 1921 and is often a consolation prize for horses beaten in the English version run earlier in May. Since the Second World War four horses have won both: Right Tack (1969), Don't Forget Me (1987), Tirol (1990) and Rodrigo de Triano (1992). Other notable winners include colts who went on to land the Derby – Hard Ridden (1958), Santa Claus (1964) and **Grundy** (1975) – and **Triptych**, who in 1985 became the first filly ever to win the race.

Similarly, the *Irish One Thousand Guineas* (one mile, for three-year-old fillies), first run in 1922, is closely connected with the English, though no filly has won both. None the less, plenty of top-notch performers have won this, including, over the last couple of decades, the likes of Al Bahathri (1985), Sonic Lady (1986), In The Groove (1990), Kooyonga (1991), Marling (1992) and Ridgewood Pearl (1995: she won the Breeders' Cup Mile later that year).

The **Irish Derby**, pinnacle of the Irish Classic programme, is described in its own entry below.

The *Irish Oaks* (one and a half miles, for three-year-old fillies) was first run in 1895, though its distance was one mile until 1915. Since 1945 nine Oaks winners at Epsom have gone on to score at The Curragh: Masaka (1948), Altesse Royale (1971), Juliette Marny (1975), Fair Salinia (1978), Blue Wind (1981), Unite (1987), Diminuendo (1988: she dead-heated with Melodist at The Curragh), User Friendly (1992) and Ramruma (1999). The great **Dahlia** burst into the big time when displaying an astonishing turn of foot to win this race in 1973.

There is a significant difference between the *Irish St Leger* (one and three-quarter miles, first run in 1915) and its English counterpart at Doncaster: the Irish version is now open to horses over the age of three. That great change came about in 1983, when the race went to the four-year-old filly Mountain Lodge, and since then several top-class stayers have taken this valuable prize, including dual winners **Vintage Crop** (1993–4), Oscar Schindler (1996–7) and Kayf Tara (1998–9). Last horse to win the English and Irish St Legers in the same year was Touching Wood in 1982.

IRISH CHAMPION STAKES

Group One; three-year-olds and upwards;
1¼ miles (Leopardstown)

Cast an eye down the list of recent winners of the Irish Champion Stakes, and consider whether any race run in Europe can boast a more consistently high quality. Scroll back further down the roll of honour and the idea that this has always been a race of the highest order grows. The Irish Champion Stakes began life as the Joe McGrath Memorial Stakes at Leopardstown in 1976, when it was won by that year's Irish Derby winner Malacate. Other notable winners in the early years included Kings Lake (1981), Assert (1982) and the ultra-tough mare Stanerra (1983). In 1984 the race was transferred to Phoenix Park and became the Phoenix Champion Stakes. The first running under that name, at the time the most valuable race ever run in Ireland, went to **Sadler's Wells**, then a top-class 10-furlong racehorse and now the most influential sire of the age. Commanche Run won in 1985, **Triptych** in 1987, Indian Skimmer in 1988 and subsequent Arc winner Carroll House in 1989, but Phoenix Park racecourse was closed after the 1990 running and the race returned to Leopardstown, where it has enjoyed a golden period. Suave Dancer, winner in 1991, won the Arc that year, while the 1992 running produced one of the greatest races of the modern era, with old rivals Dr Devious, winner of the Derby, and St Jovite, who had beaten him in the Irish Derby, locked in battle all the way up the straight. At the line it was impossible to say which had won, but Dr Devious had prevailed by the tiniest of margins. The late 1990s saw victories for three resounding advertisements for keeping horses in training to a mature age – five-year-old **Pilsudski** in 1997, six-year-old Swain in 1998, and five-year-old **Daylami** in 1999, while the 2000 running produced **Giant's Causeway's** fifth Group One victory on the trot – or, in his case, on the relentless head-down gallop. Whichever way you look at it, the Irish Champion Stakes – the only Irish leg of the **Emirates World Series** – is one of the highlights of the year.

IRISH DERBY

Group One; three-year-olds; 1½ miles
(The Curragh)

The Irish Derby was first run in 1866, but it was not until 1962 that a large injection of prize money from the Irish Sweeps propelled it to its present position as one of the great races of the European season – often a keenly anticipated showdown between the winners of the Epsom Derby and the Prix du Jockey-Club. By the time the race is run, at the very end of June or very beginning of July, the middle-distance three-year-old form is getting sorted out, and a typical Irish Derby consists of a fairly small but very high-class field. Since 1962 13 horses have won at both Epsom and The Curragh: Santa Claus (1964), **Nijinsky**

Irish Champion Stakes winners since 1990

1990	Elmaamul	3	W. Hern GB	W. Carson	2–1F	8
1991	Suave Dancer	3	J. Hammond FRA	C. Asmussen	4–6F	7
1992	Dr Devious	3	P.Chapple-Hyam GB	J. Reid	7–2	8
1993	Muhtarram	4	J. Gosden GB	W. Carson	7–1	10
1994	Cezanne	5	M.Stoute GB	M. Kinane	7–2	8
1995	Pentire	3	G. Wragg GB	M. Hills	9–4F	8
1996	Timarida	4	J. Oxx	J. Murtagh	3–1	6
1997	Pilsudski	5	M. Stoute GB	M. Kinane	5–4F	7
1998	Swain	6	S. bin Suroor GB	L. Dettori	6–4F	8
1999	Daylami	5	S. bin Suroor GB	L. Dettori	6–4	7
2000	Giant's Causeway	3	A. O'Brien	M. Kinane	8–11F	7

Irish Derby winners since 1990

1990	Salsabil	3	J. Dunlop GB	W. Carson	11–4	9
1991	Generous	3	P. Cole GB	A. Munro	evensF	6
1992	St Jovite	3	J. Bolger	C. Roche	7–2	11
1993	Commander In Chief	3	H. Cecil GB	Pat Eddery	4–7F	11
1994	Balanchine	3	H. Ibrahim GB	L. Dettori	5–1	9
1995	Winged Love	3	A. Fabre FRA	O. Peslier	5–1	13
1996	Zagreb	3	D. Weld	P. Shanahan	20–1	13
1997	Desert King	3	A. O'Brien	C. Roche	11–2	10
1998	Dream Well	3	P. Bary FRA	C. Asmussen	2–1F	10
1999	Montjeu	3	J. Hammond FRA	C. Asmussen	13–8F	10
2000	Sinndar	3	J. Oxx	J. Murtagh	11–10F	11
2001	Galileo	3	A. O'Brien	M. Kinane	4–11F	12

(1970), **Grundy** (1975), The Minstrel (1977), Shirley Heights (1978), **Troy** (1979), **Shergar** (1981), Shahrastani (1986), Kahyasi (1988), Generous (1991), Commander In Chief (1993), Sinndar (2000) and **Galileo** (2001). Of those, Nijinsky, Grundy, The Minstrel, Troy, Shergar, Generous and Galileo went on the same season to win the King George at Ascot. (In the same period nine Derby winners were beaten at The Curragh: Larkspur (1962), Charlottown (1966), **Sir Ivor** (1968), Blakeney (1969), Roberto (1972), Empery (1976), Teenoso (1983), Quest For Fame (1990) and Dr Devious (1992). Other horses to have won the Irish Derby and King George are **Ballymoss** (Irish Derby 1957, King George 1958), Ragusa (1963), Meadow Court (1965), St Jovite (1992) and **Montjeu** (Irish Derby 1999, King George 2000). Salsabil was the first filly since Gallinaria in 1900 to win the Irish Derby when taking the 1990 running under Willie Carson. In 1994 Balanchine – like Salsabil coming to The Curragh after winning the Oaks – became the second.

IRISH GRAND NATIONAL

Grade One steeplechase: five-year-olds and upwards: 3 miles 5 furlongs (Fairyhouse)

The Irish Grand National, first run in 1870, has been won by some very great chasers – not least the beloved **Desert Orchid** himself,

Irish Grand National winners since 1990

1990	Desert Orchid	11	D. Elsworth GB	R. Dunwoody	evensF	14
1991	Omerta	11	M. Pipe GB	A. Maguire	6–1	22
1992	Vanton	8	M. O'Brien	J. Titley	13–2	23
1993	Ebony Jane	8	F. Flood	C. Swan	6–1	27
1994	Son Of War	7	P. McCreery	F. Woods	12–1	18
1995	Flashing Steel	10	J. Mulhern	J. Osborne	9–1	18
1996	Feathered Gale	9	A. Moore	F. Woods	8–1	17
1997	Mudahim	11	Mrs J. Pitman GB	J. Titley	13–2	20
1998	Bobbyjo	8	T. Carberry	P. Carberry	8–1	22
1999	Glebe Lad	7	M. O'Brien	T. P. Rudd	8–1CF	18
2000	Commanche Court	7	T. Walsh	R. Walsh	14–1	24
2001	Davids Lad	7	A. Martin	T. Murphy	10–1	19

who was running in his only steeplechase outside England when winning in 1990, an almighty blunder at the last fence failing to dislodge the tenacious Richard Dunwoody.

Ann Ferris was the first lady jockey to ride the winner of the Irish Grand National when partnering Bentom Boy to victory in 1984. Her sister Rosemary Stewart finished third on Dawson Prince.

Only three horses in history have won both the Irish National and the Grand National at Aintree: Ascetic's Silver (Irish 1904, Aintree 1906), Rhyme 'N' Reason (Irish 1985, Aintree 1988) and Bobbyjo (Irish 1998, Aintree 1999). **Tom Dreaper** trained 10 winners of the race, including his three greatest horses: **Prince Regent** (1942), **Arkle** (1964 – the race immediately following his first Cheltenham Gold Cup) and **Flyingbolt** (1966). Dreaper's son Jim trained 1974 winner Colebridge and Brown Lad to win three times: 1975, 1976 and 1978.

IRISH NATIONAL STUD
Web: irish-national-stud.ie
The Irish National Stud is located at Tully, near the town of Kildare and not far from The Curragh. Stallions standing there in 2001 include Ashkalani, Croco Rouge, Desert Prince, Indian Ridge and Priolo. Part of the stud houses the Irish Horse Museum, where the star exhibit is the skeleton of **Arkle**, while the star living exhibits are two great Irish horses enjoying their retirement: **Vintage Crop** and the much-loved hurdler Danoli.

IRON
Stirrup iron (which is usually made of aluminium or carbon fibre).

ISTABRAQ
When Istabraq won the Smurfit Champion Hurdle at Cheltenham in March 2000 he was joining an elite group of horses to have landed the hurdling crown three times: **Hatton's Grace** (1949–51), **Sir Ken** (1952–4), **Persian War** (1968–70) and **See You Then** (1985–7). Had not the foot-and-

mouth epidemic intervened and caused the cancellation of the 2001 Cheltenham Festival, it was odds-on that he would have created Turf history by making it four. Istabraq, by the great sire **Sadler's Wells**, was initially owned by Sheikh Hamdan Al Maktoum and trained for his Flat campaign by John Gosden. From his first outing as a two-year-old, at Doncaster in November 1994, to his last race on the level at Haydock Park in June 1996, he ran 11 races on the Flat, winning twice. At the July sales at Newmarket in 1996 he was sold for 38,000 guineas to **J. P. McManus**, with the intention that he would be trained for a hurdling campaign by John Durkan, Gosden's assistant trainer, about to set out on his own. But Durkan had tragically contracted leukaemia – from which he was to die in January 1998 – and Istabraq went instead to **Aidan O'Brien**. He first ran over hurdles at Punchestown in November 1996, finishing second to Noble Thyne, then won his next five races that season, including a roof-raising effort to take the Royal & SunAlliance Hurdle at the Cheltenham Festival. In the 1997–8 season he won four in a row (including the AIG Europe Champion Hurdle at Leopardstown) before going to Cheltenham for his first Champion. He started 3–1 favourite and won by 12 lengths from stable companion Theatreworld. Although defeated in his next race – beaten a head by Pridwell in desperate going for the Aintree Hurdle – he was clearly a very high-class hurdler, and went through the 1998–9 term unbeaten in seven races, taking his second Champion Hurdle, with Theatreworld again runner-up. All looked set fair for Istabraq's joining that elite with a third Champion Hurdle, which he duly won in March 2000 from Hors La Loi III. The 2000–1 season, which was expected to raise him to hurdling immortality, proved a disappointment. Not only was the Champion Hurdle not run, but Istabraq managed to win only one race, the AIG Europe Champion Hurdle at Leopardstown in January 2001; he fell at the last flight at Leopardstown in both his other races. It was a season best forgotten; but Cheltenham 2002 and that magical fourth Champion Hurdle still beckoned, both for a horse who is undeniably one of the all-time hurdling greats and for jockey Charlie Swan, who has ridden Istabraq in all his hurdle races.

ITALY

Of the five nations that participate in the European pattern, Italy is lowest in the pecking order, and the top Italian races are regularly farmed by raiders from overseas. For example, of the 25 Pattern races run in Italy in 2000, British-trained horses won seven and German-trained another six. No Italian-trained horse has won Italy's most prestigious race, the Derby Italiano, since 1988. On the other hand, Italy has clearly had a significant influence on the sport beyond its own shores – through horses such as the great **Ribot** and 1988 Arc winner Tony Bin, trained in Italy by Luigi Camici, through trainers such as **Luca**

Cumani, and especially through the world-wide fame and appeal of Milan-born **Frankie Dettori.**

There are 20 racecourses in Italy, of which the best known to British and Irish racing fans are the Capannelle in Rome and San Siro in Milan, which between them stage all the country's eight Group One races: the Premio Presidente della Repubblica (Rome in May), Oaks d'Italia (Milan in May), Derby Italiano (Rome in May: Michael Jarvis-trained Morshdi won in 2001), Gran Premio di Milano (Milan in June), Premio Vittorio di Capua (Milan in October), Gran Premio del Jockey Club Italiano (Milan in October), Gran Criterium (Milan in October) and Premio Roma (Rome in November).

The ruling body of Italian racing is UNIRE (Unione Nazionale Italiano dei Reunioni Equitazione), which controls Flat racing, steeplechasing and trotting.

J

JACKPOT
Tote bet which involves selecting the winners of the first six races at the designated Jackpot meeting. If there is no winner the pool is carried forward to the next Jackpot meeting.

JADE
Name used (not very frequently these days) for an ungenuine horse.

JAMSTICK
Slang term – mostly used by jockeys – for the winning post.

JAPAN
Since the 1980s Japan has made huge strides to establish itself as a major player in world horse racing and breeding. Japanese owner–breeders have been buying heavily at the big European and and American yearling sales, and many top racehorses have gone to Japan as stallions.

When 1975 Derby winner **Grundy** ended up in Japan after failing to make his mark as a stallion in England, his departure was seen as a considerable come-down, and for a while the idea persisted that a stallion went east only if he could not succeed in Europe or the USA. **Dancing Brave**, syndicated for £14 million to stand as a stallion in Newmarket on his retirement from the track in 1986, was later sold to Japan at a valuation of just £3 million – then had the last laugh by producing 1993 Derby winner Commander In Chief from his third crop sired in England. Commander In Chief himself was one of five consecutive Derby winners of the 1990s to go to Japan. Generous (Derby 1991) stood in England for a while before being exported; Dr Devious (1992) stood in Japan and later returned to Europe to stand at the **Coolmore Stud**; Erhaab (1994) was exported there at the end of his three-year-old career; and **Lammtarra** (1995) stood for one season at the Dalham Hall stud in Newmarket before being sold to Japan for $30 million. A sign of the strength in depth of the stallions available to Japanese breeders is the roll-call of sires standing at the country's studs in 2001: it includes Arc winners Carnegie, Helissio and Tony Bin, King George winners Opera House and Pentire, Irish Derby and Prix du Jockey-Club winner Dream Well, El Condor Pasa, **Arazi**, **Pilsudski** and the great American horse Sunday Silence, winner of the 1989 Kentucky Derby and currently the predominant stallion in Japan.

A significant move in the effort to make Japan a major player was the establishment of the **Japan Cup** as an international event in 1981, and much more recently Japanese horses have started to make their mark overseas. Seeking The Pearl became the first Japanese-trained horse ever to win a European Group One race when lifting the Prix Maurice de Gheest at Deauville in 1998; Taiki Shuttle won the Prix Jacques le Marois on the same course just a week later; and Agnes World won the Prix de l'Abbaye in 1999, and in July 2000 became the first Japanese-trained horse to win a race in England when taking the July Cup. Japan-trained El Condor Pasa was narrowly beaten by Montjeu in the 1999 Prix de l'Arc de Triomphe.

Japan has also been stimulating the internationalisation of jump racing. The first running of the Nakayama Grand Jump over two miles four and a half furlongs in Tokyo in April 2000 carried a first prize equivalent to £478,300, making it easily the most valuable jumping race in the world: Boca Boca, trained in France by **François Doumen**, was a narrow runner-up to locally trained Gokai, with The Outback Way, trained in Herefordshire by **Venetia Williams**, picking up £119,219 by finishing third.

On the human front, the public face of Japanese racing is the hugely popular jockey **Yutaka Take**, whose move to France in 2001 has made him more familiar to European racing fans.

There are 10 racecourses in Japan, of which the best known is Fuchu in Tokyo, home of the Japan Cup.

JAPAN CUP

Grade One invitation race; three-year-olds and upwards; 1½ miles (Fuchu, Tokyo)

The Japan Cup, currently the Japanese leg of the **Emirates World Series** is the world's most valuable race on turf. First run in 1981 and timed to attract the best horses from both northern and southern hemispheres, its huge prize money draws the best middle-distance horses from around the world. Its first three runnings firmly established its credentials, with the winners coming from overseas – Mairzy Doates (1981) and Half Iced (1982) from the USA and the great mare Stanerra (1983) from Ireland – and the sixth running in 1986 brought the first victory by an English-trained horse, when Clive Brittain's seven-year-old gelding

Jupiter Island, ridden by Pat Eddery, had a furious battle with another English raider, Guy Harwood's Allez Milord, before prevailing by a neck. Since then England has won the Japan Cup twice more, with **Singspiel** (1996) and **Pilsudski** (1997), both trained by Michael Stoute, but the race comes very late in the year for European runners who have been on the go since the spring, and has seen some notable defeats of horses simply being taken to the well once too often: 1999 Arc winner Montjeu, for instance, could finish only fourth in the Japan Cup that autumn.

The 2000 Japan Cup was the third most valuable race run in the world that year (after the **Dubai World Cup** and Breeders' Cup Classic), with the winning owner getting the equivalent of £1,636,132.

JARVIS FAMILY

The record books of Flat racing in Britain are awash with the name Jarvis, one of Newmarket's most influential and longest-established racing families. William A. Jarvis (1852–91) trained 1892 Two Thousand Guineas winner Bona Vista. Of his sons, William Jarvis won the One Thousand Guineas with Scuttle in 1928 and the One Thousand Guineas and Oaks with Godiva in 1940 and trained for two kings, George V and George VI: *his* son Ryan Jarvis trained good horses such as Lomond (1966 Ebor Handicap winner, not the 1983 Two Thousand Guineas

Japan Cup winners since 1990

1990	Better Loosen Up	5	D. Hayes *AUS*	M. Clarke	52–10	15
1991	Golden Pheasant	5	C. Whittingham *USA*	G. Stevens	172–10	15
1992	Tokai Teio	4	S. Matsumoto	Y. Okabe	9–1	14
1993	Legacy World	4	H. Mori	H. Koyauchi	115–10	16
1994	Marvellous Crown	4	M. Osawa	K. Minai	96–10	14
1995	Lando	5	H. Jentzsch *GER*	M. Roberts	135–10	14
1996	Singspiel	4	M. Stoute *GB*	L. Dettori	66–10	15
1997	Pilsudski	4	M. Stoute *GB*	M. Kinane	36–10	14
1998	El Condor Pasa	3	Y. Ninomiya	M. Ebina	5–1	15
1999	Special Week	4	T. Shirai	Y. Take	24–10	14
2000	TM Opera O	4	I. Iwamoto	R. Wada	1–2F	16

winner) and the fine sprinter Absalom. Another of William A. Jarvis's sons was Basil Jarvis (1897–1957), who won the 1923 Derby with Papyrus. Jack Jarvis (1887–1968), yet another son of William A., won nine Classics between 1923 (Ellangowan in the Two Thousand Guineas) and 1953 (Happy Laughter in the One Thousand Guineas), including the Two Thousand Guineas and Derby in 1939 with Blue Peter and the 1944 Derby with Ocean Swell. Of the current crop of Jarvises, most successful is Michael Jarvis (born 1938), son of the jump jockey Andrew Jarvis and trainer of such horses as 1989 Arc winner Carroll House, 2000 Prix du Jockey-Club winner Holding Court, Beldale Flutter, Bob Back and Easter Sun; Ameerat in the 2001 One Thousand Guineas was his first Classic winner in England. William Jarvis, son of Ryan, also trains in Newmarket: his best horse has been Grand Lodge, beaten a short head by Mister Baileys in the 1994 Two Thousand Guineas and winner of the St James's Palace Stakes that year. Alan Jarvis trains at Aston Upthorpe near Didcot in Oxfordshire.

JEBEL ALI
Racecourse in Dubai – close to the centre of Dubai city – built on land reclaimed from the desert and opened in 1991.

JOCKED OFF
A jockey who loses a ride to another jockey has been 'jocked off'. Lester Piggott had a reputation for being a master of the craft, and some of his alleged jockings off are as much part of racing folklore as his big-race victories. He controversially came in for the winning ride on Roberto in the 1972 Derby at the expense of the colt's regular partner Bill Williamson, and took over from Luca Cumani's stable jockey Darrel McHargue on Commanche Run to win his record-breaking twenty-eighth Classic in the 1984 St Leger. Piggott's response to criticism on this front was typically laconic: 'It is part of a jockey's job to get on to the best horses, and if that involves ruffling a few feathers, so be it.'

JOCKEY
In 2000 there were some 412 professional jockeys licensed by the Jockey Club:

- 108 Flat;
- 127 **apprentices**;
- 85 jumps;
- 92 **conditional**.

In addition, some 440 were licensed as amateurs.

In August 2001, riding fees are:

- £70.55 per ride on the Flat;
- £96.40 per ride over jumps.

As well as riding fees, jockeys (other than amateur jockeys) placed in a race earn a percentage of the prize money, depending on

Champion Flat jockeys in Britain since 1975

year	jockey	wins
1975	Pat Eddery	164
1976	Pat Eddery	162
1977	Pat Eddery	176
1978	W. Carson	182
1979	J. Mercer	164
1980	W. Carson	166
1981	L. Piggott	179
1982	L. Piggott	188
1983	W. Carson	159
1984	S. Cauthen	130
1985	S. Cauthen	195
1986	Pat Eddery	176
1987	S. Cauthen	197
1988	Pat Eddery	183
1989	Pat Eddery	171
1990	Pat Eddery	209
1991	Pat Eddery	165
1992	M. Roberts	206
1993	Pat Eddery	169
1994	L. Dettori	233
1995	L. Dettori	211
1996	Pat Eddery	186
1997	K. Fallon	202
1998	K. Fallon	204
1999	K. Fallon	202
2000	K. Darley	155

the nature of the race and the placing they achieve, and may also be given a 'present' by a grateful owner. Some jockeys have a retainer with a particular stable or an individual owner: for example, Richard Quinn is stable jockey for Henry Cecil in 2001, and Richard Hughes is retained by leading owner Khalid Abdullah to ride his horses. The retaining owner or trainer will have 'first claim' on that jockey's services.

The contrast between the earning potential of a Flat jockey and a jump jockey can be immense. Never mind that the basic fee is more over the jumps: the prospect of earnings from a percentage of prize money is significantly higher on the level. Champion jockey Tony McCoy's 775 mounts in the 2000-1 jumps season earned owners £1,435,893. Champion jockey Kevin Darley's 997 mounts during the 2000 Flat season earned owners £2,305,418.

Against earnings are set considerable expenses – principally for equipment and for travel. The decentralised nature of racing in Britain means that jockeys must undertake an immense amount of travelling – a typical annual itinerary would involve 50,000 miles, mostly by car, sometimes by plane – while the leading international jockeys engage in mind-boggling travel plans.

Alongside travel, the constant bugbear of a jockey's life is weight, and most riders have to subject themselves to fierce discipline in order to keep their weight low. The traditional diet by which a jockey kept appetite at bay used to be champagne and cigars, though in in these more health-conscious days the reality is more likely to be a very small break-fast of tea and toast, no lunch (though perhaps a bar of chocolate for energy) and a light supper. (The weight range in National Hunt races is around 2st higher than for the Flat, reflecting the jumping game's origins in the hunting field, where underfed riders are not a common sight.) These days many racecourse changing rooms have saunas in which jockeys can lose the last few pounds. The aim, of course, is to maintain a starvation diet and at the same time keep the body fit and strong, for to control over 1,000lb of horseflesh through a race demands a level of athleticism which participants in many other sports would envy. (*See* **wasting**.)

See also **amateur jockeys**; **apprentices**; **conditional jockeys**; **falls**; **lady jockeys**.

JOCKEY CLUB

42 Portman Square. London W1H 0EN
Tel.: 020 7486 4921
Fax: 020 7935 8703
E-mail: info@thejockeyclub.co.uk
Web: www.thejockeyclub.co.uk

The Jockey Club, which was the sole governing body of racing until the **British Horseracing Board** was set up in 1993 and

Champion jump jockeys in Britain since 1974–5

season	jockey	wins
1974–5	T. Stack	82
1975–6	J. Francome	96
1976–7	T. Stack	97
1977–8	J. J. O'Neill	149
1978–9	J. Francome	95
1979–80	J. J. O'Neill	115
1980–1	J. Francome	105
1981–2	J. Francome/ P. Scudamore	120
1982–3	J. Francome	106
1983–4	J. Francome	131
1984–5	J. Francome	101
1985–6	P. Scudamore	91
1986–7	P. Scudamore	123
1987–8	P. Scudamore	132
1988–9	P. Scudamore	221
1989–90	P. Scudamore	170
1990–1	P. Scudamore	141
1991–2	P. Scudamore	175
1992–3	R. Dunwoody	173
1993–4	R. Dunwoody	197
1994–5	R. Dunwoody	160
1995–6	A. P. McCoy	175
1996–7	A. P. McCoy	190
1997–8	A. P. McCoy	253
1998–9	A. P. McCoy	186
1999–2000	A. P. McCoy	245
2000–1	A. P. McCoy	191

which remains responsible for such matters as discipline, the Rules of Racing and the licensing of participants, dates back to the middle of the eighteenth century. Racing was then in a parlous state. Rules were practically non-existent, corruption and doping were widespread and criminality was rife, and the Jockey Club came into being in Newmarket around 1750 in an attempt to bring some sort of order to the sport. Originally it was more concerned with arranging matches and settling bets, but in due course it began to publish rules (its first recognisable order was issued in 1758) and generally establish authority over the running of races at Newmarket. A tendency developed for other racecourses to refer their disputes to the Jockey Club, and its influence grew steadily over the next century until it became the ruling body of the sport.

Today the Jockey Club formulates, enforces and administers the Rules of Racing. It investigates possible breaches of those Rules and hands out punishment to offenders. It licenses jockeys and trainers and ensures that they behave within the Rules, both on the racecourse and at training establishments, and is closely concerned with the safety and welfare of horses and riders. The Rules are extensive, and in order to ensure that they are all adhered to the Club has its own security service. The Club appoints stewards to control individual race meetings and see that the Rules are observed, and supplies racecourse officials such as judges, starters and veterinary officers.

The Jockey Club – whose main base is now in London, though it still maintains the Jockey Club Rooms in Newmarket High Street – has a 'board of directors' known as the Stewards (including the Senior Steward and the Deputy Senior Steward), who are elected from the members and who serve for a period of three years (four years for the Senior and Deputy Senior Stewards), and approximately 120 individual members (each elected by the existing members). Until comparatively recently the Jockey Club was the epitome of the male bastion, but in 1966, after years of resistance, it agreed to grant training licences to women – the first being Florence Nagle, who had to go to the Court of Appeal in order to secure the right. Another breakthrough occurred in December 1977, when the Countess of Halifax, Mrs Priscilla Hastings and Mrs Helen Johnson Houghton became the first women to be elected to membership.

JOCKEYS' ASSOCIATION

39B Kingfisher Court, Hambridge Road,
  Newbury, Berkshire RG14 5SJ
Tel.: 01635 44102
Fax: 01635 37932
E-mail: jockeys@jagb.co.uk
Web: www.jockeysassociation.co.uk

Trade association which looks after the interests of jockeys, both Flat and jumping.

JOEL, JIM

Jim Joel's colours of black, scarlet cap were a familiar sight on British racecourses for decades. Born in 1894, he won the first of his five Classics with Picture Play in the 1944 One Thousand Guineas. **Royal Palace** won him the Two Thousand Guineas and Derby in 1967 (which helped him become leading owner on the Flat that year), and his two other Classics came with Light Cavalry (St Leger 1980) and Fairy Footsteps (One Thousand Guineas 1981), while other prominent Joel horses on the Flat included Connaught, West Side Story, Major Portion, Welsh Pageant and Predominate. He was twice leading owner over jumps (1979–80 and 1986–7) and became the first owner since **Raymond Guest** to have owned both a Derby winner and a Grand National winner when Maori Venture won the 1987 National. His other good jumpers included chasers The Laird, Summerville and Buona Notte and the hurdler Beacon Light. Jim Joel, who bred most of his horses (though not Maori Venture) at his Childwick Bury Stud near St Albans, died in March 1992 at the age of 97.

JOHN HENRY

Over a career spanning eight seasons, John Henry won 39 of his 83 races and earned

$6,597,947. The gelding was voted Horse of the Year in 1981 (when he won the **Arlington Million** by a nose from The Bart) and 1984 (when he won a second Arlington Million from Royal Heroine), and his other victories included the Oak Tree International, the Sword Dancer Stakes and the Turf Classic (beating All Along in 1984); he was beaten a neck by Luca Cumani-trained Tolomeo in the 1983 Arlington Million. Acclaimed by jockey **Bill Shoemaker** (who rode him to many victories) as 'the toughest little dude I've ever seen', John Henry was retired in 1985 and took up residence in the Kentucky Horse Park near Lexington, where he still draws the crowds.

JOHNSON, RICHARD

From a farming and racing background (his mother is a **permit holder**), Richard Johnson was born in Herefordshire in July 1977 and joined trainer David Nicholson as an apprentice at the age of 16. He rode his first winner on Rusty Bridge at Hereford on 30 April 1994, since when he has risen rapidly through the ranks to the point where he has become the principal rival to **Tony McCoy** for the jump jockeys' championship: he finished runner-up to McCoy in 1997–8, 1998–9, 1999–2000 and 2000–1. He won his first Cheltenham Gold Cup on Looks Like Trouble in 2000.

JOHNSTON, MARK

Web: www.markjohnston.racing.com

Mark Johnston was born in 1959 and qualified as a vet before taking out his first training licence in 1987. His only Classic winner has been Mister Baileys in the 1994 Two Thousand Guineas, but he has trained many other top horses, notably the popular white-faced stayer Double Trigger (winner of the Ascot Gold Cup in 1995 and triple winner of the Goodwood Cup), Royal Rebel (Ascot Gold Cup winner 2001), Lend A Hand, Branston Abby, Double Eclipse, Fruits Of Love, Quick Ransom, Bijou d'Inde and Yavana's Pace.

JOINT

A course bookmaker's 'joint' is the stand in the betting ring from which he plies his trade.

JOLLY

Betting slang for the favourite ('the jolly old favourite').

JUDDMONTE FARMS

Web: www.juddmonte.co.uk

The bloodstock operation owned by **Khalid Abdullah**, which consists of Juddmonte Farms in Berkshire, Banstead Manor Stud in Newmarket, and studs in Ireland and Kentucky.

JUDGE

Official whose task is to announce the names of the horses in the order of their finishing, from the evidence of his or her view of the race high up in the judge's box and aided as appropriate by the **photo finish**. The judge's decision is final unless an objection or stewards' enquiry brings about an alteration of the placings. If a mistake occurs, it can be corrected by the judge within five days or by the Stewards of the Jockey Club within 14 days (though that's not much consolation for punters who may have missed out on a legitimate winner). The judge's other main responsibility is to declare the **distances** between the horses.

JULY CUP

Group One; three-year-olds and upwards; 6 furlongs (Newmarket, July Course)

Centrepiece of the Newmarket July Meeting, the July Cup is one of the triple peaks of the European sprinting year, along with the Nunthorpe Stakes and the Prix de l'Abbaye. The race was first run in 1876, and in its very early days horses were expected to be much more versatile than today: before the turn of the century the race was by both a Derby winner (Melton in 1886) and an Oaks winner (Memoir in 1891). Two much more recent July Cup heroes had also run in the Derby: 1987 winner Ajdal, who had run behind Reference Point at Epsom before connections realised that his forte was sprinting, and 1992 winner Mr Brooks, who had run last in the 1990 Derby behind Quest for Fame. Dual winners of the July Cup since the Second World War are the flying grey **Abernant**

July Cup winners since 1990

1990	Royal Academy	3	M. V. O'Brien *IRE*	J. Reid	7–1	9
1991	Polish Patriot	3	G. Harwood	R. Cochrane	6–1	8
1992	Mr Brooks	5	R. Hannon	L. Piggott	16–1	8
1993	Hamas	4	P. Walwyn	W. Carson	33–1	12
1994	Owington	3	G. Wragg	Paul Eddery	3–1	9
1995	Lake Coniston	4	G. Lewis	Pat Eddery	13–8F	9
1996	Anabaa	4	Mme C. Head *FRA*	F. Head	11–4	10
1997	Compton Place	3	J. Toller	S. Sanders	50–1	9
1998	Elnadim	4	J. Dunlop	R. Hills	3–1F	17
1999	Stravinsky	3	A. O'Brien *IRE*	M. Kinane	8–1	17
2000	Agnes World	5	H. Mori *JAP*	Y. Take	4–1F	10
2001	Mozart	3	A. O'Brien *IRE*	M. Kinane	4–1F	18

(1949 and 1950) and Right Boy (1958 and 1959), while the roll of honour enshrines the names of most of the great sprinters – such as Thatch (1973), Lianga (1975), Lochnager (1976), Moorestyle (1980), Marwell (1981), Sharpo (1982), Habibti (1983), Chief Singer (1984), Never So Bold (1985) and Cadeaux Genereux (1989). With its stiff uphill finish, the July Cup demands more than sheer speed, and is often a target for horses reverting to sprinting after racing over a mile.

JUVENILE

Two-year-old racehorse.

K

KEENELAND

Web: www.keeneland.com

Racetrack in Lexington, Kentucky, founded in 1936 and best known for its yearling sales: the premier US sale takes place here in September. It was at Keeneland that the horse later named Seattle Dancer was sold as a yearling in 1985 for $13.1 million, still a world record. One of the major races here is the Bluegrass Stakes, a leading trial for the **Kentucky Derby** which has been won by many horses who have gone on to land the 'Run for the Roses'.

KELLEWAY, PAUL

Born in 1940, Paul Kelleway rode his first winner on Golovine on the Flat at Haydock Park in October 1955, but it was as a fearless and grittily determined jump jockey that he made his name. He won two Champion Hurdles on the great Bula in 1971 and 1972, the Cheltenham Gold Cup on What A Myth in 1969, and the Two Mile Champion Chase (now the Queen Mother Champion Chase) on **Crisp** in 1971, and towards the end of his career won back-to-back Scottish Nationals on Barona in 1975 and 1976. In all he rode 392 winners. In 1977 he switched to training. While never having the luxury of acquiring the most expensive yearlings, Kelleway's Newmarket yard punched well above its weight with such horses as Swiss Maid (winner of the 1978 Champion Stakes), Madam Gay (named after his daughter, and winner of the 1981 Prix de Diane), and speedy two-year-old Risk Me. Paul Kelleway died of cancer in April 1999 at the age of 58. His daughter Gay Kelleway has the distinction of being the first lady jockey to ride a winner at Royal Ascot: Sprowston Boy in the 1987 Queen Alexandra Stakes.

KELSO (1)

Kelso, Roxburghshire TD5 7SX
Tel.: 01668 281611
Fax: 01668 281113
E-mail: trish@saleandpartners.co.uk
Web: www.kelso-races.co.uk

Set in the heart of the border country, Kelso is one of those small rural jumping tracks which encapsulate the appeal of the **gaffs**. The original grandstand, built by the fifth Duke of Roxburgh when he established racing on this site in the early 1820s, is a wonderful construction of stone and ironwork and still forms part of the racecourse facilities, though it is now surrounded by a higgledy-piggledy collection of more modern (and far less distinguished) buildings.

The hurdle course and the chase course diverge on the run away from the stands, with the hurdle course cutting inside. Over hurdles the left-handed circuit is about one and a quarter miles round and pretty sharp, while the chase course is a furlong longer and puts a premium on good jumping, as the fences here are well made and several are set on the downhill stretch along the back. The run-in from the last fence, on an elbow which avoids the two fences closest to the stands, is uphill and over two furlongs long – a very tiring proposition for a horse trying to get home in heavy ground.

KELSO (2)

The gelding Kelso won 39 of his 63 starts and dominated American racing for half a decade. He was Horse of the Year five times in a row from 1960 to 1964; won the Jockey Club Gold Cup in each of those five years; won the Woodward Stakes three times; landed the 'Handicap Triple Crown' at Aqueduct (Metropolitan, Suburban and

Brooklyn) in 1961; and as a seven-year-old in 1964 won the Washington, DC International at Laurel Park at the fourth attempt after being runner-up three times previously. He won three races as an eight-year-old (including the Whitney Stakes) and ran once at nine before being retired to his owner Mrs Allaire duPont's Woodstock Farm, where a plaque on the wall outside his box read, 'The most durable horse in racing history'. Having spent much of his retirement hunting with the local hounds, Kelso died in 1983 at the age of 26.

KEMPTON PARK

Staines Road East. Sunbury-on-Thames.
  Middlesex TW16 5AQ
Tel.: 01932 782292
Fax: 01932 782044
E-mail: kempton@rht.net
Web: www.kempton.co.uk

Kempton Park has undergone two major transformations since the early 1970s. First a new 'clubhouse', incorporating the weighing room, was built, and the old parade ring around which giants such as **Arkle**, **Mill House** and **Mill Reef** had walked was resited. Then the layout was revamped again in time for Boxing Day 1997. The inside of the grandstand was completely re-ordered, its crowning glory a glass-fronted panoramic restaurant along the lines of similar constructions at Wolverhampton and Cheltenham, and behind that grandstand was built a new parade ring, overlooked by the Philip Blacker statue of **Desert Orchid**, who won the King George VI Chase, Kempton's flagship event, no fewer than four times (1986, 1988, 1989 and 1990), and landed another three races here.

Kempton Park was opened in 1878, three years after the success of the park course experiment at nearby Sandown Park, and although it has never attracted the passionate devotion which Sandown regulars have for their stamping ground, it deserves its place among the major tracks of the land. The circuit here is in the shape of a right-handed triangle, about one mile five furlongs round, intersected by a straight course for five- and six-furlong sprints, with the Jubilee Course – 10 furlongs in length – forming a long spur which joins the round course just before the home turn three and a half furlongs out. The Jubilee course has slight undulations, but otherwise Kempton is flat. Over jumps the course provides a very fair test, though speed and quick, accurate jumping are more important than sheer stamina: it is often thought, for instance, that a horse who could not get more than two and a half miles at Cheltenham would be able to stay the three-mile trip here.

Despite the generally high standard of racing, Kempton does not have a Group One race on the Flat: its best-known events on the level are handicaps – the two-mile Queen's Prize run at the Easter meeting (which also features two good three-year-old races in the Masaka Stakes and the Easter Stakes, both over one mile) and the Jubilee Handicap over one mile on May Bank Holiday Monday. But if the Flat racing programme is not out of the very top drawer, jumping at Kempton is right up there with the best. The three-mile **King George VI Chase** on Boxing Day is the most important weight-for-age staying chase of the season apart from the Cheltenham Gold Cup and has been won by most of the chasing greats. The Christmas meeting – one of the great racing occasions of the year, with a huge and hugely enthusiastic crowd – also has the Christmas Hurdle for the cream of the hurdlers. In January the course stages the Lanzarote Hurdle, named after the 1974 Champion Hurdle hero who won eight races here, and in February the **Racing Post Chase**, one of the very best handicap steeplechases of the year: Rough Quest won in 1996 and five weeks later landed the Grand National, while Desert Orchid's performance in winning under 12st 3lb in 1990 is widely considered the best of his distinguished career.

KENTUCKY DERBY

First leg of the **US Triple Crown**, the Kentucky Derby (run over 1¼ miles at Churchill Downs in Louisville, Kentucky, on the first Saturday in May) is *the* American horse race, one of the great occasions in world sport and an event steeped in tradition. That tradition is underpinned by its venue, beneath the famous twin spires of Churchill Downs; by its accompanying tipple, the lethal mint julep; by the communal spine-tingling singing of 'My Old Kentucky Home' as the runners come out on to the track; and by the placing of a garland of roses around the neck of the winning horse, a tradition begun in 1896 which in 1925 occasioned one journalist to call the race 'The Run for the Roses', a nickname which has stuck.

'Until you go to Kentucky and with your own eyes behold the Derby, you ain't never been nowheres and you ain't never seen nothin'!'

Irwin S. Cobb

'This Kentucky Derby, whatever it is – a race, an emotion, a turbulence, an explosion – is one of the most beautiful and satisfying things I have ever experienced.'

John Steinbeck

The Kentucky Derby was first run in 1875 over one and a half miles, being reduced to its present distance of 10 furlongs in 1896. As the race became linked with the **Preakness** and **Belmont Stakes** to form the Triple Crown, so its appeal grew, and the opening of the infield in 1938 gave the opportunity for huge masses to attend the race: the 1974 running was watched by a crowd of 163,628, the largest attendance ever at an American racecourse. The infield, described by Hunter S. Thompson as 'a boiling sea of people', adds to Kentucky Derby tradition by providing a bacchanalia of drinking and other debauchery in contrast with the cream of Kentucky society in the Clubhouse.

In 1986 Bold Arrangement, trained by Clive Brittain, became the first ever British-trained runner in the Kentucky Derby. He finished second to Ferdinand.

(For Kentucky Derby winners since 1990, *see* **US Triple Crown**.)

KILBEGGAN

Loughnagore, Kilbeggan, Co. Westmeath
Tel.: 0506 32176
Fax: 0506 32125
E-mail: kilbegganracecourse@eircom.net

Kilbeggan, which was scheduled to stage just six days' racing in 2001 and is one of the least-used Irish racecourses, is the only track in Ireland which stages National Hunt racing alone. The circuit is right-handed, nine furlongs round, quite undulating with a rise to the winning post. Racing was first held in Kilbeggan in 1840, and the present course has been in use continually (with the exception of the Second World War) since 1901.

KILDANGAN STUD

One of the leading studs in Europe, Kildangan is situated near Monasterevin in Co. Kildare and owned by Sheikh Mohammed's **Darley Stud Management**. It is also used as a breaking and training centre for Darley and **Godolphin** yearlings. Stallions announced as standing there in 2001 are: Bachir, Cape Cross, In The Wings, King's Best, Lend A Hand, Pennekamp and Xaar.

KILLARNEY

Killarney, Co. Kerry
Tel.: 064 31125
Fax: 064 31860

When Lester Piggott rode at Killarney for the first time in July 1991 he was asked if he had ever ridden in a more scenic setting. He replied: 'I've seen worse.' That ringing endorsement – a prelude to Lester's riding a treble for his old comrade-in-arms Vincent O'Brien – would be shared by all but the most stony-hearted visitor to Killarney, for this must be one of the most gloriously situated racecourses anywhere in the world, the lakes and mountains forming a spectacular backdrop. There are two meetings here each year – in May and July – and both draw huge crowds to a course notable not only for its setting but also for its informal atmosphere. The circuit is a left-handed oval approximately nine and a half furlongs round.

KINANE, MICHAEL

No jockey currently riding can boast a success record in the major international races to match that of Michael Kinane. By the end of July 2001 he had ridden the winners of seven Classics in England – Two Thousand Guineas on Tirol (1990), Entrepreneur (1997), King Of Kings (1998); Derby on Commander In Chief (1993) and **Galileo** (2001); Oaks on Shahtoush (1998) and Imagine (2001); eight Irish Classics, including the 2001 Irish Derby on Galileo – his first victory in the race, at his eighteenth attempt; the King George VI and Queen Elizabeth Diamond Stakes four times – Belmez (1990), King's Theatre (1994), **Montjeu** (2000) and Galileo (2001); the Prix de l'Arc de Triomphe twice – Carroll House (1989) and Montjeu (1999); the Melbourne Cup (**Vintage Crop**, 1993); the Japan Cup (**Pilsudski**, 1997); and the Belmont Stakes (Go And Go, 1990), the first European-based rider to have ridden the winner of a US Triple Crown race. Son of Tommy Kinane, who won the 1978 Champion Hurdle on Monksfield, Michael Kinane was born in Cashel, Co. Tipperary, on 22 June 1959, served his apprenticeship with Liam Browne at The Curragh, and rode his first winner on Muscari at Leopardstown in March 1975. He was champion apprentice in Ireland in 1978, and in 1984 joined trainer **Dermot Weld**. The same year he became champion jockey in Ireland for the first time: in all he has been Irish champion on eleven occasions – 1984–9, 1991–4 and 1999.

KINCSEM

Foaled in Hungary in 1874, Kincsem ran in 54 races and was never beaten. She won in her native country, in Austria, Germany, Czechoslovakia and France, and on her one visit to England took the 1878 Goodwood Cup as outsider of three runners.

KING GEORGE VI AND QUEEN ELIZABETH DIAMOND STAKES

Group One; three-year-olds and upwards; 1½ miles (Ascot)

The 'King George' is the midsummer highlight of the Flat season in Great Britain, a race designed to pitch the cream of middle-distance three-year-olds – especially horses who have won or run well in the Derby or Irish Derby – against their elders, and has many claims to being one of the major events of the world racing year. It comes at a time of the year when the three-year-olds should have sorted themselves out; the trip of one and a half miles is the classic European middle distance; the Ascot course is one of the fairest in Europe; and the prize money is considerable: £435,000 to the winning owner in 2001.

Brainchild of Sir John Crocker Bulteel, Clerk of the Course at Ascot, the race was

King George VI and Queen Elizabeth Diamond Stakes winners since 1990

1990	Belmez	3	H. Cecil	M. Kinane	15–2	11
1991	Generous	3	P. Cole	A. Munro	4–6F	9
1992	St Jovite	3	J. Bolger IRE	S. Craine	4–5F	8
1993	Opera House	5	M. Stoute	M. Roberts	8–1	10
1994	King's Theatre	3	H. Cecil	M. Kinane	12–1	12
1995	Lammtarra	3	S. bin Suroor	L. Dettori	9–4F	7
1996	Pentire	4	G. Wragg	M. Hills	100–30	8
1997	Swain	5	S. bin Suroor	J. Reid	16–1	8
1998	Swain	6	S. bin Suroor	L. Dettori	11–2	8
1999	Daylami	5	S. bin Suroor	L. Dettori	3–1	8
2000	Montjeu	4	J. Hammond FRA	M. Kinane	1–3F	7
2001	Galileo	3	A. O'Brien IRE	M. Kinane	1–2F	12

first run to mark the Festival of Britain in 1951. That inaugural running attracted 19 runners (the largest field in the history of the event) whose class would set the tone for the future of the race: they included the current Derby winner Arctic Prince, the current Arc winner Tantieme, the current St Leger winner Scratch II, both that season's Guineas winners, Belle Of All and Ki Ming, and Wilwyn, who the following year would win the first Washington, DC International. But the race was won by none of these, going to Supreme Court, who won at 100–9 and never raced again. Tulyar in 1952 became the first Derby winner to land the King George, since when the Epsom–Ascot double in the same season has been pulled off by Pinza (1953), **Nijinsky** (1970), **Mill Reef** (1971), **Grundy** (1975 – 'The Race of the Century' described in his entry), The Minstrel (1977), **Troy** (1979), **Shergar** (1981), Reference Point (1987), **Nashwan** (1989), Generous (1991), **Lammtarra** (1995) and **Galileo** (2001). **Royal Palace** (1968) and Teenoso (1984) won the King George the year after winning the Derby. The sheer quality of the race is attested by such winners, but the King George has also produced shocks – such as the defeat of 5–2 on favourite **Petite Etoile** by Aggressor in 1960 and the even more sensational overturning of Derby winner Santa Claus – at 13–2 on the shortest-priced runner in the history of the race – by Nasram II in 1964. Every King George winner is a very special horse, but mention should be made of **Brigadier Gerard**, who won in 1972 – and survived a stewards' enquiry after wandering towards runner-up Parnell – over a distance palpably too long for him; of **Dancing Brave**, who took decisive on revenge on his Epsom conqueror Shahrastani in 1986; and of **Dahlia** (1973 and 1974) and **Swain** (1997 and 1998), the only two horses to have won the race twice. Swain has the additional distinction of being the oldest horse to land the King George: six in 1998.

The King George has been sponsored by the diamond company De Beers since 1972, and carried the 'Diamond' in its title since 1975.

KING GEORGE VI CHASE

Grade One steeplechase: five-year-olds and upwards: 3 miles (Kempton Park)

The pivotal point of the jumping year and the first championship race for staying chasers, after which all eyes are fixed on Cheltenham, the King George VI Chase is for most racing fans an integral part of Christmas celebrations. On Boxing Day you blow away the cobwebs at Kempton Park, where the traditional showpiece has almost invariably produced a race to revive the most hung-over spirits.

The 2000 Pertemps King George VI Chase won by First Gold was worth £87,000 to the winning owner. The first running of the race in 1937, named to honour the king who had acceded to the throne on 11 December 1936 following the abdication of his brother Edward VIII, was worth £392 and was run in February. That first running was won by Southern Hero, the second by Airgead Sios – and then the war intervened. When racing resumed after the hostilities the King George was switched to Boxing Day to avoid proximity to the Cheltenham Gold Cup and Grand National, and soon emerged as a championship race in its own right, with Gold Cup winners such as Fortina, **Cottage Rake** (winner in 1948) and Silver Fame taking part: in 1950 the last-named was beaten by Manicou in a highly popular result, for the winning owner was Queen Elizabeth, wife of the monarch after whom the race was named.

As befits a true championship race, the King George has produced plenty great winners and memorable occasions, happy and sad:

King George VI Chase winners who had won the Cheltenham Gold Cup the same year

1948	Cottage Rake
1963	Mill House
1965	Arkle
1974	Captain Christy
1984	Burrough Hill Lad
1989	Desert Orchid
1999	See More Business

King George VI Chase winners since 1990

1990	Desert Orchid	11	D. Elsworth	R. Dunwoody	9–4F	9
1991	The Fellow	6	F. Doumen FRA	A. Kondrat	10–1	8
1992	The Fellow	7	F. Doumen FRA	A. Kondrat	evensF	8
1993	Barton Bank	7	D. Nicholson	A. Maguire	9–2	10
1994	Algan	6	F. Doumen FRA	P. Chevalier	16–1	9
1995*	One Man	8	G. Richards	R. Dunwoody	11–4F	11
1996	One Man	8	G. Richards	R. Dunwoody	8–13F	5
1997	See More Business	7	P. Nicholls	A. Thornton	10–1	8
1998	Teeton Mill	9	Miss V. Williams	N. Williamson	7–2	9
1999	See More Business	9	P. Nicholls	M. Fitzgerald	5–2F	9
2000	First Gold	7	F. Doumen FRA	T. Doumen	5–2	9

* run in January 1996 at Sandown Park

- **Arkle** winning in 1965 (a running marred by the death of the great two-mile chaser Dunkirk) and being caught by Dormant the following year when crippled by a foot injury;
- **Desert Orchid**'s runaway victory at 16–1 in 1986: in all the great grey won the King George four times, in 1986, 1988, 1989, 1990;
- triple winner **Wayward Lad** (1982, 1983, 1985);
- dual winners Halloween (1952, 1954), **Mandarin** (1957, 1959), **Pendil** (1972, 1973), **Captain Christy** (1974, 1975), Silver Buck (1979, 1980), The Fellow (1991, 1992), **One Man** (the 1995 race run at Sandown in January 1996, and 1996) and See More Business (1997, 1999);
- John Francome's two victories, on Wayward Lad in 1982 and Burrough Hill Lad in 1984.

KITE
Betting slang for a cheque.

KNIGHT, HENRIETTA
Sister-in-law of Lord Vestey, chairman of Cheltenham racecourse, Henrietta Knight trains at West Lockinge, near Wantage in Oxfordshire. She took out her first trainer's licence in 1989, and among her big-race wins counts Edredon Bleu's thrilling victory over Direct Route in the Queen Mother Champion Chase at Cheltenham in 2000 and Karshi winning the Stayers' Hurdle at Cheltenham in 1997. She is married to former champion jump jockey **Terry Biddlecombe**.

KRONE, JULIE
Julie Krone was born in 1963 and brought up on a farm in Michigan, where by the age of three she was already undertaking five-mile rides alone on her pony Daisy. Her first winner as a jockey was on Lord Farkle on 12 February 1981 at Tampa Bay. Her 1,000th winner came in August 1987, and the following spring she became the winningmost lady jockey in racing history. She was the first – and to date the only – woman rider to win a US Triple Crown race, partnering Colonial Affair to land the Belmont Stakes in 1993, and the first to win riding titles at US tracks, being top jockey at Monmouth Park and Meadowlands in 1987. In July 1992 she made a high-profile visit to Redcar, where she rode three winners from five mounts. Julie Krone retired from the saddle early in 2000, having ridden 3,545 winners in the USA.

L

LADY TRAINERS AND JOCKEYS

Ladies were first officially granted licences to train in 1966, when Florence Nagle and Norah Wilmot won a long-running battle with the Jockey Club following a verdict handed down by the Court of Appeal. Female riders were first allowed to ride in races under Jockey Club Rules in 1972: the first ladies' race was the Goya Stakes at Kempton Park on 6 May that year. A little under four years later, in early 1976, ladies – who had long ridden in **point-to-points** – were given clearance to ride under National Hunt Rules. Since 1975 women have been able to ride as professional jockeys, and there are currently some 40 professional female riders licensed by the Jockey Club: the majority of these are apprentices, with only four fully fledged Flat and three fully fledged jump jockeys operating in 2000.

LAMBOURN

The second most important training centre in Britain, after Newmarket, Lambourn sits in the heart of the West Berkshire Downs, not far from Wantage – nor from Newbury racecourse. While Newmarket is dominated by the Flat, Lambourn is more heavily weighted towards jumping, with leading trainers such as **Nicky Henderson**, Mark Pitman, Noel Chance, Nick Gaselee, Charlie Mann and Oliver Sherwood having yards in the area. Best-known Flat trainer in Lambourn is Barry **Hills**, while **Peter Walwyn** trained here for most of his career. **Fred Winter** and **Fulke Walwyn**, two giants

---

Ladies first . . .

- First lady officially credited as trainer of a winner under Jockey Club Rules: Norah Wilmot with Pat at Brighton on 3 August 1966.
- First lady to ride a winner under Jockey Club Rules: Meriel Tufnell on Scorched Earth in the Goya Stakes at Kempton Park on 6 May 1972.
- First lady to ride a winner under National Hunt Rules: Diana Thorne (now Mrs Nicky Henderson) on Ben Ruler in a hunter-chase at Stratford on 7 February 1976.
- First lady jockey to ride in the Grand National: Charlotte Brew on Barony Fort (who refused four fences out) in 1977.
- First lady jockey to complete in the Grand National: Geraldine Rees on Cheers in 1982.
- First lady to ride a winner at the Cheltenham Festival: Caroline Beasley, on Eliogarty in the Foxhunters' Chase in 1983.
- First lady to train the winner of the Grand National: Jenny Pitman with Corbiere in 1983.
- First lady to train the winner of a Classic in England: Criquette Head with Ma Biche in the 1983 One Thousand Guineas.
- First lady to train the winner of the Cheltenham Gold Cup: Jenny Pitman with Burrough Hill Lad in 1984.
- First lady to win a race over the Grand National course at Aintree: Caroline Beasley, on Eliogarty in the Fox Hunters' Chase in 1986.
- First lady to ride a winner at Royal Ascot: Gaye Kelleway, on Sprowston Boy in the Queen Alexandra Stakes in 1987.
- First lady to ride in the Derby: Alex Greaves, on Portuguese Lil in 1998.

of jumps training a generation ago, both had their yards in Upper Lambourn. The highly popular Lambourn Open Day, when most of the local trainers open their yards to the public in aid of charity, takes place every year on Good Friday.

LAMINITIS

In the horse's foot, the pedal bone is connected to the wall of the hoof by a layer of sensitive tissues called the laminae. If these tissues become inflamed the horse will be in great pain, as the horny outside of the hoof cannot expand to accommodate the swelling associated with the inflammation. Though laminitis is most common in overweight ponies, it can occur in racehorses as a result of overfeeding or severe infections; it is treated with painkillers and appropriate adjustment of diet.

LAMMTARRA

Runner of just four races, his record in 1995 alone was enough to secure him a place in the history books. He was the first Derby winner to have a Derby winner (Nijinsky, 1970) for a sire and an Oaks winner (Snow Bride, awarded the 1989 race on the disqual-ification of Aliysa after the post-race dope test) for a dam, and he is the only horse apart from **Mill Reef** in 1971 to have won the Derby, King George and Prix de l'Arc de Triomphe. A flashy chestnut with a mind of his own – he had a habit of planting himself on the gallops and could be mulish at the stalls – Lammtarra was owned by Saeed Maktoum al Maktoum (son of Maktoum Al **Maktoum**) and trained as a two-year-old by Alex Scott, who sent him out to win his sole outing in 1994, the Washington Singer Stakes at Newbury. After Scott was murdered in September 1994 the colt was switched to the care of Saeed bin Suroor at the Godolphin operation, and in June 1995 was delivered late by Walter Swinburn to land the Derby by a length from Tamure, with Presenting third. Lammtarra was the first horse to win the Derby on his seasonal debut since Grand Parade in 1919 and clocked a time of 2 minutes 32.31 seconds, beating the record set by Mahmoud in 1936. Swinburn lost the ride on Lammtarra (no one would say why), and it was Frankie Dettori who drove him to a gutsy win from Pentire in the King George and an equally sterling effort to land the Arc from Freedom Cry. Retired to stud unbeaten, Lammtarra stood for the 1996 covering season at Dalham Hall Stud before being exported to Japan.

LASIX

Trade name for frusemide, a medication used in the treatment of horses prone to **breaking blood vessels**. It acts as a diuretic, easing pressure on the capillaries which carry blood.
See also **bute**.

LAY

A bookmaker is said to lay a horse if he takes money for it – hence bookmakers are sometimes known as layers. In common betting idiom, if you say a horse is 'worth laying', you are taking the opinion that it will not win – as opposed to 'backing' it in the expectation that it will win.

LAYDOWN

A certainty.

LAY OFF

A bookmaker lays off a bet when he reduces his liability on a horse for which he has taken money by backing it himself with another bookmaker.
See also **hedging**.

LAYTOWN

Laytown, Co. Meath (Registered office:
  9 Palace Street, Drogheda, Co. Louth)
Tel.: 041 984 2111
Fax: 041 983 7566

Laytown provides a truly unique racing experience, the only official racing on the beach in Europe. The track – a straight 10 furlongs – is marked out on the strand when the tide allows, and the races are watched from vantage points on the cliff above the beach. Laytown races take place just once a year, in the spring or early summer.

LEG (GET A)

A horse is said to have 'got a leg' if it is suffering from **tendon strain**.

LEICESTER

Oadby, Leicester LE2 4AL
Tel.: 0116 271 6515
Fax: 0116 271 1746
E-mail: lrc@eggconnect.net

Leicester racecourse is a right-handed oval a mile and three-quarters round, with a run from the home turn of about four and a half furlongs; the straight mile is downhill until about halfway, with an uphill pull to the winning post, so the course needs a horse with a fair amount of stamina. A time to pay particular attention to Leicester is towards the end of the Flat season, when it often sees well-bred but late-developing two-year-olds from the top yards: for example, Sanglamore, winner of the Prix du Jockey-Club (French Derby) in 1990, had his first outing in a Leicester maiden race in November 1989.

Two racing immortals got off the mark at Leicester. On 31 March 1921 a 16-year-old named Gordon Richards rode Gay Lord to win the Apprentices' Plate here – the first of the 4,870 winners which made him the most successful jockey in British racing history – and nearly ten years later, on 20 January 1931, the four-year-old gelding Golden Miller won the Gopsall Maiden Hurdle (worth £83 to the winner), the first of his 29 career victories which included the Grand National and five Cheltenham Gold Cups.

The chase track runs inside the Flat course down the back straight, outside the Flat course in the straight; the fences are well made and the undulations – especially that uphill finish – make this a testing course for a jumper. The run-in from the last fence to the winning post is 250 yards.

There has been racing at Leicester since the seventeenth century, and the present course at Oadby was founded in 1883. The Victorian grandstand built then was demolished and replaced in 1997 by a modern facility.

LENGTH

The length of a horse's body – the basic unit of measurement for distances between horses at the end of a race.

LEOPARDSTOWN

Foxrock, Dublin 18
Tel.: 01 289 3607
Fax: 01 289 2634
E-mail: info@leopardstown.com
Web: www.leopardstown.com

Leopardstown is one of the premier racecourses in Ireland, second only to **The Curragh** in terms of the overall prestige of its racing programme. On the Flat, the major races run here are the **Irish Champion Stakes** and the Heinx 57 Phoenix Stakes, and early in the season the course stages significant Classic trials. Over jumps, the big races in a consistently high-class programme are the AIG Europe Champion Hurdle in January, the Hennessy Cognac Gold Cup in February, and the Paddy Power Chase and Ericsson Chase in December. British visitors often observe that Leopardstown has a good deal of the feel of Sandown Park about it – suburban but spacious, well laid out, with excellent facilities and a high standard of racing. The track itself is left-handed, one and three-quarter miles round, with an uphill finish. There is a straight six-furlong sprint course on which the runners pass the post in the opposite direction from the round course.

L'ESCARGOT

The Snail – in French – defied his name and gained a lasting place in the annals of jump racing as one of only two horses who have ever won both the Gold Cup (which he landed twice) and Grand National: the other was **Golden Miller**. L'Escargot, who was bought for 3,000 guineas by trainer Dan Moore and ran in the colours of **Raymond Guest** (owner of Sir Ivor), ran in 60 races over 10 seasons, winning two races on the Flat, three hurdles (including a division of the Gloucestershire Hurdle at the Cheltenham National Hunt Meeting in 1968) and nine steeplechases. He started at 33–1 for the 1970 Gold Cup and won by one and a half lengths from French Tan, then – not having won another race in the interim – returned to Cheltenham a year later. This time 7–2 co-favourite, he won by ten lengths from Leap Frog and **The Dikler**. In all he competed at the big Cheltenham meeting in March for eight successive seasons. For years Guest had been asking Moore to acquire a horse to win him a Grand National. 'You've got one,' was the trainer's reply, and L'Escargot was eventually to prove him right. His third place in 1973 was all but unnoticed as **Crisp** and **Red Rum** ran their famous race, and in 1974 he improved a place, finishing runner-up to Red Rum. In 1975 those placings were reversed, with the 12-year-old L'Escargot staying on resolutely to beat the then dual National winner by 15 lengths. A misunderstanding between owner and trainer regarding whether the old horse had been retired or not saw him run once more – beaten a head in the Kerry National at Listowel in September 1975 – after which he was despatched to Guest's farm in Virginia, where he died at the age of 21 in 1984.

LEVELS (YOU DEVILS)
Betting slang for evens.

LEVY BOARD
Horserace Betting Levy Board
52 Grosvenor Gardens, London SW1W 0AU
Tel.: 020 7333 0043
Fax: 020 7333 0041
E-mail: hblb@hblb.org.uk
Web: www.hblb.org.uk

Founded in 1961 following the legalisation of off-course betting, the Levy Board provides racing with its major source of finance by collecting part of the betting turnover from the bookmakers (including the **Tote**) and distributing it for the greater good of the sport. The first annual levy (1962–3) raised less than £2 million; the figure for 2000–1 was expected to be in the region of £62 million. The original purpose of the Levy Board was that the proceeds it raised should be used for 'the improvement of breeds of horse, the advancement or encouragement of veterinary science or veterinary education, and the improvement of horse racing'. Today it is the last of these aims with which the Board is principally concerned – for, with off-course betting severely depleting racecourse attendances and therefore takings at the gate, courses are in great need of financial support. The Levy Board helps on several fronts. It provides grants and interest-free loans to racecourses, not only for the building of new stands and facilities but also for infrastructural improvements such as watering systems and drainage; it puts a large amount towards prize money, supplementing the contributions of owners, courses and sponsors; and it gives financial support in less visible areas, for example in providing more sophisticated technical equipment and subsidising Jockey Club Security Services and the Horseracing Forensic Laboratory, with its highly elaborate techniques for detecting doping. It also puts money into the breeding industry and veterinary science.

The Levy Board is scheduled to cease operations in September 2003 following the restructuring of the finances of British racing.

LEWIS, GEOFF
Geoff Lewis was born near Brecon in 1935 and apprenticed to Ron Smyth at Epsom: his first winner was Eastern Imp at Epsom on 23 April 1953. By the late 1960s he had become one of the leading jockeys in Britain; in 1969 he was runner-up to Lester Piggott in the jockeys' table, and the same year rode his first Classic winner, Right Tack in the Two Thousand Guineas. But as a jockey he will best be remembered for his partnership with **Mill Reef**, whom he rode in all the colt's 14 races and on whom he won 12, including the glorious sequence of Derby, Eclipse, King George and Arc in 1971. That year Lewis was the first jockey ever to ride the winners of all three big races at the Epsom Derby meeting, adding the Oaks on Altesse Royale and the Coronation Cup on Lupe to Mill Reef's Derby. He also won the One Thousand Guineas and Oaks on Mysterious in 1973, taking his overall Classic tally to five. After retiring from the saddle in 1979 he started training at

Epsom: his first runner, Concert Hall at Doncaster on 20 March 1980, was his first winner. Though he never trained a Classic winner, he handled several good horses, notably Silver Wisp (third to Dr Devious in the 1992 Derby) and Lake Coniston (winner of the July Cup in 1995). He retired from training in 1999.

LIMERICK

Greenmount Park, Patrickswell, Co. Limerick

Tel.: 061 355055

Fax: 061 355766

E-mail: info@limerick-racecourse.com

Web: www.limerick-racecourse.com

The new racecourse at Limerick, scheduled to open in October 2001 to replace the old Limerick course at Greenpark which closed in 1999, is the first course to be built in Ireland for half a century. The course is right-handed and just over a mile and a quarter round, with cambered bends intended to attract the galloping type of horse. Main race here is the Munster National.

LIMITED HANDICAP

A limited handicap is one with a narrow range of weights – the theory being that since no runner will have to concede a hefty amount to another, connections of good horses will be encouraged to enter. For example, the Samsung Electronics Scottish Champion Hurdle at Ayr in April 2001 was a limited handicap, with the highest weight stipulated to be carried 11st 10lb, and the lowest 10st 4lb – a range of just 20lb. By contrast, the novices' handicap chase on the same card had a weight range of 28lb.

LINCOLN HANDICAP

Handicap; four-year-olds and upwards; 1 mile (Doncaster)

The first big event of the Flat season began life at – guess! – Lincoln in 1853, transferring to Doncaster in 1965 after the historic course on the Carholme had closed the previous year. Back in the mists of time the race attracted some seriously good horses: **Sceptre** ran twice, beaten a head by St Maclou in 1902 and fifth the following year.

Fifty-eight horses ran in the 1948 Lincolnshire Handicap – the largest field ever to run in a Flat race in Britain.

Nowadays the Lincoln is an intensely competitive handicap which attracts a good deal of ante-post interest in the preceding weeks, and some famous gambles have been landed in the race – not least in the 2001 running, when Nimello was supported from long ante-post odds down to a very cramped 9–2 at the off. One factor militating against a serious ante-post punt on the Lincoln is the perceived effect of the draw over Doncaster's straight mile, and in an effort to combat this

Lincoln Handicap winners since 1990

Year	Horse	Age	Trainer	Jockey	Odds	Ran
1990	Evichstar	6	J. FitzGerald	A. Munro	33–1	24
1991	Amenable	6	T. D. Barron	Alex Greaves	22–1	25
1992	High Low	4	W. Haggas	J. Quinn	16–1	24
1993	High Premium	5	Mrs J. Ramsden	K. Fallon	16–1	24
1994	Our Rita	5	Dr J. Scargill	D. Holland	16–1	24
1995	Roving Minstrel	4	B. McMahon	K. Darley	33–1	23
1996	Stone Ridge	4	R. Hannon	Dane O'Neill	33–1	24
1997	Kuala Lipis	4	P. Cole	T. Quinn	11–1	24
1998	Hunters Of Brora	8	J. Bethell	J. Weaver	16–1	23
1999	Right Wing	5	J. Dunlop	T. Quinn	9–2F	24
2000	John Ferneley	5	P. Cole	J. Fortune	7–1JF	24
2001	Nimello	5	P. Cole	J. Fortune	9–2F	23

the race was run on the course's round mile in 1978: this was not considered a success, and it has reverted to the straight mile ever since.

LINGFIELD PARK

Lingfield, Surrey RH7 6PQ
Tel.: 01342 834800
Fax: 01342 832833
E-mail: info@lingfieldpark.co.uk
Web: www.lingfield-racecourse.co.uk

The image of 'Leafy Lingfield' took a knock when the laying down of the **all-weather** track turned the course's sylvan setting into a massive building site in 1989, and the existence of the artificial circuit inside the turf still takes the edge off the charm. Racing began here under National Hunt Rules in 1890, with the Flat following four years later, and it is as a Flat course that Lingfield is primarily significant today.

Left-handed and undulating, with a steep downhill run towards the final turn, Lingfield quite closely resembles the Derby course at Epsom Downs, and the Derby and Oaks Trials here, held in mid-May, are significant pointers to Epsom.

The first all-weather fixture in Britain was held at Lingfield Park on 30 October 1989.

The turf course is roughly in the shape of a left-handed triangle of a mile and a half round, with a run from the home turn of just under half a mile; races up to seven furlongs 140 yards run along a straight spur off the round course. Along the straight after the winning post the course rises to the top of the hill about six furlongs out, then descends sharply. The straight course is downhill for much of the way and considered an easy trip, and generally Lingfield is not a course which puts much premium on stamina: agility and nimbleness are more important here.

The all-weather track is just under a mile and a quarter round, with no straight sprint course, and the shortness of the home straight – two furlongs – makes it imperative for a horse to be in contention turning in.

In 1998 it was announced that jump racing at Lingfield would cease the following spring, but the winter game got a partial reprieve, and a minimal programme of National Hunt sport continues.

LISTED RACE

In the **Pattern** which grades the best races on the Flat, Listed races comes below Group Three: they are designed to identify horses of merit above the norm but below Group standard.

LISTOWEL

Listowel, Co. Kerry
Tel.: 068 22407

Listowel stages one of Irish racing's most enjoyable festival meetings, a six-day hooley in September – the timing traditionally designed to accommodate farmers looking to relax after the harvest is in. The major race at this fixture is the Kerry National. The track is left-handed and mainly flat, a little over one mile round and therefore on the sharp side and well suited to front-runners.

LLEWELLYN, CARL

A senior and highly popular figure in the weighing room, Carl Llewellyn was born in 1965 and rode his first winner on Starjestic at Wolverhampton on 14 March 1986. While never challenging for championship honours, he has ridden a succession of big-race winners, notably two Grand National heroes in the shape of the gigantic Party Politics, who beat Romany King in 1992, and the ultra-durable Earth Summit (trained by Llewellyn's principal employer Nigel Twiston-Davies), winner from Suny Bay in bottomless going in 1998. Other well-known horses he has partnered include Tipping Tim, Pegwell Bay, Dublin Flyer and Beau, on whom he won the 2000 Whitbread Gold Cup by a distance.

LOCHSONG

Owned by Jeff Smith and trained by **Ian Balding**, Lochsong won 15 of her 27 races over four seasons and became one of the most popular racehorses of the age. She did not run as a two-year-old, but at three in 1991 won two of her three races: a maiden at Redcar and an apprentice handicap at Newbury. The following year she made rapid improvement, becoming the first horse ever to win all three big sprint handicaps of the season – the Stewards' Cup at Goodwood, Portland Handicap at Doncaster and Ayr Gold Cup – and running second to Wolfhound in the Diadem Stakes at Ascot. As a five-year-old in 1993 she just kept on getting better and better, rising to the status of best sprinter in Europe by winning the King George Stakes at Goodwood, Nunthorpe Stakes and Prix de l'Abbaye (by six lengths). She started her 1994 campaign with a scorching pillar-to-post victory in the Palace House Stakes at Newmarket – 'Like a surfer hitting a good wave', enthused her rider Frankie Dettori – then kept at the very top by taking the Temple Stakes at Sandown Park and the King's Stand Stakes at Royal Ascot. Those three races were over five furlongs. When stepped up to six for the July Cup she weakened in the final furlong and finished last but one. Back at five furlongs for the King George Stakes she resumed her winning ways, then disgraced herself at York: odds-on for the Nunthorpe Stakes, she got very worked up in the paddock and, in Frankie Dettori's words, 'probably broke the track record going down to the start.'

Having expended most of her energy before the race, she finished last. There was one more moment of European glory to come – a second Prix de l'Abbaye, this time by five lengths – and then Lochsong was off to Churchill Downs for the Breeders' Cup Sprint, where she finished last of the 14 runners. She was then retired to the paddocks, sorely missed by her hordes of admirers.

LOCKINGE STAKES
Group One; four-year-olds and upwards;
1 mile (Newbury)

When the Lockinge Stakes was upgraded from Group Two status in 1995, Newbury gained its first Group One race. Such elevation was well overdue, both for the course – widely acknowledged to be one of the premier Flat tracks in the country – and for the Lockinge Stakes itself, which since its first running in 1958 has had a history of attracting some tip-top milers. The first two runnings went to the Queen's 1958 Two Thousand Guineas winner Pall Mall, who landed the odds of 6–4 on in 1958 and 2–1 on in 1959. Queen's Hussar, sire of **Brigadier Gerard**, won in 1963, and the Brigadier himself kept up the family tradition when taking the 1972 renewal as a four-year-old at 4–1 on. Other familiar names on the Lockinge roll of honour include Silly Season (1966), Habitat (1969), Sparkler (1973),

Lockinge Stakes winners since 1990

1990	Safawan	4	M. Stoute	W. R. Swinburn	5–1	6
1991	Polar Falcon	4	J. Hammond FRA	L. Piggott	3–1	4
1992	Selkirk	4	I. Balding	R. Cochrane	5–2	10
1993	Swing Low	4	R. Hannon	L. Piggott	12–1	10
1994	Emperor Jones	4	J. Gosden	L. Dettori	11–2	11
1995	Soviet Line	5	M. Stoute	W. R. Swinburn	2–1F	5
1996	Soviet Line	6	M. Stoute	T. Quinn	13–2	7
1997	First Island	5	G. Wragg	M. Hills	11–4	10
1998	Cape Cross	4	S. bin Suroor	D. O'Donohoe	20–1	10
1999	Fly To The Stars	5	S. bin Suroor	W. Supple	9–1	6
2000	Aljabr	4	S. bin Suroor	L. Dettori	8–13F	7
2001	Medicean	4	M. Stoute	K. Fallon	3–1	7

Boldboy (1974), Relkino (1977), Kris (1980), Cormorant Wood and Wassl (who dead-heated in 1984) and Selkirk (1992). Soviet Line won the first two runnings at Group One level – the third dual winner in the race's history, following Pall Mall and Welsh Pageant (1970 and 1971).

LONGCHAMP

France's principal racecourse is situated in the Bois de Boulogne in Paris and home to many of the country's biggest events – notably the **Prix de l'Arc de Triomphe**, Prix de l'Abbaye, Poule d'Essai des Poulains (French Two Thousand Guineas), Poule d'Essai des Pouliches (French One Thousand Guineas), Grand Prix de Paris, Prix du Moulin, Prix Vermeille, Prix Royal-Oak (French St Leger), Prix Ganay, Prix Lupin and Grand Criterium. There are several variations of track at Longchamp, but in simple terms the course is about one and three-quarter miles round and right-handed, with a steady climb up the back straight past the Petit Bois – the cluster of trees at the far end of the course – and, before the actual home straight, the 'false straight' which catches out many an unwary visiting jockey who is tempted to start his run too soon. The five-furlong course is straight and flat, and has its own winning post remote from the stands.

LONGDEN, JOHNNY

Born in Wakefield, Yorkshire, in 1907, Johnny Longden made an indelible mark on racing in the USA. He rode his first winner in Utah in 1927, and on his retirement in 1966 had ridden 6,032 winners in his adopted country, a world record at the time. Among the horses with which he was associated were 1943 Triple Crown winner Count Fleet, Swaps, Whirlaway and TV Lark. Longden took up training in 1967: when his colt Majestic Prince won the 1969 Kentucky Derby he became the only man ever to have both ridden and trained winners of the 'Run for the Roses'.

LONG HANDICAP

See **handicap**.

LOT

A trainer's string goes out for exercise in 'lots' – so you will often hear a lad or jockey referring to having ridden out 'first lot'.

LOTTERY

According to which Turf historian you choose to trust, Lottery's victory in the Grand Liverpool Steeplechase at Aintree in 1839 makes him the first Grand National winner – or not, as some researchers are convinced that there had been earlier runnings of the race at Aintree. Whatever the niceties of the historical record, there is no doubt Lottery was a remarkable racehorse. Owned by John Elmore, he raced for eight seasons and won five hurdle races and 16 steeplechases, and his superiority over his contemporaries was such that conditions for a race at Horncastle in 1840 stated that the event was 'open to all horses – except Mr Elmore's Lottery', a changing of the conditions which foreshadowed the superiority of **Arkle** over a century later. In similar vein, conditions for a race at Finchley (yes, Finchley) in 1842 included the stipulation: 'Lottery's entry fee £40, others £10.' Lottery's party trick was to canter up to a fully stocked lunch table and jump it without disturbing so much as a wine glass.

LUCKY 15

Bet involving four selections in four separate races, in the combinations:

- 4 singles
- 6 doubles
- 4 trebles
- 1 accumulator

If just one of your selections wins, many bookmakers pay out at twice the win odds for that horse. There is usually a bonus for picking all four winners.

LUDLOW

Bromfield, Ludlow, Shropshire SY8 2BT
Tel.: 01584 856221
Fax: 01584 856217
E-mail: br-davies@lineone.net
Web: ludlow-racecourse.co.uk

Ludlow boasts one of the quaintest buildings to be found on any British racecourse, the open-topped grandstand built in 1904. That is the good news. The bad news is that the track shares its land with a golf course and has to tolerate no fewer than four road crossings, which are covered by matting for racing but none the less serve as an additional aggravation for jockeys trying to remember their way round. For Ludlow is one of those tracks where the hurdle and chase courses diverge down the back straight, and it is not unknown for riders to take a wrong turning and incur the wrath of the stewards – to say nothing of the punters.

The right-handed course has a few minor undulations but is generally flat. The chase circuit, about one and a half miles round, has fairly tight turns and is suited to the nippy sort of horse. Down the back straight the chase course cuts across the golf course, while the back straight of the hurdles circuit runs along the far side of the golf course and has easier turns than the chasing track.

LUKAS, D. WAYNE

Darrell Wayne Lukas was born in Wisconsin in 1935. He spent a period as a high school basketball coach and started training in 1966, handling not only Thoroughbreds but **quarter horses**. Having settled in California in 1972, he built up the most powerful training establishment in the country, regularly breaking earnings records. His first winner of a Triple Crown race was Codex in the 1980 Preakness Stakes, since when there has been a steady stream of success. In 1995 he became the first trainer to send out winners of each leg of the Triple Crown with different horses – Thunder Gulch in the Kentucky Derby and Belmont Stakes, and Timber Country in the Preakness. By the completion of the Triple Crown series in 2001, Lukas had won 13 races in the series, and to 2000 he had won 16 Breeders' Cup races. Among his other famous horses have been Winning Colors (filly who won the Kentucky Derby in 1988), Lady's Secret, Open Mind, Gulch, Criminal Type, Flanders and Steinlen.

M

MAGEE, SEAN

Although he rarely rode over fences, Sean Magee was one of the top riders over hurdles in the years around the outbreak of the Second World War. Riding Dorothy Paget's hurdler Solford, he was vying for the lead at the last flight in the 1939 Champion Hurdle, only to fall. Consolation was just a year away. Solford started 5–2 favourite for the 1940 Champion Hurdle and was brought with a perfectly timed run by Magee to take the lead going to the last and win by a length and a half. The following year Solford and Magee started 7–4 on in a six-runner field for the Champion, but dropped away tamely between the final two flights and finished last.

MAGNIER, JOHN

John Magnier is one of the driving forces behind making the racing operation based at the **Coolmore Stud** in Co. Tipperary one of the major forces in European racing. Most of his horses are owned in partnership with **Michael Tabor** and many race in the colours of his wife Susan Magnier (daughter of **Vincent O'Brien**): dark blue. The best horses to have borne those colours are 2001 Derby winner **Galileo** and **Giant's Causeway**, multiple Group One winner in 2000, while the Magniers had their first Classic winner in the same silks when King Of Kings won the 1998 Two Thousand Guineas. Other good horses in whom John Magnier has had a significant share include Imagine (Oaks and Irish One Thousand Guineas 2001), Entrepreneur (Two Thousand Guineas 1997) and Shahtoush (Oaks 1998).

MAGUIRE, ADRIAN

Few Cheltenham racegoers seeing the name 'Mr A. Maguire' down to ride **Martin Pipe**-trained Omerta in the Fulke Walwyn Kim Muir Chase on the opening day of the 1991 Festival would have had much sense of the riding talent about to be unleashed on British racing. After he had brought Omerta home an 11–1 Pipe winner they started to pay more attention, and within a few years Maguire had become acknowledged as one of the very best jump jockeys of the era. One of 10 children of a green-keeper in Kilmessan, Co. Meath, he was born on 29 April 1971 and cut his riding teeth on the pony-racing circuits of Ireland: he rode his first pony-race winner at the age of 12, weighing 5st 7lb. He then started riding in point-to-points, winning the Irish point-to-point riders' championship in the 1990–1 season. His first winner under Rules was Gladtogetit in a bumper at Sligo on 11 February 1990. A month after winning on Omerta at Cheltenham he landed the Irish Grand National on the same horse, beating Cahervillahow by a short head. For the 1991–2 season Maguire moved to England to ride for Toby Balding, and the 20-year-old won the 1992 Cheltenham Gold Cup on Balding-trained 25–1 outsider Cool Ground, in a furious finish with The Fellow. In 1992–3 he finished third in the jump jockeys' championship, and in 1993–4 came second to Richard Dunwoody after a memorable tussle which left him just four winners short of the champion: his total of 194 is the highest ever recorded by a rider who did not win the title. In addition to the Gold Cup on Cool Ground, Maguire has won plenty of big races: the 1992 Hennessy Gold Cup on Sibton Abbey; the 1993 Tote Gold Trophy on King Credo; the 1993 King George VI Chase on Barton Bank; the 1994 Triumph Hurdle on Mysilv; the 1994 Queen Mother Champion Chase on Viking Flagship; the 1995 Mumm Melling Chase on the same horse, in a wonderful finish with Deep Sensation and Martha's Son; the Scottish Grand National on Baronet in 1998 and Paris Pike in 2000; and the 1998 Whitbread Gold Cup on Call It A Day.

MAHER, DANNY

Born in Connecticut in 1881, Danny Maher was champion jockey in the USA in 1898 and came to England in 1900, where he was champion jockey in 1908 and 1913. Maher rode winners of every Classic and landed nine in all – including the Derby on Rock Sand (1903), Cicero (1905) and Spearmint (1906). He died of tuberculosis at the age of 35 in 1916.

MAIDEN

A horse who has not won a race – not necessarily a young horse: Panegyrist was a maiden until winning a novices' chase at Ayr in March 1989 at the age of 14. Nor does maiden status mean that a horse is not earning his keep: Clive Brittain's colt Needle Gun had amassed £257,717 in place money from 13 outings before finally losing his maiden status when winning a small race at Yarmouth in October 1994.

MAIDEN RACE

Race for horses who have not previously won.

MAKTOUM BROTHERS

The four Maktoum brothers – Sheikh Maktoum, Sheikh Hamdan, Sheikh Mohammed and Sheikh Ahmed – have changed the face of racing in Europe and around the world over the last two decades, establishing major breeding operations, buying heavily at the yearling sales and owning some of the finest horses ever to be seen on a racecourse. The brothers are sons of the late Sheikh Rashid bin Saeed Al-Maktoum, ruler of Dubai, the tiny oil-rich state which forms part of the United Arab Emirates.

Maktoum Al Maktoum (colours: royal blue, white chevron, light blue cap) is the eldest of the four and has been ruler of Dubai since his father's death in 1991. He was the first to own a Classic winner when Touching Wood, second to Golden Fleece in the 1982 Derby,

went on to win the St Leger. Sheikh Maktoum followed up with Ma Biche in the 1983 One Thousand Guineas and Shadeed in the 1985 Two Thousand; his Shareef Dancer won the Irish Derby in 1983, and Hatoof the One Thousand Guineas in 1992 and Champion Stakes in 1993. He has also owned fine sprinters in Green Desert, Cadeaux Genereux and Royal Applause as well as Ezzoud, winner of the International Stakes in 1993 and 1994 as well as the 1994 Eclipse. Balanchine and Moonshell, early carriers of the **Godolphin** flag, won the Oaks in 1994 and 1995 respectively in Sheikh Maktoum's colours, and his son Saeed Maktoum Al Maktoum owned **Lammtarra**, winner in 1995 of the Derby, King George and Arc. Maktoum Al Maktoum's bloodstock interests are gathered under the banner of the **Gainsborough Stud**.

With the achievements of **Nashwan** (Two Thousand Guineas, Derby and King George in 1989), Salsabil (One Thousand Guineas, Oaks and Irish Derby in 1990), the brilliant sprinter **Dayjur**, Erhaab (1994 Derby) and countless other familiar names, the second oldest brother Sheikh Hamdan Al Maktoum (whose day job is as Minister of Finance in Dubai) has challenged the younger Sheikh Mohammed for the position of leading light among the brothers. Before Nashwan his best horses had been Unfuwain and the filly Al Bahathri, beaten a short head by Oh So Sharp in the 1985 One Thousand Guineas and a game winner of the Irish One Thousand. His colours of royal blue, white epaulets, striped cap, have become a familiar sight in big races all over the world: he won the Melbourne Cup with At Talaq in 1986 and Jeune in 1994. Sheikh Hamdan's breeding operation is run as the Shadwell Estate Company, the flagship of which is the Nunnery Stud near Thetford in Norfolk: Nashwan, Unfuwain and Muhtarram are resident stallions here. Sheikh Hamdan was leading owner in 1990, 1994 and 1995.

Sheikh Mohammed started developing his racing interests in earnest in the late 1970s, but had to wait until 1985 for his first Classic winner when **Oh So Sharp**, whom he had bred, took the One Thousand Guineas: she then won the Oaks and the St Leger. Sheikh

Maktoum-owned Classic winners

One Thousand Guineas
1983 Ma Biche (Sheikh Maktoum)
1985 Oh So Sharp (Sheikh
    Mohammed)
1989 Musical Bliss (Sheikh Mohammed)
1990 Salsabil (Sheikh Hamdan)
1991 Shadayid (Sheikh Hamdan)
1992 Hatoof (Sheikh Maktoum)
1995 Harayir (Sheikh Hamdan)
1998 Cape Verdi (Godolphin)
2000 Lahan (Sheikh Hamdan)
2001 Ameerat (Sheikh Ahmed)

Two Thousand Guineas
1985 Shadeed (Sheikh Maktoum)
1989 Nashwan (Sheikh Hamdan)
1995 Pennekamp (Sheikh Mohammed)
1996 Mark Of Esteem (Godolphin)
1999 Island Sands (Godolphin)

Derby
1989 Nashwan (Sheikh Hamdan)
1994 Erhaab (Sheikh Hamdan)
1995 Lammtarra (Saeed Maktoum Al
    Maktoum/Godolphin)

Oaks
1985 Oh So Sharp (Sheikh Mohammed)
1987 Unite (Sheikh Mohammed)
1988 Diminuendo (Sheikh Mohammed)
1989 Snow Bride (Saeed Maktoum Al-
    Maktoum)
1990 Salsabil (Sheikh Hamdan)
1991 Jet Ski Lady (Sheikh Maktoum)
1993 Intrepidity (Sheikh Mohammed)
1994 Balanchine (Sheikh Maktoum/
    Godolphin)
1995 Moonshell (Sheikh Maktoum/
    Godolphin)

St Leger
1982 Touching Wood (Sheikh Maktoum)
1985 Oh So Sharp (Sheikh Mohammed)
1994 Moonax (Sheikh Mohammed)
1995 Classic Cliché (Godolphin)
1996 Shantou (Sheikh Mohammed)
1998 Nedawi (Godolphin)
1999 Mutafaweq (Godolphin)

Mohammed bought **Pebbles** after she had won the One Thousand Guineas in 1984, and she went on to win the Eclipse Stakes (first filly to do so), Champion Stakes (sponsored since 1982 by the Maktoum family) and Breeders' Cup Turf in 1985 – the year that Sheikh Mohammed first became leading owner. Other good fillies to have raced in his colours (maroon, white sleeves, maroon cap, white star) include the winners of the 1987, 1988 and 1993 Oaks in Unite, Diminuendo and Intrepidity, the 1989 One Thousand Guineas winner Musical Bliss and the brilliant Indian Skimmer, winner of the 1988 Champion Stakes. He has won the King George VI and Queen Elizabeth Diamond Stakes with Belmez (1990), Opera House (1993) and King's Theatre (1994), the Prix du Jockey-Club and Irish Derby with Old Vic (1989), the Arc with Carnegie (1994), and countless other big races. He has even made an impact on the National Hunt scene, winning the Champion Hurdle with Kribensis in 1990 and Royal Gait in 1992. Like his brothers, Sheikh Mohammed maintains his own international breeding interests – notably at the **Dalham Hall Stud**, Newmarket, and the **Kildangan Stud** in Ireland – but he still buys widely at the yearling sales. Leading owner on the Flat nine times (1985–9, 1991–3, 1997), he has in recent years directed much of his energy towards establishing a world racing force in the shape of the **Godolphin** operation, the immense success of which with horses like **Daylami**, **Swain** and **Dubai Millennium** is tribute to Sheikh Mohammed's dogged pursuit of the very best.

Sheikh Ahmed (yellow, black epaulets) is the youngest of the four brothers. His best-known horses have been Wassl, winner of the Irish Two Thousand Guineas in 1983; Mtoto, who in 1987 won the Eclipse Stakes and in 1988 a second Eclipse and the King George VI and Queen Elizabeth Diamond Stakes; Possessive Dancer, winner of the Irish Oaks in 1991; and Ameerat, who in May 2001 delivered Sheikh Ahmed his first Classic in England when landing the One Thousand Guineas. Sheikh Ahmed owns the Aston Upthorpe Stud in Oxfordshire, where Mtoto stands.

MALTON

Major training centre in North Yorkshire. Well-known trainers in the area include Jimmy FitzGerald and Tim Easterby.

MANDARIN

Mandarin was in his heyday at a time when interest in National Hunt racing was rapidly expanding following a rapid injection of money from commercial companies, and his exploits earned his owner Mme Kilian Hennessy a handy amount of the sponsors' money. He was beaten a neck by Much Obliged in the first Whitbread Gold Cup at Sandown Park in 1957, won the inaugural Hennessy Gold Cup at Cheltenham in 1957, and landed a second Hennessy at Newbury in 1961. Other big chases won by the Fulke Walwyn-trained gelding include the King George VI Chase in 1957 and 1959 and the Cheltenham Gold Cup at the age of 11 in 1962: ridden by **Fred Winter**, Mandarin beat Fortria a length. But the race which linked the names of Mandarin and Fred Winter for ever in jumping history came three months after that Cheltenham triumph, in the Grand Steeple-Chase de Paris at Auteuil on 17 June 1962. Mandarin was leading at the fourth of the 21 fences on Auteuil's eccentric figure-of-eight circuit when the bit in Mandarin's mouth snapped, leaving Winter with three miles still to cover and no means of steering. They managed to keep in the race, but four fences out, Winter had to wrench his horse to the left to keep him on track. He lost several lengths and – far worse – broke down in one of his forelegs. Exhausted, half crippled and out of contact with his jockey, Mandarin somehow led over the last fence and set off up the run-in with the French horse Lumino closing rapidly. The two crossed the line together, and as the horses were led back to unsaddle, Mandarin's broken bit dangling under his neck, the result was announced: Mandarin by a head. John Oaksey wrote in the *Daily Telegraph*:

I never expect to be more moved by a man and a horse than I was by Winter and Mandarin this afternoon. Separately, they have always been superb. Together, today, taking disaster by the throat and turning it into victory, they have surely earned a place of honour that will be secure as long as men talk, or read, or think of horses.

Mandarin himself had earned more than a place in history: he had earned a pension of two bottles of stout, courtesy of Whitbread, delivered daily to the paddock in Lambourn where he lived out an honourable retirement until his death at the age of 25 in 1976. He ran in 51 races, winning two hurdles and 17 chases.

MANIFESTO

Until the days of **Red Rum**, Manifesto was regarded as the greatest Grand National horse of all. He raced for 13 consecutive seasons, and ran in the Aintree marathon no fewer than eight times:

- 1895 (aged seven): fourth behind Wild Man From Borneo
- 1896 (eight): brought down at the first fence
- 1897 (nine): won by twenty lengths from Filbert
- 1899 (11): won by five lengths from Ford Of Fyne
- 1902 (14): third, beaten six lengths, behind Shannon Lass
- 1903 (15): third, beaten 23 lengths, behind Drumcree
- 1904 (16): eighth behind Moifaa

They don't make 'em like that any more!

MAN O' WAR

This great American horse ran in 21 races in 1919 and 1920 and was beaten just once. As a two-year-old he won nine of his 10 races (losing the other to the appropriately named Upset), including the Belmont Futurity. He had not been entered in the Kentucky Derby as his doting owner Samuel D. Riddle felt the race came too early in the season, but he landed the Preakness and Belmont Stakes, winning the latter by 20 lengths from a single opponent. His final race before retiring at the end of the 1920 season was a match against 1919 Triple Crown winner Sir Barton, which Man O' War won by seven lengths.

Man O' War never started at odds against, and in three of his races in 1920 started at 100–1 on.

At stud in Kentucky he sired 1937 US Triple Crown winner **War Admiral** and 1938 Grand National winner Battleship. On the horse's twenty-first birthday Riddle sent him a cake bearing 21 candles, and when Man O' War died at the age of 30 in 1947 had him laid in state in his box, in a coffin lined with Riddle's black and gold racing colours. His grave, under a massive bronze statue of the horse, is at the Kentucky Horse Park, just outside Lexington. A fitting epitaph comes from Man O' War's groom Will Harbut, who would introduce his charge to visitors as 'the mostest hoss that ever was'.

MARE
Female horse aged five or over.

MARKET RASEN
Legsby Road, Market Rasen, Lincolnshire
LN8 3EA
Tel.: 01673 843434
Fax: 01673 844532
E-mail: marketrasen@rht.net
Web: www.marketrasenraces.co.uk

Market Rasen is an excellent course, for horse and human alike. The right-handed circuit is about 10 furlongs round, with some undulations, and its comparatively easy fences render it a good testing ground for novice chasers. The turns are quite sharp, and the terrain tends to put the handy horse at an advantage over the big strong galloper. The present course was first used in 1924, but most of the current facilities are much more recent: the two main stands, for example, were built in the 1960s. The water jump in front of the stands provides a good spectacle for the paying public, and overall this is a very racegoer-friendly course: siting the parade ring on the racecourse side of the stands makes for ease of movement between paddock, betting ring, bar and stand; the facilities are kept as up-to-date as possible; viewing is excellent; and the highly popular summer evening meetings are graced with musical entertainment.

MARLBOROUGH CUP
English equivalent of the **Maryland Hunt Cup**, the Marlborough Cup (first run 1995) takes place in May over a specially built 3-mile course with timber fences at Barbury Castle, near Marlborough in Wiltshire. It is not run under Jockey Club Rules.

MARSHALL, BRYAN
Born in 1916, Bryan Marshall was champion jump jockey in the 1947–8 season. He won the Grand National in successive years – on Early Mist in 1953 and Royal Tan in 1954, both trained by **Vincent O'Brien** – and the King George VI Chase on Rowland Roy in 1947 and the Queen Mother's Manicou in 1950, but never landed the Cheltenham Gold Cup or Champion Hurdle. After retiring from the saddle in 1954 he spent a period training, then moved into the horse transportation business. Bryan Marshall died in October 1991, aged 75.

MARTINGALE
A racing martingale consists of two metal rings attached by a leather strip: the reins are threaded through the rings under the horse's neck to keep them in place.

MARYLAND HUNT CUP
The USA's most important race over timber fences, run over four miles at Far Hills in Maryland. The first Maryland Hunt Cup winner to land the Grand National was Jay Trump in 1965, the second Ben Nevis in 1980; both had won the American race twice.

MATCH
The pitching of one horse against another, each side putting up a stake and winner taking all, was common in the eighteenth century. Some races were run in heats, often over a distance of four miles, with the winners running off for the prize. Several

famous matches have passed into racing history – notably that between **Voltigeur** and **The Flying Dutchman** at York in 1851 – and the idea persisted into the twentieth century. Papyrus, winner of the 1923 Derby, travelled to the USA for a match at Belmont Park against Kentucky Derby winner Zev, who won by five lengths. The match between the gritty Seabiscuit and 1937 Triple Crown winner **War Admiral** at Pimlico in 1938 is one of the most famous contests in American racing history (Seabiscuit won by four lengths), while the race between Ruffian and Foolish Pleasure at Belmont Park in 1975 ended in tragedy when Ruffian broke down early in the race and had to be destroyed. In April 1986 **Dawn Run**, fresh from winning the Cheltenham Gold Cup, met Buck House in a match at Punchestown and won by two and a half lengths. But plans for a modern-day match which would have set racing alight were tragically thwarted. In summer 2000, when the racing world was desperate to see the great four-year-old colts Dubai Millennium and Montjeu take each other on, Sheikh Mohammed proposed a match between the two, loser to pay winner $6 million, half going to charity. The very day after his proposal was made, Dubai Millennium fractured a leg on the gallops and was retired. In August 1988 a nine-year-old horse named Klute – not a racehorse – had convinced his owner Lesley Bruce that he was the fastest horse in the world, and she attempted to prove her point in a specially arranged match over five furlongs at Haydock Park against Jack Berry's good sprint handicapper So Careful. Klute turned out to be not quite the whirlwind performer Miss Bruce had thought: he was beaten 25 lengths. So Careful won the Ayr Gold Cup the following month, so at least Klute was demolished by a good horse, and the undaunted Miss Bruce was back for more in June 1990, over five furlongs at Catterick. Klute, now 11, faced a different Jack Berry charge, Valldemosa, but the result was the same: Berry's first, Klute nowhere (actually eight lengths behind the easing-up winner).

McCAIN, DONALD

'Ginger' McCain was born in 1930, took out a permit to train in 1952 and was granted a full licence in 1967. He combined training racehorses on a modest scale with running a used car business in Southport, Lancashire: the stable yard was behind the garage. In August 1972 at Doncaster Sales he paid 6,000 guineas on behalf of his main patron Noel Le Mare for a six-year-old gelding with modest form and bad feet, a horse who within a few years had made McCain a household name: **Red Rum**. McCain's unorthodox gallops along the Southport beach worked wonders for Red Rum's feet, and he transformed the gelding from a modest chaser to a triple Grand National winner, one of the very few racehorses who ever transcend the sport. In 1990 McCain left Southport for a new base at Cholmondeley in Cheshire.

McCARRON, CHRIS

On 28 April 2001 Chris McCarron won at Hollywood Park on a horse with the delightful name of Spinelessjellyfish to record his 7,000th domestic victory, thereby becoming the seventh jockey to reach that landmark in the USA. Best known to British racing fans as the man parachuted in to ride Best Of The Bests for Godolphin in 2000 Derby following Frankie Dettori's plane crash (they finished fourth behind Sinndar), McCarron tops the all-time prize money earning list for a US jockey. He has won the Kentucky Derby twice, on Alysheba (1987) and Go For Gin (1994), and the Breeders' Cup Classic four times, on Alysheba (1988), Sunday Silence (1989), Alphabet Soup (1996) and Tiznow (2000).

McCOY, TONY

No jockey, under either code, has made as rapid a rise to the top as Tony McCoy, and no jockey has dominated the riding scene in the way that he has since moving to Britain from Ireland in 1994. McCoy was born in Ballymena, Co. Antrim, on 4 May 1974. He served his apprenticeship with Jim Bolger in Co. Kilkenny (where he rode work on seriously good Flat horses like Jet Ski Lady and St Jovite) and rode his first winner on Legal Steps at

Thurles on 26 March 1991. Sidelined for several months by a gallops accident, he found his weight rising inexorably and turned his attention to riding over jumps. In 1994 he moved to England to join trainer Toby Balding, and in his first season broke the record for winners by a conditional jockey, scoring 74. The following season, 1995–6, he was champion jump jockey for the first time with 175 winners, and has remained at the very top of the tree ever since: champion in 1996–7 (190 winners), 1997–8 (253 – demolishing Peter Scudamore's record of 221, set in 1988–9), 1998–9 (186), 1999–2000 (245), and 2000–1 (191). He was only the sixth jump jockey – and much the quickest – to break the 1,000-winner barrier, and by the close of the 2000–1 season had ridden 1,314 winners in Britain. His strike rate in 2000–1, a season severely disrupted by the weather and the foot-and-mouth epidemic, was 25 per cent: that is, McCoy won on one in four of his rides. Much of his success is down to his partnership with the phenomenally prolific yard of trainer **Martin Pipe**, but at the root of the McCoy magic is a simple determination not to be beaten – seen countless times every season, but never more dramatically than when on Edredon Bleu in the two-mile chase at Sandown Park on Whitbread Gold Cup day 2001 he simply refused to lose: after a frenetic battle with Fadalko over the last two fences the verdict was the shortest of short heads, and it was widely agreed that no jockey other than McCoy would have won. Quality has accompanied quantity: his big-race wins include the Cheltenham Gold Cup (Mr Mulligan in 1997), Champion Hurdle (Make A Stand in 1997), and Queen Mother Champion Chase (Edredon Bleu in 2000, by a short head from Direct Route after a titanic battle from the last). When he finished third in the 2001 Grand National on Blowing Wind, having remounted after parting company from the horse at the nineteenth fence, it was the first time McCoy had completed the course in the National.

McMANUS, J. P.

John Patrick McManus, born in Limerick in 1951, has some 40 horses in training in England, Ireland and France and owns the Martinstown Stud in Co. Limerick. After a spell as a bookmaker in Ireland he built up a huge fortune on the international money markets, and deployed a good deal of that fortune as ammunition in his legendary tilts at the betting ring. He first came to the notice of British racing when at Royal Ascot in 1977 he reportedly lost £32,500 on the Coronation Stakes and £39,000 on the King Edward VII Stakes, but still ended the meeting, he said, 'about two thousand quid in front'. This man was clearly taking his betting seriously, and over the years his fame as a fearless punter playing for huge stakes has made him a true legend of the betting ring. Like most big punters he is reluctant to be too specific, so it remains speculation whether the £130,000 staked on Istabraq at 13–8 on before the 1998 Aintree Hurdle was the horse's owner's or not, but there is no denying that McManus's punting is in a different league from that of the average Channel Four Racing viewer. His deep devotion to the sport goes far beyond mere betting, and as an owner and breeder he has enjoyed considerable success. His best horse has undoubtedly been **Istabraq**, bought at the sales for 38,000 guineas after his Flat career and winner of the Champion Hurdle in 1998, 1999 and 2000, while other top horses to have raced in his colours of green and gold hoops, white cap, include Jack Of Trumps, Bit Of A Skite (Irish Grand National 1983), the good staying hurdler Le Coudray, Wylde Hide, Khayrawani, Joe Mac, Cardinal Hill, Danny Connors and Time For A Run. He bought First Gold after that horse had won the King George VI Chase in 2000 and the brilliant staying hurdler Baracouda, both trained by **François Doumen**. McManus's purchase of Jackdaws Castle, the state-of-the-art training yard in the Cotswolds where David Nicholson trained and where **Jonjo O'Neill** moved in summer 2001, further underlined his commitment to jump racing.

MEDIAN AUCTION RACE

Race on the Flat restricted to the progeny of stallions, the median (i.e. middle) price of whose offspring at public auction does not exceed the figure specified in the race conditions – in essence, a very low-grade race indeed.

MELBOURNE CUP

Run at Flemington racecourse, in the outskirts of Melbourne, on the first Tuesday in November, the Melbourne Cup brings Australia to a halt. Crowds of up to 100,000 dress up smart, casual or downright bizarre, abjure the temptations of temperance and pour into Flemington for one of the great occasions of world sport. The race they have come to attend (in a few cases, watch) is a two-mile handicap first run in 1861. The first winner was Archer, who had walked the 550 miles from his New South Wales stable to run, and understandably became something of a national hero for his efforts. Archer also won the second running, carrying 10st 2lb. Other great Australian horses won the Cup: **Carbine** under 10st 5lb in 1890; the legendary **Phar Lap** in 1930, at 11–8 on the shortest priced winner; Rain Lover twice, in 1968 and 1969. In 1993 **Vintage Crop**, trained in Ireland by **Dermot Weld** and ridden by **Michael Kinane**, became the first horse from outside Australasia to win the Melbourne Cup. Despite the cost and the wear and tear on a horse's constitution brought about by a mammoth journey, British-trained horses started to have a go: the Godolphin colt Central Park, half a length second in 1999 under Frankie Dettori at 50–1 when a late stand-in for the hotly fancied Kayf Tara, has come closest, but it's only a matter of time . . .

MELLON, PAUL

Black with gold cross front and back, black cap with gold stripe – those colours will for ever be associated with **Mill Reef**, winner of the Derby, Eclipse, King George and Arc in 1971. Paul Mellon was born in Pittsburgh in 1907 into a famously wealthy family and educated at Cambridge – whose proximity to Newmarket fuelled his early love of horse racing. Mellon's first winner as an owner was Drinmore Lad at Gatwick in 1936, and he gradually built up his racing interests, achieving big-race success with horses like Secret Step (1963 July Cup), Silly Season (1965 St James's Palace Stakes and Champion Stakes), the chaser Drinny's Double (Two Mile Champion Chase at Cheltenham in 1967 and 1968), Glint Of Gold (second to Shergar in the 1981 Derby), Diamond Shoal (Grand Prix de Saint-Cloud 1983) and Forest Flower (Irish One Thousand Guineas 1987). Mill Reef was his only winner of a Classic in England, but he had the rare distinction of owning both a Derby winner and a Kentucky Derby winner: his colt Sea Hero won the latter race in 1993. Paul Mellon died in February 1999 at the age of 91.

MELLOR, STAN

When Ouzo won the Christmas Spirit Novices' Chase at Nottingham on 18 December 1971, Stan Mellor became the first jockey in National Hunt racing history to ride 1,000 winners. Born in 1937, Mellor was champion jump jockey three times – 1959–60, 1960–1 and 1961–2 – and while he never won the Grand National, Cheltenham Gold Cup or Champion Hurdle, he enjoyed much big-race success, including the King George VI Chase on Frenchman's Cove (1964) and Titus Oates (1969) and the 1963 Two Mile Champion Chase on Sandy Abbot. His greatest hour came in the 1966 Hennessy Gold Cup, when in a rousing finish he galvanised the grey Stalbridge Colonist to collar **Arkle** halfway up the Newbury run-in and win by half a length. Arkle, conceding two and a half stone to Stalbridge Colonist, was the moral victor, but the way Mellor covered up his horse going into the last and then produced him with a flourish just after landing was a typically astute and forceful piece of jockeyship. When Stan Mellor retired from the saddle at the end of the 1972 season he had ridden a total of 1,035 winners. He took up training, and had big-race success with horses like Pollardstown (Triumph Hurdle 1979), Royal Mail (Whitbread Gold Cup 1980), Saxon Farm (Triumph Hurdle 1983) and Lean Ar Aghaidh (Whitbread Gold Cup 1987) before retiring in 2001.

MERCER, JOE

John Oaksey wrote of Joe Mercer's riding style that 'It is very hard indeed to believe that a more effective, more stylish or more aesthetically satisfying method exists of persuading a Thoroughbred horse to go faster,' and many have shared the view that Mercer was the supreme riding stylist of the modern age. Born in 1934, he was apprenticed to trainer Major Fred Sneyd, winning his first race in September 1950. He was champion apprentice in 1952, and the following year, while still an apprentice (now with R. J. Colling) he won the Oaks on Ambiguity. Two horses will always be linked with him: **Brigadier Gerard**, whom he rode in all his 18 races, winning 17, and **Bustino**, runner-up to Grundy in the famous 1975 King George, whom he also rode in all his races. But he rode plenty of other top-class horses, including Le Moss (Ascot Gold Cup 1980), **Time Charter** (King George 1983) and Kris (Sussex Stakes and Queen Elizabeth II Stakes 1979). Joe Mercer never rode a Derby winner, but he did land eight Classics in all: Two Thousand Guineas on Brigadier Gerard (1971); One Thousand Guineas on Highclere (1974) and One In A Million (1979); Oaks on Ambiguity (1953); and St Leger on Provoke (1965), Bustino (1974), Light Cavalry (1980) and Cut Above (1981). He won the jockeys' championship once – in 1979, when stable jockey to Henry Cecil – and retired from the saddle in 1985, having ridden 2,810 winners

in Britain. He is now racing manager to Sheikh Maktoum Al Maktoum.

MERCER, MANNY

Joe Mercer's older brother Manny (Emmanuel), born in 1930, won two Classics – the 1953 One Thousand Guineas on Happy Laughter and 1954 Two Thousand Guineas on Darius – and the inaugural running of the Washington, DC International in 1952 on Wilwyn. In September 1959 he was killed instantly when thrown from Priddy Fair on the way to the start at Ascot.

MIDDLE PARK STAKES

Group One; two-year-old colts; 6 furlongs
(Newmarket, Rowley Mile)

Founded by William Blenkiron, who owned the Middle Park Stud at Eltham in Kent, and first run in 1866, the Middle Park Stakes has been struggling in recent years to maintain its status as one of the season's top two-year-old races. Some very famous horses have won this race – such as **Pretty Polly** in 1903, **Bahram** in 1934 and **Brigadier Gerard** in 1970. Brigadier Gerard was one of six horses since the Second World War to win the Middle Park and then take the Two Thousand Guineas the following spring: Nearula (1952), Our Babu (1954), Right Tack (1968), Known Fact (1979) and Rodrigo de Triano (1991) were the other five. On the other hand, several winners in the last decade have failed to win at all at three: Fard, Bahamian Bounty, Hayil,

Middle Park Stakes winners since 1990

1990	Lycius	2	A. Fabre FRA	C. Asmussen	13–8F	9
1991	Rodrigo de Triano	2	P. Chapple-Hyam	W. Carson	evensF	6
1992	Zieten	2	A. Fabre FRA	S. Cauthen	5–2	6
1993	First Trump	2	G. Wragg	M. Hills	6–1	8
1994	Fard	2	D. Morley	W. Carson	33–1	10
1995	Royal Applause	2	B. Hills	W. R. Swinburn	3–1	5
1996	Bahamian Bounty	2	D. Loder	L. Dettori	7–4F	11
1997	Hayil	2	D. Morley	R. Hills	14–1	8
1998	Lujain	2	D. Loder	L. Dettori	8–11F	7
1999	Primo Valentino	2	P. Harris	Pat Eddery	100–30	6
2000	Minardi	2	A. O'Brien IRE	M. Kinane	5–6F	10

Lujain and Primo Valentino (though to be fair to the last-named, he did pick up the winning thread at four). Experience suggests that the Middle Park winner is more likely to make a sprinter than a Two Thousand Guineas winner, and horses such as Royal Applause (1995) have reached the top of the sprinting tree after winning at Newmarket.

MIDDLEHAM

Middleham, in North Yorkshire not far from Ripon, is one of the major training centres in the north of England, with such familiar names as Mark Johnston and Ferdy Murphy having their yards here.

MIESQUE

Owned by Stavros Niarchos and trained at Chantilly by François Boutin, Miesque ran 16 times over three seasons, winning 12 races and only once finishing worse than second. As a two-year-old in 1986 she won three out of four, and showed form good enough to make her 15–8 favourite for the 1987 One Thousand Guineas at Newmarket, in which she showed blistering acceleration to win from Milligram and Interval. She then won the Poule d'Essai des Pouliches, first filly to complete the English–French Guineas double since Imprudence back in 1947. Beaten by Indian Skimmer in the 10-furlong Prix de Diane, she reverted to a mile to win the Prix Jacques le Marois and Prix du Moulin before being beaten by Milligram in the Queen Elizabeth II Stakes at Ascot. Next stop was Hollywood Park for the Breeders' Cup Mile, which she won by three and a half lengths. As a four-year-old in 1988 she won the Prix d'Ispahan, beat Warning in the Prix Jacques le Marois (first horse to win that prestigious race twice), was beaten by Soviet Star in the Prix du Moulin, and then ended her career covered in glory by taking the Breeders' Cup Mile – that year at Churchill Downs – for a second time, beating the great American miler Steinlen. She thus became the first horse to win two Breeders' Cup races. As a broodmare her first foal was Kingmambo and her second East Of The Moon – both winners of French Classics.

MILDMAY. ANTHONY

Anthony Mildmay – Lord Mildmay of Flete – was an influential figure in the development and expansion of National Hunt racing after the Second World War, not least on account of his introducing the then Queen Elizabeth (later the **Queen Mother**) to the sport and persuading her to buy a horse. Anthony Mildmay was born in 1909 and started riding in point-to-points while at Cambridge University. Friendship with trainer **Peter Cazalet** encouraged him to take his racing more seriously, and he became one of the very best amateur jockeys riding. In the 1936 Grand National he rode 100–1 outsider Davy Jones and was defying those odds when in the lead approaching the second last. As he landed over that fence the buckle in his reins gave (he had not knotted them on account of Davy Jones's very long neck) and was heading for the last with no steering. Predictably, Davy Jones ran out, leaving Reynoldstown to go on and win – one of the great Grand National hard luck stories. 'For the rest of his life he loved to watch the film of the race,' recalled the racing writer Roger Mortimer, 'but its conclusion was always too much for him; after the second last fence it was his invariable custom to emit a dreadful groan and to leave the room.' Mildmay suffered another slice of desperate luck in the 1948 National. His mount Cromwell was going easily when Mildmay suffered an attack of cramp in the neck and could not move his head off the horse's mane: he managed to finish third to Sheila's Cottage, and spectators were adamant that he would have won but for that misfortune. Mildmay was champion amateur five years in succession, from 1945–6 to 1949–50: that last year his total of 38 winners was enough to take him into fifth place in the professionals' table. In May 1950 he went for a swim near his home in Devon and was never seen alive again. His name lives on through the Anthony Mildmay Peter Cazalet Chase run at Sandown Park's January meeting and the Mildmay of Flete Challenge Cup at the Cheltenham Festival.

MILL HOUSE

Mill House had the bad luck to be foaled in 1957 – the same year as **Arkle**. The two giants of 1960s steeplechasing met five times, with the score 4–1 in Arkle's favour, and those with inside knowledge of a horse's emotions were convinced that successive defeats by Arkle broke Mill House's heart. Mill House was bred in Co. Kildare and in his early years was taken hunting by none other than **Pat Taaffe**, who would become Arkle's regular rider. After three races over hurdles in Ireland in early 1961 (of which he won one) he was sold and moved to join trainer Syd Dale at Epsom, going on to the Lambourn yard of Fulke Walwyn before the 1962–3 season. It soon became clear that Mill House, a large horse with a giant stride, was exceptionally promising – so promising that he started 7–2 favourite for the 1963 Cheltenham Gold Cup, in which he turned in a powerful display of jumping and galloping under Willie Robinson to beat Fortria by 12 lengths. Only a six-year-old, Mill House was now being hailed as the second **Golden Miller**, and defeat by the young chaser all Ireland was talking about seemed unthinkable. So it proved the first time Arkle and Mill House met, in the 1963 Hennessy Gold Cup at Newbury: Mill House powered to a convincing win, with Arkle only third – the excuse being that he had slipped after the third last fence. Mill House went on to win the King George VI Chase and looked invincible, but Arkle beat him fair and square in the famous 1964 Gold Cup, and thereafter Mill House was always struggling to regain his place in the sun. The month after that Gold Cup he was beaten a neck by Dormant, to whom he was conceding 42lb, in the Whitbread. On his first outing the following season, the 1964 Hennessy, hopes were high among his band of devoted followers that he could turn the table on Arkle, but the Irish-trained horse was now moving into a different league even from Mill House: Arkle won easily, Mill House struggled home in fourth. In the 1965 Gold Cup Arkle beat Mill House out of sight. On their fifth and final meeting in the Gallaher Gold Cup at Sandown Park in

November 1965 Arkle conceded 16lb to 'The Big Horse' but, after the pair had treated the crowd to a vintage display of jumping, sprinted past Mill House going to the Pond Fence and won as he liked, Mill House finishing third. They did not meet again, and Mill House had the air of the battered and bruised ex-champion. He could still win races, but the old magic was gone, and he fell in the Gold Cup in both 1967 and 1968. Yet Mill House enjoyed one last hurrah. In the 1967 Whitbread Gold Cup, ridden by David Nicholson, he jumped with what John Oaksey described as 'a display of sustained, explosive power and agility which can seldom have been equalled', then clambered up the Sandown hill and doggedly held off Kapeno in one of the most emotional races in memory. He won only one more race – a chase worth £272 at Wincanton in September 1968 – and the following month fell in a minor steeplechase at Ludlow. He was then retired. Mill House, remembered as Arkle's big rival but a great horse in his own right, died in October 1975 at the age of 18.

MILL REEF

Bred in the United States by his owner **Paul Mellon** and trained in England by **Ian Balding**, Mill Reef graced European racing with a virtually unbroken sequence of outstanding performances in his three seasons on the track, ridden throughout by **Geoff Lewis**. His two-year-old season in 1970 yielded five wins from six outings, including wide-margin victories in the Coventry Stakes at Royal Ascot (eight lengths), Gimcrack Stakes at York (ten lengths) and Dewhurst Stakes at Newmarket (four lengths). The only blot was a short-head defeat by the brilliant My Swallow in the Prix Robert Papin at Maisons-Laffitte.

At three he took the Greenham Stakes at Newbury en route to the famous Two Thousand Guineas which pitted him against Brigadier Gerard and My Swallow: the resulting defeat by three lengths at the hands of 'The Brigadier' was the last he would ever experience. He took the Derby from Linden Tree, the Eclipse Stakes from Caro and the

King George VI and Queen Elizabeth Stakes from Ortis, and brought his brilliant three-year-old term to a glorious close with a three-length victory over Pistol Packer in the Prix de l'Arc de Triomphe. The same breathtaking acceleration was on display again in Mill Reef's first race at four, the Prix Ganay at Longchamp, taking him 10 lengths clear by the line, but in the Coronation Cup he had to plug on dourly to get home just a neck from Homeric, raising fears that all was not well with the horse. Whatever it was, Mill Reef was not to delight the racegoing public again: on 30 August 1972 he fractured a foreleg on the gallops. Happily, a combination of veterinary brilliance and equine stoicism saved him for a highly successful stud career, and among the offspring he sired at the National Stud were Shirley Heights, winner of the 1978 Derby and himself sire of a Derby winner in Slip Anchor (1985), Acamas (Prix du Jockey-Club, 1978), Fairy Footsteps (One Thousand Guineas, 1981), Wassl (Irish Two Thousand Guineas, 1983) and Reference Point (Derby, King George and St Leger, 1987). He was put down in early 1986 at the age of 18 on account of a deteriorating heart condition.

MOHAMMED, SHEIKH
See **Maktoum brothers**.

MOLONY BROTHERS
Tim and Martin Molony were two of the leading jump jockeys in the period following the Second World War. Tim (born 1919) was the elder, and started riding as a professional in 1940 after a career as an amateur. He was champion jockey in Britain for five seasons (1948–9 to 1951–2 and 1954–5) and won the Cheltenham Gold Cup on Knock Hard in 1953 and four consecutive Champion Hurdles, on Hatton's Grace in 1951 and on Sir Ken in 1952, 1953 and 1954. He rode 726 winners in Britain, and died in December 1989 at the age of 70. Martin Molony (born 1926), who rode far less in Britain than his brother, preferring to commute from Ireland, won the Irish Grand National three times (1944 on Knight's Crest, 1946 on Golden View II and 1950 on Dominick's Bar) and the 1951 Cheltenham

Gold Cup on Silver Fame, who beat Greenogue by a short head. He was remarkably versatile. In addition to his jumping successes, he won several Irish Classics and the Irish Cesarewitch twice on Hatton's Grace; he was placed in both the Oaks and the Derby at Epsom. Martin Molony was champion jump jockey in Ireland for the first time in 1946 (sharing the title with Aubrey Brabazon) and remained champion every year until his career was brought to a halt by a fractured skull in 1951. (Pat Taaffe took over as leading jockey in 1952.)

MONKEY
£500 in betting slang.

MONKSFIELD
Four years running the diminutive Monksfield, bought as a two-year-old for just 740 guineas by trainer Des McDonogh, played a major part in the finish of the Champion Hurdle. In 1977 he was beaten two lengths by **Night Nurse**, and for the following three years his duels with **Sea Pigeon** threw the Festival crowd into ecstasy. In 1978 Sea Pigeon's effort petered out on the run-in and Monksfield (ridden by Michael Kinane's father Tommy) won by two lengths to become the first entire to win the race since Saucy Kit in 1967, and the 1979 race produced one of the greatest Champion Hurdles of all. Having seen off their rivals, Monksfield and Sea Pigeon touched down together over the last and set off up the hill head to head. Sea Pigeon gained a narrow advantage, then Monksfield, this time ridden by Dessie Hughes (father of current jockey Richard), stretched his neck out even further, clawed his way back and a few strides from the line got his head in front to win by three-quarters of a length. In 1980 the tables were turned when Sea Pigeon found enough speed to beat Monksfield seven lengths. Those Champion Hurdles apart, Monksfield won many big races. His dead heat with Night Nurse in the 1977 Templegate Hurdle at Aintree is one of the greatest races the sport has seen; he won the same race outright in 1978 (from Night Nurse) and 1979 (from Kybo); and he won the Welsh Champion Hurdle in 1979.

Monksfield's owner Dr Michael Mangan was working in Newfoundland at the time of the colt's first race, a maiden plate at Punchestown in October 1974, and asked his mother-in-law in Ireland to put £10 on the horse for him on the Tote. The horse won at 25–1, but the Tote paid 647–1 – and Dr Mangan's mother-in-law had to confess that she had forgotten to put on the bet . . .

His notable defeats include third in the Irish Cesarewitch as a three-year-old in 1975, second to Peterhof in the 1976 Triumph Hurdle, and twice second in the valuable Royal Doulton Hurdle at Haydock Park (to Royal Gaye, to whom he was conceding 2st, in 1979, and to Beacon Light, conceding 13lb, in 1980). In all he ran 76 times, winning five on the Flat and 14 over hurdles. He was retired to stud in County Laois, where he died at the age of 17 in February 1989. Dessie Hughes's tribute summed up the appeal of the little horse: 'People love a horse with a big heart and they don't come any bigger than Monksfield's. It's incredible how much a horse will give if he's willing: Monksfield gave me his last breath, his last ounce, every single bit he had left. He ran his heart out and offered it without complaint.'

MONOLULU, PRINCE

Ras Prince Monolulu – real name a rather more mundane Peter McKay – was a familiar sight on racecourses for much of the twentieth century. With his baggy trousers, umbrella and ostrich-feather head-dress, he cut an unmistakable figure as he dispensed tips with his trademark cry of 'I gotta horse!' and relentless tirade of doggerel:

God made the bees
The bees made the honey
The public back the favourites
And the bookies take the money

Little was known of the man behind the act. He was born in Abyssinia in 1885 and lived an itinerant life, affecting to be the intimate of royalty and the aristocracy but in reality grubbing a meagre living and often ending up in gaol. He died in 1965, mourned by – among many racing followers – John McCririck:

I remember seeing him shortly before he died. A shabby, hunchbacked, tired old man – the feathers were drooping, the dirty outfit stank. But the myth and the legend that was Monolulu endure, and every Derby Day he's remembered and missed by thousands on Epsom Downs.

MONTJEU

Bred by the late Sir James Goldsmith, Montjeu was named after one of his French residences. Trained at Chantilly by **John Hammond**, he raced in the colours of co-owner **Michael Tabor** and won 11 of his 16 races over three seasons. Unbeaten in two outings as a two-year-old in 1998, he had a magnificent campaign in 1999, winning the Prix du Jockey-Club (by four lengths from Nowhere To Exit), Irish Derby (by five lengths from Daliapour) and Prix de l'Arc de Triomphe (showing stunning acceleration to catch El Condor Pasa close home); a mere fourth in the Japan Cup at the end of a long hard season was understandable.

Only six horses have ever won both the King George VI and Queen Elizabeth Stakes and the Prix de l'Arc de Triomphe: Ribot (Arc 1955 and 1956, King George 1956), Ballymoss (1958), Mill Reef (1971), Dancing Brave (1986), Lammtarra (1995) and Montjeu (Arc 1999, King George 2000).

His four-year-old season in 2000 divides into two halves. He strolled to an easy victory over Greek Dance and Mutafaweq in the Tattersalls Gold Cup at The Curragh, sauntered home from Daring Miss in the Grand Prix de Saint-Cloud, then turned in a superb performance in the King George VI and Queen Elizabeth Diamond Stakes, hardly coming out of a canter to beat Fantastic Light and Daliapour. It was a dazzling display, but Montjeu never reached the same heights again. The brief flicker of excitement at the prospect of a match with **Dubai Millennium** was extinguished by that colt's career-ending injury, and attention was turned to a second Arc. Montjeu came through his prep race well enough and started 5–4 on for the Arc, but the customary burst of speed was missing and he could finish only fourth behind Sinndar. Two attempts at retrieving his reputation ended in defeat: narrow in the Champion Stakes, when beaten half a length by the ultra-tough Kalanisi when looking all over the winner a furlong out, and comprehensive in the Breeders' Cup Turf, where he started favourite but ran seventh behind the same horse. He was then retired to the **Coolmore Stud**. Montjeu's career might have ended in anti-climax, but at his peak he was one of the best middle-distance colts of the age.

MOORE, GEORGE

Born in 1923, George Moore was an Australian jockey who made a big impact on British racing when riding for Noel Murless in 1967, winning the Two Thousand Guineas and Derby on Royal Palace, One Thousand Guineas on Fleet and King George VI and Queen Elizabeth Stakes on Busted. He also won the 1959 Two Thousand Guineas on Taboun (trained in France by Alec Head).

MORNING GLORY

A horse which shows great ability on the home gallops but disappoints on the racecourse.

MURLESS, NOEL

Without doubt one of the greatest trainers of the twentieth century, Noel Murless sent out 19 Classic winners and trained some of the greatest horses of the age. He was born in 1910 in Cheshire, rode a little under National Hunt Rules and learned the training trade with Hubert Hartigan. He took out his first licence in 1935, starting his operation at Hambleton in Yorkshire, and in 1947 he moved to Beckhampton to succeed **Fred Darling**. From there he relocated in 1952 to Newmarket, to the historic Warren Place at the top of Warren Hill; here he remained until retiring in 1976, when he was succeeded at the yard by **Henry Cecil**, then husband of his daughter Julie. His Classic winners included three horses who landed the Derby in Crepello (Derby and Two Thousand Guineas 1957), St Paddy (Derby and St Leger 1960) and **Royal Palace** (Derby and Two Thousand Guineas 1967; Eclipse Stakes and King George 1968); the brilliant filly **Petite Etoile** (One Thousand Guineas, Oaks and Champion Stakes, 1959; Coronation Cup 1960 and 1961); Altesse Royale (One Thousand Guineas and Oaks 1971); Mysterious (One Thousand Guineas and Oaks 1973); the Queen's first Classic winner Carrozza (Oaks 1957); and Lupe (Oaks 1970, Coronation Cup 1971). Then there was the great sprinter **Abernant**, Aunt Edith (King George 1966), Busted (Eclipse and King George 1967), Twilight Alley (Ascot Gold Cup 1963) and Connaught (Eclipse Stakes 1970). Many of these horses were ridden by Lester Piggott, who rode for the stable from 1955 to 1966. Leading trainer nine times (1948, 1957, 1959, 1960, 1961, 1967, 1968, 1970, 1973), Noel Murless died in 1987 at the age of 77.

MURTAGH, JOHNNY

A sand-blaster's son from Co. Meath, Johnny Murtagh was born in May 1970 and apprenticed to trainer **John Oxx**, with whom he has shared the greatest moments of his career. His first winner was Chicago Style at Limerick on 6 July 1987, and in 1989 he was champion apprentice in Ireland. In 1995 he was champion jockey in his native land for the first time (adding further titles in 1996 and 1998) and first made his mark on British racing when Ridgewood Pearl won the Coronation Stakes at Royal Ascot: he won the Breeders' Cup Mile on the same filly later that year, and Johnny Murtagh's career as an internationally known jockey was born. But 1995 was insignificant compared with Murtagh's year in 2000. He won no fewer than 12 Group One or Grade One races around the world, including the Derby, Irish Derby and Prix de l'Arc de Triomphe on Sinndar, trained by Oxx and owned by the **Aga Khan**, and the Champion Stakes and Breeders' Cup Turf on Kalanisi. His declaration in the afterglow of Sinndar's Derby that 'I would like to dedicate this to Mr Oxx and the Aga, because they stood by me a few years ago when I was in a bit of trouble' was poignant. That 'bit of trouble' revolved around spiralling weight which threatened to destroy his blossoming career, and after losing his position with Oxx in July 1992 he went into a steep decline and spent some time out of the sport – 'It got to the stage where I didn't care much about myself and didn't care much about those around me.' But he hauled himself out of his slump and, with the renewed support of the Aga Khan and John Oxx, started the climb back to the top – which is where he undoubtedly resides now.

MUSCLE STRAINS AND TEARS

Like any human athlete, a horse is most likely to tear or strain a muscle when tired, and getting to the point where the muscles are exhausted. Muscle strains can be treated with drugs, but the key to full recovery is physiotherapy and plenty of rest.

MUSH

Slang for a bookmaker's umbrella.

MUSSELBURGH

Linkfield Road, Musselburgh, East Lothian
EH21 7RG
Tel.: 0131 665 2859
Fax: 0131 653 2083
E-mail: info@musselburgh-racecourse.co.uk
Web: www.musselburgh-racecourse.co.uk
The racecourse formerly known as Edinburgh became Musselburgh on 1 January 1996, the new name more accurately reflecting the course's location, hard by the coast to the east of the city. The circuit is a slightly undulating right-handed oval, about a mile and a quarter round, with sharp bends: the home turn is notoriously tight, but there is a run of about four furlongs before the winning post, so horses should have time to sort themselves out. Those bends conspire against the long-striding sort of horse, and Musselburgh is essentially a place for the handy type. National Hunt racing has taken place here only since 1987. There are eight fences on the circuit (four on each straight), and the course favours front-runners.

A particular feature of Musselburgh is its climate. Being so close to the sea – which racegoers on the ground can sense, rather than actually see, beyond the back straight – the area enjoys temperate weather even when conditions are particularly wintry nearby.

MUZZLE

Horses bite, and some even manage to indulge the habit during a race. Marinsky made several attempts at savaging Relkino in the Diomed Stakes at Epsom in 1977; and when top stayer Arcadian Heights twice bit opponents in races in 1992, the punishment was uncompromising: the horse was gelded. In order to prevent damage being done, a known offender may be fitted with a net muzzle over his mouth.

N

NAAS

Woodlands Park, Tipper Road, Naas, Co. Kildare

Tel.: 045 897391

Fax: 045 879486

E-mail: goracing@naasracecourse.com

Web: www.naasracecourse.com

Naas, a 12-furlong left-handed circuit with an uphill finish, has proved a nursery for champions over the decades since the first meeting was held here in 1924. **Mill House** was bred locally – his dam Nas Na Riogh took her name from the Irish version of Naas – and ran his first two races here: he won the second, a novices' hurdle in March 1961, ridden by Pat Taaffe. **Arkle**'s second victory came in a handicap hurdle at Naas a year later. A star turn from the Flat who won here was Ragusa, who won the Ardenode Stakes in 1964. The previous season he had won the King George and St Leger, and after Naas he went on to win the Eclipse Stakes.

NAD AL SHEBA

Web: www.dubairacingclubonline.com

Principal racecourse in Dubai and home of the **Dubai World Cup**, Nad Al Sheba is situated three miles outside Dubai city. Construction of the tracks (dirt and turf) commenced in 1986, and the first meeting was held there in 1992, though there has been a busy programme of refurbishment and improvement since. The track is left-handed, approximately one and a quarter miles round, with a home straight of about three furlongs. There is a chute to provide a straight six furlongs. The grass track is situated inside the dirt track. Anyone who has had cause to complain about facilities and charges on British courses might ruminate on the fact that, to quote Nad Al Sheba's own information guide, 'General admission is free. Ample car parking facilities are available. Racegoers are issued with complimentary racecards and form guides at the entrance gates.'

NAMING OF HORSES

Horses' names are constructed in all sorts of ways, one of the most common of which is to try to combine elements from the names of the horse's sire and dam. These elements may be words in the respective names (Florida Pearl, by Florida Sun out of Ice Pearl) or segments of the individual words (Red Rum, by Quo*rum* out of Ma*red*), or reflect aspects of their meaning, wittily construed (Wait For the Will, by Seeking The Gold out of You'd Be Surprised). Then there are names which advertise a company (Gearys For Strip, Amtrak Express, Mister Baileys); names which reflect personal associations (Dorans Pride, out of Marians Pride, and owned by Tom Doran); and names which have a significance for the people who choose them that is far from obvious to anyone else.

The naming of racehorses in Great Britain is very carefully controlled by **Weatherbys**, who receive applications for around 12,000 new names every year, and several criteria are strictly applied in ruling what is and is not acceptable.

Names must not be longer than 18 characters and spaces. This explains those conflations, sometimes impenetrable at first sight, such as Thethingaboutitis, Blessingindisguise, Goldengirlmichelle, Dontdressfordinner or Sirarthurpendogget.

Names cannot be made up of figures or initials. Thus a name such as E.S.B., winner of the 1956 Grand National, would no longer be acceptable; however, initials can be spelled out phonetically to produce such names as Jay Em Ess or Ahraydoubleyou.

Names cannot start with a character other than a letter (*see* **'Iggins**), nor can they, following a recent amendment, be 'made up entirely of, or including initials, figures, hyphens [so 1998 Derby winner High-Rise got in just in time], full-stops, commas, signs, exclamation marks [there was a good horse in the 1950s called By Thunder!], inverted commas, forward or backward slash, colon and semi-colon'.

Names cannot be used which are already on the *Register of Horse Names*. This list contains some quarter of a million currently registered names. The names thus precluded include those of any racehorse up to five years after its death or at the age of 20, whichever is sooner; of any broodmare for 10 years after her death or 10 years after the last recorded year in which she foaled or was covered, or at the age of 30, whichever is the sooner; and of any stallion 15 years after his death or 15 years after the last recorded year in which he covered mares, or at 35 years of age, whichever is the sooner.

Names cannot be used which are on the *International and Domestic Lists of Protected Names*. These compendia protect particularly celebrated horses against their names being sullied by lesser animals in future generations. The Domestic List of Protected Names consists of the winners of all five English Classics, the Ascot Gold Cup, the Grand National, the Cheltenham Gold Cup, the Champion Hurdle and the King George VI Chase. Thus you could not call your new horse Arkle – nor could you get round the rule by calling him The Arkle or Aarkle or Aachel or Ark'll, since names deemed unacceptably close to protected names are politely declined. The list is subject to amendment – the Champion Hurdle, for instance, was added too late to prevent another Lanzarote racing in England – and cannot protect every well-known racehorse who has not won one of the specified races. Baronet was a grand old handicapper on the Flat who won the Cambridgeshire in 1978 and 1980; another Baronet is a tough grey chaser who won the 1998 Scottish National. Recent years have seen several horses whose names revived memories of not so long ago and enraged purists, including Dunkirk, Predominate, Hornbeam, Brown Lad and Crisp. But help is at hand: a new rule prohibits the registering of 'names, in the opinion of the Stewards of the Jockey Club, of well-known horses'.

Names are not allowed 'whose meaning, pronunciation or spelling' – to quote the official Jockey Club Rule – 'may be thought obscene or insulting or, in the opinion of the Stewards of the Jockey Club, may cause offence'. This rule has caused all sorts of complications, and all sorts of ingenuity on the part of naughty owners and trainers determined to pull a fast one over Weatherbys. Snurge, the 1990 St Leger winner whose globe-trotting exploits for a while made him the highest-earning horse in British racing history, owes his appellation to the schooldays nickname of his owner Martyn Arbib – but the horse might have had to bear a more anodyne name had a dictionary of slang been consulted before Snurge was allowed through. Other names have successfully run the gauntlet. Muff Diver ran in Britain and Ireland during the late 1970s and early 1980s. A two-year-old bearing the name Who Gives A Donald, trained by Colin Tinkler, ran in 1989, while Mary Hinge was an inmate of Julie Cecil's stable in the mid-1990s. (Sometimes a name has to be assessed for its potential as a Spoonerism – a phrase where the first elements of the words are swapped.) And then there is the curious case of Wear The Fox Hat. A two-year-old filly was registered with that name and entered in a race at Folkestone in March 1995. The Jockey Club was not comfortable with the name and insisted that an alternative be produced. She was renamed Nameless. But no problem was perceived with a two-year-old in 2001 by Pursuit Of Love out of My Discovery and named Geespot.

Names are not allowed which would cause confusion in the administration of racing or betting. So don't try to name your horse 'Photo Finish', 'Stewards' Enquiry' or 'Bar'.

Naming racehorses to promote commercial organisations has led to some strange names – and plenty of publicity for the companies.

Moorestyle, that great sprinter ridden by Lester Piggott to numerous victories in the early 1980s, was owned by Moores International Furnishings Ltd; Sunday Sport Star was owned by David Sullivan and used (with other similarly named horses) to promote his newspapers, while Davidgalaxy Affair and Hellcatmudwrestler reflect Mr Sullivan's cinematic ventures; Mister Baileys, 1994 Two Thousand Guineas winner, was named to promote his owners Baileys Horse Feeds; and the 'Gearys' horses – Gearys For Strip, Gearys Cold Rolled, and so on – were named for a steel finishing company.

A complicating factor in the naming of racehorses, and one becoming more acute as racing becomes more international, is that two horses from different countries can be given the same name. In Great Britain, the names of horses born overseas carry a suffix to indicate their country of foaling: thus the 2001 Oaks was won by Imagine (IRE). In the normal course of events these suffixes do not matter, but it can happen that two horses with the same name line up for the same race. In August 1979 Ginistrelli (USA) won a maiden race at Yarmouth, with Ginistrelli fourth; and in June 1994 the same course saw Averti (IRE) and Averti (USA) both running unplaced in the same race.

After all the rules, regulations and complications, a quick bout of name-calling:

- **Arkle** was named after a mountain overlooking the Scottish estate of his owner Anne, Duchess of Westminster. Another of the Duchess's fine chasers trained by Tom Dreaper was Ben Stack, also named after a mountain near the estate, as was 1967 Grand National winner **Foinavon.** Among other well-known chasers, **The Dikler** was named after a stream in Gloucestershire . . . Rubstic was named after the Swedish equivalent of the Brillo Pad . . . Garrison Savannah is the name of the racecourse in Barbados . . . Aldaniti was named after the four grandchildren of his breeder Tommy Barron: Alastair, David, Nicola and Timothy . . . But comedian Freddie Starr's post-Grand

National assertion in 1994 that Miinnehoma is Gaelic for 'lick my bollocks' can be put down to the euphoria of victory.

- While some names suggest grandeur and aspiration, others are more downbeat. A horse named Toilet was unplaced in the race at Leicester in 1921 in which the great jockey Gordon Richards rode his first winner on Gay Lord . . . A horse glorying in the name Keith's Fridge raced in the 1970s . . . The Pub ran in a novice hurdle at Sedgefield in January 1996 . . . Grunge was in training with David Murray Smith in 1998 . . . Richard Hannon trained Sid in the early 1970s, while Eric was a good stayer who won the Chester Cup in 1972.

- The names of many horses in the great dynasty founded by **Northern Dancer** (himself by Native Dancer) perpetuate the theme of the theatre and dancing. **Nijinsky** and Nureyev are sons of Northern Dancer, as is **Sadler's Wells**, now the most influential sire in the world. Another generation on, the names of many of Sadler's Wells' offspring continue the theatrical connection: In The Wings, Entrepreneur, Opera House, King's Theatre, Royal Ballerina, Carnegie, French Ballerina, Theatreworld. Singspiel is by In The Wings out of Glorious Song: a **Singspiel** is a sort of opera which combines song and dialogue.

- Fortytwo Dee, a jumper with Tony Carroll a couple of years ago, was owned by the bra manufacturer Triumph International. Her sire was Amazing Bust.

- Her Majesty the Queen has a reputation for naming her horses with particular wit and ingenuity. Here are a few examples from the royal string: Mister Glum by Ron's Victory out of Australia Fair; Arabian Story by Sharrood out of Once Upon A Time; Rash Gift by Cadeaux Genereux out of Nettle; Whitechapel by Arctic Tern out of Christchurch; Feel Free by Generous out of As You Desire Me.

- The 1812 Two Thousand Guineas was won by a horse named Cwrw – the only winner of an English Classic whose name contained no vowels.

- Kybo, a top hurdler in the late 1970s, was owned by Isidore Kerman and named in a curious way. When Kerman was away at boarding school his mother would send him letters which ended with the instruction KYBO – maternal shorthand for 'Keep Your Bowels Open'.

You do not have to own a horse to register a name. For a fee payable to the BHB, Weatherbys will reserve a name for you against the moment when you have a horse to bear it.

NAP
Newspaper tipster's best bet of the day.

NASHWAN
The only horse ever to have won the Two Thousand Guineas, Derby, Eclipse Stakes and King George VI and Queen Elizabeth Diamond Stakes in the same season. (**Royal Palace** won these four races in different seasons: Two Thousand Guineas and Derby in 1967, Eclipse and King George in 1968.) Owned and bred by Hamdan Al **Maktoum**, Nashwan is by Blushing Groom and out of Height Of Fashion, the mare bought from the Queen for £1.2 million in 1982, and he was ridden in all his races by **Willie Carson**. Nashwan ran just twice as a two-year-old in 1988, winning well enough at Newbury and Ascot to suggest that he was a horse of some potential. But it was a home gallop in April 1989 that convinced all of trainer **Dick Hern**'s yard that he was a seriously good colt and triggered a mammoth plunge in the ante-post market both for the Two Thousand Guineas and the Derby. Nashwan went to Newmarket for the Guineas – for which he started 3–1 favourite – without a previous run, but his devouring stride saw him home by a length and a half from Exbourne. That performance made him hot favourite for the Derby, and on the day he started at 5–4, justifying those odds with a wondrous display of power galloping to score a five-length victory from Terimon and Cacoethes. Next stop Sandown Park for the Eclipse, and another five-length victory from Opening Verse, with Indian Skimmer third. Now established as one of the best middle-distance horses of recent memory, Nashwan started at 9–2 on for the King George at Ascot but had to fight hard to register a neck victory over Cacoethes after a doughty struggle through the final furlong. Attention then switched to the Prix de l'Arc de Triomphe, but Nashwan spoiled the plot by getting beaten for the first time in his life when third to Golden Pheasant in his prep race, the Prix Niel. Soon Arc plans were ditched, but there remained hope that he would redeem his reputation in the Champion Stakes. A high temperature five days before the race put paid to that idea, and he was retired to stand at Sheikh Hamdan's Nunnery Stud in Norfolk. His syndication at a value of £18 million made him, at the time, the most valuable stallion ever to stand in Britain.

NASSAU STAKES
Group One; fillies and mares aged three and upwards; 1¼ miles (Goodwood)

Although the Nassau Stakes achieved Group One status only with the 1999 running, it had long been one of the best middle-distance events of the mid-season for fillies and mares, often a target for those who have run well in – or even won – the Oaks. The race was first run in 1840, named on account of the friendship between the 5th Duke of Richmond (on whose estate the course was situated) and the Dutch royal family – the House of Orange and Nassau. Initially it was run over one mile: the distance went up to one and a half miles in 1900 and back to its present 10 furlongs in 1911. The Nassau was restricted to three-year-old fillies before being opened up to older generations in 1975, and Roussalka immediately became the first dual winner by landing both the 1975 and 1976 runnings. Her feat was emulated by the grey Ruby Tiger in 1991 and 1992. The extensive roll of honour features several famous names, including La Fleche in 1892 (she won the One Thousand Guineas, Oaks and St Leger the same year), **Sceptre** (1902), **Pretty Polly** (1904), Book Law (1927: she won the St Leger and was paternal grand-dam of **Arkle**), Aunt Edith (1965; she won the 1966 King George), and Alborada, who won as a three-year-old in

Nassau Stakes winners since 1990

1990	Kartajana	3	M. Stoute	W. R. Swinburn	11–2	6
1991	Ruby Tiger	4	P. Cole	T. Quinn	11–4	6
1992	Ruby Tiger	5	P. Cole	T. Quinn	2–1	7
1993	Lyphard's Delta	3	H. Cecil	W. Ryan	10–1	9
1994	Hawajiss	3	M. Stoute	W. R. Swinburn	4–1JF	9
1995	Caramba	3	R. Hannon	M. Roberts	5–2F	6
1996	Last Second	3	Sir M. Prescott	G. Duffield	7–4F	8
1997	Ryafan	3	J. Gosden	M. Hills	9–4F	7
1998	Alborada	3	Sir M. Prescott	G. Duffield	4–1	9
1999	Zahrat Dubai	3	S. bin Suroor	G. Stevens	5–1	8
2000	Crimplene	3	C. Brittain	P. Robinson	7–4F	7
2001	Lailani	3	E. Dunlop	L. Dettori	5–4F	7

1998: she went on to win the Champion Stakes that year and again in 1999.

NATIONAL HORSERACING MUSEUM

99 High Street, Newmarket, Suffolk CB8 8JL
Tel.: 01638 667333
Fax: 01638 665600
Web: www.nhrm.co.uk

Appropriately situated next to the Jockey Club Rooms in Newmarket, the National Horseracing Museum was opened in 1983 to record and celebrate racing's rich history. Star exhibits include the skeleton of **Eclipse**, the stuffed head of 1896 Derby winner **Persimmon** (owned by the then Prince of Wales), the pistol with which **Fred Archer** shot himself, and examples of **Prince Monolulu**'s distinctive jackets. The Museum has a wonderful collection of paintings, sculptures, documents and memorabilia, and is the perfect complement to a day at Newmarket races. The Museum also organises tours of the town and the gallops.

NATIONAL HUNT

Jump racing has been formally known as National Hunt racing since the forming of the National Hunt Committee of the Jockey Club in 1866.

NATIONAL HUNT FLAT RACE

Formal name for the race popularly known as a **bumper**.

NATIONAL STUD

Newmarket, Suffolk CB8 0XE
Tel.: 01638 663464
Fax: 01638 665173
E-mail: tours@nationalstud.co.uk
Web: www.nationalstud.co.uk

The National Stud, situated on 500 acres of spacious grassland near the July Course at Newmarket, came into being when Lord Wavertree gave his stud in Co. Kildare, now the Irish National Stud, to the nation. In 1943 the National Stud was relocated to Gillingham in Dorset, with a second stud added after the war at West Grinstead in Sussex – where in 1952 the great Italian-bred colt Ribot was foaled. The National Stud then moved to purpose-built premises in Newmarket in 1967. A stud is only as good as its stallions, and the National Stud has been fortunate in standing some major names – none more important to its fortunes than 1971 Derby winner **Mill Reef**, the most influential British-based sire of his day. Other Derby winners who have stood at Newmarket since the war are Never Say Die (1954 Derby) and Blakeney (1969). The one that got away – an acquisition which could have transformed British breeding for generations – was 1970 Triple Crown hero **Nijinsky**, who ended up going to the USA after a concerted attempt to secure him for the National Stud went awry. Stallions standing at the Stud in 2001 are Bahamian Bounty, Emarati, First Trump, Great Dane, Silver Patriarch and Handsome Ridge.

NATIONAL TRAINERS' FEDERATION

9 High Street, Lambourn, Hungerford,
   Berkshire RG17 8XN
Tel.: 01488 71719
Fax: 01488 73005
E-mail: info@racehorsetrainers.org
Web: www.racehorsetrainers.org

The NTF is the trade organisation representing licensed racehorse trainers in Great Britain. The governing body consists of a council of 18 members made up of two sub-committees, one representing Flat trainers and the other jumping.

NAVAN

Proudstown, Navan, Co. Meath
Tel.: 046 21350
Fax: 046 27964

Navan has a very special place in the history of racing in Ireland, as it was here that on 20 January 1962 that the Bective Novices' Hurdle went to a 20–1 outsider registering the first win of what would become a very distinguished career indeed: his name was **Arkle**. Generally the standard of racing here is high, and the course stages some top-class jumping races, including the Troytown Chase over three miles in November and the Boyne Hurdle over three miles in February, often a warm-up for Irish staying hurdlers with an eye on the Stayers' Hurdle at Cheltenham the following month. The left-handed circuit is about one and a half miles round, with a straight six furlongs. The turns are gradual and there is a stiff uphill finish, so this is a course where stamina limitations can be exposed.

NEAR

Left-hand side – so a horse's left front leg would be its 'near fore'. (The right side is the 'off'.)

NECK-STRAP

Leather strap which goes round a horse's neck, providing an extra source of grip for the jockey.

NEED OF THE RUN

A horse described as being 'in need of the run' is not fully fit and will become fitter for that race.

NET

Betting slang for ten.

NET AND BICE

Betting slang for 12.

NEVES

Betting slang for seven: *neves* is *seven* backwards.

NEWBURY

Newbury, Berkshire RG14 7NZ
Tel.: 01635 40015
Fax: 01635 528354
E-mail: info@newbury-racecourse.co.uk
Web: www.newbury-racecourse.co.uk

If horses could talk, they would doubtless voice their approval of Newbury, as few racecourses are more user-friendly than this. The ground is usually good or thereabouts, and the shape of the course is very well suited to a horse who likes to gallop, with a very wide track about a mile and seven furlongs round, sweeping, easy left-handed bends and no extreme undulations, though there are noticeable rises and falls in the straight. There is both a straight mile and a round mile on the Flat. Over the sticks the course is paradise for the long-striding type, but jumping ability is an important factor here as the fences are very stiffly built. There are five fences down the back straight, then the 'cross fence' before turning for home and five fences in the home straight, of which the water jump in front of the stands is omitted the final time round: runners veer right-handed round an elbow close to the winning post, and an experienced Newbury jockey can effectively cut off an encroaching rival here.

The overall standard of racing at Newbury is very high, but it was not until 1995 that the course got its first Group One event on the Flat: the **Lockinge Stakes** on the straight mile, first run in 1958.

Newbury is an excellent trial ground for big races to come, and as the quintessence of a fair test is particularly popular with top trainers looking to give their two-year-olds a decent education. (The proximity of the course to **Lambourn**, the second great training centre in the land after Newmarket, underpins the quality of the horseflesh on view here.) **Brigadier Gerard** made his racecourse debut at Newbury – in the five-furlong Berkshire Stakes on 24 June 1970 – and many years later his jockey Joe Mercer explained the course's attractions for juveniles: 'It's a very good place for a horse's first race. The ground is usually good, with an excellent covering of grass, and the track is wide open, giving the inexperienced horse plenty of room.' Other famous names which have graced the Newbury racecard as first-time-out juveniles are **Shergar** in 1980 and **Lammtarra** in 1994. The course's top two-year-old races are the Mill Reef Stakes, run in September over six furlongs, and the Horris Hill Stakes, run over seven furlongs in October; notable winners of the latter include Supreme Court, Alcide, Charlottown, Kris, Kalaglow and Tirol.

Newbury also plays an important part in the early-season programmes of three-year-olds with aspirations, for whom the April meeting stages two seven-furlong events: the Greenham Stakes, a traditional trial for the colts' Classics (**Mill Reef** and Wollow both won this in the 1970s), and the Fred Darling Stakes, the equivalent trial for the One Thousand Guineas, which in the 1990s was a springboard to Newmarket success for Salsabil, Shadayid and **Bosra Sham**.

Major Flat events at Newbury for older horses are the John Porter Stakes (one and a half miles in April), Geoffrey Freer Stakes (one mile five furlongs in August), Hungerford Stakes (seven furlongs in August) and St Simon Stakes (one and a half miles in October).

Two races dominate the superb fare which Newbury stages for jump racing fans. The **Hennessy Cognac Gold Cup**, a handicap chase over three and a quarter miles at the end of November, and the **Tote Gold Trophy**, a two-mile handicap hurdle in February.

The Berkshire Stand was opened in autumn 1992 to replace the old and much-loved grandstand and is now the centrepiece of Newbury's facilities, while the new grandstand in the Tattersalls enclosure was officially opened on Hennessy Gold Cup day 2000.

Newbury racecourse was founded in 1905, when a crowd of 15,000 attended the inaugural fixture on 26 September. When the First World War broke out and racing was suspended, the course became a prisoner-of-war camp, then a hay dispersal centre, then a munitions inspection depot and finally a repair centre for tanks. Sport resumed in 1919, but 20 years later the country was at war again, and in 1942 the racecourse was taken over by the American forces as a supply depot. The turf – then as now one of the course's great glories – disappeared under a carpet of concrete and railway lines. In 1947 the course was released from war work, and racing resumed in 1949.

NEWCASTLE

High Gosforth Park, Newcastle upon Tyne
NE3 5HP
Tel.: 0191 236 2020
Fax: 0191 236 7761
E-mail:
gknowles@newcastleracecourse.co.uk
Web: www.newcastleracecourse.co.uk

Highlight of the Flat season at Newcastle is the Northumberland Plate at the end of June, one of the major long-distance handicaps of the racing calendar. The seven-furlong Beeswing Stakes, run in July, enjoys Group Three status and commemorates the famous nineteenth-century mare Beeswing, who won 51 races, including the Newcastle Cup six times.

Racing in Newcastle began on Killingworth Moor in the seventeenth century and moved to the Town Moor in 1721: the current course at Gosforth Park was established in 1882. What greets the present-day Newcastle racegoer is a course under the ownership of Stan Clarke's Northern Racing and rapidly coming out of the doldrums into which it had sunk a few years ago to re-establish itself as one of the top racecourses in the north.

The left-handed circuit is approximately triangular in shape and one and three-quarter miles round; there is a straight course for distances on the Flat of up to one mile. From the home turn to the winning post is half a mile, with a steady climb to the finish putting an emphasis on stamina. In general – and under both codes – Newcastle is a course for the stayer, as the bends are gentle and the galloping type of horse can really stretch out around here.

If the Northumberland Plate is the flagship event in the Newcastle year on the Flat, the jumpers have their own big races. The Fighting Fifth Hurdle (a limited handicap over two miles) in November is an early-season opportunity for top hurdlers, while in February the course stages a traditional Grand National trial in the Tote Northern National (formerly the Eider Chase) over four miles one furlong: the last winner of this race to go on and win the National itself was Highland Wedding in 1969.

NEWMARKET

Westfield House, The Links, Newmarket,
  Suffolk CB8 0TG
Tel.: 01638 663482 (Rowley Mile course office
  01638 662762; July Course office 01638
  662752)
Fax: 01638 663044
E-mail: newmarket@rht.net
Web: www.newmarketracecourses.co.uk

In the parlance of racing insiders, Newmarket is 'Headquarters' – largest training centre in the land and home of the **Jockey Club**, of the country's most prestigious bloodstock **sales**, of several famous studs (including the **National Stud**) and of two famous racecourses: the Rowley Mile, used for spring and autumn meetings, and the July Course for use during the summer.

The history of Newmarket as a centre of racing excellence goes back to the early seventeenth century and James I, a monarch who was devoted to hawking, hunting and riding – despite his own physical drawbacks: according to turf historian Richard Onslow, James 'was slovenly, generally unwashed, and having a tongue too big for his mouth was constantly slobbering and dribbling'. On a hunting trip in the vicinity of Newmarket, the King was struck by the excellence of the terrain for his favourite sports, and had a house built there to accommodate him on his regular visits. In 1622 two of his courtiers raced their horses in a match for £100, and

Newmarket racing had begun in earnest.

When James died in 1625 he was succeeded by his son Charles I, who maintained the family devotion to outdoor pursuits and was himself a fine rider. But Charles fell foul of the executioner in January 1649 and five years later racing at Newmarket came to a halt: the Heath was ploughed up to prevent its use for hunting. After the Restoration the new King, Charles II, soon had Newmarket alive again, and spent a great deal of his time hunting and coursing there. Charles had a hack named Old Rowley, and his courtiers came to use the name of the monarch himself – a name that lives on, of course, in the Rowley Mile. The King rode in races and built himself a palace on the site where now stands the Rutland Arms. Salacious tradition insists that a tunnel led from the palace to a house across the street in which lodged Nell Gwyn.

After the founding of the Jockey Club in about 1750 Newmarket became the administrative centre of racing, and although its headquarters is now in Portman Square, London, the Club maintains an elegant presence in the Jockey Club Rooms on Newmarket High Street.

The two Newmarket Classics were both first run in the early nineteenth century – the Two Thousand Guineas in 1809 and the One Thousand Guineas in 1814 – by which time Newmarket was indisputably the leading racing community in the country. Today there are nearly 3,000 acres of training grounds around the town, administered by Jockey Club Estates, with some 50 racing stables housing 2,500 horses in training. To be in Newmarket early in the morning and watch as the various strings work on the famous training grounds of Warren Hill or The Limekilns is one of the greatest sights in the sport, and it is always a thrill to spot your favourite charges of the big trainers – Cecil, Stoute, Cumani and so many more, not least the Godolphin operation – in their home context.

The **Tattersalls** sale ring near the centre of town is the home of the top bloodstock auctions, including the sale in October when the cream of British yearlings come under the hammer.

Newmarket's two racecourses share a stretch of track for about a mile from the furthest point from the stands, mostly downhill, then divide into two separate straights. (Between these straights is the Devil's Dyke, an ancient earthwork which stretches for miles across the Heath and inside which are reputedly buried the remains of armies who had fought with and against Boadicea.)

Tradition has it that the Cesarewitch is a race which begins in Cambridgeshire and ends in Suffolk. In fact runners on the Rowley Mile do not enter Suffolk until they are pulling up after the winning post.

The Rowley Mile Course, venue of all Newmarket's Group One races except the July Cup, is two and a quarter miles long, with a right-handed bend after a mile. Thus every race here of 10 furlongs is run on a completely straight track, a configuration unique in the major racing countries. The course is exceptionally wide and the final straight mostly flat until the descent into the Dip, after which it runs uphill for the last furlong to the winning post. The Rowley Mile provides an unparalleled test for the big, long-striding horse, provided it does not get unbalanced on that final downhill run, where jockeyship is at a premium. (About a furlong from the winning post are one of the Rowley Mile's landmarks, the Bushes – now a scrawny shadow of their former selves.)

National Hunt racing at Newmarket – on a course the other side of the main road from the Rowley Mile – ceased in 1905.

Nowhere in Flat racing is there a more searching test than the Rowley Mile, which is why the course is home to no fewer than six races of Group One status:

- the first two Classics of the season in the **Two Thousand Guineas** (for colts and fillies) and **One Thousand Guineas** (for fillies only), both over one mile;

- three major two-year-old races in the autumn: **Middle Park Stakes** (six furlongs) for colts, **Cheveley Park Stakes** (six furlongs) for fillies and **Dewhurst Stakes** (seven furlongs) for colts and fillies;
- the **Champion Stakes** over one and a quarter miles, last of the great middle-distance races of the season for older horses in Britain.

The first fixture of the year on the Rowley Mile is the Craven Meeting in mid-April, the moment when the Flat season moves up a gear after a low-key start at Doncaster and lesser venues: feature races here are the Craven Stakes (Group Three, one mile) and Nell Gwyn Stakes (Group Three, seven furlongs), respectively trials for the Two Thousand and One Thousand Guineas. At the other end of the season, the first October meeting includes the Middle Park Stakes and Cheveley Park Stakes for top two-year-olds, but the big betting vehicle is the **Cambridgeshire**, a handicap over one mile one furlong which provides one of the heftiest wagering events of the whole year. Similarly, the second October meeting provides sheer class in the Dewhurst and Champion Stakes, but the great punting moment comes with the **Cesarewitch**, a gruelling marathon over two and a quarter miles.

An extensive programme of rebuilding over the last few years has greatly improved facilities for Rowley Mile patrons, and the Millennium Grandstand was officially opened by the Queen on Two Thousand Guineas day 2000.

On the July Course the run to the winning post from the right-handed turn is about two furlongs shorter than on the Rowley Mile, so that all races of up to a mile here are straight, along the course formally known as the Bunbury Mile, while longer races incorporate the bend. There are undulations for about the first three-quarters of the home straight, then the course runs downhill for about a furlong before a stiff uphill pull to the line – very similar to its companion course the other side of the Devil's Dyke. As on the Rowley Mile, the ideal horse here is the long-striding type with no doubts about stamina.

The July Course stages what for many enthusiasts is the most relaxed of all the major fixtures on the Flat, the three-day July Meeting: panama hats get their first airing of the year; as the runners take their pre-parade ring constitutional in the cooling shade of a clump of tall trees, racegoers lean on the rail by the thatched weighing-room building (there's even a thatched Tote kiosk here); Pimms ranks top of the drinks list; owners and trainers congregate in the paddock around the creeper-bedecked gazebo. Top of the bill at the July Meeting is the **July Cup** over six furlongs; the season's first Group One sprint race in Britain, while this fixture also has the Princess of Wales's Stakes (one and a half miles), often a warm-up for the King George VI and Queen Elizabeth Diamond Stakes, and important two-year-old races over six furlongs in the Cherry Hinton Stakes for fillies and the July Stakes for colts and geldings.

If the key mood of the July Course is relaxation, this is nowhere felt more keenly than at the summer evening meetings which feature, after racing, a free pop concert. The acts may not always be in the first flush of their musical impact, but thousands of racegoers stay behind to listen and bop to the music long after the last runner has been washed down and boxed up for the homeward journey.

NEWTON ABBOT

Kingsteignton Road. Newton Abbot. Devon
TQ12 3AF
Tel.: 01626 353235
Fax: 01626 336972
E-mail: enquiries@newton-abbot-races.co.uk
Web: www.newton-abbot-races.co.uk

Time was when Newton Abbot – where the present racecourse was established in 1880 – was the traditional curtain-raiser of the jumping season every August. Nowadays, with the summer jumping programme becoming embedded in the racing year, that honour lies elsewhere, but Newton Abbot's unpretentious fare remains a highly popular part of the jumping circuit in the West Country – especially with the holiday crowds who flock to the course for the summer fixtures.

The left-handed track is tight and flat, about nine furlongs round, with seven fences on the circuit and a noticeably short run-in from the last fence. Like so many of the small jumps tracks, Newton Abbot favours the speedy, nifty type of horse – which is just one reason why runners from the Somerset yard of Martin Pipe do so well here.

NEW ZEALAND

The influence of New Zealand on horse racing around the world has been most keenly felt in the area of breeding, with a succession of New Zealand-bred horses making their mark in British jump racing in particular. Moifaa, winner of the Grand National in 1904, had won several chases in his native New Zealand before being shipped to England for the big race – and, so the story goes, surviving a shipwreck off the coast of Ireland en route and being given up for lost until discovered by fishermen as he wandered around on the beach. Familiar New Zealand-breds from the last quarter of a century include the very good hurdler and chaser Grand Canyon, 1981 Whitbread Gold Cup winner Royal Mail, 1987 Hennessy and Welsh National winner Playschool, and Grand National winners Seagram (1991) and Lord Gyllene (1997).

Over the last few years New Zealand racing has been able to enjoy a true champion in the shape of the extraordinary mare Sunline. To the end of 2000 she had won 23 of her 31 races, including that year the Australian leg of the **Emirates World Series**, the Cox Plate at Moonee Valley, which she won by seven lengths and was landing for the second year running. That victory made her the highest stakes-winning horse in Australasian racing history. In 2000 she also won the Hong Kong Mile at Sha Tin, and at Nad Al Sheba on Dubai World Cup day in March 2001 showed that she was still at the top of her form at the age of six when narrowly beaten by Jim And Tonic and Fairy King Prawn in the Dubai Duty Free.

New Zealand has 56 racecourses, and the country's major race is the New Zealand Derby, run at Ellerslie, Auckland on Boxing Day – a sunny alternative to King George day at Kempton Park!

NICHOLLS, PAUL

Over the last few years trainer Paul Nicholls has been mounting a consistent challenge to the supremacy of Martin Pipe as champion jumps trainer. Runner-up to Pipe in the trainers' table in 1998–9, 1999–2000 and 2000–1 (when his charges netted win and place money of £1,129,498), Nicholls has been steadily amassing the fire-power of top horses and leading owners which will one day bring him the trainers' championship. Paul Nicholls was born on 17 April 1962 and rode as a professional jump jockey from 1980 until 1989. His 130 career winners included Broadheath in the 1986 Hennessy Cognac Gold Cup and Playschool in the 1987 Hennessy and Welsh National. He took out his first training licence in 1991, having spent time learning the trade with David Barons, and in his first decade as a trainer has handled a succession of top horses: See More Business (Cheltenham Gold Cup 1999, King George VI Chase 1997 and 1999), Call Equiname (Queen Mother Champion Chase 1999), Belmont King (Scottish National 1997), Ad Hoc (Whitbread Gold Cup 2001), Double Thriller, Earthmover and Fadalko. His yard is at Ditcheat, near Shepton Mallet in Somerset.

NICHOLSON, DAVID

David Nicholson, universally known as 'The Duke', is one of the few racing figures who have reached the very top both as jockey and as trainer. Son of 'Frenchie' Nicholson, a famed teacher of young jockeys (including Pat Eddery and Walter Swinburn), David was born on 19 March 1939, and first rode in a race at Newmarket at the age of 12 in April 1951. The horse who provided his first ride also supplied his first winner under National Hunt Rules: Fairval in a selling hurdle at Chepstow on 11 April 1955. (The same year he scored his one and only winner on the Flat when Desertcar won at Wolverhampton.) As a jump jockey he won many big races, including the Welsh Grand National three years running (Limonali in 1959 and 1961, Clover Bud in 1960), the Schweppes Gold Trophy (Elan in 1965) and the Imperial Cup (Farmer's Boy in 1960). But his greatest

victory – 'the most exhilarating ride of my life' – was on **Mill House** in the 1967 Whitbread Gold Cup. He retired from the saddle in 1974, having ridden 583 winners over jumps, to embark upon a training career which saw him handle many of the top jumping performers of the age – horses like Charter Party (Gold Cup 1988), Viking Flagship (Queen Mother Champion Chase 1994 and 1995), Barton Bank (King George VI Chase 1993), What A Buck, Broadsword, Waterloo Boy, Another Coral, Very Promising, Mysilv, Moorcroft Boy, Relkeel, Anzum and Call It A Day. He retired in 1999.

NIGHT NURSE

Although Night Nurse is not one of the quintet of horses to have won the Champion Hurdle three times, his two victories in the race during a golden age of hurdling give him sound claims to be the best hurdler of modern times. Bred in County Dublin and foaled in 1971, he was sold as a yearling for 1,300 guineas and went into training at the Yorkshire yard of **Peter Easterby**. Having shown uninspiring form on the Flat he was put over hurdles, and after a promising season as a juvenile hurdler in 1974–5 really hit the heights the following term, unbeaten in eight races and winning the 1976 Champion Hurdle from Bird's Nest, with former champions Comedy Of Errors and Lanzarote further in arrears. That season he also won the Irish Sweeps Hurdle, the Scottish Champion Hurdle and the Welsh Champion Hurdle. In the 1976–7 season he won five of his seven races. Despite drifting in the market from 5–2 to 15–2 on account of rapidly softening going which he was expected to dislike, Night Nurse turned in a storming performance to win the 1977 Champion Hurdle by two lengths from **Monksfield**, with Dramatist the same distance away third. Less than three weeks later Night Nurse and Monksfield met again at Aintree and gave the Grand National Day crowd a real treat – perhaps the greatest hurdle race in the history of sport – in the Templegate Hurdle, curtain-raiser to Red Rum's third Grand National. Night Nurse conceded 6lb to Monksfield, but refused to give in as the pair fought a famous duel from the last hurdle: at the line they were insepa-rable, the dead heat providing the perfect result to an unforgettable race. Winner of 19 hurdles, Night Nurse graduated to fences for the 1978–9 season and became a very fine staying chaser, winning 13 chases and finishing runner-up to his stable companion Little Owl in the 1981 Cheltenham Gold Cup – in those pre-Dawn Run days the closest a Champion Hurdler had yet come to landing the big Cheltenham double. He was retired on New Year's Day 1983, winner of 32 of his 64 races in nine seasons over jumps, and died in November 1998 aged 27. A fitting tribute comes from Timeform's *Chasers and Hurdlers 1982–3*: 'The sight of the immensely popular Night Nurse out in front setting a good gallop and tackling the obstacles with speed and precision was one of the finest that jumping had to offer.'

NIJINSKY

A son of **Northern Dancer**, Nijinsky was bought as a yearling in 1968 in Canada for $84,000 by Charles Engelhard and sent to **Vincent O'Brien** in Ireland. Despite proving a difficult youngster – a fussy eater, and none too keen on the routine of being trained – he won all five of his races at two: four in Ireland, then a facile success in the Dewhurst Stakes at Newmarket. His three-year-old career opened at The Curragh in April 1970 with victory over the four-year-old Deep Run, soon to become the most influential National Hunt sire of all. The Two Thousand Guineas deliv-ered an easy win from Yellow God; then came the Derby. At Epsom, in the face of uncer-tainty about his ability to cope with the nerve-racking prelims, act on the course and stay the trip, let alone beat the high-class French challenger Gyr, Nijinsky started odds against for the only time in his racing life. No worries: Nijinsky and Lester Piggott swept past Gyr in the closing stages, and a true star was born. Next came a simple win over Meadowville in the Irish Derby and a first meeting with older horses in the King George at Ascot, where Nijinsky toyed with the opposition, headed by the previous year's Derby winner Blakeney, and sauntered home

to win with contemptuous ease. The Triple Crown beckoned, but an attack of American ringworm severely debilitated the horse before the St Leger, and he arrived at Doncaster at less than his peak – not that you'd have known that from the race, which Nijinsky won hard held from Meadowville to become the first Triple Crown winner since **Bahram** in 1935.

That was a mammoth achievement, but there was more on Nijinsky's itinerary. In October 1970 he went to Longchamp to set the seal on a wonderful career in the Arc, only to veer away from Piggott's whip in a fierce tussle with Sassafras and go down by a head – the first defeat of his life. This was a crushing disappointment, but Nijinsky could not be allowed to bow out on a losing note, and 13 days after the Arc he ran again – at Newmarket in the Champion Stakes. The huge and adoring crowd that day reduced Nijinsky to a nervous wreck and he completely failed to run to his best, finishing a deeply disappointing second to Lorenzaccio. He was then retired, having won his first 11 races and lost the final two.

Despite an abortive bid to secure Nijinsky for the National Stud at Newmarket, he was sent to the USA to stand at **Claiborne Farm** in Kentucky. By the time of his death in 1992 at the age of 25 he had sired many top-class horses, including Derby winners Golden Fleece (1982) and Shahrastani (1986) – with **Lammtarra** (1995) adding a third Derby posthumously. Two other Derby winners – Kahyasi (1988) and Generous (1991) – are grandsons of Nijinsky.

NIVEN, PETER

When winning a novices' hurdle on Colourful Life at Wetherby on 9 May 2001, Peter Niven (born 1964) became only the sixth jockey in the history of jump racing to ride 1,000 winners (following, in chronological order of reaching that landmark, **Stan Mellor, John Francome, Peter Scudamore, Richard Dunwoody** and **Tony McCoy**).

NOBBLING

Slang for **doping**.

NOMINATION

A 'nomination' to a stallion at stud is a breeding right – the right to have your mare covered by that stallion.

NON-RUNNER

In betting, a single on a horse who does not run in the race is void and stakes are returned. A double when one of the horses does not run becomes a single; a treble when one of the horses does not run becomes a double; and so on. (These procedures do not apply to ante-post betting.) The most common reasons for a horse being announced a non-runner in a race are: significant change in the official going, sufficient for connections to judge that the horse's chance has been seriously undermined; injury or illness in the horse, which must be confirmed by a vet's certificate; or the horse has been declared for more than one race (as is allowed under certain circumstances) and connections have opted to run in a different race.

NON-TRIER

A horse perceived as not being given the best possible chance to win by its jockey is sometimes described as a 'non-trier'. Penalties for jockey and trainer found guilty of not trying are severe, and even the innocent party can be affected: the horse can be suspended from racing for 30 or 40 days (depending on the exact nature of the perceived transgression).

NORTHERN DANCER

Owned and bred by E. P. Taylor, Northern Dancer was the greatest horse in the history of Canadian racing. On the track he won 14 of his 18 races, including in 1964 the Kentucky Derby (beating Hill Rise a neck after a famous duel) and Preakness: he was denied a Triple Crown by his stamina limitations being exposed in the Belmont Stakes. But it was as a sire – initially in Canada, and for most of his stallion career at Taylor's Windfields Farm in Maryland – that the legend of Northern Dancer became established. Among the horses he sired were **Nijinsky**, Lyphard, Nureyev, Be My Guest, **El Gran Senor**, The Minstrel, Secreto and Shareef Dancer – though in the long run his most important son has turned out to be **Sadler's Wells**, who picked up his father's mantle as the most influential sire in the world. At the peak of his powers Northern Dancer was reputedly commanding a fee of $800,000 for his services. He retired from stud duties in 1987 and died in November 1990 at the age of 29.

NORTON'S COIN

The 1990 Cheltenham Gold Cup was expected to be a stately procession for 1989 hero **Desert Orchid**, then at the height of his powers. Instead it went to 100–1 chance Norton's Coin, trained by Sirrell Griffiths on his dairy farm near Carmarthen, where the horse was housed in a converted milking shed and where his exercise included being hacked around the farm by the Chief Constable of the Avon and Somerset Police. By the time that jockey Graham McCourt lined up Norton's Coin at the Gold Cup start, the nine-year-old had proved himself a good, though not top-bracket, chaser. He had won four of his 14 races, but 100–1 seemed about right for a horse who had been beaten out of sight by Dessie in the King George at Kempton earlier in the season: the *Sporting Life* described him as a 'no-hoper', and the form guide in the Cheltenham racecard stated that he was 'more of a candidate for last place than first'. The race boiled down to a battle over the last two fences between Desert Orchid, Toby Tobias, and the chestnut unflatteringly described by his trainer as 'a long, leeky, plain-looking horse'. Leeky or not, Norton's Coin's hour had come, and as Desert Orchid's petrol ran out, the other two got down to a fight to the line, Norton's Coin gaining the upper hand close home to win by three-quarters of a length – the longest-priced winner in Gold Cup history, and the fastest: the time of 6 minutes 30.90 seconds beat the previous record for the race, set by **Dawn Run** in 1986, by over four seconds. Norton's Coin ran in the Gold Cup twice more, starting at 16–1 when falling at the seventeenth fence in 1991 and at 33–1 when pulled up in 1992. Unusually for a Cheltenham Gold Cup winner, he ran at Royal Ascot: ridden by Lester Piggott, he finished eighth in the Queen Alexandra Stakes in 1991. Norton's Coin was retired at the age of 12 after refusing in a chase at Newbury in February 1993, his place in the history books – and in the annals of racing's unlikeliest winners – secure. He died at the age of 20 in January 2001.

NOT OFF

A horse is 'not off' if connections go into the race intending that, for whatever reason, it should not win.

NOTTINGHAM

Colwick Park, Nottingham NG2 4BE
Tel.: 0115 958 0620
Fax: 0115 958 4515
E-mail: nottingham@rht.net
Web: www.nottinghamracecourse.co.uk

Nottingham's circuit is a left-handed oval about a mile and a half round, level down the back but with some minor undulations in the home straight. Both bends are fairly tight, and the run from the home turn to the winning post is four and a half furlongs. Races over five and six furlongs are run on the straight course. Concentrate on the sharp, well-balanced horse here. Nottingham has the sort of terrain which often attracts young horses destined for great things: recent Derby winners Slip Anchor (1985) and Oath (1999) both won here as two-year-olds, as did the great filly **Oh So Sharp**, who landed the 1985 One Thousand Guineas, Oaks and St Leger.

Lester Piggott's first retirement from the saddle came at Nottingham on 29 October 1985. That afternoon he rode Full Choke to win the Willington Handicap, his 4,349th winner in Britain. His 4,350th came nearly five years later – at Chepstow on 16 October 1990.

Racing has been documented in Nottingham since the seventeenth century, with the present course in use since 1892. A new grandstand was opened in 1992. Jump racing was discontinued here after the 1995–6 season.

NOVICE

The status of 'novice' has nothing directly to do with age. In jump racing, a 'novice' is essentially a horse who has not won a race under that particular code (hurdling or steeplechasing) before that season – though changes to the timing of the new season and special alterations at the end of the 2000–1 season following foot-and-mouth disruption make a general definition impossible. There is nothing to stop novices running in – and sometimes winning – the most prestigious jump races: the most recent novice to win the Cheltenham Gold Cup was **Captain Christy** in 1974, and the most recent novice to win the Champion Hurdle was Alderbrook in 1995. On the Flat, the term 'novice' is as defined in the relevant race category: for example, a 'Novice Flat Race' is a race for two-year-olds only or three-year-olds only who have not won more than two Flat races.

NTF

See **National Trainers' Federation**.

NUNTHORPE STAKES

Group One; two-year-olds and upwards;
5 furlongs (York)

Placed between the July Cup at Newmarket and the Sprint Cup at Haydock Park in September, the Nunthorpe Stakes (named after a village some 50 miles north of York) is the middle leg of the Group One sprint races in the Flat season. A Nunthorpe Selling Stakes was run at York from 1903 to 1921, but the Nunthorpe we know today was first run in 1922. The third running in 1924 went to the flying grey filly Mumtaz Mahal, one of the fastest racehorses ever seen, and quality has remained the watchword of the race in the period since the Second World War. **Abernant** won the race in 1949 and 1950, while other post-war dual winners are Royal Serenade (1951 and 1952) and Right Boy (1958 and 1959). There have been two triple winners: Tag End (1928, 1929, 1930) and Sharpo

Nunthorpe Stakes winners since 1990

1990	Dayjur	3	W. R. Hern	W. Carson	8–11F	9
1991	Sheikh Albadou	3	A. Scott	Pat Eddery	6–1	9
1992	Lyric Fantasy	2	R. Hannon	M. Roberts	8–11F	11
1993	Lochsong	5	I. Balding	L. Dettori	10–1	11
1994	Piccolo	3	M. Channon	J. Reid	14–1	10
1995	So Factual	5	S. bin Suroor	L. Dettori	9–2	8
1996	Pivotal	3	Sir M. Prescott	G. Duffield	100–30	8
1997	Ya Malak	6	D. Nicholls	Alex Greaves	11–1	15
	Coastal Bluff	5	D. Barron	K. Darley	6–1	
1998	Lochangel	4	I. Balding	L. Dettori	6–1	17
1999	Stravinsky	3	A. O'Brien *IRE*	M. Kinane	evensF	16
2000	Nuclear Debate	5	J. Hammond *FRA*	G. Mosse	5–2F	13

(1980, 1981, 1982). Other top-notch sprinters on the list of winners over the last quarter of a century include Lochnager (1976), Solinus (1978), Habibti (1983), Never So Bold (1985), Last Tycoon (1986), Cadeaux Genereux (1989), the phenomenally fast **Dayjur** (1990, the year of his abortive bid for the Breeders' Cup Sprint) and Sheikh Albadou (1991; he won the Breeders' Cup Sprint later that year). In 1992 Lyric Fantasy, 'the pocket rocket' trained by Richard Hannon, became the first two-year-old filly to win the Nunthorpe, while another adored female, **Lochsong**, took the race in 1993. Lochsong spoiled her chance in 1994 by getting stirred up in the paddock and practically bolting to the start, leaving her with little energy left at the business end of the race. But family pride was restored when her half-sister Lochangel won in 1998. Mention must also be made of the 1997 running, when Coastal Bluff dead-heated with Ya Malak. Coastal Bluff's bridle had broken early in the race, leaving an undaunted Kevin Darley to ride an extraordinary finish without reins, and Coastal Bluff was the first Group One winner in Britain to be ridden by a lady jockey – Alex Greaves.

The Nunthorpe Stakes was run as the William Hill Sprint Championship between 1976 and 1989 before reverting to its original title.

NURSERY

Handicap for two-year-olds.

O

OAKS

Group One: three-year-old fillies: 1½ miles (Epsom Downs)

First run in 1779, the Oaks is a year older than its sibling Classic at Epsom, the **Derby**, but unlike that race has always been run over a mile and a half. It was conceived by Edward Stanley, Earl of Derby, and 'Gentleman Johnny' Burgoyne, who had commanded the defeated English troops at Saratoga in the American War of Independence, as a fillies' version of the **St Leger**, which had been founded at Doncaster three years earlier. The race was named after the house near Epsom where Stanley was living – The Oaks – and the first running went to his own filly Bridget. A little over two decades later in 1801 Eleanor became the first filly to win the Oaks and Derby, a feat matched only by Blink Bonny (1857), Signorinetta (1908; she won the Derby at 100–1 and the Oaks at 3–1) and Fifinella (1916, when both races were run at Newmarket on account of the First World War). Through the twentieth century the Oaks was won by most of the great staying fillies, from **Sceptre** and **Pretty Polly** during the century's first decade through to Salsabil, Balanchine and Ramruma during its last. In between, the Oaks figured as the middle leg of the 'fillies' Triple Crown' for (as well as Sceptre and Pretty Polly), **Sun Chariot** in 1942 (when all the Classics were run at Newmarket's July Course), Meld in 1955 and **Oh So Sharp** in 1985. Those were all fillies of great durability, but the Oaks in modern times has also seen individual displays of sheer brilliance, such as Noblesse winning by 10 lengths in 1963, a performance which sent young John McCririck, watching from the Downs, into raptures:

One fleeting vision of Noblesse, Ireland's first Oaks winner, is the last racing memory I intend having on my deathbed. Her sublime athletic grace has been captured and stored, a treasured memory in the mind, and nothing will ever match it.

Oaks winners since 1990

1990	Salsabil	3	J. Dunlop	W. Carson	2–1F	8
1991	Jet Ski Lady	3	J. Bolger *IRE*	C. Roche	50–1	9
1992	User Friendly	3	C. Brittain	G. Duffield	5–1	7
1993	Intrepidity	3	A. Fabre *FRA*	M. Roberts	5–1	14
1994	Balanchine	3	H. Ibrahim	L. Dettori	6–1	10
1995	Moonshell	3	S. bin Suroor	L. Dettori	3–1	10
1996	Lady Carla	3	H. Cecil	Pat Eddery	100–30	11
1997	Reams Of Verse	3	H. Cecil	K. Fallon	5–6F	12
1998	Shahtoush	3	A. O'Brien *IRE*	M. Kinane	12–1	8
1999	Ramruma	3	H. Cecil	K. Fallon	3–1	10
2000	Love Divine	3	H. Cecil	T. Quinn	9–4F	16
2001	Imagine	3	A. O'Brien	M. Kinane	3–1F	14

(For a list of all winners since the Second World War, *see* Classics.)

Pretty Polly started at 100–8 on when winning the 1904 Oaks – shortest SP ever returned in a Classic.

The flying French filly Pawneese won almost as easily in 1976, and Sun Princess set a new distance record of 12 lengths in 1983. Other runnings that stand out in recent memory include **Dunfermline**'s massively popular victory for the Queen in 1977 at the height of the Jubilee celebrations.

The Oaks was run at Newmarket during the First World War and Second World War.

Although the Oaks is run at the same meeting and over the same course and distance as the Derby, it is a different occasion in many ways. There is none of the hoopla of Derby Day, and the race itself is of a gentler order, with a smaller field than the Derby meaning a less breakneck pace. Having said that, the Oaks winner needs the same qualities of stamina, handiness and balance as any Derby winner – and, as with the Derby, winning the Oaks is a passport to lasting racing fame.

OAKSEY, LORD

Brough Scott described John Oaksey as 'a legend in his own saddle time', and it seems impossible to envisage a time when 'My Noble Lord' – as John McCririck addresses him with due deference – was not a much admired and much loved part of the racing scene, either as participant or as observer. Born John Lawrence in 1929, he was educated at Eton, Oxford and Yale, and was destined for a career in law until the distraction of racing proved too great. For two decades he was a top amateur jockey, winning the amateur riders' title over jumps in 1957–8 and 1970–1, and he scored many big race successes, notably the 1958 Whitbread and Hennessy Gold Cups on Taxidermist. In 1963 he rode Carrickbeg in the Grand National and led over the last fence, only to be caught in the shadow of the post by 66–1 chance Ayala and beaten by three-quarters of

a length. His descriptions in the *Sunday Telegraph* and *Horse and Hound* of how victory turned to defeat had the style, clarity and generosity characteristic of all his writing and were hailed as the best accounts ever written of riding in a big race. John was racing correspondent of the *Telegraph* for many years, combining this with a weekly column as 'Audax' in *Horse and Hound*. John's father the Hon. Geoffrey Lawrence had been presiding judge at the Nuremberg Trials of Nazi war criminals and was rewarded for his efforts with a hereditary peerage as Lord Oaksey – the title which John inherited on his father's death.

In 2001 John Oaksey was elected an honorary member of the **Jockey Club**.

OBJECTION

Since any interference in running is likely to be the subject of a stewards' enquiry, objections in the immediate aftermath of a race are fairly infrequent nowadays, though the matter of an objection is not confined to the running of the race.

According to the relevant clause in the Jockey Club Rules,

An objection to a horse on the grounds of
– interference or any act on the part of his rider, or
– his not having run the proper course, or
– the race having been run on a wrong course, or
– any other matter occurring in the race, or
– any other matter occurring before weighing in, or
– the rider not presenting himself to weigh in, or
– the rider not drawing the weight at which he weighed out, or
– any other matter in respect of which a Rule provides for an objection to be lodged under this Sub-Rule . . .

must be made to the Clerk of the Scales.

O'BRIEN, AIDAN

Born in Co. Wexford in 1969, Aidan Patrick O'Brien rode as an amateur jockey (he was champion amateur in Ireland in the 1993–4 season) and was assistant to Jim Bolger and to his own wife Anne-Marie Crowley (champion jumps trainer in Ireland in the 1992–3 season) before taking out his own licence in 1993. His first winner was Wandering Thoughts at Tralee on 7 June that year, and for good measure he scored a double that day. If such a start suggested that here was a young man in a hurry, his rise to the very top was positively meteoric. In his first season as a jumping trainer he set a prize money record, and on the Flat was leading trainer in Ireland for the first time in 1997, repeating the feat in 1999 and 2000; he was leading Flat trainer by winners in 1997. In 1994 he set an Irish record of 178 wins (both codes) in a calendar year, and broke his own record with 242 in 1995. He has been leading trainer over jumps in Ireland five times, but he decided to focus mostly on the Flat, and in 1995 moved to Ballydoyle near Cashel, Co. Tipperary, to take over the yard made famous by the great **Vincent O'Brien** (no relation). Here he is closely linked with the group of owners, headed by **John Magnier** and **Michael Tabor**, who have made the **Coolmore Stud** a potent force in world racing. As with any trainer, it is the quality of horses handled which dictates reputation, and in his his short career Aidan O'Brien is already living up to the finest traditions of Ballydoyle with horses such as 2001 Derby winner **Galileo**; his other Classic winners in England, King Of Kings (Two Thousand Guineas 1998), Shahtoush (Oaks 1998) and Imagine (Oaks 2001); and the ultra-tough **Giant's Causeway**. His only serious continuing involvement with jumping is **Istabraq**, winner of the Champion Hurdle in 1998, 1999 and 2000. At Ballydoyle, one genius of Irish racing has been succeeded by another.

O'BRIEN. VINCENT

No trainer in the history of horse racing can boast a record to match that of Michael Vincent O'Brien. Born in Co. Cork in 1917, his achievements around the world were so mighty that the bloodstock industry in Ireland would not be what it is today without him. He started training at Churchtown, Co. Cork, and his first winner was Oversway at

> ## Vincent O'Brien's Classic winners in England
>
> *Two Thousand Guineas*
> 1968 Sir Ivor
> 1970 Nijinsky
> 1983 Lomond
> 1984 El Gran Senor
> *One Thousand Guineas*
> 1966 Glad Rags
> *Derby*
> 1962 Larkspur
> 1968 Sir Ivor
> 1970 Nijinsky
> 1972 Roberto
> 1977 The Minstrel
> 1982 Golden Fleece
> *Oaks*
> 1965 Long Look
> 1966 Valoris
> *St Leger*
> 1957 Ballymoss
> 1970 Nijinsky
> 1972 Boucher

Limerick Junction (now Tipperary) on 20 May 1943. Through the 1940s and 1950s he made a considerable name for himself on the jumping scene. He won three consecutive Cheltenham Gold Cups with Cottage Rake (1948, 1949, 1950) and three consecutive Champion Hurdles with Hatton's Grace (1949, 1950, 1951), and is the only trainer ever to have sent out three consecutive Grand National winners: Early Mist (1953), Royal Tan (1954) and Quare Times (1955). He won a fourth Gold Cup with Knock Hard in 1953. He moved from Churchtown to Co. Tipperary in 1951 to begin building the legend of Ballydoyle – at first he had to make gaps in the hedges to accommodate the gallops – and in the late 1950s started to switch his attention to the Flat. O'Brien's record can hardly be done even remote justice in a summary: suffice it (barely) to say that he handled **Nijinsky**, **Sir Ivor**, **Ballymoss**, Gladness, The Minstrel, Roberto, **Alleged**, Golden Fleece, **El Gran Senor**,

Sadler's Wells, Caerleon, Royal Academy, and many, many more of the greats. He trained the winners of 16 English and 27 Irish Classics; won three Prix de l'Arc de Triomphe, three King George VI and Queen Elizabeth Stakes, 25 races at Royal Ascot and one Breeders' Cup Mile. But beyond the horses and the big wins, it was O'Brien's vision to buy yearlings with high-class pedigrees (especially the produce of **Northern Dancer**), develop them into top-class horses and then syndicate them for stud purposes, and this proved both highly successful in its own right and the making of the **Coolmore Stud**, now one of the most influential bloodstock breeding operations in the world. In 1983 his contribution to the life of his native land was recognised by his being awarded an honorary doctorate from the National University of Ireland, and in 1994 he announced his retirement, sending out his last winner, Mysterious Ways, at The Curragh on 17 September that year. He was leading trainer in Britain on the Flat in 1966 and 1977 and over jumps 1952-3 and 1953-4, and leading trainer in Ireland by prize money thirteen times and by number of winners four times. He was, to coin a phrase, simply the best.

OFF (1)

'The off' is the moment when the race actually starts. Thus a horse might be described as becoming favourite 'just before the off'.

OFF (2)

A horse is described (usually in private) as being 'off' when, according to connections, it is trying its best, and **'not off'** when – perish the thought! – it is, for whatever reason, not trying its best.

OFF (3)

Right-hand side: a horse's 'off fore' is its right-hand front leg (while its 'near hind' is its left-hand back leg).

OFF THE BIT

See **on the bit**.

OGDEN, SIR ROBERT

Leading owner over jumps in the 1996-7, 1999-2000 and 2000-1 seasons, Sir Robert Ogden has some 30 horses in training in Britain with a variety of trainers. The best-known to have raced in his colours (mauve and pink check, white sleeves) include Squire Silk, Edelweis du Moulin, Marlborough, Fadalko and the 2001 Whitbread Gold Cup winner Ad Hoc. His business interests include land reclamation and estate development, and he was knighted in June 2001 for services to charity.

OH SO SHARP

This filly by Kris was owned by **Sheikh Mohammed**, trained by **Henry Cecil** and ridden in her three Classics by **Steve Cauthen**. She ran in nine races in 1984 and 1985 and was beaten only twice. As a two-year-old she won a maiden race at Nottingham, the Solario Stakes at Sandown Park and the Hoover Fillies' Mile at Ascot. She started her three-year-old campaign in 1985 by winning the Nell Gwyn Stakes at Newmarket, then won the One Thousand Guineas in a finish of two short heads with Al Bahathri and Bella Colora and the Oaks by six lengths from **Triptych**. Such a record made her a filly of the very highest order, but she was defeated on her next two outings – beaten a neck by Petoski in the King George VI and Queen Elizabeth Diamond Stakes at Ascot and three-quarters of a length by Commanche Run in the Benson and Hedges Gold Cup at York. But she ended her career on a triumphant note when taking the St Leger from Phardante, becoming the first horse since Nijinsky in 1970 to win three Classics, and the first filly to do so since Meld in 1955. She was then retired to stud duties.

ONE MAN

Winner of 20 of his 35 races, One Man was bred in Ireland. Foaled in 1988, he was sold for 4,000 Irish guineas as an unbroken three-year-old and made his racing debut in an Irish point-to-point where he distinguished himself by running out. He then went into training in Bishop Auckland, Co. Durham, with Arthur

Stephenson, and at the dispersal sale in May 1993 following Stephenson's death was sold for 68,000 guineas to toy manufacturer John Hales and sent to the late Gordon Richards's yard. He won three novice hurdles, but really came into his own when put over fences, running up a sequence of five wins in 1993–4 before disappointing in the Sun Alliance Chase at Cheltenham. The following season he announced his arrival in the top bracket with a convincing win in the Hennessy Cognac Gold Cup at Newbury, then failed to complete the course on two subsequent outings. The 1995 King George VI Chase was relocated to Sandown Park after the Kempton Boxing Day fixture had succumbed to the weather, but the change made no difference to One Man, who under Richard Dunwoody produced a display of dazzling authority to leave Monsieur Le Cure and Master Oats toiling in his wake as he powered up the Sandown hill.

One Man now became a very warm order for the 1996 Cheltenham Gold Cup, and despite doubts about his stamina over the longer trip started 11–8 favourite. Coming down the hill he looked to be well in contention, but after the entrance to the straight he folded in a matter of strides, barely managed to clamber over the final fence and finished a desperately tired sixth behind Imperial Call.

A year later he was back for another crack at the Gold Cup, having easily won a second King George (safely restored to Kempton on Boxing Day 1996) in record time to invite inevitable comparisons with another dashing grey who excelled at the Sunbury track: **Desert Orchid**. But his running in the 1997 Gold Cup was uncannily similar to the previous year's: after closing on Mr Mulligan between the last two fences he went out like a light and again finished sixth. Now it was not just One Man's stamina that was being called into question, but his resolution: was he ducking the issue?

One Man's first two outings in the 1997–8 term saw him sticking to his guns well enough when beating Barton Bank at Wetherby and Viking Flagship at Huntingdon,

but he then seemed to lose his way again: in the race he was beginning to make his own, the King George, toiling in the rain-softened ground, he could finish only fifth behind See More Business. Next stop Ascot, for a facile win, then it was back to Cheltenham – not for the Gold Cup this time but to make a pitch for the two-mile title, the Queen Mother Champion Chase. Deserted by Richard Dunwoody and now ridden by Brian Harding, who had partnered the horse in much of his work at home, One Man produced a fluent display of jumping that kept him in the vanguard throughout, and as the field came down the hill the same old question nagged: would he collapse again? The answer was an emphatic negative. One Man was not stopping, and to whoops of joy from the crowd he soared over the last and set off up the hill to beat Or Royal. It was one of the great Cheltenham moments.

The following month's clash in the Mumm Melling Chase at Aintree between One Man and Strong Promise – who had run a marvellous race to finish second to Cool Dawn in the Gold Cup – was keenly anticipated. Swinging out down the back straight One Man was leading and well in command, but at the ninth fence he seemed to jink to the right and lunge at the obstacle, taking a very heavy fall and breaking a tibia. He was put down immediately, and 3 April 1998 went down as one of the blackest days in modern jumping history. Timeform's *Chasers and Hurdlers* captured the contrasting moods of One Man's last two races: 'It is very hard to imagine this sport experiencing anything better or anything worse.'

ONE THOUSAND GUINEAS
Group One; three-year-old fillies; 1 mile
(Newmarket, Rowley Mile)

The One Thousand Guineas is the youngest Classic, first run in 1814, five years after the first Two Thousand Guineas. Ten fillies were entered for the the initial running at a subscription of 100 guineas each – hence One Thousand Guineas – and a filly named Charlotte beat four opponents. That race was run over the Ditch Mile, a flatter and easier terrain than the Rowley Mile, and it was not until the early 1870s that the race was moved to its current home. The early years saw very small fields for the race, including in 1825 a **walkover** – unique in Classic history. Like the Oaks, the One Thousand Guineas in the first years of the twentieth century benefited from a golden period for fillies, with both **Sceptre** (1902) and **Pretty Polly** (1904) winning on their way to further Classic glory.

When French trainer Criquette Head landed the One Thousand Guineas in 1983 with Ma Biche she was the first lady ever to train a Classic winner in England.

The race was run on the July Course during the Second World War, and marked its return to the Rowley Mile in 1946 with a royal victory in the shape of George VI's filly Hypericum. George's daughter Queen Elizabeth II won the One Thousand Guineas with Highclere, who beat Polygamy by a short head in 1974. **Petite Etoile** in 1959 proved one of the classiest winners of the race since the war, and with hindsight it is hard to decide which is more surprising: that she was deserted by trainer Noel Murless's stable jockey Lester Piggott and ridden in the race by Doug Smith, or that she started at 8–1. The last 15 years have seen many high-class performances in the One Thousand Guineas,

including the brilliant **Miesque** in 1987 (she went on to record back-to-back victories in the Breeders' Cup Mile), Salsabil setting up a sequence of big-race victories in 1990, and **Bosra Sham**'s brilliant turn of speed despite an interrupted preparation in 1996.

O'NEILL, JONJO
Web: www.jonjooneill.com

John Joe O'Neill was born in Co. Cork on 13 April 1952, served his apprenticeship with Michael Connolly at The Curragh and rode his first winner Lana at that racecourse on 9 September 1970. He moved to England in 1973 to ride for trainer Gordon Richards, becoming champion jump jockey for the first time in the 1977–8 season with 149 winners, a record at the time. He followed up with a second championship in 1979–80, and in all rode 885 winners over jumps in Britain before retiring from the saddle. Jonjo never rode the Grand National winner – he never actually completed the course in eight attempts – but he landed two Champion Hurdles, on **Sea Pigeon** in 1980 and **Dawn Run** in 1984, and two Cheltenham Gold Cups, on Alverton in 1979 and Dawn Run in 1986. Dawn Run's Gold Cup victory was one the great moments in jumping history, and a statue of the mare, Jonjo's arm aloft in victory, stands at the foot of the Cheltenham parade ring. In all he won 15 races on Sea Pigeon,

---

One Thousand Guineas winners since 1990

1990	Salsabil	3	J. Dunlop	W. Carson	6–4F	10
1991	Shadayid	3	J. Dunlop	W. Carson	4–6F	14
1992	Hatoof	3	Mme C. Head *FRA*	W. R. Swinburn	5–1	14
1993	Sayyedati	3	C. Brittain	W. R. Swinburn	4–1	12
1994	Las Meninas	3	T. Stack *IRE*	J. Reid	12–1	15
1995	Harayir	3	W. Hern	R. Hills	5–1	14
1996	Bosra Sham	3	H. Cecil	Pat Eddery	10–11F	13
1997	Sleepytime	3	H. Cecil	K. Fallon	5–1	15
1998	Cape Verdi	3	S. bin Suroor	L. Dettori	100–30JF	16
1999	Wince	3	H. Cecil	K. Fallon	4–1F	22
2000	Lahan	3	J. Gosden	R. Hills	14–1	18
2001	Ameerat	3	M. Jarvis	P. Robinson	11–1	15

(For a list of all winners since the Second World War, *see* Classics.)

including the short-head decision from Donegal Prince in the 1979 Ebor Handicap, while another famous jumper he partnered often was **Night Nurse**. On quitting the saddle Jonjo took up training, and was soon making the scoreboard on the big occasions, saddling his first Royal Ascot winner in 1990 (Gipsy Fiddler in the Windsor Castle Stakes) and his first Cheltenham Festival winner in 1991 (Danny Connors in the Coral Golden Hurdle Final). But there was a darker side: he was diagnosed with cancer, which he faced with characteristic spirit and humour – and won through. In summer 2001 he relocated from his yard near Carlisle to take over at Jackdaws Castle in Gloucestershire following the purchase of that yard by **J. P. McManus**, one of his leading patrons.

ON THE BIT

A horse is considered to be 'on the bit' when going easily within itself, not pulling against its bit, and 'off the bit' when being rousted along by the jockey. ('On the bridle' and 'off the bridle' are virtually synonymous with 'on the bit' and 'off the bit'.)

ON THE NOD

Horses' heads move up and down as they run, and a finish described as 'on the nod' is one so close that the winner will be the horse whose nose happens to be in the right position on the line.

ON THE SHOULDERS

Betting slang for 9–2 (from the **tic-tac** sign).

OPEN DITCH

Steeplechase fence preceded by a ditch. A steeplechase must include at least one open ditch for every mile of its distance. The most famous open ditch in racing is the Chair, 15th fence on the Grand National course at **Aintree**. (In Ireland an open ditch is known as a 'regulation'.)

ORBY

First Irish-trained horse to win the Derby – which he did in 1907. He was owned by 'Boss' Croker and trained by Frederick MacCabe – whose achievement at Epsom prompted one overcome old Irish lady to greet him: 'Thank God and you, sir, we have lived to see a Catholic horse win the Derby.'

ORMONDE

Owned and bred by the first Duke of Westminster and trained by John Porter, Ormonde ran 14 times between 1885 and 1887 and was never beaten. As a juvenile he won three races, including the Dewhurst Stakes, then as a three-year-old in 1886 won the Two Thousand Guineas, Derby (ridden by **Fred Archer**), St James's Palace Stakes and Hardwicke Stakes at Royal Ascot, St Leger (thus landing the Triple Crown), Great Foal Stakes and Champion Stakes at Newmarket and the Free Handicap. At four he took the Rous Memorial Stakes at Ascot, the Hardwicke Stakes again and the Imperial Gold Cup at Newmarket. After standing at stud for a short time in England he was exported to Argentina, and from there sold on to California. He was put down in 1904 at the age of 21.

O'SULLEVAN, SIR PETER

Born in Kenmare, Co. Kerry, in 1918, Peter O'Sullevan joined the Press Association as racing correspondent in 1944 and wrote for the *Daily Express* from 1950 to 1986, building a reputation as one of the shrewdest and best-connected racing journalists of the age. It was in 1946 that he made his first race broadcast for the BBC, and he commentated on the first live televised Grand National in 1960, since when his honeyed tones have provided the soundtrack for many of racing's greatest moments – Grundy and Bustino, Red Rum's third Grand National, the Gold Cups of Dawn Run and Desert Orchid. The 'Voice of Racing' retired from commentating after calling home Suny Bay the winner of the Hennessy Cognac Gold Cup in November 1997. But however much his voice has made him a household presence, there has always been much more to Peter O'Sullevan than simply the commentating. He has worked tirelessly for many racing charities, has seen his autobiography *Calling the Horses* top the best-seller list (a phenomenon all but unheard-of with a racing book) in 1989, and has owned some notable horses. His best horse was the great sprinter Be Friendly, winner of the Prix de l'Abbaye, King's Stand Stakes at Royal Ascot, Ayr Gold Cup and twice the Vernons November Sprint Cup at Haydock Park, while the other top-class performer to carry his colours of black, yellow cross-belts and cap was Attivo, winner in 1974 of the Triumph Hurdle, Chester Cup and Northumberland Plate. Having been awarded the OBE in 1976 and CBE in 1991, O'Sullevan was knighted in the Queen's Birthday Honours in June 1997. Hugh McIlvanney, doyen of British sportswriters, famously wrote: 'His admirers are convinced that had he been on the rails at Balaclava he would have kept pace with the Charge of the Light Brigade, listing the fallers in precise order and describing the riders' injuries before they hit the ground.'

OUT OF THE HANDICAP

A horse is described as 'out of the handicap' if in the initial weights for a **handicap** race it is allotted a weight lower than the lowest rung of the weights specified to be carried in that race. If the weights are raised that horse might be brought into the handicap, but if they are not raised to a level which will do so, then it will be running 'out of the handicap'.

Try this as an example. When the weights for the 2001 Grand National were first published, See More Business was allotted top weight of 12st. A little further down the handicap came Beau on 11st 1lb, and Red Marauder on 10st 2lb. Much further down came Smarty with 9st 5lb, and further still was Art Prince with 8st 13lb. After the various forfeit stages, the horse with the highest weight in the original handicap who was declared as a runner was Beau, and as the conditions of the race stipulated that the highest weight to be carried must be not less than 11st 10lb, he had to carry that weight – 9lb higher than his original allotment. Since a handicap is all about differentials in weight, all the other horses all had to be raised 9lb as well, putting Red Marauder on 10st 11lb and Smarty on 10st exactly. Since

the conditions of the race also demanded that the lowest weight carried be 10st, Smarty had now moved from 'out of the handicap' to that state of grace called 'in the handicap' – that is, he would be racing off a weight which preserved the differentials between him and the horses weighted higher. But no horse could carry less than 10st – so the conditions stipulated – and Art Prince now had to carry the same weight as Smarty in the race, rather than maintain the 6lb advantage allotted by the original or 'long' handicap: Art Prince was, in the jargon, 6lb 'wrong' in relation to all the horses originally weighted at or above the same level as Smarty, or 6lb 'out of the handicap'. Simple, eh?

OUTCROSSING

In **breeding**, outcrossing is the opposite of **inbreeding**, so that neither of a horse's parents have ancestors in common in their recent pedigree.

OVER-BROKE

See **over-round**.

OVERREACHING

When a horse is galloping, the hind feet come very close to the front feet at the end of each stride, and when tired or at full stretch towards the end of the race the horse may strike into the back of a forefoot with a hind foot, cutting himself just above the heel of the front foot with the front edge of the hind shoe. When this happens the horse is said to have overreached, and the resulting cut is called an overreach.

OVER-ROUND

The odds for each horse in a race can be expressed as a percentage (for example, even money is 50%, 6–4 against is 40%, 3–1 on is 75%), and in strictly mathematical terms those percentages should add up to 100, since that is the true sum of the probabilities. The book for a race is said to be over-round when (as is customary) those percentages add up to more than 100 per cent, thereby giving the bookmaker his theoretical profit. For example, the combined percentages of the starting prices for the Gala Group Scottish National in April 2001 came to 134, meaning that in theory bookmakers would pay out £100 for every £134 they took in stakes. The importance of this for the punter is that with an over-round book the odds are so constructed that he or she cannot back every horse in the race and be guaranteed a profit. Books tend to be more over-round in competitive handicaps with big fields such as the Scottish National: in the seven-runner Greenham Stakes run at Newbury on the same day as the Scottish National, the book was over-round by just 11 per cent. When the percentages add up to *under* 100 per cent, that book is 'over-broke': the punter can back every horse and be guaranteed a profit.

OVER THE TOP

A horse is described as 'over the top' if it is past its peak and has had too much racing, for the season or at least for the time being: in this case it can no longer be expected to run to its best form. Being over the top can sometimes be detected before a race through close paddock inspection – the horse may appear listless or edgy, or have a 'stary' coat – but is more likely to become apparent only in the race.

OVERWEIGHT

Weight carried by the horse, over and above that specified in the conditions of the race, if the jockey cannot get down to the prescribed weight. Normally connections would not want the horse to carry more than it needs, but occasionally a top jockey will be booked for a lowly weighted horse even though he or she cannot do that weight: the extra poundage will be offset by the extra experience and skill of the rider.

OWNERS

Racehorse ownership covers a very wide range of operations, backgrounds and means. Ownership of the very best horses on the Flat is mostly confined to a very small number of immensely rich people who build up huge strings of superbly bred horses by their own breeding operations and by shelling out unconscionable amounts of money at the

Leading owners on the Flat since 1975	
1975	Dr C. Vittadini
1976	D. Wildenstein
1977	R. Sangster
1978	R. Sangster
1979	Sir M. Sobell
1980	S. Weinstock
1981	H.H. the Aga Khan
1982	R. Sangster
1983	R. Sangster
1984	R. Sangster
1985	Sheikh Mohammed
1986	Sheikh Mohammed
1987	Sheikh Mohammed
1988	Sheikh Mohammed
1989	Sheikh Mohammed
1990	Sheikh Hamdan Al Maktoum
1991	Sheikh Mohammed
1992	Sheikh Mohammed
1993	Sheikh Mohammed
1994	Sheikh Hamdan Al Maktoum
1995	Sheikh Hamdan Al Maktoum
1996	Godolphin
1997	Sheikh Mohammed
1998	Godolphin
1999	Godolphin
2000	H.H. the Aga Khan

yearling sales, so that big race after big race after big race is being fought out by jockeys sporting the colours of **Godolphin** or one of the **Maktoum** brothers, or **Michael Tabor** or **Khalid Abdullah**. On the other hand, regulations concerning partnerships (for between two and 20 people) and racing clubs mean that thousands of 'ordinary' people can now enjoy a genuine involvement with ownership for a fairly small outlay. Racing clubs (whose members make a one-off payment for a share) are increasingly popular among those with limited means but unlimited aspirations and dreams, and there are plenty of examples of big races being won by small owners. Over jumps, the biggest prizes can go to the smallest owners: for one spectacular example, see **Norton's Coin**.

Leading owners over jumps since 1974–5	
1974–5	R. Guest
1975–6	P. Raymond
1976–7	N. Le Mare
1977–8	Mrs O. Jackson
1978–9	Snailwell Stud Co. Ltd
1979–80	H. J. Joel
1980–1	R. J. Wilson
1981–2	Sheikh Ali Abu Khamsin
1982–3	Sheikh Ali Abu Khamsin
1983–4	Sheikh Ali Abu Khamsin
1984–5	T. Kilroe and Son Ltd
1985–6	Sheikh Ali Abu Khamsin
1986–7	H. J. Joel
1987–8	Miss J. Reed
1988–9	R. Burridge
1989–90	Mrs Harry J. Duffey
1990–1	P. Piller
1991–2	Whitcombe Manor Stables
1992–3	Mrs J. Mould
1993–4	Pell-Mell Partners
1994–5	Roach Foods Ltd
1995–6	A. Wates
1996–7	R. Ogden
1997–8	D. Johnson
1998–9	J. P. McManus
1999–2000	R. Ogden
2000–1	R. Ogden

An extra dimension has been added to ownership – and an extra grotesquerie to the **naming** of horses – by allowing commercial companies to own racehorses, sometimes (though not always) for advertising purposes.

There are over 18,000 owners registered with the Jockey Club. When registration (which in 2000 cost £47.75 plus VAT for an individual) is accepted, the owner deposits money in an account with Weatherbys. To this will be added winnings, and from it will be deducted entry fees and fees to the jockey. (Training fees are paid directly to the trainer.) When deductions exceed additions the owner must top up the account. But what are the chances of making a profit by owning a horse? Few owners are in it for monetary gain, and most are well aware that the odds are stacked against their prospering from this pursuit. It will cost at least £10,000 a year to keep a horse in training – considerably more if the animal is with one of the top Flat trainers. With prize money at its current levels, a horse at the lower rank is clearly unlikely to pay its way, and around two-thirds of all horses in training fail to win a race at all.

(In the tables of winning owners opposite amounts of prize money earned are not given, for the simple reason that sources for such information tend to differ – by amounts small enough not to make any difference to who is considered leading owner – and thus consistency is impossible.)

OXX, JOHN

Born in 1950, John Oxx learned his trade as assistant to his trainer father John Oxx senior. On the latter's retirement he took over the yard at Currabeg, near The Curragh in Co. Kildare, and sent out his first winner Orchestra at Phoenix Park on 31 March 1979.

Sinndar, John Oxx's Derby winner in 2000, was his first ever runner in the race.

His best horse to date has been Sinndar, winner of the Derby, Irish Derby and Prix de l'Arc de Triomphe in 2000, but he also hit the international jackpot with the tough filly Ridgewood Pearl, who in 1995 won the Irish One Thousand Guineas, Coronation Stakes and Breeders' Cup Mile. Enzeli, trained like Sinndar for his principal patron the Aga Khan, won the Ascot Gold Cup in 1999.

P

PACEMAKER

A horse whose role in a race is to ensure a strong and even gallop, to the benefit of another runner (usually but not necessarily from the same stable and in the same ownership) who is not a front-runner but needs a 'truly run' race. The pacemaker is not designated in any formal sense, but their use is officially acknowledged: a Jockey Club instruction reads that 'The Stewards of the Jockey Club are of the opinion that when horses run as pacemakers, their riders and their trainers are not in breach of the Rules of Racing provided that the horses are ridden out to a finish and do not deliberately cause any interference to other runners in the interests of another horse in the same ownership or from the same stables.' Pacemakers have their own footnotes in racing history. The use of Highest and Kinglet as pacemakers for **Bustino** was instrumental in making the 1975 King George VI and Queen Elizabeth Diamond Stakes 'The Race of the Century' (see **Grundy**), and Riboson, pacemaker for Bustino in the 1974 St Leger, was such a good horse in his own right that he stayed on to finish third. Nor is it unheard of for the pacemaker to confound the game plan completely and win: Cape Cross was pacemaker for fellow Godolphin colt Kahal in the 1998 Lockinge Stakes at Newbury, yet kept on stoutly to win a Group One prize at 20–1. Some pacemaker!

PADDOCK

The paddock is the popular name for what is formally known as the parade ring: the railed area of a racecourse where the horses, having been saddled, are walked round until, on a given signal, they are mounted by the jockeys and led out on to the course.

PADDOCK INSPECTION

Getting a good look at the horses in the paddock before the race is one of the essentials of successful betting, and no one is more skilled at assessing horses than John Francome. These are his basics of paddock inspection, as given in *The Channel Four Racing Guide to Racehorses*:

As with any athlete, assessing the overall physical condition of a horse is partly a matter of subjective judgement. But generally you're looking for a horse with an intelligent and alert outlook and a bold eye (or, ideally, two!). Many horse-watchers take great account of the ears, as long ears supposedly indicate genuineness and courage. ('Lop' ears which flop forwards are traditionally a sign of an exceptionally genuine character.) The ears should point slightly inwards. The carriage of the head should be high, and the shoulder well sloped to give maximum drive to the forelegs. The neck should be well muscled. A deep chest is a good sign – lots of room for heart and lungs – but always avoid flab: like any human, a horse with too much of a tummy is not fit. A fit horse exudes muscularity and power, just like a fit human athlete. The back should be on the short rather than the long side and the quarters – the powerhouse of the equine system – round and full of muscle. A good tip is to check a horse from behind: look for the 'hard marks' – grooves either side of the tail – that indicate peak muscular condition.

In the summer you'll want your fancy to have a shiny, well-groomed coat: a 'stary' coat – dull and patchy – is not a good sign. Always stand with the sun behind you. View each horse from an identical angle. It's uncanny how the horse with the healthiest looking coat invariably runs the best.

Look for the signs which indicate whether a horse is likely to act on the prevailing going. Large feet are often suited to soft going, small feet to firmer ground.

How does the horse walk? It is often said that a horse that walks well will gallop well, and you can learn a lot from the walking action about how an individual will use himself in the faster paces. Look for a fluid gait, where the horse is covering a good deal of ground with every stride. Try to see if he is 'tracking up', with the hind foot overlapping or falling in front of the print left by the front foot on the same side. This is easier said than done, especially if you are watching on television, but in any case concentrate on whether the horse is walking loosely and easily or clattering round with a more mincing stride. The latter does not of course mean that the horse will not win – some fine horses have not been good walkers – but as a rule a loose walk is a much better sign than a more constricted gait. Listen as they walk by: you can hear the plodders. In studying the walk, as in all other aspects of assessing horses, the more you do it the better you'll get at it.

If the horse is jig-jogging round the paddock rather than walking calmly beside its handler, consider why. Horses that do this seldom run well in staying races, where a calm and resolute demeanour usually pays dividends. In most cases the bobbing up and down is a sign of keenness, but sometimes it's an indication of jangling nerves. How do you know which? Since the horse is not available for a pre-race interview, you have to deduce what you can of his mental state from his physical condition. Have a good, lingering look to check whether there appear to be signs of agitation. Disinclination to be led round quietly – pulling against his handler – is one telling sign, as are twitching the ears and swishing the tail. Another is sweating. Some horses sweat up before a race in sheer anticipation of what lies ahead, and should not be discounted on those grounds. With others, sweating is definitely a bad sign, as it indicates that the horse is wasting nervous energy and will not be able to give his best in the race. Normally, sweating around the ears and eyes is not encouraging. A lather of frothy sweat between the back legs is a certain sign the animal will not run to its best. Sweating on the neck, on the other hand, is often a sign of keenness (a bit like an actor getting keyed up before a performance). And, at the risk of stating the obvious, bear in mind that on a very hot day any horse is much more likely to be sweating than on a cold day . . . Most importantly, get to know your horses. With some, such as that terrific miler of a few years back Zilzal, you're worried if they're not sweating.

As well as having a close look at the runners in the paddock, try to watch them going down to the start. You can see from how a horse strides out whether he is liking the ground. On firm ground, the horse who goes to post gingerly or in a scratchy fashion is not likely to want to exert himself and stretch out on that surface in the race. A high knee action often indicates a liking for wet ground, a daisy-cutting action the opposite. But whatever the going, the real eye-catcher is the horse who seems to float over the ground, expending the minimum energy to cover the maximum distance.

Never force yourself to like a horse. There's always another race, and you'll be kicking yourself if you back a loser when you know deep down that you didn't like what you saw in the paddock.

Pay attention to which horse wins the 'Best Turned Out' award which is now a parade ring feature of so many races. Often the best turned out proves to be the winner, and this is no coincidence.

Familiarise yourself with individual horses as much as you can. The more you know, the more useful will be the evidence of your own eyes.

Flat or jumps, paddock observation is most effective in the early part of the season when fitness is both at a premium and most obvious to the beholder.

Bear in mind that different physical types are suited by different races. If before a race you like two horses equally, go for the one better built for the job in hand.

PADDOCKS

A filly or mare is described as being 'retired to the paddocks' when she is giving up racing in favour of a career as a **broodmare**.

PAGET, DOROTHY

They just don't make 'em like Dorothy Paget any more. Rich, fat and eccentric – and all three to an astonishing degree – she raced on a vast scale, financing her love of the Turf from the fortune she had inherited at the age of 20. Once an accomplished horsewoman herself, riding side-saddle in point-to-points, her curious lifestyle included obsessive eating, and she soon weighed in at over 20st. She disliked human company – especially men, whose proximity reportedly inclined her to vomit – and surrounded herself with a bevy of female minders. She kept odd hours, dining at 7 a.m., sleeping through the day and getting up for breakfast at 8.30 p.m., then spending the night consuming vast meals and phoning her trainers. She expected them to be adaptable to such eccentricities, but (not surprisingly) her tyrannical ways led to friction: horses would be shuffled around among yards at her whim. But her nomadic string included some star performers, notably **Golden Miller**, who won the Cheltenham Gold Cup five times from 1932 to 1936 and remains the only horse to have won the Gold Cup and Grand National in the same year: 1934. (When she planted a kiss on Golden Miller's nose after one of his victories, a racegoer suggested that this was probably the first occasion on which she had kissed a member of the opposite sex: 'And he's a gelding,' pointed out another.) She owned 1940 Gold Cup winner Roman Hackle; Insurance, winner of the Champion Hurdle in 1932 and 1933; and two other Champion Hurdle winners: Solford (1940) and Distel (1946). She also owned Straight Deal, who took the wartime Derby at Newmarket in 1943, and Mont Tremblant, winner of the Cheltenham Gold Cup as a novice in 1952. Dorothy Paget was an inveterate punter: her largest stake was reputed to have been £160,000, on an 8–1 on chance. To say that it duly obliged (which it did) seems to underplay the magnitude of the wager. But her curious daily routine made orthodox punting rather awkward, and such was the trust with which she was regarded by one of her bookmakers that he allowed her to phone him in the evening and bet on races which had already taken place. Stories of the Paget eccentricity are legion, but one which would appeal to any racing fan whose afternoon's sport has been spoiled by the car breaking down on the way to the races concerns an incident shortly after the Second World War. En route to a race meeting, accompanied by her secretary, her car seized up. The only other vehicle in sight was a butcher's delivery van; this she instructed her secretary to purchase on the spot, and was reported to have arrived at the racecourse sitting between two carcasses. She had been alarmed by the breakdown, and thereafter never drove anywhere without a second car following her in case of a repetition. For long journeys a third car would follow the second, just in case the back-up vehicle broke down as well. Dorothy Paget – truly a big owner – died aged 54 in 1960.

PARADE

Many big races are preceded by a parade of the runners down the course past the stands, thus allowing racegoers without access to the paddock to have a good look at the horses, and punters to have a last-minute asssessment of how a particular horse is behaving. An alternative to the standard parade is having the runners canter down in racecard order at set intervals – such as ten seconds.

PARADE RING AND PRE-PARADE RING

The parade ring is the formal name for the racecourse paddock. The pre-parade ring is the area where the horses are walked around before being taken to the saddling boxes, and at most courses provides a less hectic setting for close study of the runners than the parade ring itself. At some courses the pre-parade ring is particularly atmospheric: at Newmarket's July Course, for example, it is sited among the tall trees.

PARDUBICE

This racecourse, in the Czech Republic about 90 miles east of Prague, is home to one world-famous race, the Velka Pardubice run in October. Commonly described as the Czech version of the Grand National, the Velka Pardubice mixes orthodox steeplechasing and cross-country over a distance of around four and a quarter miles – some of it across a ploughed field – and 32 obstacles, which include The Moat (a huge water jump), a six-foot upright bank, a stone wall and the famous Taxis. English jockey Guy Lewis first rode in the race in 1996:

From the take-off side the Taxis looks inoffensive enough – the sort of stiff hedge you'd think nothing of on a day's hunting. It's on the landing side that the full horror hits you: an enormous ditch with a long sloping lip out of it. Your horse wouldn't know about this until he was clearing the hedge, so you'd have to ride like the clappers into the fence and pray that you had enough momentum to clear the ditch.

The Velka Pardubice was first run in 1874, when it was won by an English jockey named Sayers on Frantome. The first British-ridden winner of modern times was Stephen's Society, ridden by amateur jockey Chris Collins in 1973. Lambourn trainer Charlie Mann won the race on It's A Snip in 1995, and leading British and Irish jockeys are becoming a more common sight in this unique race. Risk Of Thunder, winner of the La Touche Cup at **Punchestown** six years in a row, was runner-up in 1999.

PARI-MUTUEL

Name for totalisator betting used in France (and in the USA). In French, the phrase literally means 'mutual wager'.
See also **pool betting**.

PARK COURSES

See **racecourses; Sandown Park**.

PARK TOP

Owned by the Duke of Devonshire and trained by Bernard van Cutsem, Park Top won 13 of her 24 races in four seasons between 1967 and 1970. Bought as a yearling for 500 guineas and too backward to race as a juvenile, she started her racing career as a three-year-old in 1967, winning at Windsor, Newbury, Royal Ascot (the Ribblesdale Stakes) and Brighton before running unplaced in the Prix Vermeille. At four she won two more races (at Brighton and Longchamp), but it was not until she was five that she really came into her own: in 1969 she won the Prix de la Seine, the Coronation Cup and the Hardwicke Stakes, was controversially beaten by Wolver Hollow in the Eclipse Stakes, and then, ridden by Lester Piggott, beat Crozier in the King George. Horse and jockey teamed up again to land the Prix Foy at Longchamp en route to the Prix de l'Arc de Triomphe, where she came very late and was beaten three-quarters of a length by Levmoss. Lester Piggott later wrote that 'I got a great deal of stick from local racegoers and the press for overdoing the waiting tactics on her, and for once the criticism hit home: I was very annoyed with myself that day, as I knew deep down that had I made my move sooner I would certainly have won.' She had probably not got over the Arc when second to Flossy in the Champion Stakes. Park Top remained in training in 1970: she won La Coupe at Longchamp, was given too much to do by Piggott when runner-up to Caliban in the Coronation Cup, won the Cumberland Lodge Stakes at Ascot and ended her career running third in the Prix Royallieu. She then retired to the paddocks and died in May 1989 at the age of 25.

PASSPORTS (HORSES')

At birth every Thoroughbred is issued with a chart logging its breeding and physical characteristics. Once it is named it has a passport giving date of foaling, name, colour and distinguishing marks, which must accompany it to every race meeting at which it runs.

PASTERN

Part of the horse's leg just below the fetlock joint and above the hoof.
See also **split pastern**.

PATENT

Bet combining three different horses in different races in seven separate wagers – three singles, three doubles and one treble:

- 3 singles on A, B and C;
- 3 doubles: A with B, A with C and B with C;
- 1 treble: A with B with C.

A £1 win Patent will cost you £7; a £1 each-way Patent costs £14. Say you have a £1 win Patent and all three selections come in at 2–1; your winnings are:

- £6 (three £1 singles each winning at 2–1); plus
- £24 (three £1 doubles with each horse winning at 2–1); plus
- £26 (a £1 treble with each horse winning at 2–1), producing a total of £56.

If two of the horses win at 2–1 while the third loses, you would still make a profit. You win £4 (two £1 singles each winning at 2–1) plus £8 (one £1 double with each horse winning at 2–1): total winnings £12. But of your seven bets four (one single, two doubles, one treble) have lost, so your profit is £12 less £4: £8.

PATTERN (FLAT)

Pattern races, or Group races, are the elite contests of Flat racing: a series of tests for the best horses at all ages and at different distances, together they give the season its carefully constructed form, ensuring top-class and competitive racing on a Europe-wide scale. The idea was born in the mid-1960s in response to worries about the lack of balance between British and French racing, and the Duke of Norfolk's Pattern of Racing Committee recommended in 1965 a system to embrace England, Ireland and France. (Germany and Italy joined later.) The aim of the Pattern was not to invent races but to grade existing races in such a way, according to the report of the Committee, as 'to ensure that a series of races over the right distances and at the right time of the year are available to test the best horses of all ages and . . . to

---

Group One races in Great Britain 2001

(see separate entries for each)

Two Thousand Guineas (Newmarket)
One Thousand Guineas (Newmarket)
Lockinge Stakes (Newbury)
Coronation Cup (Epsom Downs)
Oaks (Epsom Downs)
Derby (Epsom Downs)
St James's Palace Stakes (Royal Ascot)
Prince of Wales's Stakes (Royal Ascot)
Gold Cup (Royal Ascot)
Coronation Stakes (Royal Ascot)
Eclipse Stakes (Sandown Park)
July Cup (Newmarket)
King George VI and Queen Elizabeth
    Diamond Stakes (Ascot)
Sussex Stakes (Goodwood)
Nassau Stakes (Goodwood)
International Stakes (York)
Yorkshire Oaks (York)
Nunthorpe Stakes (York)
Sprint Cup (Haydock Park)
St Leger (Doncaster)
Fillies' Mile (Ascot)
Queen Elizabeth II Stakes (Ascot)
Cheveley Park Stakes (Newmarket)
Middle Park Stakes (Newmarket)
Dewhurst Stakes (Newmarket)
Champion Stakes (Newmarket)
Racing Post Trophy (Doncaster)

---

ensure that the horses remain in training long enough and race often enough to be tested properly for constitution and soundness.' In addition to this noble aim in pursuit of the excellence of the Thoroughbred breed, the existence of the Pattern guarantees enthusiasts a constant stream of high-class racing throughout the season and makes it difficult for the best horses from several countries to avoid meeting each other regularly. The recommended system was finally implemented in 1971, with the Pattern races divided into three groups:

- *Group One*: Classics and other races of major international importance (in the USA the equivalent is Grade One);

Other European Group One races 2001

Ireland
Irish Two Thousand Guineas (The Curragh)
Irish One Thousand Guineas (The Curragh)
Tattersalls Gold Cup (The Curragh)
*Irish Derby (The Curragh)
Irish Oaks (The Curragh)
Phoenix Stakes (Leopardstown)
Moyglare Stud Stakes (The Curragh)
*Irish Champion Stakes (Leopardstown)
Irish St Leger (The Curragh)
National Stakes (The Curragh)

France
Prix Ganay (Longchamp)
Poule d'Essai des Poulains (Longchamp)
Poule d'Essai des Pouliches (Longchamp)
Prix Lupin (Longchamp)
Prix Saint-Alary (Longchamp)
Prix d'Ispahan (Longchamp)
Prix du Jockey-Club (Chantilly)
Prix Jean Prat (Chantilly)
Prix de Diane (Chantilly)
Grand Prix de Paris (Longchamp)
Grand Prix de Saint-Cloud (Saint-Cloud)
Prix Maurice de Gheest (Deauville)
Prix Jacques le Marois (Deauville)
Prix Morny (Deauville)
Prix du Moulin (Longchamp)

(asterisked races indicate separate entries)

Prix Vermeille (Longchamp)
Prix de la Salamandre (Longchamp)
Prix Marcel Boussac (Longchamp)
Prix de l'Abbaye (Longchamp)
*Prix de l'Arc de Triomphe (Longchamp)
Prix de l'Opera (Longchamp)
Prix du Cadran (Longchamp)
Grand Criterium (Longchamp)
Prix de la Foret (Longchamp)
Prix Royal-Oak (Longchamp)
Criterium de Saint-Cloud (Saint-Cloud)

Italy
Premio Presidente della Repubblica (Rome)
Oaks d'Italia (Milan)
Derby Italiano (Rome)
Gran Premio di Milano (Milan)
Premio Vittoria di Capua (Milan)
Gran Premio del Jockey Club Italiano (Milan)
Gran Criterium (Milan)
Premio Roma (Rome)

Germany
Deutsches Derby (Hamburg)
Deutschland Preis (Dusseldorf)
Grosser Dallmayr-Preis (Munich)
Grosser Erdgas-Preis (Gelsenkirchen)
Grosser Preis von Baden (Baden-Baden)
Preis von Europa (Cologne)

- *Group Two*: races of international importance just below championship level;
- *Group Three*: primarily domestic races regarded as preparatory contests for the higher groups (such as Classic trials).

Group One races are always run without penalties on a weight-for-age-and-sex basis, whereas penalties can apply in Groups Two and Three races, based on previous performance in Pattern races.

Below Group races are Listed races, a set of races designed to identify racehorses of superior merit but below Group standard.

The Pattern is fluid, allowing the status of a particular race to be altered if appropriate: thus the Prince of Wales's Stakes at Royal Ascot was upgraded from Group Two to Group One in 2000, whereas Doncaster's Flying Childers Stakes was downgraded from Group One to Group Two in 1979.

There were 110 Pattern races run in 2000 in Great Britain, with 27 at Group One level, 29 at Group Two and 54 at Group Three.

PATTERN (NATIONAL HUNT)

While jump racing is not part of the European Pattern described above, a separate Pattern was introduced to the winter game in 1990 to give more of a structure to the jumps season. The jumping Pattern divides into three grades:

Grade One scheduled races over jumps 2000–1

Tingle Creek Chase (Sandown Park)
Long Walk Hurdle (Ascot)
Feltham Novices' Chase (Kempton Park)
*King George VI Chase (Kempton Park)
Christmas Hurdle (Kempton Park)
Finale Junior Hurdle (Chepstow)
Challow Hurdle (Newbury)
Tolworth Hurdle (Sandown Park)
Cleeve Hurdle (Cheltenham)
Scilly Isles Novices' Chase (Sandown Park)
Ascot Chase (Ascot)
Supreme Novices' Hurdle (Cheltenham)
Arkle Chase (Cheltenham)
*Champion Hurdle (Cheltenham)
Royal & SunAlliance Novices' Hurdle
 (Cheltenham)
*Queen Mother Champion Chase
 (Cheltenham)
Royal & SunAlliance Chase (Cheltenham)
Festival Bumper (Cheltenham)
*Triumph Hurdle (Cheltenham)
*Gold Cup (Cheltenham)
Melling Chase (Aintree)
Sefton Novices' Hurdle (Aintree)
Maghull Novices' Chase (Aintree)
Aintree Hurdle (Aintree)

(asterisked races indicate separate entries)

- *Grade One*: the major weight-for-age races in different categories and over different distances (thus a staying hurdler would have two Grade One events: the Long Walk Hurdle at Ascot in December and the Stayers' Hurdle at Cheltenham in March);
- *Grade Two*: races just below championship standard;
- *Grade Three*: includes the major handicap hurdles and steeplechases.

PEBBLES

Adored by the racing public, with good reason. Over three seasons between 1983 and 1985 she never gave of less than her best, won eight of her 15 career starts, and has two notable distinctions: she was the first filly ever to win the Eclipse Stakes, and the first British-trained horse to win a Breeders' Cup race. Trained at Newmarket by **Clive Brittain**, Pebbles first raced in the colours of Greek shipping magnate Captain Marcos Lemos. She won two of her six races as a two-year-old and showed her best form when runner-up at 33–1 to Desirable in the Cheveley Park Stakes. At three in 1984 she won the Nell Gwyn Stakes at Newmarket and then won the One Thousand Guineas by three lengths – after which she was sold by Lemos to **Sheikh Mohammed**, though she remained with Clive Brittain. In the Sheikh's maroon and white colours she ran second to Katies in the Coronation Stakes and was beaten a neck in the Champion Stakes. Kept in training as a four-year-old in 1985, Pebbles blossomed from a very good filly to a great one. She won the Trusthouse Forte Mile at Sandown Park, was surprisingly beaten by Bob Back in the Prince of Wales's Stakes at Royal Ascot (though she had 1984 St Leger winner Commanche Run behind her in third), and won the Eclipse Stakes by two lengths from subsequent Arc winner Rainbow Quest. She was then rested in preparation for an autumn campaign, which consisted of two great races. In the Champion Stakes at Newmarket she was only third choice in the market as a major showdown between Commanche Run and that year's runaway Derby winner Slip Anchor was avidly anticipated – but Pebbles put the colts in their place, showing a devastating turn of foot to win by three lengths from Slip Anchor. The Breeders' Cup was then in its infancy, having been first run only the year before, and Pebbles's attempt at the Turf at Aqueduct in 1985 was seen as a typical example of Clive Brittain's sense of adventure. Accompanied to New York by her constant companion, the gelding Come On The Blues (who had won the Royal Hunt Cup at Royal Ascot that year), and ridden by Pat Eddery, Pebbles started 11–5 favourite for the Turf. She had to be snatched up to avoid scrimmaging on the final bend, but then shot into the lead halfway up the home stretch and went half a length up. Steve Cauthen on Strawberry Road started to close relentlessly, but the filly stuck her neck out and made for the line, and the wire came in time: she won by a neck to land Sheikh Mohammed $900,000 – which at the prevailing exchange rate came to £629,371, then the greatest amount ever won by a British-trained horse in a single race. Though the original intention was to keep her in training, Pebbles did not run again, and she was much missed. Timeform's *Racehorses of 1985* hit the right note: 'Pebbles acts as a tonic to any race in which she competes.'

PECK ON LANDING
A chaser or hurdler is said to 'peck on landing' over an obstacle if its nose touches or almost touches the ground before it rights itself.

PEGGY'S PET
In the hallowed annals of all-time British losers and never winners, Peggy's Pet comes one below **Quixall Crossett** and one above **Amrullah**. Trained for most of his career by Peter Poston, Peggy's Pet posted a career record of nought from 94 starts – Flat, hurdles and chases – between 1962 and 1969. He was also defeated in 17 point-to-points.

PENALTY
A penalty in racing is extra weight. In a **handicap**, it indicates extra weight (in addition to the allotted handicap weight) to be carried by a horse who has won since the weights were originally published. For example, the conditions for the Mitsubishi Shogun Handicap Chase run at Sandown Park on Whitbread Gold Cup day, 28 April 2001, specified: 'Penalties, after April 22nd, a winner of a steeplechase 5lb' – that is, had the horse won after that date, he would have to carry 5lb above his allotted handicap weight. (With some handicaps, such as the Whitbread itself, no penalties apply once the original weights have been published.) The term also applies in a conditions race when the weight to be carried depends on past performances at certain levels. For example, when Nuclear Debate ran in the Temple Stakes at Sandown Park on May Bank Holiday Monday 2001 he had to carry 7lb above the basic weight for a horse of his age as the conditions stipulated such a penalty for the winner of a Group One race, which he was.

PENALTY VALUE
Total sum of prize money won by the winner's connections, before mandatory deductions: it is this sum which is used in calculating penalties for future races which relate to race value. *See also* **prize money**.

PENDIL
Trained for most of his career by **Fred Winter**, Pendil won the King George VI Chase twice (1972 and 1973) and many other big races, but the bottom line of his career is regret that this splendid chaser failed in two attempts at the most prestigious jump race of all, the Cheltenham Gold Cup. In 1973 he started 6–4 on favourite on the strength of 11 consecutive victories, took the lead at the second last fence, skipped over the last and looked all over the winner as he strode away from his rivals up the hill – only to tie up close home and allow **The Dikler** to get up and beat him a short head. The following year, an even hotter favourite at 13–8 on, he was travelling smoothly just behind the leaders coming down the hill for the final time – but could not get out of the way when High Ken fell in front of him at the third last fence and brought him down. Those two Gold Cup setbacks were his only defeats in three seasons between autumn 1971 and spring 1974, when his victories included those two King Georges, the 1972 Arkle Trophy, the 1972 Black and White Whisky Gold Cup at Ascot, the 1973 and 1974 Yellow Pages Chase at Kempton (now the Racing Post Chase) and the 1973 Massey-Ferguson Gold Cup at Cheltenham (now the Tripleprint Gold Cup). He started the 1974–5 term with three wins (including beating **Tingle Creek** in the Sandown Pattern Chase), but **Captain Christy** (who had won the 1974 Gold Cup when Pendil was brought down) spoiled his bid for a third King George when winning by eight lengths at Kempton. Pendil was then beaten by Shock Result at Newbury and finished third to Cuckolder in the Yellow

Pages, despite breaking down. Off the course for nearly two years, he reappeared at Kempton Park in late December 1976 a few days before his twelfth birthday: ridden by **John Francome**, he surprised and delighted the jumping fraternity by making a winning return, starting at 10–1 and beating Spanish Tan and the Queen Mother's good chaser Game Spirit in a three-horse race. Two subsequent wins, beating Fort Devon at Kempton and What A Buck in a two-horse race at Wincanton, fuelled unlikely dreams of winning that richly deserved Gold Cup after all. He ran third to Don't Hesitate in the Yellow Pages in February 1977 and was reportedly on course for Cheltenham, only for a fall on the road to end his career. He had won six hurdles and 21 chases. Pendil – whose most unusual physical characteristic was a pair of horny lumps on his forehead – spent an honourable retirement at the Wiltshire farm of journalist and BBC racing presenter Jonathan Powell, and died in September 1994 aged 29.

PENETROMETER

The penetrometer was originally devised for road-builders to measure the depth of asphalt, and is now used in many racing countries – notably France – to determine the state of the **going**. (Not in Britain, though, where on most courses the Clerk of the Course's stick being thrust into the ground was good enough for our grandfathers and is good enough now.) A penetrometer consists of a calibrated hollow metal rod, down the shaft of which is dropped a heavy ball; the reading is determined by how far that ball penetrates the soil.

PERMIT HOLDER

A permit holder is a person entitled to train, under National Hunt Rules, only horses which are the property of his or her immediate family (as opposed to a 'public trainer' who can train horses for anyone). Permit holders operate small time but do have their moments: Sirrell Griffiths, trainer of **Norton's Coin**, 100–1 winner of the 1990 Cheltenham Gold Cup, is a permit holder, as was Frank Gilman, owner and trainer of 1982 Grand

National winner Grittar, and as is Norman Mason, owner and trainer of 2001 National hero Red Marauder.

PERSIAN WAR

The period since the war has been rich in great hurdlers, but for many people Persian War was simply the best. He won the Champion Hurdle in 1968, 1969 and 1970 and was second to Bula in 1971. He also won the Daily Express Triumph Hurdle, the Sweeps Hurdle in Ireland, the Schweppes Gold Trophy and the Welsh Champion Hurdle, and in building up his remarkable record showed himself as tough and resilient a horse as any that has raced under National Hunt Rules.

When Brough Scott was a professional jockey he was closely connected with Persian War's trainer Colin Davies. Though Brough never rode Persian War in a race, he did get to ride work on the great horse:

I once rode him in a gallop in France over a mile and three-quarters with two good Flat horses. At a mile they were cantering over him but he just tried and tried and was actually going away at the finish. It was the bravest piece of work I ever experienced.

Persian War was bred by Jakie Astor and trained on the Flat by Dick Hern, winning over two miles. He was sold to the Lewes trainer Tom Masson in the autumn of 1966 and early the following year, having been sold on to David Naylor-Leyland, was bought by Henry Alper, an insurance assessor who had been watching racing from Newbury on television and was smitten by the horse's performance when winning a small novice hurdle. In Alper's claret and blue colours – reflecting his other passion, West Ham United – and under the care of trainer Brian Swift at Epsom, Persian War won the Victor Ludorum Hurdle at Haydock and the Triumph Hurdle at Cheltenham. By the following spring the horse was being trained by Colin Davies at Chepstow, and he put up a superb performance to win the Schweppes Gold Trophy at

Newbury under 11st 13lb, a crushing burden for a five-year-old and still a weight-carrying record for the race. Then came the Champion Hurdle at Cheltenham, for which Persian War started 4–1 second favourite: he beat the favourite Chorus II by four lengths, and became the first hurdler to be voted Horse of the Year. The following season he started a heavily backed 6–4 favourite for the Champion, run in heavy going (his first victory had been on firm); again he won by four lengths. Less than three weeks later he won the Welsh Champion Hurdle on rock-hard ground. For the 1970 Champion, run on yielding going, he was again a short-priced favourite at 5–4, despite not having won a race for 11 months, and he strode up the Cheltenham hill in majestic style to beat Major Rose by one and a half lengths. Alper was a somewhat capricious owner, and by the time of the 1971 race Persian War had moved trainers once more – to Arthur Pitt – and had won the Irish Sweeps Hurdle at Fairyhouse. Despite a gallant effort, however, a fourth Champion Hurdle victory was not to be; he went under by four lengths to the king of the new generation, Bula. Persian War was soon on the move yet again, and it was from Dennis Rayson's yard at Exning that he went to the last of his 18 victories in a £374 hurdle at Stratford in June 1972. He was finally retired at the age of 11 and died in 1984, aged 21.

PERSIMMON

Owned and bred by the Prince of Wales (later Edward VII) and trained by Richard Marsh, Persimmon won the Coventry Stakes at Royal Ascot first time out as a two-year-old in 1895, then the Richmond Stakes at Goodwood, before running third in the Middle Park Stakes.

Persimmon's severed and stuffed head is one of the choice exhibits at the National Horseracing Museum in Newmarket.

In 1896 he missed the Two Thousand Guineas and went straight to the Derby, in which he was ridden by Jack Watts and started at 5–1: after a fierce struggle with odds-on favourite St Frusquin, Persimmon won by a neck. St Frusquin, receiving 3lb, turned the tables in the Princess of Wales's Stakes at Newmarket, but Persimmon went on to win the St Leger and the Jockey Club Stakes, and as a four-year-old in 1897 he won the Ascot Gold Cup by eight lengths and the Eclipse Stakes. He was champion sire twice, the most famous of his offspring being the great filly **Sceptre**, one of his first crop. Persimmon died at the age of 15 in 1908.

PERTH

Scone Palace Park, Perth, Perthshire
  PH2 6BB
Tel.: 01738 551597
Fax: 01738 553021
E-mail: sam@perth-races.co.uk
Web: www.perth-races.co.uk

The most northerly racecourse in Britain, Perth opened in 1908, although there had been racing in the area in the eighteenth century. It enjoys a glorious setting in the wooded parkland of Scone Palace, hard by the River Tay, and the river comes into its own when feeding the watering system which irrigates the course and thus makes possible its participation in the summer jumping programme. The downside of this location is that the track is particularly vulnerable to waterlogging, and the number of abandoned fixtures here has been a source of great frustration over recent years: the April festival meeting, high point of the Perth racing year, was completely washed out both in 1999 and 2000. The track is a right-handed circuit of about a mile and a quarter round, the home straight longer than the back. It is mostly flat, with two tight turns and the other two much more gradual, and as a short circuit tends to favour the handy sort of horse. Front-runners can do well here.

PESLIER, OLIVIER

Often characterised as 'the Frankie Dettori of France', as his ebullient and articulate demeanour matches that of the Italian, Olivier Peslier was born in January 1973 and rode his first winner on Cavallo d'Oro at Rouen in March 1989. He was champion jockey in France for the first time in 1996 and has repeated the feat three times since, in 1997, 1999 and 2000. He won the Prix de l'Arc de Triomphe three years running – on Helissio (1996), Peintre Celebre (1997; he took the Prix du Jockey-Club on the same horse that year) and Sagamix (1998) – and won the Derby on High-Rise (1998: 'the summit of my career') and the Irish Derby on Winged Love in 1995.

PETITE ETOILE

A distinctive grey filly owned by Prince **Aly Khan** and trained by **Noel Murless**, Petite Etoile started her glittering career in May 1958 at the less than glamorous racecourse of Manchester (which closed in 1963), beaten eight lengths by her solitary opponent Chris. She then won the Star Stakes at Sandown Park, was beaten in the Molecomb Stakes at Goodwood, and returned to Sandown to win the Rose Stakes. She seemed to be a good filly but nothing out of the ordinary, and it was no great surprise when the following spring Murless's stable jockey **Lester Piggott** opted to ride Collyria rather than Petite Etoile in the One Thousand Guineas. The grey went into the first fillies' Classic having won the Free Handicap at Newmarket under top weight, but none the less she started at 8–1 for the One Thousand: ridden by **Doug Smith**, she stormed up the hill to win by a length from the favourite Rosalba. Next stop the Oaks. Piggott had got the message by now and was in the saddle, but she still started at 11–2, her stamina being very much in doubt. Again Petite Etoile confounded the doubters, winning easily from the favourite Cantelo (who went on to win the St Leger). She then won the Sussex Stakes, Yorkshire Oaks and Champion Stakes, ending her three-year-old season unbeaten in six races (of which five now enjoy Group One status, though the Pattern was not in existence at the time). She ran only three times at four, winning at Kempton Park, landing the Coronation Cup cheekily from 1959 Derby winner Parthia, then sensationally failing to catch Aggressor in the King George VI and Queen Elizabeth Stakes and going down by half a length. Riders in the

stand blamed Piggott for giving her too much to do, but his view was that she failed to get home. She raced again as a five-year-old in 1961, winning a second Coronation Cup (narrowly from Vienna) and three lesser races, but blotted her copybook when beaten at Kempton in the Aly Khan Memorial Gold Cup (named for her owner, who had been killed in a car crash shortly before she won the Oaks) and ended her racing career on a downbeat when beaten half a length by Le Levanstell in the Queen Elizabeth II Stakes. She retired the winner of 14 of her 19 races, but as a broodmare produced nothing which remotely approached her own ability. Petite Etoile died in 1978 at the age of 22.

PHAR LAP

Your horse getting stuffed is one thing. Your horse getting stuffed by a taxidermist and placed in a museum is quite another. That's what happened to Phar Lap; but then Phar Lap was no ordinary horse. Foaled in New Zealand and sold as a yearling in 1928 for 160 guineas, he ran 51 races between 1929 and 1932 and won 37, including as a three-year-old the AJC Derby, the Craven Plate and the Victoria Derby before finishing third in the Melbourne Cup; he then won the AJC Plate. At four he won 14 of his 16 races and landed the 1930 Melbourne Cup: despite carrying 9st 12lb he started at 11–8 on, shortest-priced favourite in the history of the race, and won by three lengths. By the time of his third Melbourne Cup in 1931 he had won another eight races as a five-year-old and become a national hero, but weight is no respecter of popular adulation and the 10st 10lb he had to carry in the Cup proved too much. That 1931 Melbourne Cup proved his last race in Australia, and he was shipped off for a new career in the USA. In March 1932 he faced 1929 Preakness winner Dr Freeland and nine other opponents in the Agua Caliente Handicap at Agua Caliente in Mexico, close to the US border: he won easily, but two weeks later, on 5 April 1932, he died. Rumours abounded that he had been poisoned, but the exact cause of his end was never properly established.

Phar Lap's ability had much to do with his

size. A magnificent chestnut nicknamed 'The Red Terror', he stood over 17 hands and had a girth which measured 79in. After his death his heart was removed and weighed: it tipped the scales at $14\frac{1}{2}$ lb. His stuffed body is the star exhibit of the Melbourne Museum, and his skeleton is in the Dominion Museum in Wellington, New Zealand.

PHOENIX PARK

Before it closed in 1990 Phoenix Park in Dublin was one of the major courses in Ireland, home of the Phoenix Champion Stakes.

PHOTO FINISH

The photo finish has always been based on the principle of photographing runners as they pass through a very narrow field of vision, and these days calls on the very latest in photographic technology. Two digital cameras are fixed in place in the photo-finish booth high in the stand – one to cover the whole width of the track and the other to focus on that part of the course furthest away from the camera in order to make maximum use of the strip of mirror (6in wide by 6ft tall) which is attached to the far winning post and which allows the judge to see what is happening from the far side of the course if the horses are so close together that the view from the judge's box does not afford enough information. The pictures these cameras produce are made up of millions of tiny dots, and the 'line' is a vertical column the equivalent of one dot wide which is photographed 2,000 times per second, building up the photo-finish picture in a computer as the horses go through. In the old days film had to be processed before the judge could deliver his or her verdict. Now the judge simply has to examine the image, which is instantly presented on the monitor, with a vertical white line added to represent the winning line. The aim is to announce the result of the photo finish within 20 seconds – compared with a delay of several minutes under the old system.

The prototype photo-finish camera – based on the notion of photographing moving objects through a slit onto a continuous strip of film – was first used to decide placings in a race in the Grand Metropolitan Handicap at Epsom on 22 April 1947: the winner Star Song was a length to the good, but the judge needed to consult the photo before deciding that Parhelion was second, a head in front of Salubrious. In 1949 the photo was first called upon to decide the outcome of a Classic race in England when Nimbus beat Abernant a short head in the 1949 Two Thousand Guineas at Newmarket. Later that season it was first used to determine the outcome of the Derby, when the judge called for the evidence of the camera before announcing Nimbus the winner by a head from Amour Drake, with Swallow Tail another head away in third.

PIGGOTT, LESTER

Born on Guy Fawkes Day, 5 November 1935, Lester Keith Piggott was 12 when scoring his first victory, on The Chase in a selling handicap at Haydock Park on 18 August 1948. He rode his last winner in Britain, Palacegate Jack, at the same course some 46 years later on 5 October 1994: by then he was 58 years old. The career spanned by those two Haydock winners was altogether remarkable. Piggott took the jockeys' championship eleven times (1960, 1964–71, 1981–2); he won a record number of 30 English Classics (including the Derby nine times) and hundreds of other big races at home and abroad; and his career tally of 4,493 domestic winners on the Flat makes him the second most successful jockey (behind **Gordon Richards**) in British Turf history. In addition, he won 20 races over hurdles (including the 1954 Triumph Hurdle on Prince Charlemagne) and over 800 races overseas.

Lester was bred for the sport: father Keith was a jockey and then a trainer (his Ayala beat John Oaksey on Carrickbeg to win the 1963 Grand National), grandfather had ridden the winners of two Grand Nationals, and mother was a member of the famous jockey-producing Rickaby dynasty. His genes thus bursting with horsemanship, Piggott was the complete rider: a superb judge of pace, fearless, almost unbeatable in a close finish, hard on a horse when he thought it necessary yet unsurpassed at coaxing the best out of a reluctant or non-staying partner, completely cool yet fiercely competitive. This last aspect of his character led him into trouble on many occasions, not least when at the age of 18 in 1954 he fell foul of the Royal Ascot Stewards for his riding of Never Say Die (on whom he had won his first Derby that year) in the King Edward VII Stakes. Piggott had supposedly ridden danger-ously in going for a gap just after the turn into the home straight, and the incident is still, nearly 50 years later, the subject of debate and disagreement. He was suspended from riding until further notice, the Stewards of the Jockey Club (to whom the case was referred) advising him that they had 'taken notice of his dangerous and erratic riding both this season and in previous seasons, and that in spite of continuous warnings, he continued to show complete disregard for the Rules of Racing and for the safety of other jockeys'. Never one to overreact to anything, Piggott put such rever-sals behind him, and in 1955 replaced Sir Gordon Richards (who had retired in 1954) as first jockey to **Noel Murless** – the top riding job in British racing. The partnership won several Classics and saw Piggott take his first jockeys' title in 1960, but it was not a formal arrangement, and when in 1966 Piggott decided to ride **Vincent O'Brien**'s Valoris in the Oaks rather than the Murless runner, Varinia, Murless announced that their partnership was over. Valoris duly won the Classic, and Piggott and Murless patched up their differences, enabling the jockey to ride several other big winners for the stable. In 1967 he won the jockeys' championship as a freelance, and in 1968 deepened his already close association with the Vincent O'Brien stable, putting in one of his most brilliant performances in producing **Sir Ivor** with a dazzling burst of finishing speed to win the Derby. In 1970 he landed the Triple Crown with **Nijinsky**, though he was criticised by some riders in the stand for coming too late on the colt in the Prix de l'Arc de Triomphe when beaten a head by Sassafras. Controversy surrounded Piggott again before the 1972 Derby, in which he replaced **Bill Williamson**

Lester Piggott's 30 Classic winners

Two Thousand Guineas (5 times)
- 1957 Crepello
- 1968 Sir Ivor
- 1970 Nijinsky
- 1985 Shadeed
- 1992 Rodrigo de Triano

One Thousand Guineas (2)
- 1970 Humble Duty
- 1981 Fairy Footsteps

Derby (9)
- 1954 Never Say Die
- 1957 Crepello
- 1960 St Paddy
- 1968 Sir Ivor
- 1970 Nijinsky
- 1972 Roberto
- 1976 Empery
- 1977 The Minstrel
- 1983 Teenoso

Oaks (6)
- 1957 Carrozza
- 1959 Petite Etoile
- 1966 Valoris
- 1975 Juliette Marny
- 1981 Blue Wind
- 1984 Circus Plume

St Leger (8)
- 1960 St Paddy
- 1961 Aurelius
- 1967 Ribocco
- 1968 Ribero
- 1970 Nijinsky
- 1971 Athens Wood
- 1972 Boucher
- 1984 Commanche Run

as rider of Roberto. Whether this was a case of Piggott's jocking off the other rider or whether he was an innocent bystander as the owner exercised his right to have whichever partner he could get for his horse, Piggott produced one of his most inspired finishes to get Roberto home by a short head from **Rheingold** – and the same determination was in evidence when he drove The Minstrel home a neck ahead of Hot Grove in the 1977

Derby, having won his seventh Derby on the French-trained Empery in 1976.

Towards the end of the 1980 season O'Brien and Piggott parted company, and in 1981 Piggott became stable jockey to **Henry Cecil** at Warren Place, the Newmarket yard where he had had such a long association with Noel Murless. The new arrangement got off to a flying start when Piggott rode Fairy Footsteps to take the One Thousand Guineas – just days after he had been dragged under the front door of the Epsom stalls by Winsor Boy, an accident which left the jockey with a severely injured ear. He was champion jockey for the last time in 1982, and for what was announced as his final season in 1985 returned to freelance status. Amid emotional scenes at Nottingham on 28 October 1985 Lester Piggott, having ridden what everybody (including the man himself) thought was his final domestic winner, Full Choke, retired . . .

In 1986, his first year as a trainer at Eve Lodge, Newmarket, he sent out 30 winners, including Cutting Blade in the Coventry Stakes at Royal Ascot, and 1987 won the Italian Oaks with Lady Bentley. Lester Piggott had always been an enigmatic character, and stories of his carefulness with money were part of the fabric of racing gossip for decades. But few people were prepared for the revelation that he was being investigated for possible tax fraud, and the shock when he was convicted and sentenced to three years in prison in October 1987 reverberated throughout the racing world. His OBE, awarded in the 1975 New Year Honours, was stripped from him. He was released on parole on 24 October 1988, a year and a day after conviction, and that seemed to be that – a sad coda to an extraordinary sporting career.

Then, from quite out of the blue in October 1990, Lester was back in the saddle. It was a measure of Piggott's standing in the sport that once the racing world had recovered from the shock, it seemed to accept his presence as completely normal – despite the fact that when on 15 October 1990 he had his comeback ride at Leicester he was three weeks short of his fifty-fifth birthday. The following day he rode Nicholas, trained by his wife Susan, to win a six-furlong race at Chepstow, and the winner-machine was back in action. On the Saturday of the following week he was at Belmont Park to replace the injured John Reid on Vincent O'Brien's Royal Academy in the Breeders' Cup Mile, and showed that the old magic was still very potent when bringing the colt with an exquisitely timed late run on the outside to get up and beat Itsallgreektome by a neck. In May 1992 he won his thirtieth English Classic when Rodrigo de Triano took the Two Thousand Guineas, but even Piggott's extraordinary career could not go on for ever, and by 1994 rides were beginning to dwindle. Without any fanfare or formal announcement, 'The Long Fellow' (as he had been affectionately known on account of his height, unusual for one of his calling) was gone – this time, with the exception of the occasional charity race, for good.

The 30 Classic winners are listed in the box, but to put Piggott's career into true perspective consider that in addition to those Classics he won the King George VI and Queen Elizabeth Stakes seven times; the Prix de l'Arc de Triomphe three times; Ascot Gold Cup 11 times; Irish Derby five times; Coronation Cup nine times; Eclipse Stakes seven times; July Cup 10 times; International Stakes (under various names) five times; Nunthorpe Stakes seven times; Champion Stakes five times – and in all rode the winners of 16 Irish Classics, seven French Classics and 114 races at Royal Ascot. But then again, he never won the Cambridgeshire . . .

PILSUDSKI

If horses qualified for air miles, Pilsudski would never have to pay for a flight: in four seasons' action he raced in Britain, Ireland, France, Germany, Canada and Japan. His career was testament to the extraordinary ability of trainer **Sir Michael Stoute** to improve horses as they get older, and more evidence that keeping top Flat horses in training to the age of five can hugely enhance their reputations. Bred by his owner **Lord Weinstock**, Pilsudski first saw a racecourse as a two-year-old in 1994, running sixth and eighth in maiden races at Newmarket and Leicester – hardly an auspicious first act to one of the great careers of modern racing. He started his three-year-old career running second in a maiden race at Ripon and spent the rest of the season in handicaps, winning the Duke of Cambridge Handicap at the Newmarket July Meeting and the Tote Gold Trophy at Goodwood. Good form, but can this be the right Pilsudski? His four-year-old career answered that by demonstrating remarkable improvement. He was beaten by stablemate **Singspiel** (another great late developer) in the Gordon Richards Stakes at Sandown Park, returned to that course to win the Brigadier Gerard Stakes, disappointed when eighth behind First Island in the Prince of Wales's Stakes at Royal Ascot, then won the Royal Whip at The Curragh and the Grosser Preis von Baden, ran a fine race when five lengths second to runaway winner Helissio in the Arc and rounded off a magnificent season when, ridden by Walter Swinburn, he beat Singspiel, **Swain** and Shantou in the 1996 Breeders' Cup Turf at Woodbine, Toronto.

Time was when such a season would have been considered enough to justify retirement to a lucrative life at stud, but this is a more enlightened age and Pilsudski was kept in training to race again as a five-year-old in 1997. He justified that decision magnificently. After running a remote third to Helissio in the Prix Ganay and a close second to Predappio in the Hardwicke Stakes at Royal Ascot, he beat Derby winner Benny The Dip and the great filly **Bosra Sham** (who had encountered trouble in running) in the Eclipse Stakes, was beaten a length by Swain in the King George (with Helissio and Singspiel behind), slammed Irish Derby winner Desert King in the Irish Champion Stakes, was five lengths runner-up in the Arc for a second year, this time behind Peintre Celebre, then ended his British racing career when maintaining a grinding gallop to beat Loup Sauvage in the Champion Stakes. But still Pilsudski was not finished, and he wound up in the best possible style when winning the Japan Cup at Tokyo by a neck from local horse Air Groove. Winner of ten of his 22 races and a horse of

remarkable consistency in the highest class – not to mention the small matter of approaching £3 million in win and place prize money – he was retired to stand as a stallion in Japan. Punters could do with a few more like him!

PIMLICO

Opened in 1870, Pimlico – in Baltimore, Maryland – is the second oldest racetrack in the USA (after **Saratoga**). The major race run here is the **Preakness**, second leg of the **US Triple Crown**. The Pimlico circuit is one mile round, and the turf course was installed in 1954.

PINCAY, LAFFIT

Born in Panama on 29 December 1946, Laffit Pincay junior rode his first winner in his native country in 1964, and his first in the USA on Teacher's Art at Arlington Park, Chicago, in July 1966. On 10 December 1999, at the age of 52, he won on Irish Nip at Hollywood Park to register his 8,834th US victory and become the winningmost jockey in racing history, beating the record held by **Bill Shoemaker**. Among his big wins have been the 1984 Kentucky Derby on Swale, six Breeders' Cup races, and seven consecutive wins on the great Affirmed in 1979. By the end of May 2001 he had ridden 9,152 winners.

PINHOOKING

The business of buying foals and then selling them on as yearlings can be very profitable, as it cuts out the costs of breeding and of keeping the pregnant mare. The most notable horse of recent years to have been pinhooked was 1991 Derby winner Generous, sold as a foal for 80,000 Irish guineas at the Goffs' December Sales in 1988 and then sold on as a yearling in 1989 for 200,000 Irish guineas.

PIPE, MARTIN

When 8–1 on favourite Through The Rye won the Sponsor A Race At Folkestone Juvenile Novices' Hurdle at Folkestone on 4 February 2000, Martin Pipe was registering his 2,989th winner – Flat and jumps – to become the winningmost trainer of all time in Britain, passing the record previously held by Arthur Stephenson. He achieved the feat a little short of 25 years after sending out his first winner: Hit Parade (ridden by Len Lungo, now himself a trainer) in a selling hurdle at Taunton on 9 May 1975. The son of a West Country bookmaker, Martin Pipe was born on 29 May 1945 and rode in point-to-points (winning one) and as an amateur under Rules until breaking his thigh in a fall at Taunton in December 1972. He took out a training licence in 1977 and landed his first big race when Baron Blakeney won the Daily Express Triumph Hurdle at Cheltenham in 1981 at 66–1. But it was towards the end of the 1980s that his extraordinary dominance of National Hunt training started to bite, culminating in the remarkable 1988–9 season when for the first time he was champion trainer, winning nearly £600,000 in prize money from 208 winners: the previous record had been 120 winners trained by **Michael Dickinson** in 1982–3. He broke his own numerical record with 224 winners in 1989–90, and broke it again with 230 in 1990–1. Pipe has been leading trainer by number of winners every year since 1985–6, and champion trainer by prize money 11 times (every year since 1988–9 with exception of 1993–4 and 1994–5, when David Nicholson amassed more win and place earnings).

Numerical domination is one thing, but Pipe has had plenty of quality alongside the quantity. He won the Grand National in 1994 with Miinnehoma and the Champion Hurdle in 1993 with Granville Again and in 1997 with Make A Stand – two of the 25 winners he has had at the Cheltenham Festival, the best record of any current trainer. (Nicky Henderson has had 24.) Pipe has won the Welsh National with Bonanza Boy (1988 and 1989), Carvill's Hill (1991), Run For Free (1992) and Riverside Boy (1993); Scottish Grand National with Run For Free (1993); Irish Grand National with Omerta (1991); Whitbread Gold Cup with Cache Fleur (1995); and Hennessy Cognac Gold Cup with Strands Of Gold (1988) and Chatam (1991). Other top jumpers he has handled include

Beau Ranger, Sabin du Loir, Aquilifer, Cyborgo, Rolling Ball, Balasani, Olympian, Champleve, Pridwell, Kissair, Rushing Wild, Challenger du Luc, Unsinkable Boxer, Cyfor Malta, Gloria Victis and Blowing Wind. On the Flat he has had four winners at Royal Ascot, and in 1999 landed the Northumberland Plate and Doncaster Cup with Far Cry – just touched off by Kayf Tara in the 2000 Ascot Gold Cup.

Martin Pipe built his reputation on devotion to detail, paying much more attention to such matters as blood testing and the chemical balance of the equine metabolism than had hitherto been common, and his version of 'interval training' at his yard at Nicholashayne, Somerset – working horses uphill, then letting them walk down before cantering or galloping up again – has produced exceptionally fit runners. When Pipe broke the all-time winners record, Sir Peter O'Sullevan gave him this tribute: 'When you think what he started from and how he was prepared to do it his way and ignore precedent while picking the brains of those he admired, it's a great achievement. He's broken the mould and has been the most remarkable innovator.'

PIPE-OPENER

A gallop to clear a horse's wind. The term may also be used when a horse is not expected to be fully fit for a race, and rather is being run to get it fit for a later race.

PITMAN, JENNY

Born Jennifer Harvey on a Leicestershire farm in June 1946, Jenny Pitman – or 'The Cuddly One', as a doting John McCririck long ago named her – started working in a racing yard at the age of 15 and married jockey **Richard Pitman** at 19 in 1965. Her training career began with point-to-pointers, and she took out her first full licence in 1975; her first win under National Hunt Rules came when Biretta was awarded a novices' hunter-chase at Fakenham on 26 May 1975 on the disqualification of first-past-the-post Urlanmore. Her final winner under Rules was Scarlet Emperor at Huntingdon on 29 May 1999. In between she sent out 797 winners and, by dint of her forceful personality as much as her undoubted skills as a trainer, became the highest-profile lady trainer there has been. She was the first of her sex to win the Grand National, with Corbiere in 1983, and landed a second National with Royal Athlete in 1995. She was the first lady to win the Cheltenham Gold Cup, with her greatest horse Burrough Hill Lad in 1984, and gained a second when Garrison Savannah, ridden by her son, Mark, short-headed The Fellow in 1991. (Garrison Savannah very nearly became the only horse apart from Golden Miller to win Gold Cup and Grand National the same year, when leading up most of the Aintree run-in only to be caught close home by Seagram.) Jenny Pitman's other big race wins included the Welsh National three times (Corbiere 1982, Burrough Hill Lad 1983, Stearsby 1986), King George VI Chase (Burrough Hill Lad 1984), Scottish Grand National (Willsford 1995), Hennessy Cognac Gold Cup (Burrough Hill Lad 1984) and Irish Grand National (Mudahim 1997).

On her retirement her yard, Weathercock House in Lambourn, was taken over by the younger of her two sons, Mark (born 1966), whose short training career to date has already produced a Grand National runner-up (Smarty in 2001), a Hennessy Cognac Gold Cup winner (Ever Blessed 1999) and a very high-class performer in Monsignor, who won the Royal & SunAlliance Novices' Hurdle at Cheltenham in 2000.

Mrs Pitman married her long-time assistant David Stait in July 1997.

PITMAN, RICHARD
Born in 1943, Richard Pitman rode 470 winners over jumps (and, he is always keen to point out, some 5,000 losers) in a riding career which lasted from 1961 to 1975 and included a long period as first jockey to trainer Fred Winter. Pitman won many big races, including the Champion Hurdle (Lanzarote, 1974), King George VI Chase twice (Pendil, 1972 and 1973), Whitbread Gold Cup (Royal Toss, 1970) and Hennessy Gold Cup (Charlie Potheen, 1972) and rode other great horses

such as Killiney and Bula. But as a jockey Richard Pitman is probably best remembered for two races he lost in spring 1973: the Cheltenham Gold Cup, when his mount **Pendil** was caught on the line by The Dikler, and the unforgettable Grand National when front-running **Crisp** was caught close home by Red Rum. Since retiring from the saddle Richard Pitman has worked as a presenter for BBC television racing coverage, and has written many books, including several thrillers.

PLACE (IN BETTING)
In betting, the exact definition of 'place' depends on the number of runners. For the great majority of bookmakers (and for the Tote), a horse is placed if it

- finishes in the first two in a race of five, six or seven runners;
- finishes in the first three in a race of eight or more runners;
- finishes in the first four in a handicap with sixteen or more runners.

These stipulations can vary from one bookmaker to another, and some pay out on the fifth place in very competitive big races. Shop around for the best terms.

PLACED
Whatever the exact nature of the betting terms, a horse is said to have been placed if it finishes in the first three.

PLACEPOT
Tote bet requiring the selection of horses to be placed in the first six races (or, for any race with fewer than five runners, to win). The Placepot operates at all meetings.

PLAIN FENCE
In steeplechases, a plain fence is the standard obstacle – not an **open ditch**, nor a **water jump** – usually constructed of birch packed together in a wooden frame. On the take-off side is an apron of gorse, sloped to encourage horses to jump. The minimum allowed height for a plain fence is 4ft 6in.

PLANT

A horse is said to 'plant' when it stands stock still and refuses to move.

PLATE (1)

In racing jargon, a plate is a horseshoe. At home most horses are fitted with iron-based shoes, which are replaced with much lighter aluminium plates for races. A plate is attached to the hoof with thin nails driven into the wall of the hoof, though some horses with very sensitive feet are fitted with stick-on shoes attached with a strong glue. Royal Academy was wearing stick-on shoes when winning the Breeders' Cup Mile under Lester Piggott in 1990. A horse who has lost a shoe has 'spread a plate'.

PLATE (2)

'Plate' as a race title is rarely heard these days – though it survives in the occasional race name such as the Northumberland Plate at Newcastle. A selling plate was the old name for what is now commonly called simply a **selling race**.

PLATE (3)

Racing colloquialism for saddle.

PLATER

A 'plater' is specifically a horse which usually runs in **selling races** (selling plates), and generically describes a horse of very low ability.

PLUMPTON

Plumpton Green, East Sussex BN7 3AL
Tel.: 01273 890383
Fax: 01273 891557
E-mail: plumptonracecourse@dial.pipex.com
Web: www.plumptonracecourse.co.uk
One of the most hair-raising sights in jump racing is a field of raw novice chasers hammering at breakneck speed down the back straight at Plumpton, a stretch of racecourse guaranteed to have any sane racegoer sending thanks to heaven that the task of piloting these horses is left to others. The runners take a fence as they enter that back straight, then face a long and steeply downhill run to the next, so that by the time they reach it they are usually going like bats out of hell – with inevitable consequences for poor jumpers. At just 9 furlongs round, with tight left-handed bends and marked undulations – the downhill rush of the back straight is balanced by the uphill pull from the home turn – Plumpton is a course which much favours the handy, quick-jumping horse: the slower type, once adrift from the rest of the field, has little chance to make up ground here.

Like its neighbour Fontwell Park, Plumpton (where racing has been held since 1884) is very much a place for course specialists – human as well as equine.

POINT-TO-POINT

Sometimes described as racing 'between the flags', point-to-point races are steeplechases run under the auspices of the local hunt, usually over farmland (though some use the facilities of proper racecourses). Most hunts stage an annual point-to-point to raise funds, and the strong local flavour at these events gives them a special atmosphere. Many good steeplechasers have used the point-to-point field as a nursery before graduating to racing under Rules, and at the other end of a racing career old chasers can often be spotted enjoying themselves away from the serious business of 'official' racing. Professionals are not allowed to ride in point-to-points, but many top jockeys (and indeed trainers, including **Martin Pipe**) have cut their riding teeth between the flags.

POLITICS

There has long been a close link between the worlds of horse racing and politics. The great nineteenth-century Turf reformer **Lord George Bentinck** gave up the Turf for politics, but many have managed to combine the two quite happily. The 5th Earl of Rosebery was Prime Minister only from 5 March 1894 to 22 June 1895, but in that time managed to own two Derby winners: Ladas in 1894 and Sir Visto in 1895; he also won the premier Classic with Cicero in 1905, and 11 Classics in all. Sir Winston Churchill was 75 before he became a keen racing man, then owned many good horses, including the grand grey stayer Colonist, who won 13 races (including the Winston Churchill Stakes at Hurst Park in 1951) and ran second and fourth in the Ascot Gold Cup; High Hat, who beat Petite Etoile at Kempton Park in 1961 and ran fourth in the Prix de l'Arc de Triomphe; and Vienna, who won six races and was placed in the St Leger (1960), Coronation Cup, Hardwicke Stakes, Champion Stakes and Prix Ganay, and sired the 1968 Arc winner Vaguely Noble. Michael Oakeshott, one of the leading political theorists of the twentieth century, was co-author with Guy Griffith of one of the wittiest books ever written about racing, *A Guide to the Classics* (1936).

Sir Winston Churchill's racing colours — pink, chocolate sleeves and cap — are perpetuated in the scarf of Churchill College, Cambridge. He sold his best horse, Colonist, before the popular grey went to stud, explaining that he did not wish to live off the immoral earnings of a horse.

More recently, racing has appealed to many political figures who are regularly seen on British racecourses. Robin Cook, Foreign Secretary in Tony Blair's first government, is an avid racegoer and wrote a successful newspaper tipping column for the *Glasgow Herald* until affairs of state intervened (at which point the column was taken over by Scottish National Party leader Alex Salmond). Robin Oakley, former political editor of the BBC, writes a regular racing column for *The Spectator*.

PONTEFRACT
Park Lane, Pontefract, West Yorkshire
WF8 1LE
Tel.: 01977 702210
Fax: 01977 600577
E-mail: info@pontefract-races.co.uk
Web: www.pontefract-races.co.uk
Racing at Pontefract dates back to at least the seventeenth century. During the Civil War, Cromwell's soldiers laid siege to Pontefract Castle, the last royalist stronghold, but despite this distraction the local race meeting went ahead, and over the succeeding centuries

racing was a regular feature of local social activity. The present stands date back to 1919.

Pontefract is a good place to spot stars of the future running in comparatively humble surroundings. Silver Patriarch, short-head second in the 1997 Derby and winner of that year's St Leger, won a 10-furlong maiden race for two-year-olds here in October 1996, and 1998 Derby winner High-Rise opened his three-year-old campaign at the course.

Stamina is the watchword at Pontefract, with its left-handed circuit of about two miles, marked gradients and long uphill run over the last three furlongs. There is no straight course, and the run from the sharp home bend is about two furlongs: in sprint races a horse needs to break smartly to avoid being cut off at that bend, so beware of slow starters here. Also, pay particular attention to jockeys with a good Pontefract record: this is a tricky course for horse and rider alike, and experience can be a crucial factor. Pontefract was a horseshoe-shaped track until the two ends were joined up in 1983 to form what is now the longest Flat racing circuit in the country. The distance of 2 miles 5 furlongs 122 yards is the second longest Flat trip in Britain (the longest being the 2 miles 6 furlongs of the Queen Alexandra Stakes at Royal Ascot).

PONY
Betting slang for £25.

POOL BETTING
The concept behind pool betting – as opposed to fixed-odds betting – is straightforward: all the money wagered goes into a 'pool', which is then shared out among the winners. (The office sweep is a simple example of pool betting.)
See also **Tote; pari-mutuel.**

PORTMAN SQUARE
No. 42 Portman Square, London W1 (near Baker Street), houses the London offices of the **Jockey Club**, where most of that organisation's activities are carried on, including the Disciplinary Committee. So when you hear after some racecourse enquiry that the matter

has been 'referred to Portman Square', it is being passed on to head office for the Disciplinary Committee to deal with.

POULE D'ESSAI DES POULAINS
French equivalent of the Two Thousand Guineas: see **France**.

POULE D'ESSAI DES POULICHES
French equivalent of the One Thousand Guineas: see **France**.

PREAKNESS
Middle leg of the **US Triple Crown**, the Preakness Stakes is run at Pimlico (in Baltimore, Maryland) over a distance of one mile, one and a half furlongs, two weeks after the Kentucky Derby. The race, named after a local equine hero who had won twice at the inaugural Pimlico meeting in 1870, was first run in 1873 (two years before the first **Kentucky Derby** and six years after the first **Belmont Stakes**). Before 1889 it was run over a mile and a half, and was not run between 1891 and 1893 while racing at the track was suspended. Apart from Triple Crown winners, perhaps the most famous Preakness winner was **Man O' War** in 1920: he had not run in the Kentucky Derby, but went on to land the Belmont.

For winners since 1990, see **US Triple Crown**.

In 1973 journalist Bob Marisch of the *Baltimore Sun* was moved to verse by his local race:

The Derby is a race of autocrat sleekness
For horses of birth to prove their worth to
run in the Preakness.
The Preakness is my weakness.

PRENDERGAST, PADDY
The reputation of Paddy Prendergast stands second only to that of **Vincent O'Brien** in the ranks of great Irish trainers. Born in County Carlow in 1909, Prendergast rode as a jump jockey in England without conspicuous success before starting training in 1940 with just two horses. But his operation steadily grew, and he scored the first of 17 wins in Irish Classics in 1950 when Princess Trudy took the Irish One Thousand Guineas; the same year Prendergast – widely known as 'P.J.' or 'Darkie' – won the first of his four Irish Derbies with Dark Warrior. He had scored his first winner in England in 1945, but his profile increased significantly in 1951 when his colt Windy City won the Gimcrack Stakes at York and topped the Free Handicap (in so doing achieving a **Timeform** rating of 142, the highest ever accorded to a two-year-old). Prendergast was a master at sending juveniles from his base at The Curragh to land the big two-year-old races in England: in all he won the Gimcrack Stakes four times, Champagne Stakes at Doncaster five times and Coventry Stakes at Royal Ascot six times. His first Classic in England came with Martial in the 1960 Two Thousand Guineas, followed by Noblesse, scintillating winner of the 1963 Oaks, Ragusa in the 1963 St Leger and Pourparler in the 1964 One Thousand Guineas. The only Classic he did not win in England was the Derby, though he was third with Ragusa (to Relko in 1963) and second with Meadow Court (to Sea Bird II in 1965); both went on to win the Irish Derby and the King George VI and Queen Elizabeth Stakes. Prendergast also won the Eclipse Stakes with Khalkis (1963) and Ragusa (1964), the Sussex Stakes with Carlemont (1965), the Nunthorpe Stakes with My Beau (1954) and Floribunda (1961), and the Queen Elizabeth II Stakes with Linacre (1964) and World Cup (1968). He was leading trainer in Britain three times – 1963, 1964 and 1965. Paddy Prendergast died on the last day of Royal Ascot (where he had trained 22 winners), 22 June 1980. His sons Kevin and Paddy junior are current trainers at The Curragh.

PRESCOTT, SIR MARK
Sir Mark Prescott, Baronet, was born in March 1948 and rode as an amateur under both codes. After acting as assistant trainer to Jack Waugh he took out his first licence in 1971, since when he has established a strong reputation as one of the shrewdest trainers

around. While he has enjoyed Group One success with such horses as the grey filly Alborada, winner of the Champion Stakes in 1998 and 1999, and 1996 Nunthorpe Stakes winner Pivotal, he built his immense popularity with punters through well-planned touches in the big handicaps, winning the Ebor with Hasten To Add in 1994 and the Cambridgeshire with Quinlan Terry in 1988 and Pasternak in 1997 (backed from 11–1 in the morning to a starting price of 4–1: his win reportedly cost bookmakers £5 million). Sir Mark also hit the headlines when training the two-year-old Sprindrifter to win 13 races (10 of them in a row) in 1980, equalling the twentieth-century record for a two-year-old set by Nagwa in 1975.

PRETTY POLLY

Foaled near The Curragh in 1901 at the stud of her breeder Major Eustace Loder, she was sent to Newmarket trainer Peter Purcell Gilpin and won her first race as a two-year-old in 1903 at Sandown Park by 10 lengths. She returned to that course to win the prestigious National Breeders' Produce Stakes, started at 33–1 on for her next race (which she won) and ended her juvenile career unbeaten in nine outings, including the Champagne Stakes at Doncaster and the Cheveley Park Stakes and Middle Park Plate (precursor of today's Middle Park Stakes) at Newmarket. Her three-year-old debut in 1904 came in the One Thousand Guineas, which she won easily. At Epsom she beat three rivals to take the Oaks at 100–8 on. She then won the Coronation Stakes at Royal Ascot and the Nassau Stakes at Goodwood before going to Doncaster for the St Leger: starting at 5–2 on, she duly won, and for good measure took the Park Hill Stakes at the same meeting two days later. Unbeaten and apparently unbeatable, Pretty Polly was sent over to Longchamp to put the best French horses in their place in the Prix du Conseil Municipal. In heavy going which did not suit her and after a bad trip across the Channel, she was beaten by Presto II. The defeat caused a sensation; but at the end of October the beloved filly had found the winning thread again and took the Free

Handicap at Newmarket despite bearing a burden of 9st 7lb. At last it was decided that she had done enough for 1904.

Pretty Polly is commemorated in two races named after her – at Newmarket and The Curragh.

Pretty Polly went through her four-year-old career unbeaten, winning the Coronation Cup, Champion Stakes, Limekiln Stakes and Jockey Club Cup. She remained in training at five, but after winning the March Stakes at Newmarket and the Coronation Cup ended her career on quite the wrong note with a narrow defeat by Bachelor's Button in the Ascot Gold Cup. This was no time for impartiality, and the *Sporting Life* wore its heart on its sleeve: 'Alas, and again Alas! Pretty Polly beaten! Lamentations as sincere as they were loud were heard on every hand after the race was over.' In all she had won 22 of her 24 races.

At stud Pretty Polly had limited success in the short term, but left a lasting mark as the ancestor of such horses as consecutive Derby winners St Paddy and Psidium, and as great-great-great-granddam of **Brigadier Gerard**. She was put down at the age of 30 in 1931.

PRICE, RYAN

Born in 1912, Ryan Price rode over 100 point-to-point winners before becoming private trainer to Lord Nunburnholme in Yorkshire in 1937. After distinguished war service as a commando he resumed his training career in Sussex – at Wisborough Green and Lavant, moving to Findon in 1951. His major triumphs over jumps were winning the Champion Hurdle three times with Clair Soleil (1955), Fare Time (1959) and Eborneezer (1961); the Grand National with Kilmore (1962); and the Cheltenham Gold Cup with What A Myth (1969). He won the Schweppes Gold Trophy four times – with Rosyth in 1963 and 1964, Le Vermontois in 1966 and Hill House in 1967 – and in doing so attracted controversy by the bucket-load (*see* **Tote Gold Trophy**). He was leading National Hunt trainer five times: 1954–5, 1958–9, 1961–2, 1965–6 and 1966–7. In the early 1970s Price scaled down his involvement in National Hunt racing, passing that side of the Findon operation to his erstwhile stable jockey Josh Gifford while himself concentrating on the Flat. He had already had a fair measure of success on the level – he won the Cesarewitch three times in the 1960s, with Utrillo (1963), Persian Lancer (1966) and Major Rose (1968) – but the 1970s saw him competing for the Classics. He won two, the Oaks with Ginevra in 1972 and the 1975 St Leger with Bruni (by 10 lengths), and in 1974 his colt Giacometti scored an 'Each-Way Triple Crown' when placed in the Two Thousand Guineas (second to Nonoalco), Derby (third to Snow Knight) and St Leger (second to Bustino). Ryan Price's other big-race victories on the Flat included the 1973 Nunthorpe Stakes with Sandford Lad, 1974 Champion Stakes with Giacometti, and 1976 Ebor Handicap with Sir Montagu.

Famously formidable, Price had his softer side, as a young journalist named Alastair Down discovered on a visit to Sussex to interview him:

On the journey excitement turned to more than mild consternation as I realised that one young journalist was going to be very late indeed. Arriving an hour behind schedule I was expecting a bollocking straight out of the top drawer. Instead I received numerous gin and tonics and a whole morning of the great man's time.

After all the chat I asked if we could go up on to the Downs and see his old warriors in retirement – What A Myth, Major Rose, Charlie Worcester, Persian Lancer and Le Vermontois.

I recall racing up a rough old cart track in a large Merc at what seemed about 60 mph and getting out at the edge of an apparently empty field. But after an ear-splitting shout of 'Come on you boys!' the place suddenly came to life as the horses responded to that inimitable roar and ambled up over the skyline to greet him.

He loved those horses and his obvious affection for them and gratitude for what they had done for him taught me an important lesson about racing and racing people. It is impor-

tant because it helps draw a crucial line between those who love racing and those who love racehorses. To most trainers – and it is usually the best trainers – the horses are more important than the racing.

Ryan Price retired in 1982 and died in 1986.

PRICEWISE
Daily column in the *Racing Post* which compares prices from a range of bookmakers and suggests bets of particular value.

PRICKER
See **brush pricker**.

PRINCE OF WALES'S STAKES
Group One; four-year-olds and upwards; 1¼ miles (Royal Ascot)
The Prince of Wales's Stakes did not attain Group One status until the 2000 running, and the same year the race was confined to four-year-olds and older: hitherto three-year-olds had been eligible. Few quibbled about its being raised to the top level, as this 10-furlong event traditionally held on the opening day of Royal Ascot (moved to the Wednesday in 2000) has long been a very high-class race. It was first run in 1862 to honour the then Prince of Wales – later Edward VII – who had taken over many of the public and social duties of his mother Victoria, in mourning following the death of Albert in 1861. Derby winners Iroquois (1881), Galtee More (1897), Jeddah (1898), Ard Patrick (1902), Sansovino (1924) and **Hyperion** (1933) won the Ascot race within a month of triumph at Epsom, but after the Second World War the Prince of Wales's Stakes disappeared from the Royal Ascot programme until being revived in 1968 in anticipation of the inauguration of Prince Charles as Prince of Wales the following year. The race's new lease of life could hardly have begun better: the 1968 running went to 1967 Derby winner **Royal Palace**, the next two runnings to 1968 Derby runner-up Connaught and the 1972 race to the mighty **Brigadier Gerard**, whose jockey Joe Mercer had been badly shaken in a plane crash two days before: 'I'm convinced the

Prince of Wales's Stakes winners since 1990

1990	Batshoof	4	B. Hanbury	Pat Eddery	2–1F	8
1991	Stagecraft	4	M. Stoute	S. Cauthen	6–4F	6
1992	Perpendicular	4	H. Cecil	W. Ryan	20–1	11
1993	Placerville	3	H. Cecil	Pat Eddery	11–2	11
1994	Muhtarram	5	J. Gosden	W. Carson	6–4F	11
1995	Muhtarram	6	J. Gosden	W. Carson	5–1	6
1996	First Island	4	G. Wragg	M. Hills	9–1	12
1997	Bosra Sham	4	H. Cecil	K. Fallon	4–11F	6
1998	Faithful Son	4	S. bin Suroor	J. Reid	11–2	8
1999	Lear Spear	4	D. Elsworth	M. Kinane	20–1	8
2000	Dubai Millennium	4	S. bin Suroor	J. Bailey	5–4	6
2001	Fantastic Light	5	S. bin Suroor	L. Dettori	100–30	9

Brigadier knew I wasn't right that day. It's as if he said to me before the race: "Just sit tight, I'll get you through." He looked after me – didn't pull, and absolutely sluiced in, beating Steel Pulse, who went on to win the Irish Derby, by five lengths.' Other notable winners since then include Ela-Mana-Mou (1980, en route to landing the King George on the same course the following month), dual winner Mtoto (1987 and 1988, after which he won the King George) and **Bosra Sham**, who turned in a spectacular performance to win the 1997 running by eight lengths. Even more spectacular was another eight-length victory in the race's first Group One incarnation, when **Dubai Millennium** ran his opponents into the ground in 2000.

PRINCE REGENT

Arkle had won his second Cheltenham Gold Cup before his trainer **Tom Dreaper** would concede that 'Himself' was as good a chaser as an earlier Dreaper star – Prince Regent, winner of the 1946 Gold Cup and a heroic loser of two Grand Nationals.

Foaled in 1935, Prince Regent suffered a career disrupted by the war (no Cheltenham National Hunt Meeting in 1943 or 1944), and by the time he got to run in the Gold Cup at the age of 11 he was probably past his best: he beat Poor Flame by five lengths, but on dismounting jockey Tim Hyde told Dreaper, 'It took me a moment or two to beat that fellow

today, Tom.' Nevertheless, three weeks later Prince Regent started 3–1 favourite for the 1946 Grand National despite carrying 12st 5lb. He took up the running at second Valentine's and was still leading at the last fence, but the weight took its toll and he was passed on the run-in by Lovely Cottage and Jack Finlay. In finishing third, seven lengths behind the winner, Prince Regent had turned in a gargantuan performance at the weights. The following year, a 12-year-old, he again started favourite: he carried 12st 7lb, and finished fourth behind Caughoo. In the 1948 National he was carried out by a loose horse at second Becher's. However, Prince Regent did win twice over the National fences – the Champion Chase in November 1946 and the Becher Chase a year later. In all he won 18 of his 41 races over fences (including the 1942 Irish Grand National under 12st 7lb).

PRIX DE DIANE

French equivalent of the Oaks: see **France**.

PRIX DE L'ARC DE TRIOMPHE

Group One; three-year-olds and upwards;
1½ miles (2400 metres) (Longchamp)

Highlight of the year for Flat racing in Europe, the Prix de l'Arc de Triomphe was first run in its current guise in 1920 (though there had been a selling race bearing that name some years before). But it was not until after the Second World War that the race started to grow in status towards its present pinnacle. First English-trained winner after the war was Migoli, trained by Frank Butters, in 1948, and the following decade saw dual victories for the great Italian horse **Ribot** in 1955 and 1956. **Ballymoss** in 1958 was the first Irish-trained winner of the Arc, and the towering performance of the 1960s came in 1965 when the incomparable **Sea Bird II** won by six lengths from Prix du Jockey-Club winner Reliance despite veering diagonally across the track in the final furlong.

Le Paillon, winner of the Prix de l'Arc de Triomphe in 1947, had finished second to National Spirit in that year's Champion Hurdle.

Three years later **Vaguely Noble** won almost as impressively, beating **Sir Ivor** three lengths, and Sir Ivor's trainer and jockey Vincent O'Brien and Lester Piggott suffered an even more painful Arc reverse in 1970 when **Nijinsky** came too late to catch Yves Saint-Martin on Sassafras. The 1971 Arc saw **Mill Reef** at his brilliant best – beating Pistol Packer three lengths – and throughout the seventies and eighties the first Sunday in October in the Bois de Boulogne produced memorable moments: **Rheingold** giving Lester Piggott that long-awaited first victory in 1973; **Allez France** and **Yves Saint-Martin** in 1974; an astonishing last-furlong run up the rail from 119–1 shock winner Star Appeal

(ridden by Greville Starkey) in 1975; Lester scoring back-to-back wins on **Alleged** in 1977 and 1978, and on Ardross just failing to catch Akiyda in 1982; **Walter Swinburn** and All Along in 1983; three consecutive wins for Pat Eddery on Rainbow Quest (1985), **Dancing Brave** (1986) and Trempolino (1987); Italian-trained Tony Bin and John Reid in 1988. Since then Eddery's feat of three wins in a row has been matched by **Olivier Peslier** on Helissio (1997), Peintre Celebre (1998) and Sagamix (1999), while **Lammtarra** (1995) and Sinndar (2000) emulated Sea Bird II and Mill Reef by adding the Arc to the same year's Derby. El Condor Pasa added a new dimension to the race in 1999 when very nearly becoming the first Japanese-trained winner: he had pulled well clear of the field and for a moment looked like holding on, until Michael Kinane and **Montjeu** went into overdrive and cut him down close home. No recent running has better advertised the essence of the Arc: a true championship event for the best turf horses in the world.

PRIX DU JOCKEY-CLUB

French equivalent of the Derby: *see* **France**.

PRIX ROYAL-OAK

French equivalent of the St Leger: *see* **France**.

PRIZE MONEY

The prize money for a race consists of stakes put up by the owners of the entered horses,

---

Prix de l'Arc de Triomphe winners since 1990

Year	Horse		Trainer	Jockey	Odds	Ran
1990	Saumarez	3	N.Clement	G. Mosse	15–1	21
1991	Suave Dancer	3	J. Hammond	C. Asmussen	37–10	14
1992	Subotica	4	A. Fabre	T. Jarnet	88–10	18
1993	Urban Sea	4	J. Lesbordes	E. Saint-Martin	37–1	23
1994	Carnegie	3	A. Fabre	T. Jarnet	3–1CPF	20
1995	Lammtarra	3	S. bin Suroor *GB*	L. Dettori	21–10F	16
1996	Helissio	3	E. Lellouche	O. Peslier	18–10F	16
1997	Peintre Celebre	3	A. Fabre	O. Peslier	22–10F	18
1998	Sagamix	3	A. Fabre	O. Peslier	5–2JF	14
1999	Montjeu	3	J. Hammond	M. Kinane	6–4CPF	14
2000	Sinndar	3	J. Oxx *IRE*	J. Murtagh	6–4	10

plus added money, from sources such as sponsors, the racecourse, and the Levy Board. It is distributed to the connections of the **placed** horses according to regulations set down by the British Horseracing Board, the distribution varying depending on the category of race and the number of placed horses' connections to be rewarded. (In recent years prizes in some big races have gone to horses placed as far down as sixth, rather than just to the customary first four.) Around 60 per cent of the total prize money goes to the winner, the exact proportion depending on the nature of the race. Connections of each of the first four horses receive mandatory percentages (which are separate from any 'presents' which the owner may wish to give jockey or trainer), and the regulations also allow for percentages to industry training, to the Jockeys' Valets' Attendance Fund, and to the Jockeys' Association Pension Fund. (The percentage for a winning jump jockey is higher than that for a Flat jockey, but if an amateur jockey qualifies for a percentage that sum goes to the British Horseracing Board.)

Prize money won in Britain in 2000 totalled £71.69 million, made up of
• £33.28 million from the Levy Board
• £26.71 million from racecourses and sponsors
• £11.06 million from owners' stake money
• £0.64 million from the Divided Fund (money supplied to cover the additional cost of divided races).

The prize money for the winning owner is expressed in terms of 'Penalty Value', which is the amount to be used for calculations should that winning horse be subject to a **penalty** under the conditions of a future race (and is the amount used for calculating prize money won by trainers, and so on). Penalty Value is the profit made by the winner's connections – that is, their portion of the total prize money less the owner's original stake money.

PROHIBITED SUBSTANCES

'Prohibited substances' are those substances which, if detected in a horse's system by the post-race dope test, will, in normal circumstances, lead to disqualification. The Jockey Club defines these as:

• *Substances capable at any time of acting upon one or more of the following mammalian body systems: the nervous system; the cardiovascular system; the respiratory system; the digestive system; the urinary system; the reproductive system; the musculoskeletal system; the blood system; the immune system except for licensed vaccines; the endocrine system.*
• *Endocrine secretions and their synthetic counterparts.*
• *Masking agents.*

Some substances are subject to 'threshold levels' – that is, a limited (and defined) amount may be identified in the horse's system without penalty.

PULL

A horse is said to be 'pulling' if it refuses to settle and strains at the bit. On the other hand, a horse 'pulling double' is going very easily indeed. A horse with a 'pull in the weights' with another horse has a weight advantage compared with the weights the two have been allotted in an earlier race. A jockey 'takes a pull' to restrain a horse who is inclined to go faster than his rider wishes at that particular point. A notable example of this was Richard Dunwoody holding back Miinnehoma on the run-in of the 1994 Grand National until the very last moment, aware that the brakes should not be released too soon or his horse might idle in front. Jim McGrath (the Australian version) in his *Daily Telegraph* report called it 'a ride at which future generations of steeplechase riders will look back and wonder: How did he have the "bottle" to take a pull after jumping the last fence in a National?' Yet another sense is that of 'pulling a horse' – that is, deliberately restraining it in order to prevent it running on its merits and fool the handicapper.

PULL UP

A horse is pulled up ('P' in a form line) during a race when, for whatever reason (exhaustion, injury, or simply recognising a hopeless cause) its rider (or sometimes the horse itself) considers it appropriate to down tools and cease competing. A runner is also described as pulling up after the winning post.

PUNCHESTOWN

Naas, Co. Kildare
Tel.: 045 897704
Fax: 045 897319
E-mail: racing@punchestown.com
Web: www.punchestown.com

Punchestown racecourse was founded in 1793 and is now Ireland's premier jumping circuit, home of the great Irish National Hunt Festival in late April or early May – the Irish equivalent of the Cheltenham Festival, it attracts plenty of horses who have performed heroics at Prestbury Park a few weeks earlier. (The Punchestown Festival was sadly cancelled in 2001 due to what was considered the unraceable state of the ground, and the major races were relocated to Fairyhouse and Leopardstown.) Showpiece of the Festival, which began in 1854 as a two-day fixture for the Kildare Hunt Club and is now scheduled for four days, is the La Touche Cup run over four miles one furlong of the course's famous cross-country course, which involves the runners clearing banks, stone walls and a mind-boggling array of other unorthodox obstacles: when Risk Of Thunder won this famous old race in May 2000 he was doing so for the sixth year in succession – the first horse in Ireland to win the same race six years in a row. Other big races at the Festival include the BMW Chase over two miles, the Heineken Gold Cup over three miles one furlong (Commanche Court won this in 2000 after winning the Irish Grand National), the Swordlestown Cup Novices' Chase over two miles (Tiutchev landed this in 2000 in the wake of winning the Arkle Trophy at Cheltenham) and the Shell Champion Hurdle over two miles (won by **Istabraq** in 1999). Punchestown, which also stages a limited programme on the Flat, is a right-handed circuit about two miles in circumference.

Q

QUADPOT

Tote bet in which you pick four horses to be placed in the four designated races (the third, fourth, fifth and sixth legs of the Placepot). The Quadpot is therefore a means of keeping your interest going (at a cost) if your Placepot has gone down on the first or second legs.

QUARTER HORSE

A horse bred to run in quarter-mile mile races in America.

QUARTER MARKS

The brush pattern – often consisting of diamonds, or squares like a chessboard – which a careful and horseproud groom can produce on the horse's quarters.

QUARTERS

The muscle mass in a horse's body over the pelvis.

QUEEN ALEXANDRA STAKES

At two and three-quarter miles, the Queen Alexandra Stakes, closing race on the final day of Royal Ascot, is the longest Flat race run in Britain.

QUEEN ELIZABETH II

The extensive interest which Her Majesty the Queen has shown in horse racing was inherited from her father George VI (whose best horse was **Sun Chariot**, winner of the fillies' Triple Crown in 1942). One of her wedding presents on her marriage to Prince Philip in 1947 was a filly foal named Astrakhan, given by the Aga Khan, and in 1949 the then Princess Elizabeth registered her first racing colours – scarlet, purple hooped sleeves, black cap. Astrakhan delivered her first victory on the Flat when winning the Merry Maidens Stakes at Hurst Park on 15 April 1950, though the Princess had already tasted great success with the chaser Monaveen, owned jointly with her mother: he raced in the Princess's colours and won many good races (and finished fifth in the 1950 Grand National) before being killed at Hurst Park on New Year's Day 1951. After her accession to the throne in 1952 the Queen took over the royal colours (purple, gold braid, scarlet sleeves, black velvet cap, gold fringe) and concentrated on the Flat. She very nearly hit the jackpot just four days after her Coronation in June 1953 when her colt Aureole ran second to Pinza in the Derby. Aureole matured into a top-class four-year-old, winning the King George VI and Queen Elizabeth Stakes in 1954 (having again found Pinza too good for him in the 1953 running), and had a fine career at stud, siring the 1960 Derby and St Leger winner St Paddy and two other winners of the St Leger in Aurelius and Provoke. The Queen's first Classic winners were Carrozza, who snatched the Oaks by a short head under Lester Piggott in 1957, and Pall Mall, winner of the Two Thousand Guineas in 1958. Highclere won the One Thousand Guineas in 1974 and then took the Prix de Diane at Chantilly. (Highclere was the dam of Height Of Fashion, who won good races in the royal colours before being sold to Sheikh Hamdan Al **Maktoum** and proving herself one of the great broodmares of recent times, producing **Nashwan** and Unfuwain.) In 1977, the Queen's Jubilee year, **Dunfermline** fittingly provided two more English Classic victories in the Oaks and – after an unforgettable duel with **Alleged** – the St Leger. Thus the Queen has won five Classics, but no Derby.

At the start of the 2001 Flat season the Queen had 16 horses in training, divided among trainers Sir Michael Stoute (responsible for Her Majesty's filly Flight Of Fancy, runner-up to Imagine in the 2001 Oaks), Richard Hannon and Roger Charlton.

QUEEN ELIZABETH II STAKES

Group One: three-year-olds and upwards:
1 mile (Ascot)

Given the quality of every running, it is surprising to note that the Queen Elizabeth II Stakes was accorded Group One status only in 1987, when it was elevated from Group Two to form the centrepiece of Ascot's Festival of British Racing.

Markofdistinction in the 1990 Queen Elizabeth II Stakes was Frankie Dettori's first Group One victory in Britain. His second came in the very next race: Shamshir in the Brent Walker Fillies' Mile.

By then the race had firmly established itself as one of the top events in Europe for milers. The first three runnings all went to France (Hafiz in 1955, Cigalon in 1956, Midget II in 1957) and the roll of honour contains most of the great milers of the age. **Brigadier Gerard** won the Queen Elizabeth II Stakes twice – by eight lengths at 11–2 on as a three-year-old in 1971, and by six lengths from Sparkler in 1972 immediately following the only defeat of

his career, by Roberto at York. The other dual winner was the filly Rose Bowl (1975 and 1976), while the enduring quality of the race is attested by the victories of such horses as Romulus (1962), Linacre (1964), Derring-Do (1965), Reform (1967), Kris (1979), Known Fact (who beat Kris a neck in a famous finish in 1980), To-Agori-Mou (1981), Teleprompter (1984), Shadeed (1985), Warning (1988), Zilzal (1989), Selkirk (1991) and **Dubai Millennium** (1999). And special mention must be made of 1996 winner Mark Of Esteem – third leg of **Frankie Dettori's** Magnificent Seven.

QUEEN MOTHER

A mark of the very special place which Queen Elizabeth the Queen Mother holds in the affections of jump racing – and the place of jump racing in the affections of the Queen Mother – was the presence of her horses The Argonaut and Braes Of Mar at the parade held in London in July 2000 to mark her one hundredth birthday. More than any other individual, the Queen Mother was responsible for raising the status of the jumping game from that of a poor relation to the Flat to the position it enjoys today, and a succession of famous horses have carried her colours (blue, buff stripes, blue sleeves, black cap, gold tassel) to victory in top races: Manicou, The Rip, Silver Dome, Makaldar, Laffy, Double Star, Gay Record, Antiar,

Queen Elizabeth II Stakes winners since 1990

1990	Markofdistinction	4	L. Cumani	L. Dettori	6–1	10
1991	Selkirk	3	I. Balding	R. Cochrane	10–1	9
1992	Lahib	4	J. Dunlop	W. Carson	8–1	9
1993	Bigstone	3	E. Lellouche *FRA*	Pat Eddery	100–30	9
1994	Maroof	4	R. Armstrong	R. Hills	66–1	9
1995	Bahri	3	J. Dunlop	W. Carson	5–2	6
1996	Mark Of Esteem	3	S. bin Suroor	L. Dettori	100–30	7
1997	Air Express	3	C. Brittain	O. Peslier	9–1	9
1998	Desert Prince	3	D. Loder	O. Peslier	100–30F	7
1999	Dubai Millennium	3	S. bin Suroor	L. Dettori	4–9F	4
2000	Observatory	3	J. Gosden	K. Darley	14–1	12

Oedipe, Escalus, Inch Arran, Colonius, Isle Of Man, Game Spirit, Sunyboy, Tammuz and The Argonaut among them. Two others in particular recall notably memorable, and very different, occasions. Special Cargo, who won the Grand Military Gold Cup at Sandown Park three times, will always be remembered for his last-gasp victory in the Whitbread Gold Cup on the same course in 1984, a race which many people regard as the finest steeplechase of all time. And the fate of her **Devon Loch** in the 1956 Grand National will be for ever the epitome of defeat snatched out of the jaws of victory. For having seen off his rivals in the world's greatest steeplechase with a superb display of jumping, Devon Loch (ridden by **Dick Francis**) was bounding up the Liverpool run-in to certain triumph in front of his owner and the young Queen and Princess Margaret when, 50 yards from the winning post, he seemed to leap at an imaginary obstacle and slid down to the turf, leaving E.S.B. to stride past and take the race. No one can say for sure why he did it: Dick Francis thinks that the crescendo of noise greeting a winner who would have been the most popular victor in the history of the race scared the horse: 'I have never heard in my life such a noise. It rolled and lapped around us, buffeting and glorious, the enthusiastic expression of love for the Royal Family and delight in seeing the Royal horse win.'

Whatever the reason for Devon Loch's sensational slither, the Queen Mother stifled her disappointment: 'Well, that's racing!' she is said to have exclaimed, and wrote a few days later to the horse's trainer **Peter Cazalet**, 'We will not be done in by this, and will just keep on trying.'

By the end of the 2000–1 jumps season the Queen Mother had owned the winners of 447 races, and her continued presence on the racecourse – for example, she presented the trophy for the 2001 Whitbread Gold Cup at Sandown Park on the final day of the season – proved a source of continuing delight to all connected with racing.

QUEEN MOTHER CHAMPION CHASE
Grade One steeplechase; five-year-olds and upwards; 2 miles (Cheltenham)

The Queen Mother Champion Chase is one of the great sights of the National Hunt Festival at Cheltenham – a small field of the *crème de la crème* of two-mile chasers hurtling round that famous circuit, jumping at breathtaking speed, hammering down the hill to the final turn and invariably producing a rousing finish. This is a race never won easily, and over the last few years has produced two of the great showdowns of the age – Barnbrook Again edging out Waterloo Boy in 1990, and the titanic struggle in 2000 before Edredon Blue beat Direct Route by a short head. Badsworth Boy (1983, 1984, 1985) is the sole triple winner, while dual

Queen Mother Champion Chase winners since 1990

1990	Barnbrook Again	9	D. Elsworth	H. Davies	11–10F	9
1991	Katabatic	8	A. Turnell	S. McNeill	9–1	7
1992	Remittance Man	8	N. Henderson	J. Osborne	evensF	6
1993	Deep Sensation	8	J. Gifford	D. Murphy	11–1	9
1994	Viking Flagship	7	D. Nicholson	A. Maguire	4–1	8
1995	Viking Flagship	8	D. Nicholson	C. Swan	5–2F	10
1996	Klairon Davis	7	A. Moore *IRE*	F. Woods	9–1	7
1997	Martha's Son	10	T. Forster	R. Farrant	9–1	6
1998	One Man	10	G. Richards	B. Harding	7–2	8
1999	Call Equiname	9	P. Nicholls	M. Fitzgerald	7–2	13
2000	Edredon Bleu	8	Miss H. Knight	A. P. McCoy	7–2	9
2001	no race (foot-and-mouth epidemic)					

winners are Fortria (1960, 1961), Drinny's Double (1967, 1968), Royal Relief (1972, 1974), Skymas (1976, 1977), Hilly Way (1978, 1979), Pearlyman (1987, 1988), Barnbrook Again (1989, 1990) and Viking Flagship (1994, 1995). Other notable heroes include **Flyingbolt** (1966 – he ran third in the Champion Hurdle the following day), **Crisp** (1971), Remittance Man (1992) and **One Man**, who raised the Cheltenham roof when winning in 1998. The race began life in 1959 as the National Hunt Two Mile Champion Chase Trophy, and the Queen Mother's name was incorporated in the title in 1980, the year of her eightieth birthday.

QUINN, RICHARD

Thomas Richard Quinn was born in Stirling, Scotland (birthplace of **Willie Carson**) in 1961 and rode his first winner on Bolivar Baby at Kempton Park on 21 October 1981. He was champion apprentice in 1984 and rode as stable jockey to trainer Paul Cole, for whom he won his first Classic on Snurge in the 1990 St Leger, before losing that position for the 1991 season to Alan Munro – who then proceeded to enjoy a glorious year on Cole's Derby winner Generous. Quinn won widespread respect for the way he reacted to that disappointment, and continued to notch up a prolific quantity of winners. He became first jockey to Henry Cecil when the trainer fell out with Kieren Fallon in the 1999 season, and won the 2000 Oaks on Cecil's Love Divine, gaining his third Classic win on Millenary in that year's St Leger. He finished runner-up to Kieren Fallon in the 1999 jockeys' championship, and was again runner-up – to Kevin Darley – in 2000.

QUIXALL CROSSETT

Web: www.quixall-crossett.co.uk

No horse in the history of British racing has a record to match that of Quixall Crossett. When the 16-year-old bay gelding was pulled up in the Ropewalk Chambers Maiden Chase at Southwell on 22 July 2001, he was running for the 100th time in his racing career – and losing for the 100th time, in a sequence stretching back to February 1990.

The second part of Quixall Crossett's name comes from High Crossett Farm, near Chop Gate in North Yorkshire, where he is trained. The first part reflects trainer Ted Caine's regard for Albert Quixall, flaxen-haired Sheffield Wednesday, Manchester United and England forward in the late 1950s.

There has been the occasional close call. In May 1998 Quixall Crossett suddenly found a real turn of foot in a chase at Wetherby and over the last three fences was rapidly catching the leader, odds-on favourite Toskano. The post came just in time and his record remained intact by two lengths. His indefatigable trainer Ted Caine would brook no criticism of his most famous charge – 'He doesn't get in anybody's way' – and the fame of Quixall Crossett had spread far and wide long before the century was achieved: he has his own fan club (of which the author of this book is privileged to be Honorary President) and his own website. After that Southwell defeat there was talk of retirement in the air, but whatever the future holds, the legend that is Quixall Crossett will live on.

(*See* **Peggy's Pet, Amrullah, Zippy Chippy**)

R

RACECOURSE ASSOCIATION (RCA)

Winkfield Road, Ascot, Berkshire SL5 7HX
Tel.: 01344 625912
Fax: 01344 627233
E-mail: info@rcarcl.co.uk
Web: www.comeracing.co.uk

The RCA is the trade organisation representing the interests of Britain's 59 racecourses, including the provision of information and training, market support services and the pursuit and coordination of race sponsorship.

RACECOURSE HOLDINGS TRUST (RHT)

23 Buckingham Gate, London SW1E 6LB
Tel.: 020 7828 6090
Fax: 020 7963 9044
E-mail: rht@rht.net
Web: www.rht.net

Racecourse Holdings Trust, initially established in 1964 to ensure the future of Cheltenham racecourse, is a subsidiary of the Jockey Club which owns and/or operates 13 tracks: Aintree, Carlisle, Cheltenham, Epsom Downs, Haydock Park, Huntingdon, Kempton Park, Market Rasen, Newmarket, Nottingham, Sandown Park, Warwick and Wincanton.

RACECOURSES

There are 59 racecourses in Great Britain (60 if you count separately the two courses – Rowley Mile and July Course – at Newmarket), from Perth in the north to Newton Abbot in the south, Yarmouth in the east to Bangor-on-Dee in the west. Some stage Flat racing only, some jump racing only, and some offer both; three have **all-weather** tracks. There are five courses in Scotland – Ayr, Hamilton Park, Kelso, Musselburgh and Perth – and two in Wales – Bangor-on-Dee and Chepstow. The remaining 52 are in England.

The variety which characterises Britain's racecourses is reflected in their history. Many developed from festivals and fairs held in towns around the country – at Chester, for example, there has been racing on the Roodeye continuously since the early sixteenth century, when the race for the Silver Bell formed part of the city's Shrove Tuesday celebrations. Newmarket's position as a centre for racing and training grew out of its popularity with sporting monarchs from the early seventeenth century. Ascot took the eye of Queen Anne as a likely spot for an afternoon's sport, and the first royal meeting was held in 1711. Later in the eighteenth century regular racing became established at such familiar venues as York, Doncaster and Epsom.

Originally racecourses were sited on common land. You had to pay for admission to the stands and enclosures, but outside these anyone could turn up and witness the action without charge – much as you can today at such courses as Newmarket or York. Then, late in the nineteenth century, came the notion of the 'park' course, where the whole racecourse area was enclosed within a fence and everyone paid to get in – the idea being that such a restriction would stabilise course finances (thereby improving the general level of prize money) and rid the racecourse of unruly elements. In the wake of the successful innovation at Sandown Park came other park courses in the London suburbs: Kempton Park at Sunbury-on-Thames opened in 1878 and Hurst Park, near Hampton Court Palace, in 1890. Although there has been no completely new racecourse – that is, at a fresh location –

since the opening of Taunton in 1927, the establishment of the all-weather courses at Southwell (opened 1989) and Wolverhampton (1993) produced what are in effect new courses: new siting, new stands and facilities, new track.

RACEFORM

Compton, Newbury, Berkshire RG20 6NL
Tel.: 01635 578080
Fax: 01635 578101
E-mail: raceform@raceform.co.uk
Web: www.raceform.co.uk

Raceform Ltd publishes the official form books for Flat racing (*Raceform*) and jumping (*Chaseform*), the details of which are verified with the official return prepared by the Clerk of the Scales at each meeting. These are published for the **British Horseracing Board** through the season in weekly or twice-weekly sections which build up into the complete form picture, and at the end of each season the whole form is published in an annual. The form book contains an extraordinary wealth of detail, including comments in running as well as pointers to the future, along with all the relevant information about each race (time, distances, weights, betting, etc.). Raceform has a team of expert race-readers who attend every meeting in Britain (and many of the big occasions abroad) and report on the performance of every horse. (Channel Four Racing's Mike Cattermole worked as a Raceform race-reader.) In addition to the form books, Raceform publishes a range of other books, including *Racehorse Record* and the annual *Horses In Training*.

RACEGOERS' CLUB

Winkfield Road, Ascot, Berkshire SL5 7HX
Tel.: 01344 625912
Fax: 01344 627233
E-mail: info@rcarcl.co.uk
Web: www.racegoersclub.co.uk

The principal aims of the Racegoers' Club, founded in 1968 and now under the management of the **Racecourse Assoc-iation**, are to encourage people to go racing and to promote racegoers' interests and involvement. Among the benefits it offers members are entrance charge concessions on all British racecourses, stable visits, private marquees at big meetings and social events. The Club has a representative on the important Industry Committee of the British Horseracing Board, and Sir Alex Ferguson is currently Honorary President.

RACEHORSE OWNERS' ASSOCIATION (ROA)

60 St James's Street, London SW1A 1LE
Tel.: 020 7408 0903
Fax: 020 7408 1662
E-mail: info@roa.co.uk
Web: www.racehorseowners.net

The ROA represents the interests of racehorse owners and provides its members with information on all aspects of owning, including veterinary matters, sponsorship, VAT, etc. Two members of the **British Horseracing Board** are nominated by the ROA, which also represents owners on the major racing committees.

RACETECH

88 Bushey Road, Raynes Park, London
   SW20 0JH
Tel.: 020 8947 3333
Fax: 020 8879 7354
E-mail: admin@racetech.co.uk
Web: www.racetech.co.uk

RaceTech is the trading name of Racecourse Technical Services Ltd, now in the ownership of the **Racecourse Association**. The company's brief is to provide technical support for horse racing at all racecourses licensed by the Jockey Club, and the company is currently responsible for the provision and operation of **starting stalls, photo finish**, race timing, the **camera patrol**, and public address and radio communications. RaceTech also supplies closed-circuit television coverage at most courses, provides racecourse cable installations, feeds pictures to other broadcasting concerns (including the BBC, Channel Four Racing, **Satellite Information Services** and the Racing Channel). In addition, the company provides and operates the huge Tote-sponsored screens which have become a regular feature of many racecourses, mobile information units in the betting ring, and equipment for electronic sectional timing at the Rowley Mile course at Newmarket. It advises developing racing nations on the technical matters which are such a vital element of the modern sport and uses its unique film archive both for private use – sales to owners, trainers and punters – and commercial publication through compilation tapes of the season's sport. One of the biggest outside-broadcast operations in British television, with six mobile control rooms supported by 17 camera hoist vehicles, RaceTech operates principally from its base in Raynes Park and maintains regional bases for its technical vehicles at Warwick, York and Newmarket.

RACING CALENDAR

Weatherbys Group Ltd, Sanders Road,
Wellingborough, Northamptonshire
NN8 4BX
Tel.: 01933 440077
Fax: 01933 270300
E-mail: pubsdept@weatherbys-group.com
Web: www.weatherbys-group.com

Published weekly, the Racing Calendar is the official organ of the British Horseracing Board, containing such information as the outcomes of stewards' enquiries, alterations to the rules, conditions of all forthcoming races at home and the major events abroad, and entries and weights for early-closing races.

RACING CHANNEL

Satellite House, 17 Corsham Street, London
N1 6DR
Tel.: 020 7696 8944
Fax: 020 7608 2229

An offshoot of **Satellite Information Services** which on a daily basis provides extensive racing coverage for subscribers with satellite or cable television, the Racing Channel started broadcasting in 1995.

RACING POST

1 Canada Square, Canary Wharf, London
E14 5AP
Tel.: 020 7293 3000
Fax: 020 7293 3758 (editorial)
E-mail: editor@racingpost.co.uk
Web: www.racingpost.co.uk

The Racing Post, following the demise of the **Sporting Life** in 1998 the sole daily racing newspaper in Britain, was first published in 1986. It contains programmes and form details for all domestic racing and all significant racing overseas, backed up with a mind-boggling array of statistics, advice and articles. Several of the Channel Four Racing team have worked for the Post: Brough Scott has been editorial director from the outset; John McCririck wrote the sorely missed 'At Large' column for several years; and Alastair Down is a regular columnist. Since 1999 the Post has been available online.

Racing Post Chase winners since 1990

1990	Desert Orchid	11	D. Elsworth	R. Dunwoody	8–11F	8
1991	Docklands Express	9	K. Bailey	A. Tory	7–2	9
1992	Docklands Express	10	K. Bailey	A. Tory	6–1	11
1993	Zeta's Lad	10	J. Upson	J. White	11–1	12
1994	Antonin	6	Mrs S. Bramall	J. Burke	7–1	16
1995	Val d'Alene	8	F. Doumen FRA	A. Kondrat	11–2	9
1996	Rough Quest	10	T. Casey	R. Dunwoody	3–1JF	9
1997	Mudahim	11	Mrs J. Pitman	R. Farrant	14–1	9
1998	Super Tactics	10	R. Alner	A. Thornton	4–1	7
1999	Dr Leunt	8	P. Hobbs	R. Dunwoody	3–1F	8
2000	Gloria Victis	6	M. Pipe	R. Johnson	100–30F	13
2001	Young Spartacus	8	H. Daly	R. Johnson	9–1	15

RACING POST CHASE

Grade Three handicap steeplechase:
five-year-olds and upwards; 3 miles
(Kempton Park)

Before the Second World War the race now run as the Racing Post Chase was the Coventry Chase – the great **Easter Hero** won in 1928 – and since the war the race in its various guises has gone to some very familiar names, including Cheltenham Gold Cup winner Mont Tremblant (1952), **Crisp** (1972) and **Pendil** (1973 and 1974). The first running under *Racing Post* sponsorship in 1988 went to Rhyme 'N' Reason, who later that season won the Grand National. The second produced a remarkable performance from Peter Scudamore on Bonanza Boy, who seemed to be struggling at the home turn and was only third at the last fence but then rallied to catch Gainsay close home. And the third produced what for many pundits was the finest performance that **Desert Orchid** ever put up, jumping flamboyantly under 12st 3lb pounds and storming up the straight to win by eight lengths from Delius and trigger a rapturous reception from his legion of fans. The diminutive Docklands Express won back-to-back runnings in 1991 and 1992, while another notable winner in the 1990s was Rough Quest in 1996: like Rhyme 'N' Reason, for him the Racing Post Chase was a stepping stone to Grand National glory later the same season. No such glory awaited poor Gloria Victis: his brilliant victory as a novice in 2000 put him on course for a bold attempt at the Gold Cup, but he fell at the second last when still in contention for the Cheltenham showpiece and was killed.

RACING POST TROPHY

Group One; two-year-olds; 1 mile (Doncaster.)
The race now run as the Racing Post Trophy began life in 1961 as the Timeform Gold Cup, brainchild of Timeform's founder **Phil Bull**, who was convinced that the lack of a top-class two-year-old race over one mile was a serious omission from the racing programme. It became the Observer Gold Cup in 1965, the William Hill Futurity in 1976 and the Racing Post Trophy in 1989. To underline Bull's point, the first running in 1961 contained the following year's Derby winner, though you would have had to be pretty clairvoyant to identify that horse as Larkspur, who finished out with the washing behind Miralgo. Hethersett, the next year's St Leger winner, was fifth. The 1962 race went to the brilliant Paddy Prendergast-trained filly Noblesse, runaway winner of the 1963 Oaks. Ribocco won in 1966 and took the St Leger in 1967. **Vaguely Noble** won by a street in 1967 and landed the Arc in 1968. Green Dancer was the first French-trained winner in 1974. **Shergar** was runner-up to Beldale Flutter in 1980. But the first horse to set the seal on Phil Bull's vision and win this race and the Derby was Reference Point in 1986 and 1987. Deserted by stable jockey Steve Cauthen, who

Racing Post Trophy winners since 1990

1990	Peter Davies	2	H. Cecil	S. Cauthen	2–1JF	4
1991	Seattle Rhyme	2	D. Elsworth	C. Asmussen	2–1F	8
1992	Armiger	2	H. Cecil	Pat Eddery	5–4F	10
1993	King's Theatre	2	H. Cecil	W. Ryan	9–2	9
1994	Celtic Swing	2	Lady Herries	K. Darley	evensF	8
1995	Beauchamp King	2	J. Dunlop	J. Reid	11–4	4
1996	Medaaly	2	S. bin Suroor	G. Hind	14–1	9
1997	Saratoga Springs	2	A. O'Brien *IRE*	M. Kinane	9–2	8
1998	Commander Collins	2	P. Chapple-Hyam	J. Fortune	2–1F	6
1999	Aristotle	2	A. O'Brien *IRE*	G. Duffield	10–1	9
2000	Dilshaan	2	M. Stoute	J. Murtagh	14–1	10

opted to ride the other Henry Cecil runner Suhailie, Reference Point was ridden at Doncaster by Pat Eddery and won by five lengths. Cauthen would not make the same mistake again, riding Reference Point to land the Derby, King George and St Leger in 1987. King's Theatre, winner in 1993, landed the King George in 1994 after finishing runner-up to Erhaab in the Derby, but the performance of the 1990s was undoubtedly Celtic Swing's in 1994. Ridden by Kevin Darley, he barrelled up the straight to set a distance record for the race of 12 lengths – indeed, a record for any Group One two-year-old race ever run in Britain – and raise premature visions of a Triple Crown in 1995. That was not to be, but his Racing Post Trophy victory was one of the greatest individual efforts of the decade. Phil Bull has been well and truly vindicated.

RAG

Betting slang for outsider.

RAILS BOOKMAKERS

Betting with bookmakers is not usually allowed in the Members' enclosure of a racecourse, so the larger companies have representatives who maintain a position by the rail dividing Members from the main betting ring in the Tattersalls (or grandstand) enclosure, and take bets – some in cash, many in credit – from the members on the other side of it. Much of the serious punting is done here with these 'rails bookmakers', though it is only very recently that rails bookies have been allowed to display their prices on boards like Tatts bookmakers: hitherto they were confined to shouting the odds.

RANGY

Of a horse – long in its frame.

RATED STAKES RACE

A 'rated stakes' is a handicap on the Flat where the range of weights is limited to 14lb. For example, the race before the 2001 Sagitta Two Thousand Guineas at Newmarket was the Countrywide Steel & Tubes Rated Stakes, a handicap in which the weights ranged from 9st 7lb down to 8st 7lb.

RATINGS

Every horse in training, once it has run three times, is given an official rating by the **handicappers** of the British Horseracing Board, in the range 0–140 on the Flat and 0–175 over jumps. Each point on this scale is equivalent to a pound in weight: that is, Horse A, rated 121, is deemed to be one pound 'better' than Horse B, rated 120, which in turn means that were they to race against one another with Horse A carrying 9st 2lb and Horse B carrying 9st 1lb, they should theoretically dead-heat. The official rating is revised every week, going up or down or staying the same depending both on how the horse has performed and on whether a race in which he has run has proved to be of better quality than originally considered. So, should a horse win off a particular rating, or 'mark', and there is time to run again before he is re-handicapped – that is, his official rating is revised – connections may well be tempted to give him another race during that period if a suitable opportunity arises. In some cases a **penalty** – an additional weight to be carried if the horse has won a race since the last revision – will apply to take account of the improvement not yet reflected in the official ratings. So when you hear a Channel Four pundit refer to a horse having 'won off 99', and relating that to his current mark, he or she is referring to the horse's official rating. And reference to a '0–90 handicap' means a handicap for horses rated no higher than 90.

In addition to the official ratings, there are lists of ratings maintained by organisations such as the *Racing Post*, Timeform and Raceform, and many serious punters maintain their own: when their opinion is significantly at odds with that of the official ratings, that could be the opportunity for a touch.

RCA

See **Racecourse Association**.

REDCAR

Redcar, Cleveland TS10 2BY
Tel.: 01642 484068
Fax: 01642 488272
E-mail: enquiries@redcarracing.co.uk
Web: www.goracing.co.uk

Two straights each six furlongs long, joined by two well-rounded left-hand bends to make up a perfectly flat circuit of one mile five furlongs, and a straight mile – Redcar offers an excellent course for the galloping type of horse. The present course was first used in 1871, before which racing used to take place on the nearby sands. Under the direction of Leslie Petch, an enterprising and influential Clerk of the Course, Redcar's status grew steadily in the post-war years: for a while the Vaux Gold Tankard, first run in 1959, was the most valuable handicap in Europe.

Princess Anne – now the Princess Royal – rode her first winner on the Flat at Redcar: Gulfland in the Mommessin Stakes on 5 August 1986.

Today the course's main races are the Zetland Gold Cup, on Spring Bank Holiday Monday, and the very valuable Two-Year-Old Trophy run in October – worth £93,177 to the winner in 2000.

RED RUM

Foaled in 1965 in Co. Kilkenny, Red Rum was sold as a yearling for 400 guineas to trainer and former champion jump jockey Tim Molony. His first race was a two-year-old selling plate at Liverpool in April 1967, the day before the famous **Foinavon** Grand National: ridden by Paul Cook, Red Rum dead-heated for first place with Curlicue. There were to be nine more runs on the Flat for this future jumping hero, and two of them he won outright.

Sold on to Mrs Lurline Brotherton (who had owned 1950 Grand National winner Freebooter), Red Rum was briefly trained by Tommy Stack, who would re-enter his story for its greatest moment. Although he won over hurdles and fences his racing potential was clouded by the foot disease pedalostitis, and in August 1972 he was bought at the Doncaster sales for 6,000 guineas on behalf of millionaire Noel Le Mare by **Donald – 'Ginger' – McCain**, who combined training racehorses with his second-hand car business in Southport, Lancashire. The move to the coast transformed Red Rum. Being trained on the sands and galloping through the sea worked wonders on his foot problems, and by Grand National day 1973 he had become one of the leading staying chasers in the north – so good that he started 9–1 joint favourite for the National alongside the joint top weight, the Australian chaser **Crisp**.

Red Rum, ridden by Brian Fletcher, did not endear himself to every racing fan that day, catching Crisp just short of the winning post after the Australian horse had built up a huge lead and put up the bravest front-running performance ever seen in the National. Receiving 23lb from Crisp, the winner got home by three-quarters of a length in a time which demolished the course record; and the majority of observers thought it a cruel injustice that the front-runner had not held on. That said, Red Rum had shown great persistence as Crisp's only serious pursuer, and great agility and economy jumping the Aintree fences.

A year later, with Crisp sidelined, Red Rum galloped home from **L'Escargot** to become the first dual National winner for nearly 40 years. That year he himself carried top weight of 12st, and three weeks later went on to win the Scottish National under 11st 13lb to prove himself an exceptional horse.

Lester Piggott rode Red Rum in the Earl of Sefton's Stakes at Liverpool in March 1968: they were beaten a short head.

Red Rum showed good form away from Liverpool – he was beaten only a short head in the 1973 Hennessy Gold Cup at Newbury as well as winning that Scottish National – but saved his best for Aintree, and, after finishing runner-up to L'Escargot in 1975 and Rag Trade in 1976, lined up for his fifth consecutive National in 1977. **Tommy Stack**, formerly his trainer, was by then his established jockey, and despite the horse's advancing years – he was now 12 – Red Rum was strongly fancied for a unique third win in the race: he started at 9–1. After front-runner Andy Pandy had fallen at second Becher's there was only going to be one winner, and over the last two fences Red Rum shook off the challenge of Churchtown Boy to romp home by 25 lengths, as the crowd went wild and **Peter O'Sullevan** delivered one of his most famous commentaries: 'He's coming up to the line, to win it like a fresh horse in great style. It's hats off and a tremendous reception – you've never heard one like it at Liverpool!'

It was to be Red Rum's last run in the race. In 1978 he was being prepared for his sixth National when on the eve of the big day a leg injury ruled him out, and, winner of 27 of his 110 races, he was retired – from racing, but not from public appearances: for years thereafter Red Rum, a genuine equine celebrity and the first British racehorse whose commercial potential was seriously tapped, was a familiar sight opening betting shops or leading the Grand National parade. He was a star, and brought jump racing – and the Grand National in particular – to a wider public than it had previously attracted.

Over the course of his racing career Red Rum passed through the hands of no fewer than five trainers: Tim Molony, Bobby Renton, Tommy Stack, Tony Gillam and Ginger McCain.

Red Rum's particular qualities as a Grand National horse were his balance and cleverness: never a flamboyant jumper, he was nimble enough to swerve out of trouble and keep up his relentless gallop. He died in October 1995 at the age of 30 and is now buried – where else? – by the winning post at Aintree.

REFUSE

In a steeplechase or (less often) a hurdle, a horse is said to refuse (noted as 'R' in a form line) when it decides not to jump the obstacle. Sometimes this will occur out of sheer caprice or cussedness; sometimes there will be a very good excuse. For example, Blowing Wind was officially described as refusing at the nineteenth fence in the 2001 Grand National. What actually happened was that just as he was about to take off he was slammed into by a loose horse, dislodging Tony McCoy (who

then remounted to finish third) – hardly any fault of the horse that he 'refused'. When a horse **plants** himself at the start and declines to go forward, that is reported in the form book as 'refused to race'.

REGULATION

In Ireland, term for the steeplechase fence known in Britain as an **open ditch.**

REID, JOHN

Long hailed as one of the most stylish and accomplished jockeys on the Flat scene, John Reid was born in Co. Down on 6 August 1955 and served his apprenticeship with Verly Bewicke at Didcot. His first winner was Eyry at Goodwood on 16 May 1973. In 1978 he joined trainer Fulke Johnson Houghton, for whom he struck big-race glory with Ile de Bourbon in that year's King George VI and Queen Elizabeth Diamond Stakes and in the 1979 Coronation Cup. He won the Irish Derby on Sir Harry Lewis and the Prix de l'Arc de Triomphe on Italian-trained Tony Bin in 1988, the July Cup on Royal Academy in 1990 (while he was stable jockey to **Vincent O'Brien**) and landed a second King George on **Swain** in 1997. John Reid's first Classic winner was On The House, trained by Harry Wragg, in the 1982 One Thousand Guineas, but his greatest moment came when Dr Devious stayed on to win the 1992 Derby. Further Classic success has come with Las Meninas in the 1994 One Thousand Guineas and Nedawi in the 1998 St Leger.

REMINDER

When a jockey gives a horse a smack with the whip to keep its mind on the job before the race comes to the boil, that is sometimes referred to as a 'reminder'.

REMOUNTING

'There are fools, damn fools, and those who remount in steeplechases,' goes the old racing adage, and the history of chasing is peppered with heroic feats of remounting – most recently when Blowing Wind and Papillon were remounted in the 2001 Martell Grand National. Both horses had been separated from their riders at the nineteenth fence, but when their jockeys Tony McCoy and Ruby Walsh realised that only two horses were continuing, and that third and fourth prizes were there for the taking, they remounted and set off in forlorn pursuit of Red Marauder and Smarty. Blowing Wind finished third (netting his owner £55,000) and Papillon fourth (£25,000). Before that eventful renewal, the last horse to finish in the first three in the Grand National after being remounted was Loving Words, remounted by Richard Hoare to finish third behind Grittar in 1982 after falling four out. The rules regarding remounting are quite straightforward: a jockey is allowed outside assistance to get back into the saddle, but must resume the race from the point where horse and rider were separated. Common sense, rather than the rule book, dictates that a remounting jockey needs to be confident that the horse has done itself no damage before deciding to continue in the race. There are plenty of instances of jockeys remounting and winning: for example, Capability Brown fell three fences out in a novice chase at Chepstow in January 1993 but his rider Peter Scudamore vaulted straight back into the saddle and they went on to win by 30 lengths. Carl Llewellyn and Sure Metal performed a similar feat on the same course in December 1987 after falling at the final fence when so comprehensively clear of their rivals that Carl could remount and still win by 10 lengths.

RETAINER

Sum paid by a trainer or owner to have first claim on a jockey's riding services. A rider might have a first retainer with one trainer and a second with another – the first taking priority over the second should a clash arise. It is becoming increasingly common for top jockeys to be retained by a big owner rather than by a stable: for example, Richard Hughes was retained by Khalid Abdullah for 2001 (except for horses trained by Henry Cecil, whose retained stable jockey Richard Quinn would keep the rides on Abdullah-owned horses). The amount of each retainer must be registered at Weatherbys' *Racing Calendar*

office: Lester Piggott's undeclared demand for the 1982 season for a sum of £45,000 from trainer Henry Cecil's owners over and above his registered retainer of £10,000 set in motion the events which led to his imprisonment for tax fraud.

RETIREMENT (HORSES)

For the majority of racehorses not destined for a life at stud, career opportunities do not exactly abound. For ex-Flat horses in particular, past their usefulness on the Turf but still young in terms of physical development and experience, the transition from the hothouse atmosphere of a racing yard to the chill wind of the outside world can be difficult. For ex-jumping horses, often older, bigger and more experienced, the range of options may be slightly broader. The 1983 Grand National winner Corbiere had an honourable crack at show jumping, winning several classes. Another Grand National winner, Mr Frisk, turned his hand to eventing, as did 1973 Cheltenham Gold Cup winner **The Dikler** who, remarkably for such a large and headstrong racehorse, proved a dab hand at the dressage stage. A few suitably built ex-racehorses have found employment as a polo ponies.

Few Thoroughbreds are temperamentally suited to conversion from racehorse to riding-school hack, though many find good homes with more experienced riders, and it is common for ex-chasers to enjoy a stint following hounds in their twilight years. (Hunting has also proved a highly effective pick-me-up frequently used for horses in training who have become jaded or bored.) Closely related to hunting is **point-to-point** racing, and former racehorses are a common sight in the point-to-point field (which can also serve as a nursery for aspiring chasers).

Grand Canyon, a marvellous chaser in the mid-1970s and dual winner of the **Colonial Cup** in South Carolina, joined the Household Cavalry, but was not an unqualified success: habits acquired as a racehorse were not easily shrugged off, and Grand Canyon took exception to being required to perform very specific turns or trot in a suitably stately manner.

Eventually he too was retired to a more congenial life in the hunting field.

Among the plum retirement jobs for Thoroughbreds is that of trainer's hack or schoolmaster to a stable's young horses. **Devon Loch** had a stint in such a role with Noel Murless, **Tingle Creek** with Tom Jones, dual Champion Hurdler Comedy Of Errors with Mercy Rimell, and that fine chaser What A Buck with David Nicholson, who explains: 'The horse is living in an environment to which he is accustomed and is kept fit and busy.' Special Cargo, the Queen Mother's 1984 Whitbread Gold Cup winner, was tried out as Julie Cecil's hack but soon disgraced himself by setting off up the gallops with the two-year-olds – not the idea at all – and was promptly despatched to a more placid retirement home at Sandringham. Other old hands, such as Path Of Peace and Shiny Copper, have played their part in educating the next generation of jockeys at the **British Racing School** at Newmarket or its sister school at Doncaster.

Red Rum, a celebrity on the racetrack, became equally feted off it, his services much in demand for personal appearances opening supermarkets and betting shops, and a similar devotion to public service has kept **Desert Orchid** busy. Some ex-racehorses – including familiar National Hunt names Gainsay and South Parade – have found a new niche as police horses. Casamayor, fourth in the 1979 Cheltenham Gold Cup, carried the Commissioner of Police at the Trooping the Colour and got stuck in during the Wapping riots in 1986.

Yet, for all the pleasure afforded by the sight of an old racehorse picking at grass in a field or beautifully turned out for Trooping the Colour, some have a less pleasant time of it once their racing careers are over. Even well-known horses suffer from neglect, and in recent years a few high-profile cases have stimulated an increase in concern about the fate of ex-racehorses. Walnut Wonder, a good hurdler and chaser, won 14 races and over £90,000 in prize money, but still found himself on equine Skid Row: arthritic, skinny and with failing sight, he was found in a small paddock without food or shelter, and his plight was reported to the RSPCA. He was taken in by the Glenda Spooner Trust (now part of the International League for the Protection of Horses), where his condition revived. Every racehorse deserves a better fate than neglect, but it is still particularly poignant to learn of a Grand National winner who hit the lows. Hallo Dandy, who beat Greasepaint and Corbiere at Liverpool in 1984, was retired after running unplaced in the 1986 National and leased by his owners for hunting. He spent the next few years following hounds, but by 1994 this magnificent chaser was showing serious physical deterioration, and it was even contemplated that he should be put down. Enter a rescuer in the shape of Carrie Humble, founder of the **Thoroughbred Rehabilitation Centre**, then based in Kendal, a charity dedicated to re-educating unwanted racehorses and finding them new owners in different walks of life. Ms Humble reported that Hallo Dandy 'had given up the ghost' – but an infusion of tender loving care brought about a striking restoration, and this grand old campaigner continues to be the flagship of the Centre in its new quarters near Preston, Lancashire.

REVELEY, MARY

From her yard at Saltburn, Cleveland, Mary Reveley has sent out a regular stream of winners under both Flat and jumping codes – the only lady trainer to be as successful at the one as the other. She took out her first licence in 1982 and now regularly has a complement of around 100 horses in her care. On the Flat her biggest wins have come in Newmarket's big autumn handicaps: the redoubtable gelding Mellottie won the Cambridgeshire in 1991 (having been runner-up in 1990), and Mrs Reveley struck twice in the Cesarewitch in the 1990s, with Old Red in 1995 and Turnpole in 1997. Her best jumpers have been Cab On Target, a brilliant hurdler and useful chaser, the hurdler Marello, and the staying chasers Seven Towers and Into The Red.

RHEINGOLD

Owned by Henry Zeisel and trained by Barry Hills, Rheingold was one of the best middle-distance horses of the 1970s, but in some quarters is more remembered for his short-head defeat by Roberto in the 1972 Derby than for his big wins. Ridden at Epsom by Ernie Johnson, he just gave best after a relentless Lester Piggott barrage with the whip had forced Roberto up in the last few strides. In all Rheingold won nine of his 17 races over three seasons: one out of four as a juvenile, three out of six (including the Dante Stakes and the Grand Prix de Saint-Cloud) at three, and five out of seven during a triumphant campaign as a four-year-old in 1973 which saw him win the John Porter Stakes at Newbury, Prix Ganay at Longchamp, Hardwicke Stakes at Royal Ascot, Grand Prix de Saint-Cloud again and then the Arc. Starting at pari-mutuel odds of nearly 8–1, he ran out a convincing winner, beating **Allez France** by two and a half lengths and giving **Lester Piggott** the first of his three Arc winners.

RHT
See **Racecourse Holdings Trust**.

RIBOT
Bred by the Marchese Incisa della Rochetta and the great Italian breeder Federico Tesio (who died before the colt ever raced), Ribot was foaled in 1952 at the English National Stud (then in West Grinstead, Sussex), and went into training in Italy with Ugo Penco. As a two-year-old and three-year-old he won seven races without experiencing defeat, but Italy could not muster sufficiently stiff opposition to test the horse fully, and in the autumn of 1955 he travelled to Paris for the Prix de l'Arc de Triomphe, his first race outside his home country. His reputation had preceded him but he started at almost 9–1 before being steered home by his regular jockey Enrico Camici to win by three lengths from Beau Prince II. He then won one more race in Italy to bring his score by the end of 1955 to nine out of nine.

As a four-year-old in 1956 Ribot came to England for the only time in his career, defying soggy going to land the King George VI and Queen Elizabeth Stakes at Ascot, beating High Veldt by five lengths. Later that year he returned to Longchamp for a second Arc and won by six lengths from Irish Derby winner Talgo. He was then retired, unbeaten in 16 races.

Ribot stood as a stallion for one year in England before moving to Italy and then to the United States, where he remained until his death in 1972: it had been the intention to return him to Europe, but the horse had become very difficult to manage and the idea of undertaking such a journey was vetoed. Among Ribot's offspring were Arc winners Molvedo and Prince Royal II, and English Classic winners Ribocco, Ribero, Ragusa, Long Look and Boucher.

RICHARDS, GORDON
When Gordon Richards died in September 1998 at the age of 68, jump racing in Britain lost one of its giants, a man who had trained some of the most popular chasers of the time. No relation of his famous namesake **Sir Gordon Richards**, he took out his first licence in 1964 and sent out over 2,000 winners. He won the Grand National twice – with Lucius in 1978 and Hallo Dandy in 1984 – but his greatest horse was the hugely popular grey **One Man**, winner of the Queen Mother Champion Chase, Hennessy Cognac Gold Cup and King George VI Chase twice. Other notable horses to have been trained by Richards (who for most of his career was based at Greystoke Castle, near Penrith in Cumbria) include Playlord (Scottish Grand National 1969), Titus Oates (King George VI Chase 1969; Whitbread 1971), Dark Ivy, Unguided Missile, The Grey Monk and Addington Boy.

RICHARDS, SIR GORDON
Gordon Richards's career total of 4,870 winners from 21,815 rides has never been in danger of being exceeded. He was champion jockey 26 times (1925, 1927–9, 1931–40, 1942–53) and rode the winners of 14 Classics. Born in Shropshire on 5 May 1904, one of 12 children of a miner, he had his first ride in public in 1920 and his first winner, Gay Lord, in an apprentice race at Leicester, in April 1921. (On returning to unsaddle he

was asked why he had taken the horse so wide round the bends, and he replied that he had been told that Gay Lord needed a longer trip.) He was champion jockey for the first time in 1925, and for the 1932 season accepted a retainer from the immensely powerful **Fred Darling** stable at Beckhampton: he subsequently rode for the stable until Darling's retirement in 1947. In 1933 Richards's seasonal total of winners was a record-breaking 259. On 3 October that year he won on his last ride at Nottingham, then all six races at Chepstow the next day, and the first five at Chepstow the day after. In the sixth race he was aboard a 3–1 on shot called Eagle Ray: 'I did not think that I could possibly be beaten,' he wrote, but Eagle Ray finished third, beaten a head and a neck. Gordon Richards had ridden the winners of 12 successive races, still a world record.

Brough Scott on Gordon Richards (on the Injured Jockeys' Fund Calendar for 2001):

One day, it must have been about 1950, my father took me to Brighton to watch him. A tiny, serious-looking man so big in the chest and short in the leg that if he had not been such a legend you would almost have thought him a circus dwarf. In the saddle he should have been something of a pea on a drum but even by the time he left the paddock I could see he was part of the horse beneath. When he cantered down, loose rein and upright, it was obvious.

But it was the finish that was fantastic. Before or since there has never been anything like it. When things got tough going to the furlong pole Gordon started shovelling away as if he was shooing a dog into a kennel. He stood bolt upright and threw the reins forward and waved his whip in tempo. With anyone else the horse would have rolled all over the South Downs. With Gordon, eight stone of solid Shropshire muscle on top of little legs of Hercules, it was the clamp of victory.

In 1947 he set a fresh record with 269 winners, but the same year saw one of his most sensational defeats, on Tudor Minstrel in the Derby. Tudor Minstrel had won the Two Thousand Guineas by eight lengths and seemed a certainty for the Epsom race, starting at 7–4 on, but refused to settle and could finish only fourth. Richards finally got his desperately sought-after victory in the Derby at the 28th attempt with Pinza in 1953, just four days after he had been knighted in recognition of his services to racing – the first and to date the only jockey to have been so honoured. Pinza and Richards went on to win the King George VI and Queen Elizabeth Stakes. In 1954 Richards was forced to retire after the Queen's filly Abergeldie reared and fell on him in the paddock at Sandown Park on Eclipse Stakes day, causing severe injuries.

His career as a trainer produced several very good horses, including Pipe of Peace, winner of the Middle Park Stakes in 1956 and third to Crepello in both the Two Thousand Guineas and the Derby the following year; Court Harwell, second to Ballymoss in the 1957 St Leger; and Reform, who beat Taj Dewan and Royal Palace in the Champion Stakes in 1967. His final year of training was 1969, after which he acted as racing manager for Sir Michael Sobell and for **Lady Beaverbrook**. Gordon Richards died on 10 November 1986 at the age of 82. A model of integrity and modesty, he was loved by the racing community and punters alike.

RICK
In betting slang, a mistake.

RIDING OFFENCES
The phrase 'riding offences' covers a variety of issues, many of them contentious and frequently highlighted. For example, the question of whether a 14-day suspension for a jockey dropping his hands before the finish is sufficient punishment came up again at the Chester May Meeting in 2001 when Darryl Holland eased up too soon on Island House and allowed Adilabad to get up and win. The principal riding offences are, in descending order of seriousness:

- intentional interference, if the rider purposely interferes with another horse or rider: the horse must be disqualified;
- reckless riding, if the rider shows no regard to the consequences of his actions and/or the risk to others and, in particular, the danger of injury to other horses or riders: the horse must be disqualified;
- irresponsible riding, when interference is caused by some manoeuvre of the rider and where it ought to have been obvious to the rider that interference would be the result: the horse must be placed behind the horse or horses affected by the interference, unless the interference is considered minor;
- careless riding, if the rider fails to take reasonable steps to avoid causing interference or causes interference by misjudgement or inattention: if the interference is judged to have improved the placing of the horse doing the interfering, then that horse must be placed behind the horse or horses with which it interfered.

If interference is deemed to be accidental, no offence has been committed by the rider – though if accidental interference is judged to have improved the placing of the horse doing the interfering, then that horse must be placed behind the horse or horses with which it interfered.

Other offences for which a rider would be punished include:

- misuse of the whip (*see* **whip rules**);
- failure to ride the horse out approaching the finish;
- mistaking the race distance and either riding a finish a circuit too early or failing to ride a finish at all;
- deliberately preventing a horse winning;
- purposely not riding out a horse who would have won;
- intentionally not asking a horse for an effort;
- failure to weigh in;
- schooling in public;
- continuing on a lame or exhausted horse;
- failure to draw the correct weight;
- objecting frivolously.

A scale of punishments applies to each offence, and suspensions start nine days after the day of transgression.

RIG

A 'rig' is a male horse in which one of the testicles has not descended properly, or an imperfectly gelded horse. A notable rig of recent years was the very good miler Selkirk, whose form improved dramatically after his equipment had been properly aligned. In the 1991 Queen Elizabeth II Stakes at Ascot he beat the good Irish filly Kooyonga, whose trainer Michael Kauntze wryly observed afterwards: 'If I'd been running around all my life with an inflamed testicle and it was suddenly sorted out, I'm sure I'd run faster.'

RIMELL, FRED

Born in 1913, Fred Rimell was apprenticed to his trainer father Tom (who trained 1932 Grand National winner Forbra) and rode 63 winners on the Flat before switching to National Hunt. He was champion jump jockey four times – 1938–9, 1939–40, 1944–5 (sharing the title with Frenchie Nicholson) and 1945–6 – and won the 1945 Champion Hurdle on Brains Trust, but his career was cut short when he broke his neck twice in 1947. He had taken out his first training licence in 1945, and by the time of his sudden death in 1981 had been responsible for a galaxy of big winners rivalled only by **Fulke Walwyn** and **Fred Winter:**

- Grand National four times: E.S.B. (1956), Nicolaus Silver (1961), Gay Trip (1970) and Rag Trade (1976);
- Cheltenham Gold Cup twice: Woodland Venture (1967) and Royal Frolic (1976);
- Champion Hurdle twice: Comedy Of Errors (1973 and 1975);
- Triumph Hurdle three times: Coral Diver (1969), Zarib (1972), Connaught Ranger (1978);
- Welsh Grand National four times: Creeola II (1957), Glenn (1968), French Excuse (1970), Rag Trade (1976);
- Mackeson Gold Cup four years running: Jupiter Boy (1968), Gay Trip (1969 and 1971), Chatham (1970);

- Two Mile Champion Chase: Another Dolly (1980);
- Scottish Grand National: The Fossa (1967);
- Whitbread Gold Cup: Andy Pandy (1977).

He was leading trainer five times: 1950–1, 1960–1, 1968–9, 1969–70 and 1975–6. On his death the Rimell stable at Kinnersley, near Severn Stoke in Worcestershire, passed to his widow Mercy Rimell, who continued the tradition of winning big races when training Gaye Brief to win the 1983 Champion Hurdle. She stopped training at the end of the 1988–9 season.

RING
The area where the principal racecourse bookmakers operate.

RINGER
A horse substituted surreptitiously for another horse in a race. Many of the big **coups** of betting history have concerned ringers. For example, the famous Francasal coup at Bath in 1953 involved switching Francasal for a much speedier horse named Santa Amaro, and in March 1982 suspicions were aroused when Flockton Grey won a two-year-old maiden race at Leicester by 20 lengths – but turned out not to be Flockton Grey at all, but a three-year-old named Good Hand. (The term has entered non-racing language in the phrase 'dead ringer'.)

RING INSPECTOR
Official on hand in the betting ring after each race to arbitrate in disputes.

RIPON
Boroughbridge Road, Ripon, North Yorkshire HG4 1UG
Tel.: 01765 602156
Fax: 01765 690018
E-mail: jmk@hutchbuch.demon.co.uk
Web: www.ripon-races.co.uk
In shape and nature Ripon is reminiscent of Redcar (though the circuit here is right-handed) – long straights, sharp but well-rounded bends. The round course

measures about 13 furlongs, and the longest straight distance here is six furlongs, started from a spur. There is a dip a furlong from home and a few other minor undulations, making this a course on the sharp side.

Ripon has seen several racecourses since the sport was first recorded as taking place in the area in the mid-seventeenth century, and the first meeting at the present course took place in August 1900. Nowadays, with its catchment area encompassing the gentility of nearby Harrogate, Ripon has a very relaxed atmosphere, a mood reflected in the course facilities: lots of well-kept flower beds here. The course also has its own resident fish and chip shop.

Ripon's major race is the six-furlong Great St Wilfrid Handicap (named for the town's patron saint), run in August.

ROA
See **Racehorse Owners' Association**.

ROARING
See **whistling and roaring**.

ROBERTS, MICHAEL
When Michael Roberts, born in Cape Town on 17 May 1954, won the 1992 Flat jockeys' championship with 206 winners, he was the first South African ever to land that title. He learnt his trade at the South African Jockeys' Academy, riding his first winner on Smyrna at the Pietermaritzburg Turf Club on 30 August 1969 at the age of 15, and became champion jockey in South Africa in the 1972–3 season. In all he was champion in his native country 11 times. His first season in Britain was 1978, when he rode 25 winners (the first was Pakeha at Ayr on 3 April); he returned in 1986, and it took him only until 1994 to notch up his 1,000th winner in Britain. By then he had made his mark in the big races: on Mtoto he won the 1987 and 1988 Eclipse Stakes and 1988 King George, and his first Classic came with Mystiko in the 1991 Two Thousand Guineas, followed by Intrepidity in the Oaks in 1993 (the year he was retained jockey to **Sheikh Mohammed**). Other notable horses ridden to big-race victory by Michael Roberts include Lando (Japan Cup 1995), Indian

Skimmer (Phoenix Champion Stakes and Champion Stakes 1988), Opera House (Coronation Cup and King George 1993), Lyric Fantasy (Nunthorpe Stakes 1992), Terimon (International Stakes 1991) and Barathea (Irish Two Thousand Guineas 1993).

ROBINSON, WILLIE

George William Robinson – better known as Willie – was born in 1934 and rode his first winner at Navan in 1955. For much of his riding career he combined jumps with the Flat, and on 100–1 outsider Paddy's Point came second to Hard Ridden in the 1958 Derby. In the early 1960s he moved to England to join trainer **Fulke Walwyn**, and by 1964 had become only the third jockey since the war to have won the Grand National, Cheltenham Gold Cup and Champion Hurdle, taking the 1962 Champion Hurdle on Anzio, 1963 Gold Cup on **Mill House** and 1964 National on Team Spirit; for good measure he added a second Champion Hurdle in 1965 on Kirriemuir. (All four horses were trained by Walwyn.)

The four jockeys since the Second World War to have won the Grand National, Gold Cup and Champion Hurdle are:

Fred Winter: Grand National on Sundew (1957) and Kilmore (1962), Gold Cup on Saffron Tartan (1961) and Mandarin (1962), Champion Hurdle on Clair Soleil (1955), Fare Time (1959) and Eborneezer (1961);

Bobby Beasley: Grand National on Nicolaus Silver (1961), Gold Cup on Roddy Owen (1959) and Captain Christy (1974), Champion Hurdle on Another Flash (1960);

Willie Robinson: Grand National on Team Spirit (1964), Gold Cup on Mill House (1963), Champion Hurdle on Anzio (1962) and Kirriemuir (1965);

Richard Dunwoody: Grand National on West Tip (1986) and Miinnehoma (1994), Gold Cup on Charter Party (1988), Champion Hurdle on Kribensis (1990).

A highly stylish rider, Robinson won many other big races, including the Hennessy Gold Cup three times (Mandarin 1961, Mill House 1963, Man Of The West 1968) and the King George VI Chase (Mill House 1963). He retired in 1970.

ROGUE

Name given to an ungenuine horse, a horse not to be trusted to show the best of his or her ability.

ROSCOMMON

Racecourse Road, Roscommon,
  Co. Roscommon
Tel.: 0903 63494 (26231 racedays)
Fax: 0903 63608

Roscommon is a right-handed circuit about one and a quarter miles round. Racing first took place in this area in 1837, and has been continued on a regular basis since 1885.

ROUF

Betting slang for 4–1.

ROUS, ADMIRAL HENRY

Born in 1791, Admiral John Henry Rous was elected to the Jockey Club in 1821 and became a Steward in 1838, gaining a huge reputation as a **handicapper**: he left a lasting legacy to racing by working out the first **weight-for-age scales**. Rous became public handicapper in 1855 and pursued his duties energetically, watching races from the top of the stand with a large telescope and rushing down after the race to see which horses were blowing most. At Newmarket he would watch from the Bushes, about two furlongs from the winning post, and was in the habit of roaring at non-trying jockeys as they came by. Probably the most influential of all Turf administrators, he was instrumental in the transformation of racing from the ill-structured days of the early nineteenth century towards the organised sport that we now enjoy. Rous, whose most famous racing advice was to 'Keep yourself in the best company and your horses in the worst,' died in 1877.

ROWLEY MILE

See **Newmarket**.

ROYAL ASCOT
See **Ascot**.

ROYAL PALACE
Bred and owned by **Jim Joel** and trained by **Noel Murless**, Royal Palace won two of his three outings as a two-year-old in 1966 (notably the Royal Lodge Stakes at Ascot) and as a three-year-old in 1967 proclaimed himself a top-class horse. He won the Two Thousand Guineas and Derby (ridden in both by Australian jockey **George Moore**) and would have been a very warm order to secure the Triple Crown in the St Leger had not an injury ruled him out of the Doncaster race. As it was, his only other run as a three-year-old was third to Reform in the Champion Stakes.

The meeting of Royal Palace and Sir Ivor in the 1968 Eclipse Stakes was the first time two successive Derby winners had faced each other since Ard Patrick and Rock Sand in the same race in 1903.

At four in 1968 he was unbeaten, winning the Coronation Stakes (now the Gordon Richards Stakes) at Sandown Park, Coronation Cup, Prince of Wales's Stakes at Royal Ascot, Eclipse Stakes (in a thrombotic finish with French raider Taj Dewan and Derby winner **Sir Ivor**) and the King George VI and Queen Elizabeth Stakes – in which he incurred an injury which caused him to be retired. In all he won nine of his 11 races. As a sire his best offspring were **Dunfermline** (1977 Oaks and St Leger) and triple Champion Hurdle winner **See You Then**. Royal Palace died in 1991 at the ripe old age of 27.

ROYALTY
That horse racing is widely referred to as 'The Sport of Kings' advertises the close connection between royalty and the Turf – a connection which goes back a long way. Charles II, the first English king to show a real enthusiasm for organised racing, holds the distinction of being the only reigning monarch to ride the winner of an official horse race. His patronage of Newmarket established the town as the centre of British racing, and Charles won The Plate there in 1671 and 1674: 'I do assure you the king won by good horsemanship,' wrote Sir Robert Carr of his second victory – no favouritism there, then. James II had little time on the throne, but his successor William of Orange bred racehorses, and won a £500 match at Newmarket with a horse who bore the engaging name of Stiff Dick. It was Queen Anne who next exerted great royal influence on the Turf, establishing Ascot racecourse in 1711: the Queen Anne Stakes remains the traditional opening race at Royal Ascot. George II's third son, the Duke of Cumberland, bred Herod and **Eclipse**, and George IV instituted the Royal Procession at Ascot. Queen Victoria bred the winners of 11 Classics, though she never set foot on a racecourse after the death of Prince Albert. Her son the Prince of Wales founded the Sandringham Stud and bred **Persimmon**, who won the Derby for him in 1896, and Diamond Jubilee, who repeated the feat in 1900. As King Edward VII he won his third Derby with Minoru in 1909 – the only time the winner of the 'Blue Riband of the Turf' has been owned by the reigning monarch. George V was less keen than his father, though he won the One Thousand Guineas in 1928 with Scuttle, but George VI, who had shown little interest in racing until his accession, won five Classics: in 1942 the brilliant **Sun Chariot** took the One Thousand Guineas, Oaks and St Leger; in the same year the King won the Two Thousand Guineas with Big Game; and in 1946 the One Thousand was his again with Hypericum. The considerable racing achievements of the **Queen** and the **Queen Mother** are dealt with in their own entries, but mention must be made here of two of the Queen's children. The Prince of Wales rode a few times over fences in the 1980–1 season, taking a well-publicised tumble from Good Prospect at the Cheltenham National Hunt Festival. Under pressure to give up such a dangerous pursuit, he was quoted as saying: 'I wish people could only understand the real thrill, the challenge of steeplechasing. It's part of the great British way of life, and none of the sports I've done

bears any comparison.' (The Prince of Wales also rode in a charity race at Plumpton in March 1980, when his mount Long Wharf, owned by Paul Mellon, went off 13–8 favourite. But the form of the horse and high birth of his rider counted for nothing as Long Wharf failed to peg back 14–1 shot Classified, ridden by none other than our very own Derek Thompson. Tommo's breeches, borrowed from trainer Nicky Henderson, could not confine his excitement and split along the flies in the closing stages of the race, occasioning one newspaper to headline this perpetrator of disgraceful *lèse majesté* as 'The outsider who flashed past the Prince'.) The Princess Royal became an accomplished amateur jockey under the tutelage of trainer David Nicholson, and rode regularly under both codes. In 1987 she won the top ladies' race of the season, on Diamond Day at Ascot, for Michael Stoute on Ten No Trumps; and the following year she took (appropriately) the Queen Mother's Cup at York on Insular, an eight-year-old gelding of whom his rider generously conceded: 'Insular knows more about racing than I do. I just sat and let him get on with it.'

The Royal Studs in Norfolk are three separate establishments – the Sandringham, Wolferton and Polhampton Studs. Principal stallion for 2001 is Royal Applause, while the Royal Studs have in recent times housed two very influential stallions: 1978 Derby winner Shirley Heights and 1974 St Leger winner **Bustino**.

RULE 4

Betting is regulated by rules laid down by the Tattersalls Committee. Rule 4 addresses the problem of the distortions in the betting market which occur if one (or more) of the runners is withdrawn shortly before the race – for example, when a horse refuses to enter the starting stalls: betting will have started in earnest on that race and there may be no time to make a new book. In such instances, money staked on the horse withdrawn is returnable to the punters. The shorter the price of that horse at the time of withdrawal, the greater the distortion of the market, so

Rule 4 sets out a scale whereby a deduction is made from all winning bets in that race, the size of the deduction depending on the price of the withdrawn horse at the time of withdrawal. Rule 4 also applies when a horse is deemed by the starter not to have taken part in the race.

RULES

The official Rules of Racing are published by the **Jockey Club**. The phrase 'under Rules' is often used to denote 'official' racing, as opposed to **point-to-points**, which are not run under Jockey Club Rules.

RUN FREE

A horse is said to be running free if it is going too fast for its own good and the good of its backers: by refusing to settle it is wasting valuable energy rather than conserving it for a finishing effort.

RUN-IN

On a jumps track, the run-in is the stretch of the course between the last fence or hurdle and the winning post. The length of the run-in can vary slightly from meeting to meeting on a particular course depending on the exact siting of the final obstacle, and significantly from course to course: understandably, the shape of a finish on a course with a long run-in may change dramatically between the last obstacle and the post, and a stiffly uphill run-in such as at Sandown Park or Cheltenham adds significantly to the drama. The shortest run-in on a British racecourse is the 150 yards at Taunton; the longest the half-mile or so that Cartmel runners must travel from the last obstacle to the post – a disconcerting experience for a racegoer to witness, as the runners cross the last going away from the stand. Several courses have a run-in which involves veering around a fence not to be jumped on the final circuit – the water jump at Market Rasen or Newbury, say – but there is no doubt that the most famous of all run-ins is that at Aintree, where the runners veer right around the Elbow to avoid taking the Chair fence again. This notorious stretch of land, on which the complexion of many a Grand National finish has metamorphosed wildly, has its own place in racing literature, at the opening of the description by John Lawrence (now Lord Oaksey) of his heartbreaking finish on runner-up Carrickbeg in the 1963 National:

There are 494 yards between the last fence and the winning post in the Grand National at Aintree – and, for about 480 of them, I was, last Saturday afternoon, the happiest man in the world. But the last battle is the only one to count – and for that, for those final, ghastly fourteen yards, Carrickbeg and I had nothing left . . .

RUN OUT

A horse has run out when in a jump race it veers past an obstacle or, on the Flat or over jumps, takes the wrong course (say by going the wrong side of a running rail). One of the most famous examples of a horse running out came in the 1936 Grand National when **Anthony Mildmay**'s reins came apart at the second last fence, leaving him with nothing to steer 100–1 chance Davy Jones – who ran out at the last.

RUN UP LIGHT

A horse is said to have 'run up light' when it looks thinner than ideal, and lacking in physical substance.

S

SADDLE

A racing saddle is far cry from any you'll find in the tack room of your local riding school. For one thing, it will be constructed to be as light as possible – and may be made from synthetic material rather than leather. Most jockeys have several saddles and select one for each race according to the weight to be carried: the smallest might weigh as little as 8oz, though that will increase once it is 'made up' with stirrup leathers, irons and girths.

SADLER'S WELLS

There was no better illustration of the prepotent status of Sadler's Wells as a stallion than the results of the two Classics at Epsom Downs in June 2001. The first three fillies home in the Oaks – Imagine, Flight Of Fancy and Relish The Thought – were all by Sadler's Wells, and the day after Imagine's victory **Galileo** became the first Derby winner sired by him. Galileo's victory raised to 45 the number of individual Group One or Grade One winners sired by this phenomenal horse – a world record. There's no argument: Sadler's Wells is the greatest stallion of the modern age.

Sadler's Wells covered 196 mares during the 2000 breeding season. His covering fee for 2001 was reportedly 200,000 Irish guineas (about £161,000).

A son of **Northern Dancer** owned by **Robert Sangster** and trained by **Vincent O'Brien**, Sadler's Wells was a very good racehorse but could not be considered one of the modern greats. He was foaled in 1981, and in an 11-race career over two seasons won six, notably, as a three-year-old in 1984, the Irish Two Thousand Guineas, Eclipse

Stakes (beating 1982 Oaks winner **Time Charter**) and Phoenix Champion Stakes; he was also runner-up to Darshaan in the Prix du Jockey-Club and to Teenoso in the King George. He was then retired to stand at the **Coolmore Stud** in Co. Tipperary, and has been champion sire every year since 1990 with exception of 1991, when Caerleon, sire of Derby and King George winner Generous, topped the list. Galileo and Imagine are just the latest top horses by Sadler's Wells, whose offspring also includes such star performers as Old Vic (Prix du Jockey-Club and Irish Derby 1989), Salsabil (One Thousand Guineas, Oaks and Irish Derby 1990), Opera House (Coronation Cup, Eclipse and King George 1993), Entrepreneur (Two Thousand Guineas 1997), King Of Kings (Two Thousand Guineas 1998), Dream Well (Prix du Jockey-Club and Irish Derby 1998), King's Theatre (King George 1994), Intrepidity (Oaks 1993), Moonshell (Oaks 1995), Barathea (Irish Two Thousand Guineas 1993 and Breeders' Cup Mile 1994), In The Wings (Irish Derby 1990, and himself sire of **Singspiel**), Carnegie (Prix de l'Arc de Triomphe 1994), **Montjeu** (Prix du Jockey-Club and Arc 1999, King George 2000), and – to show that his influence also stretches to the jumping game – triple Champion Hurdler **Istabraq**.

SAGARO

The only horse ever to have won the Ascot Gold Cup three times, Sagaro was bred in Ireland by his owner Gerry Oldham, trained in France by **François Boutin** and ridden in all three Gold Cups by **Lester Piggott**. As a four-year-old in 1975 he beat Mistigri by four lengths (though the runner-up was subsequently demoted for interference); in 1976 he won by a length from Crash Course; and in

1977 he cantered in on a tight rein, the Piggott posterior set nonchalantly at its highest setting, by five lengths from Buckskin. Among his other big-race wins were the 1974 Grand Prix de Paris, when he beat **Bustino**, and the Prix du Cadran in 1976. In all he won 10 of his 24 races and was out of the frame only three times. He died in 1986 at the age of 15, and his name is commemorated in the Sagaro Stakes, run at Ascot in the spring.

SAINT-CLOUD

Located in the suburbs of Paris, it is the only French racecourse apart from Longchamp, Chantilly and Deauville to stage Group One races – the Grand Prix de Saint-Cloud over one and a half miles in late June or early July (won by **Montjeu** in 2000), and two big two-year-old races in November: the Criterium International and the Criterium de Saint-Cloud over one and a quarter miles.

SAINT-MARTIN, YVES

Born in 1941, Yves Saint-Martin was champion jockey in France 15 times, won 29 French Classics (including the Prix du Jockey-Club nine times) and all five Classics in England. His first ride in public in 1958 ended ignominiously – he fell off – but the same year he rode his first winner, on Royalic at Le Tremblay, and embarked on a career which by the time of his retirement in 1987 had brought him over 3,300 winners. His Classic winners in England were Nonoalco (Two Thousand Guineas 1974), Altesse Royale (One Thousand Guineas 1971), Flying Water (One Thousand Guineas 1976), Relko (Derby 1963), Monade (Oaks 1962), Pawneese (Oaks 1976) and Crow (St Leger 1976).

He also won the King George VI and Queen Elizabeth Stakes on Match III (1962) and Pawneese (1976) and the Champion Stakes on Flying Water (1977), Vayrann (1981) and Palace Music (1984) – though he was beaten in the 1973 and 1975 Champion Stakes on the greatest horse he ever partnered, **Allez France**. Daniel Wildenstein's great filly was one of Saint-Martin's four winners of the Prix de l'Arc de Triomphe: she won in 1974, while his other three Arcs came with

Sassafras (conqueror of Nijinsky in 1970), Akiyda (who beat Ardross in 1982) and Sagace (1984). Saint-Martin won two Breeders' Cup races: the inaugural Turf in 1984 on Lashkari and the 1986 Mile on Last Tycoon. His son Eric Saint-Martin has taken over the family mantle: he won the 1993 Arc on Urban Sea.

SAIS A CHING

Betting slang for 6–5.

SALES

See **breeding**.

SALISBURY

Netherhampton, Salisbury, Wiltshire SP2 8PN
Tel.: 01722 326461
Fax: 01722 412710
E-mail: biburyclub@salisburyracecourse.fs.net
Web: www.salisburyracecourse.co.uk

Queen Elizabeth I went racing at Salisbury in 1588 – supposedly on her way to see Sir Francis Drake just before his encounter with the Spanish Armada – and several of the all-time great horses have competed here, including **Gimcrack**, **Eclipse** and (somewhat more recently) **Mill Reef**, who made a winning first racecourse appearance here in May 1970. The Bibury Club, founded in 1681 at Burford in Oxfordshire and the oldest racing association in the world, moved to Salisbury in 1899 and established the present course, situated high on a hill above the town.

Steve Cauthen rode his first winner in Britain at Salisbury: Marquee Universal, trained by Barry Hills, in the Grand Foods Handicap on 7 April 1979.

The layout is similar to that of **Hamilton Park**: a straight (though in Salisbury's case that straight is decidedly dog-legged, with a right-handed elbow at about the five-furlong marker) to which is attached a right-handed loop. Races up to one mile use the straight; longer races take in the loop, so that the longest distance run here, one and three-quarter miles, is started in front of the stands, with the runners going away from the spectators before negotiating the loop and returning to the straight seven furlongs out. The first part of the loop is downhill, but most of the straight is decidedly uphill, and this is a very testing course.

SALMAN, AHMED
See **Thoroughbred Corporation**.

SALMAN, FAHD
Fahd Salman, who died suddenly in July 2001 at the age of 46, was a Saudi prince and Deputy Governor of the Eastern Province of Saudi Arabia, with extensive racing interests around the world. The best horse to have carried his colours (dark green) since he had his first winner in 1982 was Generous, who won the Derby, Irish Derby and King George VI and Queen Elizabeth Diamond Stakes in 1991 (and, lest we forget, landed the 1990 Dewhurst Stakes at 50–1, which with that great racing tool of hindsight must have been one of the bets of all time). Further Classic success came to Prince Fahd with Ramruma (1999 Oaks, plus the Irish Oaks and Yorkshire Oaks), while he also won the Irish Oaks with Knight's Baroness in 1990 and the Irish St Leger with Ibn Bey in 1990, and owned many other good horses such as Bint Pasha and Zoman. His breeding interests operated under the name Newgate Stud. Prince Fahd was the son-in-law of **Khalid Abdullah** and older brother of Ahmed Salman, owner of the **Thoroughbred Corporation**.

SANDOWN PARK
Esher, Surrey KT10 9AJ
Tel.: 01372 463072
Fax: 01372 465205
E-mail: sandown@rht.net
Web: www.sandown.co.uk

The Sandown Park circuit is a right-handed oval about one mile five furlongs round, with the separate five-furlong course starting the far side of the home turn and having its own winning post a couple of hundred yards from the stands: the sprint course is quite straight, and rises steadily throughout. From the winning post on the round course the track climbs uphill into a fairly sharp right turn, then goes steeply downhill towards the back straight, which is level. At the far end of that straight the runners start to engage the very long, sweeping home turn which leads towards the entrance to the home straight about four furlongs out, and from there it is a steady uphill climb until the ground levels out shortly before the line. Long straights and easy bends make Sandown a place for the galloping horse, and the incline up to the winning post – on both the round and the sprint courses – puts the emphasis on stamina. This is a testing course, and the horse must get the trip.

Chasers here must be good jumpers, as the Sandown Park fences are very well constructed. There are 11 on the circuit, of which seven are in the back straight; the fence in the front of the stands is an open ditch on the near side, a plain fence (the last) on the far side.

Take a two-mile chase as an example of the nature of the jumping course. The runners start near the entrance to the home straight and jump a plain fence and then the open ditch in front of the enclosures before climbing past the post and turning downhill. Acceleration on that downhill stretch makes the next fence especially trappy, but having survived that they swing into the back straight for those seven fences in a row – plain, plain, open ditch and water jump, then the Railway Fences, the key phase of any chase at Sandown: three plain fences, taken parallel to the railway line, set so close together that a horse must meet the first right to ensure a smooth passage over all three. The runners then negotiate the long right-handed curve before straightening out towards the Pond Fence, three from home. Get this right and you have the momentum for the final part of the race; get it wrong and you're struggling. After the Pond Fence the runners turn towards the second last, jump that, then take the last, a furlong from home, before knuckling down to tackle the desperately steep climb to the line. The complexion of so many chases at Sandown has changed as the horses hit that incline, and so often an apparently hopeless cause turns into victory. Chasers approach the winning line at Sandown at a different angle from hurdlers or runners on the Flat, which is why they have a separate winning post.

The hurdle course follows the line of the Flat track for most of the way, down the back straight switching from inside the chasing course to outside before passing the water jump. At the home turn it follows the Flat rather than the chasing circuit, and therefore the run from the last is not so steep as for the chasers.

Three Channel Four Racing presenters have ridden the winner of Sandown Park's big handicap hurdle, the Imperial Cup: John Oaksey on Flaming East in 1958, Brough Scott on Persian Empire in 1968, and John Francome on Prayukta in 1980.

On the Flat, Sandown Park hosts just one Group One event: the **Eclipse Stakes**, run over a mile and a quarter in early July, which is the first opportunity of the season for the cream of the three-year-old crop to take on the older generation at Group One level. Whatever the outcome, the relative merits of the generations are much more obvious after the running of the Eclipse, which makes it a pivotal event in the calendar. Sandown's other big Flat races come in the spring. The Classic Trial over one and a quarter miles at the April meeting – on the same day as the Whitbread Gold Cup – has enjoyed a fine record in showing up horses who will run prominently in the Derby. Shirley Heights was second in the race in 1978, and for the following three years the winner – **Troy**, Henbit, **Shergar** – went on to land the Derby; Shahrastani did likewise in 1986. The meeting on Spring Bank Holiday Monday features the Temple Stakes over five furlongs and the Henry II Stakes over two miles, a good trial for the Ascot Gold Cup. The second day of the May meeting includes the Brigadier Gerard Stakes over a mile and a quarter, and the National Stakes for two-year-olds over five furlongs. In August, Sandown stages Variety Club Day, one of the big charity race days of the year.

Sandown's principal jumping race is the **Whitbread Gold Cup** at the end of April – on a day which combines top-class jumping with top-class Flat racing to draw enormous crowds to the Esher track. (Since 2000 Whitbread Day has officially marked the end of the jumping season, and awards are made to the appropriate champions at the end of the day's sport.) The quality of jump racing at Sandown Park is consistently high throughout the winter. An excellent card on a Saturday in early December has the two-mile **Tingle Creek** Chase, which commemorates the flying chaser whose spectacular jumping was seen to such effect at the course in the 1970s. January sees the **Anthony Mildmay**, **Peter Cazalet** Memorial Chase (three miles five and a half furlongs) which commemorates the famous amateur rider and legendary trainer who were two of the giants of National Hunt racing. February has the Agfa Diamond Chase, a high-class handicap over three miles and half a furlong, and the Agfa Hurdle (two miles and half a furlong), a good Champion Hurdle trial. The Grand Military Meeting, with its centre-piece the Grand Military Gold Cup (a three mile and half a furlong chase for amateur riders), comes just before the Cheltenham Festival in March. Feature race on the second day of this meeting is the valuable Imperial Cup, a handicap hurdle over two miles and half a furlong which dates back to 1907.

The founding of Sandown Park, where the first meeting was run in 1875, represents a milestone in the history of British racegoing, for this was the first 'park' course, where the whole racecourse area was enclosed and everyone had to pay to get in (admission half a crown), rather than watch from common ground. One consequence of this was that the course could have more control over who came in, with the result that ladies could go racing without their sensibilities being assailed by foul-mouthed riff-raff: according to one early observer of this new phenomenon, Sandown Park was the only course 'where a man could take his ladies without any fear of their hearing coarse language or witnessing uncouth behaviour'. In a song current at the time a lady gleefully anticipated 'a lark in the light or the dark – my silly old man's at Sandown Park'. But silly her for not going with him.

SANGSTER, ROBERT

With some 160 broodmares around the world and horses in training in England, Ireland, the USA and Australia, Robert Sangster remains a major force in world racing – though his fortunes have been somewhat subdued of late as the **Maktoum brothers** and the **Coolmore Stud** operation have emerged as the biggest players on the global stage. Since Chalk Stream trained by Eric Cousins, won a Haydock Park handicap for the 24-year-old Sangster back in 1960, he has owned or co-owned some of the very best horses of recent decades, including:

* The Minstrel (Derby, Irish Derby and King George 1977)
* **Alleged** (Prix de l'Arc de Triomphe 1977 and 1978)
* Detroit (Arc 1980)
* Beldale Ball (Melbourne Cup 1980)
* Golden Fleece (Derby 1982)
* Lomond (Two Thousand Guineas 1983)
* Caerleon (Prix du Jockey-Club 1983)
* **El Gran Senor** (Two Thousand Guineas and Irish Derby 1984)
* **Sadler's Wells** (Irish Two Thousand Guineas, Eclipse Stakes and Phoenix Champion Stakes 1984)
* Rodrigo de Triano (Two Thousand Guineas, Irish Two Thousand Guineas, International Stakes and Champion Stakes 1992)
* Las Meninas (One Thousand Guineas 1994)
* Assert, Solford, Pas de Seul, Hawaiian Sound, Turtle Island and many more . . .

Sangster changed the face of racing by appreciating and responding to its international dimension. In the early 1970s he founded with **John Magnier** the Coolmore Stud in Co. Tipperary, and in 1975 formed a syndicate of big owners (including Stavros Niarchos and Danny Schwartz) to breed and race horses, most of whom represented the best American blood, to be trained by **Vincent O'Brien**. The first crop – not all of which raced in Sangster's colours (emerald green, royal blue sleeves, white cap, emerald green spots) – included The Minstrel, Be My Guest, Artaius, Godswalk and Alleged. Sangster's own Swettenham Stud has bred many fine horses (such as Dibidale, El Gran Senor and Sadler's Wells), but with the Coolmore operation in full swing his breeding interests started to spread all over the world, and he now has studs in Ireland and Australia (though he is no longer directly involved with Coolmore). In 1984 he purchased the famous training establishment at Manton in Wiltshire, with first **Michael Dickinson** (who departed in 1986), then **Barry Hills**, then Peter Chapple-Hyam and now **John Gosden** as the resident trainer. Robert Sangster has been leading owner on the Flat in Britain five times: 1977, 1978, 1982–4.

SANTA ANITA

Located in the Los Angeles suburb of Arcadia, this is one of the main tracks in California. The course staged the third Breeders' Cup in 1986 – the year **Dancing Brave** proved so disappointing in the Turf – and 1993, and is due to host again in 2002.

SARATOGA

Web: www.nyra.com
The oldest racetrack in the USA, having opened in 1863. This course has seen some remarkable results. **Man O' War** suffered his only defeat in 21 races here, beaten by Upset (*sic*) in the Sanford Memorial Stakes in 1919. In 1930 Triple Crown winner Gallant Fox was beaten in the Travers by 100–1 rag Jim Dandy. And in 1973 the immortal **Secretariat** started at 10–1 on for the Whitney Handicap and was beaten by a horse named Onion. The 1978 Travers saw yet another duel between that year's Triple Crown winner **Affirmed** and **Alydar**, runner-up to him in all three Triple Crown races: a crowd of over 50,000 packed into Saratoga's tasteful but not over-large stands to see Affirmed pass the post first – and then be disqualified in favour of Alydar. Saratoga, in upstate New York, races only during August.

SATELLITE INFORMATION SERVICES

Satellite House, 17 Corsham Street, London N1 6DR

Tel.: 020 7253 2232

Fax: 020 7251 3737

SIS is the service which transmits televised pictures of racing into betting shops. The company made its first live transmission – to a limited number of shops – in May 1987, and now transmits to some 11,000 subscribers around the world.

SAVILL, PETER

Peter Savill, whose business interests are primarily concerned with magazine publishing, became Chairman of the British Horseracing Board in 1998 on the resignation of Lord Wakeham. As an owner his best horse has been Celtic Swing, winner of the 1994 Racing Post Trophy by 12 lengths, and in 1995 of the Prix du Jockey-Club, while his colours (maroon, light blue sleeves, light blue cap, maroon diamond) have also been carried by 2001 Ascot Gold Cup winner Royal Rebel and by the popular and prolific handicapper Chaplin's Club. His breeding interests are based at two studs in Co. Wicklow, and he has horses in training in Britain, France and Singapore.

SCEPTRE

No horse has ever won all five English Classics, but Sceptre came closest. In 1902 she won the Two Thousand Guineas, One Thousand Guineas, Oaks and St Leger and finished fourth in the Derby, and by any standards must be ranked not only one of the all-time greats, but one of the toughest racemares ever.

Bred in the purple by the 1st Duke of Westminster – her sire was 1896 Derby and St Leger winner **Persimmon** and her dam was a full sister to the great **Ormonde** – Sceptre was sold by public auction following the Duke's death in 1899 and bought for 10,000 guineas, a massive amount at the time, by Robert Sievier, a notorious gambler.

As a two-year-old she won the Woodcote Stakes at Epsom and the July Stakes at Newmarket before coming third in the Champagne Stakes at Doncaster, but at the end of that season her trainer Charles Morton became private trainer to J. B. Joel, and Sievier decided to train Sceptre himself. Although well aware that he had a Classic filly on his hands, Sievier could not resist a gamble, and Sceptre's first race as a three-year-old in 1902 was the Lincoln Handicap: overtrained by Sievier's assistant, Sceptre was beaten by the four-year-old St Maclou.

Despite that reverse, she thrived physically thereafter, and by the time of the Two Thousand Guineas was at her peak. She won the first Classic in record time and followed up two days later in the One Thousand despite losing a shoe at the start. In the Derby she started even-money favourite but could only finish fourth behind Ard Patrick, and yet after just one day's rest came out again to win the Oaks.

Between the Oaks and St Leger, Sceptre's schedule ran as follows: Grand Prix de Paris (beaten); Coronation Stakes at Royal Ascot (beaten); the following day the St James's Palace Stakes (won); Sussex Stakes at Goodwood (beaten); Nassau Stakes at Goodwood (won). No wonder she looked worn out by the time of the St Leger – but she won the final Classic by three lengths to claim a unique place in British racing history: the only other horse whose name features on the roll of honour of four Classics is Formosa, who in 1868 won the One Thousand Guineas, Oaks and St Leger and dead-heated in the Two Thousand Guineas. Surely no horse ever deserved a rest more; but two days after the Leger poor Sceptre was out again – to be beaten in the Park Hill Stakes.

Her four-year-old season in 1903 again began in the Lincoln: this time she could finish only fifth, and following the race was sold to provide some temporary alleviation of Sievier's chronic financial problems. Her new owner, William Bass, sent her to the great trainer Alec Taylor at Manton, and gradually she started to thrive once more. She won the Hardwicke Stakes at Royal Ascot and then played a leading role in one of the greatest races ever, beaten a neck in the Eclipse Stakes by Ard Patrick, the horse who had won the Derby in her year, with 1903 Derby winner Rock Sand third. That autumn Sceptre not only won the Champion Stakes but beat Rock Sand – by then winner of the Triple Crown – to land the Jockey Club Stakes.

As a five-year-old she failed to run up to her best – who could blame her? – and was beaten in the Coronation Cup, Ascot Gold Cup and Hardwicke Stakes. She retired winner of 13 of her 25 races.

At stud she bred four winners but was somewhat disappointing: Relko in 1963 was the first horse in her direct female line to win the Derby. She died in 1926.

SCHOOLING

Teaching chasers and hurdlers to jump by putting them over obstacles on the home gallops, and then keeping that ability ticking over – though many National Hunt trainers are reluctant to school their charges during the season unless racecourse performance suggests that a refresher course is necessary. Young and inexperienced horses often learn how to jump in a 'loose school', jumping over a line of poles without a rider to build up confidence before facing a proper obstacle.

SCOOP6

A weekly Tote bet which every Saturday involves predicting the winners of six designated races, all of which are normally shown on Channel Four Racing. Money bet is pooled and distributed among the week's successful punters, who are then eligible to increase their winnings substantially by predicting the winner of the designated 'bonus race' the following Saturday. There is a consolation dividend for those who fail to come up with all six winners but manage to find six placed horses. With a minimum bet of £2, the Scoop6 holds out the prospect of huge winnings from a very small outlay, and the excitement which builds up as punters go for the bonus can make for gripping television.

SCOPE (1)

A horse is said to have 'scope' if it looks likely to develop and mature – that is, if it looks

likely to improve physically. 'Scopey' is sometimes to used to describe a gangly or 'unfurnished' young horse who can be expected to fill out and grow.

SCOPE (2)

To 'scope' a horse is to subject its airways to endoscopic assessment by feeding a tube through its nostrils and down to its lungs, so that a sample of fluid from the pulmonary area can be brought up and examined. If the fluid shows traces of blood, that suggests that the horse is liable to **break blood vessels**.

SCORE

Betting slang for £20.

SCOTT, BROUGH

See **Channel Four Racing**.

SCOTTISH GRAND NATIONAL

Grade Three handicap steeplechase; five-year-olds and upwards; 4 miles 1 furlong (Ayr)

Highlight of the jumping year at Ayr, the Scottish Grand National began life as the West of Scotland Grand National at Bogside (about 14 miles north of Ayr) in May 1867, over three miles. In 1881 the distance was increased to three miles seven furlongs and the name changed to the Scottish Grand National, and between the two world wars three horses won both the Scottish race and 'the real thing' at Aintree: Music Hall (1920, Grand National 1922), Sergeant Murphy (1922, Grand National 1923) and Kellsboro Jack (1935, Grand National 1933). But the greatest Scottish National horse of the period was Southern Hero, first horse to win three times: 1934, 1936 and (at the age of 14) 1939; he was also second in 1937 and 1938. Southern Hero's treble was emulated after the Second World War by Queen's Taste (1953, 1954 and 1956). Merryman II won at Bogside in 1959 and the Grand National in 1960, but perhaps the most memorable race at Bogside after the war was the 1964 running, when Popham Down beat the great hunter-chaser Freddie, who was conceding 22 pounds, by half a length as, according to *The Field*, 'the crowd erupted to an uninhib-

Scottish Grand National winners since 1990

1990	Four Trix	9	G. Richards	D. Byrne	25–1	28
1991	Killone Abbey	8	A. Stephenson	C. Grant	40–1	18
1992	Captain Dibble	7	N. Twiston-Davies	P. Scudamore	9–1	21
1993	Run For Free	9	M. Pipe	M. Perrett	6–1	21
1994	Earth Summit	6	N. Twiston-Davies	D. Bridgwater	16–1	22
1995	Willsford	12	Mrs J. Pitman	R. Farrant	16–1	22
1996	Moorcroft Boy	11	D. Nicholson	M. Dwyer	20–1	20
1997	Belmont King	9	P. Nicholls	A. McCoy	16–1	17
1998	Baronet	8	D. Nicholson	A. Maguire	7–1	18
1999	Young Kenny	8	P. Beaumont	B. Powell	5–2F	15
2000	Paris Pike	8	F. Murphy	A. Maguire	5–1JF	18
2001	Gingembre	7	Mrs L. Taylor	A. Thornton	12–1	30

ited roar audible in Arran.' (Popham Down achieved racing immortality of a sort three years later as the horse who precipitated the infamous pile-up in **Foinavon**'s Grand National.) Bogside closed in 1965 – Brasher (ridden by Jimmy FitzGerald, now a leading trainer) was the last winner of the Scottish Grand National there – and the race transferred to Ayr, where it has become one of the great spectacles of the jumping season. **Red Rum** won in 1974 just three weeks after his second National victory at Aintree (John Oaksey was runner-up on Proud Tarquin) and is the only horse to have won both races in the same season: his statue now overlooks the paddock area at Ayr. Other horses to have won both the Scottish Grand National at Ayr and the Grand National are Little Polveir (Ayr 1987, Aintree 1989) and Earth Summit (Ayr 1994, Aintree 1998), and there have been two dual winners at Ayr: Barona (1975 and 1976) and Androma, trained by Brasher's rider Jimmy FitzGerald (1984 and 1985).

SCRATCH

Withdraw a horse from a race.

SCRUBBED ALONG

A horse is being 'scrubbed along' when its jockey is vigorously pushing away (in a movement reminiscent of scrubbing a floor) to make it keep going.

SCUDAMORE FAMILY

When Peter Scudamore retired after riding Sweet Duke to victory at Ascot on 7 April 1993 he held two major riding records. His career total of 1,678 winners made him the winningmost jockey in the history of British jump racing, and his 221 winners in 1988–9 was a record for a single season. Both totals have since been surpassed (by Richard Dunwoody and Tony McCoy respectively), but Scu remains one of the greats of modern jumping history. He was champion jockey eight times (itself a record): 1981–2 (when he shared the title with John Francome), and every season from 1985–6 to 1991–2. Although he never won the Grand National (third on Corbiere in 1985 his best placing) or the Cheltenham Gold Cup, he landed the Champion Hurdle twice, on Celtic Shot in 1988 and Granville Again in 1993. He is now assistant trainer to Nigel Twiston-Davies and a racing presenter for BBC television.

On 25 October 1998 the three generations of riding Scudamores all took part in the same event, a charity race at Wincanton in aid of the Injured Jockeys' Fund. Michael Scudamore, at 66, rode the winner Barneys Bell – his first winner for 32 years.

Peter's father Michael Scudamore (born 1932) was himself a leading jockey, second in the championship table in 1956–7. He won the Cheltenham Gold Cup on Linwell in 1957 and the Grand National on Oxo (1959), and retired in 1966 following a bad fall to take up a career as a trainer: his Bruslee won the Mackeson Gold Cup in 1974.

Peter's son Tom Scudamore (born May 1982) is keeping up the family tradition: he started riding in point-to-points at the age of 16 and was champion amateur under Rules for the 2000–1 season.

SEA BIRD II

Although Sea Bird II ran just eight races in his life, only one of them in England, there is no serious disputing that he was the very best horse to have run on the Flat in Europe since the Second World War, nor that he was one of the all-time greats. He may not have pleased purist paddock-watchers – he was a bright chestnut with a thin white blaze, two white stockings and an excitable temperament – but could he gallop!

Sea Bird was bred in France by his owner M. Jean Ternynck and trained at Chantilly by Etienne Pollet. Although his sire Dan Cupid was a son of the great American horse Native Dancer, his dam Sicalade came from humbler stock – so humble that she was sold for the equivalent of £100 for butcher's meat before her illustrious son ever raced.

In three outings as a two-year-old, Sea Bird won twice and was then beaten in the Grand Criterium at Longchamp by his stable companion Grey Dawn – but he was never beaten again.

Sea Bird opened his three-year-old campaign with a facile victory in the Prix Greffulhe at Longchamp, following up with a six-length rout of Diatome in the Prix Lupin at the same course. Sights were then set on the Derby, for the only occasion on which the horse would race beyond his native shores. Starting hot favourite at 7–4 and ridden by Australian jockey Pat Glennon, Sea Bird hacked up at Epsom, sweeping into the lead hard held inside the final furlong to become one of the easiest Derby winners ever. His margin over Meadow Court may have been a mere two lengths, but Sea Bird had never come off the bridle to achieve it. Indeed, Glennon subse-

quently reported that his only worry during the race was how to pull up his mount beyond the winning post! His reputation as a racehorse of exceptional merit secured, Sea Bird then won the Grand Prix de Saint-Cloud, after which it was announced that the Prix de l'Arc de Triomphe would be his last race.

That 1965 Arc saw one of the best fields ever assembled for any horse race, including Derby runner-up Meadow Court, who since his defeat at Epsom had won the Irish Derby and the King George VI and Queen Elizabeth Stakes at Ascot; Reliance II, winner of the Prix du Jockey-Club and the second best three-year-old in France; Diatome, runner-up in the Prix du Jockey-Club and later that year winner of the Washington, DC International; Anilin, the best horse in Russia; and the American challenger Tom Rolfe, winner of the Preakness Stakes.

It all boiled down to a duel up the Longchamp straight between Reliance and Sea Bird – and while Reliance was a great horse, Sea Bird was a superlative one. The two came clear of their rivals, then Sea Bird just surged away, veering to the outside of the track but still recording a six-length verdict over Reliance, who was himself five lengths ahead of the third horse Diatome. It was a monumental performance, a race against which lesser horses would have to be judged.

Retired the winner of seven of his eight races, Sea Bird II stood as a stallion in the United States for five years before returning to France, where he died in 1973. He achieved little at stud to compare with his supremacy as a racehorse, though his offspring included the very good French colt Gyr, second to Nijinsky in the 1970 Derby, and two great favourites: **Allez France**, winner of the Arc in 1974, and **Sea Pigeon**, dual Champion Hurdler in 1980 and 1981.

SEA PIGEON

Although he won the Champion Hurdle twice, Sea Pigeon was bred to be a high-class performer on the Flat. His one race as a two-year-old in 1972, in which he won the Duke of Edinburgh Stakes at Ascot, did nothing to dispel the hopes of owner–breeder Jock

Whitney and trainer **Jeremy Tree** that the colt (a son of 1965 Derby winner Sea Bird II) had Classic pretensions, but although Sea Pigeon did get to the Derby line-up in 1973, in the event he could finish only seventh behind Morston. After failing to win at all as a three-year-old, the colt was gelded and subsequently sold to Pat Muldoon, for whom he was trained by first **Gordon Richards** and later **Peter Easterby**.

In a hurdling career which began at Newcastle in November 1974 and ended at the same course in November 1981, Sea Pigeon won 21 of his 40 starts, and ran in five consecutive runnings of the Champion Hurdle. Fourth behind **Night Nurse** in 1977, he returned to Cheltenham a year later for the first of his series of titanic Champion Hurdle duels with **Monksfield**. Three years running the pair came to the last flight locked together. In 1978 Monksfield asserted up the run-in and won by two lengths; in 1979 the two had a desperate duel from the last before Monksfield again got the upper hand to win by three-quarters of a length; but in 1980 Sea Pigeon finally managed to turn the tables, going clear of his rival to win by seven lengths under **Jonjo O'Neill**.

By the time of the 1981 running Monksfield had been retired. **John Francome**, who had come in for the ride on the 11-year-old Sea Pigeon as Jonjo had been sidelined through injury, presented the Cheltenham crowd with a typical piece of artistry. Sea Pigeon was a horse who tended to idle in front and needed producing at the very last minute, so John let Daring Run and Pollardstown lead over the last before easing past them inside the last hundred yards to win cosily – a riding performance of exceptional cool-headedness. (Sea Pigeon was one of only two 11-year-olds ever to win the Champion Hurdle, the other being Hatton's Grace in 1951.)

In addition to his two Champion Hurdles, Sea Pigeon won many other big races over jumps, including the Scottish Champion Hurdle at Ayr twice, the Welsh Champion Hurdle at Chepstow and the Fighting Fifth Hurdle at Newcastle twice. It was undoubtedly a great record; but the root of Sea Pigeon's appeal was his versatility, and a distinguished Flat career (16 wins) was being played out in parallel with the winter game. Sea Pigeon won the Chester Cup twice, the Vaux Gold Tankard at Redcar three times, the Moët and Chandon Silver Magnum for amateur riders at Epsom and the Doonside Cup at Ayr – but his greatest moment on the level was winning the 1979 Ebor Handicap at York. Ridden by Jonjo O'Neill and carrying the crushing burden of 10st (the highest weight carried to victory in the famous handicap in the twentieth century), Sea Pigeon won by a short head from Donegal Prince.

Sea Pigeon was retired shortly before the 1982 Champion Hurdle, winner of 37 of his 85 races. He spent most of his retirement at Slingsby in Yorkshire, where he died in 2000 at the ripe old age of 30.

SECRETARIAT

A massively built chestnut colt – hence his nickname 'Big Red' – Secretariat was trained throughout his racing career by Lucien Laurin. He first ran as a two-year-old in July 1972, finishing fourth, then proceeded to win his next eight races (though he was disqualified after one) and was voted Horse of the Year. His three-year-old career in 1973 kicked off with two easy victories; then there was a defeat (reason: infected boil in his mouth) in the Wood Memorial at Aqueduct; then it was off to the Kentucky Derby at Churchill Downs, first leg of the US Triple Crown. Secretariat smashed **Northern Dancer's** course record when winning the 'Run for the Roses' from Sham, then despatched the same horse in the second leg, the Preakness Stakes at Pimlico (nearly breaking the track record). Two down, one to go – and Secretariat was already a national hero, a welcome distraction from the unfolding saga of Watergate. The Triple Crown had not been won since **Citation** had achieved the feat a quarter of a century earlier in 1948, but Secretariat looked a shoo-in for the final leg, the Belmont Stakes over one and a half miles, and started 10–1 on favourite. A crowd of 70,000 crammed into Belmont Park to see 'Big Red' on his date with destiny, and few of them expected him to lose; but fewer still could have expected what they were to witness – possibly the greatest individual performance in racing history.

A mark of the magnitude of Secretariat's performance in the 1973 Belmont Stakes is that 5,617 winning on-course tote tickets for that race – value $14,597 – were not cashed in. Punters were keeping them as mementoes of an unrepeatable occasion.

Ridden by Ron Turcotte, Secretariat shot out of the starting gate from his inside berth and set out to make all, with Sham trying to take issue. They passed the stands at a searing pace and swung round the clubhouse turn, drawing a gasp from the crowd as the time for the first quarter was posted: 23.6 seconds, a breakneck pace for such a long race. Down the back straight Sham fell away, leaving Secretariat in glorious isolation. After a mile had been run the chestnut was seven lengths ahead, and his lead was still building rapidly – so rapidly that he was over 20 lengths clear by the turn into the home stretch. The crowd went wild as Secretariat barrelled home, and at the wire the winning margin from Twice A Prince was an astonishing 31 lengths – and another course time had been shattered. An astounding performance, perfectly summed up by American racing writer Charlie Hatton: 'He could not have moved faster if he had fallen off the grandstand roof.'

Secretariat ran six more times, winning four, including the Arlington Invitational, the Man O' War Stakes (on grass) and the Canadian International Turf Championship, to bring his career tally to 16 victories from 21 races. He was then retired to Claiborne Farm in Kentucky, where he died in 1989 at the age of 19. Among his offspring is Betty's Secret, dam of 1984 Derby winner Secreto and of triple Champion Hurdle winner **Istabraq**.

SECTIONAL TIMING

Horses are not necessarily running faster at the end of a race than at other points, and plotting the time taken to run each portion can be very revealing with regard to how the race was run. Sectional timing is mostly carried out by dedicated specialists who write up their findings in the racing press, but recent years have seen experimentation with sectional timing equipment installed on the racecourse. In 1997 Newmarket's Rowley Mile became the first course to have **RaceTech** install and operate an electronic sectional timing system (though the all-weather track at Wolverhampton has its own sectional timing equipment, and there are plans for similar systems at the other all-weather courses Lingfield Park and Southwell).

SEDGEFIELD

Sedgefield, Stockton-on-Tees, Cleveland
TS21 2HW
Tel.: 01740 621925
Fax: 01740 620663
E-mail: enquiries@sedgefield-
racecourse.com
Web: www.sedgefield-racecourse.com

The town – or rather the constituency – of Sedgefield was sprung to national prominence in May 1997 when the local MP, one Tony Blair, became Prime Minister. Long before then the local racecourse had been famous as the only British jumping track where the final fence in a steeplechase was an open ditch, but that distinction was removed a few years ago when the decision to do away with the water jump in the straight provided the opportunity – readily taken – to rearrange the configuration of fences and make the final obstacle, as everywhere else, a plain fence. Sedgefield's circuit is left-handed, about one and a quarter miles round. It undulates markedly, and is essentially sharp – a track for the handy horse. The run-in from the final fence is about 200 yards.

Organised racing at Sedgefield can be dated as far back as 1846, with racing in the locality much earlier than that. Nowadays no one would pretend that Sedgefield provides high-class racing, but its extremely strong base of local support makes it yet another of jumping's great **gaffs**.

SEE YOU THEN

When See You Then, owned by the Stype Wood Stud and trained by **Nicky Henderson**, won the 1987 Champion Hurdle, he was following **Hatton's Grace, Sir Ken** and **Persian War** to become the fourth triple winner of the hurdling championship. (**Istabraq** became the fifth in 2000.) See You Then, who suffered from chronic leg trouble and was very lightly raced, was runner-up to Northern Game in the 1984 Triumph Hurdle and the following year won his first Champion by seven lengths from Robin Wonder in a record time for the race. (This was the running when odds-on favourite Brownes Gazette, ridden by Dermot Browne, whipped round at the start and lost enough ground to forfeit any real chance.)

See You Then's first Champion Hurdle was a highly lucrative chance ride for Steve Smith Eccles: at the last minute he replaced intended rider John Francome, who had had a bad fall from The Reject in the Arkle Chase immediately before the Champion and gave up the rest of his rides that day, leaving Smith Eccles to form a partnership with the horse which extended to all three Champion victories.

In 1986 See You Then won by seven lengths from 1983 winner Gaye Brief, and in 1987, after just one preliminary race, by one and a half lengths from the American-trained Flatterer. In 1988 hopes were high that See You Then could become the first ever quadruple winner, but he broke down badly in his prep race at Wincanton and was retired.

SELLING RACE

The lowliest form of racing in Britain, a selling race (or 'seller') is a race in which the winner is sold at auction (with a reserve laid down) directly after the race, and in which other runners may be 'claimed' (bought) for an amount previously advertised. The owner of the winner may buy back the horse (in which case it is said to be 'bought in'), but even in this case a percentage of the proceeds of the sale goes to the racecourse.

SETFAST

Common name for the condition *azoturia*, manifested by muscular spasm which at its worst causes the horse's muscles to seize up completely.

SEX ALLOWANCE

In racing, the sex allowance is not a daily sum paid by Channel Four to John McCririck for essential research into social interaction but the weight concession made in certain races to fillies and mares to reflect their supposed weakness in relation to the male of the species: for example, in the Derby colts carry 9st, fillies carry 8st 9lb, an allowance of five pounds.

SHEEPSKIN NOSEBAND

The standard reason for fitting a sheepskin noseband is to encourage a horse to look further ahead, stretch out its feet and keep its nose down, but for some trainers it is a stable custom. (Ian Balding's horses, for example, tend to sport them.) A variation is the fitting of sheepskin attachments to the side of the bridle – again to encourage the horse to look ahead (as with **blinkers**).

SHERGAR

It is Shergar's fate to be remembered less for his glittering racing career than for what befell him after he had retired from the track. On the night of 8 February 1983, shortly before his second season standing as a stallion, he was abducted from the Aga Khan's Ballymany Stud, just outside Newbridge near The Curragh in Co. Kildare, and never heard of again. Ransom demands from his kidnappers – widely assumed to be the IRA on a fund-raising drive – drew no response, and it is assumed that the horse was killed a few days after his kidnapping.

But if Shergar's end was tragic, his brief period on the racecourse was epic.

Bred by his owner the **Aga Khan** and trained by **Michael Stoute**, Shergar – a bay colt notable for the large white blaze down his face – raced just twice as a two-year-old, winning at Newbury and then finishing runner-up to Beldale Flutter in the William

Hill Futurity (now the Racing Post Trophy) at Doncaster. A promising start, but it was his first appearance at three which really raised eyebrows – a 10-length victory in the Guardian Classic Trial at Sandown Park. The previous three runnings of the Classic Trial had thrown up the winner of the Derby – Shirley Heights had run second in 1978, then Troy and Henbit had each won the Sandown race – and Shergar's victory made him a serious Epsom candidate, a position which solidified after he had won the Chester Vase by 12 lengths. Such was the impression which Shergar made in these two races that after Chester the late Richard Baerlein of the *Observer* famously observed of Shergar's chance in the Derby: 'Now is the time to bet like men.'

Not for a moment on Derby Day did Richard Baerlein seem likely to be proved wrong. Ridden by 19-year-old **Walter Swinburn** having his first ride in the premier Classic, Shergar was cantering all over his rivals for the first half of the race, then eased his way to the front soon after entering the straight and scampered clear of Glint Of Gold for a 10-length victory – the longest winning distance ever in the Derby. Next came the Irish Derby. Walter Swinburn was suspended, so **Lester Piggott** (who had ridden the colt in both his two-year-old races) came in for an armchair spare ride. The pair won unchallenged by four lengths, but it was the manner of the victory which made it memorable: Shergar passed his rivals in a hack canter to win with ridiculous ease. No three-year-old could get near him, so it was time to face older horses such as Master Willie and Light Cavalry in the King George VI and Queen Elizabeth Diamond Stakes at Ascot. Here too Shergar won easily, by four lengths from Madam Gay.

He then had a rest until the St Leger, expected to be a doddle en route to Paris for the Prix de l'Arc de Triomphe. Instead, it was a disaster: Shergar failed to show his true spark at Doncaster and faded in the final quarter of a mile to finish a labouring fourth behind Cut Above. Arc plans were shelved, and he did not race again. His career had consisted of eight races, of which he had won six.

Shergar had just one season at stud – too little time to assess his long-term potential as a stallion – before they came for him that February night.

SHOEMAKER, BILL

Born in Texas in 1931, Bill Shoemaker rode 8,833 winners in the USA in a famous career which lasted from 1949 until 1990, and was the world's winningmost jockey from September 1970 (when he beat **Johnny Longden**'s record of 6,032) until December 1999, when his total was passed by **Laffit Pincay junior**. Shoemaker won 11 US Triple Crown races, including the Kentucky Derby four times (Swaps 1955, Tomy Lee 1959, Lucky Debonair 1965 and Ferdinand 1986), the Breeders's Cup Classic on Ferdinand in 1987 and the Arlington Million on **John Henry** in 1981, while other famous horses he rode included Forego, Round Table, Ack Ack and **Spectacular Bid**.

At Ascot in September 1982 Bill Shoemaker rode against Lester Piggott in a match race for charity: Shoemaker on Princes Gate beat Piggott on Spanish Pool by a length and a half. And in June 1989 he rode three heats against Peter Scudamore at Cheltenham as part of his round-the-world farewell tour: Scu won 2–1.

He was champion rider in North America in terms of races won five times: 1950, 1953, 1954, 1958 and 1959. He rode one winner at Royal Ascot – Sikorsky in the 1984 Bessborough Handicap – but his best-remembered ride in Britain was on Hawaiian Sound, caught close home and beaten a head by Shirley Heights in the 1978 Derby. After commencing a training career, in 1991 he was involved in a car crash which left him paralysed from the neck down.

SHOES (HORSES')

See **plate (1)**.

SHOULDER

Betting slang for 7–4 (from the **tic-tac** sign).

SHOW BUSINESS

There are plenty of connections between the worlds of show business and racing. Here are a few:

- Edward VII's mistress Lily Langtry was an actress whose horses raced under the *nom de course* 'Mr Jersey'.
- George Formby was an apprentice jockey before setting out on his unlikely career of ukelele-playing screen hero: he rode in Lord Derby's colours at the age of 10 but never partnered a winner.
- 1932 Derby winner April The Fifth was owned and trained by Tom Walls, star of many Aldwych farces.
- Bing Crosby owned Meadow Court, second to Sea Bird II in the 1965 Derby and later that season winner of the Irish Derby (after which the crooner treated the crowd at The Curragh to an impromptu rendition of 'When Irish Eyes Are Smiling') and the King George VI and Queen Elizabeth Stakes.
- Errol Brown of pop group Hot Chocolate owned the good chaser Gainsay, trained by Jenny Pitman.
- 1994 Grand National winner Miinnehoma was owned by comedian Freddie Starr.
- Gregory Peck owned several good horses who ran in Britain, including the chasers Different Class (third in the 1968 Grand National) and Owen's Sedge.
- Actors James Bolam and Sue Jameson owned Credo's Daughter, a highly popular chasing mare in the 1970s.
- Benny Andersson of Abba has horses with John Dunlop.
- Other well known showbiz personalities who have owned racehorses include Paul McCartney, Des O'Connor, Enn Reitel, Sting and Rick Wakeman.
- Composer Andrew Lloyd Webber has seen his and his wife Madeleine's colours carried to many big race successes on horses like Crystal Music (Fillies' Mile 2000), hurdlers Bacchanal (Stayers' Hurdle 2000) and Dusty Miller and chasers Uncle Ernie, Black Humour and Raymylette. Lady Lloyd-Webber has built up the Watership Down Stud into one of the most successful breeding operations in the country: the stud was vendor of the highest-priced yearling sold in Europe in 2000 – the **Sadler's Wells** colt sold at Tattersalls in Newmarket for 3.4 million guineas.

SHOWCASE RACE

One race a day is designated the 'showcase race' by the major bookmakers, who guarantee to give early prices on that race and feature it in their advertising in order to stimulate betting turnover. The showcase race is usually the sort of competitive handicap so beloved of the bookies, but a very big non-handicap – such as the Derby – could be so designated.

SILVER RING

Traditional name for the cheap enclosure on racecourses – so called because the paupers in there tended to bet with silver rather than banknotes.

SINGAPORE

Over the last few years Singapore, with its state-of-the-art racecourse Kranji, has made great strides in establishing itself as one of the major racing nations of the world, hosting extremely well endowed races to attract high-class runners from Europe, the USA and Australasia. Most valuable race is the Singapore Airlines International Cup, worth the equivalent of £694,981 to the winning owner when landed by **Luca Cumani**-trained Endless Hall from **François Doumen**-trained Jim And Tonic in May 2001. The local Triple Crown consists of the Queen Elizabeth II Cup, the Singapore Cup and the Singapore Gold Cup.

SINGLE

A bet on one horse in one race.

SINGSPIEL

Owned by Sheikh Mohammed Al-**Maktoum** and trained by **Michael Stoute**, Singspiel made a major contribution to the golden period of the late 1990s when the Flat saw some tip-top older horses kept in training. As a two-year-old in 1994 he won one of his three races and was runner-up to the mighty juvenile Celtic Swing (beaten eight lengths) at Ascot. At three Singspiel won only once – the Troy Stakes at Doncaster – but showed top-class form when going down narrowly in four big races: beaten a neck by Pentire in the Classic Trial at Sandown Park, a neck by Valanour in the Grand Prix de Paris, a neck by Halling in the Eclipse Stakes and a short head by Pentire in the Great Voltigeur Stakes at York. In 1996 as a four-year-old Singspiel made huge improvement. He won four races, including the Canadian International at Woodbine (beating Chief Bearhart) and the Japan Cup, and finished runner-up to **Swain** in the Coronation Cup (beaten a neck) and to stable companion **Pilsudski** in the Breeders' Cup Turf. The following year, 1997, saw Singspiel land the Dubai World Cup from the American-trained Siphon and the Coronation Cup by five lengths from Dushyantor, before finishing fourth behind Swain, Pilsudski and Helissio in the King George. He then won the International Stakes at York from Irish Derby winner Desert King, Derby winner Benny The Dip and top filly Bosra Sham in what proved his final race: while being prepared for the Breeders' Cup Turf he suffered a serious leg injury and was retired, winner of nine of his 20 races. He now stands as a stallion at the Dalham Hall Stud in Newmarket.

SIRE

Father of a horse. Tables of leading sires in Britain and Ireland combined, based on the amount of prize money won by their offspring, are compiled every season under both codes. On the Flat, **Sadler's Wells** has been champion sire every year since 1990 with the exception of 1991, when Caerleon took the honours. Over jumps two sires have dominated the list in recent times: Deep Run, champion sire every season between 1979–80 and 1992–3, and Strong Gale, who was champion jumping sire every season since then until 2000–1, when Be My Native topped the table.

SIR IVOR

'Of all my nine Derbys, Sir Ivor's was the most exciting,' declared **Lester Piggott**, and whenever Piggott is pressed to say which was the greatest horse he ever rode, Sir Ivor tends to get the nod. American-bred, Sir Ivor was owned by **Raymond Guest** and trained in Ireland by **Vincent O'Brien**. He won three of his four races as a two-year-old in 1967, including the Grand Criterium at Longchamp, and – after wintering in Pisa – at three in 1968 took the Two Thousand Guineas Trial at Ascot before heading for the Guineas itself, in which he beat Petingo and Jimmy Reppin. He started 5–4 on for the Derby, but looked held by Connaught until Piggott conjured an extraordinary turn of foot from him inside the final furlong to sweep by and win by a length and a half. Sir Ivor was clearly a horse of the highest order, but he proceeded to lose his next four races: ridden by Liam Ward, he was runner-up to Piggott-partnered Ribero in the Irish Derby; third to **Royal Palace** and Taj Dewan in a closely fought finish to the Eclipse Stakes; beaten half a length by Prince Sao in the Prix Henry Delamarre at Longchamp; and a three lengths runner-up to **Vaguely Noble** in the Arc. The winning thread was picked up with an easy victory over Locris in the Champion Stakes, and then Sir Ivor headed to the USA for the Washington, DC International, the first Derby winner to race in North America since Papyrus in 1923. He duly won, but Piggott's style of covering up the horse and producing him at the last minute brought a hail of criticism from the local press, not used to the unorthodox ways of Europe's greatest jockey. Piggott himself was characteristically unperturbed, observing that 'I knew a bit more about Sir Ivor than they did.' Sir Ivor did not run again, retiring to stud – for two years in Ireland and then at Claiborne Farm in Kentucky – winner of eight of his 13 races. His offspring included 1976 Arc winner Ivanjica and the top-class American horse Bates Motel, while his son Cavo Doro – bred by Lester Piggott – was runner-up to Morston in the 1973 Derby. Sir Ivor died in November 1995 at the age of 30: at the time he was the oldest surviving Derby winner.

SIR KEN

Along with only four others horses, **Hatton's Grace**, **Persian War**, **See You Then** and **Istabraq**, Sir Ken has the distinction of winning three Champion Hurdles. Bred in France and trained by Willie Stephenson, he first won the championship as a five-year-old in 1952, beating Noholme by two lengths, following up in 1953 by two lengths from Galatian at 5–2 on, and in 1954 by a length from Impney at 9–4 on. In all three he was ridden by Tim Molony. Sir Ken returned to Cheltenham in 1955 but could finish only fourth behind the new champion Clair Soleil. In all he won 20 of his 28 races over hurdles (including the first 16), plus four from 12 when he graduated to steeplechasing – including the Cotswold Chase (now the Arkle) at the big Cheltenham meeting in 1956. In 1957 Sir Ken became the first Champion Hurdler to run in the Gold Cup (he fell), and the following year he was retired. In 1964, at the age of 17, he was out hunting with the Puckeridge Hounds when he dropped dead.

SKINNER

Betting slang for a horse not backed at all: if he wins the bookmakers pay out nothing.

SLEEPER

Uncollected winnings.

SLIGO

Cleveragh, Sligo, Co. Sligo
Tel.: 071 62484 (racedays) or 071 83342
Fax: 071 83342

Sligo is the heart of Yeats country. The one-mile right-handed racetrack, hard by Ben Bulben in one of the most scenic settings in Irish racing, is the home of Connacht National and the Guinness Hurdle.

SLIP

If a broodmare is said to have 'slipped' her foal, she has miscarried.

SLOAN, TOD

Born in Bunker Hill, Indiana in 1874, James Forman Sloan – named 'Tod' by his father on account of his diminutive size – revolutionised British race riding by popularising what is now the universal jockey's seat based on very short stirrup leathers, the jockey crouched up over his mount's neck rather than in a much more upright posture. 'He rides like a monkey on a stick,' wrote the famous contemporary society magazine *Vanity Fair*, 'but he wins races.' Sloan had not invented the style (which was deemed to be effective as it cut down wind resistance on a jockey during a race), but he made it a common sight on English racecourses, and he enjoyed a good deal of success. He was a brilliant judge of pace and a fine tactician, and mastered the art of riding a race from the front: to 'do a Tod Sloan' became rhyming slang for going out on your own – hence 'on your Tod'. Between 1897 and 1900 Sloan rode 254 winners (including one Classic winner – Sibola in the 1899 One Thousand Guineas) from 801 mounts in England, and in 1899 earned the huge retainer of £5,000 from Lord William Beresford. But he fell foul of the Jockey Club on account of his betting, and his licence to ride was not renewed. He was deported from England in 1915 for running an illegal gaming house in London, and died in the charity ward of a Los Angeles hospital in 1933.

SMIRKE, CHARLIE

Born in 1906, Charlie Smirke was apprenticed to Epsom trainer Stanley Wootton. He partnered his first winner in April 1922 and his last in November 1959. In between he rode the winners of 11 Classics:

- *Two Thousand Guineas*: My Babu 1948, Palestine 1950;
- *One Thousand Guineas*: Rose Royale II 1957;
- *Derby*: Windsor Lad 1934, Mahmoud 1936, Tulyar 1952 and Hard Ridden 1958 (when he was 51; it was one of only three winners that season);
- *St Leger*: Windsor Lad 1934, Bahram 1935, Tulyar 1952 and Never Say Die 1954.

Arrogant, brash and nerveless, Charlie Smirke was popular with punters but often less so with trainers for whom he rode. There is a story of a tout approaching trainer Frank Butters on the Newmarket gallops during the Second World War:

'Have you heard the news, Mr Butters? Charlie Smirke's been awarded the VC in Sicily.'

'Really, what for?'

'For stopping a German tank.'

'I'm not surprised. When he was riding for me he would stop anything.'

Other big-race success included Migoli in the 1947 Eclipse Stakes and 1948 Prix de l'Arc de Triomphe, Irish Derby on Turkhan (1940) and Fraise du Bois (1951), Tulyar in the 1952 Eclipse and King George VI and Queen Elizabeth Stakes, and Worden II in the 1953 Washington, DC International. His career suffered a major interruption when he was banned after his mount Welcome Gift refused to start at Gatwick in August 1928, his exclusion lasting until October 1933. Charlie Smirke died in 1993 at the age of 87.

SMITH, DOUG AND EPH

Born in 1917, Doug Smith was apprenticed to Fred Sneyd and rode his first winner in 1932. He won the Two Thousand Guineas on Our Babu in 1955 and the Queen's Pall Mall in 1958, and the One Thousand Guineas on Hypericum (owned by King George VI) in 1946 and **Petite Etoile** in 1959. Among other famous horses he partnered was the great stayer **Alycidon**, on whom he won the Ascot Gold Cup, Goodwood Cup and Doncaster Cup in 1949. He took the Gold Cup again the following year on Supertello, and excelled in staying races: in addition to those two Gold Cups he won the Doncaster Cup six times, Cesarewitch six times, Northumberland Plate three times and Goodwood Cup three times. Champion jockey five times (1954, 1955, 1956, 1958 and 1959), he retired in 1967 having ridden 3,112 winners in Britain (at the time second only to **Gordon Richards** as winningmost jockey in British racing history).

He then turned to training, in which role he enjoyed more Classic success with Sleeping Partner, winner of the 1969 Oaks, but gave up in 1979 to become a bloodstock agent, and in 1989 was found dead in his Newmarket swimming pool at the age of 71.

Doug Smith's older brother Eph Smith (born 1915) had a riding career which stretched from 1929 to 1965 and brought him 2,313 domestic winners, including the Derby and St Leger in 1939 on Blue Peter and the 1953 St Leger on Premonition. Eph Smith died in 1972.

SMITH, TOMMY

Born in 1919, Tommy Smith was arguably the greatest trainer in Australian racing history, winning over 7,000 races. For 33 consecutive seasons from 1952 to 1985 he headed the Trainers' Premiership in Sydney, and won it for the last time in 1989. He landed the **Melbourne Cup** twice, with Toporoa in 1955 and Just A Dash in 1981, but his greatest horses were Tulloch, who won 36 of his 53 races in the 1950s and only once finished out of the first three, and Kingston Town, who won 30 out of 41, including the **Cox Plate** three years in a row (1980–2), and was the first Australian horse to win more than A$1 million in stakes. Tommy Smith died in September 1998 at the age of 79.

SNAFFLE

The simplest design of **bit** – two metal bars joined in the middle and attached to rings.

SNIP

On the face of a brown, bay or black horse, a small strip of white hair just above the muzzle.

SOBELL, SIR MICHAEL

See **Lord Weinstock**.

SOCK

Short extent of white hair above the hoof of a bay, brown or black horse.

SOFT PALATE DISEASE

A horse with a soft palate complaint 'swallows his tongue': the horse gurgles and suddenly slows right up, then gets his breath back.

What has happened is that the junction between the larynx and the soft palate has become unsealed, causing the passage of air to be obstructed. This usually happens when the horse is under pressure at the climax of a race; once he can swallow and reseal the junction, he recovers. The use of a tongue-strap can be an effective counter to this condition: by keeping the tongue in a forward position, it helps to maintain the essential seal between larynx and soft palate.

SORE SHINS
As with **fractures of the knee** or **stress fractures**, sore shins are most common among young racehorses. Fast work or racing on hard ground puts great stress on the legs, and can result in inflammation of the shins.

SOUTH AFRICA
There are 13 racecourses within South Africa (and two in Zimbabwe), the best-known of which in Britain are Turffontein (Johannesburg), Kenilworth (Cape Town) and Clairwood (Durban): when domestic racing is scarce, sport from South Africa is often beamed into British betting shops. While the country does not currently figure prominently on the international racing stage, South African influence has been keenly felt in Europe through the achievements of the country's finest jockey **Michael Roberts**. Basil Marcus is another South African rider who has become well known in Britain (via Hong Kong), and his brother Anton Marcus is leading rider in their homeland: he was champion jockey in the 1999–2000 season with a total 120 winners clear of the runner-up. South Africa's most celebrated race is the July Handicap, which takes place at Greyville (Durban).

SOUTHWELL
Rolleston, Newark, Nottinghamshire NG25 0TS
Tel.: 01636 814481
Fax: 01636 812271
E-mail: info@southwell-racecourse.co.uk
Web: www.southwell-racecourse.co.uk
Until the advent of all-weather racing in 1989 there was little to be said about Southwell.

A very minor jumping track which had opened in 1898, it provided modest sport for a mostly local clientele. The acquisition of the course in the 1980s by Ron Muddle, who had earlier brought a new lease of life to Lingfield Park, paved the way for the installation of an all-weather track. Unlike at Lingfield, where the all-weather track was fitted into the existing turf circuit, at Southwell a completely new circuit was laid out and new facilities built. The all-weather track is laid out very much on the model of American circuits: left-handed, 10 furlongs round and completely flat, with five-furlong races starting from a spur. From the home bend to the winning post is about three furlongs. There is no turf racing on the Flat here, but jumping continues on turf on a course positioned inside the all-weather track, which makes it rather remote from the spectators.

SPECTACULAR BID
Winner of 26 of his 30 races between 1978 and 1980, the grey Spectacular Bid was one of the very best American horses of the modern age. He won the Kentucky Derby and Preakness in 1979 but failed to stay when third to Coastal in the Belmont Stakes: his only other defeat in 1979 was by 1978 Triple Crown winner **Affirmed** in the Jockey Club Gold Cup.

SPEED (HORSES')
The speed at which racehorses travel obviously relates to the distance and the **going**. In the fastest modern British race on record, the Tadworth Handicap over five furlongs at Epsom on 2 June 1960, the winning horse Indigenous averaged over 41 miles per hour – though that race was timed by hand, generally regarded as less reliable than the electrical timing now in widespread use. The average speed of a top-class two-mile hurdler through a race on good going is in the region of 30 miles per hour and of a Grand National winner in heavy going around 25 miles an hour. When Galileo won the 2001 Derby in 2 minutes 33.27 seconds – second fastest time in the history of the race – he posted an average speed of just over 35 mph.

SPLINT

Splint bones are small bones between the knee and the fetlock, and a 'splint' is the common name for a bony enlargement of one of these, caused by a kick or by stress on the bones and ligaments. It may look unsightly but does not usually interfere seriously with the horse's long-term prospects.

SPLIT PASTERN

The pastern is the region consisting of three bones between a horse's fetlock joint and hoof, and a split pastern is a condition to which young horses are especially susceptible. Repeated concussion causes a hairline fracture vertically through the centre. The injury is usually treated by inserting compression screws across the fracture, but the horse will be out of action for several months.

SPONSORSHIP

Commercial sponsorship, which now puts well over £11 million a year into British racing, has long been an essential ingredient of the sport, and now extends to jockeys and training stables as well as race meetings and indiviual races. The first commercially sponsored race in England was the **Whitbread Gold Cup** at Sandown Park in April 1957 (the first Hennessy Gold Cup followed at Cheltenham in November the same year), while the longest-standing sponsorship on the Flat is the John Smith's Cup at York, first run as the Magnet Cup in July 1960; the Classics have been sponsored only since 1984. Some major sponsors support not just big races but a whole meeting – for example, the Derby meeting at Epsom Downs is supported by Vodafone – while racecourses have benefited from commercial support (for example, the Fosters Enclosure at Cheltenham). Loosen ing of the regulations in 1995 heralded sponsorship of jockeys' silks and breeches (which has led to problems when the riders' endorsements clash with the race sponsor) and of stables and saddlecloths. The main area of racing which staunchly resists sponsorship is Royal Ascot, where none of the races is commercially underwritten.

SPORTING LIFE

The *Sporting Life*, for well over a century the principal daily racing newspaper, was first published in 1859 and ceased publication in May 1998. John McCririck worked for the *Life* from 1972 to 1984, Alastair Down was Associate Editor, and both Mike Cattermole and Simon Holt also wrote for the paper.

SPREAD A PLATE

A horse is said to have 'spread a plate' when it has loosened or lost one of its shoes.

SPREAD BETTING

The essence of spread betting is wagering on a range – a 'spread' – of possibilities. Most sporting events are decided by numbers – runs in cricket, goals in soccer, points in rugby – and the spread better backs his or her view on what those numbers will be. So if the spread-betting firm is of the opinion that the total number of points scored in a rugby international will be 29, it may quote '28–30'. If you think the match will produce more points than 29, you 'buy' at 30; if fewer than 29, you 'sell' at 28. The punter makes the decision to buy (the higher figure) or sell (the lower) and stipulates the stake, but here's the rub: your profit or loss on the bet is calculated by measuring the difference between the price at which you bought or sold and the actual result, and multiplying your stake by that figure. So, unlike in fixed-odds betting, your losses are not confined to the amount you have staked. If you buy the spread at £10 and the total number of points is 25, you lose £50: 30 minus 25 equals 5. But if you sell the spread at £10 and the total number of points is 25, you win £30 (28 minus 25). Racing applications of spread betting include:

- backing a horse to score points according to the bookmaker's advertised scale – for example, all four major spread betting companies quoted Galileo at 19–22 on the morning of the 2001 Vodafone Derby, on the scale of 50 points if the colt won, 30 if runner-up, 20 if third and 10 if fourth: had you bought Galileo for £10 a point you would have won £280 (stake times 50 points for winning, less the 22 of the spread), while had he been unplaced you would have lost £190;

- total winning distances at an individual race meeting;
- performances of favourites at a meeting, with market leaders scoring points on an advertised scale;
- the distance by which one named horse will beat another, wherever they actually finish in the race;
- betting on the jockeys' index: back or oppose your selected jockey, so that every ride he has on the card is running for you;
- favourites: back or oppose the favourites for a whole programme without having to pick which horse will actually win.

One of the attractions of spread betting is that you can back your opinion if you think the horse in question will lose, as well as if you think he will win. (In the example above, you would have 'sold' Galileo if you felt he was going to finish unplaced.) The danger, of course, is that the more wrong you are, the more you will lose (though in bets such as those relating to distance a ceiling is usually imposed). Two other points to remember. You cannot have a spread bet in a betting shop or on the racecourse – only through an account with one of the spread bookmakers. And if you get it so comprehensively wrong that you cannot afford to pay up, beware: unlike with

orthodox betting, you can be sued for the debt by your bookmaker. (And he, should it come to it, can be sued by you.)

SPRING DOUBLE

Traditional name for the two big handicaps run in the spring: the **Lincoln Handicap** and the **Grand National**.

SPRINGER

A springer in the betting market is a horse whose price is shortening rapidly.

SPRINT CUP
Group One; three-year-olds and upwards; 6 furlongs (Haydock Park)

The only Group One race run at Haydock Park, the Sprint Cup was first run on the last day of the 1966 season as the Vernons November Sprint Cup, won by **Peter O'Sullevan**'s Be Friendly, then a two-year-old and ridden by apprentice Colin Williams. The following year Be Friendly – by then one of the best sprinters around – won again, this time ridden by **Scobie Breasley** to beat Mountain Call a neck. In 1968 Be Friendly, fresh from winning the Prix de l'Abbaye at Longchamp, was back for the treble on what promised to be an emotional occasion: Scobie Breasley's last day in the saddle. But the fog descended on Haydock Park and the race was cancelled. (The race was switched from the November gloom to the more temperate weather of early

Sprint Cup winners since 1990

Year	Winner	Age	Trainer		Jockey	SP	Ran
1990	Dayjur	3	W. Hern		W. Carson	1–2F	9
1991	Polar Falcon	4	J. Hammond *FRA*		C. Asmussen	13–2	6
1992	Sheikh Albadou	4	A. Scott		B. Raymond	9–4JF	8
1993	Wolfhound	4	J. Gosden		M. Roberts	7–2	7
1994	Lavinia Fontana	5	J. Dunlop		J. Weaver	11–2	8
1995	Cherokee Rose	4	J. Hammond *FRA*		C. Asmussen	5–1	6
1996	Iktamal	4	E. Dunlop		W. Ryan	10–1	11
1997	Royal Applause	4	B. Hills		M. Hills	15–8F	9
1998	Tamarisk	3	R.Charlton		T. Sprake	13–2	13
1999	Diktat	4	S. bin Suroor		L. Dettori	13–8F	16
2000	Pipalong	4	T. Easterby		K. Darley	3–1	13

September in 1979.) The Sprint Cup soon became an established target for top sprinters, going to such familiar names as Lianga (who beat Roman Warrior in 1975), the popular gelding Boldboy (who won at the age of seven in 1977), Absalom (1978), Double Form (**Geoff Lewis**'s last riding winner in Britain when winning in 1979), Moorestyle (1980), Habibti (1983), Green Desert (1986) and Ajdal (1987). The Sprint Cup was raised to Group One status in 1988 (when the race was run on Haydock's new straight six furlongs rather than the round course) and the first two runnings at the top level went to colts owned by Khalid Abdullah: Dowsing (1988) and Danehill (1989). Star turns in the 1990s were **Dayjur** (1990), who scorched home in the Sprint Cup en route to winning the Prix de l'Abbaye and sensationally losing the Breeders' Cup Sprint, and Sheikh Albadou, who when he won this in 1992 had already won the 1991 Breeders' Cup Sprint.

SQUIGGLE
See **Timeform squiggle**.

STABLE LADS' WELFARE TRUST

20B Park Lane, Newmarket, Suffolk CB8 8QD
Tel.: 01638 560763
Fax: 01638 560831
E-mail: racingcharities@charity.vfree.com
Charity for the benefit of stud and stable staff and their dependants.

STABLE STAFF
There are around 4,000 staff employed on a full-time basis by racing stables in Britain – working as stable lads and lasses, head lads, travelling head lads, blacksmiths, box drivers, secretaries, gallop men, yardmen, feedmen, work riders, hostel keepers and in all sorts of other roles. The daily routine of a stable lad – who might be required to look after as many as five or six horses – would typically involve arriving at the yard around 6.30 a.m.; mucking out boxes and giving the horses a light grooming; riding out first lot around 7.30 a.m.; breakfast; riding out second lot at about 10 a.m., and possibly third lot after that; grooming the horses more thoroughly; taking a break in the early afternoon before returning at around 4 p.m. to prepare for evening stables, when the trainer goes round and looks at each horse; and finishing at about 6 p.m. That routine is varied by trips to the races, but working in a racing stable is hard graft for low reward.

STACK, TOMMY
Born in Co. Kerry in November 1945, Tommy Stack worked as an insurance clerk in Dublin until the lure of racing, caught from his school-friend Barry Brogan, who became a top jockey, led to his working at the yard run by Brogan's father Jimmy. He moved to England in 1965 to join trainer Bobby Renton, and started to ride as an amateur, his first winner under Rules coming on New Money at Wetherby on 2 October 1965. He turned professional in 1967 and for a while combined riding and training: in the latter role he was for a short time in charge of a six-year-old gelding named **Red Rum**, who along with the rest of the Stack string came into the charge of Anthony Gillam when Stack decided to concentrate on riding, becoming first jockey to the powerful Arthur Stephenson stable in 1974. He was champion jockey for the first time in the 1974–5 season and topped the table again in 1976–7, and the latter season brought his greatest moment as a jockey when he partnered Red Rum to his historic third Grand National victory in April 1977. Stack retired from the saddle in 1978 (soon after winning the Whitbread Gold Cup on Strombolus) and worked in the bloodstock business before taking out a permit to train in 1986 and a full licence in 1988, winning his first Classic in England with Las Meninas in the 1994 One Thousand Guineas. Tommy Stack was hit by a life-threatening bout of meningitis in 1999 but recovered well enough to resume his training career at his yard at Golden, not far from Cashel in Tipperary.

STALE (1)
A horse 'stales' when he urinates.

STALE (2)
A horse described as 'stale' has had too much racing.

STALLION

Male horse kept for breeding purposes.

STANDARD TIMES

Compiled by Raceform for each distance at each racecourse as a mark against which to judge the pace of a race and assess the effect of the going. A race time under standard is faster than the norm, over standard slower than the norm: thus Galileo's Derby-winning time of 2 minutes 33.27 seconds in 2001 was described in the form book as '–5.21': that is, 5.21 seconds faster than the standard time for a mile and a half at Epsom.

STAR

Small patch of white hair on the forehead of a bay, brown or black horse.

STARKEY, GREVILLE

Born in 1939, Greville Starkey was apprenticed to Harry Thomson Jones at Newmarket and rode his first winner on Russian Gold at Pontefract in 1955, becoming champion apprentice in 1957. Between then and his retirement from the saddle in 1989 he won five Classics: 1964 Oaks on Homeward Bound, 1978 Derby on Shirley Heights, 1978 Oaks on Fair Salinia, 1981 Two Thousand Guineas on To-Agori-Mou, and 1986 Two Thousand Guineas on Dancing Brave. He also won the Prix de l'Arc de Triomphe on Star Appeal (1975) and King George VI and Queen Elizabeth Diamond Stakes on Kalaglow (1982).

STARTER

The starter's principal responsibilities are:
- to make sure that all the runners are at the start;
- to see that they start from the correct draw (in a Flat race);
- to supervise the loading (with stalls) or the lining up;
- to dispatch the runners.

He or she can order the exclusion from the race of an unruly runner and will report any rider guilty of misconduct to the stewards of the meeting.

STARTING GATE

While almost every race on the Flat is started from starting stalls, jump races are started from a starting gate. This takes the form of either a tape strung across the course, lowered into position once the runners have arrived at the start and raised to start the race when the starter pulls a lever, or a stretch of elasticated tape pulled across the course and released to start the race.

STARTING PRICE

The price (odds) at which the horse is officially judged to have started the race. The SP is arrived at by a team of official starting price reporters who monitor price fluctuations in the main racecourse betting ring and agree the SPs by consensus as soon as the race is started. Not every SP reflects a price which has actually been available in the ring. For example, the returned SP of 1990 Champion Hurdle winner Kribensis was the highly unusual 95–40: this indicates that a roughly equal number of Cheltenham layers had him at 9–4 and 5–2 at the off, and the returned SP splits the difference to arrive at 95–40. By the same token, 85–40 is halfway between 2–1 and 9–4. If one horse in a race is a complete certainty (rare but not unknown) and there is no meaningful betting in the ring, no starting price is returned.

STARTING STALLS

Starting stalls are used for all races on the Flat, though they may be dispensed with in adverse circumstances such as high winds or very heavy going, when their use would be impractical or unsafe. (They are not used for National Hunt races, where with a minimum race distance of two miles there is less necessity for the whole field to break together.) Stalls have been in use in most of the major racing countries since the early 1960s, but were not introduced to Britain until 1965, when they were first used in the Chesterfield Stakes for two-year-olds on Newmarket's July Course on 8 July 1965: the race was won by Track Spare, ridden by Lester Piggott.

After further tentative use at Newmarket during the remainder of the 1965 season, stalls started appearing at other racecourses in 1966, and the first Derby started by stalls was the 1967 running won by **Royal Palace**.

Wolverhampton racecourse has been using its own design of starting stalls since 1998. The bays are 17 per cent wider than the standard design and thus more inviting for the horses.

Standard stalls come in 10-bay units which are manoeuvred around the racecourse, and between courses, by specially modified Land Rovers. At each meeting the stalls are supported by a team of nine professional horse handlers – eight handlers under the direction of a team leader – whose function is to load the horses into the stalls as rapidly and efficiently as possible, taking into account the different needs of different horses: some need to go in late as they will fret if in the stalls too long, others require particularly sensitive handling. Before the runners start to enter the stalls, all the front gates are locked in a closed position by means of spring-loaded latches linked to an electrical locking system, and the opening mechanism is tested before each race. Once all the runners are installed and the gates at the rear of each bay closed, the starter presses the electrical release mechanism which unfastens the latch on each gate simultaneously.

STEAMER
Horse gambled on significantly on the morning of the race.

STEEPLECHASE
The word 'steeplechase' derives from the occasion in 1752 when Cornelius O'Callaghan and Edmund Blake rode their horses in a race from the parish church at Buttevant in Co. Cork across country to the steeple of St Leger Church in Doneraile, some four and a half miles away – and four and a half miles just happens to be the distance of the most famous steeplechase, the Grand National.
See also **fences**.

STEVENS, GARY
Long one of the most successful riders in the USA, Gary Stevens (born in Idaho in 1963) made a big impact on the British racing scene when riding as stable jockey to **Michael Stoute** in the summer of 1999. He won on his first ride in Britain that year and on his last, and in all rode 45 winners from 210 rides – notably an eight-length victory on Royal Anthem in the International Stakes at York. Just when it seemed as if Stevens would be the natural successor to **Steve Cauthen** as an American rider who wowed British fans, he announced that he would be returning to the USA to ride over there for the **Thoroughbred Corporation** – and not long after that came news that severe knee trouble was forcing him into premature retirement. However, Stevens did return to the saddle (ascribing his recovery to 'new supplements and herbal remedies'), and was still going strong in 2001, when his big-race victories included the Preakness and Belmont Stakes on Point Given. He has won the Kentucky Derby three times (Winning Colors 1988, Thunder Gulch 1995, Silver Charm 1997), seven Breeders' Cup races, the 1991 Japan Cup on Golden Pheasant and the 1998 Dubai World Cup on Silver Charm.

STEWARDS
Racecourse stewards are unpaid officials responsible at every race meeting for seeing that the Rules are adhered to, and expected to take action if they are not. Appointments are made by the racecourse and approved by the Stewards of the Jockey Club (a body of men not to be confused with racecourse stewards), and there must be at least four stewards for every meeting. Their remit includes the power to abandon races or the whole meeting, and they have jurisdiction over conduct of all officials, owners, trainers and jockeys while the meeting is in progress.

STEWARDS' ENQUIRY
Racecourse stewards can call an enquiry after a race to look into possible interference which may affect the placings or to investigate other ways in which the race might not have been

fairly or properly contested. The standard procedure is for the jockeys involved to be called in, shown film of the race and asked to put their case; then they wait outside while the stewards deliberate, being called back in to hear the verdict and (if appropriate) learn their punishment. Racecourse stewards are empowered to suspend a jockey for up to 14 days (depending on the nature of the transgression): if they want to impose a heftier penalty (say for repeated offences) they report the matter to the Stewards of the Jockey Club in London (a procedure popularly known as 'referring the case to **Portman Square**').

STEWARDS' SECRETARY

The stewards' secretary – the stipendiary steward, or 'stipe' – is an official who provides racecourse stewards with advice relating to the conduct of the meeting and interpretation of the Rules of Racing. Some well-known former jockeys have become stipes, including Paul Barton, Simon Cowley, Robert Earnshaw and Phil Tuck.

STIFLE

A horse's stifle is the large joint at the upper end of the hind leg, between the hock and the hip.

STIPENDIARY STEWARD

See **stewards' secretary**.

ST JAMES'S PALACE STAKES

Group One; three-year-old colts; 1 mile
(Royal Ascot)

First run in 1834, the St James's Palace Stakes has had Group One status only since 1988. Until the Second World War the race was regularly a target for the Derby winner, and notable names who have won the Ascot race after Epsom include **Bend Or** (1880), **Ormonde** (1886) and Triple Crown winners Rock Sand (1903) and **Bahram** (1935), while the great filly **Sceptre**, fourth in the Derby, won this in 1902. Since the war the race has become more closely linked to the Two Thousand Guineas: last horse to win both races was To-Agori-Mou in 1981, who was following in the hoofprints of **Tudor Minstrel** (1947), Palestine (1950), Nearula (1953), Right Tack (1969), **Brigadier Gerard** (1971) and Bolkonski (1975). Many Two Thousand Guineas runners-up have found consolation in the St James's Palace Stakes, including the great miler Kris (1979), Chief Singer (1984) and, over the last few years, Grand Lodge (1994) and **Giant's Causeway** (2000).

ST LEGER

Group One; three-year-old colts and fillies;
1 mile 6 furlongs 132 yards (Doncaster)

The St Leger is the oldest Classic. First run in 1776, it is senior to the Oaks by three years and the Derby by four. The race was inaugu-

St James's Palace Stakes winners since 1990

1990	Shavian	3	H. Cecil	S. Cauthen	11–1	8
1991	Marju	3	J. Dunlop	W. Carson	7–4F	7
1992	Brief Truce	3	D. Weld *IRE*	M. Kinane	25–1	8
1993	Kingmambo	3	F. Boutin *FRA*	C. Asmussen	2–5F	4
1994	Grand Lodge	3	W. Jarvis	M. Kinane	6–1	9
1995	Bahri	3	J. Dunlop	W. Carson	11–4F	9
1996	Bijou d'Inde	3	M. Johnston	J. Weaver	9–1	9
1997	Starborough	3	D. Loder	L. Dettori	11–2	8
1998	Dr Fong	3	H. Cecil	K. Fallon	4–1	8
1999	Sendawar	3	A. de Royer-Dupré *FRA*	G. Mosse	2–1F	11
2000	Giant's Causeway	3	A. O'Brien *IRE*	M. Kinane	7–2F	11
2001	Black Minnaloushe	3	A. O'Brien *IRE*	J. Murtagh	8–1	11

St Leger winners since 1990

1990	Snurge	3	P. Cole	T. Quinn	7–2	8
1991	Toulon	3	A. Fabre *FRA*	Pat Eddery	5–2F	10
1992	User Friendly	3	C. Brittain	G. Duffield	7–4F	7
1993	Bob's Return	3	M. Tompkins	P. Robinson	3–1F	9
1994	Moonax	3	B. Hills	Pat Eddery	40–1	8
1995	Classic Cliché	3	S. bin Suroor	L. Dettori	100–30F	10
1996	Shantou	3	J. Gosden	L. Dettori	8–1	11
1997	Silver Patriarch	3	J. Dunlop	Pat Eddery	5–4F	10
1998	Nedawi	3	S. bin Suroor	J. Reid	5–2F	9
1999	Mutafaweq	3	S. bin Suroor	R. Hills	11–2	9
2000	Millenary	3	J. Dunlop	T. Quinn	11–4F	11

(For a list of all winners since the Second World War, *see* Classics.)

rated by Colonel Anthony St Leger, a distinguished soldier (later Governor of St Lucia) who lived at Park Hill, near Doncaster, and who decided that the novelty of a race over two miles confined to three-year-olds would make good sport. So the new event was run on 24 September 1776 at Cantley Common, moving to its present home on the nearby Town Moor (and carrying the name St Leger for the first time) in 1778: the distance was reduced to just short of one mile seven furlongs in 1814, where (give or take a few yards) it has remained since. The first Derby winner to land the St Leger was Champion in 1800, and thereafter the race grew in stature as the idea of 'The Classics' took hold and the notion became established that the ideal three-year-old Thoroughbred would have the speed to win over a mile at Newmarket in the spring, the agility and increasing stamina to win over a mile and a half at Epsom in early summer, and the staying power and constitution to win over more than one and three quarter miles at Doncaster in the autumn. Only 15 colts and nine fillies have ever managed that stiff programme (*see* **Triple Crown**).

Since the Second World War the St Leger has had its ups and downs, with the growing stature of the Prix de l'Arc de Triomphe, run in early October, presenting a serious rival for the attentions of the best horses – to such an extent that for a period it was suggested that the Doncaster race might follow the example of the Irish St Leger and be opened to older horses. Such heresy died away, and the race has reasserted its position as one of the key moments of the racing year. If you need convincing, think of these big St Leger moments from the last 25 years:

- **Dunfermline** beating **Alleged** after that long-drawn-out duel in 1977;
- Sun Princess and **Willie Carson** in 1983;
- Commanche Run holding off Baynoun to give **Lester Piggott** his record-breaking twenty-eighth Classic in 1984;
- **Oh So Sharp** and **Steve Cauthen** landing the fillies' Triple Crown in 1985;
- Cauthen again in 1987, as Reference Point becomes the sixth post-war Derby winner to land the St Leger (after Airborne 1946, Tulyar 1952, Never Say Die 1954, St Paddy 1960 and **Nijinsky** 1970);
- Willie Carson driving home Minster Son in 1988, the first time a Classic had been won by a horse bred by its rider;
- Classic Cliché winning in 1995 to give **Frankie Dettori** his 1,000th winner in Britain . . .
- . . . and Silver Patriarch winning in 1997 to give **Pat Eddery** his 4,000th winner in Britain.

STOCKING

A length of white hair above the hoof of a bay, brown or black horse.

STORE

A horse who is not broken in or put into training at a young age but left to mature until four or five. The term is mostly heard with regard to jumpers.

STOUTE, SIR MICHAEL

Born in Barbados (where his father was chief of police) in 1945, Michael Stoute moved to Britain at the age of 19 to join the Yorkshire stable of Pat Rohan; he followed up with spells at Newmarket with Doug Smith and Tom Jones before setting up there on his own account in 1972. His first Classic success came with Fair Salinia in the 1978 Oaks, since when he has become established as one of the very best – arguably *the* best – Flat trainer of the age in Britain. The astonishing array of Stoute equine talent has included:

- **Shergar** (Derby, Irish Derby and King George VI and Queen Elizabeth Diamond Stakes 1981)
- Shahrastani (Derby and Irish Derby 1986)
- **Pilsudski** (Breeders' Cup Turf 1996, Eclipse Stakes, Irish Champion Stakes, Champion Stakes and Japan Cup 1997)
- **Singspiel** (Japan Cup 1996, Dubai World Cup, Coronation Cup and International Stakes 1997)
- Opera House (Coronation Cup, Eclipse Stakes and King George 1993)
- Ezzoud (International Stakes 1993 and 1994, Eclipse Stakes 1994)
- Entrepreneur (Two Thousand Guineas 1997)
- Shadeed (Two Thousand Guineas and Queen Elizabeth II Stakes 1985)
- Kalanisi (Champion Stakes and Breeders' Cup Turf 2000)
- Shareef Dancer (Irish Derby 1983)
- King's Best (Two Thousand Guineas 2000)
- Marwell (King's Stand Stakes, July Cup and Prix de l'Abbaye 1981)
- Doyoun (Two Thousand Guineas 1988)
- Ajdal (July Cup, Nunthorpe Stakes and Sprint Cup 1987)
- Zilzal (Sussex Stakes and Queen Elizabeth II Stakes 1989)
- Musical Bliss (One Thousand Guineas 1989)
- Sonic Lady (Irish One Thousand Guineas, Coronation Stakes, Sussex Stakes and Prix du Moulin 1986)
- Unite (Oaks and Irish Oaks 1987)
- Golan (Two Thousand Guineas 2001)

Michael Stoute was the only trainer in the twentieth century to win a Classic in five successive seasons, scoring with Shadeed (Two Thousand Guineas 1985), Shahrastani (Derby 1986), Unite (Oaks 1987), Doyoun (Two Thousand Guineas 1988) and Musical Bliss (One Thousand Guineas 1989).

Golan was the tenth Classic winner trained by Michael Stoute, while horses like Opera House, Singspiel, Kalanisi and Pilsudski advertise one of his particular strengths: the ability to keep on improving certain horses as they get older. He modestly explains that it takes him a long time to get to know his horses, but whatever his secret, having such horses around at four, five or even six years of age has hugely enhanced the appeal of the Flat over the last decade. Michael Stoute, who was knighted for his services to tourism in his native Barbados in 1998, has been leading trainer on the Flat in Britain six times: 1981, 1986, 1989, 1994, 1997, 2000. He has also made his mark on the jumping code, training Sheikh Mohammed's grey Kribensis to win the Triumph Hurdle in 1988 and the Champion Hurdle in 1990.

STRATFORD-UPON-AVON

Luddington Road, Stratford-on-Avon, Warwickshire CV37 9SE
Tel.: 01789 267949
Fax: 01789 415850
E-mail: info@stratfordracecourse.net
Web: www.stratfordracecourse.net

Stratford racecourse is in the shape of a left-handed triangle, one and a quarter miles round and mostly flat, with tight bends which favour the handy horse over the galloping type. The straight is about two furlongs long and the run-in from the last fence under a furlong, so it is imperative for a horse to be in contention at the final bend.

In 1967 the Horse and Hound Cup was won by Cham, ridden by John Lawrence – now Lord Oaksey. They won by one and a half lengths from Royal Phoebe, ridden by a young amateur rider named Brough Scott.

Stratford has been the site of racing since the eighteenth century, and today the course stages sport of a fairly modest quality – though the Horse and Hound Cup retains its position as one of the year's most valuable and prestigious hunter-chases: its roll of honour includes the names of many of the great hunter-chasers, including triple winner Baulking Green (1962, 1963 and 1965) and quadruple winner Credit Call (1971, 1972, 1973 and 1975).

A new grandstand was opened in 1997.

STRESS FRACTURES

Stress fractures in the lower limb, particularly the **cannon bone**, are common in young horses, whose bones are not mature, and are often caused by repeated concussion of the limbs on a hard surface – hence the danger of running two-year-olds on firm going. (**Sore shins** in cannon bones are a form of stress fracture.) Older horses are considerably less prone to stress fractures as their bones are much harder.

STRIKE RATE

Term used, usually of a jockey or trainer, to express the ratio of winners to runners. **Tony McCoy**'s strike rate for the 2000–1 jumps season was 25 per cent: he had won 191 races from 775 rides.

STRINGHALT

A muscular condition manifested by the horse making a very exaggerated stride – or 'hyper-flexing' – with one or both of its hind legs. Stringhalt is usually most apparent in the walk, and may disappear in the faster paces. It will not necessarily affect how a horse will run.

STRIPE

Thin length of white hair down a brown, bay or black horse's nose.

ST SIMON

Trained by Matthew Dawson and bought by the Duke of Portland as a two-year-old for just 1,600 guineas, St Simon was one of the all-time giants of the Turf, despite never running in a Classic. He was unbeaten in nine races. In 1883 he won his first race as a two-year-old by six lengths and his second the following day; by the end of his juvenile career had won five out of five. As a three-year-old in 1884 St Simon had just four races, winning them all, including the Ascot Gold Cup by 20 lengths and the Goodwood Cup by the same distance, starting at 100–7 on. At stud, where he sired the winners of 571 races, St Simon became almost uncontrollable. When he was given a cat in his stable to calm him down, he hurled the creature against the wall of his box and killed it. He dropped dead in 1908, aged 27.

STUDS

The factories of the bloodstock business, with some 300 stud farms producing the 5,000 or so Thoroughbred foals born in Britain every year. They range from the huge establishments of the super-rich owner–breeders to working farms where the owner will keep a mare or two and breed for fun. Many studs do not stand stallions but house only mares.

See also **breeding; Coolmore Stud; Maktoum brothers; National Stud.**

SUN CHARIOT

Trained by **Fred Darling** at Beckhampton, Sun Chariot was bred at the **National Stud** (then in Ireland) and leased for her racing career to King George VI. She won all four of her races as a two-year-old (including the Middle Park Stakes), and on her first outing at three blotted her copybook by finishing third at Salisbury before getting back into the winning groove at the same course. Sun Chariot then won three Classics – all run at Newmarket's July Course on account of the Second World War – and was ridden in all three by **Gordon Richards**. She started at evens for the One Thousand Guineas and won by four lengths; won the Oaks despite veering off to the left as the tapes rose and giving her rivals a huge start; and won the St

Leger by three lengths from Derby winner Watling Street. Winner of eight of her nine races despite an increasingly volatile temperament, Sun Chariot was then retired: as a broodmare her best offspring was the Queen's colt Landau. She died in 1963, and is commemorated in the Sun Chariot Stakes, run at Newmarket in October.

SUNDAY RACING

The first race meeting on a Sunday under Jockey Club Rules in Great Britain took place at Doncaster on 26 July 1992. No cash betting could be allowed for that or the other experimental Sunday meetings over the next couple of years, but a change in the law allowed bookmakers to be legally in attendance at the Garth and South Berks Hunt point-to-point at Tweseldown on 15 January 1995, and the first Sunday race meeting under Rules with cash betting took place at Newmarket on 7 May 1995 (the day Harayir won the One Thousand Guineas). Following those tentative early moves Sunday racing become a regular feature of the summer, with 14 consecutive Sundays scheduled between 3 June and 2 September 2001 out of a total of 20 Sunday fixtures for the whole year.

SUPER HEINZ

Bet combining seven selections in 120 bets:

- 21 doubles
- 35 trebles
- 35 four-horse accumulators
- 21 five-horse accumulators
- 7 six-horse accumulators
- 1 seven-horse accumulator.

SUPER YANKEE

Bet combining five selections in 26 bets:

- 10 doubles
- 10 trebles
- 5 four-horse accumulators
- 1 five-horse accumulator

Also known as a 'Canadian'; see **Yankee**.

SUPPLEMENT

For some big races a horse who, for whatever reason, has not been entered at the initial **entry** stage can be 'supplemented' in return for a large fee. For example, a horse could be supplemented for the 2001 Derby up to a week before the race at a cost of £75,000.

SURCINGLE

Strap fitted over the top of the saddle and under the horse's belly, to complement the girth in keeping the saddle in place.

SUROOR, SAEED BIN

Born in 1967, Saeed bin Suroor took out his first training licence in Dubai in 1994 (having had an earlier career as a policeman), and in 1995 replaced Hilal Ibrahim as principal trainer for the **Godolphin** operation, overseeing the horses in Dubai during the winter and at its Newmarket base for the rest of the year. The few years since his appointment have seen a phenomenal number of big races credited to his name:

- each Classic in England at least once: Two Thousand Guineas with Mark Of Esteem (1996) and Island Sands (1999); One Thousand Guineas with Cape Verdi (1998); Derby with **Lammtarra** (1995); Oaks with Moonshell (1995); St Leger with Classic Cliché (1995), Nedawi (1998) and Mutafaweq (1999);
- King George VI and Queen Elizabeth Diamond Stakes four times in five years, with Lammtarra (1995), **Swain** (1997 and 1998) and **Daylami** (1999);
- Eclipse Stakes three times in four years with Halling (1995 and 1996) and Daylami (1998, when Godolphin and Saeed bin Suroor also had the second horse Faithful Son and the third Central Park);
- International Stakes in successive years with Halling (1995 and 1996);
- Irish Champion Stakes in successive years with Swain (1998) and Daylami (1999);
- Ascot Gold Cup three times in five years with Classic Cliché (1996) and Kayf Tara (1998 and 2000);

- Coronation Cup twice in three years with Daylami (1999) and Mutafaweq (2001);
- Breeders' Cup Turf with Daylami (1999);
- Dubai World Cup in successive years with Almutawakel (1999) and **Dubai Millennium** (2000).

Saeed bin Suroor was champion trainer in Britain in 1996, 1998 and 1999.

SUSSEX STAKES

Group One: three-year-olds and upwards:
1 mile (Goodwood)

The Sussex Stakes is the first Group One race of the Flat season in Britain where the best three-olds can face their elders over one mile. It was first run over one mile in 1878 (though Goodwood had staged a six-furlong two-year-old race named the Sussex Stakes since 1841), and confined to three-year-olds until 1959 (and to three- and four-year-olds from 1960 to 1974). Whatever the age range, it has invariably attracted a top-class field, and its roll of honour since the Second World War contains the cream of milers: Two Thousand Guineas winners My Babu (1948), Palestine (1950), **Brigadier Gerard** (1971), Bolkonski (1975) and Wollow (1976); One Thousand Guineas winners **Petite Etoile** (10–1 on when winning in 1959), Humble Duty (1970), On The House (1982) and Sayyedati (1995: she had won the Classic two years earlier); and other great milers like Romulus

(1962), Reform (1967), Kris (1979), Chief Singer (1984), Warning (1988) and Zilzal (1989). Marling won by a head from Selkirk in 1992 after a stirring duel, but no less memorable was the gutsy performance of **Giant's Causeway** to win by three-quarters of a length from Dansili in 2000.

SWAIN

A son of **Nashwan**, Swain posted a record of remarkable performances in big races all round the world. He was bred by **Sheikh Mohammed**, in whose colours he started his racing career in 1995 as a three-year-old trained in France by **André Fabre**, winning five in a row (including the Grand Prix de Deauville) before finishing third to **Lammtarra** in the Prix de l'Arc de Triomphe. The following year he won the Coronation Cup at Epsom and the Prix Foy at Longchamp and finished fourth behind Helissio in the Arc and third behind **Pilsudski** and **Singspiel** in the Breeders' Cup Turf. Relocated to the **Godolphin** team to be trained by **Saeed bin Suroor**, Swain won just once as a five-year-old in 1997, but this was a wonderful victory over Pilsudski, Helissio and Singspiel in the King George: ridden by John Reid, he started at 16–1 and at the line had a length to spare over Pilsudski. That year he ran a third time in the Arc, finishing seventh behind Peintre Celebre. The decision to keep Swain in training as a six-year-old in 1998 was well

Sussex Stakes winners since 1990

1990	Distant Relative	4	B. Hills	W. Carson	4–1	7
1991	Second Set	3	L. Cumani	L. Dettori	5–1	8
1992	Marling	3	G. Wragg	Pat Eddery	11–10F	8
1993	Bigstone	3	E. Lellouche *FRA*	D. Boeuf	14–1	10
1994	Distant View	3	H. Cecil	Pat Eddery	4–1	9
1995	Sayyedati	5	C. Brittain	B. Doyle	11–2	6
1996	First Island	4	G. Wragg	M. Hills	5–1	10
1997	Ali-Royal	4	H. Cecil	K. Fallon	13–2	9
1998	Among Men	4	M. Stoute	M. Kinane	4–1	10
1999	Aljabr	3	S. bin Suroor	L. Dettori	11–10F	8
2000	Giant's Causeway	3	A. O'Brien *IRE*	M. Kinane	3–1JF	10
2001	Noverre	3	S. bin Suroor	L. Dettori	9–2	10

rewarded. He started his campaign by running a stupendous race in the Dubai World Cup, beaten a short head by 1997 Kentucky Derby and Preakness winner Silver Charm after a memorable tussle. He was then runner-up to Silver Patriarch in the Coronation Cup and third in the Hardwicke Stakes at Royal Ascot before returning to Ascot to become only the second horse ever to land the King George twice – the first was Dahlia – and the oldest winner of the race. Ridden this time by **Frankie Dettori**, he won well from Derby winner High-Rise, Royal Anthem and his own stable companion **Daylami**. Next stop Leopardstown for a brilliant victory over Alborada and Xaar in the Irish Champion Stakes (Swain's first win over a mile and a quarter), and then it was off to the world's richest race that year, the Breeders' Cup Classic at Churchill Downs. It was asking a great deal of Swain to take on Silver Charm and the best dirt horses in North America, but he very nearly pulled it off, mounting a furious challenge up the home stretch until veering away from Frankie Dettori's whip inside the final furlong and finishing third behind Awesome Again and Silver Charm, beaten three-quarters of a length and a neck. The controversy that raged over Dettori's ride – should he have switched his whip to the other hand, or put it down as soon as the horse came off a straight line? – could not change the result, and Swain's wonderful career had ended with a defeat. That career had brought him eight wins from 20 races, and he retired to stud in Kentucky.

SWALLOWING THE TONGUE
See **soft palate disease**.

SWINBURN, WALTER
'That's it, lads – I'm finished!' With those words to fellow jockeys in the weighing room at Kempton Park on 22 April 2000, one of the great riding careers came to an end. Walter Swinburn was never one to go chasing around for jockeys' championships, but his record in the big races around the world was exceptional, and some of the horses he rode rank with the very highest: **Lammtarra**, Marwell,

All Along – and of course **Shergar**. Son of top Irish jockey Wally Swinburn (who won three Irish Classics and was champion jockey in Ireland in 1976 and 1977), Walter was born in Oxford on 7 August 1961. He was apprenticed to Frenchie Nicholson – father of David Nicholson and famous nurturer of young riding talent – and rode his first winner on Paddy's Luck at Kempton Park on 12 July 1978. In 1981 he joined trainer **Michael Stoute** and that June, at the age of 19, steered Shergar to his famous 10-length victory in the Derby. His Classic haul in England totalled eight: the Two Thousand Guineas on Doyoun in 1988; One Thousand Guineas on Musical Bliss in 1989, Hatoof in 1992 and Sayyedati 1993; Derby on Shergar in 1981, Shahrastani in 1986 (beating **Dancing Brave**) and Lammtarra in 1995; and Oaks on Unite in 1987 (he was also first past the post in 1989 on the Aga Khan's Aliysa, subsequently disqualified after failing the post-race dope test).

Walter also won the King George VI and Queen Elizabeth Diamond Stakes on Shergar (1981); Prix de l'Arc de Triomphe and Washington, DC International on All Along (1983); Eclipse Stakes on Ezzoud (1994) and Halling (1995); Ascot Gold Cup on Indian Queen (1991); Irish Derby on Shareef Dancer (1983) and Shahrastani (1986); International Stakes on Shardari (1986), Ezzoud (1993 and 1994) and Halling (1995); July Cup on Marwell (1981), Green Desert (1986) and Ajdal (1987); Champion Stakes on Hatoof (1993); Sussex Stakes on Sonic Lady (1986) and Zilzal (1989); and many more big races. But there was also a downside: in February 1996 a horrendous fall from a two-year-old filly in Hong Kong caused him multiple injuries, from which he made a remarkable recovery to end that year with one of his greatest triumphs, on **Pilsudski** in the Breeders' Cup Turf at Woodbine. His last winner was Sir Francis at Brighton on 13 April 2000, and he joined the Channel Four Racing team soon after retiring from the saddle. He rode 1,391 winners in Britain.

SYNDICATION
The dividing of the ownership of a stallion

into shares. **Shergar**, for example, was syndicated in 40 shares at £250,000 per share – a valuation of £10 million: his owner the Aga Khan kept six shares, while the remaining 34 were sold to other breeders.

SYSTEMS (BETTING)

Betting systems provide a sort of template for your punting, a framework that dictates how and when you put your money on. Not many people bet only according to a system, but most regular punters have a few schemes they like to bear in mind, from supposedly logical notions such as backing the top weight in a nursery (a handicap for two-year-olds), on the basis that it is demonstrably the best horse in the race, to wholly illogical ones such as betting on greys or on a horse whose racecard number coincides with the date of Granny's birthday. Among the most regularly followed systems are:

- backing favourites (around a third of all races are won by the market leader, but you won't make a profit out of backing them blindly);
- blindly backing horses ridden by a particular jockey (sometimes it works, sometimes it doesn't; had you staked £1 on every one of champion jockey Kevin Darley's 997 rides during the 2000 Flat season you would have backed 155 winners, but ended the year £209.83 down);
- backing particular trainers at particular courses – e.g. Martin Pipe at any of the West Country tracks.

In the *Channel Four Racing Guide to Form and Betting*, Big Mac shared some of insights about betting systems:

If there were a system that worked, everyone would have twigged by now. But it does no harm to have a few which might throw up the odd winner, and these are the ones I would recommend:

- *Back the horse that won the same race last year. Many of the relevant factors – type of race, course, distance, time of year – are in its favour.*

- *Back horses blinkered or visored for the first time.*
- *Back the outsider of three. There's more logic to this than might be apparent at first, as races with very small fields are often run at a false pace, making a less predictable result more likely, and when punters concentrate on the first two in the betting there may be value to be had from the outsider.*
- *If a top jockey is riding at his absolute minimum weight, back his horse. He wouldn't have given up even his meagre breakfast if the creature had no chance!*
- *In handicaps, restrict yourself to horses running off their old mark when their new rating will be higher. They are clearly improving, and should be caught before their official reassessment is dictating the weight they carry.*
- *In amateur and apprentice races, go for the most experienced and best jockey, whatever he or she is riding.*
- *Consider the effect of the draw sensibly. If a race is run on extremes of going and the draw has a marked effect, concentrate on the favoured side for all bets, including forecasts.*
- *When studying a maiden race, find out whether any of the runners are engaged in big races later in the season: those that are must be highly rated by connections.*
- *Back the animal whose stable has sent it the longest distance for the race.*
- *If a stable has more than one runner in a race, go for the outsider. They won't come in too often, but when they do rewards can be great.*
- *Totally illogically, support horses with the same initials in forecasts.*
- *And, just as bad, go for any horse whose racecard number is the same as its starting stall position.*

But never get hooked on a system. It removes the flexibility – and a lot of the fun – from your punting. And whatever you do, don't forget that telegram wired home by the roulette player: 'System working well – send more money!'

T

TAAFFE, PAT

Son of trainer Tom Taaffe (who won the 1958 Grand National with Mr What), Pat Taaffe was born in Rathcoole, Co. Dublin, in 1930. He rode his first point-to-point winner while still a schoolboy, then became an amateur jockey, notching up his first winner under Rules on Ballincorona at Phoenix Park on Easter Saturday 1946. He joined trainer **Tom Dreaper** in 1949, and their partnership became a legend of jump racing: together they won the Cheltenham Gold Cup three times with the immortal **Arkle** (1964–6) and a fourth time with Fort Leney in 1968. Other famous victories on Arkle included the 1964 and 1965 Hennessy Gold Cups, 1965 King George VI Chase, 1965 Whitbread Gold Cup and 1965 Gallaher Gold Cup: in all he rode the greatest of all chasers to 24 of his 27 career victories, including all his 22 steeplechase wins. But ironically neither of his Grand National winners was trained by Dreaper: he won on Quare Times in 1955 for **Vincent O'Brien** and on Gay Trip in 1970 for **Fred Rimell** (after Rimell's stable jockey Terry Biddlecombe had been injured). Taaffe won the Irish Grand National six times (including on Arkle in 1964 and **Flyingbolt** in 1966) and a host of other big races. He was champion jockey in Ireland in 1952 and 1953, and his total of 25 winners at the Cheltenham National Hunt Festival remains a record. He retired from the saddle in 1970 to take up training, and his new career produced one exceptional horse: **Captain Christy** won the King George VI Chase twice (1974 and 1975) and the 1974 Cheltenham Gold Cup, making Taaffe only the second man to have both ridden and trained a Gold Cup winner. (Danny Morgan had ridden the winner Morse Code in 1938 and trained winner Roddy Owen in 1959, and the feat was matched in 1978 by **Fred Winter**.) Pat Taaffe was not the most stylish rider ever seen over fences, but he was one of the most effective, and widely acknowledged to be the complete horseman in a golden age of jump jockeys. The church for the memorial mass at Kill, Co. Kildare, following his death on 7 July 1992, was packed to hear the priest quote Ted Walsh's tribute to one of the all-time great Irish horsemen: 'As gentle as a lamb off a horse, a lion in the saddle.'

TABOR, MICHAEL

Born in east London, where his later business interests included bookmaking, Michael Tabor started owning horses in the 1970s – on a comparatively modest scale until the 1990s, when his activities expanded to the extent that his colours (royal blue, orange disc, orange and royal blue striped sleeves and cap) became one of the most familiar sets of silks on the world racing stage. He won the Kentucky Derby and Belmont Stakes in 1995 with Thunder Gulch, and his first Classic winner in England came with Entrepreneur in the 1997 Two Thousand Guineas. But the best horse to have raced in his colours has been **Montjeu**, winner of the 1999 Prix de l'Arc de Triomphe and 2000 King George. Tabor's influence, however, stretches well beyond horses carrying his own colours: he is closely involved with the group of owner-breeders who operate from the **Coolmore Stud** in Co. Tipperary, and many of the big winners achieving big-race success in the colours of Mrs Susan Magnier (such as **Giant's Causeway,** 1998 Two Thousand Guineas winner King Of Kings or 2001 Oaks heroine Imagine and Derby hero **Galileo**) are part-owned by Tabor.

TAILED OFF

A horse well behind the rest of the field is described as being 'tailed off'.

TAKE, YUTAKA

Yutaka Take was born in 1969, son of trainer Kunihiko Take, and rode his first winner on Dyna Bidhop at Tokyo on 7 March 1987. By the end of 2000 he had ridden some 1,900 domestic winners, been champion jockey in Japan 11 times, and established himself as a true sporting superstar. Since moving more towards the centre of the international racing stage he has established the happy knack of winning on his first ride at big racecourses: at Newmarket (where he won the 2000 July Cup on Agnes World, the first Japanese jockey to win a Group One race in Britain), at Nad Al Sheba in Dubai (where he won the Dubai Sheema Classic on Stay Gold by a nose from Fantastic Light in March 2001), at Deauville and at Saint-Cloud. In June 2000 he transferred his base from Japan to California, and in 2001 moved to join trainer John Hammond at Chantilly.

TATTERSALLS (1)

Terrace House, Newmarket, Suffolk CB8 9BT
Tel.: 01638 665931
Fax: 01638 660850
Web: www.tattersalls.com

Founded in 1766 by Richard Tattersall, Tattersalls is the leading bloodstock auction company in Britain and the largest in Europe, also staging sales through its Irish offshoot at Fairyhouse. Approximately 17 sales a year see some 10,000 horses – foals, yearlings, horses in training, broodmares, etc. – going through the sale ring, but the biggest occasion of the Tattersalls year is the Houghton Yearling Sale at Newmarket in October: at this sale in 2000 the average price of the 141 yearlings sold was 233,886 guineas, and the most expensive lot, a colt by **Sadler's Wells** out of Darara, went for 3.4 million guineas. In all Tattersalls sold over £137 million worth of horseflesh in 2000.

TATTERSALLS (2)

The public enclosure at a racecourse where the betting ring is located – popularly abbreviated to 'Tatts'. (The name derives from the days when betting was carried on at Subscription Rooms in London founded by Richard Tattersall; *see* **Tattersalls (1)**.)

TATTERSALLS RULES

The Tattersalls Committee is the organisation which lays down the rules concerning betting (of which the best known to the day-to-day punter is **Rule 4**).

TAUNTON

Orchard Portman, Taunton, Somerset TA3 7BL
Tel.: 01823 337172
Fax: 01823 325881

With its notoriously tight bends, which until recent cambering work improved them could become very slippery in wet conditions, Taunton is not universally popular among jockeys. But as another of those staunchly unpretentious tracks catering to a strong and enthusiastic base of local support, it forms an integral part of the West Country jumping scene.

Taunton stages races over four miles two and a half furlongs, the longest distance in the calendar apart from the four and a half miles of the Grand National.

The right-handed circuit is sausage-shaped, with a run-in from the last fence of just 150 yards. The water jump is just beyond the stands, which denies spectators the full benefit of the spectacle which these obstacles are assumed to offer, but generally the viewing here is good. National Hunt racing at the present course began in 1927, though there had been racing in the town of Taunton as early as 1802.

TAX

The first introduction of betting tax to Britain by Chancellor of the Exchequer Winston Churchill in 1926 caused a strike of bookmakers at Windsor racecourse, and lasted no longer than 1929. It was in October 1966 that betting tax returned, brought in by Chancellor James Callaghan, and ever since then tax, and the calculation of its effect on winnings, has been the bane of the off-course punter. The niceties of how the tax is calculated are irrelevant to the punter adding 9 per cent to his stake or deducting it from his returns – and in any case a more enlightened Chancellor has now come along in the shape of Gordon Brown, who announced in his March 2001 Budget that betting duty would be abolished from 1 January 2002 – and bookmakers expected to be betting tax-free from October 2001.

TBA
See **Thoroughbred Breeders Association**.

TEASER
At a stud, the teaser is the (usually sterile) stallion used to check that the mare about to be covered is ready for what awaits her. He flirts with the mare across a 'trying board' over which they are introduced, and when the handlers are happy that the mare is responsive to male attention, the poor teaser is led off while the mare is covered by the stallion with which she is being mated. (The point of this is to avoid the risk of injury and inconvenience to the covering stallion should the mare not be ready.) Occasionally the teaser gets a piece of the action for himself. In 1986 the broodmare Branitska, due to be covered by Wolver Heights at the Stetchworth Stud in Newmarket, declined to cooperate. 'Branitska just would not take to Wolver Heights at all,' recalled stud owner Bill Gredley, 'and kicked him like mad. In the end we brought the teaser forward, and because she stood still for him we thought, "Why not?"' The offspring, well named Call To Arms, was beaten a neck at 66–1 in the 1989 Dewhurst Stakes.

TELEVISION, RACING ON
Horse racing is the most televised sport on terrestrial television in Britain: cumulative domestic terrestrial audiences are approximately 400 million – 450 million when Sky and the **Racing Channel** are added to the calculation – and some ten million watch the Grand National. The history of televised racing goes back to 1931, when John Logie Baird experimented with transmitting the Derby, four years after the Derby and Grand National had first been broadcast on radio in 1927. In 1932 the Epsom victory of April The Fifth was broadcast to an audience at the Metropole Cinema in Victoria, London. Live televising of racing to domestic receivers commenced tentatively in 1946, and when the independent television network began in 1955 coverage increased, culminating in the 'ITV Seven', in which seven races from two courses were shown each Saturday afternoon. The ITV coverage shifted to Channel Four in 1984, while the BBC has maintained its presence at some of the big occasions – notably the Grand National, Royal Ascot and Goodwood – and from 2001 has resumed broadcasting the Derby, which it left to the independent network after 1979. Sky Television began its coverage of evening racing in 1993, and the Racing Channel has been broadcasting to subscribers since 1995. After a sometimes acrimonious period of negotiation, the future of televised racing – on both terrestrial and non-terrestrial channels – was finally settled in June 2001, when 49 of Britain's 59 racecourses signed a £307 million deal for their media rights with Go Racing (to be renamed Attheraces), a consortium formed by **Channel Four**, Arena Leisure and Sky.

TEMPERAMENT
Thoroughbreds tend to be much more highly strung, nervous and sometimes downright perverse than breeds designed for less hectic forms of work, and their temperamental quirks can be the bane of the punter's life. A horse can effectively throw away his chance in a race by 'boiling over' – getting himself worked up into a lather of nervous agitation – during the preliminaries. The history of racing is peppered with instances of good horses whose athletic ability is at odds with their temperament, and occasionally a volatile nature gets the upper hand. Remember that great sprinter Lochsong. Her explosive manner of running – riding her was 'like a surfer hitting a good wave', said Frankie Dettori – endeared her to the racing public, but part of that explosiveness was a tempera-

ment geared to going as fast as she could. The same temperament got the better of her at York in August 1994 before the Nunthorpe Stakes, when she became very worked up in the parade ring, was almost uncontrollable on the way to the start, and then, having sacrificed all her energy to her nerves, ran a terrible race. Some horses 'plant' – that is, refuse to move when called upon to do so – which can be disastrous at the start of a race. The extremely high-mettled Lammtarra had a habit of doing this out on the gallops. And do you remember that exasperating chaser Vodkatini, a brilliant chaser when he put his mind to it, but as often as not a surly character who would just dig in his heels and refuse to set off? Yet the 'Iron Horse' himself, Giant's Causeway, who won five Group One races in a row in 2000 and battled like a lion in every one, was occasionally fractious at the starting stalls, and no one doubted *his* honesty.

Some horses try to pull themselves up in a race when they feel that enough is enough: remember Derring Rose or Riverside Boy? Some try to bite their opponents during a race: remember Arcadian Heights and Marinsky? (If not, *see* **muzzle**.) Other notoriously mean and moody horses include the great chaser **Flyingbolt** – 'He would eat you as soon as look at you' was the consensus regarding his sour temperament from those in Tom Dreaper's yard with the bruises to support their view. And Celtic Shot, winner of the Champion Hurdle in 1988, had little time for that nonsense about other animals providing a calming influence. Turned out in a field, he amused himself by picking any available sheep up in his teeth and savaging it. Those sheep would not take much persuading that the Thoroughbred temperament can exact a heavy cost. Yet that very spirit is an essential part of the make-up of the racehorse – the 'high-mettled racer'. And plenty of great racehorses have had a temperament, both at home and on the track, to match their status: the peerless **Arkle** was serene, gentle, and kind to children.

Temperament in a racehorse is hereditary, passed on through the genes, with the result that certain sires are noted for producing horses with questionable temperament: the great Italian horse **Ribot**, for instance, imprinted too many of his stock with dubious temperamental characteristics.

TENDON STRAIN
See **breaking down**.

T.H.
In betting slang, 8–1.

THE DIKLER
John Oaksey's description of The Dikler as 'a constant source of entertainment, excitement, inspiration and occasionally exasperation to the jumping world' could not be bettered: this imposing white-faced gelding trained by Fulke Walwyn attracted a devoted following through his racing exploits and his tearaway style of going about his business, but occasionally showed signs of having a mind of his own – such as the occasion at Ascot in 1976 when he showed new jockey Bill Smith who was boss by planting himself at the start and refusing to race. But when he was good he was very very good.

After making his name in the point-to-point field The Dikler (named after a stream in Gloucestershire) won 14 of his 53 races under Rules, including the Cheltenham Gold Cup in 1973 (when, ridden by Ron Barry, he snatched the race from hot favourite **Pendil** right on the post to win by a short head), the 1971 King George VI Chase (from Spanish Steps, Titus Oates and **L'Escargot**) and, controversially, the 1974 Whitbread Gold Cup, which he was awarded in the stewards' room after Proud Tarquin, ridden by John Oaksey, was judged to have interfered with him on the run-in. (The Dikler ran in seven consecutive Cheltenham Gold Cups: 1970 (fell behind L'Escargot); 1971 (third to L'Escargot); 1972 (third to Glencaraig Lady); 1973 (won from Pendil); 1974 (second to **Captain Christy**); 1975 (pulled up behind Ten Up); 1976 (eighth behind Royal Frolic).)

The Dikler ran twice in the Grand National: fifth behind L'Escargot in 1975 and sixth behind Rag Trade the following year, at the grand old age of 13. On his retirement The

Dikler, notoriously headstrong when racing, found a new career in the controlled discipline of three-day eventing, excelling at the dressage stage. A great horse and a great character, he was put down in 1984 at the age of 21.

THE FLYING DUTCHMAN

Though he won the Derby and St Leger in 1849 and the Ascot Gold Cup in 1850, The Flying Dutchman is best remembered for the famous match race against 1850 Derby and St Leger winner **Voltigeur** at York in the spring of 1851. In front of a crowd of over 100,000 he had to concede $8^{1}/_{2}$ lb to the other horse, a year younger, and started marginally favourite for the two-mile contest. Voltigeur set the pace but could never properly shrug off his rival, and inside the final hundred yards The Flying Dutchman forged past for a hard-earned victory by just under a length.

THE TETRARCH

Nicknamed 'The Spotted Wonder' on account of his blotchy grey colour, The Tetrarch ran only as a two-year-old in 1913, but he did enough in his one season racing to prove himself one of the fastest racehorses ever seen in Britain. Bred in Ireland and trained at Stockbridge by Atty Persse, he first saw a racecourse at the Newmarket Craven Meeting in spring 1913, winning a maiden race by four lengths in a canter. He then won the Woodcote Stakes at Epsom, the Coventry Stakes at Royal Ascot (by 10 lengths), the National Produce Stakes at Sandown Park (by a mere neck, having been hampered at the start and losing a great deal of ground), the Rous Memorial Stakes at Goodwood, the Champion Breeders' Foal Stakes at Derby and the Champagne Stakes at Doncaster. Plans for a three-year-old career were thwarted by injury and he was retired to stud in Co. Kilkenny. His pronounced lack of interest in sex was not helpful in his new career, but he did get three St Leger winners and the brilliantly fast sprinters Tetratema and Mumtaz Mahal. The Tetrarch died in 1935 at the age of 24, and in his old age part of his daily routine was to be ridden to the local post office with the letters. **Steve Donoghue**, who rode The Tetrarch in all his races, described him as 'the nearest thing to a bullet in animal shape that I ever met'.

THICK 'UN

Betting slang for a large bet.

THINKER

Beware if the horse you fancy has been described 'a thinker': the term suggests that he has his own ideas about racing, and will put his best hoof forward only if he chooses to.

(The term is not to be confused with the horse The Thinker, who won the Cheltenham Gold Cup in 1987 and was considered completely genuine.)

THIRSK

Station Road, Thirsk, North Yorkshire YO7 1QL
Tel.: 01845 522276
Fax: 01845 525353
E-mail: info@thirskraces.fsnet.co.uk
Web: www.thirskracecourse.net

Racing has taken place at Thirsk since 1855, and although it may not be one of the major Flat venues, it is such a good test of a young racehorse that the course regularly forms the target of a raid from one of the major trainers based in the south: runners from John Dunlop's stable in Arundel, nearly 300 miles away, have a good strike rate here, and most Thirsk racecards include a fair number of runners from Newmarket, 185 miles distant.

Professional punter Paul Cooper took lucrative advantage of the effect of the Thirsk draw in the Dick Peacock Sprint Trophy over six furlongs on 20 May 1989. Aware that high numbers were favoured in sprints here, he permed high-drawn horses in Tricasts. There were twenty-three runners, and the result was:

1 Miss Daisy (drawn 21) at 20–1
2 Halvoya (drawn 23) at 25–1
3 Roysia Boy (drawn 22) at 33–1

The Tricast paid £13,673.17 to a £1 unit, and Cooper won around a quarter of a million pounds.

A left-handed oval a little over a mile and a quarter round, with minor undulations in the straight but otherwise pretty flat, Thirsk is on the sharp side but essentially a very fair course. Although its most valuable race is traditionally the Thirsk Hunt Cup run in May, the course also stages a significant Classic Trial at the April meeting. In 1972 High Top won the equivalent race with the filly Waterloo third, and two weeks later High Top won the Two Thousand Guineas and Waterloo the One Thousand. Tap On Wood won the race in 1979 en route to beating Kris and Young Generation in the Two Thousand Guineas.

The St Leger was transferred from Doncaster to Thirsk (and renamed the Yorkshire St Leger) for the 1940 running on account of the war.

THOMAS PINK GOLD CUP

Grade Three handicap steeplechase; five-year-olds and upwards; 2 miles 4½ furlongs (Cheltenham)

A race by any other name . . . the Thomas Pink Gold Cup, first sponsored by the shirt-making company in 2000, is the old Mackeson Gold Cup in a new guise, having been run as the Murphy's Gold Cup between 1996 and 1999 – but whatever the name, this remains the first big steeplechase of the new season, the moment when jumping really comes into its own. The Mackeson Gold Cup was one of the pioneers of sponsored jump races, first run in 1960 (over two miles until the distance was increased in 1967) and thus the third of the big drink-sponsored chases, after the Whitbread and Hennessy Gold Cups (both first run in 1957). Those early days saw the Mackeson go to some of the great two-milers, including Fortria (1960 and 1962) and Dunkirk (1965, carrying 12st 7lb). Gay Trip won the 1969 Mackeson and in 1970 landed the Grand National over a distance two miles further. Other notable names on the roll of honour include dual winners Half Free (1984 and 1985) and Bradbury Star (1993 and 1994); Bachelor's Hall, who won the Mackeson in 1977 and within six weeks had added the Hennessy and King George VI Chase; Pegwell Bay (1988) and Senor El Betrutti (1997), the only two horses to have won this and the similar race at Cheltenham's December meeting (now the Tripleprint Gold Cup) in the same year; and the hugely popular Dublin Flyer (1995).

THOROUGHBRED BREEDERS' ASSOCIATION

Stanstead House, The Avenue, Newmarket,
  Suffolk CB8 9AA
Tel.: 01638 661321
Fax: 01638 665621
E-mail: info@tbassoc.demon.co.uk

Usually known by its initials TBA, this is the trade association representing racehorse breeders in Britain.

Thomas Pink Gold Cup winners since 1990

Year	Winner	Age	Trainer	Jockey	SP	Ran
1990	Multum In Parvo	7	J. Edwards	N. Williamson	12–1	13
1991	Another Coral	8	D. Nicholson	R. Dunwoody	15–2	15
1992	Tipping Tim	7	N. Twiston-Davies	C. Llewellyn	11–2F	16
1993	Bradbury Star	8	J. Gifford	D. Murphy	13–2	15
1994	Bradbury Star	9	J. Gifford	P. Hide	5–1	14
1995	Dublin Flyer	9	T. Forster	B. Powell	4–1JF	12
1996	Challenger du Luc	6	M. Pipe	R. Dunwoody	7–1	12
1997	Senor El Betrutti	8	Mrs S. Nock	J. Osborne	33–1	9
1998	Cyfor Malta	5	M. Pipe	A. McCoy	3–1F	12
1999	The Outback Way	9	Miss V. Williams	N. Williamson	9–1	14
2000	Lady Cricket	6	M. Pipe	A. McCoy	5–1F	15

THOROUGHBRED CORPORATION

The racing operation of Prince Ahmed Salman (younger brother of **Fahd Salman** and nephew of **Khalid Abdullah**) races on a worldwide scale. To date the best horses to carry the familiar light green and white colours are 2001 Preakness and Belmont Stakes winner Point Given, 1999 Derby winner Oath, Dr Fong (St James's Palace Stakes 1998), Royal Anthem (Canadian International 1998, International Stakes 1999), Sharp Cat, Anees (Breeders' Cup Juvenile 1999), and Spain (Breeders' Cup Distaff 2000). The Thoroughbred Corporation, whose racing manager in Britain is former champion jockey **Willie Carson**, has around 100 horses in training and 30 broodmares around the world.

THOROUGHBRED REHABILITATION CENTRE

Poplar Grove Farm, Nateby, near Preston,
  Lancashire PR3 0LL
Tel.: 01995 605007
Fax: 01995 605006
E-mail: thoroughbredrehabilitationcentre
  @btopenworld.com
Web: www.equine-world.co.uk/trc

The Thoroughbred Rehabilitation Centre is a charity devoted solely to the welfare and rehabilitation of former racehorses. It was founded in 1991 by Carrie Humble, who had become concerned about the fate of racehorses once their competitive career was over: 'Some of the fortunate ones go on to a new life where they are lucky enough to find a home with knowledgeable horse-loving people. A few make stallions or broodmares if they're good enough to breed from. But what about the rest? Those no-hopers or youngsters who never made it to the top – what about them? A life of misery? An endless life of salerooms? An early death? It struck me that this was a miserable waste of good animals. With the right approach and schooling, many could have a fresh start and continue to bring pleasure and fulfil a very useful role for many years to come.' The TRC's most famous inmate – and only permanent resident – has been 1984 Grand National winner Hallo Dandy, who had fallen on hard times and became the charity's flag-bearer. Patrons of the TRC include Sir Peter O'Sullevan, Frankie Dettori and John Oaksey.

THREE-PARTS BROTHERS (OR SISTERS)

Two colts who share a dam and a paternal grandsire are known as three-parts brothers. For example: Commander Collins, winner of the Racing Post Trophy in 1998, is a three-parts brother to Colonel Collins, third in both Two Thousand Guineas and Derby in 1994. They share the dam Kanmary and each is by a son of Northern Dancer – El Gran Senor in the case of Colonel Collins, Sadler's Wells in the case of Commander Collins.

THUMB, WITH THE

In betting slang, 'with the thumb' means the price is being taken, and likely to shorten.

THURLES

Thurles, Co. Tipperary
Tel.: 0504 22253 (racedays 0504 23272)
Fax: 0504 23245
E-mail: thurles@iol.ie

There has been racing in the Thurles area since the mid-eighteenth century. The current track is a right-handed oval of about one and a quarter miles, quite undulating in nature, with the final stretch uphill. Main race here is the Kinloch Brae Chase over two and a half miles, run in late January or early February.

TIC-TAC

Sign language of the betting ring, by which course bookmakers communicate information and transmit bets. The term also refers to an individual purveyor of this arcane activity.

TIE-BACK

See **whistling and roaring**.

TIME CHARTER

Owned by Robert Barnett and trained by Henry Candy, Time Charter was one of the most popular fillies of the mid-1980s. She won two of her five races as a two-year-old in 1981, and in 1982 developed into a top-class staying filly, running second to On The House in the One Thousand Guineas and winning four races, including the Oaks (by a length from Slightly Dangerous), the Sun Chariot Stakes (by three-quarters of a length from Stanerra) and the Champion Stakes (by seven lengths from Prima Voce). As a four-year-old she was even better, winning the King George VI and Queen Elizabeth Diamond Stakes from Diamond Shoal and the Prix Foy from All Along – to whom she was fourth in that year's Arc, beaten little more than a length. Time Charter remained in training at five, taking the 1984 Coronation Cup in a canter from Sun Princess but failing to win again: she was beaten a neck by **Sadler's Wells** in the Eclipse, ran fourth behind Teenoso in the King George, and ended her career running down the field behind Sagace in the Arc, after suffering an interrupted preparation. In all she won nine of her 20 races, including Group One races in three separate seasons.

TIMEFORM

Timeform House, Northgate, Halifax,
  Yorkshire HX1 1XE
Tel.: 01422 330330
Fax: 01422 398017
E-mail: timeform@timeform.com
Web: www.timeform.com

The largest company in the world devoted to the publication of form, Timeform was founded by the late **Phil Bull**, whose strictly logical approach to the business of betting on racehorses transformed the nature of the battlefield on which punter takes on bookmaker. Timeform produces a wide variety of publications, notably the annuals *Racehorses* (which lists and discusses every runner on the Flat) and *Chasers and Hurdlers* (for jumpers); the daily Timeform Racecard, which provides detailed runner-by-runner analysis of every race at every meeting, and rates the chances of each horse according to Timeform's own ratings; the weekly *Black Book*, with up-to-date commentaries and ratings; and *Timeform Perspective*, which includes the result of every race run in Britain and Ireland and major races overseas and focuses on pointers for the future. Timeform also provides services by telephone and on-line.

TIMEFORM SQUIGGLE

Timeform's rating for a horse is sometimes accompanied by a printer's mark indicating some aspect of that horse's make-up beyond the basic level of form. The most notable of these is the '§' sign – popularly known as the 'Timeform squiggle' – which indicates a horse considered 'unreliable (for temperamental or other reasons)'. A horse completely beyond the pale could be awarded the double squiggle – §§ – which denotes a horse 'so temperamentally unsatisfactory as to be not worth a rating'. The famous loser **Amrullah** was awarded the double squiggle for both chases and hurdles.

TINGLE CREEK

The sight of Tingle Creek standing off the Railway Fences at Sandown Park was enough to warm the cockles of the coldest winter day, and this white-faced chestnut had a huge following throughout a career that saw him win 23 of his 52 races in Britain and Ireland, and never fall. Trained at Newmarket by Harry Thomson Jones, Tingle Creek was bred in the USA and first raced in Britain in 1972. A wonderfully flamboyant jumper who attacked his fences with a truly breathtaking gusto, he was in his element at Sandown Park and won the Sandown Pattern Chase – now named the Tingle Creek Chase in his honour – three times, on each occasion setting a new course record. He ran in the Two Mile Champion Chase four times, but Cheltenham was not his ideal course and the best he could manage in the two-mile championship was runner-up to Royal Relief in 1974. After winning the Pattern Chase in November 1978 he was retired, taking on a new role as a schoolmaster for Tom Jones's two-year-olds. Tingle Creek died in October 1996 at the age of 30.

TIPPERARY

Limerick Junction, Co. Tipperary
Tel.: 062 51357
Fax: 062 51303

Opened in 1916 and named Limerick Junction until 1986, Tipperary is a flat left-handed course ten furlongs round, with a straight five-furlong chute. The course has Ireland's only Group race run outside The Curragh or Leopardstown – the Coolmore Concorde Stakes (Group Three) – but also stages some top-class jumping, notably the John James McManus Memorial Hurdle run over two miles in October. The race was founded in 1997 by **J. P. McManus** in honour of his late father, and J.P.'s legendary hurdler **Istabraq** appropriately won the first three runnings. In 1997 he beat Cockney Lad; in 1998, when the race was transferred to Cork as Tipperary was waterlogged, he beat Master Beveled; and in 1999, back at Tipperary, he sauntered away from Limestone Lad.

TIPS
In betting slang, 11–10 (from the **tic-tac** sign).

TISSUE
Racecourse bookmakers' forecast of how the betting will open, prepared by a form expert employed by the bookies.

TM OPERA O
When the four-year-old colt TM Opera O, trained in Japan by Ichizo Iwamoto, won the 2000 Japan Cup, he took his lifetime earnings to the dollar equivalent of $12,677,309, beating the previous record held by **Cigar**, who had accumulated just short of $10 million. In all TM Opera O won eight races from eight outings in 2000, five of them at Group One level.

TON
Betting slang for £100.

TONGUESTRAP
During a race a horse under pressure might 'swallow its tongue'. To prevent this the trainer will sometimes fit a tonguestrap to keep the tongue in a forward position and prevent its being swallowed. The fitting of a tonguestrap must be notified at the time of declaration for the race, and will be indicated in the racecard in the morning paper by 't'.

TOP OF THE HEAD
In betting slang, 9–4 (from the **tic-tac** sign).

TOTE
Horserace Totalisator Board, Tote House, 74 Upper Richmond Road, London SW15 2SU
Tel.: 020 8874 6411
Fax: 020 8874 6107
E-mail: info@tote.co.uk
Web: www.tote.co.uk

The Tote, introduced to Britain in 1929, operates on a very simple principle. All the money bet on all the horses in a race goes into a pool. Following the race, this pool is shared out among all those who have placed winning bets, after deductions have been made to cover running costs, including contributions to racecourses and to the Betting Levy. So the essence of betting with the Tote is that the punter is betting against fellow punters rather than against a bookmaker. Odds fluctuate according to the pattern of betting, and there are separate pools for the different sorts of bet. A simple example will show how this works.

Say the Win pool for a race consists of £10,000, of which one thousand £1 bets have been staked on the horse which wins:

pool	£10,000
deduction	£1,600
payout	£8,400
dividend	£8.40 per £1 ticket

The dividend (or 'Tote return') is declared to a £1 unit and includes the stake, so the actual winnings in the above example are £7.40, odds equivalent of 7.4–1. All the other pools operate in the same way as the Win pool.

Tote screens at racecourses (and in those betting shops where you can have a direct Tote bet) will show you approximate Tote odds as the betting takes place before a race, but you cannot know exactly what the dividend will be until after the race, and this is the crucial difference between betting with the Tote and with a bookmaker: with a bookmaker you bet either at **starting price** or at the price which he quotes you or has displayed, and your bet remains at that price regardless of how many other people place bets after you, and at what odds; with the Tote you will not know when you make the bet precisely what the return will be, as it will be affected by all the people who place their bets after you. Off course you have even less chance of seeing the likely return: it is not possible for the television viewer to know how the Tote odds are looking just before the race, and some off-course betting shops do not bet at Tote odds. Because Tote and bookies operate on different principles, their odds usually differ; but neither side is consistently favoured by the discrepancy.

The Tote (currently state-owned, though privatisation is in prospect) is a prominent presence as a race sponsor – notably of the Cheltenham Gold Cup, Chester Cup, Ebor Handicap, Cambridgeshire and Cesarewitch, Becher Chase, Tote Gold Trophy (formerly the Schweppes), Tote Northern National (formerly the Eider Chase) and – from 2001 – the Ayr Gold Cup. In all the Tote provides well over £2 million a year in race sponsorship, and its profits go back into racing.

The Tote is divided into four parts. The Tote Credit Club has offices on all racecourses in Britain and a telephone betting centre in Wigan for the use of its 50,000 members; the Tote Racecourse Division oversees Tote windows on all courses; Tote Bookmakers operates betting shops throughout the country; and Tote Direct, whereby some off-course bookmakers provide terminals taking Tote bets, the stakes being transmitted to the racecourse pools.

Tote bets are:

- *Win*: Bet on one horse to come first. (The record win dividend was £341 2s 6d to a two-shilling stake on Coole at Haydock Park on 30 November 1929: the Tote odds of over 3,410–1 compared with a starting price of 100–8: just over 12–1.)
- *Place*: Bet on a horse to be placed: first or second in races of five, six or seven runners; first, second or third in races of eight runners or more; first, second, third or fourth in handicaps of 16 runners or more. (The record place dividend was £67.32 to 10p on Strip Fast (started 66–1), second in an apprentice race at Nottingham on 31 October 1978.)
- *Exacta*: In races of three or more runners, pick two horses to finish first and second in the correct order.

- *Trifecta*: Pick the first three home in the designated race in correct order. (*See separate entry.*)
- *Jackpot*: Pick the winners of the first six races at the designated Jackpot meeting. If there is no winner the pool is carried forward to the next Jackpot meeting. (Record Jackpot dividend was £273,365.80 to £1 at Newmarket on 2 October 1993.)
- *Placepot*: Pick horses to be placed in the first six races (or, for any race with fewer than five runners, to win). The Placepot operates at all meetings. (Record Placepot dividend was declared at Newbury on 16 May 1998: £41,255.80 to a £1 stake.)
- *Quadpot*: Pick horses to be placed in the final four legs of the Placepot. (Record Quadpot dividend was £2,119.30 to £1 at Ascot on 15 June 1994.)
- *Tote Multibet*: Double, treble, accumulator, Patent, Yankee etc.
- **Scoop6**: *see separate entry.*

TOTE GOLD TROPHY

Grade Three handicap hurdle; four-year-olds and upwards; 2 miles ½ furlong (Newbury)

It must be very aggravating for the sponsors, whose support has made the Tote Gold Trophy the most valuable handicap hurdle run in Europe, that some diehards *still* refer to the race as 'The Schweppes', when the last running of the race as the Schweppes Gold Trophy was back in 1986. The race began life (as the Sch . . . you know who) in 1963 at Liverpool, when it was won by Rosyth, trained by **Ryan Price** and ridden by Josh Gifford. After just one running on that very tight hurdle circuit it transferred to the much more spacious arena of Newbury in 1964 – and was again won by Rosyth, a victory so at odds with the horse's most recent form that Price's training licence was suspended until the end of the season. Licence duly restored, Price won the race again with Le Vermontois in 1966 and for a fourth time in 1967 with Hill House, whose win again put the trainer in hot water, as the gelding had been running indifferently earlier that season. Then Hill House's dope

Tote Gold Trophy winners since 1990

1990	Deep Sensation	5	J. Gifford	R. Rowe	7–1	17
1991	abandoned (frost)					
1992	Rodeo Star	6	N. Tinkler	G. McCourt	15–2	15
1993	King Credo	8	S. Woodman	A. Maguire	10–1	16
1994	Large Action	6	O. Sherwood	J. Osborne	9–2	11
1995	Mysilv	5	C. Egerton	J. Osborne	9–4F	8
1996	Squire Silk	7	A. Turnell	P. Carberry	13–2	18
1997	Make A Stand	6	M. Pipe	C. Maude	6–1	18
1998	Sharpical	6	N. Henderson	M. Fitzgerald	10–1	14
1999	Decoupage	7	C. Egerton	J. McCarthy	6–1	18
2000	Geos	5	N. Henderson	M. Fitzgerald	15–2	17
2001	Landing Light	6	N. Henderson	M. Fitzgerald	4–1F	20

test proved positive to the steroid cortisol, and for months the case dragged on as Price tried to clear his name – which he eventually did when it was shown that the horse generated his own cortisol. Hill House became famous as The Horse Who Made His Own Dope, and the Schweppes Gold Trophy became synonympous with intrigue and sensation. Since those days the race has settled into a more respectable middle age, but remains one of the most keenly contested handicap hurdles of the year and a very big betting race. Two horses have gone on from this race to win the Champion Hurdle – **Persian War** (1968: he won the Champion that year and for the following two seasons) and Make A Stand (who won both races in 1997).

TOUT

A tout was an individual whose station in life was surreptitiously to watch horses on the home gallops and deliver information about their well-being or otherwise to the appropriate quarters, usually bookmakers. (Probably the most famous touts in racing history were those who arrived too late to watch **Eclipse** gallop on Banstead Downs.) The modern equivalent is a 'workwatcher' or 'gallops watcher' and tends to be a respectable racing journalist writing gallops reports for the press, rather than a fellow skulking in the bushes.

TOWCESTER

London Road, Towcester, Northamptonshire
NN12 7HS
Tel.: 01327 353414
Fax: 01327 358534
Web: www.towcester-racecourse.co.uk

Located in the beautiful countryside of Lord Hesketh's Northamptonshire estate, Towcester (pronounced 'Toaster') is a course which gives the impression of space – a right-handed circuit of one and three-quarter miles round, good long straights, and a very easy bend out of the back towards the turn for home. A horse can really stretch out here, and the downhill run from the bend after the winning post is countered by a long, hard slog out of the back, which taxes stamina to its limits. Towcester, especially in heavy ground, is no place for faint-hearted horses. The present course was laid out in 1928 – though there was racing in the area in the nineteenth century – but the facilities have been constantly improved (a new grandstand was opened in 1997), the viewing is very good, and this remains an exceptionally pleasant venue for racegoing. It is also the ideal place to take a racing newcomer who wishes to get some flavour of the sport without the bustle of a bigger track.

TRAINERS

There are some 700 racehorse trainers in Great Britain licensed by the Jockey Club.

<table>
<tr><th colspan="2">Leading trainers on the Flat since 1975
(by prize money won)</th></tr>
</table>

1975	P. Walwyn
1976	H. Cecil
1977	M. V. O'Brien *IRE*
1978	H. Cecil
1979	H. Cecil
1980	W. Hern
1981	M. Stoute
1982	H. Cecil
1983	W. Hern
1984	H. Cecil
1985	H. Cecil
1986	M. Stoute
1987	H. Cecil
1988	H. Cecil
1989	M. Stoute
1990	H. Cecil
1991	P. Cole
1992	R. Hannon
1993	H. Cecil
1994	M. Stoute
1995	J. Dunlop
1996	S. bin Suroor
1997	M. Stoute
1998	S. bin Suroor
1999	S. bin Suroor
2000	M. Stoute

Of this number, some 200 are '**permit holders**', licensed to train for steeplechases, hurdle races and National Hunt Flat races only horses which are the property of the trainer or his (or her) immediate family. Horses are trained all over the country and in a variety of settings: **Red Rum**'s stable was behind a second-hand car showroom on a busy street in Southport, and he galloped on the local beach. ('If a horse has ability,' said his trainer Ginger McCain, 'you can train it up the side of a mountain or down a mineshaft.') A complete contrast is the magnificent training estate of Manton in Wiltshire, where John Gosden now trains. And there are towns and villages which revolve around racehorse training. The major one in Britain is

Newmarket, which houses around 50 trainers and about 2,500 horses in training. **Lambourn** in Berkshire is the home of some 40 trainers; the Yorkshire towns of **Malton** and **Middleham** are other major centres.

The number of horses which a trainer has in his or her care varies enormously. John Dunlop had 198 horses listed as being in his charge in *Horses in Training* for 2001. The top jumping trainers tend to maintain smaller establishments than their equivalents on the Flat: Martin Pipe had 103 for 2001. Some permit holders had only a couple. Likewise, the amount of money trainers bring in for their patrons varies enormously. The *Racing Post* statistics for

<table>
<tr><th colspan="2">Leading trainers over jumps since 1974–5
(by prize money won)</th></tr>
</table>

1974–5	F. Winter
1975–6	F. Rimell
1976–7	F. Winter
1977–8	F. Winter
1978–9	M. H. Easterby
1979–80	M. H. Easterby
1980–1	M. H. Easterby
1981–2	M. Dickinson
1982–3	M. Dickinson
1983–4	M. Dickinson
1984–5	F. Winter
1985–6	N. Henderson
1986–7	N. Henderson
1987–8	D. Elsworth
1988–9	M. Pipe
1989–90	M. Pipe
1990–1	M. Pipe
1991–2	M. Pipe
1992–3	M. Pipe
1993–4	D.Nicholson
1994–5	D.Nicholson
1995–6	M. Pipe
1996–7	M. Pipe
1997–8	M. Pipe
1998–9	M. Pipe
1999–2000	M. Pipe
2000–1	M. Pipe

the 2000 Flat season, covering every trainer who earned prize money that year, shows that Sir Michael Stoute's charges brought in £2,963,712 in win and place money in Britain alone, while at the other end of the table sits W. de Best-Turner with earnings of £143. The jumps table for the 2000–1 season takes in every trainer who sent out at least one winner: Martin Pipe's horses earned £1,356,517, while Mrs B. L. M. Sillars had a strike rate of 50 per cent (one winner from two runs) but earned only £1,347.

(In the tables of winning trainers overleaf amounts of prize money earned are not given, for the simple reason that sources for such information tend to differ – by amounts small enough not to make any difference to who is considered leading trainer – and thus consistency is impossible.)

TRAIN ON, TRAIN OFF

A horse is said to have 'trained on' between one season and the next – most commonly, between its two-year-old and three-year-old seasons – if it has developed to such an extent that it shows, or can be expected to show, the same level of form as before. The key time for the punter to assess this is on that horse's first appearance at three: has it grown and matured since last year, or does it look small compared with the other horses in the paddock? A horse who has 'trained off' has had too much racing – enough to push it **over the top** – and no longer holds its form.

TRALEE

Ballybeggan Park, Tralee, Co. Kerry
Tel.: 066 7126148 (racedays 066 7126188)
Fax: 066 7126090

Dawn Run notched up the first of her 21 career victories at Tralee. Ridden by her 62-year-old owner Mrs Charmian Hill, she won the Castlemaine Flat Race for amateur riders on 22 June 1982 – Mrs Hill's last ride in public before her licence was revoked on the grounds of her age and various earlier injuries.

Tralee racecourse was once a deerpark belonging to the family of Daniel O'Connell – in whose memory the course stages the Liberator Handicap – and is overlooked by the Slieve Mish mountains. The August Festival Meeting coincides with the Rose of Tralee contest and lasts six days. The left-handed circuit is nine furlongs round, with a stiff climb towards the home turn.

TRAMORE

Waterford and Tramore Racecourse, Tramore, Co. Waterford
Tel.: 051 381425
Fax: 051 390928

The racecourse serving the city of Waterford was founded in 1911, and is best known for the four-day festival meeting in August. The course itself is a tight, undulating one-mile right-handed circuit. Among the major races here are the Waterford Crystal Noel Griffin Memorial Hurdle and the Charmian Hill Memorial Chase: the latter is named after the owner of the great mare **Dawn Run**.

TRAVELLING

Jockey-speak for a horse going well in a race.

TREBLE

Bet on three different horses in different races. If the first wins, returns – winnings plus stake – go on to the second, and if that wins the total goes on to the third. A simple way of calculating returns from a treble is to add one point to each winning odds, multiply the three and deduct one from the total: so a £5 treble on three horses who all win at 2–1 gives a return of £135 – winnings of £130 plus your £5 stakes returned.

TREE, JEREMY

Born in 1925, Jeremy Tree was assistant to Dick Warden in Newmarket before starting to train in his own right at Beckhampton in 1952. In a long and distinguished career he won four Classics – the Two Thousand Guineas with Only For Life (1963) and Known Fact (1980, on the disqualification of Nureyev) and the Oaks with Juliette Marny (1975) and Scintillate (1979). Rainbow Quest won the 1985 Coronation Cup and the same year was awarded the Prix de l'Arc de Triomphe on the disqualification of Sagace; Sharpo was one of the best sprinters of the age, winning the Nunthorpe Stakes at York three years running (1980–2) and the Prix de l'Abbaye in 1982; and John Cherry was a very tough and high-class stayer, winning the Cesarewitch under 9st 13lb in 1976.

Jeremy Tree died in 1993 at the age of 67.

Jeremy Tree was once asked to address the Turf Society at Eton College. Apprehensive about what his talk might consist of, he phoned Lester Piggott for advice:

'Lester, I've been asked to talk to the racing society at Eton. What should I tell them?'

'Tell 'em you've got flu ...'

TRIAL RACES

Several races are acknowledged to be effectively trials for big races in the future, in the sense that you can expect some horses aiming at those bigger races to take in the so-called 'trials' as part of their preparation. Thus in Britain the recognised trials for the **Derby** are the Two Thousand Guineas (which is of course a major race in its own right), Classic Trial at Sandown Park, Chester Vase, Dee Stakes at Chester, Derby Trial at Lingfield Park, Dante Stakes at York and Predominate Stakes at Goodwood. The recognised trials for the **Oaks** are the One Thousand Guineas, Pretty Polly Stakes at Newmarket, Cheshire Oaks at Chester, Oaks Trial at Lingfield Park, Musidora Stakes at York and Lupe Stakes at Goodwood. In Dubai, **Godolphin** stages trial races – run under racing conditions but not 'official' races – to sort out its horses early in the season. The 'Arc trials' run at Longchamp in September are the Prix Foy and the Prix Niel (won in 1998, 1999 and 2000 by that year's Arc winner).

TRICAST

Bet involving the selection of the first three in correct order, in handicaps of eight or more declared runners and no fewer than six actual runners. A computer calculates the dividend. (The Tote equivalent is the **Trifecta**.)

TRIFECTA

Tote bet involving the selection of the first three home in the designated race in correct order. Although a punter could make just one selection of three horses to finish 1, 2, 3, most prefer permutations: to perm the finishing orders of three horses requires six bets, four horses 24 bets, five horses 60 bets, and so on. (The first ever Trifecta, on the Vodafone Stewards' Cup at Goodwood on 1 August 1998, attracted a pool of £127,909, and the dividend for nominating Superior Premium to beat Ansellman with Eastern Purple third was £6,311.00 to a £1 stake – compared with the bookmakers' tricast on the same race paying £4,192.88.)

TRIPLE CROWN

To land the Triple Crown a horse needs to win the Two Thousand Guineas over one mile in the spring, the Derby over a mile and a half in early summer, and the St Leger over an extended mile and three-quarters in the autumn. Just 15 colts have ever achieved this: West Australian (1853), **Gladiateur** (1865), Lord Lyon (1866), Ormonde (1886), Common (1891), Isinglass (1893), Galtee More (1897), Flying Fox (1899), Diamond Jubilee (1900), Rock Sand (1903), Pommern (1915), Gay Crusader (1917), Gainsborough (1918), **Bahram** (1935) and **Nijinsky** (1970). Nine fillies have won the Fillies' Triple Crown of One Thousand Guineas, Oaks and St Leger: Formosa (1868: also Two Thousand Guineas), Hannah (1871), Apology (1874), La Fleche (1892), **Sceptre** (1902: also Two Thousand Guineas), **Pretty Polly** (1904), Sun Chariot (1942), Meld (1955) and **Oh So Sharp** (1985).
See also **US Triple Crown**.

TRIPTYCH

The flag-bearer of the internationalisation of horse racing, between 1984 and 1988 Triptych ran in 41 races (35 of them at Group One level) over five seasons in six countries. She won 14 races, nine of them at Group One or Grade One. Her wins at the highest level were:

- 1984 Prix Marcel Boussac;
- 1985 Irish Two Thousand Guineas (first filly ever to win this race);

- 1986 Champion Stakes;
- 1987 Prix Ganay, Coronation Cup, International Stakes, Phoenix Champion Stakes and Champion Stakes;
- 1988 Coronation Cup.

In addition, she was runner-up to Oh So Sharp in the 1985 Oaks, third to Commanche Run in the 1985 Benson and Hedges Gold Cup, second to Saint Estephe (beaten a short head) in the 1986 Coronation Cup, second to Dancing Brave in the 1986 Eclipse, third to Dancing Brave in the 1986 King George and Arc, second to Shardari in the 1986 International Stakes, third to Mtoto in the 1987 and 1988 Eclipse, third to Reference Point in the 1987 King George, third to Trempolino in the 1987 Arc, fourth in the 1987 Japan Cup, and fourth in the 1988 Breeders' Cup Turf. She had two owners (Alan Clore and Peter Brant), four trainers (David Smaga, David O'Brien, John Gosden – for whom she did not race – and Patrick-Louis Biancone) and 15 jockeys, and raced in England, Ireland, France, the USA, Canada and Japan. No surprise that she attracted the epithet of 'Iron Lady' (a sobriquet she shared with the incumbent in 10 Downing Street during her career); but her retirement as a broodmare was cruelly cut short. In the early hours of 24 May 1989, only a few months after she had retired from the track, she was with other mares in a paddock at Claiborne Farm, Kentucky, where she had been covered by Mr Prospector. The nightwatchman doing his rounds in a truck seems to have alarmed the mares into a stampede, and it was reported that Triptych had panicked and crashed into the back of the vehicle. She died of severe bleeding on the way to the veterinary clinic – a tragic end to a truly wonderful horse.

TRIUMPH HURDLE

Grade One hurdle; four-year-olds; 2 miles (Cheltenham)

The Triumph Hurdle, championship race for four-year-old hurdlers, was first run at Hurst Park in 1939, relocating to Cheltenham when that course (near Hampton Court) closed in 1962. While it is a notoriously difficult contest for ante-post punters to unravel, the Triumph Hurdle has produced some special memories. Since the first running at Cheltenham in 1965 (the race was not run in 1963–4) the only horses to have won the Triumph and gone on to take the Champion Hurdle are **Persian War** (1967, Champion 1968–70) and Kribensis (1988, Champion 1990), though dual Champion Hurdler **Monksfield** was second in 1976 and triple Champion Hurdler **See You Then** second in 1984. Other landmark races saw **Peter O'Sullevan**'s grand little stayer Attivo win in 1974 despite demolishing the final hurdle,

---

Triumph Hurdle winners since 1990

1990	Rare Holiday	4	D. Weld *IRE*	B. Sheridan	25–1	30
1991	Oh So Risky	4	D. Elsworth	P. Holley	14–1	27
1992	Duke Of Monmouth	4	S. Sherwood	M. Richards	33–1	30
1993	Shawiya	4	M. O'Brien *IRE*	C. Swan	12–1	25
1994	Mysilv	4	D. Nicholson	A. Maguire	2–1F	28
1995	Kissair	4	M. Pipe	J. Lower	16–1	26
1996	Paddy's Return	4	F. Murphy	R. Dunwoody	10–1	29
1997	Commanche Court	4	T. Walsh *IRE*	N. Williamson	9–1	28
1998	Upgrade	4	N. Twiston-Davies	C. Llewellyn	14–1	25
1999	Katarino	4	N. Henderson	M. Fitzgerald	11–4F	23
2000	Snow Drop	4	F. Doumen *FRA*	T. Doumen	7–1F	28
2001	no race (foot-and-mouth epidemic)					

Baron Blakeney come in at 66–1 in 1981 to supply a first big-race victory for a little-known West Country trainer named **Martin Pipe**, and Solar Cloud in 1986 give trainer **David Nicholson** and jockey **Peter Scudamore** the first Festival winner either of them had scored.

Lester Piggott rode the winner of the Triumph Hurdle on Prince Charlemagne at Hurst Park in 1954 – one of his 20 career victories over hurdles.

TRIXIE
A Trixie bet is a **Patent** without the singles – that is, three horses combined in three doubles and one treble.

TROY
Troy's giant stride eating up the Epsom straight to demolish his rivals in the 200th Derby in 1979 is one of the great Epsom racing memories, and he has to be accounted one of the best middle-distance horses of the last quarter of a century. Owned and bred by Sir Michael Sobell and **Lord Weinstock** and trained by **Dick Hern**, Troy was ridden in all his races by **Willie Carson**. As a two-year-old in 1978 he won two out of four and showed great promise when runner-up to Ela-Mana-Mou in the Royal Lodge Stakes at Ascot – promise underlined on his first outing at three, when he won the Classic Trial at Sandown Park. He tuned up for Epsom by winning the Predominate Stakes at Goodwood, then embarked on a glorious midsummer campaign which saw him land the Derby (by seven lengths from Dickens Hill), the Irish Derby (with Dickens Hill again runner-up, this time four lengths behind), the King George (from Gay Mecene) and the Benson and Hedges Gold Cup at York (from Crimson Beau). After that sequence he looked a good thing for the Prix de l'Arc de Triomphe, but could finish only third behind Three Troikas. He was retired to stand as a stallion at the Highclere Stud in Berkshire, but tragically died from a perforated gut in 1983, after just three covering seasons.

TUBING
See **whistling and roaring.**

TUCKED UP
A horse described as 'tucked up' looks too thin behind the saddle to be at his best. It is often a sign of mental agitation, and a symptom of being **over the top**.

TUDOR MINSTREL
In 1947 Tudor Minstrel started at 7–4 on for the Derby, shortest-priced favourite for the premier Classic since the Second World War: ridden by **Gordon Richards**, he refused to settle, ran out of stamina and finished fourth behind Pearl Diver. That was a rare blot on a brilliant career in which Tudor Minstrel, owned and bred by J. A. Dewar and trained by **Fred Darling**, won eight of his 10 races including the 1947 Two Thousand Guineas (by eight lengths) and St James's Palace Stakes, and was widely considered the best miler of modern times until **Brigadier Gerard**. (**Timeform** rated both Brigadier Gerard and Tudor Minstrel at 144. Only **Sea Bird II**, at 145, has ever prompted a higher assessment.) He died in 1971, aged 27.

TURF CLUB
Web: www.turfclub.ie

Irish equivalent of the Jockey Club, founded in the late eighteenth century and now based at The Curragh. The first volume of the *Irish Racing Calendar* was published in 1790, but there is evidence that the Turf Club existed at least six years earlier than that.

TURKEY
Turkey is not one of the major racing nations of the world, but occasionally horses well known in European racing end up there as stallions. Doyoun, sire of two Breeders' Cup Turf winners in **Daylami** (1999) and Kalanisi (2000), now stands at the Turkish National Stud, where he was exported in 1998 before his two most famous sons had made their mark. Another well-known horse exported to Turkey as a stallion is 1996 St James's Palace Stakes winner Bijou d'Inde. Turkey's premier racecourse is Veliefendi.

TWINS

Thoroughbred twins are rare, for while as many as 30 per cent of conceptions result in twins, in most cases the vet will 'pop' one of the eggs to ensure that only one foal is born. The reasoning behind this is that each twin would probably be significantly weaker than a single offspring, though there have been examples of successful racing twins. On the human front, notable racing twins include Michael and Richard **Hills**, both top jockeys.

TWISTON-DAVIES, NIGEL

Nigel Twiston-Davies famously does not give interviews. He prefers to let his horses do the talking – horses of the calibre of **Earth Summit**, only horse ever to win the Grand National (1998), Welsh Grand National (1997) and Scottish Grand National (1994); Beau, winner of the 2000 Whitbread Gold Cup by a distance; Tipping Tim, winner of the 1992 Mackeson Gold Cup; Captain Dibble, winner of the 1992 Scottish Grand National; Upgrade, winner of the 1998 Triumph Hurdle; Mrs Muck, Young Hustler, Sweet Duke, Kerawi, Frantic Tan and plenty more. Born in 1957, Twiston-Davies rode as an amateur (17 winners under Rules) and learned the training trade with Richard Head, Fred Rimell, Kim Bailey and David Nicholson. He took out his first licence in 1981, and trains at Naunton in Gloucestershire, not far from Cheltenham, where his assistant trainer is **Peter Scudamore**.

TWO THOUSAND GUINEAS

Group One; three-year-old colts and fillies;
1 mile (Newmarket, Rowley Mile)

There were 23 entries for the new race over one mile at Newmarket in spring 1809, at 100 guineas each, the entry fees rounding down to . . . two thousand guineas. The race has long outstripped that monetary value – the 2001 running won by Golan was worth £174,000 to the winning owner Lord Weinstock – and has for nearly two centuries been established as not only the first Classic of the year in which colts may run, but a race which often sets the tone for the whole season.

In its very early years the Two Thousand Guineas was characterised by small fields (in both 1829 and 1830 it was literally a two-horse race), but as the Classic framework to the season became ingrained through the nineteenth century it became second only to the Derby as a test of a three-year-old.

First horse to win the Two Thousand Guineas and go on to win the Derby was Smolensko in 1813, and he has been followed by plenty of others – including, since the Second World War, Nimbus (1949), Crepello (1957), **Royal Palace** (1967), **Sir Ivor**

Two Thousand Guineas winners since 1990

1990	Tirol	3	R. Hannon	M. Kinane	9–1	14
1991	Mystiko	3	C. Brittain	M. Roberts	13–2	14
1992	Rodrigo de Triano	3	P. Chapple-Hyam	L. Piggott	6–1	16
1993	Zafonic	3	A. Fabre *FRA*	Pat Eddery	5–6F	14
1994	Mister Baileys	3	M. Johnston	J. Weaver	16–1	23
1995	Pennekamp	3	A. Fabre *FRA*	T. Jarnet	9–2	11
1996	Mark Of Esteem	3	S. bin Suroor	L. Dettori	8–1	13
1997	Entrepreneur	3	M. Stoute	M. Kinane	11–2	16
1998	King Of Kings	3	A. O'Brien *IRE*	M. Kinane	7–2	18
1999	Island Sands	3	S. bin Suroor	L. Dettori	10–1	16
2000	King's Best	3	M. Stoute	K. Fallon	13–2	27
2001	Golan	3	M. Stoute	K. Fallon	11–1	18

(For a list of all winners since the Second World War, *see* Classics.)

(1968), **Nijinsky** (1970: he also won the St Leger and thus the **Triple Crown**) and **Nashwan** (1989). The Two Thousand Guineas is often the stage for a contest which commands a lasting place in racing's collective memory – for example:

- **Brigadier Gerard** beating **Mill Reef** and My Swallow in 1971;
- Tap On Wood giving **Steve Cauthen** his first Classic win in England in 1979;
- Known Fact getting the race on the controversial disqualification of the brilliant Nureyev (who never raced again) in 1980;
- **El Gran Senor** striding imperiously away from Chief Singer and Lear Fan in 1984;
- **Dancing Brave** as imperious in 1986;
- Rodrigo de Triano giving **Lester Piggott** his thirtieth and last Classic victory in 1992: 'How long can you go on?' asked Brough Scott in the post-race interview, to which the laconic reply was, 'I've got a ride in the sixth';
- **Zafonic**'s burst of sheer power in 1993;
- Mark Of Esteem and **Frankie Dettori** beating Even Top and Bijou d'Inde in a desperate finish in 1996;
- **Sir Michael Stoute**'s pair King's Best and Golan each showing a devastating turn of foot in 2000 and 2001.

U

UNDER STARTER'S ORDERS

The condition 'under starter's orders' applies at the start of a race when the Starter is satisfied that the field is ready to go, and is the point where all bets stand. This state used to be indicated by the raising of a white flag ('The white flag's up – they're under starter's orders') but that practice has been discontinued.

UNFURNISHED

Used to describe a horse less than fully mature physically – for instance, an awkwardly built or gangly youngster.

UNITED ARAB EMIRATES

Of the seven sheikhdoms in the United Arab Emirates, Sharjah was the first to stage serious Thoroughbred racing, with the course at the Sharjah Racing and Equestrian Club opening in 1983. But by far the most influential in world racing terms is Dubai, with its two state-of-the-art racecourses (**Nad Al Sheba** and **Jebel Ali**), major international racing programme (including the **Dubai World Cup**, richest race in the world), many racing stables (of which the best known in the West is Al Quoz, Dubai base of the **Godolphin** operation) and studs. Credit for that influence goes to the drive and vision of the **Maktoum** brothers – and principally to Sheikh Mohammed – who within a very short space of time have made the tiny oil-rich state one of the leading players in world racing. Sheikh Maktoum bin Rashid Al Maktoum is Vice President and Prime Minister of the UAE and ruler of Dubai, Sheikh Mohammed is Crown Prince of Dubai and Defence Minister. The principal racecourses in Abu Dhabi are the Abu Dhabi Equestrian Club and Ghantoot. Emirates Airlines is sponsor of the **Emirates World Series**.

UNITED RACECOURSES

United Racecourses Ltd (URL) was formed in 1966 to take over ownership of **Epsom** and **Sandown Park**, adding **Kempton Park** in 1972. The company is now a subsidiary of **Racecourse Holdings Trust** (RHT), itself a subsidiary of the Jockey Club.

UNSEATED RIDER

A chaser or hurdler is deemed to have unseated its rider when the jockey is dislodged without the horse having actually fallen. Whether a parting of the ways is officially described as a fall or unseated rider ('U' in a line of form) can be a contentious matter, as unseated can be attributed to human error, a fall to equine.

UP THE ARM

Betting slang for 11–8 (based on the **tic-tac** sign).

USA

The influence of the United States of America on horse racing around the globe has been immense. Many of the world's finest studs are situated in Kentucky; America's racetracks host some of the sport's biggest occasions, notably the Kentucky Derby and the Breeders' Cup; and American jockeys have made their mark in countries thousands of miles from their native shores. Thoroughbred racing is one of the most popular spectator sports in the USA, although by British standards the courses themselves are somewhat uniform: all the major tracks are left-handed ovals where the principal events are run on dirt – only a few championship races in the USA take place on turf. Racing is administered on a state-by-state basis which can lead to inconsistencies, for example in the matter of whether certain drugs are permitted to be given to horses. Although there are no on-course bookmakers, some states allow off-track betting (a betting office is known as an OTB) at the odds determined on the course by the totalisator system in operation. (Some states, such as South Carolina, stage horse racing – usually steeplechase meetings – but do not allow betting.)

The history of racing in the USA is peppered with the names of legendary horses such as **Man O' War, Kelso, Buckpasser, Northern Dancer, War Admiral,** Seabiscuit, **Citation, John Henry, Secretariat,** Seattle Slew, **Affirmed, Spectacular Bid** and, more recently, **Cigar.**

Fourstars Allstar, trained by Leo O'Brien, became the first US-trained winner of a European Classic when taking the Irish Two Thousand Guineas at the Curragh in May 1991. Lonesome Glory, trained by Bruce Miller, became the first US-trained horse to win a jumps race in Great Britain when winning the Chris Coley Racing Hurdle at Cheltenham in December 1992.

Many American jockeys have made a big impact on European racing. That impact has been provided most tellingly in Britain by **Tod** **Sloan** and champions **Danny Maher** and **Steve Cauthen** and in France by **Cash Asmussen,** while the increasing internationalisation of the sport made leading US-based riders such as **Bill Shoemaker** and more recently **Gary Stevens, Chris McCarron** and **Jerry Bailey** familiar to European racing fans. The winningmost jockey in US – and world – racing history is **Laffit Pincay jnr.**

While the backbone of the domestic racing year in the USA remains the **US Triple Crown,** North America is now a frequent port of call for leading Europe-based horses, attracted by many hugely valuable prizes. The annual **Breeders' Cup** is the unofficial world championship of racing, while the racing year in the USA bristles with other opportunities for raiders such as the **Arlington Million** and the Turf Classic at Belmont Park.

Bloodstock breeding in the USA is big business, with some 50,000 foals being registered every year and a Thoroughbred population of over half a million horses. The spiritual home of racing in the USA is Kentucky, where most of the famous American stud farms – including **Claiborne,** Gainesway, Calumet, Ashford, Spendthrift and Three Chimneys – are located. Other major Thoroughbred breeding states are Virginia, California, Maryland, New York and Florida.

Betting terms in the USA

With racing from the USA becoming increasingly familiar to punters in the UK, not only on account of regular broadcasts of the Breeders' Cup but with a generally higher level of television coverage of American racing, it may be useful to have a brief explanation of the main betting terms in that country. Remember that all American on-course betting is carried out on a pari-mutuel – pool – basis.

Win	Back the horse to win.
Place	Back the horse to come first or second.
Show	Back the horse to come first, second or third (assuming the number of runners allows for a payout on the third horse).
Exacta	Pick the first two finishers in correct order. (Also called a perfecta.)
Trifecta	Pick the first three in correct order.
Quinella	Pick the first two finishers in either order.
Pick Three, Pick Six, Pick Nine	Bets in which the winners of all the included races must be selected.

US TRIPLE CROWN

The Triple Crown, most highly prized achievement in American horse racing, consists of three races on dirt for three-year-old colts, geldings and fillies:

- **Kentucky Derby** over $1^1/4$ miles at Churchill Downs, Kentucky, on the first Saturday in May;
- **Preakness Stakes** over 1 mile $1^1/2$ furlongs at Pimlico, Maryland, two weeks after the Kentucky Derby;
- **Belmont Stakes** over $1^1/2$ miles at Belmont Park, New York, three weeks after the Preakness.

Just 11 horses have won the Triple Crown: Sir Barton (1919), Gallant Fox (1930), Omaha (1935), War Admiral (1937), Whirlaway (1941), Count Fleet (1943), Assault (1946), Citation (1948), Secretariat (1973), Seattle Slew (1977) and Affirmed (1978).

UTTOXETER

Wood Lane, Uttoxeter, Staffordshire ST14 8BD

Tel.: 01889 562561

Fax: 01889 562786

E-mail: info@uttoxeterracecourse.co.uk

Web: www.uttoxter.racecourse.co.uk

The circuit at Uttoxeter is about a mile and a quarter round, and to describe it as 'left-handed' is not telling the whole story, for the back straight of this popular Staffordshire course includes a marked right-hand kink – so that a horse on the inside in the early part of that stretch will find himself on the outside, only to regain the inner as the field tacks across to approach the home turn. Despite that unusual characteristic, this is essentially a galloping track, where the dour stayer can plug on resolutely – and in no event will his resolution be more needed than the Midlands Grand National, the major race of the Uttoxeter year. Usually held on the Saturday immediately following the Cheltenham National Hunt Festival in March, the Midlands National is run over a distance of four and a quarter miles: a true slog, and any horse which performs well in this event must come into consideration for the Aintree marathon a couple of weeks later. The last Grand National winner to land the Midlands National was Rag Trade, who won the Uttoxeter race in 1975 and beat Red Rum at Liverpool the following year. The Thinker, winner of the 1987 Cheltenham Gold Cup, won the race in 1986. Lord Gyllene, winner of the 1997 National, had run second in the race in his outing before Aintree in the colours of Stan Clarke, whose enterprise had been so vital in reviving the fortunes of the track in the 1980s and 1990s. Uttoxeter's other major race is the Classic Novices' Hurdle, run in November over two miles four and a half furlongs, which usually attracts a good-class field.

US Triple Crown race winners since 1990

	Kentucky Derby	Preakness	Belmont Stakes
1990	Unbridled	Summer Squall	Go And Go
1991	Strike The Gold	Hansel	Hansel
1992	Lil E Tee	Pine Bluff	A P Indy
1993	Sea Hero	Prairie Bayou	Colonial Affair
1994	Go For Gin	Tabasco Cat	Tabasco Cat
1995	Thunder Gulch	Timber Country	Thunder Gulch
1996	Grindstone	Louis Quatorze	Editor's Note
1997	Silver Charm	Silver Charm	Touch Gold
1998	Real Quiet	Real Quiet	Victory Gallop
1999	Charismatic	Charismatic	Lemon Drop Kid
2000	Fusaichi Pegasus	Red Bullet	Commendable
2001	Monarchos	Point Given	Point Given

Racing took place in the area in the eighteenth century and has been held on the current course since 1907, but Uttoxeter today has a very modern feel. The Prince Edward Grandstand, symbol of the resurgence of the course's fortunes after many years as a jumping backwater, was opened in 1995, since when there has been an ongoing process of improvement, with a newly designed paddock and unsaddling area.

V

VAGUELY NOBLE

By far the best offspring of Sir Winston Churchill's good horse Vienna, Vaguely Noble was one of the last crop bred by Major Lionel Holliday before his death in 1965. By the time the colt came to the sale ring as part of the dispersal of Holliday's estate, Vaguely Noble was officially the second-best two-year-old in England. Trained as a juvenile by Walter Wharton, he was narrowly beaten in his first two races in 1967, at Newcastle and Doncaster, then won a maiden race at Ascot by 12 lengths and the Observer Gold Cup (forerunner of the Racing Post Trophy) at Doncaster by seven lengths. He was clearly a racehorse of the highest class, and at the sale at Newmarket in December 1967 fetched 136,000 guineas, then a world record for any Thoroughbred at auction. For his three-year-old campaign in 1968 Vaguely Noble – now co-owned by Robert Franklyn and **Nelson Bunker Hunt** – was trained at Chantilly by Etienne Pollet and ran all his races in France. He won the first two easily, was unexpectedly beaten into third in the Grand Prix de Saint-Cloud, won the Prix de Chantilly and then lined up in one of the best Arc fields ever assembled, with eight individual Classic winners including the great Two Thousand Guineas and Derby winner **Sir Ivor**. Vaguely Noble treated the opposition with disdain, jockey **Bill Williamson** needing only to push him out to win by a facile three lengths. He was then retired, winner of six of his nine races, and stood as a stallion at the Gainesway Farm in Kentucky until his death in April 1989. The cream of his offspring were the outstanding racemare **Dahlia**, Nobiliary (the filly who ran second to Grundy in the 1975 Derby), 1976 Derby winner Empery and 1977 Coronation Cup winner Exceller.

VALET

The jockey's valet (always pronounced *vallett* in a racing context) is a key player in the changing room. For a percentage of the riding fees earned by the jockeys in his care, the valet transports clothing and equipment from meeting to meeting, lays it out in readiness for the jockeys' arrival and washes it after their departure, ready to be transported to the next meeting. But the valet usually does much more than the mundane chores, acting as nursemaid, confidant and personal assistant in a variety of ways. Best-known valet over the last few years has been John Buckingham, who had his own moment of improbable glory as a jockey when riding **Foinavon** to 100-1 success in the 1967 Grand National. Chris Maude, rider of Young Hustler and many other good horses as a jockey, took over Buckingham's valeting business in 2001.

VALUE (IN BETTING)

In a betting context, value is that elusive phenomenon of a horse's odds being markedly longer than you think they should be, given your assessment of its chance. Time to commandeer the wisdom of form expert Jim McGrath from Channel Four Racing's *Form and Betting* guide:

Exactly what constitutes 'value' for the punter is a subjective matter, but here's an example. Take a big field of handicappers. You look at the race with a view to picking the winner, and you find five horses with a real chance: it's difficult to divide them. If you take under 4–1 about any of those you need your head examining. But say one of them is on offer at 8–1 or more – win or lose, that's value. It's as simple as that: a horse represents value when the odds on offer are longer than you think constitute his chance. If you constantly back horses who are bad value, in the long term you will lose.

VERSATILITY

Racehorses tend to be specialists, but there are many instances of versatility. Of the horses with individual entries in this book, for example, the likes of **Brown Jack**, **Hatton's Grace** and **Sea Pigeon** won big races both on the Flat and over hurdles. There's even been a Classic winner who won over hurdles and fences: Aurelius, winner of the 1961 St Leger, who proved a failure at stud and returned to racing. Plenty of trainers have excelled under both codes, and so have jockeys: **Lester Piggott** won 20 hurdle races, **Willie Robinson** rode a Derby runner-up as well as many big winners over jumps, and more recently Richard Hughes has shown that a top rider need not confine himself to one code. But the palm for versatility must go to a horse named Threadbare, who on three successive racing days in August 1973 won a handicap hurdle over two miles at Newton Abbot, a handicap chase over the same course and distance, and an apprentice handicap over nine furlongs on the Flat at Wolverhampton.

VINTAGE CROP

A chestnut gelding owned by Dr Michael Smurfit and trained in Ireland by **Dermot Weld**, Vintage Crop has the singular distinction of being the first horse trained outside Australasia to win the **Melbourne Cup**, which he achieved at the age of six under **Michael Kinane** in 1993, winning by three lengths at 14–1. He returned to Flemington for the Cup in 1994 (seventh behind Jeune after injuring a leg the day before the race) and 1995 (third to Doriemus). Vintage Crop also has the distinction of being the first horse to win a Classic in successive years, taking the Irish St Leger (opened to older horses in 1983) in 1993 and 1994, and his other big-race victories include the 1992 Cesarewitch, which he won by eight lengths under Walter Swinburn. In addition to the 16 races he won on the Flat, he won twice over hurdles and finished sixth to Granville Again in the 1993 Champion Hurdle. A statue of this magnificent advertisement for Irish racing now stands at The Curragh racecourse, and the old fellow himself resides nearby at the Irish National Stud.

VIRUS

'The virus' in racing parlance is a term that covers a variety of respiratory conditions caused by a viral infection of some kind, all of which can spread rapidly in stable yards and on racecourses; often the first sign of the presence of the virus is a lacklustre race performance. Equine flu is a severe viral respiratory infection: its major symptom is a dry cough – hence the horror of coughing in a racing stable – accompanied by high temperature and a nasal discharge. It usually takes a horse two to three weeks to recover, after which he will need a period of convalescence. The particular horror of the virus is that once it affects one horse in a stable, it can spread very quickly among the other inmates, and it is not unknown for a stable badly affected to shut up shop while the affliction works its passage. Less severe versions of the malady can simply take the edge off the horses' performance for a while, and when a stable is out of form, a bout of some version of the virus is often the cause.

VISION (IN HORSES)

The horse has the largest eyes of any land mammal, and uses them in a very different way from a human. Eyes set on the side rather than the front of the head afford a field of vision of very nearly 360 degrees in which to be constantly on the look-out for predators. Research has shown that each eye has an individual field of vision of 146 degrees, with a 65-degree binocular field straight ahead and a 3-degree blind spot immediately to the rear. The horse's nose creates a small blind spot on the ground in front of him – with the consequence that a horse taking a fence at speed cannot actually see the jump at the moment of take-off: he is depending on the image of that jump seen two or three strides before, on the approach. (Often a horse will turn his head slightly as he jumps.)

Blinkers or a **visor** severely reduce the field of lateral vision and thus shut out distractions, focusing the horse's sight to the front.

VISOR

Form of blinkers where a narrow slit is cut in each of the cups over the eyes, allowing the horse a small degree of lateral vision.

VOLTIGEUR

Bred at Hartlepool, Voltigeur won his only outing as a two-year-old at Richmond (Yorkshire) in 1849 and next time out won the 1850 Derby. He then dead-heated with Russborough for the St Leger, winning the run-off, and two days later beat **The Flying Dutchman** – winner of the Derby and St Leger the previous year – in the Doncaster Cup. He met The Flying Dutchman again in their famous match race at York in May 1851 and was beaten a length. The following year Voltigeur won the Flying Dutchman Handicap at York, and it is at that course that Voltigeur is commemorated in the running of the Great Voltigeur Stakes at the August meeting. As a stallion his most notable achievement was to sire Two Thousand Guineas winner Vedette, grandsire of St Simon. Voltigeur died after being kicked by a mare in 1874.

Voltigeur's best friend was a cat, who, once the horse was rugged up, would sit for hours on his back.

W

WALKOVER

A walkover is a one-horse race. 'If only one horse is declared a runner,' states the Rule, '. . . or two horses are so declared but one is withdrawn prior to the start, the race shall be deemed a "walk over". In such case it shall not be necessary for the horse to "walk over" the entire course but that horse shall be ridden past the Judge's box and then shall be deemed the winner.'

Point-to-pointers Rossa Prince and Mister Chippendale share the extremely dubious distinction of having failed to win a walkover. In May 1990 Rossa Prince bolted while being saddled and could not be caught in time to meet the demands of the regulations, and in April 1994 Mister Chippendale forfeited his walkover prize when his rider omitted to weigh in.

A jockey must weigh out and weigh in for a walkover in the normal way. Races which attract very low entries are these days reopened, and walkovers are very rare.

WALL-EYED

The iris in the eye of a 'wall-eyed' horse is excessively light. The condition, unusual but not unknown in Thoroughbreds, is not detrimental to the horse's sight, but some horse-watchers dislike it.

WALSH FAMILY

Ted Walsh, Channel Four Racing's guru on all things relating to the Irish racing scene, was a highly successful amateur jockey – top amateur in Ireland 11 times and winner of four races at the Cheltenham Festival, including the 1979 Two Mile Champion Chase on Hilly Way. As a trainer – operating from a small yard in Kill, Co. Kildare – he is best known for winning the 2000 Grand National with Papillon, ridden by his then 20-year-old son Ruby. He has also won the 1997 Triumph Hurdle and 2000 Irish Grand National with Commanche Court. Ruby Walsh has rapidly established himself as one of the most stylish young jockeys on the jumps scene: after Papillon's Grand National, his biggest win in England came on Ad Hoc in the 2001 Whitbread Gold Cup.

WALWYN, FULKE

Born in Monmouthshire in 1910, Fulke Walwyn began riding in races while serving with the 9th Lancers. He was leading amateur three times and won the 1936 Grand National on Reynoldstown, after which he turned professional: he enjoyed a brief association with the great **Golden Miller**, whom he rode twice (winning once) in the autumn of 1936. Walwyn's riding career was cut short when he fractured his skull (for the second time) in a fall at Ludlow in 1938 which left him unconscious for a month. He started training in Lambourn – moving to his famous Saxon House yard in 1944 – and was leading trainer for the first time in the 1946–7 season. On the death of **Peter Cazalet** in 1973 he took over as trainer for the **Queen Mother**. But the true glory of Fulke Walwyn's incomparable career can only be expressed through his big-race winners: Cheltenham Gold Cup four times (Mont Tremblant 1952, **Mandarin** 1962, **Mill House** 1963, **The Dikler** 1973); Grand National (Team Spirit 1964); Champion Hurdle twice (Anzio 1962, Kirriemuir 1965); Grand Steeplechase de Paris (Mandarin 1962); King George VI Chase five times (Rowland Roy 1947, Mandarin 1957 and 1959, Mill House 1963, The Dikler 1971), Whitbread Gold Cup seven times (Taxidermist – ridden by **John Oaksey** – 1958, Mill House 1967, Charlie Potheen 1973, The Dikler 1974, Diamond Edge 1979 and 1981, Special Cargo 1984); Hennessy Gold Cup seven times (Mandarin 1957 and 1961, Taxidermist – again ridden by John Oaksey – 1958, Mill House 1963, Man Of The West 1968, Charlie Potheen 1972, Diamond Edge 1981); Schweppes Gold Trophy (Tammuz, owned by the Queen Mother, 1975); and Scottish National twice (Rowland Roy 1947, Popham Down 1964). Add in the names of Game Spirit, Ten Plus, Dramatist and Gay George, and there's no doubt that Fulke Walwyn was the finest trainer of jumpers the sport has yet seen. Leading trainer for five seasons (1946–7, 1947–8, 1948–9, 1957–8 and 1963–4), he retired in June 1990. Fulke Walwyn died in February 1991 at the age of 80.

WALWYN, PETER

Peter Tyndall Walwyn – first cousin of **Fulke Walwyn** – was born in 1933. He was assistant trainer to Geoffrey Brooke at Newmarket in the early 1950s, worked with Helen Johnson Houghton (Fulke Walwyn's twin sister) – who was not allowed to hold a trainer's licence on account of her gender – and in 1960 moved to train in his own right at Windsor House, Lambourn, relocating in 1965 to Seven Barrows, just outside the town. His first Classic winner was Humble Duty, who won the 1970 One Thousand Guineas in a canter by seven lengths, and he landed the other fillies' Classic with Polygamy in 1974. But Peter Walwyn's greatest horse was undoubtedly **Grundy**, winner in 1975 of the Derby, Irish Two Thousand Guineas, Irish Derby and, most famously, the King George VI and Queen Elizabeth Diamond Stakes in which he beat Bustino. Other good horses he trained included Linden Tree (1970 Observer Gold Cup, and second to Mill Reef in the 1971 Derby), Rock Roi (first past the post in two Ascot Gold Cups and disqualified both times – for failing the dope test in 1971 and for interference in 1972), Shoemaker, Buckskin, Habat, Charlie Bubbles, English Prince (1974 Irish Derby), Patch, Pasty, Oats

(third in the 1976 Derby), Crow, Orange Bay (short-headed by The Minstrel in the 1977 King George at Ascot), Classic Example, Formidable, Sporting Yankee (1976 William Hill Futurity), Vitiges (1976 Champion Stakes), Dactylographer (1977 William Hill Futurity), Camden Town, Stalker and Relief Pitcher. By the time of his last Group One winner in Britain – Hamas in the 1993 July Cup – he was back in Windsor House, having swapped premises with the previous incumbent Nicky Henderson in 1992. Leading trainer in 1974 and 1975, he retired at the end of the 1999 season having trained 1,783 winners on the Flat in Britain (plus eight steeplechases and 23 hurdle races). On his retirement he was appointed an honorary member of the Jockey Club. But for all the great horses and quantity of winners, Peter Walwyn's huge popularity was rooted in his perceived eccentricity – he was widely known as 'Basil Fawlty', a nickname with which he was not displeased – and the firmness of his opinions over a range of issues. He has made no secret of his aversions, as avowed in his autobiography *Handy All the Way*:

For many years there has been a small number of people whom I have disliked, because, in my opinion, they have done us wrong. I have always had an inkling that it would be good to have a bus to take them all over Beachy Head. It would not be very big; it would have a regulator to make sure it would go at a uniform speed, and it would have no brakes. It would be a double-decker, and the top storey, with the best view, would be reserved for the main culprits. Willie Carson would have an upstairs seat; Alec Wildenstein would definitely be the driver, and the doors would be firmly locked to make sure the inmates could not escape.

WAR ADMIRAL

Owned by Samuel Doyle Riddle (owner of his sire **Man O' War**) and trained by George Conway, War Admiral won the US Triple Crown winner in 1937. He won 21 of his 25 races, one of those four defeats coming in the famous **match** with Seabiscuit.

WARNING OFF

Warning off – the correct term these days is to be rendered a 'disqualified person' – is the ultimate sanction for anyone who seriously transgresses the Rules of Racing. A person who has been 'warned off' is forbidden to enter any racecourse or any licensed racing premises, such as a training yard.

WARWICK

Hampton Street, Warwick CV34 6HN
Tel.: 01926 491553
Fax: 01926 403223
E-mail: warwick@rht.net
Web: www.warwickracecourse.co.uk

Racing at Warwick is first mentioned in 1714, and these days the course is a popular venue under both codes. The left-handed circuit is about one and three-quarter miles round; five-furlong sprints start from a spur off the main course and involve a left-hand dog-leg after about half the trip where the spur joins the main course. With marked but not severe undulations, Warwick is basically sharp in nature and puts the emphasis on speed and agility rather than sheer galloping power. The steeplechase track runs inside the Flat and has 10 fences, five of them in a good long run down the back straight.

In May 1985 John Francome and Lester Piggott rode a match race at Warwick for charity. Lester on The Liquidator beat John on Shangoseer by three-quarters of a length.

Spectators' enjoyment is a little hampered by the runners disappearing from view for a while down the back, but patrons have every chance of seeing top horses on jumping days here – especially the pre-Cheltenham fixture in February when the card includes the Kingmaker Novices' Chase. A new grandstand was opened in 2000.

WASTING

A jockey 'wastes' to lose weight in order to ride at the allotted level. These days he or she is likely to do this through a combination of factors: carefully controlled intake of food and liquid, judicious periods spent in the sauna, and possibly 'pee pills' – diuretics – to reduce liquid through regular urination. That last method is frowned upon as it can weaken the body, and even more frowned upon is the practice known as 'flipping' – eating as much as you can, then nipping off to the bathroom to throw it all up. Trainer John Gosden observed: 'One night an owner of mine complained that he didn't mind buying one dinner for the jockey, but he resented it when the same jockey returned from the bathroom to order a second lobster and repeat the process.' **Steve Cauthen** reportedly lived off grapes while fighting his ultimately losing battle with the scales, **Fred Archer** took a specially prepared diuretic concoction, and **Lester Piggott**, whose usual riding weight of 8st 5lb was about two stone below his natural body weight, characteristically evolved his own procedure, described in his autobiography:

The simplest way to lose weight is to eat less. Beyond that you can remove the excess poundage primarily by emetics (such as Fred Archer's famous mixture, which reputedly had the effect of dynamite) or sweating. Back then [the late 1950s] we didn't have saunas so had to make our own arrangements: hot baths were always very effective, but you can't do much else while sitting in the bath, and I needed to find a way of losing weight while engaged in other activities – specifically, the long stretches of driving to the races. My solution was to wear a plastic running suit, which covered me from foot to neck, and turn the heater in the car on full blast for the duration of the journey. I got my weight down, but my passengers didn't always enjoy their lifts.

WATER JUMP

While the water jump situated in front of the stands is a spectacular and popular feature of many jumping courses (Newbury, for example, Haydock Park or Aintree), the inclusion of such an obstacle in a steeplechase is no longer required by the rules. Many courses have taken the opportunity to remove the water jump – often considered an unfair and dangerous fence – and there have been few complaints.

WAYWARD LAD

A standing dish in the big chases of the mid-1980s, Wayward Lad ran in five consecutive Cheltenham Gold Cups (1983 to 1987) and five consecutive runnings of the King George VI Chase (1982 to 1986), and in all won 28 of his 55 races. Bred in Ireland and sold as a yearling for 2,500 guineas, then as a three-year-old for 5,250 guineas, he went into training with Tony **Dickinson** (and subsequently came under the care of Tony's son Michael and widow Monica). In his first season, 1979–80, Wayward Lad won six of his eight races over hurdles, and graduated to chasing in 1980–1, winning four from eight including the West of Scotland Pattern Novices' Chase at Ayr and the Welsh Champion Chase at Chepstow, though he was unplaced in the Sun Alliance Chase at Cheltenham. Wayward Lad had done enough to pronounce himself a high-class chaser, a claim underlined the following season when he won six out of seven, including the Lambert and Butler Premier Chase Final at Ascot, the Timeform Chase at Haydock and the Welsh Champion Chase for a second time. In 1982–3 he competed in the very top bracket: third in the Mackeson Gold Cup, second in the Kennedy Construction Gold Cup at Cheltenham (now the Tripleprint), and first – ridden by **John Francome** – in the King George VI Chase, beating Fifty Dollars More and stable companion Silver Buck; his only other outing that season was to run third in the famous Dickinson-dominated 1983 Cheltenham Gold Cup, with two stable companions, Bregawn and Captain John, leading him home and two others, Silver Buck and Ashley House, following him. Wayward Lad was now in his prime, and he won a second King George (this time ridden by Robert Earnshaw) in 1983 when beating Brown Chamberlin, though he was pulled up behind Burrough Hill Lad when 6–4 favourite for the Gold Cup. A third King George was denied him in 1984 when he finished last of three behind Burrough Hill Lad and he was unplaced behind Forgive'N Forget in the 1985 Gold Cup, but he ended the 1984–5 term on a good note by winning the valuable Whitbread Gold Label Cup at Aintree. Having won the Charlie Hall Chase at Wetherby for a second time in November 1985, in December he started at the insulting price of 12–1 for the King George, and after a tremendous duel with Combs Ditch from the last fence prevailed by a neck to become the first horse to win the prestigious Boxing Day race three times. (Only **Desert Orchid**, with four, has bettered Wayward Lad's King George record.) His next race was the 1986 Cheltenham Gold Cup, which for a few moments up the final hill he looked certain to win as he surged past Forgive'N Forget after the last – only for **Dawn Run** to find that astonishing final burst and deny him. By the time of the 1986 King George, Wayward Lad was a few days short of his twelfth birthday, and past his best: he finished unplaced behind the new star Desert Orchid. In the 1987 Gold Cup – the running delayed by an hour and half after a blizzard had covered Cheltenham in snow – Wayward Lad again looked to have every chance at the last fence, then ran out of puff and finished fifth behind The Thinker. One race remained for him, and he ended his racing days in perfect fashion with a smooth win in the Whitbread Gold Label Cup at Aintree.

Wayward Lad's highly distinguished career had an unpleasant epilogue. An acrimonious dispute over the horse's future led to his entering the sale ring in May 1987 to dissolve the partnership of his owners, and this great horse's future was in serious doubt until he was knocked down for 42,000 guineas to Monica Dickinson, who sent him to the USA for an honourable retirement under the watchful eye of her son Michael, by then training in Maryland. Graham Bradley, who won many races on Wayward Lad, described him as the horse 'who had almost everything' before elaborating: 'He had very high cruising speed with the ability to quicken off it and inject pace that could settle a race very quickly. He was majestic over a fence.'

WEATHERBYS

Sanders Road, Wellingborough,
Northamptonshire NN8 4BX
Tel.: 01933 440077
Fax: 01933 440807
E-mail: e-mail@weatherbys-group.com
Web: www.weatherbys-group.com

Weatherbys, working under contract to the **British Horseracing Board**, is racing's secretariat, implementing the rules and regulations and generally ensuring that the day-to-day running of the sport goes as smoothly as is feasible. Among the particular functions for which Weatherbys is responsible are:

- registration of **owners**
- registration and administration of the **naming of horses**
- registration and administration of **racing colours**
- accounts
- publication of the fixture list and conditions of races
- publication of the *Racing Calendar*
- **entries** and declarations
- allocation of weights and determination of eligibility for races
- the **draw** for Flat races

A family firm whose history stretches back to the eighteenth century, Weatherbys is nowadays involved in a number of commercial areas. It has its own bank, and every registered owner must have an account either with the BHB or with Weatherbys Bank. From this account will be deducted entry fees, and to it will be added prize money won, after mandatory deductions have been made including percentages for jockey, trainer, and so on. Jockeys and trainers may have their own accounts with Weatherbys, and for jockeys who do so riding fees will be transferred directly from the owner's to the rider's account. Weatherbys also publishes its own titles, including *The Stallion Book* and *The Statistical Record*; produces racecards for the majority of British meetings; is one of the country's leading bloodstock insurance agencies; compiles catalogues for many bloodstock sales companies (including **Tattersalls**); and offers marketing services and a travel agency.

WEAVER

A horse 'weaving' in its box – that is, swaying from side to side – is showing signs of nervous agitation.

WEIGHED-IN SIGNAL

When the jockeys have weighed in and there is no stewards' enquiry or objection to be decided, the announcement 'weighed in' is given and the result stands. It is at this point that bets can be settled – though in practice most course bookmakers will pay out before the weighed-in signal, unless there is some expectation of a change in the placings. (In Ireland the equivalent announcement is 'Winner all right.')

WEIGHING OUT, WEIGHING IN

Since it is essential that each horse in a race carries the weight allotted to it by the conditions of that event, jockeys weigh out – by sitting on the scales under the watchful eye of the Clerk of the Scales – before a race and weigh in afterwards. Included in the rider's weight when weighing out are everything that the horse is to carry except the jockey's crash helmet (which is exempt from the weighing in order to remove the temptation to wear a dangerously light helmet), his whip, the bridle, blinkers (or equivalent), breastplate or breast-girth, martingale, neck-strap or muzzle, and anything worn on the horse's legs: so what is weighed out is the jockey, his clothing (though an allowance of 2lb is made for the body protector worn under the silks– hence a jockey weighing out at 9st will actually register 9st 2lb on the scales), saddle and weight-cloth. If the correct weight is registered, the saddle with its related equipment is then passed to the trainer (or his representative) who will go off to saddle the horse. Directly after the race all jockeys who have ridden in a race may be required to weigh in (unless prevented by injury), at the discretion of the Clerk of the Scales, and the jockeys of all placed horses must do so: a placed horse whose jockey, for whatever reason, fails to weigh in will be disqualified. So will a jockey whose weight at weighing in is different from that at weighing out, though a jockey is allowed to fall 1lb below the weighed-out weight to take into account the possible slimming effects of his exertions. A jockey who weighs in at 2lb or more over the weighed-out weight is reported to the stewards.

WEIGHING ROOM

The weighing room is the inner sanctum of the racecourse, with entry firmly restricted to those with legitimate business there. The term strictly covers the area where the jockeys are weighed in and weighed out under the jurisdiction of the Clerk of the Scales, but in general parlance 'the weighing room' covers the area which includes the jockeys' changing room, stewards' room and other administrative functions directly concerned with the running of the race.

WEIGHT (OF HORSE)

A Thoroughbred foal weighs 80–120lb at birth, and a mature racehorse in training hits the scales at around 1,100lb – about half a ton (or around 500 kilos). Weight can be a very telling indication of the race fitness and general well-being of a racehorse, and many trainers regularly check their charges on an equine weighbridge to monitor their condition and assess when a particular individual is coming to his ideal 'racing weight'. (In Japan racehorses are publicly weighed at the track and the weights announced – thus making knowledge of an individual horse's weight another weapon in the punter's betting armoury.) On a race day, the stress of travel and the race itself can cause a horse to lose as much as 40lb: the less weight lost, the better the horse has come out of the race.

WEIGHT-CLOTH

If a jockey in his silks plus the saddle does not make up the required weight the horse should be carrying, the difference will be added by using a weight-cloth, which goes under the saddle and has pockets into which can be slipped lead weights.

WEIGHT-FOR-AGE

Formally, any race which is not a **handicap** is a weight-for-age race, the weights which each horse will carry relating to the published 'weight-for-age scales' published by the British Horseracing Board. The Flat weight-for-age scale (originally devised by **Admiral Henry Rous** in the nineteenth century) expresses the number of pounds that it is deemed the average horse in each age group falls short of maturity at different dates and at different distances. Since a young horse will not be as mature as an older, he will carry less weight than his elder in order to even up their chances: for example, under the current Flat scale a three-year-old running against a four-year-old over five furlongs in late March would receive 12lb from his elder; by early July, when the difference in maturity will have diminished, that concession will be down to 5lb, and by October they will be competing at level weights. The jumping weight-for-age scales work on a similar basis.

WEINSTOCK, LORD

Arnold Weinstock, whose business career saw him become managing director of the vast electrical company GEC, married the daughter of GEC's chairman Sir Michael Sobell, and the partnership between Sobell and Weinstock as owner–breeders was one of the most successful of the modern age. They bought **Dorothy Paget**'s Ballymacoll Stud in Ireland in 1960, since when a stream of big-race winners have carried the famous colours of pale blue, yellow and white checked cap:

- **Troy** (Derby, Irish Derby, King George and Benson and Hedges Gold Cup 1979);
- Ela-Mana-Mou (Eclipse Stakes and King George VI and Queen Elizabeth Diamond Stakes 1980);
- Sun Princess (Oaks, Yorkshire Oaks and St Leger 1983);
- Spectrum (Irish Two Thousand Guineas, Champion Stakes 1995);
- **Pilsudski** (Breeders' Cup Turf 1996; Eclipse Stakes, Irish Champion Stakes, Champion Stakes and Japan Cup 1997);

- Greek Dance (Grosser Dallmayr-Preis 2000);
- Golan (Two Thousand Guineas 2001).

Ela-Mana-Mou raced in 1980 in the name of Lord Weinstock's only son Simon, who was closely involved the bloodstock business until his death at the tragically early age of 44 in May 1996.

WELD, DERMOT

Dermot Weld was born in Surrey in 1948 and qualified as a vet. He rode as an amateur for many years, partnering his first winner at the age of 15 and winning the prestigious Moët & Chandon Silver Magnum – the 'Amateurs' Derby' – at Epsom on Lane Court in 1975: he was champion amateur in Ireland on the Flat in 1969, 1971 and 1972. Having learnt the trade with his father Charlie Weld and the great Australian trainer **Tommy Smith**, he took over his father's yard at Rosewell House, The Curragh, in 1972, since when he has sent out big-race winners on four continents. He won his only Classic in England with Blue Wind in the 1981 Oaks and has won all five Irish Classics, including the Irish Derby with Zagreb in 1996. But Weld's greatest achievements have been in pushing out the frontiers of international racing. He was the first trainer from outside North America to win a US Triple Crown race when Go And Go won the **Belmont Stakes** in 1990, and – an even

more startling breakthrough – the first trainer from outside Australasia to win the **Melbourne Cup**, with **Vintage Crop** in 1993. He also won the Hong Kong Invitation Bowl in 1991 with Additional Risk. As if that were not enough, he has made his mark on the jumping game, winning the Triumph Hurdle with Rare Holiday in 1990, the Irish Grand National with Perris Valley in 1988 and sending out Greasepaint to finish second to Hallo Dandy in the 1984 Grand National, and has won the Galway Plate twice and the Galway Hurdle three times. On the Flat, he has been champion trainer in Ireland by prize money eight times (1983, 1985, 1989, 1990, 1993, 1994, 1996, 1998). In terms of the number of winners trained he has been leading trainer in Ireland no fewer than 18 times between 1972 (his first season) and 2000, and he has saddled more winners than any other Irish trainer.

WELSH NATIONAL

Grade Three handicap steeplechase; five-year-olds and upwards; 3 miles 5½ furlongs (Chepstow)

First run as the Welsh Grand National at Cardiff in 1895 (over two and a half miles), the Welsh National is one of the oldest jump races in the calendar. After moving to Newport for the 1948 running, it found a settled home – and its current distance – at Chepstow the following year. The first

Welsh National winners since 1990

1990	Cool Ground	8	R. Akehurst	L. Harvey	9–2	14
1991	Carvill's Hill	9	M. Pipe	P. Scudamore	9–4F	17
1992	Run For Free	8	M. Pipe	M. Perrett	11–4JF	11
1993	Riverside Boy	10	M. Pipe	R. Dunwoody	6–4F	8
1994*	Master Oats	8	K. Bailey	N. Williamson	5–2JF	8
1995	abandoned (frost)					
1996	abandoned (frost)					
1997	Earth Summit	9	N. Twiston-Davies	T. Jenks	25–1	14
1998	Kendal Cavalier	8	N. Hawke	B. Fenton	14–1	14
1999	Edmond	7	H. Daly	R. Johnson	4–1	16
2000	Jocks Cross	9	Miss V. Williams	B. Crowley	14–1	19

* run at Newbury in January 1995

Chepstow running in 1949 was won by Fighting Line, ridden by **Dick Francis**, and Francis won the race again in 1956 on the remarkable **Crudwell**, who got home by a head from Billy Budd. Until the 1960s the race was usually run at Easter, but when it moved to February it became a major trial for the Grand National: Rag Trade in 1976 won at Chepstow and then beat Red Rum at Aintree. (After too many abandonments of the February fixture, the race was shifted to December for the 1979 running.) The only other horses to have won the Welsh National and Grand National are Corbiere (Chepstow 1982, Aintree 1983) and **Earth Summit** (Chepstow 1997, Aintree 1998), while two have won the Welsh National and Cheltenham Gold Cup: Burrough Hill Lad won at Chepstow in December 1983 and the Gold Cup in March 1984, and Master Oats won the 1994 Welsh National (actually run at Newbury in January 1995 as Chepstow was unraceable on the original date) and the Gold Cup the following March. Bonanza Boy in 1988 and 1989 is the only horse to have won back-to-back Welsh Nationals. The other dual winner since the war was Limonali in 1959 and 1961. But arguably the greatest Welsh National display came in 1991 when Carvill's Hill, trained by **Martin Pipe** and ridden by **Peter Scudamore**, took the lead early on and turned in an astonishing display of galloping and jumping, going further and further ahead to beat Party Politics by 20 lengths: some pundits thought it a display not bettered since the days of Arkle. The following year Pipe saddled the first four home when Run For Free beat Riverside Boy, Miinnehoma and Bonanza Boy.

WERTHEIMER FAMILY

The Wertheimer brothers – Alain and Gerard – are the sons of Jacques Wertheimer, son of Pierre Wertheimer, who won the 1956 Derby with Lavandin and died in 1965. The family colours – royal blue, two white seams on the reverse side of the silks and a single central stripe down the front, white sleeves and cap – have also been seen on two winners of the Prix de l'Arc de Triomphe (Ivanjica 1976 and Gold River 1981) and on 1993 Breeders' Cup Turf winner Kotashaan, while other good horses to have carried those colours include Riverman (owned by Pierre's widow), Green Dancer, Val de l'Orne, Dancing Maid, Gay Mecene and Kistena. Recent Wertheimer *frères* winners in England include Gold Splash (Coronation Stakes 1993) and Pas de Reponse (Cheveley Park Stakes 1996). The Wertheimer fortune comes from the Chanel cosmetic empire.

WESTMINSTER, ANNE, DUCHESS OF

Anne, Duchess of Westminster, was born Nancy Sullivan in Co. Cork and became the fourth wife of the second Duke of Westminster in 1947. (He died in 1953.) Her colours of yellow, black hoop, black cap with yellow tassel will for ever be associated with the immortal **Arkle**, whom she bought as a three-year-old in 1960 for 1,150 guineas. But she has had many other good horses, notably Ben Stack, who won 10 races including the Two Mile Champion Chase in 1964, the 1975 Cheltenham Gold Cup winner Ten Up and 1985 Grand National winner Last Suspect. At one point she owned the notorious **Foinavon** – though she had sold him before he won the 1967 Grand National at 100–1.

WETHERBY

York Road, Wetherby, West Yorkshire LS22 5EJ
Tel.: 01937 582035
Fax: 01937 580565
E-mail: info@wetherbyracing.co.uk
Web: www.wetherbyracing.co.uk

Yorkshire's sole jumps-only track is a left-handed 12-furlong oval circuit with good long straights and little in the way of undulation. The fences are very well built, and this is a course for the long-striding, clean-jumping, galloping type of horse. It is no coincidence that the late lamented **One Man** was in his element here, his three course wins including back-to-back victories in 1996 and 1997 in the Charlie Hall Memorial Chase – an important early-season event for top-class three-mile chasers.

Wetherby's other major steeplechases are both run at the Christmas meeting: the Rowland Meyrick Handicap Chase (named after a famous former Clerk of the Course) over three miles one furlong on Boxing Day, and the Castleford Chase for two-milers the following day: winners of the Castleford Chase include such greats as **Tingle Creek**, Badsworth Boy, Pearlyman, Waterloo Boy (twice) and Viking Flagship. If those are the main races here, the overall standard of racing is high, with owners and trainers attracted by what is essentially a very fair course.

Racing was first held on the current track in 1891, though there had been jump meetings at a previous course in Wetherby, on the banks of the River Wharfe, since the 1840s. With a new weighing room complex and new members' stand, the course is investing heavily in its future.

WEXFORD

c/o B. J. Doyle and Co. Ltd. 5 Selskar Street.
Wexford. Co. Wexford
Tel.: 053 42307 (racedays) or 051 421681
Fax: 051 421830

With just seven days' racing scheduled for 2001, Wexford is not one of Ireland's busiest racecourses, but the overall standard of sport here under both codes is good. The course, which was first used in 1951, is a right-handed, undulating circuit of nine furlongs' circumference.

WHIPPER IN

During the running of a race you will sometimes hear the runner at the rear of the field referred to as 'whipping them in' or being the 'whipper in'. The phrase comes from fox hunting, where the whipper in rounds up dawdling hounds and drives them back into the main pack.

WHIP RULES

The use of the whip has long been a contentious issue in racing. At the Cheltenham Festival in 1980 Irish jockey Tommy Ryan received a three-month ban for excessive use of the whip on two winning horses, Mountrivers and Drumlargan: with regard to the latter, Ryan usefully explained that 'With the money our lads had on this one I should have been lynched if we'd got beat.' At the same meeting Joe Byrne received similar punishment for over-enthusiastic belting of Batista, narrowly beaten in the Triumph Hurdle. Few who saw those races would have quibbled with the verdict that the whip was used excessively, but since then there have been plenty of more borderline cases, where a stirring finish to a big race has been marred by punishment to the jockeys: Graham McCourt after winning the Cheltenham Gold Cup on Norton's Coin in 1990, for example; Hywel Davies (Barnbrook Again) and Richard Dunwoody (Waterloo Boy) after the 1992 Queen Mother Champion Chase; or Adrian Maguire (Cool Ground) in the same year's Cheltenham Gold Cup. Maguire summed up the jockey's dilemma in such circumstances: 'I was excessive, but you don't think of that during the Gold Cup and I wouldn't have won otherwise.' On the Flat, high-profile cases include Olivier Peslier's two-day suspension after winning the 1998 Derby on High-Rise; in the same year a stupendous finish to the International Stakes at York, when One So Wonderful (Pat Eddery) beat Faithful Son (Frankie Dettori) by a short head, with Chester House (Kieren Fallon) another short head behind in third, saw all three riders banned. In July 2000 both George Duffield and Pat Eddery received suspensions after a pulsating Eclipse Stakes finish on Giant's Causeway and Kalanisi.

Regulations and guidelines regarding use and abuse of the whip have been subjected to various changes over the last few years. For a while a specified number of strokes over a specified distance was suggested as the trigger for racecourse stewards to instigate an enquiry, but this is no longer the case. Since there is so much confusion over the issue, it is worth quoting the official Instruction in the *Orders and Rules of Racing* for 2001:

The Stewards of the Jockey Club will not tolerate abuse of the horse and consider its welfare, and the safety of the rider, to be paramount. The whip should be used for safety, correction and encouragement only and they therefore advise all riders to consider the following good ways of using the whip which are not exhaustive:

(a) Showing the horse the whip and giving it time to respond before hitting it;

(b) Using the whip in the backhand position for a reminder;

(c) Having used the whip, giving the horse a chance to respond before using it again;

(d) Keeping both hands on the reins when using the whip down the shoulder in the backhand position;

(e) Using the whip in rhythm with the horse's stride and close to its side;

(f) Swinging the whip to keep a horse running straight.

The Stewards of the Jockey Club have asked Stewards to consider holding an enquiry into any cause where a rider has used his whip in such a way as to cause them concern and publish the following examples of uses of the whip which may be regarded as improper riding:

(1) Hitting horses:
  to the extent of causing injury;
  with the whip arm above shoulder height;
  rapidly without regard to their stride, i.e.
    twice or more in one stride;
  with excessive force;
  without giving the horse time to respond.

(2) Hitting horses which are:
  showing no response;
  out of contention;
  clearly winning;
  past the winning post.

(3) Hitting the horse in any place except:
  on the quarters with the whip in either
    the backhand or forehand position;
  down the shoulder with the whip in the
    backhand position;
  unless exceptional circumstances prevail.

(4) Hitting horses:
  with excessive frequency.

When examining cases of excessive frequency, the Stewards will consider all the relevant factors such as:

(a) whether the number of hits was reasonable and necessary over the distance they were given, taking into account the horse's experience;

(b) whether the horse was continuing to respond; and

(c) the degree of force that was used; the more times a horse has been hit the stricter will be the view taken over the degree of force which is reasonable.

It is emphasised that the use of the whip may be judged to be proper or improper in particular circumstances which have not been included above . . .

Few would dispute that tightening up the whip rules has improved the standard of jockeyship.

WHISTLING AND ROARING

These are noises caused by paralysis of the vocal cords in the larynx. When an affected horse breathes in, the cords flap around in the airway, making noises and obstructing the incoming air. The surgical operation sometimes carried out to remove the vocal cords and ventricles in such cases – to improve the airflow through the larynx – is known as hobdaying, after its originator Sir Frederick Hobday, former Principal of the Royal College of Veterinary Surgeons. That good hurdler Relkeel was hobdayed in 1998, and showed that the operation had left no ill effects when battling to victory in the Bonusprint Bula Hurdle at Cheltenham on his reappearance.

An alternative way of dealing with the problem is to insert a metal tube in the trachea (windpipe) below the larynx to allow the air to bypass the obstruction; this is known as 'tubing', and a horse that has been tubed can be identified by a small hole on the underside of the neck. The 1992 Grand National winner Party Politics, who suffered various wind infirmities over the years, is a prominent example of a tubed horse; he had also undergone a 'tie-back' operation, in which the paralysed muscle in the larynx is replaced with elastic material which keeps the larynx open permanently. Another example is that grand sprinter Coastal Bluff, still winning races at the age of nine in 2001 despite having been tubed.

WHITBREAD GOLD CUP

Grade Three handicap steeplechase; five-
year-olds and upwards; 3 miles 5½ furlongs
(Sandown Park)

The first running of the Whitbread Gold Cup
in April 1957 marked an historic moment in
British racing – the advent of commercial
sponsorship. Increased television coverage of
racing made the sport a highly attractive
proposition for commercial companies, and
the vision of Colonel Bill Whitbread (who had
himself twice ridden in the Grand National in
the 1920s) opened up a brave new world for
National Hunt racing, with sponsors rapidly
appreciating the potential in setting up the
new races which would transform and hugely
enhance the sport. The first Whitbread was
won by Much Obliged: the official margin of
his victory over **Mandarin** was a neck, but
many who saw the finish were convinced that
Mandarin had won. (This was before jump
racing at Sandown Park had the benefit of the
photo finish.) The second running in 1958
went to John Lawrence (now **John Oaksey**)
on Taxidermist, with Mandarin second again,
and the third in 1959 to Done Up, who beat
– guess! – Mandarin, by a short head. (Done
Up was ridden by Harry Sprague, who usually
confined himself to hurdles and rarely rode
over fences. On his way up Sandown's
Rhododendron Walk after the race he was so
exhausted that he vomited, spewing out his

top set of false teeth. Legend has it that
winning trainer **Ryan Price** scrabbled around
in the dirt and eventually located the missing
gnashers.)

The history of the Whitbread is heaving
with memorable occasions:

- 1960 Gold Cup winner Pas Seul giving 21lb
  to Grand National winner Nicolaus Silver
  and beating him four lengths in 1961;
- **Arkle** and Pat Taaffe skipping clear of
  Brasher (ridden by Jimmy FitzGerald, now
  a leading trainer) in 1965;
- not a dry eye in the house as **Mill House**,
  so often defeated by Arkle, had his last
  hurrah when beating Kapeno in 1967:
  'The Big Horse' had been caught close
  home by Dormant, to whom he was
  conceding 42lb, in the 1964 race;
- John Oaksey and Proud Tarquin losing the
  race in the stewards' room in 1974 after a
  controversial battle up the hill with Ron
  Barry on **The Dikler**;
- the astonishing climax in 1984 when
  Diamond Edge (going for his third win in
  the race) was fighting a ferocious duel with
  Lettoch and Plundering when *whoosh!* up
  the far side stormed the Queen Mother's
  Special Cargo to snatch the race in a finish
  of two short heads;
- **Desert Orchid** setting Sandown on a roar
  when pulling away from Kildimo up the
  hill in 1988;

Whitbread Gold Cup winners since 1990

1990	Mr Frisk	11	K. Bailey	Mr M. Armytage	9–2F	13
1991	Docklands Express	9	K. Bailey	A. Tory	4–1JF	10
1992	Topsham Bay	9	D. Barons	H. Davies	9–2	11
1993	Topsham Bay	10	D. Barons	R. Dunwoody	10–1	13
1994	Ushers Island	8	J.H. Johnson	C. Swan	25–1	12
1995	Cache Fleur	9	M. Pipe	R. Dunwoody	10–1	14
1996	Life Of A Lord	10	A. O'Brien *IRE*	C. Swan	12–1	17
1997	Harwell Lad	8	R. Alner	Mr R. Nuttall	14–1	9
1998	Call It A Day	8	D. Nicholson	A. Maguire	8–1	19
1999	Eulogy	9	R. Rowe	B. Fenton	14–1	19
2000	Beau	7	N. Twiston-Davies	C. Llewellyn	6–1F	20
2001	Ad Hoc	7	P. Nicholls	R. Walsh	14–1	25

- Mr Frisk winning in 1990 to become the only horse to have won the Grand National and the Whitbread;
- Beau winning by a distance in 2000 after a display of front-running power which left his rivals toiling.

The 1973 Whitbread Gold Cup won by Charlie Potheen was run at Newcastle as development work was in full swing at Sandown.

With a past like that, no wonder all roads lead to Sandown Park for the Whitbread on the last Saturday in April.

WHITTINGHAM, CHARLIE

Born in 1913, Charlie Whittingham took out his first training licence in California in 1934 and went on to become one of the greatest trainers of the twentieth century. At 73, he was the oldest trainer of a Kentucky Derby winner when Ferdinand landed the 1986 running, and broke that record three years later with the great Sunday Silence. (Both horses won the Breeder's Cup Classic.) Other well-known horses he has handled include **Dahlia**, Ack Ack (US Horse of the Year in 1971), Perrault, Estrapade and Golden Pheasant. Charlie Whittingham was known as 'The Bald Eagle' on account of his lack of hair – possibly caused by contracting malaria when serving in the US Marines during the Second World War. When applying for training credentials at the New York tracks he gave his hair colour as brown, explaining: 'That's the way I remember it.' Charlie Whittingham died in April 1999, aged 86.

WILDENSTEIN, DANIEL

First, the good news. Some top-notch horses have carried the colours (royal blue, light blue epaulets and cap) of French art dealer Daniel Wildenstein:

- four winners of the Prix de l'Arc de Triomphe: **Allez France** (1974), All Along (1983: she also won the Turf Classic and Washington, DC International in the USA and the Rothmans International in Canada, and was the first foreign horse to

be voted Horse of the Year in the USA); Sagace (1984, and disqualified after passing the post first in 1985); and Peintre Celebre (1997: he won the Prix du Jockey-Club the same year);
- winners of three Classics in England in 1976: Flying Water (One Thousand Guineas: she also won the 1977 Champion Stakes), Pawneese (Oaks: she won the King George that year) and Crow (St Leger: he won the Coronation Cup in 1978);
- 1975 July Cup winner Lianga;
- top milers Bigstone and Steinlen and top stayer Buckskin;
- Arcangues, 133–1 winner of the Breeders' Cup Classic in 1993.

The less good news is that over the years Wildenstein *père et fils* – Daniel's son Alec is closely involved in the family's racing operation – have not exactly endeared themselves to racing fans, due to their habit of removing their horses from a trainer when adversity or disagreement strikes. When in May 2001 André Fabre learned that he was to lose the 42 Wildenstein horses in his stable, he was joining a distinguished group of trainers, including fellow Chantilly trainer **John Hammond** and, in England, **Peter Walwyn** and **Henry Cecil**. Walwyn lost his Wildenstein horses in 1978 after the owner expressed dissatisfaction with Pat Eddery's riding of Buckskin in the Ascot Gold Cup. 'I was sad to lose the horses,' wrote Walwyn, 'but relieved that I would no longer have to train for such unpleasant and ungrateful people' – and Alec Wildenstein secured his place on Walwyn's bus heading for Beachy Head (*see* **Walwyn, Peter**).

The Wildenstein string in England went to Henry Cecil, and in due course that relationship soured. Again jockeyship was at the root of the problem: the Wildensteins took against Cecil's jockey Lester Piggott (who later described them as 'inveterate bad losers') and demanded he be taken off their horses. This led to Piggott's losing the Cecil post to Steve Cauthen at the end of the 1984 season, but the Wildenstein horses were on their way again in 1985, removed from Cecil and relocated to France. Walter Swinburn was another who incurred the Wildensteins' displeasure, losing the ride on All Along after they had disapproved of the way he rode her in the 1984 Rothmans International. Daniel Wildenstein (who owns the very good French chaser Kotkijet, winner of the 2001 Grand Steeple-Chase de Paris), was leading owner in Great Britain in 1976.

WILLIAMS, VENETIA

Since the retirement of Jenny Pitman the mantle of jump racing's most prominent lady trainer has passed to Venetia Williams, whose yard is at Kings Caple, near Hereford. She rode as an amateur jockey between 1986 and 1988, riding 10 winners, and learned her training skills as assistant to John Edwards, after time with Martin Pipe and Barry Hills and spells in Australia and the USA. Since taking out her first licence in 1995 she has made rapid progress to the top through the achievements of such horses as Teeton Mill (Hennessy Cognac Gold Cup and King George VI Chase 1998), the diminutive but indefatigable staying hurdler Lady Rebecca, winner of the Cleeve Hurdle at Cheltenham three years running (1999–2001), Jocks Cross (Welsh National 2000), The Outback Way and Bellator.

WILLIAMSON, BILL

Nicknamed 'Weary Willie' on account of his laid-back approach to his calling, Bill Williamson is perhaps best remembered in Britain as the rider jocked off by **Lester Piggott** (or, strictly, by owner John Galbreath) for the winning ride on Roberto in the 1972 Derby. But he had considerable success in Europe, winning two Classics in England – One Thousand Guineas on Abermaid in 1962 and Night Off in 1965 – along with plenty of other big races, such as the Ascot Gold Cup (Levmoss 1969), Sussex Stakes (Le Levanstell 1961), Queen Elizabeth II Stakes (Le Levanstell 1961), Nunthorpe Stakes (Deep Diver 1972), Yorkshire Oaks (Lynchris 1960), Cambridgeshire (Tarqogan 1965), Champion Stakes (Arctic Storm 1962), and the Timeform Gold Cup (forerunner of the Racing Post

Trophy) three times (Miralgo 1961, Hardicanute 1964 and Vaguely Noble 1967, by which time the race was the Observer Gold Cup). He won the Prix de l'Arc de Triomphe two years running, on **Vaguely Noble** in 1968 and Levmoss in 1969, while his greatest triumph in his native Australia was landing the 1952 Melbourne Cup on Dalray. Born in 1922, Bill Williamson rode his first winner at the age of 15 in 1937 and was six times leading jockey in the state of Victoria before moving to Ireland in 1960 and to Britain two years later. He died in 1979.

WILLIAMSON, NORMAN

Of jockeys currently riding, only **Tony McCoy** shares Norman Williamson's distinction of having ridden the winner of the Champion Hurdle and Cheltenham Gold Cup in the same year: Williamson achieved the feat on Alderbrook and Master Oats in 1995, and before that you have to go back to Fred Winter on Eborneezer and Saffron Tartan in 1961. Norman Williamson was born in Mallow, Co. Cork, on 16 January 1969 and served his apprenticeship as an amateur rider with **Dermot Weld**. His first winner was Jack And Jill at Clonmel on 19 May 1988. He moved to England in 1989 to ride as stable jockey for John Edwards, winning big races on horses like Monsieur Le Cure and Multum In Parvo (Mackeson Gold Cup 1990). In 1993 he joined **Kim Bailey**, and was in only his second season with the then Lambourn-based trainer when landing his famous double for the yard, while his association with the Herefordshire yard of **Venetia Williams** has brought more big-race success, including the Hennessy Cognac Gold Cup and King George VI Chase on Teeton Mill in 1998.

WINCANTON

Wincanton, Somerset BA9 8BJ
Tel.: 01963 32344
Fax: 01963 34668
E-mail: wincanton@rht.net
Web: www.wincantonracecourse.co.uk

Wincanton – where racing has been held since the late nineteenth century – is a perennial favourite among West Country jumping enthusiasts and really comes into its own in the spring, staging several races guaranteed to provide serious pointers to the National Hunt Festival at Cheltenham in March. The Jim Ford Challenge Cup over three miles one and a half furlongs at the late February meeting is a traditional warm-up for the Gold Cup (**Desert Orchid** won the race in 1987), and at the same meeting the Kingwell Hurdle (two miles) provides a major Champion Hurdle trial; Dessie won this too, in 1984. Other classy Wincanton races include the Desert Orchid South-Western Pattern Chase (two miles five furlongs), run at the late October meeting, and generally the standard of sport here is high – significantly classier than at the other West Country courses of Newton Abbot, Exeter and Taunton.

From an equine point of view Wincanton is a very fair track – 11 furlongs round, right-handed, with easy bends and well-made fences, a good test both for the long-striding horse and the handier type. The undulations are not too severe, though the downhill run to the cross fence before the turn into the straight can find some jockeys going faster than they would ideally like.

WINDSOR

Windsor, Berkshire SL4 5JJ

Tel.: 01753 865234

Fax: 01753 830156

E-mail: office@windsorracing.co.uk

Web: www.windsorracing.co.uk

Windsor is a town oozing history, and it is no surprise that racing has been taking place here since at least the time of Henry VIII, with the present site used since 1866. A programme of evening fixtures was initiated in 1964, and nowadays the course is hugely popular with the crowds who swarm in on Monday evenings through the summer. Never mind the quality of the racing – this is the place for a jolly night out eating and drinking in the tree-filled enclosures, with perhaps the occasional glimpse of horse or jockey to remind revellers that they are at a sporting event. With a new grandstand opened in 1995, facilities for the 'ordinary' racegoer here are significantly better than they were a

few years ago, though the viewing remains less than ideal.

The course, a figure-of-eight about a mile and a half round, is quite flat, and at five furlongs the home straight is long enough to give a horse time to sort himself out after all those bends.

Windsor bookmakers staged a strike in 1926 in protest against the imposition of a betting tax by Winston Churchill, then Chancellor of the Exchequer.

Jumping, long an integral part of racing at Windsor, was discontinued in 1998: the last meeting over the sticks there was on 3 December that year.

WINDSUCKER

A 'windsucker' is a horse that sucks air into its stomach while gnawing an object (such as its manger or box door) – in an attempt to quell mental agitation.

WINNER ALL RIGHT

The announcement heard on Irish racecourses to signal that the result of the race stands is 'winner all right'– equivalent to the 'weighed in' announcement in Britain.

WINTER, FRED

Fred Winter is the only man in jump racing history to have both ridden and trained winners of the Grand National, Cheltenham Gold Cup and Champion Hurdle:

- *Grand National*: rode Sundew (1957) and Kilmore (1962); trained Jay Trump (1965) and Anglo (1966);
- *Cheltenham Gold Cup*: rode Saffron Tartan (1961) and Mandarin (1962); trained Midnight Court (1978);
- *Champion Hurdle*: rode Clair Soleil (1955), Fare Time (1959) and Eborneezer (1961); trained Bula (1971 and 1972), Lanzarote (1974) and Celtic Shot (1988).

Son of the trainer also called Fred Winter, who as a jockey had won the 1911 Oaks on Cherimoya, he was born in 1926 and began a career as a Flat jockey, riding his first winner at the age of 13 on Tam O'Shanter at Salisbury on 15 May 1940. Increasing weight forced a move to National Hunt, and he rode his first winner over jumps on Carton at Kempton Park on 27 December 1947. (Curiously, the same horse was the first winner ever ridden by Winter's lifelong friend Dave Dick.) Carton was the first of 923 jumping winners that Fred Winter rode during a famous career. By the time of the last – Vultrix at Wolverhampton on 25 March 1964 – he had etched his name deep into the history of the sport.

Fred Winter's total of 121 winners for the 1952–3 season was then a record for a jump jockey. In the very first race of the 1953–4 term, a novices' chase at Newton Abbot, his mount Cent Francs fell at the first fence, breaking the jockey's leg and putting him out of action for the entire season.

In addition to two Grand Nationals, two Cheltenham Gold Cups and three Champion Hurdles, he won the King George VI Chase three times (Halloween 1952 and 1954, Saffron Tartan 1960), the Triumph Hurdle twice (Clair Soleil 1953 and Cantab 1961) and many other big races. But the one victory for which he will most be remembered is the epic 1962 Grand Steeple-Chase de Paris on **Mandarin**. A rider of supreme strength, style and determination, he was champion jockey four times: 1952–3, 1955–6, 1956–7 and 1957–8. He took out a trainer's licence for the 1964–5 season and made a spectacular start, winning the Grand National in each of his first two seasons, and was soon showing that his training career would be no less dominant than his riding. The 1970s saw a period when his Uplands yard in Upper Lambourn contained, at the same time and housed in a stretch of boxes appropriately known as 'Millionaires' Row', five great horses:

- **Pendil**, winner of the King George VI Chase in 1972 and 1973 and beaten a short head by The Dikler in the 1973 Gold Cup;
- **Crisp**, winner of the Two Mile Champion Chase in 1971 and hero of that famous

1973 Grand National when caught on the line by Red Rum;
- Bula, winner of the Champion Hurdle in 1972 and 1972 and one of the few great hurdlers to make a successful transition to fences;
- Lanzarote, winner of the Champion Hurdle in 1974 and killed in the 1977 Gold Cup;
- Killiney, brilliant novice chaser killed at Ascot in 1973.

John Francome spent his entire riding career with Fred Winter. He joined Uplands in October 1969, became first jockey to the stable in 1975 and still held that position when retiring in April 1985. He rode Midnight Court to win Winter his only Gold Cup in 1978.

Fred Winter was leading jumps trainer eight times: five years in a row between 1970–71 and 1974–5, then 1976–7, 1977–8 and 1984–5. In September 1987 he suffered a serious fall and a stroke at his Lambourn home, and although Celtic Shot won the Champion Hurdle in his name later that season (the horse's preparation having been handled by his assistant Charlie Brooks) he was forced to retire – a true legend of the sport.

WITHERS
Top of a horse's shoulder, immediately in front of the saddle.

WOLVERHAMPTON
Dunstall Park, Gorsebrook Road, Wolverhampton, West Midlands WV6 0PE
Tel.: 01902 421421
Fax: 01902 716626
E-mail: dunstall@parkuk.freeserve.co.uk
Web: www.dunstallpark.co.uk

After serving as a low-grade dual-purpose track for over a century, Wolverhampton underwent a complete makeover in the early 1990s. The old stands and old circuit were discarded, and a new all-weather track was first used on 27 December 1993: that afternoon the course staged two races under floodlights, the first time horse racing in Britain had been illuminated. Wolverhampton was the somewhat unlikely venue for ushering British racecourses into a new era – a fact underlined by the £15.7 million development which went alongside the new track, including a 370-seat glass-fronted panoramic restaurant in the manner of American tracks.

The left-handed all-weather circuit at Dunstall Park is extremely compact at just under a mile round, with no straight course. The bends are quite tight and the run from the home turn to the winning post just two furlongs, so the ability to lay up with the pace and be thereabouts turning in is of paramount importance here. National Hunt racing resumed at Wolverhampton, with two steeplechases on a new turf track on the outside of the all-weather, on 11 May 1997.

WOODBINE

The premier racecourse in Canada, in Toronto. The Breeders' Cup was held here in 1996 – the only time that event has left the USA – while the major international race run here is the **Canadian International**, over one and a half miles on turf in October: recent winners include **Singspiel** (1996), Royal Anthem (1998) and Mutafaweq (2000). Woodbine is the only major North American racetrack where the turf course is on the outside of the main dirt course.

WORCESTER

Pitchcroft, Worcester, Worcestershire WR1 3EJ
Tel.: 01905 25364
Fax: 01905 617563
E-mail: info@worcester-racecourse.co.uk
Web: worcester-racecourse.co.uk

Worcester is an excellent place to spot the equine stars of the future, as its long straights, easy bends and well-sited fences make it a good course for novice chasers. For all runners, young or old, it provides a fair test, and suits the strong galloper with plenty of stamina. The left-handed circuit is one mile five furlongs round and very flat, and a particular hazard is that if a horse goes too wide at the home turn he can end up in the adjacent

River Severn: it has been known to happen! That river is the cause of Worcester's greatest problem – the danger of flooding. The Severn has to rise only a little for the course to become submerged, and waterlogging is a constant risk.

The current track was laid out in 1880, though there had been racing at this site long before then, and the course used to stage racing on the level: the last Flat meeting was on 20 August 1966.

WORK

In training parlance, 'work' is when a horse is asked to gallop seriously, rather than just canter. Most trainers would schedule two mornings a week as work mornings.

WRAGG, GEOFF

Geoff Wragg, born in 1930 and son of **Harry Wragg** (for whom he worked for 30 years as assistant), was the first trainer to have won the Derby in the first season he held a licence. Teenoso, ridden by Lester Piggott, brought him this distinction in 1983 and went on to win the Grand Prix de Saint-Cloud and King George VI and Queen Elizabeth Diamond Stakes in 1984; Wragg won a second King George with Pentire in 1996. Other top horses trained at Abington Place, his Newmarket yard, include Marling (Cheveley Park Stakes 1991, Irish One Thousand Guineas, Coronation Stakes and Sussex Stakes 1992), Most Welcome (Lockinge Stakes 1989), Arcadian Heights (Ascot Gold Cup 1994) and Owington (July Cup 1994).

WRAGG, HARRY

Harry Wragg, born in 1902, was one of the few men to have followed a career at the top as a jockey with a second career at the top as a trainer. He rode his first winner in 1919, and by the end of his time in the saddle in 1946 had ridden 1,762 in Britain. His 13 Classic victories included the Derby three times – on Felstead in 1928, Blenheim in 1930 and Watling Street in 1942. Had he not been a contemporary of **Gordon Richards** he would certainly have been champion jockey many times, but he landed the title just once:

in 1941, taking advantage of Richards being sidelined by injury. As a jockey he was famed for his judgement of pace and for his ability to sit coolly for the moment to make his challenge: hence his nickname, 'The Head Waiter'. On his retirement from the saddle he set up as a trainer in Newmarket, gaining his first licence in 1947, and sent out six Classic winners: Darius (Two Thousand Guineas 1954), Psidium (Derby 1961), Abermaid (One Thousand Guineas 1962), Full Dress II (One Thousand Guineas 1969), Intermezzo (St Leger 1969) and On The House (One Thousand Guineas 1982). Harry Wragg died in 1985.

WRIST

Betting slang for 5–4 (from the **tic-tac** sign).

WYNDBURGH

Trained first by Rhona Oliver and then by her husband Ken, Wyndburgh has the unique distinction of having finished second in the Grand National three times without ever winning the race. He was second to Sundew in 1957, beaten eight lengths; a desperately unlucky second to Oxo in 1959, beaten a length and a half after his jockey Tim Brookshaw had to ride from second Becher's without stirrups, an iron having broken; and second to Kilmore in 1962, beaten ten lengths, at the age of 12. In all he ran in the big Aintree race six years in succession. Apart from those seconds, he started favourite in 1958 but could finish only fourth behind Mr What; fell at first Becher's in 1960; and was sixth behind Nicolaus Silver in 1961. A true Liverpool specialist, he won the Grand Sefton Chase over the National fences in 1957 and is commemorated with a plaque in the runner-up berth of the Aintree unsaddling enclosure.

X Y Z

X

No horse whose name begins with X has ever won the Derby or Grand National.

XAAR

Owned by **Khalid Abdullah** and trained in France by **André Fabre**, Xaar had the same connections as his sire Zafonic, and like his father turned in a power-packed display in the Dewhurst Stakes, Britain's top two-year-old race. Indeed, Xaar's seven-length demolition of Tamarisk in the 1997 Dewhurst was widely judged one of the very best performances ever seen from a two-year-old. It was his fourth victory from five races as a juvenile, and it made him one of the shortest-priced winter favourites for the Two Thousand Guineas in living memory. But, as so often, top-class two-year-old form did not lead on to Classic glory. His 1998 campaign proved a severe disappointment. After narrowly and unimpressively winning the Craven Stakes, he started 11–10 on for the Two Thousand Guineas but could finish only fourth. He was then second in a race at Deauville and third to **Swain** in the Irish Champion Stakes before being sold to **Godolphin**, in whose colours in 1999 he was third to Lear Spear in the Prince of Wales's Stakes at Royal Ascot and a neck second to Compton Admiral in the Eclipse Stakes. Very good form – but nothing like the sensational Xaar we saw in the 1997 Dewhurst.

YANKEE

Bet which combines four different horses in different races in 11 bets (so a £1 win Yankee costs £11). The horses are connected in

- six doubles
- four trebles
- one four-horse accumulator.

See also **Super Yankee; Lucky 15**.

YARMOUTH

Jellicoe Road, North Denes, Great Yarmouth, Norfolk NR30 4AU
Tel.: 01493 842527
Fax: 01493 843254

Yarmouth is the nearest 'away' Flat track to Newmarket, and trainers at Headquarters who are not keen to expose their young horses too soon to the yawning spaces of the Rowley Mile or the July Course often take promising two-year-olds there. So it can be a good place for picking out embryo stars.

Dubai Millennium, then trained by David Loder, ran his first race at Yarmouth: the South Norfolk Caterers Maiden Stakes on 28 October 1998. Ridden by Frankie Dettori, he started 9–4 on favourite and won by five lengths.

The track is a narrow left-handed oval about one and three-quarter miles round, with distances from five furlongs to one mile run up the straight, and apart from minor undulations the track is flat. With its long straights, this is essentially a fair course, and although the bends are quite sharp there is enough time up the home straight to reach a decent position from which to mount a finish. Thus it is a course for the long-striding, galloping type of horse. The sandy soil drains quickly, so the going is rarely heavy.

The current track was established after the previous site, further down the coast, was given over to redevelopment in 1920: there had been racing on that spot since the early eighteenth century.

YEARLING

A horse in the second year of its life: officially a foal becomes a yearling on 1 January following its foaling.

YORK

York YO2 1EX
Tel.: 01904 620911
Fax: 01904 611071
E-mail: info@yorkracecourse.co.uk
Web: www.yorkracecourse.co.uk

Like the great city itself, racing at York is wrapped in history. There were horse races here in Roman times, when in AD 208 the ageing emperor Severus laid out a course on what is now known as the Knavesmire – the vast tract of common land just outside the city centre which later served, among other uses, as the site of common executions: three robbers were hanged there on the morning of 16 August 1731, and the same afternoon the first official race meeting took place on the Knavesmire. The highwayman Dick Turpin was hanged here in 1739, again prior to the afternoon's sport. In 1851 a crowd of over 100,000 watched the famous match between **The Flying Dutchman** and **Voltigeur**, each of whom had won a Derby and a St Leger. At five, The Flying Dutchman was a year older than his rival and had to concede $8^1/_2$ lb in the two-mile race: he won by a length.

Today York shows due deference towards history – there is a very fine racing museum at the course which can be visited on race days – but in other respects is the model of a modern racecourse. The new grandstand, opened in 1996, has gone down very well with the public in the Tattersalls enclosure, while members in the County Stand likewise have very up-to-date facilities. Terraces afford excellent viewing of the large parade ring (which now incorporates the unsaddling enclosure), and the pre-parade takes place on a quiet, tree-lined lawn adjacent to the paddock. There is a sort of friendly grandeur to York which makes it a wonderful place to go racing.

The course itself is highly appreciated by jockeys and trainers, who consider it as fair a test of the Thoroughbred racehorse as there is – easy left-hand bends, wide track and long straights rendering it ideal for the long-striding galloper. York's circuit is in the shape of a warped horseshoe, with two miles the longest distance on offer. Runners in a race of that distance start to the right of the stands and undertake a long gallop until making a gradual left-hand turn a little under 10 furlongs from home: this takes them into a shorter straight which leads to the home turn, about four and a half furlongs out. There is a straight course for five- and six-furlong races, and seven-furlong races start on a separate spur, joining the straight by means of a very gentle dog-leg bend to the left. The course is completely flat.

Although the standard of racing at York is uniformly high, the three-day meeting in mid-August is its best fixture – and one of the very best of the whole Flat year.

Each of the three days has a Group One race. Tuesday sees the **International Stakes** over a mile and a quarter, which links with the earlier Eclipse Stakes and later Champion Stakes as the three big 10-furlong races of the British Flat racing season. Wednesday has the **Yorkshire Oaks**, very often the next outing for horses who have won or run well in the Oaks or Irish Oaks, but above all Wednesday is Ebor day, when York stages its most famous race, the **Ebor Handicap** over one and three-quarter miles. Thursday features the **Nunthorpe Stakes**, the only five-furlong Group One sprint of the year in Britain.

Other major races at the August Meeting include a serious St Leger trial in the Great Voltigeur Stakes (one and a half miles) and two races over six furlongs for two-year-olds: the Lowther Stakes for fillies and the Gimcrack Stakes for colts and geldings. To the owner of the winner of the Gimcrack goes the opportunity of sounding off with a speech at the Gimcrack Dinner in December.

York's other can't-miss meeting is in May, featuring important Classic trials over a mile and a quarter: the Dante Stakes is a major unraveller of clues for the Derby (recent winners of both races include Shirley Heights, Shahrastani, Reference Point, Erhaab and Benny The Dip) while the Musidora Stakes serves the same purpose in relation to the Oaks (winners of both include Diminuendo and Reams Of Verse). The Yorkshire Cup (one and three-quarter miles) at the May Meeting is an early-season outing for the top stayers.

Yorkshire Oaks winners since 1990

1990	Hellenic	3	M. Stoute	W. Carson	100–30	6
1991	Magnificent Star	3	M. Moubarak	A. Cruz	16–1	7
1992	User Friendly	3	C. Brittain	G. Duffield	8–11F	8
1993	Only Royale	4	L. Cumani	R. Cochrane	10–1	8
1994	Only Royale	5	L. Cumani	L. Dettori	15–2	7
1995	Pure Grain	3	M. Stoute	J. Reid	11–10F	8
1996	Key Change	3	J. Oxx *IRE*	J. Murtagh	7–1	9
1997	My Emma	4	R. Guest	D. Holland	7–1	8
1998	Catchascatchcan	3	H. Cecil	K. Fallon	2–1F	6
1999	Ramruma	3	H. Cecil	Pat Eddery	5–6F	11
2000	Petrushka	3	M. Stoute	J. Murtagh	5–4F	6

Two other York fixtures which should be mentioned are the Timeform Charity Day in June, from which down the years over £2 million has been raised for various charities, and the Saturday in mid-July featuring what in 1998 was named the John Smith's Cup after over three decades as the Magnet Cup, first run in 1960 and supported by the oldest continuous sponsorship on the Flat.

YORKSHIRE OAKS

Group One: fillies and mares 3 years and upwards: 1½ miles (York)

The Yorkshire Oaks is the natural late-summer target for horses who have run prominently in the Oaks and Irish Oaks, and the list of winners is full of horses who have pulled off the Epsom–York or The Curragh–York double, with an even more distinguished group of just four fillies who have won all three races: Fair Salinia (1978), Diminuendo (1988: she had dead-heated at The Curragh), User Friendly (1992) and Ramruma (1999). This distinguished quartet apart, fillies who have won the Oaks and Yorkshire Oaks since the Second World War are Frieze (1952), **Petite Etoile** (1959), Homeward Bound (1964), Lupe (1970), Mysterious (1973), Sun Princess (1983) and Circus Plume (1984).

The Yorkshire Oaks was confined to three-year-old fillies until being opened up to older generations in 1991. Four-year-old Only Royale took advantage of the revised conditions to become the first four-year-old to win in 1993 – and followed up with a repeat win as a five-year-old in 1994.

ZAFONIC

This colt ran only seven times in his life, but one of those races produced a display of sheer galloping power which no one who witnessed it is ever likely to forget. A handsome son of the American sire Gone West, owned by **Khalid Abdullah** and trained in France by **André Fabre**, Zafonic was unbeaten in four outings as a two-year-old in 1992, notably a demolition of Kingmambo in the Prix de la Salamandre at Longchamp and then an equally authoritative display to win the Dewhurst Stakes at Newmarket – such a comprehensive victory that he became the shortest-priced winter favourite for the Two Thousand Guineas since Tudor Minstrel in 1947. Ante-post vouchers on Zafonic sustained many a punter through the winter months – not least one John McCririck, who made no secret of the fact that he had lumped on for the Guineas at a working man's price. Despite causing his supporters a momentary wobble when losing his unbeaten record to Kingmambo in his prep race, the Prix Djebel at Maisons-Laffitte, Zafonic started 6–5 on favourite for the 1993 Two Thousand Guineas and never gave his supporters a moment's anxiety, storming home under Pat Eddery to win by three and a half lengths from Barathea in record time for the course. He ran only once more, putting in a below-par performance when unplaced in the Sussex Stakes at the Goodwood July Meeting. Post-race examination revealed an 'exercise-induced pulmonary haemorrhage' – that is, he had broken a blood vessel, and was not asked to exert himself again. He is now standing as a stallion at his owner's Banstead Manor Stud at Newmarket.

ZILBER, MAURICE

During the 1970s the name Maurice Zilber – based in France but an Egyptian who had been born (in 1919) in India – featured prominently in the results of big races, through the exploits of horses trained for his major patron **Nelson Bunker Hunt**. His biggest victory in Britain (and only English Classic) came with Empery in the 1976 Derby, but he was also responsible for such familiar horses as **Dahlia**, Nobiliary and Youth before moving to the USA to continue his training career there. He is now back training in France. Zilber received this assessment from Lester Piggott: 'I have to say that Maurice Zilber could be downright impossible in the matter of riding plans: you never knew for sure that you were riding his horse until you got up on it in the paddock – and even then it would not have surprised me to find another jockey up there!'

ZIPPY CHIPPY

The **Quixall Crossett** of the USA – a horse who has achieved fame and a loyal following through running frequently but failing to win a single race, including a contest over 40 yards against a minor league baseball player. After his eighty-fifth defeat in 1998 he was barred from competing at his regular track, Finger Lakes in upstate New York: the stewards announced that they were banning him 'for the protection of the public'. But Zippy Chippy (who had been acquired by his trainer Felix Monserrate in exchange for an old van) has soldiered on, and by February 2001 his losing run, unblemished by victory, had reached 89. In March 2001 he beat a Standardbred horse who was pulling a bike and driver and had a 20-length start, getting up to win the 40-yard race by a neck – but that was an exhibition, and Zippy Chippy's 0 for 89 record remained intact.

In this updated edition of the *Channel Four Racing Guide to Form and Betting*, Jim McGrath and John McCririck pool their considerable wisdom to equip punters with all the information vital for the battle with the bookmakers. McGrath explains how to weigh all the different factors affecting each horse's chance, while McCririck offers a guide through the steaming jungle of the betting ring, describing all the different bets, systems and strategies. Don't bet without it.

ISBN 07522 1970 7   £5.99

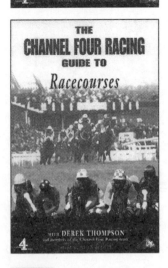

In the *Channel Four Racing Guide to Racehorses* John Francome – former champion jump jockey and famed judge of a horse – shares his wisdom. This guide reveals how to spot a good horse, explains the breeding business, and also tells the history of the Thoroughbred, taking in some of the greatest equine personalities along the way.

ISBN 07522 1399 7   £9.99

Covering all fifty-nine British racecourses and including sections on major racecourses around the world, the *Channel Four Racing Guide to Racecourses* includes all the vital information to help you plan your day at the races and reveals which sort of horse suits which course. Introduced by Derek Thompson and containing course diagrams, this is the essential companion to racing's fields of dreams.

ISBN 07522 2198 1   £9.99

 You can order your copies direct from Channel 4 Books by calling 01624 84 44 44. Postage and packing is free in the UK.